What Determines Savings?

What Determines Savings?

Laurence J. Kotlikoff

The MIT Press
Cambridge, Massachusetts
London, England

This book was set in Palatino by Asco Trade Typesetting Ltd., Hong Kong, and printed and bound by Halliday Lithograph in the United States of America.

Library of Congress Cataloging-in-Publication Data

Kotlikoff, Laurence J.
  What determines savings? / Laurence J. Kotlikoff.

   p.   cm.
  Bibliography: p.
  Includes index.
  ISBN 0-262-11137-3
  1. Saving and investment. I. Title.
HB843.K68   1989   88-9091
 339.4′3—dc19   CIP

To my parents, Harold and Vivienne Kotlikoff, my sister Barbara, and my brother Michael for their steadfast support and encouragement.

And to my co-authors and treasured friends, Alan Auerbach, Michael Boskin, John Shoven, Avia Spivak and Lawrence Summers.

Contents

    with Avia Spivak and Lawrence H. Summers

18 Public Debt and United States Saving: A New Test of the
    Neutrality Hypothesis (1985)   455
    with Michael J. Boskin

19 An Examination of Empirical Tests of Social Security and Savings
    (1983)   479
    with Alan Auerbach

    References   499
    Sources   523
    Index   525

Preface

Understanding what determines savings has been the main goal of my research since graduate school. This volume collects nineteen studies bearing directly or indirectly on the determinants of savings. I wrote eleven of the articles myself and the other eight with coauthors. Of the nineteen studies, four have not been published previously and eight were published in journals or books that may not be readily available or well known to students of savings.

As a group the articles consider the role in wealth accumulation of saving for retirement, saving for bequests and other intergenerational transfers, and precautionary saving. They also address the savings effects of fiscal policy, social security, and demographic change. And they examine the empirical validity of different theories of saving behavior. Several key findings in this volume are:

US wealth accumulation is primarily the consequence of intergenerational transfers as opposed to life cycle saving for retirement.

The extent of risk sharing among family members is a subtle but potentially important determinant of aggregate savings.

The precautionary saving response to a small probability of major future health expenditures can easily account for a third of total savings in life cycle economies.

Consumption decisions of altruistically linked individuals depend on collective resources, not on the distribution of resources.

Individuals can become altruistically linked simply by caring for the same person. Hence altruistically linked groups are likely to be quite large.

Structural tax changes, increases in government consumption, and intergenerational redistribution are policies that can have substantial effects on national saving.

Investment incentives are more effective than savings incentives as a means to stimulate wealth accumulation.

Investment incentives induce capital losses on existing assets. This produces a subtle but potentially major redistribution across generations and stimulates saving.

From the perspective of neoclassical economics the conventional budget deficit is an inherently arbitrary accounting construct that is wholly unreliable for assessing the effects of fiscal policy on savings.

If young and old generations implicitly bargain through the political system over their financing of government consumption, debt will be neutral (i.e., will not crowd out savings) even in the life cycle model.

Baby booms and baby busts and changes in retirement ages and life expectancy are demographic and economic events that can greatly alter wealth accumulation.

There is no evidence of systematic irrational undersaving by American households.

In contrast to at least one version of the Barro model, aggregate consumption appears to depend on the age distribution of resources.

Because of aggregation and simultaneity problems, conventional time-series consumption functions are likely to provide little or no evidence concerning the underlying nature of intertemporal preferences or the impact of fiscal policies, such as Social Security, on savings.

An analysis of contingent bequests indicates that the wealth elasticity of bequest is less than unity.

Although the essays in this book cover many of the major determinants of savings, they certainly do not cover them all. In the interest of providing a comprehensive picture of current knowledge of savings determinants, the introduction presents a brief and selective review of the savings literature. Because several of the articles collected here are themselves lengthy reviews of portions of this literature, the introduction gives shorter shrift to issues surveyed in this book.

Part I: Saving Motives

In addition to the introduction, this book has four parts. Part I, entitled "Saving Motives," contains six chapters. The first four chapters consider saving for life cycle motives and intergenerational transfers. Chapters 5 and 6 examine precautionary motives for savings. Chapter 1, coauthored with Lawrence H. Summers, suggests that intergenerational transfers rather than life cycle motives play the predominant role in US wealth accumulation. Chapter 2, surveys the recent literature on the importance of intergenerational transfers to savings, pointing out the wide variety of evidence supporting the importance of intergenerational transfers in the process of wealth accumulation.

The third chapter demonstrates that altruistic concern for one's children and their spouses implies altruistic linkages with the in-laws of one's children as well as linkages with everyone with whom such in-laws are linked. The chapter suggests that, if altruism exists, the number of individuals who are altruistically linked will be very large. Redistribution within such large altruistic clans will have no effect on savings or other economic variables.

The fourth chapter, coauthored with Avia Spivak, provides an explanation for intergenerational transfers that has nothing to do with altruism. In the absence of well-functioning annuity markets, children can help hedge the life span uncertainty of their parents by agreeing to support their parents if they live longer than expected in exchange for receiving their parents' wealth in the form of a bequest if they die sooner than expected. These arrangements need not be explicit, and they can be self-enforcing. Chapter 4 shows that the economic risk associated with life span uncertainty is remarkably important; nonaltruistic parents who do not have access to fairly priced or close to fairly priced annuity insurance have large incentives to enter into risk-sharing arrangements with their children.

Depending on the bargaining between parents and children, life span risk sharing may give rise to positive expected net transfers from parents to children. In comparison with an economy with perfect private insurance, an economy with family annuity markets and positive expected net transfers can accumulate substantially more wealth. This is one of the lessons of chapter 5, coauthored with Avia Spivak and John B. Shoven. This chapter also considers extended family longevity risk sharing in altruistic settings.

Chapters 4 and 5 compare the amounts of wealth that would be accumulated in a market setting with actuarially fair annuity insurance and a family risk-sharing setting that, because of the smaller number of participants, is less than actuarially fair. Because there is less insurance available in the family insurance setting, there is also more savings, reflecting in large part the precautionary savings motive.

Chapter 6 also examines precautionary saving motives. The risk considered here is uncertain future health expenditures. In addition to showing a substantial precautionary demand for savings in the absence of fair insurance, this chapter points out that certain institutional substitutes for fair insurance, such as an asset-tested Medicaid program, can greatly alter (reduce in the case of Medicaid) aggregate wealth.

Part II: Fiscal Policy and Savings

Fiscal policy, the focus of part II, can greatly influence wealth accumulation. Although the saving impact of fiscal policies within static Keynesian models is widely understood, their impact in dynamic neoclassical models is not. Chapter 7 discusses the recent literature on this issue and uses the Auerbach-Kotlikoff 55-period life cycle simulation model (Auerbach and Kotlikoff 1987) to compare the saving impact of tax cuts, changes in the tax structure, and changes in government consumption. Chapter 8 and chapter 9, coauthored with Alan J. Auerbach, also use the Auerbach-Kotlikoff model but consider the savings impact of intergenerational redistribution, including deficit finance and investment incentives.

One message of chapters 7 through 9 is that a variety of fiscal policies may be structurally quite similar if not identical, yet may imply quite different time paths of government deficits. This raises the question of whether official deficits are meaningful measures of fiscal policy. Chapter 10 argues forcefully that, from the perspective of neoclassical economics, the deficit should be discarded as a measure of fiscal policy; the chapter points out that the "deficit" is a noneconomic arbitrary accounting construct that bears no necessary relationship to the fundamental stance of fiscal policy.

The last essay in part II is chapter 11. This chapter points out that the standard life cycle model's prediction that intergenerational redistribution affects savings is based on the implicit assumption that older generations can coerce younger generations. Suppose that one drops this arbitrary assumption and instead assumes that young and old generations implicitly negotiate through the political process over the size and financing of government consumption. In this case there will be no net intergenerational redistribution. Deficit finance can arise in this model, but it has no consequences for savings.

Part III: Social Security, Demographics, and Savings

This part examines how Social Security and demographics separately and jointly affect savings. Chapter 12 is an early use of simulation methods to study the savings effects of government policy. The study demonstrates that an unfunded Social Security system can dramatically reduce an economy's long-run stock of wealth. Chapter 13, coauthored with Alan J. Auerbach, uses the Auerbach-Kotlikoff model to study the short-run and long-run effects of unfunded Social Security, baby booms and baby busts, and unfunded Social Security in the presence of a baby boom followed by a baby bust. The results suggest that changes in fertility rates can, through time, have major effects on wealth accumulation. In addition, rapid and prolonged reductions in fertility rates can have a severe impact on Social Security finances, although they may alleviate other financial pressures on the government.

Work spans and life spans are additional demographic and economic outcomes and choices that are of major importance to wealth accumulation. Chapters 12 and 14 demonstrate within the life cycle model the sensitivity of the long-run stock of wealth to changes in the age of retirement and the age of death.

Part IV: Empirical Analyses of Savings Determinants

The five essays of this part test various saving models and thereby shed light on underlying determinants of savings. Chapter 15 uses the Parnes panel survey to study the saving response to Social Security predicted by the life cycle model. The results provide mixed support for that model. The results should, however, be viewed cautiously because of several short-comings in the data.

Chapter 16 examines the wealth elasticity of bequests. The size of this elasticity is an important determinant of the transmission of inequality through time and the rates of growth and saving. Surprisingly the size of this important elasticity has been little studied. Chapter 16 presents a new approach to studying the wealth elasticity of bequests. The idea is simply to look at the bequest that survey respondents would leave if they died at the time of the survey. The chapter contains fairly strong evidence that the wealth elasticity of bequests is less than unity for the broad middle class.

Chapter 17, coauthored with Avia Spivak and Lawrence H. Summers, considers from a broader perspective the rationality of saving decisions. The objective in this study is to learn what fraction of the public significantly undersaves for retirement. A finding that a large fraction of the public significantly undersaves would cast doubt on neoclassical models that rely on the assumption of rational choice. The method used to assess undersaving compares the level of affordable old-age consumption with indirect estimates of the actual level of consumption when young. A finding that affordable old-age consumption is much smaller than the level of consumption when young would suggest inadequate saving. The study's results, however, provide no prima facie case that a large fraction of households significantly undersaves.

Chapter 18 was coauthored with Michael J. Boskin. This chapter presents a test of an important implication of Robert Barro's (1974) model of intergenerational altruism, namely, that consumption of altruistically linked individuals depends on the sum, not the distribution, of resources. Boskin and I test this proposition using US time-series data by considering whether aggregate consumption depends on the age distribution of resources as proxied by the age distribution of income. After controlling for demographics, we find that the age distribution of income remains a significant explanatory variable, contradicting at least our specification of the Barro model.

The final chapter, chapter 19, is coauthored with Alan J. Auerbach. This paper points out some serious problems with a number of recent time-series studies of consumption and Social Security and related time-series consumption analyses that ignore issues of aggregation and simultaneity. To demonstrate these problems, Auerbach and I simulate the introduction of unfunded Social Security using our life cycle simulation model. We then use the data from this simulation to estimate the time-series consumption regressions reported in the literature. Notwithstanding the fact that our data correspond perfectly to the theory being tested, the regression analysis based on these perfect data produces coefficients that would conventionally be read as rejecting both the life cycle model and Social Security's predicted impact on the life cycle model.

Acknowledgments

I have been extremely privileged to work with Alan Auerbach, Michael Boskin, John Shoven, Avia Spivak, and Larry Summers. In our joint research these individuals were excellent partners, and they brought creativity, energy, enthusiasm, wit, fun, and occasionally good grammar. I learned a great deal from each of them, and I treasure each as a close friend.

I also want to acknowledge Martin Feldstein as a strong source of inspiration in my research. Marty was my thesis adviser and has remained a close friend and adviser. His interest in savings sparked my own, and his blend of policy-oriented theoretical and empirical economics greatly influenced my own style of research.

I am very grateful to the government agencies and private research institutions that provided research support for the studies contained in this volume. These government agencies and research institutions are the National Science Foundation, the National Institute of Aging, the Department of Health and Human Services, the National Academy of Sciences, the National Bureau of Economic Research, the Brookings Institution, the International Monetary Fund, the Hoover Institution, the American Enterprise Institute, the Foundation for Research in Economic Education, the Center for Economic Policy Research, the Carnegie-Rochester Conference Series, and the Pinchas Saphir Institute.

What Determines Savings?

Introduction: What Determines Savings?

Economists have long been interested in savings for several important reasons. Savings constitutes the supply of capital, which with labor represent the two primary inputs to production. Savings or nonhuman wealth, together with human wealth, determine which individuals or families, which regions, and which nations are rich or poor. And savings, which equals the sum of past saving (nonhuman wealth accumulation), influences current saving of both human and nonhuman wealth; indeed, savings is the central economic link connecting the past, the present, and the future.

The study of savings brings together analysis of consumption choice, labor supply, demographics, economic growth, and government policy. This joint analysis raises, in turn, other issues, such as the nature of preferences, the rationality of expectations, the degree of economic risks, the completeness of insurance markets, and the role of credit institutions. While it would be convenient if each of these influences on savings could be understood one at a time and in partial equilibrium, such is typically not the case. On the contrary, since savings depends, in part, on a large array of interrelated economic choices and since these choices are intertemporal in nature, understanding savings requires a dynamic general equilibrium framework.

Recent research on savings has built on the seminal contributions of Solow (1956) and Modigliani and Brumberg (1954) and the growth theory literature of the 1960s. Some of this research involves new models of consumption choice [e.g., Barro (1974)]; some involves new tests of intertemporal optimization [e.g., Hall (1981)]; some involves new empirical approaches [e.g., Feldstein (1974c)]; some uses simulation analysis [e.g., Auerbach and Kotlikoff (1987)]; and some is based on economic experiments [e.g., Johnson, Kotlikoff, and Samuelson (1987)]. The new research has made real progress: The simulation analyses have helped to distinguish potentially important from potentially unimportant determinants of savings; the empirical research has demonstrated a much greater role of inter-generational transfers in US savings than was previously believed to be the case; the theoretical research has demonstrated the importance for savings of economic ties within the family; and the experimental research has raised questions about the ability of individuals to make rational intertemporal choices.

Fortunately or unfortunately, this research progress has, on balance, increased the number of factors that have been identified as playing a major role in determining the amount of savings. Take, as an example, the recent analysis of nonaltruistic bequests that arise when annuity insurance cannot be purchased on the market and is not provided by the government or by employers. Kotlikoff and Spivak (1981), Davies (1981), Eckstein, Eichenbaum, and Peled (1983), Hubbard (1984a,b), Abel (1985), and Kotlikoff, Spivak, and Shoven (this volume) demonstrate the considerable additional savings that can result because of nonaltruistic bequests. For example, according to Kotlikoff, Spivak, and Shoven's results, the absence of annuity insurance or a close substitute can mean as much as a doubling of savings in life cycle economies.

Discovering more factors that can significantly affect savings exacerbates the problem of determining empirically which factor or combination of factors is most important in understanding any particular change in saving behavior. Consider, for instance, the question of why the US saving rate in the postwar period is roughly two-thirds the rate observed between 1870 and 1930. The list of possible explanations includes (1) increased provision of health insurance, disability insurance, unemployment insurance, and annuity insurance that reduced the need for precautionary savings, (2) an increase in government consumption and distortionary taxation, (3) a decline in altruistically motivated bequests to children, (4) an increase in subjective time preference rates, (5) deficit finance by the federal government, both explicit and implicit (such as unfunded social security), (6) a reduction in the labor supply of younger workers because of increased college attendance, (7) welfare programs that reduce the risk of abject poverty and precautionary savings to avoid poverty, and (8) the asset tests of Medicaid and other welfare programs that reduce incentives to save.

Each of these factors may have played a major role in reducing saving. Indeed, as a group they may more than explain the decline in saving. Hence one also needs to consider events that may have increased saving and offset this set of potential saving deterrents. Postwar factors that should have increased US saving include (1) the prolonged baby bust that started in the early 1960s, (2) the increase in life expectancy, (3) the increase in early retirement, (4) the increased earnings of young and middle-age women, (5) the decline in family financial support, (6) the increased risk and cost of nursing home institutionalization, (7) government subsidization of pension and similar forms of saving, and (8) historically high real after-tax returns during the 1980s.

Extended lists of this kind are a start in considering questions such as the postwar decline in US saving, but it is a far cry from such lists to the empirical knowledge needed to assess to relative contributions of different factors to changes in savings. Such empirical knowledge is a long way off not only because more and better data are needed but also because some issues of great importance to savings are surprisingly difficult to test. The value of a review of knowledge concerning savings is not, therefore, to say precisely what determines actual savings. The value is to identify key determinants, to indicate what is known about their savings effects, and to indicate areas for future research. In this survey I first identify eight principal determinants of savings within a general framework. I then review the state of knowledge concerning each of these savings determinants. In the final section I indicate directions for future research.

A Framework for Analysis

To organize the discussion, I find it useful to consider the accumulation of wealth in a two-period overlapping generations (OLG) model with a single good. The one-good two-period OLG model is the simplest way to consider intertemporal choices. Its use places no restrictions on behavior; for example, in making consumption choices agents can have life cycle intertemporal preferences à la Modigliani and Brumberg (1954), they can have altruistic preferences à la Barro (1974), or they can have Keynesian preferences.

Consider first the model in the absence of government, and assume that members of each generation are identical. Agents are adults for two periods, corresponding to youth and old age. New adults appear at the beginning of each period at which time they, together with old adults (their parents), go to work with the capital supplied by the old adults. At the end of each period output is produced, factors are paid, consumption occurs, and intergenerational and intragenerational private transfers are made. At the beginning of any period the young adults have no wealth, since they do not receive any income or transfers until the end of the period. All wealth at the beginning of any period is held by the current old generation. The assets of each old person at time $t + 1$, A_{t+1}, equal the assets they accumulated when young, i.e., at the end of time t. As indicted in equation (1), this accumulation equals the labor earnings received by each young adult at time t, E_{yt}, plus the net intergenerational transfers received by each young adult at time t, I_t, less the consumption by each young adult at time t, C_{yt}.

$$A_{t+1} = E_{yt} + I_t - C_{yt}. \tag{1}$$

The consumption when young, C_{yt}, of each member of generation t (those who are young adults at time t) is constrained by

$$C_{yt} + A_{t+1} \leqslant E_{yt} + I_t. \tag{2}$$

If young adults at time t are unable to borrow against their future labor earnings or their possibly positive net future transfers from their children ($I_{t+1} < 0$), constraint (3) will also apply:

$$A_{t+1} \geqslant 0. \tag{3}$$

Th second-period budget constraining consumption of members of generation t when old, C_{ot+1}, and their transfers I_{t+1} to their children is

$$C_{ot+1} + I_{t+1} \leqslant A_{t+1}(1 + r_{t+1}) + E_{ot+1}, \tag{4}$$

where E_{ot+1} is the labor earnings of the elderly at $t + 1$ and r_{t+1} is the second period return on savings accumulated in the first period. If the elderly in period $t + 1$ are retired, E_{ot+1} equals 0. Second-period labor earnings and the rate of return may be uncertain from the perspective of the first period.

While this framework is simple, it is sufficient to point out a number of determinants of savings. To focus attention on the determinants of the economy's savings at time $t + 1$, A_{t+1}, let us assume that (2) holds with equality and rewrite the equation as

$$A_{t+1} = w_{yt}L_{yt} + I_t - C_{yt}, \tag{2'}$$

where we replace E_{yt} by the wage at time t paid to young workers, w_{yt}, multiplied by the supply of labor of young workers at time t, L_{yt}.

The Nature of the Consumption Function

There are three principal alternative theories of consumption: the life cycle model of Modigliani and Brumberg (1954) and Ando and Modigliani (1963), the Barro (1974) model, and the Keynesian model. Friedman's (1957) permanent-income model of consumption might be viewed by some as a distinct theory of consumption, but it seems consistent with either the life cycle or Barro model. In brief, the life cycle model, or at least a stylized version of it, views young adults as caring only about their first- and second-period levels of consumption and leisure. Since there is no bequest motive, in the absence or presence of life span uncertainty but with perfect annuity markets, I_t in (2') will be 0. If life cycle agents are not liquidity constrained, i.e., (3) is not binding, they will make their decision about C_{yt} and L_{yt} taking full account of the second-period budget constraint (4). In the absence of uncertainty, taking account of equation (4) means properly discounting future labor earnings in determining one's first-period consumption and labor supply decisions.

The Barro model views individuals as caring not only about their own welfare but also about their children's. Since children care about grandchildren and grandchildren care about great grandchildren, etc., caring about one's children translates into caring about all future descendants. This intergenerational altruism toward one's descendants provides a motive for positive values of intergenerational transfers I_t. Of course, altruism could run in the opposite direction, with children caring about their parents, in which case one would expect negative values of I_t. The degree of foresight assumed in the Barro model is far greater than that in the life cycle model; in the Barro model young individuals at time t have to take into account their own current and future labor earnings and inheritance in deciding how much to consume, but they also have to take into account the future labor earnings and consumption of all their descendants.

The Keynesian model, in contrast to the other two, is not based on an optimization problem; rather it simply asserts that agents consume some fraction of their current incomes and some other fraction of their assets. In time series regressions the estimated marginal propensity to consume out of income is typically close to unity, while the estimated marginal propensity to consume out of wealth is a fairly small fraction. Since Keynesian agents apparently do not consume all their lifetime resources, the Keynesian model also suggests a positive value of I_t in (2').

While there is no formal justification for the Keynesian model, the informal argument rests on some combination of liquidity constraints [equation (3)] and myopia. Clearly, in an economy with positive wealth, not all consumers can be liquidity constrained, but, depending on the distribution of wealth and the timing of labor earnings over the life cycle, a significant fraction of consumers may be liquidity constrained. The notion that consumers are to some extent myopic seems to reflect the view that many consumers will fully or partially ignore the future because the future is highly uncertain and because planning for an uncertain future is a complex and difficult problem.

The Shape of the Age-Consumption Profile

Regardless of which consumption model governs choices, the ratio of C_{yt} to C_{ot+1}, holding constant the present value of lifetime consumption expenditures $[C_{yt} + C_{ot+1}/(1 + r_{t+1})]$, the level of transfers I_t, the interest rate r_{t+1}, and the values of earnings E_{yt} and E_{ot+1}, is an important determinant of savings. According to (2'), a decision by agents to consume more when young, which they finance by consuming less when old, means a lower stock of savings. In simple formulations of the life cycle model in which labor supply is exogenous, one can change just the shape of the age-consumption profile by changing the rate of time preference or the intertemporal elasticity of substitution. In the Barro model there are also ways of changing the shape of the age-consumption profile without changing E_{yt}, E_{ot+1}, r_{t+1}, or I_t. For example, in the Boskin and Kotlikoff (this volume) version of the Barro model, the shape of the age-consumption profile is controlled by age-specific utility weights.

The Keynesian model does not share this feature (often referred to as Ricardian equivalence) of non-liquidity-constrained neoclassical models that the timing of consumption over the life cycle is potentially independent of the timing of exogenous income. In the Keynesian model a present value neutral change in exogenous income that increases income when young and decreases income when old produces an increase in consumption when young. Stated differently, in the Keynesian model the shape of the age-consumption profile depends critically on the shape of the age-income profile.

In addition to changes in agents' general preferences for current as opposed to future consumption, there are other kinds of preference changes that may change the ratio of consumption when young to consumption when old and influence savings. Suppose, for example, that individuals are interested in consuming particular goods in their second period, such as the services from an owner-occupied house. As the demand for second-period housing services rises, agents will save more when young by reducing C_{yt}. As a consequence, total savings in the economy will rise.

The Shape of the Age-Earnings Profile

Just as the time path of consumption can change in neoclassical models without altering the time path of labor earnings, the time path of labor earnings can change with no change in the time path of consumption or the amount of intergenerational transfers. Present-value neutral changes in the timing of labor earnings that involve increased earnings when young, E_{yt}, but leave C_{yt} and I_t unchanged will, according to (2'), raise savings.

Of course, many determinants of the shape of the age-earnings profile also affect the present value of earnings. One example is investment in human capital. The decision to spend more time in school or in training when young may be viewed in this model as lowering E_{yt} in order to raise E_{ot+1}. The decline in E_{yt} lowers savings, and, if the human capital investment has the effect of raising the present value of lifetime earnings, the investment will also likely increase C_{yt} in the life cycle and Barro models. In the Keynesian model the consumption response to increased human capital investment could well be a decline in C_{yt}. In all three models, however, increased human capital investment is likely to imply decreased investment in nonhuman capital, i.e., decreased savings.

The age of retirement is a second important determinant of the age-earnings profile. A decline in the age of retirement can be viewed within the two-period model as a reduction in E_{ot+1}. Presumably, agents who retire earlier will consume less (save more) when young to make up for the loss in earnings in old age (at least in neoclassical models). The reduction in C_{yt} means an increase in savings, holding E_{yt} and I_t fixed. Viewing bequests and inheritances as fixed in response to changes in lifetime earnings may not, however, be appropriate. If bequests are desired because of intergenerational altruism, agents are likely to reduce their bequests in old age and their first- and second-period consumption in response to an earlier retirement. The effect of lower bequests and inheritances could outweigh the reduction in C_{yt} and spell an ultimate net increase in savings (Skinner 1985b). On the other hand, if inheritances arise because annuity insurance is incomplete and agents die before they consume all their assets, the initial higher savings of the first generation that begins to retire early will lead to more, not fewer, bequests to the next generation, as some of the additional assets are passed on to the next generation. This process could lead to more, not less savings in the long run.

A third determinant of the shape of the age-earnings profile is the rate of secular productivity growth. Clearly productivity growth raises savings by raising real wages. In terms of (2') the value of W_{yt} will be larger because of productivity growth. But higher rates of productivity growth also mean steeper age-earnings profiles; wages in the second period of each agent's life will be higher than in the first because of the secular productivity growth. As a consequence, C_{yt} will likely rise by a greater percentage than W_{yt}. In addition, the labor supply response to higher wages in the second period is likely to be a decline in first-period labor supply and an increase in second-period labor supply. Hence, the increase in savings resulting from productivity growth is likely to be less than proportional to the increase in the first-period wage W_{yt}.

Changes in Real Interest Rates

As stressed by Summers (1981a), changes in real interest rates, holding constant the present value of resources, represent uncompensated changes in the relative price of current and future consumption. But real interest rate changes also change the present value of human wealth through the discount factors [$1 + r_{t+1}$ in equation (4)]. In conventional life cycle and Barro models an increase in interest rates typically leads to a decline in consumption when young. In terms of equation (2′), this means an increase in savings. If labor supply is also subject to choice, an increase in interest rates is likely to increase current labor supply relative to future labor supply. Thus E_{yt} is likely to rise when interest rates, ceteris paribus, increase.

The effect of higher interest rates on savings in the Keynesian model is less clear. For young agents who initially have no assets, a higher interest rate will not mean higher first-period income and consequently will not affect C_{yt} through that channel. On the other hand, the amount of inheritance I_t received from one's parents might increase.

In thinking about interest rate changes one must keep in mind that, except for small open economies in which the interest rate is set from abroad, a change in real interest rates is typically associated with a simultaneous change in real wages. Since real wage changes can independently influence savings, analyses of the effects of interest rate changes on savings need to control for changes in real wages.

Intergenerational Transfers

If the intergenerational transfer to the young at time t increases because of increased altruism by their parents, then I_t in (2′) will rise. If the other terms on the right-hand side of (2′) remain unchanged, savings will increase as well. The response of young agents to a larger inheritance is likely to be an increase in their own consumption when young and old and an increase in the bequests to their children. The young may also reduce somewhat their labor supply when young and old. Since the young will spend only a fraction of the increased inheritance on C_{yt}, the net impact on savings of an increase in I_t is likely to be positive. Of course, the young at time t may also experience an increased desire to bequeath. In this case the increase in savings associated with a higher value of I_t may be larger.

Intergenerational transfers may also reflect the absence of an actuarially fair market in annuity insurance. In the two-period model presented so far, there is no uncertainty about the data of death. But the model can easily be altered to include the case when a fraction of each generation dies at the beginning of the second period. Obviously, those who die will have zero end-of-second-period consumption and earnings. Hence the budget constraints (2) and (3) need to be reconsidered. Suppose that we view the variables in these equations as describing the average amounts of consumption, earnings, and assets per individual in generation t. Then the constraints are valid, and savings is still determined by equation (2').

To see this point, suppose that the strict (no intentional bequest) life cycle model holds and that there is an actuarially fair annuities market. In this case no one will make bequests, and I_t and I_{t+1} will be 0. If one takes equations (2) and (4) as holding with equality and combines them by substituting out for A_{t+1}, the resulting equation states that the average (expected) value of consumption when young of members of generation t plus the average (expected) value of consumption when old of members of generation t equals the average (expected) present value of generation t's earnings when young and old. This is precisely the result one expects of a fair annuities market; rather than leaving any resources to the next generation, a fair annuities market transfers the assets of those in generation t that die early to those that survive to the end of their second period. Hence the present value of total generation t realized consumption divided by the size of generation t equals the present value of total generation t realized earnings divided by the size of generation t.

If annuity markets are imperfect or, in the limit, nonexistent, bequests are likely to arise despite the lack of a bequest motive. In this case I_t and I_{t+1} will be positive and should be viewed as the average amount of inheritance received and the average amount of bequests made by members of generation t. Thus, in contrast to the case of a perfect annuity market, A_{t+1} in (2') is likely to be larger because I_t is positive. True, the average value of C_{yt} in (2') may also be larger, reflecting the positive average value of inheritance I_t and the possible desire to hedge the uncertainty of the date of death by consuming more when young. But, on balance, the effect of imperfect annuity insurance is likely to raise savings, potentially by a large amount.

Uncertainty

While the positive effect on savings of lifetime uncertainty in the absence of annuity insurance works primarily through an increase in I_t, a reduced value of C_{yt} is often the source of precautionary saving in response to other types of uninsured uncertainties. Earnings uncertainty is one example; consider a mean preserving spread of the value of E_{ot+1}. Although Sandmo (1970) has shown that the response of C_{yt} to uncertainty in E_{ot+1} is theoretically ambiguous, the response that seems most plausible empirically is a decline in C_{yt}, and, according to (2'), an increase in savings. Other types of uncertainty, such as uncertainty concerning future government taxes and transfers and uncertainty concerning future health expenditures, is also likely to lead to significant precautionary savings (e.g., see chapter 6).

Clearly, the provision of various forms of insurance, such as unemployment and disability insurance, is likely to reduce the amount of precautionary savings. But even when formal insurance markets do not exist, insurance may nonetheless be available. The reason is that families can self-insure; that is, they can form an implicit, incomplete insurance market (see chapter 4 for an example). For instance, with earnings uncertainty the ability of a spouse to increase his or her earnings in case the other spouse suffers a loss in earnings constitutes implicit earnings insurance. Family insurance of this kind can reduce the precautionary demand for savings.

Demographics

Obviously, since equation (2') describes the assets per elderly in the two-period economy, the product of the population size of generation t and A_{t+1} determines the total amount of savings. Since the real wage and the real interest rate depend on capital per worker, assuming a constant returns to scale technology, the amount of savings per worker a_{t+1} expressed in (5) is the focus of most discussions of savings and population growth:

$$a_{t+1} = (E_{yt} + I_t - C_{yt})/(1 + n). \tag{5}$$

In (5) the term n stands for the population growth rate; that is, for each old person there are $1 + n$ young people at any point in time. Holding E_{yt}, I_t, and C_{yt} constant, an increase in n leads to a decline in assets per worker. In general equilibrium this effect would feed back to lower real wages and raise the real rate of return. The net impact of these factor price changes is likely to be a further reduction in savings per worker.

A second important effect of population growth on saving per worker involves the added consumption expenditures and loss of female earnings from raising more children. While the model so far has ignored children and has treated agents as effectively being born into adulthood, this unrealistic

treatment can be easily modified. Suppose that we model young adults as having young children whose consumption is included in C_{yt}. Then the increase in children per young adult will mean an increase in C_{yt} and, possibly, a decline in E_{yt} because of mothers' time out of the labor force. The explanation for the higher value of C_{yt} is the following: While the increased consumption expenditures on children will necessitate a reduction in the adult parent's consumption both when young and when old, on balance, C_{yt}, which now includes expenditures on children, will increase. Stated differently, the increase in children per young adult leads to a shift in the age-consumption profile toward more consumption in the first period. The higher value of C_{yt} and the possibly lower value of E_{yt} provide an additional reason why population growth reduces saving per worker.

While these effects of demographics on savings are easy to see, demographic change can have more subtle effects on saving. Consider the effect on savings of an increase in divorce rates. The uncertainty about the longevity of one's marriage and therefore the extent of support by one's spouse may lead each spouse to accumulate more human capital when young to hedge the possibility of being divorced and self-sufficient in the future. As mentioned, increased human capital accumulation is likely to occur at the expense of nonhuman capital accumulation. On the other hand, uncertainty about divorce could raise, rather than lower savings; young agents may try to hedge themselves against future divorce by lowering C_{yt}. In general, the actual or potential size of one's family helps determine the extent of possible implicit family insurance. And the smaller the extent of family insurance, the greater the motive for precautionary savings.

Fiscal Policy

Extending the Analytical Framework
So far I have not introduced fiscal policy into the savings framework. While there are several notational choices for discussing fiscal policy, the use of certain notation and accounting conventions can blur the fundamental similarities of a variety of fiscal policies (see chapters 7 through 10). To avoid any possibility of fiscal illusion, assume that fiscal policy works in the following manner: In each period t the government simply orders the young generation to purchase an amount G_t per young person of consumption for the government. The government in period t also orders the old generation to transfer an amount Z_t per young person to the young generation. With these assumptions and the simplifying assumption of zero population growth, the amount of savings per old person at time $t + 1$ can

be written as

$$A_{t+1} = w_{yt}L_{yt} + I_t + Z_t - C_{yt} - G_t. \tag{6}$$

And, assuming either that A_{t+1} is positive or that there are no liquidity constraints, the present value budget constraint is now

$$C_{yt} + \frac{C_{ot+1}}{1 + r_{t+1}} + \frac{I_{ot+1}}{1 + r_{t+1}} + G_t + \frac{Z_{t+1}}{1 + r_{t+1}}$$

$$= w_{yt}L_{yt} + \frac{w_{ot+1}L_{ot+1}}{1 + r_{t+1}} + I_t + Z_t. \tag{7}$$

Equation (6) suggests two important possible effects of fiscal policy on savings. One involves the effects of redistributing across generations, and the other involves the effects of increases in government consumption.

Intergenerational Redistribution
Consider first the issue of intergenerational redistribution in a pure life cycle model in which I_t and I_{t+1} are 0. Holding G_t fixed, suppose that at the beginning of time t the government orders the elderly to increase their end of time t required transfers Z_t to the young. Also suppose that there is no change in Z_{t+1}. This policy will then lead to an increase in A_{t+1}; to see this, note that Z_t in (6) rises. Although C_{yt} will also increase, if second-period consumption is a normal good, the increase in C_{yt} will be less than the increase in Z_t, and A_{t+1} will increase. Next, examine the effect of an ongoing transfer from the old to the young in which Z_t, Z_{t+1}, Z_{t+2}, etc. are all increased by a fixed amount. Equations (6) and (7) indicate that this policy will also increase savings but in future periods as well as period $t + 1$. According to (7) an equal increase in Z_t and Z_{t+1} implies an expansion of the present-value budget opportunities and will lead to an increase in C_{yt}; but the increase in C_{yt} will be smaller than when Z_{t+1} is fixed. Again, from (6), A_{t+1} rises because Z_t increases more than C_{yt} (and more than $w_{yt}L_{yt}$ falls, if L_{yt} is variable). The same reasoning indicates that A_{t+2}, A_{t+3}, etc. are all larger because of the government's intergenerational redistribution. The change in savings will have general equilibrium implications for the time path of wage rates and interest rates, but these changes in factor prices are likely to reinforce the partial equilibrium effects on the time path of savings.

In the Barro model temporary or permanent increases in the time path of Z_t will have no effect on savings because the time path of I_t will adjust to exactly offset changes in Z_t. For example, suppose that the government orders an increase in the time path of the Z_t's in which Z_t, Z_{t+1}, Z_{t+2}, etc.

all increase by a fixed amount. In the Barro model, I_t, I_{t+1}, I_{t+2}, etc. will all be reduced by the same fixed amount, leaving the time path of assets (the A_t's) unchanged. The intuition here is that in the Barro model families are otherwise transferring resources across generations. Since the government's policy does not alter the total resources of the intergenerationally altruistic extended family, the family will simply offset the government's policy by returning in terms of private transfers the resources it was forced to transfer by the government.

If one models Keynesian consumption behavior as involving agents who consume a fixed fraction, say θ, of their income plus government transfers (but not including private transfers), then an increase in Z_t in the Keynesian model will likewise have no effect on A_{t+1}. To see this, note that C_{yt} will rise by $\theta \Delta Z_t$. But I_t in (6) will fall by $(1 - \theta)\Delta Z_t$. And since Z_t in (6) rises by ΔZ_t, the net impact on A_{t+1} is 0. Unlike the life cycle model in which the marginal propensity to consume of the old is unity and exceeds the marginal propensity to consume of the young, in the Keynesian model the marginal propensities to consume of the young and old are equal; hence redistribution between the young and the old has no effect on savings.[1]

Increases in Government Consumption

The second policy to consider is changes in G_t. In practice, increases in government consumption will likely involve concomitant changes in the time path of the Z_t's; that is, the government will typically spread the burden of paying for an increase in its consumption over all generations, including the initial old generation. But since changes in the time path of the Z_t's have just been discussed, it may help to clarify effects by discussing changes in G_t holding the time path of the Z_t's fixed.

In the life cycle model a one-time increase in G_t holding the Z_t's fixed will, in general, lead to a temporary decline in savings. In (6), A_{t+1} declines because G_t rises by more than the associated decline in C_{yt}; if C_{ot+1} is a normal good, members of generation t will pay for the higher G_t by reducing C_{ot+1} and C_{yt}. Hence C_{yt} will fall by less than G_t. In addition, L_{yt} is likely to increase if first-period leisure is also a normal good. In contrast to a one-time increase in government consumption, a permanent increase in the time path of the G_t's will permanently lower savings in the life cycle model. There will be temporary changes in factor prices for the temporary increase in government consumption and permanent changes in factor prices for permanent increases in government consumption. These general equilibrium factor price response will, in general, reinforce the partial equilibrium effects of changes in the time path of the G_t's on savings.

The impact of a temporary increase in G_t in the Barro model is also a short-term reduction in savings. The Barro dynastic family will adjust their intergenerational transfers, the time path of the I_t's, to spread the burden of paying of the temporary increase in G_t over all current and future family members. As a consequence, in the formula for A_{t+1} the reduction in G_t will lead to a much smaller offsetting reduction in C_{yt} than in the life cycle model. In addition, I_t will increase somewhat, but the likely net impact will be a decline in A_{t+1}. On the other hand, if the increase in government consumption is permanent, there may be no effect on savings. Suppose, for example, that labor is inelastically supplied and that the Barro family responds to a permanent increase of ΔG in the time path of the G_t's by reducing its total consumption each period ($C_{yt} + C_{ot}$) by the same amount ΔG. In this case total private plus government consumption is unchanged, as is national income. Since national saving equals national income less total consumption, national saving is unaffected by the policy. In terms of equation (6), the increase in G_t is exactly offset by a decline in C_{yt} and an increase in I_t, leaving A_{t+1} unaffected. If labor supply is variable, the Barro family may increase its labor supply rather than fully absorb the increase in government consumption through a decline in its consumption. In this case savings may again be unaffected, depending on the precise responses.

The Keynesian model predicts temporary and permanent declines in savings from temporary and permanent increases in government consumption, respectively, still assuming no change in the time path of the Z_t's. The decrease in disposable income leads young Keynesian agents to reduce C_{yt} by a fraction θ of the increase in G_t, but the net effect, according to equation (6), is a reduction in A_{t+1} by $(1 - \theta)\Delta G_t$.

Intragenerational Redistribution
In addition to the income effects of intergeneration redistribution (the Z_t's) policy and government consumption (the G_t's) policies, lump sum intragenerational redistribution has income effects that may alter savings. Consider at time t lump sum transfers from type A young individuals to type B young individuals. In the life cycle model if the B individuals have larger marginal propensities to consume goods (a flatter age-consumption profile) and leisure (a steeper age-earnings profile), this policy will raise the average value of C_{yt} and lower aggregate savings.

In the Barro model the story is quite similar, but one must consider how the preferences of the Barro family to which individual A belongs differ from those of the Barro family to which individual B belongs. If the Barro family containing individual B has larger marginal consumption and leisure propensities than the Barro family containing individual A, the redistribution will also reduce A_{t+1}. For example, if the Barro family receiving the transfer discounts the utility of future generations at a higher rate than the Barro family providing the transfer, the redistribution will reduce subsequent aggregate bequests and lower current saving.

Finally, in the Keynesian model, the time t redistribution will lower A_{t+1} if person B's marginal propensity to consume exceeds person A's. Even if the policy is discontinued after time t, it is likely to permanently reduce the time path of savings through its impact on the time path of the average value of the I_t's.

Distortionary Taxation

To this point the issue of distortionary taxation has been skirted by assuming that the government can simply command each young generation to purchase G_t and each old generation to transfer Z_t to the contemporaneous young generation. To add distortionary taxation to the analysis, consider distortionary taxes that are compensated in a lump sum manner to the individuals paying the distortionary taxes in the period the taxes are paid. In contrast to the Z_t's and G_t's, policies that have only income effects, these compensated distortionary taxes have only incentive effects. In combination with a proper choice of the Z_t's, G_t's, and intragenerational redistribution policies, these compensated distortionary taxes can be used fully to describe any actual fiscal policy. To see this point most clearly for neoclassical consumption theories, recall that any fiscal policy will ultimately affect individual behavior through its effects on the individual's budget constraint. Changes in an individual's budget constraint will produce movements from one indifference curve to another. But such movements can always be decomposed into a substitution effect plus an income effect.

The compensated distortionary taxes that are of most interest to a discussion of savings are compensated capital income taxes, compensated labor taxes, and compensated consumption taxes. Consider first the effects of compensated taxes in the life cycle model, and ignore changes through time in distortionary taxes. In a two-period model in which labor supply is exogenous, a compensated capital income tax leads to an increase in C_{yt} and a decrease in C_{ot+1} and, according to (6), decreases savings. If labor supply is endogenous, compensated capital income taxes are likely to increase C_{yt} and to decrease L_{yt}, also implying a decline in savings. Time-invariant compensated labor income taxes and compensated consumption taxes distort consumption-leisure choices and are likely to lead to a reduction in L_{yt} and C_{yt}. The likely net effect on savings from time-invariant compensated labor or consumption taxes is negative.

If the compensated labor or consumption taxes differ across the two periods, these taxes will distort not only the choice between consumption and leisure at a point in time but also the choice between consumption when young and consumption when old and the choice between leisure when young and leisure when old. For example, if the compensated tax rate on second-period consumption exceeds that on first-period consumption, this difference in tax rates acts, in part, like a compensated capital income tax in that it raises the price of future consumption relative to current consumption.

The effects of compensated taxes in the Barro model on first- and second-period consumption and leisure are similar. But in the Barro model one must also consider how voluntary intergenerational transfers will be affected. Since such transfers facilitate the consumption of future members of the altruistic family, a time-invariant capital income tax raises the price of Barro family consumption beyond period $t + 1$ relative to consumption at time t. Hence the impact of a time-invariant compensated tax on capital income is likely to be a reduction in I_t in equation (6) that reinforces the likely increase in C_{yt} and decline in L_{yt} in reducing savings. Time-invariant compensated labor or consumption taxes are also likely to reduce the time path of the I_t's. The reason is that the Barro family will substitute leisure, both today and in the future, for consumption, both today and in the future.

In the Keynesian model, or at least a simplified version of the Keynesian model, relative prices of current and future consumption and leisure do not influence consumption decisions. Hence, since they also do not affect disposable income, compensated taxes appear to have no savings effects in the Keynesian model.

Translating Actual Fiscal Policies into Paths of Z_t's and G_ts, Intragenerational Redistribution, and Compensated Distortionary Taxes
While space does not permit a lengthy categorization of fiscal policies in terms of the fundamental components just discussed, it may be useful to provide a few translations. To make the examples concrete, consider the recent Reagan fiscal policy. It combined income tax cuts, major reductions in future Social Security benefits, reductions in tax progressivity, a short-lived (six-year) shift from income toward consumption taxation, and a reduction in federal government consumption as a share of net national product (Boskin and Robinson 1987).

The last of these five policies can be disposed of quickly since it corresponds to an at least temporary decline in the time path of the G_t's. The income tax cut that produced the large official federal deficits can be viewed as a combination of an at least temporary reduction in compensated capital income and labor income taxes combined with an ongoing reduction in the Z_t's; that is, the deficit can be viewed as transferring to current generations from future generations by reducing the amount each generation is forced by the government to hand back to the succeeding generation.

The reduction in future Social Security benefits, in contrast, can be viewed as increasing the Z_t's, starting at time $t + 1$ (where a period stands for a generation). Since Social Security is unfunded, the 1983 cut in the future Social Security benefits of baby boomers means a smaller redistribution to them from their children and smaller subsequent redistributions from later to earlier generations; it means larger values of the Z_t's starting with Z_{t+1}. Using this more basic fiscal policy language makes clear that the 1983 Social Security policy is an intergenerational redistribution policy that offsets the intergenerational redistribution associated with the Reagan tax cuts.

The changes in tax progressivity can be described as compensated reductions in capital and labor income tax rates plus intragenerational redistribution from high- to low-income households. And the 1981 shift toward consumption taxation in the Economic Recovery Tax Act, which was reversed in the 1986 Tax Reform Act, can be understood as combining a short-lived reduction in compensated capital income taxes with a short-lived increase in Z_t that reflects the policy's short-lived likely effects on the asset values of existing capital [see Summers (1981b) and chapter 9].

As discussed in Kotlikoff (1988), the combination of these policies appears, at least from a life cycle perspective, to have provided a small stimulus to savings. This view differs, of course, from most popular accounts of the Reagan fiscal policy that have focused almost exclusively on the federal deficits of this period.

A Review of Knowledge Concerning Savings Determinants

Time Series Evidence Concerning the Consumption Function

Time series consumption regressions represent one set of studies bearing on the true nature of the consumption function. These regressions typically relate aggregate consumption to disposable income, aggregate wealth, the real interest rate, and measure of government policy, such as government debt. As a rule these studies report significant coefficients for disposable income and wealth, but the coefficients on the interest rate and government policy variables are sensitive to the precise specification of the regression and the dates of the sample.

It is quite difficult to interpret the results of the standard time series regressions with respect to alternative models of savings. The reason is that these regressions seem to mix various models rather than choose one as a null hypothesis that can be tested. An example of this problem is the time series literature that purports to test the effects of Social Security on savings by including Social Security wealth among the set of regressors. This literature includes the studies of Feldstein (1974c), Barro (1978a,b), Darby (1979), and Leimer and Lesnoy (1980). The results of this body of research can be summarized with one word, ambiguous. Even if the results all agreed, it would be difficult to know precisely what had been learned; as pointed out in chapter 19 and Williamson and Jones (1983), if the life cycle model is taken as the null hypothesis in these studies, the models are misspecified because of the inability to aggregate the behavior of different age groups. Chapter 19 shows that these time series regression procedures would reject the life cycle model even using data taken from a pure life cycle economy. An alternative view of these regressions is that the Barro model is the null hypothesis. But in this case the regressions are also misspecified because they use disposable income rather than the present value of human wealth and because they ignore the government's intertemporal budget constraint.

A different time series literature that is relevant for distinguishing neoclassical models from the Keynesian model is the Euler equation study of Hall (1978) and closely related studies of Sargent (1978), Flavin (1981), Mankiw, Rotemberg, and Summers (1982, 1983), Davidson and Hendry (1981), Daly and Hadjimatheou (1981), Cuddington (1982), Bilson (1980), Muellbauer (1982), and others. These papers test intertemporal expected utility maximization, specifically its implication that the Euler error is uncorrelated with previous information. A rejection of this null hypothesis would rule out neoclassical consumption models. But, as stressed by King (1983), tests of the Euler equation require specifying the explicit form of preferences, and rejection of the Euler equation may simply reflect an incorrect formulation of preferences. In addition, analysis of the Euler relationship using time series data requires the questionable assumption that one can aggregate the Euler equations of millions of households into a single relationship that is based on per capita consumption.

The time series tests of the Euler equation have provided mixed results. Hall's (1978) results are generally supportive of the Euler equation's implication that past information does not predict the evolution of the marginal utility of consumption. On the other hand, Flavin (1981) and Mankiw, Rotemberg, and Summers (1982) reject the equation's implication. While the studies subsequent to Hall's use the same consumption time series and as such are not independent tests of the Euler proposition, it is clear that the time series Euler relationship is not robust.

Another time series approach to testing neoclassical consumption functions that is closely related to the Euler equation tests involves estimating the volatility of income changes and determining whether consumption responses to that income volatility are too small or too large. Flavin's (1981) study provides an early comparison of income and consumption changes. She finds that consumption responses are excessively volatile. Other studies, such as Kotlikoff and Pakes (1988), West (1987), and Campbell and Deaton (1987) show that consumption is not sufficiently sensitive to changes in income. The jury is clearly still out on this question. The research by Mankiw and Shapiro (1985), Deaton (1986), Campbell and Deaton (1987), and West (1987) points out that conclusions about excessive sensitivity of consumption to income changes hinge critically on how one models the income process.

A fourth approach is to use time series data to estimate a structural model of consumption. This is possible for certain simple versions of the Barro model because this model aggregates much more nicely than the life cycle model. Chapter 18, a joint study will Michael Boskin, illustrates this approach. This study determines the optimal consumption plan for a Barro dynasty, with a known future course of demographic change, that faces uncertainty with respect to labor earnings and rates of return. The joint distribution of earnings and rates of return is estimated empirically and used to calculate the optimal annual consumption path. This predicted time path of consumption is then compared with actual consumption. While the fit is fairly good, the study goes on to consider whether the deviation between the actual time path of consumption and the predicted time path depends on proxies for the age-distribution of resources. As demonstrated in chapter 3, in the Barro model or other models in which individuals are altruistically linked, the distribution of resources within altruistically linked clans of individuals does not influence the distribution or level of consumption of such individuals. Chapter 18 reports a rejection of this proposition; the level of aggregate consumption appears, in part, to be determined by the age-distribution of resources. While the chapter 18 results cast doubt on the Barro model, they are certainly not definitive; the analysis may be subject to aggregation bias if different Barro clans have different preferences. In addition, the specification of preferences and uncertainty may be inappropriate.

A fifth type of time series research on consumption includes articles by Poterba (1987a,b) and Wilcox (1987a,b). These event studies compare monthly changes in consumption expenditure to specific one-time changes in disposable income. The goal is to determine whether the consumption changes are larger than would be suggested by neoclassical consumption functions. Poterba (1987a) and Wilcox (1987b) report evidence of sizable consumption responses that are consistent with a view that roughly one-quarter of households are Keynesian consumers. Wilcox (1987a), on the other hand, reports small consumption responses to disposable income changes—the kind of responses suggested by neoclassical models. Even if these three studies agreed, one might question whether the result was picking up something other than Keynesian behavior. The aggregation problems in these kinds of analyses seem as troublesome as the problems in other time series consumption studies.

In sum, problems of aggregation make reliance on macroeconomic time series tests of microeconomic behavior highly suspect. And the time series evidence that seems least suspect permits no strong conclusion about the nature of consumption preferences.

Cross Section and Panel Studies of Consumption

Much of the recent consumption research based on microeconomic data involves tests of Hall's (1978) Euler error proposition. This research has paid special attention to the possibility that some consumers are liquidity constrained. The conclusion that emerges from a number of studies including Hall and Mishkin (1982), Hayashi (1982, 1984, 1985), Shapiro (1986), Zeldes (1985), Runkle (1983), and Lawrence (1983) is that roughly 20 percent of US households are liquidity constrained. These households are among the poorest in the economy and presumably account for much less than 20 percent of US consumption.

Not all studies support the conclusion that even 20 percent of households are liquidity constrained or otherwise act like Keynesian consumers. In a recent and careful panel analysis of consumption, Altonji and Siow (1986) develop a regression equation that nests both the life cycle and Keynesian models. They conclude that "the vast majority of households obey the life cycle model" (p. 319). They also point out that failure to account for measurement error in income may lead one inappropriately to accept the Keynesian model. Finally, their tests of the pure life cycle model against a life cycle model with liquidity constraints "do not show much evidence against the perfect capital markets assumption" (p. 322).

Most of the Euler tests based on microeconomic data can be viewed as testing both the Barro and the life cycle models against the Keynesian liquidity-constrained alternative. What is missing in this literature are tests of the Barro model against the life cycle model. The reason for this is the lack of data on either the consumption or income of extended families. As suggested in chapter 3 and by Bernheim and Bagwell (1986), who independently reached the same conclusion, the extended family may be very, very large because of altruistic linkages arising from marriage across otherwise distinct extended families. One approach to testing the Barro model against alternatives that does not require extended family data is the study by Abel and Kotlikoff (1988). This study shows that, under the assumptions of homothetic and time separable utility, the Barro clan will respond to shocks to the incomes of its members by having the consumption of all members increase or decrease by the same percentage. With some weak additional assumptions, this proposition implies that the average percentage change in household consumption within an age cohort should be the same for all age cohorts.

Testing the Barro model by comparing average percentage changes in consumption across age cohorts is particularly advantageous because it is nonparametric; in determining whether the average consumption of different age cohorts move together, Abel and Kotlikoff place no restrictions on preferences beyond the assumptions of homotheticity and time separability. In particular, each Barro clan can have quite different preference parameters.

The null hypothesis of their test is that cohort differences in the average percentage change in consumption are due simply to sampling and measurement error. Alternative hypotheses, suggested by the life cycle model, are that (1) the percentage changes in the average consumption of any two cohorts are more highly correlated the closer in age are the two cohorts and (2) the variance in the percentage change in consumption is a monotone function of the age of the cohort. Their US Consumer Expenditure Survey data for the 1980s fail to reject the null hypothesis of equal average percentage changes in consumption. Indeed, their results provide fairly strong support for the intergenerational altruism model as opposed to the life cycle model.

In addition to the microeconomic-level Euler equation literature, there is a short literature that tests the life cycle model's implication that Social Security reduces private savings. This literature includes Feldstein and Pellechio (1979), chapter 15, Kurz (1981), Blinder, Gordon, and Wise (1981), and Diamond and Hausman (1984). The results here are mixed; some studies and aspects of some studies support the life cycle model's predictions. Others are at odds with its predictions. For example, in considering the savings response to Social Security, Blinder, Gordon, and Wise also test whether the marginal propensity to consume rises with age as predicted by the life cycle model (at least under certainty). They find no evidence that such is the case. In contrast to other microeconomic empirical research, much of the data used in this literature are quite weak. Since the key social security variables are constructed based on estimates of future labor earnings and since many of these data sets report only current earnings, the critical Social Security variables are often estimated based on current earnings. Hence these variables are measured with error—error that is correlated with other resource variables in the regressions.

To summarize the findings based on microeconomic data, the strongest empirical evidence supports neoclassical models over the Keynesian liquidity-constrained alternative for most US households. For a minority, about 20 percent, the Keynesian liquidity-constrained model is probably most appropriate. Determining which neoclassical formulation best describes the consumption behavior of most US households remains an important task but a task that may require extended family data as well as the construction of statistical frameworks that nest both the life cycle and Barro models.

Testing the Rationality of Life Cycle Consumption Choice

The assumption that consumers make rational choices is a maintained hypothesis that is rarely tested in empirical research, although it is viewed by many as implausible [e.g., Thaler and Sheffrin (1981)]. One way to explore the issue of rationality is through experiments. Johnson, Kotlikoff, and Samuelson (1987) report an experiment in which subjects are paid to answer a computerized consumption questionnaire. The experiment is non-salient in that subjects are not rewarded for their answers. Despite this feature, subjects appeared to take the experiment seriously and took their time to answer the questionnaire. The questionnaire asks subjects to place themselves in a simple life cycle setting, one in which they are single, are of a given age, face no uncertainty, face a given life span, have a given amount of initial assets and a given stream of labor earnings, and can borrow and lend at a fixed real interest rate. As the computer changes the parameters of the life cycle setting, it solicits consumption choices.

The questions in the experiment are designed to test rational choice and to elicit information about preferences. The questionnaire intersperses, in a subtle manner, seventeen pairs of cases in which the present value of resources is the same but the mix between human and nonhuman wealth differs. Many of the subjects clearly undervalued future earnings streams, a result that is suggested by the Keynesian model. Indeed, the subject's responses suggest a widespread inability to make coherent and consistent consumption decisions. Errors in consumption decision making appear to be substantial and, in many cases, systematic. In addition, the experiment's data strongly reject the standard time-separable homothetic life cycle model of consumption choice.

While this type of research is in its infancy, these findings raise serious questions about the ability of the typical person to make consumption choices that, at least on average, mimic the results of highly complex dynamic optimization problems.

A second way to consider consumer rationality is to examine whether households' saving and insurance decisions are grossly at odds with what one would expect sensible people to do. Diamond (1977) and Kotlikoff, Spivak, and Summers (this volume) examine the adequacy of savings, and Holden, Burkhauser, and Myers (1986), Myers, Burkhauser, and Holden (1986), Auerbach and Kotlikoff (1987), and Hurd and Wise (1987) consider whether the amount of life insurance households purchase is adequate. The method Kotlikoff, Spivak, and Shoven used to consider the adequacy of savings is to compare, albeit inferentially, the level of consumption in old age with the level of consumption when young. Evidence of dramatically lower levels of consumption when old relative to consumption when young would suggest either remarkably poor planning or extreme poor fortune. While Diamond reports that a significant fraction of US elderly have small or zero amounts of net worth, Kotlikoff, Spivak, and Summers show that, once one takes account of Social Security, pensions, and labor earnings, there is no evidence of widespread irrational undersaving. Quite the contrary, they find surprisingly few elderly households who appear to have saved far too little.

The research on life insurance purchase leads, however, to the opposite conclusion. Here it seems quite clear that most US couples, in which one spouse is the principal earner, are underinsured and a significant fraction are dramatically underinsured. In addition, households fail to adjust their purchase of life insurance in response to survivor insurance provided by Social

Security, suggesting that they improperly value Social Security's provision of insurance.

In sum, the initial experimental evidence and the analyses of life insurance holdings raise real questions as to the ability of consumers to make complex intertemporal consumption choices consistently and coherently. When juxtaposed with the microeconomic and time series evidence, the resulting picture concerning the true nature of the consumption function is quite mixed. Given the reservations about the time series studies, one should probably given strongest weight to the cross section and panel studies, which, on balance, strongly support the neoclassical view; but research on consumer rationality and casual introspective give one considerable pause.

How Changes in the Shapes of Age-Earnings and Age-Consumption Profiles Affect Savings

An Illustration from the Auerbach-Kotlikoff Simulation Model
The importance of the shape of consumption profiles is demonstrated in Tobin's (1969) and subsequent simulation studies of life cycle savings. There has been much less analysis of the savings effects of changes in the shapes of age-earnings profiles on savings. The Auerbach-Kotlikoff dynamic life cycle simulation model (henceforth, the AK model) is convenient for illustrating the effects of changes in preferences that influence both age-earnings and age-consumption profiles. The AK model, which is described in detail in Auerbach and Kotlikoff (1987), is a pure life cycle model, which solves for the economy's perfect foresight general equilibrium transition path from one steady state to another. Agents life for 55 periods, face no uncertainty, and have a time-separable CES utility function in consumption and leisure. There are two factors of production, capital and labor, and the production function is also CES.

Equations (8) and (9) indicate, respectively, how the growth of consumption and leisure as one ages in the AK model are related to the model's preference parameters and factor prices:

$$C_t = [(1 + r_t)/(1 + \delta)]^\gamma (v_t/v_{t-1}) C_{t-1}, \tag{8}$$

$$l_t = [(1 + r_t)/(1 + \delta)]^\gamma (v_t/v_{t-1})^{-\rho} (w_t^*/w_{t-1}^*)^{-\rho} l_{t-1}, \tag{9}$$

where

$$v_t = [1 + \alpha \rho w_t^{*(1-\rho)}]^{(\rho-\gamma)/(1-\rho)} \tag{10}$$

and

$$w_t^* = (w_t e_t + \mu_t).$$ (11)

In these equations w_t and r_t are the wage rate per effective unit of labor and the interest rate, respectively, in period t. In the presence of taxes these factor prices need to be modified appropriately. The terms γ, ρ, δ, and α are, respectively, the intertemporal elasticity of substitution, the static elasticity of substitution, the time preference rate, and a leisure share parameter that enters the CES utility function. The term w_t^* is the worker's effective wage at time t. It equals the sum of μ_t, the shadow wage on the constraint on nonnegative labor supply plus the product of the economy-wide wage per unit of effective labor w_t and e_t, which determines the age profile of effective labor supply; that is, the e_t profile permits workers to become more productive over the life cycle.

According to equations (8) and (9), the larger δ is, the time preference rate, the flatter the age-consumption profile and the steeper the age-earnings profile (since the age-leisure profile is flatter)—both of which reduce savings. The values of the other taste parameters influence the effects of changes in δ on the slopes of the age-consumption and age-earnings profiles. Next consider simultaneous increases in γ and ρ under the assumptions that γ and ρ are equal and that w_t^* does not change over the life cycle. In this case the growth rates of consumption and leisure over the life cycle are identical, and, assuming that r_t exceeds δ, increases in γ steepen the age-consumption profile and flatten the age-earnings profile over the life cycle—both of which stimulate savings. When γ and ρ are not equal, the effect of increases in γ will also depend on the shape of the age-effective wage profile. The shape of the e_t profile, on which the shape of w_t^* in part depends, is based on estimates for the United States by Welch (1979). The e_t profile peaks at age 30 (corresponding to a real world age of about 50), and wages at that age are 45 percent greater than at age 1 (a real world age of 21).

Table 1 reports the impact in the AK model of different values of γ and δ on steady-state aggregate savings, national income, aggregate labor supply, the wage per effective unit of labor input, and the interest rate. The table assumes a 15 percent proportional income tax, a value of ρ of 0.8, a value of α of 1.5, and a Cobb-Douglas production function in which capital's income share is 0.25. The changes in preference parameters in the table are not small in terms of their effects on behavior. For example, when γ equals 0.25, a value of ρ of 5 percent rather than 1.5 percent means a growth rate of consumption that is almost 60 percent larger.

Table 1
Effects on steady-state savings and other variables of changes in the shapes of age-earnings and age-consumption profiles

| Parameters | | | | | | |
γ	δ	Savings	Income	Labor supply	Wage rate	Interest rate (%)
0.25	0.015	95	25	19.1	1.00	7
0.10	0.015	45	21	19.3	0.82	12
0.50	0.015	148	29	19.2	1.11	5
0.25	0.050	55	22	19.2	0.87	10
0.25	−0.030	202	31	19.3	1.20	4

As demonstrated by table 1, savings is highly sensitive to variations in preferences that influence the shapes of age-earnings and age-consumption profiles. When the intertemporal elasticity of substitution γ increases from 0.25 to 0.50, savings increases by more than 50 percent. When the rate of time preference δ increases from 1.5 percent to 5 percent, savings declines by almost half.

The Effects of Liquidity Constraints on the Age-Consumption Profile and Savings

A recent simulation study of savings and liquidity constraints by Hubbard and Judd (1986a,b) provides a sense of the possible importance of liquidity constraints. This research, which follows in the footsteps of earlier work by Tobin and Dolde (1971a,b), indicates that liquidity constraints can play a major role in the determination of savings. Simulations in the Hubbard and Judd 55-period life cycle model in which young individuals are liquidity constrained for nine years (from age 20 to 29) indicate that the liquidity constraints could raise aggregate savings by as much as one-third. These results, like all simulation analyses, are sensitive to assumptions. In this case the assumption that all young individuals are liquidity constrained for extended periods seems rather strong. It ignores the possibility that the young can borrow from their parents and other relatives. By omitting intergenerational transfers, their model also ignores the possibility that some of the young inherit sufficient assets or receive large enough gifts (such as college tuition) that liquidity constraints are not binding.

The data, at least for the United States, indicate that young households on average have positive net worth. Hence it may be more appropriate to model liquidity constraints along the lines of Lawrence (1983), in which only a segment of individuals, those in occupations with steep age-earnings profiles, are liquidity constrained. Lawrence's simulation analysis suggests a smaller effect on aggregate savings of liquidity constraints.

Zeldes's (1986) analysis, on the other hand, suggests that certainty models are likely to understate the savings effects of liquidity constraints. Zeldes demonstrates that, when future labor earnings are uncertain, consumers may increase their current saving, not because they are currently liquidity constrained but because they may be liquidity constrained in the future. With the use of simulation techniques, Zeldes demonstrates that possible future liquidity constraints can have a nontrivial impact on current consumption and aggregate savings.

The Importance of Intergenerational Transfers to Savings

Chapter 2 provides an extensive review of recent research on the importance of intergenerational transfers to savings. As the chapter demonstrates, a wide variety of evidence suggests that intergenerational transfers play a major role, if not a predominant role in US wealth accumulation. Other studies, including Hayashi (1986), indicate that the same is true for Japan. The literature indicates (1) that the shapes of age-consumption and age-earnings profiles are far different from those needed to generate considerable life cycle savings [e.g., Darby (1979) and chapter 1], (2) that the elderly dissave far less than is predicted by the life cycle model [e.g., Mirer (1979), Bernheim (1986), and Danziger et al. (1983)], (3) that the distribution of wealth can only be explained by significant intergenerational transfers [e.g., Atkinson (1971), Oulton (1976)], (4) that the elderly fail to purchase annuity insurance even on actuarially fair terms (Bernheim et al. 1985), (5) that savings has been unresponsive to changes in the length of retirement, and (6) that life cycle simulation studies with reasonable parameter values predict far less wealth than is actually observed (e.g., chapter 13).

Knowing that intergenerational transfers are important and knowing why they arise are two different things. As mentioned, the recent simulation literature on nonaltruistic bequests suggests that much of non-life-cycle intergenerational transfer wealth could potentially be traced to imperfections in annuity insurance arrangements. But true intergenerational altruism —the desire to improve the circumstances of one's descendants—is surely a major, if not the major, factor in explaining savings resulting from intergenerational transfers. As chapter 2 observes, sorting out altruistic from nonaltruistic motives in intergenerational transfers appears to require data on the extended family, not simply data on individual households.

In general, the limited data on bequests and inter vivos transfers also makes studying intergenerational transfers difficult. But one source of data on bequests appears to have been underutilized. This is data taken from living respondents on their current net worth plus face value of life insurance. Together these pieces of information determine the bequest a living survey respondent would leave (ignoring burial and related costs) if the respondent were to die at the time of the survey. As chapter 16 stresses, since life span is uncertain, individuals choose a level of bequests at each point in their lives; that is, there is not a single planned terminal bequest but rather age-specific bequests contingent on dying at that age. Chapter 16 examines such contingent bequests and reaches a surprising conclusion, namely, that the elasticity of bequests with respect to lifetime resources is less than unity. This finding implies that redistribution from the lifetime rich to the lifetime poor will increase saving. It also suggests that, as countries grow, their wealth to income ratios will decline.

Precautionary Savings

The nascent literature on precautionary savings represents one of the most promising frontiers of research on savings. Life cycle simulation studies have examined precautionary savings resulting from uncertain life span [e.g., Davies (1981) and chapters 4 and 5], labor earnings uncertainty [e.g., Barsky et al. (1987), Zeldes (1986), and Skinner (1986)], and uncertain health expenditures (chapter 6). The conclusion flowing from these studies is that each of these forms of uncertainty can explain a substantial amount of precautionary savings. For example, Zeldes's (1986) and Skinner's (1986) results suggests earnings uncertainty could easily raise total savings by 25 percent. The simulations reported in chapter 6 suggest that precautionary savings resulting from health expenditure uncertainty could raise savings by one-third.

The literature also indicates that the degree of insurance against income, expenditures, life span, and other risks can greatly influence the amount of precautionary savings. Take, for example, the case of uncertain health expenditures. Table 2, extracted from chapter 6, indicates how insurance and Medicaid arrangements can alter aggregate savings. The table reports results on a 55-period life cycle simulation model in which individuals between ages 20 and 55 have a constant annual probability of becoming ill. If they become ill once and are cured, they will not become ill again. The cost of the cure of the illness is parameterized as a multiple of annual earnings. The table considers four different situations. The first

Table 2
Aggregate savings under different health expenditure regimes

Regime	Base case[a]	Cure costs = 2.5 × annual earnings	Annual illness probability = 0.01
Self-payment	1,008,670	869,710	1,136,140
Fair insurance	891,521	828,212	822,061
Live with it	527,017	527,017	682,301
Medicaid	222,062	325,871	626,383

a. Cure costs equal 5 times annual earnings, and annual illness probability equals 0.05.

case is "self-payment." In this economy there is no health insurance and individuals self-insure. In the second case actuarially fair health insurance is available. In the third case individuals choose (because of a preference parameter) to live with the sickness if they become ill rather than take the cure. And in the fourth case there is no insurance but there is a Medicaid program that has a 100 percent asset tax on its recipients.

Table 2 considers the base case in which the probability of the illness is 5 percent per year starting after age 20, and the cost of the cure is five times annual earnings. The second case involves a cost of the cure equal to $2\frac{1}{2}$ year's earnings. And the third case lowers the annual probability of the illness from 5 percent to 1 percent.

A comparison of the "live with it" regime and the "self-payment" regimes indicates the potential importance of precautionary savings. In the "live with it" regime there is no uncertainty about future health expenditures because, when people become ill, they simply live with the ailment rather than have the cure. The "fair insurance" regime has much less savings than the "self-payment" regime reflecting the reduction in precautionary saving when insurance is available. Savings in the "fair insurance" regime exceeds savings in the "live with it" regime because, even though agents are insured, there is a steepening of the age-consumption profile in the "fair insurance" regime relative to the "live with it" regime, reflecting the consumption health expenditures on the cure in old age. And the increased savings of young agents explains the increase in savings in "fair insurance" relative to "live with it." Savings in the Medicaid regime is remarkably small, even when the illness probability is only 1 percent per year. The prospect of having all one's assets confiscated by a Medicaid system is clearly a major saving disincentive.

Given the ability of families to self-insure and the lack of data exploring implicit family insurance arrangements, it is difficult to know how much to make of the precautionary savings motive. The extent of precautionary savings becomes even more difficult to assess in light of another form of insurance, namely government insurance. Government insurance includes social security, which often provides real annuities, life insurance, and disability insurance, Medicaid and Medicare, and welfare programs, which insures against poverty. Some fiscal policies can provide significant if subtle forms of insurance. For example, Merton (1983) points out that an un-funded social security system in which benefits are adjusted in response to labor earnings can pool earnings risks across generations. And Eaton and Rosen (1980), Varian (1980), Chan (1983), Barsky et al. (1987), and Kimball and Mankiw (1987) show that a progressive income tax can provide earnings insurance.

More theoretical and simulation research is needed to explore how well families and government policies hedge uncertain earnings and health expenditures and other uncertainties, such as uncertain rates of return and uncertain dates of retirement because of disability. But pinning down em-pirically the extent of precautionary savings will require new surveys that examine two issues: first, the nature of implicit family insurance arrange-ments and, second, the extent of subjective uncertainties. This latter issue has been thoroughly finessed in the precautionary savings literature by simply assuming the nature of subjective probability distributions.

One approach to determining the extent of subjective uncertainty that does not require eliciting survey responses about probability distributions is proposed by Eden and Pakes (1981) and Kotlikoff and Pakes (1988). These papers demonstrate how one can infer the degree of earnings un-certainty from information on consumption. Their technique, however, does not appear to generalize to other types of uncertainty. And in the presence of other uncertainties besides labor earnings, their technique may give an inaccurate picture of earnings uncertainty.

Demographic Change and Savings

Simulation analyses have been the main vehicle for demonstrating the importance of demographics to savings. Table 3 provides an illustration; it summarizes some findings of chapter 14, which considers the response of savings to changes in life span and the age of retirement in a 55-period life cycle model. The table reports capital-labor ratios for different ages of death and retirement. The parametrization of this model is similar to that of the AK model and is detailed in chapter 14. The table indicates that savings can be quite sensitive to the lengths of work and life spans.

Table 3
Capital-labor ratios for various life spans and work spans

Age of retirement	Age of death			
	50	70	80	100
40	6.89	13.29	15.99	20.46
50		10.23	11.27	17.02
60		8.02	10.13	14.22
70			8.80	11.85
80				10.15

Table 4
Effects of a baby bust on saving rates

Year	Fraction of population at specified ages				Saving rate (%)
	1–20	21–40	41–60	61–75	
0	0.50	0.28	0.15	0.07	7.6
20	0.37	0.36	0.20	0.09	7.9
50	0.28	0.28	0.28	0.16	3.0
70	0.26	0.27	0.27	0.21	0.0
110	0.27	0.27	0.27	0.21	− 1.5
150	0.27	0.27	0.27	0.20	0.0

Holding the age of retirement at 60, an increase in the model's age of death from 70 to 80 raises the capital-labor ratio and quantity of savings (since labor supply is inelastic in this model) by more than 25 percent. Reductions in the age of retirement can also have important savings effects. Holding the age of death at 70, a reduction in the age of retirement from 60 to 50 leads to a 27 percent increase in the capital-labor ratio.

A second illustration of the impact of demographics on savings is given in table 4, which draws on findings from chapter 13. This chapter uses the AK model to study how baby booms and baby busts affect the economy's general equilibrium transition path. The parameters of this model are described in chapter 13, but they are quite similar to those underlying table 1. Table 4 depicts the effects on the age structure of the economy over a 150-year period of a year zero reduction in fertility rates from one that produces a 3 percent annual population growth rate to one that produces no population growth. The table also indicates how the demographic transition affects national saving rates. Once the transition begins, saving rates in the first few years (not included in the table) fall slightly. Then they rise through year 20 to a value above that in the initial steady state. There follows a decline in saving rates, which reach negative values in the year 110. Between years 110 and 150 the saving rate rises to its ultimate steady-state value of 0.

The initial drop in the saving rate is unrelated to concurrent demographic changes, which in the first few years are unimportant, but is related to anticipated general equilibrium increases in future wages. These projected increases in budget opportunities resulting from capital deepening stimulate higher current consumption and lower current saving. The subsequent increase in the saving rate between years 1 and 20 reflects the drop in fertility. The drop reduces the number of children and the importance of their dissaving, that is, their consumption. By year 20 the fraction of the population between 20 and 60 has increased from 45 percent to 56 percent, and this group is doing more saving because there are fewer children to feed. By year 70, however, the decline in birth rates has affected the size of the young and middle-age adult saving population so that there are relatively more elderly dissavers. This leads temporarily to a slightly negative saving rate. The ultimate steady-state saving rate is 0 because the population growth rate is 0, and savings per capita is constant in the steady state. The final steady-state wage rate is 11 percent larger than the initial steady-state wage, reflecting the permanent capital deepening resulting from the permanent drop in fertility.

Despite the importance of demographic change to savings, as indicated by these two illustrations, there has been limited research on this subject. Research by Barro and Becker (1987, 1988) and several other researchers has just begun to link fertility decisions and long-run savings behavior. Research by Noguchi (1986) has begun to explore the interactions of nonaltruistic bequests and demographic change. And studies such as that in chapter 13 have begun to examine the connections among demographic change, fiscal policy (including social security), and savings. But little or no work has been done on the more subtle influences of demographics on savings. For example, no one has yet considered how changes in family size influence family insurance and thereby the extent of precautionary savings. No one has explored how increases in divorce rates affect saving behavior. And no one has explored how a strong trend toward the elderly living alone, rather than with their children, affects the demand for old age housing and aggregate savings. These and related questions present some fruitful areas for additional research.

Fiscal Policy's Effects on Savings

Chapter 7 presents an extensive review of fiscal policy effects on savings. The main message of this chapter is that fiscal policies can greatly influence savings. This message may be contrasted with an earlier view that fiscal policies, such as reductions in capital income tax rates, have ambiguous saving effects. Chapter 7 points out that many policies, such as a shift in the tax structure, can be decomposed into compensated tax changes plus income effects. The impact of compensated tax changes on savings are unambiguous, and the income effects of shifts in the tax structure often reinforce the effects of the compensated tax changes. The discussion distinguishes four types of policies: changes in the tax structure holding constant the time path of government consumption, tax-financed changes in government consumption, intergenerational redistribution, and intragenerational redistribution. Each of these policies, with the exception of intragenerational redistribution, appears to be capable of generating major changes in national savings.

The fiscal policy literature, since chapter 7 was written, has begun to explore models with uncertainty [e.g., Barsky et al. (1984)] and models in which individuals are liquidity constrained [e.g., Hubbard and Judd (1986)]. Both of these elements can significantly influence fiscal policy effects on savings. Take, as an example, an increase in income tax progressivity. In a certainty model increased tax progressivity would likely reduce savings because of the increased disincentives to work and save. But there is a second reason savings might fall in a world of earnings uncertainty, namely, the increased tax progressivity may improve risk sharing and thereby reduce precautionary savings.

More research along these lines can be expected. In addition, it seems likely that uncertain fiscal policy will, itself, be identified as a reason for additional precautionary savings [e.g., Eaton (1981)]. Understanding the source of changes in fiscal policy may lead to the incorporation of explicit models of government decisions. Chapter 11 presents one such model—a life cycle model in which government decisions reflect the outcome of bargaining between young and old generations. Fully modeling government decisions can lead to some surprising results. In chapter 11 the specification of government decision making implies that debt is neutral even in the life cycle model.

Conclusion and Suggestions for Additional Research

One way to describe the current state of knowledge about savings is that a great deal is known at a theoretical level about savings determinants taken one at a time. Much less is known about the interactions of these determinants, and too little is known at an empirical level about the true causes of savings. As is often the case in economics, the theory seems to have advanced well beyond the empirical research. Unfortunately the theoretical progress has dimmed the prospects for quick empirical resolution of the major outstanding questions concerning savings. The theory has pointed out a number of subtle but powerful determinants of savings on which little data are available. These include the extent of family and government insurance, the degree of intra- and intergenerational altruism, and the nature of subjective probability distributions. New data will be needed to assess these issues, but some of this data will be difficult to collect. For example, it will be a challenge to elicit meaningful statements from workers about their subjective probabilities of getting laid off from their job, of finding a new job if they are laid off, of the salary on their new job, etc. It will also be a challenge to elicit information on who is and who is not altruistically linked; the extent to which family members are currently making transfers to one another is insufficient for assessing altruistic linkages since family members may plan to make such transfers in the future or be willing to make such transfers in emergencies.

Even with the best data, answering some savings questions seems quite difficult. Consider trying to distinguish altruistic family behavior from selfish family risk pooling. In both settings one will observe intrafamily transfers. In both settings one will observe that each family member's consumption depends on collective resources. And in both settings family members will surely state that they care for one another. The selfish risk-sharing family will differ from the altruistic family in that the distribution of consumption across different members will in the selfish model depend on the distribution of resources; for example, members with more wealth will consume more. But in the altruistic model different members may consume more than others because their utility is weighted differently. If these utility weights are correlated with resource position, it may be quite hard to tell whether, for example, the elderly members of the extended family are consuming more because they are old or because they are the ones with most of the wealth.

In sum, the question of what determines savings is like a good jigsaw puzzle. It has a large number of pieces. Some of the pieces have been found.

Those that are available do not immediately fit together, but not all the combinations have yet been tried. The pieces that are missing are not necessarily in the bottom of the box and indeed may be mixed up with identical looking pieces in some other jigsaw puzzle. While it is easiest to keep playing with the pieces at hand, the puzzle may never be solved without the tedious task of looking in the other boxes. While the outlines of the puzzle are getting clearer, the precise picture it displays remains well worth the search.

Note

1. If the Keynesian model specifies that the young consume a fraction θ of their disposable income, including their private transfers, while the old consume a fraction θ of their income, before private transfers, there will be an increase in A_{t+1}, when Z_t increases, by an amount $\theta^2 \Delta Z_t$.

I   Saving Motives

Introduction

This section explores the following motives for saving: life cycle saving for retirement, saving for intergenerational transfers, precautionary saving resulting from life span uncertainty, and precautionary saving resulting from uncertain health expenditures. The extent of life cycle savings for retirement can be studied by examining the shapes of age-earnings and age-consumption profiles. If these profiles do not exhibit significant "hump" saving before retirement, then life cycle savings will be small. If wealth is nonetheless substantial, then intergenerational transfers must be the main explanation for wealth accumulation. Chapter 1 uses this methodology to decompose total US wealth into life cycle and intergenerational savings. In addition to this technique of distinguishing life cycle wealth from intergenerational transfer wealth, there are other approaches to answering this question. These other approaches are reviewed in chapter 2.

The analysis of precautionary savings requires an understanding of the saving response to different insurance arrangements, including risk sharing among family members. Risk sharing among family members can be an important form of insurance. Such risk sharing arises automatically when family members are altruistically linked (they care for one another). But even selfish family members will find it in their interest to pool risks with one another. As a prelude to discussing risk sharing among altruistic extended family members, chapter 3 examines whether intermarriage between altruistic extended families leads to altruistic linkages across the extended families. It also considers the implications of altruistic linkages for consumption decisions.

Chapter 4 starts from assumptions opposite to those in chapter 3; rather than assume family members care for one another, chapter 4 assumes that family members are perfectly selfish. Chapter 4 shows that, their selfishness notwithstanding, family members will self-insure against life span risk when actuarially fair annuity insurance is unavailable. This self-insurance will give rise to voluntary inter- and intragenerational transfers among family members.

Chapter 5 considers the amount of precautionary savings and intergenerational transfers that arise in economies in which families pool life span risk. The chapter also examines the implications of this savings and intergenerational transfers for the distribution of wealth. A third question explored is the effect of Social Security's provision of annuity insurance on precautionary savings in an economy in which life span risk is otherwise insured only within families.

A different form of precautionary saving, precautionary saving for uncertain health expenditures, is discussed in chapter 6. In contrast to the focus on family insurance in chapters 4 and 5, the focus here is on the amount of precautionary savings arising under different institutional insurance arrangements, including actuarially fair market insurance, actuarially unfair market insurance, and government insurance provided by a Medicaid program.

Although chapters 4, 5, and 6 examine precautionary saving in response to only two types of uncertainty, life span uncertainty and health expenditure uncertainty, the findings have implications for precautionary saving for other types of risks. Specifically, these chapters indicate that the precise amount of precautionary savings critically depends on both family risk sharing and government insurance institutions.

The specific questions addressed in this part are:

1. How important is life cycle savings to US wealth accumulation?

2. How much of US savings can be explained by intergenerational transfers?

3. What are the shapes of US age-earnings and age-consumption profiles?

4. Do the elderly dissave at rates suggested by the life cycle model?

5. Has US saving been responsive to changes in the length of retirement as suggested by the life cycle model?

6. Can the distribution of wealth be explained by life cycle savings?

7. Can realistic life cycle simulation models reproduce observed ratios of aggregate wealth to aggregate income?

8. What motivates intergenerational transfers?

9. How does intermarriage between extended families affect altruistic linkages?

10. How does uninsured life span uncertainty affect age-consumption profiles?

11. How well can family risk sharing against life span uncertainty substitute for perfect insurance?

12. How much precautionary savings and intergenerational transfers arise when life span is uncertain and fair annuities are unavailable?

13. Can perfections in market annuity insurance greatly reduce savings?

14. How do intergenerational transfers arising from imperfect annuity insurance affect the distribution of wealth?

15. If life span risk sharing among families reflects selfish motives, how does family bargaining between young and old family members alter the amount of precautionary savings?

16. How does uncertainty concerning future health expenditures affect individual and aggregate savings?

17. By how much does precautionary health expenditure savings decline in response to health insurance?

18. Is the asset test of Medicaid a potentially important saving deterrent?

The major findings in this part are:

1. Intergenerational transfers account are a major, and probably the major explanation for US savings.

2. US longitudinal age-earnings and age-consumption profiles do not exhibit the shapes needed to produce significant life cycle "hump" savings.

3. If it could be enforced, a law that prohibited all intergenerational transfers could well reduce US wealth by as much as 50 percent in the long run.

4. A wide variety of evidence points to the importance of intergenerational transfers in US savings, including findings that the elderly dissave little, if at all, that the distribution of US wealth is highly skewed, that US saving is unresponsive to changes in the length of retirement, and that realistic life cycle simulation models do not predict observed wealth to income ratios.

5. The explanation for US intergenerational transfers remains an important puzzle.

6. In altruistically linked extended families the consumption of individual family members depends on collective family resources and not on the distribution of resources within the extended family.

7. Intermarriage between altruitically linked extended families leads to altruistic linkages across the extended families with the implication that consumption of any member of these families depends on the combined

resources of all families and not on the distribution of resources across or within families. Hence redistribution among members of altruistically megaextended families has no effect on anyone's consumption.

8. The finding about intermarriage and altruism suggests that, if there are altruistic extended families, they are likely to be extremely large mega-extended families.

9. Although family annuity insurance markets are incomplete, even small families can substitute by more than 70 percent for a perfect annuities market.

10. Given adverse selection and transactions costs, family risk pooling may be preferred to public annuity insurance.

11. In the absence of public annuities, life span risk sharing provides powerful incentives for marriage and family formation.

12. Family life span risk sharing can have an important effect on the shape of age-consumption profiles.

13. In nonaltruistic economies in which families pool life span risk, the nature of family bargaining can be a key determinant of aggregate savings.

14. Perfecting life span insurance arrangements in public markets or through social security can sharply lower savings in both intergenerationally atruis-tic and life cycle economies in which family insurance is the alternative to public or government insurance.

15. In altruistic economies perfecting annuity insurance can greatly influence inequality; indeed, switching from imperfect family insurance to perfect market or government insurance can mean the difference between absolute inequality and absolute equality.

16. Precautionary saving for uncertain health expenditures appears capable of explaining a large amount of aggregate savings. Adding uncertain health expenditures to a stylized life cycle simulation model raises long run savings by almost one-third.

17. Introducing actuarially fair health insurance to the stylized economy reduces steady-state wealth by 12 percent.

18. Switching from the fair health insurance regime to a regime in which only a Medicaid program with a 100 percent assets test is available reduces steady-state wealth by 75 percent.

1

The Role of Intergenerational Transfers in Aggregate Capital Accumulation

with Lawrence H. Summers

During the past quarter century, the life-cycle hypothesis (Modigliani and Brumberg 1954; Ando and Modigliani 1963) has emerged as the principal theory of aggregate saving in the American economy. It has stimulated a vast quantity of research testing and exploring its implications. Despite this effort, the importance of lifetime consumption smoothing to the process of capital accumulation remains unresolved.[1] This paper presents evidence that the pure life-cycle component of aggregate US savings is very small. American capital accumulation results primarily from intergenerational transfers. Distinguishing the roles of life-cycle savings and intergenerational transfers in the capital accumulation process is crucial to a number of economic issues. Economic models that incorporate intergenerational transfers can generate strikingly different results for a number of major economic questions, including the burden of the national debt, the impact of social security on savings, the incidence of taxation, the perpetuation of the inequality of wealth, and the optimal structuring of taxes to promote economic growth (see, e.g., Diamond 1970; Atkinson 1971; Feldstein 1974a–d; Oulton 1976; Calvo, Kotlikoff, and Rodríguez 1979).

This paper has two objectives. The first is simply to answer an accounting question, namely, can life-cycle savings alone account for the US capital stock? The second goal is to answer an economic question: If, ceteris paribus, there were no intergenerational transfers, how large would the US capital stock be? That is, if all such transfers were taxed in a confiscatory way, by how much would capital accumulation be reduced? We find that life-cycle savings cannot explain the capital stock in an accounting sense and that in the absence of intergenerational transfers the US capital stock would be substantially smaller.

Journal of Political Economy 89(4):706–32 (1981). © 1981 by The University of Chicago. Reprinted with permission.

Our findings are based on a new methodological approach.[2] In particular, a variety of historical US data detailing population, labor earnings, consumption, and government taxes and transfers are used to directly estimate the shapes of historic age-earnings and age-consumption profiles. These profiles are combined with data on rates of return to calculate a stock of life-cycle wealth. This stock of life-cycle wealth is compared with aggregate wealth holdings in the United States. If there were no intergenerational transfers, the stock of life-cycle wealth would exactly equal total US wealth. When intergenerational transfers occur, these two stocks differ by an amount equal to the stock of net received transfers. Hence, comparing total wealth with life-cycle wealth indicates whether the life-cycle model alone can explain aggregate US capital formation. We find that lifetime consumption and earnings profiles do not exhibit the kind of shapes needed to generate substantial life-cycle savings. Log linear approximations to these profiles suggest that growth rates of real earnings slightly exceed growth rates of real consumption over the lifetime. Since the life-cycle theory strongly relies on a lifetime growth rate of consumption in excess of the growth rate of earnings, the life-cycle theory of savings with no intergenerational transfers is a very poor description of the process of capital accumulation in the US economy.

Our findings are in agreement with recent studies by White (1978) and Darby (1979) and rationalize other stylized facts about the US economy at odds with the life-cycle theory. Mirer presents evidence from social security data that "the aged do not run down their wealth during their lifetime" (1979, p. 442). Indeed, after he adjusts for intercohort differences in wealth at retirement, Mirer finds "that wealth clearly increases with age" (1979, p. 442). Darby points out that, although the ratio of expected retirement years to expected life span increased by 67 percent from 1890 to 1930, aggregate savings rates showed no increase during this period as would be predicated by the life-cycle theory (1979, pp. 22–28). Atkinson (1971) and Oulton (1976) construct life-cycle models to determine how much of observed British inequality of wealth may be explained by this theory. The answer is, very little. After taking into account inequality in age-earnings profiles and realized rates of return, Oulton concludes, "The results indicate that none of these factors, either singly or in combination, are capable of accounting for a substantial proportion of actual wealth inequality" (1976, p. 99).

Section 1.1 presents a theoretical framework for considering the importance of intergenerational transfers to aggregate capital accumulation. Section 1.2 discusses the procedure to estimate the stock of life-cycle wealth. The data are described in Section 1.3. Section 1.4 presents and intuitively motivates the findings. The sensitivity of the findings to reasonable possible errors in the data and estimation procedure is also considered. The fifth section attempts to account for the residual between total US wealth and the stock of life-cycle wealth using the limited information available on actual intergenerational transfers. The sixth and final section of the paper presents the conclusions and discusses some of their implications.

1.1 Life-Cycle and Transfer Wealth: A Theoretical Framework

The division of the stock of wealth, W, into life-cycle and transfer components, L and T, respectively, is easily understood by considering a 3-period model of economic growth with identical individuals in each age cohort. At a point in time, aggregate wealth in the economy is the sum of individual wealth holdings. Let W_i stand for the wealth holdings of a representative individual of age i, and let P_i stand for the population of individuals age i; then

$$W = W_1 P_1 + W_2 P_2 + W_3 P_3. \tag{1}$$

The W_i's equal, by definition, accumulated flows of net received transfers plus accumulated flows of earnings net of government taxes less government transfers less accumulated flows of consumption, where accumulation takes place at the after-tax interest rate r. Let T_{ij}^k be the net transfer received at age i from individuals age j for individuals who are currently age k. For example, T_{12}^3 represents the net transfer (which may be positive or negative) that a current 3-period-old individual received at the time he or she was 1 period old from individuals who were then 2 periods old. Let e_i^k and c_i^k represent the earnings and consumption of k-period-old individuals when they were i periods old. Assuming that earnings, consumption, and transfers occur at the end of each period, W_1, the wealth of age 1 individuals, equals zero. With this notation, W_2 and W_3 may be expressed as

$$W_2 = (T_{12}^2 + T_{13}^2)(1 + r) + (e_1^2 - c_1^2)(1 + r)$$
$$W_3 = (T_{12}^3 + T_{13}^3)(1 + r)^2 + (T_{21}^3 + T_{22}^3)(1 + r) \tag{2}$$
$$+ (e_1^3 - c_1^3)(1 + r)^2 + (e_2^3 - c_2^3)(1 + r).$$

Combining (1) and (2) yields

$$W = T + L, \tag{3}$$

where

$$T = (T_{12}^2 + T_{13}^2)(1 + r)P_2 + [(T_{12}^3 + T_{13}^3)(1 + r)^2$$
$$+ (T_{21}^3 + T_{23}^3)(1 + r)]P_3$$

and

$$L = (e_1^2 - c_1^2)(1 + r)P_2 + [(e_1^3 - c_1^3)(1 + r)^2 + (1 + r)(e_2^3 - c_2^3)]P_3.$$

Equation (3) is the fundamental accounting relationship analyzed in this paper. Transfer wealth, T, corresponds to accumulated net received transfers, while life-cycle wealth, L, corresponds to accumulated earnings less accumulated consumption. Clearly, in a world with no intergenerational transfers, T would equal zero and W would equal L. Our first goal is to establish the relative magnitudes of the two components T and L and thereby determine whether US wealth holdings can be predominantly explained by life-cycle savings. Since substantially less information is available about the values of the T_{ij}^k, most of this paper is devoted to calculating the value of L. Section 1.5 does, however, attempt to estimate T directly using fragmentary data and invoking steady-state assumptions.

If the economy is in a steady state, net intergenerational transfers received at a given age are constant through time, so that

$$T_{12} = T_{12}^2 = T_{12}^3$$
$$T_{13} = T_{13}^2 = T_{13}^3$$
$$T_{21} = T_{21}^3$$
$$T_{23} = T_{23}^3.$$

$$(4)$$

Under the assumption that population grows at a constant rate n,

$$P_1 = P_3(1 + n)^2 \quad \text{and} \quad P_1 = P_2(1 + n). \tag{5}$$

Since transfers received by age group i from age group j equal the negative of group j's transfers from age group i,

$$T_{ij}P_i = -T_{ji}P_j, \tag{6}$$

and

$$T_{12}P_1 = -T_{21}P_2. \tag{7}$$

From (4), (5), (6), and (7), T may be expressed in the steady state as[3]

$$T = P_1 \left\{ T_{13} \left[\frac{1 + r}{1 + n} + \frac{(1 + r)^2}{(1 + n)^2} \right] + T_{12} \frac{(1 + r)^2}{(1 + n)^2} + T_{23} \frac{(1 + r)}{(1 + n)^2} \right\}. \tag{8}$$

Under the assumption that $r = n$, T equals the yearly net flow of transfers from old to young cohorts, t, multiplied by the transfer-weighted age gap, g, between donors and recipients:

$$T = [P_1(T_{12} + T_{13}) + P_2 T_{23}] \cdot \left[\frac{T_{12} P_1 + 2 T_{13} P_1 + T_{23} P_2}{P_1(T_{12} + T_{13}) + P_2 T_{23}} \right] \equiv t \cdot g. \tag{9}$$

If r exceeds (is less than) n, accumulated transfer wealth will exceed (be less than) the annual flow of transfers times the weighted average age gap. Equations (8) and (9) show that the contribution of transfers to the total stock of wealth depends critically on both the volume of the annual flow of transfers and the age span of transfers. Equation (8) is invoked in Section 1.5 to directly estimate the size of T.

The second goal of this paper is to ask the economic question, How would the US capital stock, W, change if, because of changes in taxes or tastes, intergenerational transfer wealth, T, was reduced? Since consumption, leisure, and transfer decisions are jointly determined it is important to examine the possibility that changes in transfers might induce or be associated with changes in consumption and earnings paths and thus alter the life-cycle component of wealth. In addition to recognizing interdependencies between transfer wealth and life-cycle wealth, the effect of changes in transfer behavior on capital formation may be examined in both partial and general equilibrium contexts. The partial equilibrium change in W resulting from a reduction in T holds wage rates and interest rates constant and corresponds to a shift in the household supply curve of capital. This paper considers only the steady-state partial equilibrium impact of changes in transfers on the capital stock. A calculation of the general equilibrium effect requires taking account of the responsiveness of the level and shapes of earnings, consumption, and lifetime transfer profiles to changes in capital accumulation.[4]

The Steady-State Partial Equilibrium Reduction in Capital Intensity Arising from a Reduction in Intergenerational Transfers

In order to analyze the partial equilibrium reduction in the stock of wealth, we first note that life-cycle wealth, L, equals accumulated earnings minus accumulated consumption. Accumulated earnings, in turn, equals accumulated wages at full-time work minus the accumulated value of leisure.

Letting C stand for accumulated consumption, S for accumulated full-time wages, and M for the accumulated value of leisure, equation (3) becomes

$$W = T + S - M - C. \tag{3'}$$

The partial equilibrium percentage reduction in W for a percentage change in transfer wealth, T, equals

$$\frac{\partial W}{\partial T} \frac{T}{W} = \left(1 - \frac{\partial M}{\partial T} - \frac{\partial C}{\partial T}\right) \frac{T}{W}. \tag{10}$$

Equation (10) states that the proportionate reduction in the capital stock equals the share of transfer wealth in aggregate wealth, T/W, minus two additional terms indicating how accumulated earnings and accumulated consumption respond to changes in transfers.

Our analysis of the response terms $\partial M/\partial T$ and $\partial C/\partial T$ assumes that the utility of consumption and leisure is separable from the utility derived from intergenerational transfers. This assumption implies that the marginal rates of substitution between consumption and leisure at different points in time are independent of the level of intergenerational transfers. Two examples of utility functions exhibiting this property are

$$U_0 = \log C_0 + \log C_1 + \log C_2 + \log l_1 + \log l_2 + \log l_3 + \alpha \log T_{12}$$

$$+ \alpha \log T_{13} + \alpha \log T_{21} + \alpha \log T_{23} + \alpha \log T_{31} + \alpha \log T_{32} \tag{11}$$

and

$$U_0 = \log C_0 + \log C_1 + \log C_2 + \log l_1 + \log l_2 + \log l_3 + \alpha U_1. \tag{11'}$$

The term U_0 stands for the utility of a representative individual of generation zero. The terms l_1, l_2, and l_3 correspond to leisure in different periods. In (11) the individual derives utility directly from the level of net transfers. In (11') the individual derives utility from the utility, U_1, of his descendants. This is an example of an "overlapping utility function." For both types of separable utility functions the marginal rates of substitution between consumption and leisure are independent of the level of α, the preference parameter influencing the size of transfers. In addition, the first-order conditions for the optimal choice of consumption and leisure involve the equality between these marginal rates of substitution and the relative prices of consumption and leisure at different ages. Hence, neither changes in transfer preferences nor taxes on intergenerational transfers that affect only the price of transfers but not the price of consumption or leisure will alter the first-order conditions.

Given the levels of transfers, the utility-maximizing levels of consumption and leisure can be separately derived from these first-order conditions and the lifetime budget constraint given below:

$$C_1 + \frac{C_2}{1 + r} + \frac{C_3}{(1 + r)^2} + M_1 + \frac{M_2}{1 + r} + \frac{M_3}{(1 + r)^2}$$

$$= s_1 + \frac{s_2}{1 + r} + \frac{s_3}{(1 + r)^2} + T_{12} + T_{13} + \frac{T_{21}}{1 + r} + \frac{T_{23}}{1 + r}$$

$$+ \frac{T_{31}}{(1 + r)^2} + \frac{T_{32}}{(1 + r)^2}. \tag{12}$$

In equation (11), M_1, M_2, and M_3 are the values of leisure in periods 1, 2, and 3 [by value of leisure we mean the number of units of leisure times the price (wage) per unit]. The terms s_1, s_2, and s_3 are full-time wages in periods 1, 2, and 3. Equation (12) indicates that lifetime consumption and leisure are financed by full-time lifetime earnings plus net lifetime received transfers. The separability assumption implies that changes in preferences or taxes that alter the values of the T_{ij} have only an income effect on the choices of consumption and leisure over the lifetime.

We now demonstrate that this income effect of a change in transfers is identically zero for the case that r equals n.[6] Using (5) and (6) to rewrite (12), we obtain

$$C_1 + \frac{C_2}{1 + r} + \frac{C_3}{(1 + r)^2} + M_1 + \frac{M_2}{1 + r} + \frac{M_3}{(1 + r)^2}$$

$$= s_1 + \frac{s_2}{1 + r} + \frac{s_3}{(1 + r)^2} + \frac{T_{12}(r - n)}{(1 + r)} + \frac{T_{23}(r - n)}{(1 + r)^2}$$

$$+ \frac{T_{13}[(1 + r)^2 - (1 + n)^2]}{(1 + r)^2}. \tag{12'}$$

We can also write the budget constraint (12') in terms of aggregate transfer wealth per young person T', where $T' = T/P_1$:

$$C_1 + \frac{C_2}{1 + r} + \frac{C_3}{(1 + r)^2} + M_1 + \frac{M_2}{1 + r} + \frac{M_3}{(1 + r)^2}$$

$$= s_1 + \frac{s_2}{1 + r} + \frac{s_3}{(1 + r)^2} + \frac{(r - n)(1 + n)^2 T'}{(1 + r)^3}. \tag{12''}$$

As is clear from (12') and (12''), when $r = n$, lifetime consumption and leisure are financed solely out of lifetime full earnings; all of the accrued interest on received transfers, as well as the principle itself, is used to maintain steady-state transfers per head at a constant level. When $r = n$, reducing transfers has no impact on the steady-state budget constraint, and the terms $\partial M/\partial T$ and $\partial C/\partial T$ in (10) are zero (i.e., since lifetime consumption and earnings paths stay the same when $r = n$, steady-state life-cycle wealth, L, will be unaltered by changes in steady-state transfer wealth, T). Thus, any decline in transfer wealth, T, will reduce total wealth, W, dollar for dollar in partial equilibrium when $r = n$.

In the case that r differs from n, steady-state changes in the level and pattern of transfers (the T_{ij} terms) affect the steady-state budget constraint only insofar as they alter the stock of transfer wealth T. This is a general proposition that can easily be shown to hold independent of the number of periods in the model. When r exceeds n, part of lifetime consumption and leisure is financed by lifetime transfers. Again, under the separability assumption, the reduction in transfers has simply an income effect on consumption and leisure and, assuming both are normal goods, will reduce lifetime consumption and raise lifetime earnings. In (10) both $\partial M/\partial T$ and $\partial C/\partial T$ will be positive when r exceeds n. The reverse will be true when n exceeds r. It is easy to demonstrate that introducing labor-augmenting productivity growth simply requires relabeling n everywhere as the population growth rate plus the productivity growth rate. In the case of productivity growth, the steady state is characterized by a constant level of transfers per effective worker.

The value of these terms depends on the particular preferences determining the levels and shapes of consumption and leisure paths. As one example, table 1.1 gives the value of the transfer wealth-adjustment factor $[1 - (\partial M/\partial T) - (\partial C/\partial T)]$ for a particular specification of preferences for consumption and leisure and for different values of r and n. The example assumes a 55-year life span and uses the logarithmic utility function with time-preference parameter ρ and leisure-preference parameter α:[7]

$$U = \int_0^D \log C_t e^{-\rho t}\, dt + \alpha \int_0^D \log l_t e^{-\rho t}\, dt. \tag{13}$$

The l_t terms in (1.13) are units of leisure at different points in time. The calculations underlying table 1.1 are presented in Kotlikoff and Summers (1980, appendix A).

The figures in table 1.1 indicate that the response of consumption and labor supply can be quite important in determining the final partial equilibrium effect of a reduction in transfers when the interest rate differs from the economy's growth rate. For the specific logarithmic function chosen here,

Table 1.1
Transfer wealth adjustment factor

r	n	ρ	$1 - \dfrac{\partial M}{\partial T} - \dfrac{\partial C}{\partial T}$
0.02	0.01	0.02	0.73
0.02	0.01	0.03	0.71
0.02	0.02	0.02	1.00
0.02	0.03	0.02	1.40
0.02	0.04	0.02	2.00
0.03	0.01	0.01	0.58
0.03	0.01	0.05	0.48
0.03	0.02	0.03	0.71
0.03	0.03	0.03	1.00
0.03	0.04	0.03	1.43
0.04	0.01	0.01	0.45
0.04	0.01	0.07	0.30
0.04	0.02	0.04	0.49
0.04	0.03	0.04	0.70
0.04	0.04	0.04	1.00

a real interest rate this is 1 percent higher than the rate of population plus productivity growth generates total wealth response numbers approximately equal to 0.7. If, on the other hand, the rate of population plus productivity growth exceeds the real interest rate by 1 percent, reducing transfer wealth by $1.00 reduces aggregate wealth by $1.40.

For the United States the annual rate of population growth has averaged 1.40 percent from 1900 through 1974, the period of this study (see US Department of Commerce 1975, pt. 1, p. 8). Productivity growth as measured by the annual percentage change in real GNP per man-hour has averaged 2.20 percent over this period.[8] Adding 1.4 to 2.2 yields 3.6 percent as the rate of population plus productivity growth. This paper calculates a portfolio-weighted net nominal rate of return for the US economy from 1900 through 1974. After subtracting inflation, the real annual net after-tax rate of return in the US economy averaged 4.5 percent between 1900 and 1974.[9]

The fact that real interest rates have on average exceeded growth rates suggests that part of US consumption and leisure may well have been financed by interest earned on intergenerational transfers. Hence, a dollar reduction in transfer wealth can be expected to reduce aggregate wealth by reduction in transfer wealth can be expected to reduce aggregate wealth by less than \$1.00. The calculated 1 percent gap between r and n suggests that eliminating transfer wealth in the US economy would reduce total wealth by about 70 percent of the amount of transfer wealth. While the 70 percent figure is meant to be suggestive rather than precise, it appears that almost any choice of preferences would yield offset factors not far from 70 percent.[10] That is, the life-cycle offset to a change in transfer wealth is likely to be small.

1.2   The Estimation of Life-Cycle Wealth: Methodological Approach

Total life-cycle wealth in the US economy equals the sum over all living persons in the economy of life-cycle assets. Each person's life-cycle assets correspond to his or her accumulated earnings less accumulated consumption where accumulation occurs at the actually realized rates of return. If data existed detailing each person's earnings, consumption, and realized rate of return on assets at each point in time in the past, it would be easy to check whether US wealth holdings could be explained predominantly by life-cycle accumulation.

Obviously, such detailed individual specific data are not available. However, historical data for the United States on aggregate earnings, aggregate consumption, rates of return, and age-earnings and age-consumption profiles may be used to carry out this life-cycle asset computation on a cohort-by-cohort basis. This paper treats individuals of each sex within an age cohort as identical and estimates the average excess of after-tax earnings plus government transfers over consumption experienced by members of that age-sex cohort during each of their adult years in the past. These differences are then accumulated up to 1974 using historical net nominal interest rates. The total over all age-sex cohorts of these accumulated life-cycle assets is then compared with the 1974 value of total US private net worth.

Life-cycle wealth of the age-sex cohort that is age a and sex j in 1974, $L_j(a)$, is given by

$$L_j(a) \equiv \sum_{i=18}^{a} \left\{ [\bar{E}_j(a, i) + \bar{G}_j(a, i) - \bar{C}_j(a, i)] \prod_{k=i}^{a} [1 + r(a, k)] \right\} P_j(a). \qquad (14)$$

In equation (14), $P_j(a)$ stands for the number of people alive in 1974 who are age a and sex j. The terms $\bar{E}_j(a, i)$, $\bar{G}_j(a, i)$ and $\bar{C}_j(a, i)$ are, respectively, the average after-tax earnings, government transfers, and consumption of the age a–sex j cohort at the time its members were age i. Age 18 is taken as the age of adulthood. Consumption expenditures by adults on children under the age of 18 are considered to be a part of adult consumption rather than intergenerational transfers.[11] The term $r(a, k)$ is the economy-wide annual net nominal interest rate received by the age a cohort during the year the cohort's members were k years old.

Our estimate of total life-cycle assets in the economy in 1974 equals the sum over all age-sex cohorts of the estimated values of $L_j(a)$.[12] The difference between life-cycle wealth and total US wealth in 1974 is our estimate of transfer wealth.

Calculation of Longitudinal Profiles of Net Earnings, Government Transfers, and Consumption

The essential idea involved in these calculations is to use cross-sectional distribution profiles to allocate aggregate flows of net earnings, government transfers, and consumption to different age-sex cohorts in a given year. By performing this computation for each year from 1900 to 1974, we obtain the longitudinal profiles $\bar{E}_j(a, i)$, $\bar{G}_j(a, i)$, and $\bar{C}_j(a, i)$ as i varies.

To illustrate the computation for $\bar{E}_j(a, i)$, we define the following terms: $\bar{e}_t$ is the average earnings of 40-year-old male workers in year t; $g_m(a, t)$ is the ratio of average earnings of male workers at age a in year t to average earnings of 40-year-old male workers in year t; $g_f(a, t)$ is the ratio of average earnings of female workers at age a in year t to average earnings of 40-year-old female workers in year t; λ_t is the ratio of average earnings of 40-year-old female workers to average earnings of 40-year-old male workers in year t; $\alpha_m(a, t)$ is the percentage of males age a with work experience in year t; $\alpha_f(a, t)$ is the percentage of females age a with work experience in year t; H_t is total after-tax labor income in year t; $P_m(a, t)$ is the population of males age a in year t; and $P_f(a, t)$ is the population of females age a in year t. Given information on all of the above variables except $\bar{e}_t$, equation (1.14) is used to solve for $\bar{e}_t$:

$$H_t = \bar{e}_t \sum_{a=18}^{100} [g_m(a, t)\alpha_m(a, t)P_m(a, t) + \lambda_t g_f(a, t)\alpha_f(a, t)P_f(a, t)]. \tag{15}$$

Given $\bar{e}_t$, $\bar{E}_m(a, i)$ for males and $\bar{E}_f(a, i)$ for females satisfy

$$\bar{E}_m(a, i) = \bar{E}_m[a, a - (1974 - t)] = \bar{e}_t g_m(a, t)\alpha_m(a, t), \tag{16}$$

$$\bar{E}_f(a, i) = \bar{E}_f[a, a - (1974 - t)] = \bar{e}_t \lambda_t g_f(a, t)\alpha_f(a, t). \tag{17}$$

The procedure for computing the longitudinal profiles of consumption, $\bar{C}_j(a, i)$, is identical to that just described for earnings; a cross-sectional profile of relative consumption by age and sex is used to distribute aggregate US consumption in each year to different age-sex cohorts.

Calculation of Net Nominal Interest Rates Series

The interest rate term $r(a, i)$ on (14) depends only on the year t since $r(a, i) = r[1974 - (a - i)] = r(t)$. The computation is performed using two different interest rate time series. Series 1 was calculated by dividing US wealth holdings into six separate assets, estimating a rate of return series for each asset, and then weighting each asset's rate of return by its share in the US portfolio for the particular year in question.

Series 2 is based on the wealth augmentation relation

$$W_{t+1} = W_t(1 + r_t) + E_t + G_t - C_t. \tag{18}$$

Equation (18) indicates that private US net worth in year $t + 1$ equals US net worth in year t plus savings in year t. Savings in year t is, in turn, equal to net income on assets, $r_t W_t$, plus after-tax labor income and government transfers, E_t and G_t, less aggregate consumption in year t, C_t. Equation (18) is solved for r_t using time-series data on W_t, E_t, G_t, and C_t.

1.3   Description of Data Used to Calculate Life-Cycle Wealth

This section describes sources and procedures for several of our data series. Kotlikoff and Summers (1980) provide a detailed description of all the data and adjustments to the data used in calculations.

Information on compensation of employees after 1929 is obtained from the *National Income Accounts* and, for the years 1909–29, from Leven, Moulton, and Warburton (1934) and Kuznets (1941, 1946). Prior to 1909, employee compensation is imputed from Kendrick's (historal Statistic) estimates of net national product using the ratios of employee compensation to national product from 1909 to 1918.[13] The imputation of labor income to the self-employed follows Christensen (1971). The number of proprietors is multiplied by the average earnings of full-time equivalent employees. The chief bias here is simply that the self-employed may earn more or less on average than employees. To ensure that the results do not reflect a substantial underestimate of entrepreneurial earnings, the estimate of entrepreneurial earnings for each year is increased by 20 percent.

Estimates of state and federal income taxes paid on labor income were obtained from IRS *Statistics of Income* and the *National Income and Product Accounts*. Combined employer and employee social security and health insurance taxes were obtained from the *Social Security Annual Statistical Supplement* for various years.

Estimates of the age-earnings profiles for men and women were obtained by fitting separate regressions to social security estimates of median annual earnings of workers at different ages for the years 1950 through 1975.[14] The general shapes of the profiles predicated by the regressions are quite similar throughout the 1950–75 period. For the years prior to 1950, the predicted male and female age-earnings profiles for the year 1955 were used.[15]

The value of λ_t, the ratio of average earnings of 40-year-old female workers to average earnings of 40-year-old male workers in year t, was taken to be .55 throughout the period. This appears to be an upper-bound value for λ_t (see Kotlikoff and Summers 1980, p. 46, n. 35).

Values for work experience rates by age and sex, $\alpha_m(a, t)$ and $\alpha_f(a, t)$, are available only after 1959. Substantially more information, especially for the early 1900s, is available on labor force participation rates by age and sex. Regression analysis for the post-1959 period indicates that work experience rates can be predicted quite well by functions of age and labor force participation rates. This post-1959 regression was used to estimate the α function for each year from 1900 to 1974 based on labor force participation rates for the appropriate year. The labor force participation rates equal the values predicted from regressions of labor force participation rates on fifth-order age polynomials for each sex and for different census years.

While cross-sectional distribution functions by sex and age were computed for social security and medicare transfers, we assumed that other transfers, including veterans' benefits and welfare payments, were distributed in the cross-section over the years 1900–1974 according to that year's age-earnings distributions.

Total consumption expenditure, Z_t, is taken from National Income Accounts after 1929 and from Kendrick prior to 1929. Ideally one should subtract expenditures on consumer durables and add imputed rent on consumer durables to obtain true economic consumption. The difficulties of implementing this for the pre-1929 years led us to simply use the consumer expenditure series. In any case, there appears to be very little difference between the consumer expenditure series and the true economic consumption series.[16]

The cross-sectional consumption distribution functions were obtained from the 1960 and 1972–73 *Consumer Expenditure Survey* (CES) tapes.

Unfortunately, similar data are not available to generate these profiles for earlier years. Life-cycle wealth is computed using the 1972–73 cross-sectional profiles throughout the period 1900–1974. The 1960 profiles generated essentially the same level of life-cycle wealth.

In distributing total household consumption to household members, household heads and their spouses are assumed to consume equally; all other household members, including children, were allocated 50 percent of the household head's consumption. The total consumption of children under the age of 18 was then reallocated to the household head and spouse, assigning each one half of children's consumption in the case of two spouses, or giving all the children's consumption to the household head if he or she was single. The general shape of the profiles was quite insensitive to the assumption that other household members and children consume only 50 percent of the consumption level of the household head. The 50 percent assumption generated slightly more life-cycle wealth and is the one used.

Net nominal interest rate series 1 is generated from data on historical rates of return and Goldsmith and Lipsey's (1963) data on portfolio shares. From Goldsmith and Lipsey's balance sheets we constructed seven asset categories plus liabilities. These are tangible, noncorporate business assets including land and structures, residential land and structures, money, short-term claims (savings accounts and US Treasury bills), corporate stock, long-term corporate bonds, and US savings bonds. A rate of return series was calculated for each asset as well as the liabilities. A weighted rate of return was computed taking the share of each item in net worth during the period considered as the weight. The nominal rates of return were converted to after-tax nominal rates of return using average income tax rates for each year. The series 2 net nominal interest rates were computed for the post-1929 period using equation (22). Reliable net worth data are not available until 1929. In the computation the series 2 rates from the pre-1929 years are filled in with the series 1 values.

1.4 The Size of Life-Cycle Wealth

At the end of 1974 total net worth in the US economy equaled $4.154 trillion. Of the $4.154 trillion, $134 billion represent the tangible assets of nonprofit institutions (see FRB-MIT balance sheets); in 1974 nonprofit institutions owned 4.4 percent of corporate equities (SEC 1977, p. 11). Under the assumption that this percentage applies to all other financial assets, total net worth of nonprofit institutions in 1974 would equal $270 billion.[17] After subtracting $270 billion from $4.154 trillion, the 1974 net worth figure for the noninstitutional household sector is $3.884 trillion. This is the number to compare with the life-cycle wealth calculations.

In addition to presenting total life-cycle wealth of individuals, a second life-cycle wealth concept, LCW2, is calculated that adds to LCW1 an upper-bound estimate of accumulated interspousal transfers. Many economists would include within their definition of life-cycle wealth the amount of accumulation that arises from interspousal transfers. Interspousal transfers give rise to wealth accumulation, first, because wives are on average younger than husbands and, second, because females live longer than males. Since it is conceptually difficult, if not impossible, to exactly trace individual patterns of household formation that involve marriage, divorce, and death, an upper-bound estimate of the stock of interspousal accumulated transfers is added to LCW1. To be specific, at age 21 all males are assumed to marry 18-year-old females.[18] If either spouse dies prior to reaching age 75, all of his or her individual life-cycle net worth is assumed to be transferred to the surviving spouse; it was furthermore assumed that the surviving spouse does not die prior to age 75. Thus, for example, if a 40-year-old male dies in 1960 with $20,000 of life-cycle wealth, this $20,000 is transferred to a 37-year-old female who is assumed still to be alive 14 years later in 1974. The $20,000 of received transfers is accumulated up to 1974 at the prevailing interest rates and included in life-cycle wealth.

This procedure overestimates accumulated interspousal transfers for three reasons. First, not all transfers of decedents go to surviving spouses or even to surviving relatives in the same age cohort. Second, not all surviving spouses will, themselves, live until age 75. Rather, many will die much earlier, leaving the bulk of their residual wealth to children or grandchildren. Third, some decedents die without ever having married, leaving their estates to younger cohorts.

Table 1.2 reports the life-cycle wealth numbers, LCW1 and LCW2, based on interest rate series 1 and series 2, as well as constant interest rates

Table 1.2
Accumulated life-cycle wealth (in billions of dollars)

Life-cycle wealth concept	Interest rates						
	Series 1	Series 2	0.02	0.04	0.06	0.08	0.09
LCW1	−1,032	−1,229	−270	−520	−1,108	−2,526	−3,882
LCW2	502	733	186	300	446	565	557

of 2, 4, 6, 8, and 9 percent. The series 1 values for LCW1 and LCW2 are, respectively, −$1,036 and $505 billion. The series 2 figures are −$1,229 and $733 billion. These figures are strikingly small; they are even more surprising in light of assumptions made that bias the calculation toward more life-cycle wealth.[19] Under the stricter definition of life-cycle wealth, LCW1, life-cycle accumulated hump savings is a large, negative number. The allowance for interspousal transfers yields positive, but very small, estimates of hump savings. The $733 billion series 2 LCW2 figure for life-cycle wealth represents only 19 percent of the total 1974 US wealth. These small values for life-cycle wealth do not reflect the choice of interest rates; no historically reasonable constant nominal interest rate will yield significant positive life-cycle wealth. Accumulated intergenerational transfers appear to represent the bulk of the $3,884 billion of US wealth holdings in 1974. Subtraction of 733 from 3,884 gives $3,151 billion as the estimate of the 1974 stock of transfer wealth. Taking the .7 (r exceeds n by about 1 percent) adjustment factor as illustrative, entirely eliminating intergenerational transfers would reduce US wealth by about $2.2 trillion in the context of a partial equilibrium, long-run steady-state model.

To explain the large stock of US wealth, the life-cycle theory of savings must rely on a substantial excess of earnings over consumption when young followed by an excess of consumption over earnings when old. The historical reality for the United States is simply that longitudinal earnings and consumption profiles have not exhibited the kinds of shapes required for substantial life-cycle accumulation. For males, earnings profiles greatly exceed consumption profiles over most of the life cycle. For females, however, the opposite is true. Life-cycle wealth starts out negative and remains negative over all ages. Figures 1.1 and 1.2 graph longitudinal profiles of the sum of male and female average earnings plus government transfers and average consumption for two different age cohorts. The profiles are presented in real 1967 dollars. The diagrams clearly show that the male excess of earnings over consumption is essentially offset by the female excess of consumption over earnings.

Contrary to the life-cycle simulation studies that have generated substantial life-cycle wealth, the actual growth rate of lifetime consumption does not substantially exceed the actual growth rate in lifetime earnings.[20] For example, the male age cohort that reached age 18 in 1920 experienced a growth rate of 2.93 percent in real earnings between ages 18 and 65. In comparison, the male growth in real consumption between ages 18 and 72 was only 2.32 percent. For the corresponding female cohort, earnings growth was 2.23 percent and consumption growth only 1.72 percent. Real

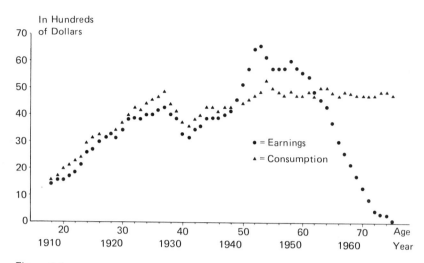

Figure 1.1
Sum of male and female longitudinal average earnings and average consumption profiles, age 18 in 1910 to age 82 in 1974.

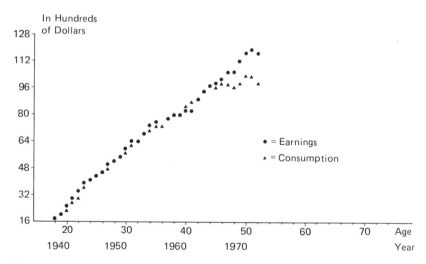

Figure 1.2
Sum of male and female longitudinal average earnings and average consumption profiles, age 18 in 1940 to age 52 in 1974.

consumption profiles are fairly flat, and real earnings profiles peak in late middle age, not at early ages. Both of these factors militate against the life-cycle theory of savings as an explanation of US wealth holdings.

The large transfer wealth value of $3.151 trillion cannot simply be explained as private transfers from old to young offsetting forced government social security and medicare transfers from young to old. Under the Barro (1974) view, introducing unfunded social security into an economy will not lead to a change in consumption but will increase private net transfers from old to young. If Barro's view is correct, it is easy to determine how large private transfers would have been with no social security and Medicare system by simply setting all historic social security and Medicare benefits and taxes to zero in the calculation. This procedure led to a series 1 value of $775 billion and a series 2 value of $1,094 billion for LCW2. Hence, even if Barro is correct in his view about unfunded social security, transfer wealth would still have exceeded $2.79 trillion in 1974 if there had never been a social security program.

One possible problem with the estimates is that the age-consumption profiles prior to 1960 may have looked substantially different from those after 1960. To explore this issue, relative consumption prior to age 40 was reduced by 10 percent and relative consumption after age 40 was increased by 10 percent. Thus, 60-year-olds were effectively assigned an extra 20 percent consumption relative to 30-year-olds in every year from 1900 to 1974. Altering consumption profiles in this manner produced values of −193 for LCW1 and 1,702 for LCW2 using series 1 and −169 for LCW1 and 2,178 for LCW2 using series 2. These numbers are still substantially smaller than the $3,884 billion of 1974 US net worth.

Another issue of concern is whether our data series on aggregate flows accurately describe US experience in the 1900s. As mentioned, to ensure against underestimation of the labor income of the self-employed, we have already increased our estimates by 20 percent. Raising this add-on factor to 30 percent increases the series 1 values of LCW1 to −679 and LCW2 to 872. It is worth noting that eliminating any self-employment add-on factor lowers LCW1 to −1,739 and LCW2 to −714.

A final data issue concerns consumption expenditures of nonprofit institutions as well as contributions of individuals to such institutions. Ideally we should subtract institutional consumption from aggregate consumption and add contributions to these institutions to arrive at total household consumption. While not all the data needed for this adjustment are available, what data are available suggest that the adjustment would be very small and would slightly lower our estimate of life-cycle wealth.[21]

The LCW2 wealth concept effectively deals with possible bias arising from differential survival probabilities between the rich and the poor. This calculation assumes that at least one member of each household survives to age 75 and attributes all household life-cycle accumulation to the surviving spouse(s). Hence, this procedure assumes that rich and poor households have identical survival probabilities, which eliminates this issue of bias.

Another type of aggregation error could arise if some households continually received higher rates of return on their assets than other households. In order to investigate this issue, one would need detailed knowledge of the joint distribution of rates of return and household consumption and earnings patterns. Unfortunately, this information cannot be obtained from existing micro data, and this fact precludes a reasonable assessment of the magnitude of this source of error.

1.5   Explaining the Residual: The Stock of Transfer Wealth

This section investigates the extent to which US data on intergenerational transfers can explain the large residual between total net worth and the estimates of life-cycle wealth. Unfortunately, there are very few data detailing nontaxed intergenerational transfers. These nonenumerated transfers take many forms. Parents who lend money at below market rates to their children for a down payment on a house or a business are engaged in an intergenerational transfer. A father who makes his son a full partner in a lucrative business can effectively transfer large sums of money with no tax lability to the IRS. Parents who fully or partially support their children through college or after college are making transfers. A grandmother's gift of her expensive wedding china and rings to her granddaughter is an intergenerational transfer. Transfers in these forms, as well as outright monetary gifts, are very rarely reported.

To obtain some idea about how large aggregate intergenerational transfer flows need to be in order to explain a \$3.151 trillion stock of transfer wealth, consider the multiperiod analogue to equation (8):

$$T = t \frac{e^{(r-n)D}}{(r-n)} [1 - e^{(n-r)(G-I)}]. \tag{19}$$

Equation (19) is a simplified expression for the steady-state stock of transfers; the formula assumes that all transfers are given at age G and received at age I. The yearly flow of intergenerational transfers is t, the age of death D, and r and n are rates of interest and population plus productivity growth, respectively. In the case $r = n$, this expression reduces to $T =$

Table 1.3
Age gap factor

Age gap ($G - I$)	$r - n$					
	−0.02	−0.01	0	0.01	0.02	0.03
20	8	13	20	31	49	78
25	11	16	25	38	59	92
30	14	20	30	45	68	103
35	17	24	35	51	76	113

$t(G - I)$, the analogue to equation (9). Table 1.3 evaluates the age gap factor, that is, the terms multiplying t for various parameter values and taking D to be 55.[22]

Exactly which age gap is appropriate is unclear.[23] An age gap of 30 allows some significant transfers to grandchildren as well as children. The age gap factor in this case for a .01 excess of r over n is 45. Hence, to explain $3,151 billion in transfer wealth, the yearly flow of transfers would have to equal 3,151 divided by 45, or $70 billion. A 2 percent differential between ($r - n$), again assuming a 30-year gap, would require only a $46 billion annual transfer flow.

The 1962 Federal Reserve Survey of Consumer Finances was used to estimate the bequest portion of the yearly transfer flow. Specifically, the distribution of net worth holdings by age, sex, and marital status was calculated. Next, 1962 mortality probabilities were applied to this distribution to arrive at an estimated distribution of bequests by age, sex, and marital status. An additional adjustment to these figures was made in order to reconcile the US aggregate net worth value estimated from the Federal Reserve tape with the FRB-MIT net worth data.

Unpublished data collected by Paul Menchik and Martin David from the Washington, D.C., Inheritance Tax File for the year 1967 reveal that males who were married at the time of their death left 10 percent of their estate to their children. Married female decedents left 19 percent of their estates to their children. The proportion left to grandchildren and other young relatives is unclear, but it probably does not exceed 2 percent for males and 4 percent for females, which represents half of the percentage contribution to other relatives. For single male decedents, 32 percent of the estate is left to children; the single female proportion is 37 percent. Again taking half of the contributions to other relatives as "distant in age" intergenerational transfers, another 22 percent can be ascribed to single males and 23 percent to single females. Using these figures and the Federal Reserve simulated bequest distributions, the estimated "distant in age" intergenerational bequest transfer flow in 1962 was $11.9 billion. Multiplying this figure by the 221.6 percent growth in the nominal value of total US net worth between 1962 and 1974 gives us an estimate of the 1974 bequest transfer flow of $26.4 billion.

In 1974 the total value of life insurance death benefits equaled $8.885 billion. In conjunction with the Menchik numbers, this raises the $26.4 billion bequest flow figure to $28.9 billion.

We also estimate the flow of intergenerational transfers from parents to children that occur in the form of financial support during college. In 1974 college enrollment totaled 8.8 million students (US Department of Commerce 1978, p. 138). In 1976 parental contributions to college-enrolled children who were taken as tax deductions averaged $1,738 (Froomkin 1977, p. 479). Assuming that non-tax dependent college-enrolled children received one-quarter of this level of support, average support from parents in 1976 was $1,270. Reducing this number by 15 percent, the growth in tuition between 1974 and 1976 (US Department of Commerce 1978, p. 165) suggests a level of college support payments of about $1,080 in 1974. This type of intergenerational transfer could then account for $10.3 billion of the total 1974 flow. Adding the 10.3 to the 28.9 leaves us with $39.2 billion of explained transfer flows.

Another component of the intergenerational transfer flow is transfers made in the form of trusts. While direct data on the value of new trusts formed in 1974 are not available, there are fiduciary income tax data for the years 1965 and 1970 that permit a rough calculation of this transfer flow component (US Internal Revenue Service 1970, p. 46). Between 1965 and 1970 the number of new trusts established each year averaged 35,098. The 1970 income of the 152,398 existing trusts in 1970 totaled $7.513 billion. The average 1970 trust had, therefore, an income of $9,985. Dividing this value by our 1970 series 1 interest rate of 0.0787 gives an estimate of the average value of a 1970 trust of $126,874. Multiplying this figure by 35,098 leads to an estimate of $4.44 billion as the value of new trusts established in 1974. After multiplying this number by 1.395 to allow for the growth in total wealth between 1970 and 1974, our estimate of the 1974 flow of intergenerational transfers in the form of trusts is $6.19 billion. This figure raises the explained transfer flow to $45.4 billion.

This $45.4 billion figure seems small compared with the $70 billion total flow needed if the stock of transfer wealth is $3.151 trillion and the age gap factor is 45. On the other hand, it is not too far from the $46 billion total flow needed if r exceeds n by 2 percent and the age gap factor is 68.

Unfortunately, before one can precisely determine the total intergenerational flow, substantially more information will have to be collected about family gift giving and support payments to children and grandchildren. These data may prove particularly difficult to obtain since we would have to estimate the value of the cedar chest passed from grandmother to grandnephew, or the family car given to son John as a college graduation present, or the value to son Alex of making him a full partner in a lucrative family business. Since the distribution of wealth is very highly skewed, such surveys need to be aimed at the intergenerational transfer payments of the very wealthy. However, the very wealth may be the least willing to disclose these types of transfers because of potential estate and gift tax liabilities.

1.6 Summary and Conclusions

The evidence presented in this chapter rules out life-cycle hump saving as the major determinant of capital accumulation in the US economy. Longitudinal age-earnings and age-consumption profiles do not exhibit the kinds of shapes needed to generate a large amount of life-cycle wealth accumulation. The view of US capital formation as arising, in the main, from essentially homogeneous individuals or married spouses saving when young for their retirement is factually incorrect.

Intergenerational transfers appear to be the major element determining wealth accumulation in the United States. Our best estimates of the 1974 stock of transfer wealth after allowing for interspousal life-cycle accumulation is approximately $3 trillion.

While these estimates of the stock of transfer wealth are quite large, totally eliminating transfers in the US economy would not necessarily reduce total US wealth by the full amount of transfer wealth. We have demonstrated within the context of a steady-state growth model that a $1.00 reduction in the stock of transfer wealth may reduce total wealth by less than $1.00 if the steady-state real interest rate exceeds the steady-state growth rate. Taking the US historical real interest and growth rates as illustrative, eliminating a $3 trillion stock of transfer wealth would reduce total US wealth by about $2.1 trillion in a steady-state context. This, however, is a partial equilibrium analysis. Substantially more research must be undertaken before we can begin to attach probable numbers to full general equilibrium responses to changes in transfers.

This chapter suggests the importance of and need for substantially more research and data collection on intergenerational transfers. Economic

models of savings that stress the homogeneity of agents and the importance of the demographic structure should give way to models that emphasize the rather massive intergenerational transfers in the US economy and
the apparent concentration of these transfers among the very wealthy.

Notes

We are indebted to R. Barro, M. Boskin, G. Chamberlain, R. Clower, M. Darby, S.
Engerman, M. Feldstein, V. Fuchs, R. Gordon, F. Learner, P. Menchik, J. Skinner,
and F. Welch for enlightening discussions. We thank the Foundation for Research
in Economic Eduction; the Department of Health, Education, and Welfare; and the
National Bureau of Economic Research for providing research support. All views
expressed here are solely those of the authors.

1. Tobin (1967) and Boskin (1978) argue that life-cycle savings are the predominant form of savings in the United States. White (1978) and Darby (1979)
argue otherwise. Tobin and Dalde (1971) provide a somewhat intermediate view.

2. Our methodological approach was influenced by and is similar to those of
Brittain (1978) and Darby (1979).

3. By examining (8), one can see that T corresponds simply to the accumulated
holdings of transfers received by people who are currently alive from people who
are currently dead.

4. Kotlikoff (1979) demonstrates that general equilibrium changes in capital intensity can be substantially smaller than partial equilibrium changes.

5. Because wage rates are held constant in this partial equilibrium analysis, $\partial S/\partial T$
equals zero.

6. In the case of a tax on transfers, the income effect of a change in transfers when
$r = n$ will be zero only for the case of a compensated tax on transfers. Compensated rather than uncompensated tax changes are the appropriate focus of studies
of government tax policies toward savings. See Diamond (1970) and Kotlikoff and
Summers (1979).

7. The utility function in (13) corresponds only to that part of total utility pertain-
ing to consumption and leisure. Any set of preferences for transfers may be added
to (13) as long as utility of consumption and leisure is separable from the utility of
transfers. The assumption of a steady state with productivity growth also requires
that the entire utility function be homothetic.

8. US Department of Commerce (1973, series A167 and A168, p. 210), and US
Department of Labor (1978, p. 336). Kendrick's series of output per man-hour is
used for the years 1900–1910, and the BLS series thereafter.

9. To obtain a real net rate of return series, we subtract the annual percentage
change in the CPI from our net nominal return series indicated in US Department

of Commerce (1975, pt. 1, pp. 210–11, table B2) and US Department of Commerce (1978, p. 490).

10. These calculations were performed for the more general isoelastic utility function. A wide range of parameter values for rates of risk aversion and time preference produced values of $[1 - (\partial M/\partial T) - (\partial C/\partial T)]$ ranging from 0.6 to 0.75 when r exceeds n by 1 percent. While it is unclear what utility function is most appropriate, these parameter values cover a wide range of different shapes of consumption and leisure profiles and, we presume, bound the likely response. The assumption implicit in these utility functions that consumption and leisure respond homothetically to changes in transfers may be inappropriate. Even if the utility function is homothetic, capital market constraints precluding borrowing when young against future earnings may make the consumption and leisure response to a reduction in transfers nonhomothetic. These capital market constraints may not be binding in the presence of transfers because the excess of consumption over earnings when young is financed by the received transfers. Eliminating or reducing transfers could make these capital market constraints binding and require proportionately less consumption and leisure when young than when old.

11. Treating consumption of children under age 18 as their own life-cycle consumption would greatly reduce our estimate of life-cycle wealth and greatly increase our estimate of transfer wealth. The age of adulthood is somewhat arbitrary, but 18 appears to be a reasonable number and of general interest.

12. Assets of children under age 18 are assumed to be completely inherited and are not included in life-cycle wealth.

13. See Leven et al. (1934, p. 155), Kuznets (1941, pp. 322–23), and Kendrick's series A6 and B61 in US Department of Commerce (1973, pp. 182, 222). Because of limitations on population estimates on individuals above age 85, we treat all individuals who are age 18 until 1907, we really do not use any data for the years prior to 1907 in this paper.

14. These and other regression results are reported in Kotlikoff and Summers (1980).

15. The year 1955 was chosen because by 1955 the social security data cover most of the private economy's work force.

16. Christensen and Jorgenson's (1973) "true" consumption series (p. 17) is very close to the NIA series for the years 1929–69. The Christensen and Jorgenson series is slightly higher for most years; using the Christensen and Jorgenson series for the post-1929 years would, therefore, lead us to calculate less life-cycle wealth.

17. See SEC (1977, p. 11). This assumes that nonprofit institutions have no liabilities.

18. The 1972–73 CES data indicate that the average age gap between husband and wife is 3 years. The number of deaths in an age-sex cohort in a particular year was obtained by multiplying age-, sex-, and year-specific death rates from the US

Census Bureau's population estimates. Historical statistics (US Department of Commerce 1975, vol. 1, death rates, series B 181–192, pp. 61–62) are smoothed. Even in the absence of marriage, our LCW2 concept would be of interest because it essentially treats individuals as if their wealth at each moment were fully annuitized; i.e., given the uncertainty of the date of death, individuals in a life-cycle model with no bequest motive would always purchase annuities. Hence, our procedure of essentially passing a cohort's bequest over to surviving members mimics the life-cycle wealth of the US economy if individuals always purchased annuities.

19. These include increasing the labor income of the self-employed by 20 percent, using a high value of .55 for the ratio of female to male earnings at age 40, assuming that the age-consumption profile is flat after age 75 and assuming that all earnings after age 75 are zero.

20. Roger Gordon has suggested to us that observed age-earnings profiles may differ from true age-earnings profiles to the extent that firms and workers are engaged in implicit contractual arrangements. Firms could pay out to workers less (more) than they truly earn when young and more (less) than they truly earn when old. Some part of a worker's life-cycle saving or dissaving would then by accomplished within the firm and would correspond to a claim (or liability) attached to the firm's assets. While we would strongly contest the empirical validity of this proposition, certainly a very upper-bound estimate of life-cycle savings with firms would be the difference between the market and replacement costs of capital in the corporate sector. Using 0.819, the average value of q over the period 1952–74 (von Furstenberg 1977) and the 1974 replacement value of corporate capital of $1.679 trillion give an upper-bound estimate of $304 billion for this effect.

21. In 1970, for example, the level of philanthropic payments of individuals totaled $16.09 billion (US Department of Commerce 1976, p. 90, lines 101 and 102) reported 1970 expenditures of institutions for religious, educational, and welfare activities totaled only $11.32 billion.

22. If we take age 18 as the age of adulthood, the value of 55 for D corresponds to a real-world age of death of 73.

23. To precisely calculate a weighted age gap we would need data detailing age of donors and recipients as well as the size of the transfers. Such data are currently unavailable.

2   Intergenerational Transfers and Savings

In recent years the role of intergenerational transfers in the process of wealth accumulation has been the subject of substantial empirical and theoretical analysis. The key question stimulating this research is, What is the main explanation for savings? Is it primarily accumulation for retirement, as claimed by Albert Ando, Richard Brumberg, and Franco Modigliani in their celebrated life cycle model of savings? Is it primarily intentional accumulation for intergenerational transfers? Or is it primarily precautionary savings, much of which may be bequeathed because of imperfections in annuity markets?

The answer to the savings puzzle has many policy implications; certain tax structures are much more conducive to some types of savings than others, and certain government insurance programs might appear less attractive if precautionary motives are the main explanation of savings. Knowledge of the primary savings mechanism would also provide the key to understanding the distribution of wealth.

Solving the savings puzzle requires first collecting the pieces and then seeing how they fit together. A major piece of the puzzle is understanding the quantitative importance of intergenerational transfers to the accumulation of wealth. As I argue, there is strong evidence that intergenerational transfers play an important and perhaps dominant role in US wealth accumulation. This does not mean, however, that intentional saving for gifts and bequests is the main saving motive. Significant intergenerational transfers could also arise in the life cycle model in the absence of well-functioning private annuity markets or close substitutes for such markets. In such a setting bequests would be involuntary and potentially quite sizable (Stiglitz and Bevan 1979; Davies 1981; and see chapter 4 of this book). Let us first look at the evidence on the importance of intergenerational transfers and then turn to the deeper question of why such transfers arise.

Journal of Economic Perspectives, forthcoming. © Reprinted with permission.

2.1   The Importance of Intergenerational Transfers to Savings

There are six types of evidence concerning the importance of intergenerational transfers to savings: (1) comparisons of total US wealth with life cycle wealth, defined as the amount of US wealth there would be in the absence of any net intergenerational transfers (the difference between total wealth and life cycle wealth is defined as transfer wealth; these calculations use age-earnings and age-consumption profiles and other data, but they do not use data on transfers since they are concerned with what wealth would be in the absence of transfers), (2) the calculation of transfer wealth using steady-state assumptions and the limited reported data on the flow of transfers, (3) zero-transfer life cycle simulation models that attempt to reproduce in a realistic manner actual wealth to income ratios or actual wealth distributions, (4) analysis of the rate of asset decumulation of the elderly, (5) evidence from annuity markets, and (6) historical evidence concerning the correlation of saving rates and changes in the length of retirement. Each type of evidence suggests an important role for intergenerational transfers in savings.

Calculation of Life Cycle and Transfer Wealth Components

Chapter 1 considered the following question: Are the US data broadly consistent with the view that intergenerational transfers play a negligible role in US wealth accumulation? Stated differently, can one reject the null hypothesis that the life cycle model fully explains US wealth? To address this question we divided total wealth W into two components, life cycle wealth L and transfer wealth T, and defined life cycle wealth of a cohort as the sum over each age of the accumulated difference between past streams of labor earnings and consumption. Total life cycle wealth equals the sum over cohorts of each cohort's life cycle wealth. Let E and C stand, respectively, for the sum over cohorts of all past accumulated earnings and all past accumulated consumption. Then

$$W = L + T \quad \text{and} \quad L = E - C. \tag{1}$$

With this definition of L, T equals the sum over cohorts of the sum of accumulated net transfers received at each age. Calculating L requires knowledge of longitudinal age-earnings and age-consumption profiles for each cohort. These profiles were derived using data for the period 1900–1974 on cross-section-relative age-earnings and age-consumption profiles and aggregate earnings and consumption. The procedure involved distributing total earnings and consumption in each year by age and sex; combining these cross-section age-sex matrices of earnings and consumption yields longitudinal profiles that are used to form E and C. In our initial paper Summers and I reported a value of L for 1974 of $733 billion, which is only 18.9 percent of total 1974 household wealth of $3,884 billion. We subsequently identified an error in the treatment of durables. In our reply to Modigliani (1984) (Kotlikoff and Summers 1986), we indicate that a proper correction for durables raises the share of life cycle wealth to 21.9 percent.[1]

While the 21.9 percent figure is quite small, it is probably an over estimate of the life cycle share of total wealth. In order to generate at least some positive value for life cycle wealth, Summers and I adjusted upward standard estimates of the labor income of the self-employed by 20 percent. Since life cycle wealth is the accumulated difference between labor earnings and consumption, larger labor earnings of the self-employed implies a larger calculated value of life cycle wealth. The ratio of self-employed workers to employees was substantially larger in the prewar period than it is today. Hence the calculated value of life cycle wealth is fairly sensitive to the estimation of the labor earnings of the self-employed. Using standard estimates would reduce life cycle wealth by about $700 billion. In addition, correcting several other intentional biases in our calculation would produce negative values for life cycle wealth. These include our assumption of a quite high ratio of female to male earnings, our assumption of zero earnings after age 75, and our assumption that the age-consumption profile is flat, rather than declining, after age 75.

It may be useful to repeat our basic explanation for why life cycle wealth is so small in the United States. Unlike simple classroom depictions of hump saving in which the age consumption is flat and the earnings profile rises to retirement, actual age-earnings and age-consumption profiles, such as those in figures 1.1 and 1.2 (see chapter 1 in this volume), have essentially identical shapes and levels before at least age 45. Between ages 45 and 60 there clearly is some hump saving in that earnings profiles exceed consumption profiles; also after age 60 the age-consumption profile clearly exceeds the age-earnings profile. However, this pattern of hump saving and dissaving (at least relative to earnings) occurs quite late in the life cycle. Hence one would not expect a large accumulation of life cycle wealth in the aggregate since the life cycle wealth of the more numerous generations below age 45 is so small. The simple fact is that consumption does not rise more rapidly through life than labor income.

An earlier study by Darby (1979), which influenced my study with Summers, used cross-section data on wealth, earnings, and consumption to divide current wealth holdings into a fraction that would be consumed and a fraction that would be transferred to succeeding generations. Darby inferred longitudinal age-consumption and age-earnings profiles from the cross-section profile and concluded that at most 29 percent of US private net worth is devoted to future consumption, with the rest destined for intergenerational transfer. White (1978) used aggregate data on the age structure of the population, age-earnings and age-consumption profiles along with a variety of parametric assumptions and concluded that the life cycle model can account for only about a quarter of aggregate saving. Although their accounting frameworks are somewhat different and although they use different data, and only cross-section data at that, Darby and White reach essentially the same conclusion as Kotlikoff and Summers because the basic shapes of US cross-section age-earnings and age-consumption profiles and the longitudinal profiles that can reasonably be inferred from the cross-section profiles are quite different from those of the textbook life cycle model.

Calculations of Life Cycle and Transfer Wealth Using Flow Data

The analyses just described directly calculate life cycle wealth and indirectly infer the stock of transfer wealth. Obviously it would be useful to corroborate these results with direct evidence on intergenerational transfers. Chapter 1 also examines the available flow data on intergenerational transfers. We presented a formula, which is valid only in the steady state, that relates the flow of transfers to the stock of transfer wealth.

There are three major problems with this method for calculating T. First, the available flow data on transfers clearly provide a lower bound estimate for total transfer flows; there are no data sources that systematically report intergenerational transfers made in the form of implicit and explicit gifts. Explicit gifts, which may be in kind as well as in cash, are clearly knowledged as such by donors and recipients. Implicit gifts, such as making one's child an equal partner in a lucrative family business or providing low interest loans to children, may not be viewed as a gift by donors or recipients and would be hard to identify in a survey. Since the US distribution of wealth is highly skewed, implicit gifts, while perhaps small in number, could be quite large in value. Hence any flow estimates of transfer wealth, particularly those of Modigliani (1988), since he ignores all nonbequest intergenerational transfers, should be viewed as potentially seriously downward biased.

The second problem with using flow data to calculate T is that the assumption of a steady state may be far from justified. It may be, for example, that the flow of intergenerational transfers in relation to the scale of the economy was much greater in the 1920s than in the 1960s and 1979s. Not only must one assume that aggregate variables have been in steady state since at least the turn of the century, but one must also assume that the age distribution of transfers is time invariant.

The third problem is that the simple formula given in equation (2), which relates transfer wealth T to the transfer flow [the formula incorporates Modigliani's (1984) correction for a small error], assumes that everyone dies at the same age D, that all transfers are received at the same age I, and that all transfers are made at the same age G. This is obviously unrealistic, and it is not clear what choice of these three ages best approximates reality. The appropriate choice of these ages depends on one's assumption about the steady-state interest and growth rates of the economy, r and n, respectively. If half of transfers are received at age 20 and half at age 60, using 40 for the approximate I would be inappropriate; transfers received at age 20 should receive more weight in the approximation formula because they are accumulated for a much longer period than transfers received at age 60 and because the accumulation formula is a nonlinear function of age.

$$T = \frac{t}{(r-n)} e^{(r-n)D} [1 - e^{(n-r)(G-I)}] e^{(n-r)I}. \tag{2}$$

To illustrate the implication of the formula, Summers and I discussed an example in which D equals 55 (a real world age of death of 73 if the age of adulthood is 18), $(G - I)$ equals 30, and $(r - n)$ equals 0.01. Because of our algebraic error, we did not assume a value for I. Using a value of I equal to 15 seems justified when r exceeds n because transfer wealth depends on the period of accumulation and the appropriate approximation to I should be smaller if r exceeds n. The resulting value of G of 45 also seems reasonable, given the fact that not all transfers are made at death. A similar statement holds for the choice of the age gap $(G - I)$; thus it seems likely that the choice of 30 for $(G - I)$ is too small, given that r exceeds n. But if we keep $(G - I)$ at 30 and choosing I equal to 15, the factor multiplying the flow of transfers t in (2) is 39. Since the estimated 1974 flow of reported transfers is $45.4 billion, the "transfer flow" lower bound estimate for T is $1,771 billion, or 46 percent of 1974 household wealth. Note that using a potentially more appropriate age gap of $(G - I)$ of 45 would yield a lower bound value of T of \$2,455 billion, or 63 percent of total wealth.

Modigliani's Critique and Calculations

Modigliani (1988) focuses to a large extent on two issues. The first is "flow" estimates of the importance of intergenerational transfers to savings, and the second is the proper definition of life cycle versus transfer wealth. Modigliani devotes little space to the main contribution of chapter 1, the direct calculation of life cycle wealth. We devoted most of our paper to the direct calculation of life cycle wealth because, as we stressed, the "flow" approach overestimates life cycle wealth as a result of the absence of data on a variety of transfer flows. In addition, as mentioned, the flow approach requires invoking steady-state and other simplifying assumptions that may not be valid.

Defining Life Cycle Weath
Our definition of life cycle wealth is motivated by the following question: Are the US data on labor earnings, rates of return, consumption, and wealth broadly consistent with the view that intergenerational transfers play a negligible role in US wealth accumulation? Stated differently, can one reject the null hypothesis that the life cycle model without intergenerational transfers fully explains US wealth? We defined life cycle wealth according to the theoretical prediction of the zero-intergenerational-transfer life cycle model, namely, as the sum over cohorts of the accumulated difference between past streams of labor earnings and consumption. We defined the difference between actual US wealth and life cycle wealth as transfer wealth.

Modigliani focuses on a different definition of the two components of life cycle wealth. He also suggests that we have "redefined" the two components. While Modigliani asserts that our definition of life cycle wealth is nonstandard, it is the definition used in the two previous extensive analyses by Tobin (1967) and Darby (1979) of the role of the pure life cycle model in US wealth accumulation. This definition is also the one chosen by Hayashi (1986) in his inquiry into life cycle and intergenerational transfer saving in Japan. Indeed, the practice of comparing the wealth predicted by the zero-intergenerational-transfer life cycle model with total wealth dates to Modigliani and Brumberg (1954).

Modigliani prefers to define life cycle wealth as L_m, where L_m equals the sum over cohorts of the sum of saving at each age and saving is defined as income less consumption. The problem with his definition is that income may include capital income earned on previously received intergenerational transfers. Hence, because income itself may reflect intergenerational transfers, the sum of saving out of income cannot be used to test with maximum power the null hypothesis that the zero-transfer life cycle model accounts for essentially all of US wealth. Stated differently, under the null hypothesis, $L_m = L$, but, if there are significant intergenerational transfers, L_m could be close to W, although both L_m and W would be substantially different from L. Indeed, Ando (1986a) reports calculations of L_m equal to 65 percent to 75 percent of W for the period 1960 to 1970, while our 1974 calculation of L is only 21.9 percent of 1974 W.

Once one finds that the data are highly inconsistent with the zero-transfer life cycle formulation, a natural behavioral question to raise is, What would be the impact on US wealth of eliminating all intergenerational transfers? We raised this economic, as opposed to accounting, issue in our 1981 paper, indicating how our definition and estimate of life cycle wealth could be used to address this unrealistic but nonetheless interesting counterfactual. The answer to this economic question is, of course, independent of accounting convention. It takes into account the changes in life cycle wealth that might arise if the intergenerational transfers were eliminated. More precisely, in a world of significant transfers some fraction of consumption and leisure may be financed out of such transfers, and their elimination could affect the value of L. Our answer to the economic question, to which we still subscribe, is that totally eliminating intergenerational transfer would in partial equilibrium reduce US wealth by at least 50 percent. This economic as opposed to accounting statement suggests a much more important role for intergenerational transfers than has generally been thought to be the case.

Bequests versus Total Intergenerational Transfers
In addition to redefining life cycle wealth, Modigliani redefines intergenerational transfers to include only bequests at death. Thus his flow calculations of the shares of life cycle and transfer wealth exclude all intergenerational transfers in the form of explicit gifts, college tuition, and implicit gifts, such as interest free loans and the transfers of businesses to children through partnership agreements. In effect, Modigliani treats any adult, regardless of age, who receives nonbequest transfers from his or her parents as a "dependent" and ascribes the consumption resulting from such transfers to the parent(s).

In contrast to this peculiar redefinition of intergenerational transfers and adulthood, chapter 1 defines the age of adulthood as age 18 and treat all payments, either in cash or in kind (including tuition payments), received from parents by children above age 18 as an intergenerational transfer. Support of children before age 18 is considered consumption by the parent. Because the consumption of children is ascribed to their parents, the choice of age of adulthood affects the shape of the age-consumption profile of adult cohorts.

Modigliani particularly objects to our labeling college tuition expenditures by parents as an intergenerational transfer. While one may argue about the proper age of adulthood, given the fungibility of money, there is no reasonable basis for labeling parental tuition support differently from parental gifts of durables, such as cars, or parental gifts of money; that is, whether the parent pays tuition or gives the child the money to pay tuition is economically equivalent. In addition, there is no reason, as Modigliani suggests, to classify somehow educational expenditures as a human as opposed to nonhuman wealth transfer. The transfer of funds to pay for education constitutes a transfer of nonhuman capital. The fact that the expenditure leads to smarter or more skilled children as opposed to, for example, fatter children is quite immaterial to the issue of tracing the origins of nonhuman wealth accumulation.

The choice of the age of adulthood is, however, arbitrary. While age 18 seems reasonable for the postwar period, it may be too old for older 1974 cohorts, some of whom were born in the last century. Many of these older generations entered the labor force at younger ages than is currently typical and they certainly had a much shorter life span. Indeed, until the 1950s labor force participation rates were calculated for the population over age 14. Had Summers and I used a younger age, such as 16, for the age of adulthood for the older cohorts that were alive in 1974, we would have reported considerably less life cycle wealth.

Simulation Studies of Life Cycle Wealth and Comparisons with
Actual Wealth Holdings

Simulation analyses also call into question the pure life cycle model. Auerbach and Kotlikoff (1987; and see chapter 13) point out, using a detailed life cycle simulation model, that realistic specification of US demographics, preferences, and fiscal institutions implies an extremely small if not negative wealth to income ratio. Their results differ from those of Tobin (1967) because of their inclusion of income taxes and social security and their more realistic assumptions concerning the growth rate of consumption over the life cycle. In order to generate substantial life cycle savings, Tobin found it necessary to assume that consumption over the life cycle grows at a much faster rate than actually observed. Tobin's calculations, which appear to come closest to replicating observed ratios of wealth to income, assume that consumption grows at a rate of 5 percent per year over the life cycle. This rate is more than twice the rate actually observed chapter 1.

Other simulation studies by Atkinson (1971a,b) and Oulton (1976) point out the difficulty of explaining wealth inequality based on the zero-transfer life cycle model. To quote Atkinson: "It is clear from the analysis that life cycle factors cannot explain the upper tail of the current distribution of wealth in Britain." Note that the upper tail of the British wealth distribution in Atkinson's study accounts for about three-quarters of total British wealth holdings. Both Atkinson and Oulton indicate that the substantial inequality in wealth relative to earnings can be explained only by intergenerational transfers. The Bevan and Stiglitz (1969) simulation study explicitly accounted for "altruistic" bequests, but just for lower-income children, and showed that even this could not account for the tail.

Asset Decumulation of the Elderly

Decumulation of wealth after retirement is an essential aspect of the life cycle theory. Yet simple cross-section tabulations of wealth holdings by age (Mirer 1979; Kurz 1984a,b) or saving rates by age (Thurow 1976; Danziger et al. 1984) do not support the central prediction that the aged dissave. Mirer and Kurz report that wealth holding tends to increase with age.

Thurow reports positive saving rates for persons in all age groups, whereas Danziger et al. report that saving rates increase with age with "the elderly spend[ing] less than the nonelderly at the same level of income and [with] the very oldest of the elderly having the lowest average propensity to consume." The most recent cross-section study of consumption rates by age is that of Ando (1986b); his regression analysis leads him to conclude that "most families follow a reasonably well defined pattern of savings and net wealth accumulation before their retirement, but they tend to dissave little after retirement."

Cross section analysis of estate data by Atkinson (1971a) and Atkinson and Harrison (1978) and panel analysis of the estates of individual cohorts by Menchik and David (1983) and David and Menchik (1985) also show that the average amount of wealth of cohorts rises in old age. Shorrocks's (1975) panel study of the estates of a single cohort in England indicates positive wealth accumulation until age 70. Hayashi's (1986) analysis of savings of Japanese cohorts in the 1970s leads him to conclude that "mean asset holdings do decline as cohorts age," and Ando (1986a) commenting on Hayashi's research on Japan and his own states that "the apparent total lack of dissaving by older households in Japan is clearly inconsistent with the life-cycle theory." Menchik and David's longitudinal analyses of American estate data is most relevant for understanding US savings behavior. They examine the estates of four birth cohorts living in Wisconsin in the period 1947–1978 and born between 1880 and 1925. In addition to studying within cohort behavior, their analyses control for the lifetime earnings of cohort members. Their results "fail to show individuals decumulating wealth in old age."

In contrast to these studies, King and Dicks-Mireaux (1982), using cross-section Canadian data, suggest a positive rate of decumulation in old age. Burbidge and Robb (1985), on the other hand, reach a somewhat different conclusion from an examination of King and Dicks-Mireaux's data. They report old age asset decumulation only for blue-collar workers. For white-collar workers the age wealth profile is flat between ages 55 and 65 and rises after age 65. Except for the study by King and Dicks-Mireaux, the only other analysis that seems to confirm the life cycle model's prediction of a declining age wealth profile is the panel regression analysis by Diamond and Hausman (1984). However, as both Bernheim (1986) and Hurd (1986) point out, their subsample from the National Longitudinal Survey may not be representative. Indeed, Diamond and Hausman begin their analysis by excluding low wealth households on the grounds that their behavior is inconsistent with the assumptions of the life cycle model. In addition, their data set is not well suited to a study of the wealth of the elderly after they retire because, even at the end of the ten-year panel, the ages of the sample range from 55 to only 69.

A number of questions can be raised about many of these analyses of the age-wealth profiles and saving rates of the aged. The cross-section and several of the cohort analyses (but not those of Menchik and David) may be biased toward a slower rate of asset decumulation because the rich live longer than the poor. In addition, the composition of the sample by age of retirement changes with the age of the sample. But these findings concerning the failure to decumulate are particularly striking since, as Bernheim

(1986) points out, the presence of future social security and pension streams increases the rate of asset decumulation implied by the life cycle model.

Probably the best analyses of asset changes among the aged are those by Hurd (1986) and Bernheim (1986), both of whom use the panel data in the Retirement History Survey. While panel analysis permits holding constant the individual household, one cannot be sure whether changes over time in wealth reflect conscious household saving decisions or are merely the result of unexpected capital gains or losses.

Bernheim considers changes in wealth over two periods, 1969–1975 and 1975–1979, for two samples of elderly, the retired and the nonretired. He also distinguishes between couples and single individuals. Bernheim's measure of wealth change is the log of the ratio of wealth at the end of the period to wealth at the beginning of the period.

For retired couples Bernheim reports a quite small average rate of asset decumulation (a small average ratio of the logs) for the first period and a small average rate of asset accumulation in the second period. Almost half of retired couples in the earlier period and almost three-fifths of couples in the latter period exhibited positive rates of asset accumulation. For nonretired couples the average rate of wealth change was positive in both periods with roughly three-fifths of the nonretired elderly engaging in positive accumulation. Nonretired single individuals also had positive accumulation on average in both periods, again with about three-fifths exhibiting positive saving. The only group whose average rate of wealth change was negative in both periods is retired single individuals. This group displayed a reasonably large rate of asset decumulation on average; but even among this group over two-fifths had positive saving.

Bernheim carefully considers these data in light of social security and private pensions and states that "the inclusion of annuities reinforces earlier findings that resources decline only slightly, if at all, after retirement" and that "the pure life cycle hypothesis fails to account for savings behavior after retirement."

Hurd reaches a different conclusion from Bernheim stating "contrary to many results from cross-section data, the elderly do dissave." However, this conclusion appears to be based on tabulations that exclude housing wealth. In addition, one may question Hurd's method of calculating wealth changes; Hurd examines the change in average wealth rather than the average change in wealth. When Hurd includes housing wealth, he reports that average total real wealth of all Retirement History Survey couples declined by only 2 percent between 1969 and 1979. For single individuals Hurd reports a decline of 22.4 percent over the ten-year period in average total wealth. The corresponding figures when housing wealth is excluded are 14.5 percent for couples and 36.4 percent for singles.

Hurd views the findings on nonhousing wealth as most informative, arguing that increases in housing wealth in the 1970s reflect unexpected capital gains. He fails to point out, however, that the reduction in non-housing wealth over the period may reflect unexpected capital losses on stocks and bonds. In addition, the elderly may well have responded to capital gains in housing by accumulating less in other forms; that is, in the absence of capital gains in housing, nonhousing wealth may have been larger.

Hurd's measure may also be more sensitive to measurement error than Bernheim's; the level of average wealth in either 1969 or 1979 may be biased because of outliers. Hurd has indicated (personal communication) that the results based on median wealth are similar, but his study, in contrast to that of Bernheim, tells us little about the distribution of wealth changes across the sample.

In sum, the panel studies of Bernheim and Hurd suggest little if any total wealth decumulation of couples and some limited total wealth decumulation of single individuals. In addition, Bernheim shows that a sizable fraction of singles and couples continue to accumulate wealth in old age. Even those panel studies that suggest wealth decumulation, on average, indicate a significant fraction of elderly households continuing to accumulate wealth. This by itself is strong evidence against the standard no-intergenerational-transfer life cycle model.

Evidence from Annuity Markets

The strict life cycle model without allowance for bequest motives makes strong predictions about the demand for annuities. Since the date of death is uncertain and since bequests provide no utility, life cycle models imply that there should be a strong demand for annuity insurance. Indeed, chapter 4 demonstrates that, for the commonly used time separable CES utility function of consumption and assuming a risk aversion coefficient of 1.75, the gain to a 55-year-old with average mortality probabilities from obtaining access to an actuarially fair annuities market is equivalent to an almost 70 percent increase in his lifetime resources in the absence of such markets.

In fact, the demand for annuities appears to be weak (Friedman and Spivak 1986). Friedman and Wahrshawsky (1984) report that the loads on annuity insurance are no higher than the loads on other frequently purchased types of insurance such as property and casualty insurance. Yet annuity purchases are a rarity. Friedman and Wahrshawsky argue that it is necessary to assume a fairly strong bequest motive to explain this behavior. Friedman and Wahrshawsky do not, however, take into account uncertainty with respect to inflation risk, which may explain the reluctance of many to purchase nominal annuities. In addition, totally "annuitizing" one's wealth might leave one illiquid and unable to pay major one-time expenses such as medical care. Still the virtual nonexistence of annuity insurance is quite surprising.

Chapter 4 advances a possible alternative explanation, namely, that families will self-insure to a large extent when annuity insurance is available only on unfavorable terms; family insurance, however, does not appear capable of fully accounting for the widespread failure to annuitize. Bernheim, Shleifer, and Summers (1986) review a number of settings in which annuities are available on a fair or even subsidized basis and report that even in these cases there is little demand for annuities. They conclude from this evidence that many consumers must have significant bequest motives. Their strongest evidence comes from TIAA-CREF's 1973 Survey of Beneficiaries. In this survey over 70 percent of beneficiaries chose plans other than those providing full annuity protection despite the fact that TIAA-CREF annuities appear to be quite close to actuarially fair.

Historical Evidence

The essential prediction of the life cycle theory is that people save to prepare for their retirement when they must dissave and consume. Without periods of retirement or at least significant decreased labor earnings at the end of life, there is no life cycle motive for saving. Yet there were substantial positive net national saving rates (net national saving divided by net national product) over the period 1870–1930, when retirement was much less common than it is today.

There was some retirement in the latter part of the last century and the pre-Depression years of this century, but the retirement rate of the elderly was small, especially when compared with current rates. During the period 1870–1930 the labor force participation rate of males 65 and older exceeded 58 percent and for much of the period it exceeded 70 percent (Moen 1987a, 1987b). In contrast, the comparable current rate for males 65 and older is 25 percent. Life expectancy for age 20 males during the period 1870–1930 appears to have been about 65; for much of the postwar period it has been above 70.

Despite this significant increase in the length of retirement, the saving rate in recent decades has been substantially smaller than that observed between 1870 and 1930. The average saving rate, defined as net national saving divided by net national product, recorded from 1870 to 1930, is close to 50 percent greater than the average saving rate in the postwar period.[2] In contrast to the life cycle model, at least one class of bequests models suggests that saving rates may fall with the life span and, ceteris paribus, length of retirement (Skinner 1985). The intuition here is that a reduction in mortality probabilities reduces the likelihood of a near-term bequest. Hence there is less of a bequest saving incentive.

Of course, much besides the length of retirement changed over the last century, so the negative correlation between the saving rate and the length of retirement may be spurious. It is therefore also useful to examine this correlation over shorter periods. During the period 1869–1891 the labor force participation rate of men 65 and older exceeded 73 percent and at times was as high as 78 percent. In contrast, the participation rate between 1902 and 1931 was below 66 percent, and for most of the period it was below 60 percent. Despite this increase in the length of retirement over the two periods, the average rate of net national saving is slightly higher in the latter period. There is also a postwar negative correlation between the length of retirement and the saving rate. Kotlikoff and Smith (1983) report that since 1950 the expected duration of retirement and other nonworking periods for the average adult has almost doubled. This change coincided with a secular decline since 1950 of almost 40 percent in the net national saving rate. Of course, the introduction of unfunded Social Security (Feldstein 1974c) and other government policies may have reduced saving since 1950, but the life cycle model would still predict a quite substantial offsetting impact arising from the change in retirement (chapter 12).

2.2   Understanding Intergenerational Transfers

Explanations for Intergenerational Transfers

Altruistic concern for one's children is the first reason one thinks of for intergenerational transfers. This concern may be expressed mathematically as the parent having direct utility for the utility of the child, as in Barro (1974) and Becker (1974). An alternative nonaltruistic model of bequests

(Yarri 1965; Blinder 1973) is that parents care about the level of the bequest per se. But a utility of the size of the bequest model seems implausible because it implies that the parent's transfer to the child is independent of the child's economic circumstances.

The altruistic model also seems somewhat implausible because it has such strong neutrality predictions. As is well known, Barro (1984) showed that intergenerational transfers by the government are completely neutralized because parents internalize the effects on all future generations of such transfers. More recently Kotlikoff (1983) and Bernheim and Bagwell (1985) independently showed that marriage may altruistically link a large number of parents and other extended family members (if not the entire planet) with the implication that intragenerational government transfers will also be entirely neutralized.

The neutrality properties of the altruistic models hold only if transferors are not constrained in their transfers. As an example of such constraints, suppose that an altruistic parent would like to transfer from her children to herself but that the parent cannot compel her children to make such a transfer; in this situation government redistribution from that parent to her child will have real effects.

An alternative view of transfers from parents to children, which has nothing to do with parental concern for children or a desire per se to leave bequests, is that parents and children form an incomplete annuities market (Kotlikoff and Spivak 1981). According to this view parents and children enter into implicit risk sharing arrangements. The risk to be shared is the parent's longevity risk. The arrangement involves parents agreeing to transfer their assets to their children at death as a quid pro quo for support payments from the children if the parents live longer than expected. Enforcement of such arrangement is enhanced by having the child make payments to the parent each year rather than waiting until the parent runs out of resources.

Chapter 5 demonstrates that significant intergenerational transfers could arise in the aggregate in a dynamic equilibrium model of imperfect family annuity insurance. Indeed, they point out that such a model could explain much of the 80–20 split of transfer and life cycle wealth reported in chapter 1. This point is important; it indicates that, although intergenerational transfers may be large in the aggregate, fundamental preferences may still correspond to those posited in the generationally selfish life cycle model.

Other researchers, including Sheshinski and Weiss (1981), Davies (1981), Eckstein, Eichenbaum, and Peled (1983), Abel (1983), and Hubbard (1984a,

1984b), have examined the potential for intergenerational transfers when no annuity insurance whatsoever, including implicit family insurance, is available. These studies also demonstrate clearly that significant intergenerational transfers can arise in the life cycle model if annuity insurance is unavailable.[3]

Even if the life span were certain, individuals may save significant sums for the possibility of substantial end-of-life medical and nursing home expenses. If such medical problems do not arise, the elderly individual may be unable to consume this nest egg before he or she dies, and consequently a bequest will arise.

Other individuals may simply strike it rich in their professions and investments and find themselves unable to consume all their resources. It is clear that consumption satiation does occur; there are enough examples of extremely wealthy individuals, many who are quite young, who are unable to consume their wealth over their lifetime, especially when one properly measures consumption as excluding expenditures on durables but including imputed rent on durables. Additional research is needed to determine how substantial windfalls influence total wealth accumulation. Although there is some contradictory evidence concerning the bequest-resource elasticity (Menchik and David 1983; and see chapter 16 of this book), this elasticity surely exceeds unity for the superwealthy.

Bernheim, Shleifer, and Summers (1985) advance a forth explanation for intergenerational transfers, namely, the implicit payment by parents to their children for providing in kind services, such as assisting them with chores and trips to the doctor. While some intergenerational transfers surely arise as payments for child-provided services, it seems quite unlikely that such transfers would be large in the aggregate.

Each of these explanations of intergenerational transfers presumably plays some role in explaining aggregate transfers; in addition, there are probably many traditional life cycle households that are well annuitized through private pensions and Social Security and, consequently leave no intergenerational transfers. This heterogeneous view of preferences and insurance arrangements is espoused by Kurz (1984a).

Empirical Analyses of Alternative Models of Intergenerational Transfers

Empirical analysis of intergenerational transfers has been greatly limited by the available data. To test models of altruism or family insurance arrangements, one needs data on the transfers, consumption choices, and resources of not only parents but also adult children; that is one needs information on the extended family. At present there are simply no suitable data sets covering the extended family.

There are, however, data on inter vivos transfers and bequests. In his analysis of 379 Connecticut estates with bequests to children with siblings, Menchik (1980) finds strong evidence that "wealth bequeathed to children is shared equally." This study confirmed earlier findings by Sussman et al. (1970) and Brittian (1978). On the other hand, Tomes's (1981) findings based on recall data from Cleveland contradict the equal bequest view; but in 1985 Menchik (1985) sampled actual probate records in Cleveland and found equal division in 93 percent of the cases. The finding of equal bequests strongly contradicts the prediction of the altruistic model, which predicts that differences in bequests would compensate for differences in children's earnings capacities. Cox (1987) reports another finding at odds with altruism, namely, that transfers are positively related to the recipient's income level.

Hurd (1986) also finds evidence against the utility of bequest model and indirectly against the altruism model. Hurd points out that parents with bequest motives should consume their end-of-life resources at a slower rate than those with bequest motives. He then compares the rate of asset decumulation of the elderly who have children with those who do not. He finds no significant difference in the rate of asset decumulation between the two groups. A contrasting finding by Friedman and Spivak (1986) is that people with more children are less likely to purchase annuities.

Bernheim, Schleifer, and Summers (1985) report that, in settings with two or more children, children of richer parents spend more time with their parents than children of poorer parents. In contrast, they find no significant impact of parental wealth on the visitation of only children. The authors view these findings as strong support for their model in which parents with two or more children credibly threaten to disinherit those children who are insufficiently attentive. These findings, while suggestive, must be viewed as preliminary; further analysis taking account of childrens' own wealth position is needed.

In addition to these microeconomic analyses of intergenerational transfers, chapter 18 uses time series data to test directly one of the key neutrality propositions of the altruism model, namely, that aggregated consumption is independent of the age distribution of resources. Their model assumes that extended families have identical Barro-type preferences and identical demographic structures. Under these assumptions aggregate household consumption depends simply on the present value of aggregate human wealth, plus national net worth, less the present value of future government consumption. It is independent of the age distribution of resources. Boskin and Kotlikoff show that, given the appropriate resource variables, the age composition of income still significantly influences aggregate consumption. Thus they reject their admittedly stylized model of intergenerational altruism.

2.3 Conclusion

Like most good puzzles, the saving puzzle has a lot of pieces, many of which do not seem to fit together. It seems well established that intergenerational transfers are sizable and that the process leading to these transfers is responsible for a sizable amount of wealth accumulation. The precise explanation for these transfers remains unclear.

Intergenerational altruism might appear the most likely candidate, but at least some stylized facts, such as the equal allocation of bequests among children, are strongly at odds with the altruism model. Other explanations involving imperfect insurance arrangements or payments for child services do not appear capable of explaining the substantial amount of transfers actually observed. Sorting out the relative contributions of different models to intergenerational transfers and the precise role of intergenerational transfers in the process of wealth accumulation remains an intriguing and exciting enterprise.

Notes

I thank Michael Hurd, James Poterba, Joseph Stiglitz, Lawrence Summers, and Timothy Taylor for helpful comments.

1. The 26 percentage point durable correction referred to by Modigliani (1988) is based on highly suspect steady-state assumptions that we do not regard as reasonable.

2. *Historical Statistics*, p. 231, and the 1987 Economic Report of the President.

3. I find these life cycle models somewhat unsatisfactory because they simply assume away annuity insurance despite the fact that life cycle agents will have substantial demands for annuities. In addition, the bequests arising in these models are arbitrarily allocated to children despite the parents' lack of a bequest motive.

3

Altruistic Linkages within the Extended Family: A Note

The proposition that the consumption of altruistically linked households depends on common as opposed to individual resources appears to be an implication of virtually all reasonable models of such behavior. If all households in the extended altruistic family share the identical utility function, this result is immediate. In this case total extended family resources determine each particular household's consumption, and the coefficients of the resources of other extended family households in a cross-section regression explaining the household's consumption should each equal the coefficient on the sampled household's own resources.

This prediction that an altruistically linked household's consumption depends only on the sum and not the distribution of extended family resources also holds for differences in preferences among altruistic households under the following two assumptions: first, that the utility function of each altruistically linked household is homothetic, and, second, that households act as Cournot-Nash agents in choosing their levels of transfers to other households; that is, they take as given the transfers of all other households in determining their own transfers.

As an example, consider the following four utility functions for households A, B, C, and D that depend on their own consumptions and possibly the utility levels of households 1, 2, and 3. In the equations A and B are both altruistic toward household 1. B is also altruistic with respect to household 3, as is D. Household C here represents a household altruistically connected to household A:

$$U_A = U_A(C_A, U_1(C_1), U_2(C_2)),$$

$$U_B = U_B(C_B, U_1(C_1), U_3(C_3)),$$

$$U_C = U_C(C_C, U_2(C_2)),$$

$$U_D = U_D(C_D, U_3(C_3)).$$

Now each household, taking transfers of other households as given, perceives that a marginal dollar contributed to a household will increase that household's consumption by a dollar. Hence the first-order conditions for determining private transfers are simply that the marginal rate of substitution of each household between its own consumption and that of other households for which it is altruistic, is unity; for example, the price perceived by A of increasing C_A by \$1 is decreasing C_1 or C_2 or $C_1 + C_2$ by \$1.

In these utility functions we have seven unknowns: C_A, C_B, C_C, D_D, C_1, C_2, and C_3. There are six first-order conditions plus the budget constraint that the sum of the consumptions must add to the total resources of the seven households. These seven equations suffice to solve for the seven unknowns. Since the utility functions are homothetic, each of the seven consumption terms is simply proportional to the total resources of the seven households. The Cournot-Nash altruistic bargaining solution implies therefore that an extra dollar of resources acquired by, for example, one's parents should have the same impact on one's consumption as directly acquiring the extra dollar. As in the case of common preferences, the cross-section consumption regression coefficients of altruistically linked household's resources should all be equal.

Although providing a sharp statistical test, this result raises the problem of defining and delimiting the altruistic family. As the example suggests, if one thinks of households D and B as being the two sets of in-laws of household 3 and household A and B as two sets of in-laws of household 1, then household A's consumption will be in part determined by household D's resources. In terms of the example, $C_A = \alpha_A R$ and $C_1 = \alpha_1 R$, where R is total and extended family resources ($R = R_A + R_B + R_C + R_D + R_1 + R_2 + R_3$) and α_A and α_1 are constants. Hence C_A/C_1 should be independent of R_A/R_1. The proportionality factors α_A and α_1 are a function not simply of the preferences of the household in question but of all households with which it is altruistically linked. As a result these variables will likely depend on the particular characteristics, such as age, of the particular household and on the size and demographic composition of its extended family.

Note

This chapter was written in 1983 and was included in a grant proposal to the Sloan Foundation. Bernheim and Bagwell (1985) independently derived the same result.

4

The Family as an Incomplete Annuities Market

with Avia Spivak

The institution of the family provides individuals with risk-sharing opportunities which may not otherwise be available. Within the family there is
a degree of trust and a level of information which alleviates three key
problems in the provision of insurance by markets open to the general
public, namely, moral hazard, adverse selection, and deception. In addition,
provision of insurance within the family may entail smaller transaction
costs than arise in the purchase of insurance on the open market. There are
a number of important risks for which the "public" market problems of
moral hazard, adverse selection, and deception are especially severe. The
risk of loss of job or earnings because of changes in the pattern of demand
or partial disability is one example. Here the ability of the public market to
determine the extent to which the individual actually suffered an earnings
loss or is simply lying about his backache is highly questionable. Other
examples are the risk of bankruptcy and the default risk on personal loans.
Many family practices in dealing with these types of risks can be explained
as implicit insurance contracts made ex ante by completely selfish family
members. Love and affection may be important for the enforcement of
some of these implicit contracts, but they need not be their sole or even
chief determinant. Healthy brother A's support for disabled brother B may
simply be the quid pro quo for brother B's past implicit promise to support
A if A became disabled instead of B.

The existing economics literature on marriage and the family [including
Becker, Landes, and Michael (1977)] has not, to our knowledge, explicitly
considered the family's role in providing insurance to family members.

This paper is concerned with family provision of insurance against the
risk of running out of consumption resources because of greater than

Journal of Political Economy 89(2):372–91(1981). © 1981 by The University of Chicago.
Reprinted with permission.

average longevity. The problem is how fast to consume over time when one does not know how long one will continue to live. Too much consumption when young may mean relative poverty later on if one lives "too long"; alternatively, excessive frugality when young involves the risk of dying without ever having satisfied one's hunger. A complete annuity market permits an individual to hedge this uncertainty of the date of death by exchanging his initial resources for a stream of payments that continue as long as the individual survives. We demonstrate here that implicit risk-sharing arrangements within marriage and the family can substitute to a large extent for the purchase of annuities in public markets. Since the number of family members involved in the risk pooling is generally small, these family risk-sharing arrangements constitute an incomplete annuities market. However, our findings suggest that even small families can substitute by more than 70 percent for a complete annuity market in pooling the risk of death. When the economic structure of society is sufficiently developed to sustain organized public insurance markets, implicit risk pooling within an incomplete family annuity market may well be preferred to public purchase of annuities because of adverse selection and transaction costs.[1] When organized insurance markets do not exist, the analysis here indicates that implicit risk-sharing arrangements can provide powerful economic incentives for marriage and family formation.

Throughout the paper individuals are assumed to be completely selfish; that is, they obtain utility only from their own consumption. One implication of this approach is that voluntary transfers from children to parents or bequests and gifts from parents to children need have nothing at all to do with altruistic feelings; rather, they may simply reflect risk-sharing behavior of completely selfish individuals. While altruism per se is not required, some level of mutual trust and honesty *is* required since elements of these arrangements are not legally enforceable.

This paper is divided into four sections, the first of which describes optimal consumption behavior for a single individual in both the presence and absence of a complete annuity market. The welfare gains from access to a complete and fair annuity market are calculated for the case of the iso-elastic utility function. This welfare gain is, in turn, decomposed into income and substitution effects. This decomposition suggests that an important component of the gains from access to complete or incomplete annuity markets is the desirability of substituting future for current consumption.

Section 4.2 develops the theoretical argument for Pareto-efficient implicit family annuity contracts and explores potential welfare gains arising from these arrangements.[2] Although the complexity of the calculations pre-cluded analysis of large families, quantitative results for families of two and three persons are presented. The analysis considers cases in which family members both do and do not have identical survival probabilities (i.e., are of similar and dissimilar ages and sexes). This framework permits us to ask whether marriage between individuals with similar survival probabilities is more efficient than marriage between individuals with dissimilar survival probabilities.

Optimal family annuity contracts involve agreements on the consumption path of each family member as well as a commitment on the part of each member to name the other members as sole heirs in his estate. Section 4.3 discusses the problems of enforcing both aspects of these agreements. Section 4.4 summarizes the paper and suggests areas for future research.

4.1 A Single Person's Consumption Plans with and without Fair Annuities[3]

In the absence of an annuity market, a single individual's consumption choice problem is to maximize his expected utility, equation (1), from current and future consumption subject to the budget constraint, equation (2):

$$EU = \sum_{t=0}^{D} P_t U(C_t), \tag{1}$$

$$\sum_{t=0}^{D} C_t R^{-t} = W_0. \tag{2}$$

The P_t's of equation (1) are probabilities of surviving from age zero through age t; P_0 equals one. The term D is the maximum longevity. For simplicity, we assume the utility function is separable in consumption (C_t) over time. In (2) R, the discount factor, is one plus the interest rate. The initial wealth of the individual is W_0; we ignore possible streams of future labor earnings or inheritances.[4]

The budget constraint written in equation (2) is identical to the budget constraint that would arise in a certainty world in which individuals never died before age D. While individuals will, on the average, die prior to age D, equation (2) reflects the nonzero probability that an individual will live through age D; that is, equation (2) is the relevant budget constraint because the individual may actually live through age D, in which case his realized present value of consumption cannot exceed his budget.

Let us now assume that the single person is free to purchase actuarially fair annuities in a complete public annuities market. The budget constraint in this case is

$$\sum_{t=0}^{D} P_t C_t R^{-t} = W_0. \tag{3}$$

In contrast with (2), (3) requires only an equality between the expected present value of consumption and initial wealth. The single individual now chooses his optimal consumption path by maximizing (1) subject to (3); he then exchanges his initial wealth W_0 with the insurance company in return for its promise to pay out the C_t stream as long as the person continues to live.

The $P_t R^{-t}$'s in (3) may be thought of as prices. Since each of the P_t's in (3), expect P_0 which equals unity, is less than one, the consumption choice in the case of a fair annuity market is equivalent to the consumption choice without an annuity market but with lower prices of future consumption. Obviously, access to a fair annuity market increases utility by expanding the budget frontier; it also alters the optimal consumption path because of the income and substitution effects resulting from the lower prices of future consumption.

The iso-elastic utility function (4) is convenient for assessing the potential gains from access to a fair public annuities market as well as the gains from family annuity arrangements:

$$EU = \sum_{t=0}^{D} P_t \frac{C_t^{1-\gamma}}{1-\gamma} \alpha^t. \tag{4}$$

In (4), γ is the constant relative risk-aversion parameter, and α is the time preference parameter. By considering different values of γ we indicate for this family of utility functions how the gains from annuities and family arrangements depend on the specification of tastes.

In the no-annuities case maximization of (4) subject to (2) leads to the consumption plan, (5):

$$C_t = \frac{W_0 (R\alpha)^{t/\gamma} P_t^{1/\gamma}}{\sum_{j=0}^{D} R^{j(1-\gamma)/\gamma} \alpha^{j/\gamma} P_j^{1/\gamma}}. \tag{5}$$

In the case of fair annuities, maximizing (4) subject to (3) leads to

$$C_t = \frac{W_0 (R\alpha)^{t/\gamma}}{\sum_{j=0}^{D} R^{j(1-\gamma)/\gamma} \alpha^{j/\gamma} P_j}. \tag{6}$$

Consumption

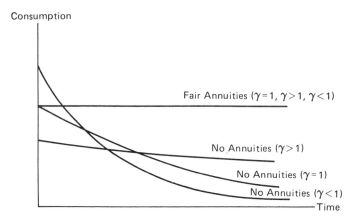

Figure 4.1
Consumption paths with and without fair annuities.

Figure 4.1 compares equations (5) and (6) for the case $R = \alpha = 1$. The ability to trade in a fair annuities market may raise or lower initial consumption, depending on whether γ is less than or greater than unity (fig. 4.1). Intuitively, the higher the degree of risk aversion, γ, the greater the concern for running out of money because of excessive longevity and, hence, the lower the initial consumption. At γ equal to infinity, equation (5) dictates equal consumption in each period.

Plugging (5) or (6) into (4), we arrive at two indirect utility functions for the no-annuity and annuity cases with initial wealth, the interest rate, and survival probabilities as arguments. These functions are presented in equations (7) and (8), respectively:

$$H_0(W_0) = \frac{1}{1 - \gamma} W_0^{1-\gamma} \left[\sum_{j=0}^{D} \alpha^{j/\gamma} R^{j(1-\gamma)/\gamma} P_j^{1/\gamma} \right]^{\gamma}, \tag{7}$$

$$V_0^*(W_0) = \frac{1}{1 - \gamma} W_0^{1-\gamma} \left[\sum_{j=0}^{D} \alpha^{j/\gamma} R^{j(1-\gamma)/\gamma} P_j \right]^{\gamma}. \tag{8}$$

The increase in utility resulting from access to fair annuities can be measured in terms of dollars. Equation (9) solves for the value of M, which represents the percentage increment in a single person's initial wealth required, in the absence of an annuity market, to leave him as well off as he would be with no additional wealth but with access to an annuities market:

$$H_0(MW_0) = V_0^*(W_0). \tag{9}$$

Table 4.1
Percentage increase in initial wealth required to obtain fair annuities utility level[a]

Age	Relative risk aversion (γ)	Males	Females
30	0.75	24.5	18.5
55	0.75	46.9	34.4
75	0.75	71.2	63.0
90	0.75	99.8	100.2
30	1.25	30.3	22.7
55	1.25	59.2	43.4
75	1.25	97.0	85.3
90	1.25	152.6	152.9
30	1.75	34.7	26.1
55	1.75	68.9	50.7
75	1.75	119.1	104.6
90	1.75	199.1	199.4

a. $\alpha = 0.99$ and $R = 1.01$.

For the iso-elastic utility function this calculation is independent of the initial level of wealth. Table 4.1 reports values of M for different ages and levels of risk aversion using both male and female survival probabilities. Friend and Blume (1975) estimate the degree of relative risk aversion from individual portfolio choices. They conclude that risk aversion, on average, exceeds unity. We present our results for risk-aversion coefficients of 0.75, 1.25, and 1.75, a range that we feel encompasses reality. The survival probabilities used in this and all subsequent calculations are actuarial estimates from the Social Security Administration.[5] Maximum longevity is taken to be 120 throughout the paper.

Table 4.1 indicates that the utility gain measured in dollars from access to an annuities market can be quite large. For a relative risk-aversion parameter value of 0.75, the gain to a 55-year-old male is equivalent to a 46.90 percent increase in his initial wealth. The utility gain is age dependent: for $\gamma = 0.75$, the 30-year-old male's gain is 24.46 percent, while the 90-year-old male's gain is 99.81 percent. Annuities are less important to young people because a large fraction of their lifetime utility from consumption is fairly certain due to their lower mortality probabilities in the immediate future. Higher levels of risk aversion naturally increase the gains from access to an annuities market. The male-female differences in the table reflect the higher male age-specific mortality rates. The calculation is somewhat sensitive to the choice of α and R. Raising the interest rate to 5 percent while holding α constant increases the age 55 wealth-equivalent factor from 46.90 to 55.57 for the case of $\gamma = 0.75$. The 90-year-old wealth equivalent is increased from 99.81 to 115.34.

Income, Substitution Effects, and Unintended Bequests

Without access to an annuity market a single, nonaltruistic individual will always die prior to consuming all his wealth and, accordingly, will make involuntary bequests. The level of these unintended bequests can be quite large. From equation (5) we calculated the consumption path as well as the corresponding wealth path for the no-annuity case. By multiplying the probability of dying at each age times the wealth at each age and discounting back to the initial age, the present expected value of these unintended bequests can be computed. For $\gamma = 0.75$, $R = 1.01$, and $\alpha = 0.99$, the present expected value of unintended bequests represents 24.47 percent of initial wealth for a single male aged 55. This number means that a 55-year-old male with no annuity market will, on average, fail to consume about one-quarter of his wealth because he is risk averse. Increasing the risk-aversion coefficient to 1.75 raises the ratio of present unintended bequests to initial wealth to 0.3583. These large unintended bequests occur despite a fairly rapid rate of consumption. Current mortality probabilities dictate a fairly rapid rate of consumption even for high levels of risk aversion. For $\gamma = 1.75$, a single male who survives to age 85 consumes at age 85 less than a third of his age 55 consumption level.[6]

The homothetic property of the iso-elastic utility function permits a decomposition of the utility gains from fair annuities into income and substitution effects. Suppose a fair insurance company approached a single, 55-year-old ($\gamma = 0.75$) male and offered to pay him 24.47 percent of his initial wealth in exchange for his naming the insurance company as his heir. The single male would take the 24.47 percent gain and, because of homotheticity, consume it according to his original no-annuity consumption path. This additional wealth would give rise to an additional 0.2447×0.2447 in present expected bequests. By letting the insurance company also pay for this second round of expected but involuntary bequests as well as further rounds, the insurance company ends up paying $32.40 = 0.2447/(1 - 0.2447)$ percent of the single individual's initial wealth. This 32.40 percent figure represents the utility gain from the pure income effect. In this scenario the individual continues to consume at the no-annuity set of prices. Since the total gain from being able to purchase fair annuities and thus face lower prices for future consumption is 46.90 percent, the income effect represents 69.08 percent and the substitution effect 30.92 percent of the total gain. Hence, the ability to alter the age consumption profile is an important part of the total welfare gain from annuities.

4.2   The Family as an Incomplete Annuities Market

Decisions by family members concerning consumption expenditures and interfamily transfers may reflect implicit though incomplete annuity contracts. In the case of marriage both individuals commonly agree to pool their resources while both marriage partners are alive and to name each other as the major, if not the sole, beneficiary in their wills. For each partner the risk of living too long is somewhat hedged by the other partner's potential death; if one partner lives to be very old, there is a high probability that his (or her) spouse has already died leaving him a bequest to help finance his consumption. While each spouse gains simply from the exchange of wills, the two can further increase their expected utilities by agreeing on a joint consumption path that takes into account each spouse's expected bequest to the other. The importance of joint consumption planning is highlighted in the case of an implicit contract between a parent and a child. Here the parent implicitly promises to name the child in his will in exchange for the child's implicit promise to care for the parent if the parent lives too long. Although the child may have zero probability of dying while the parent is still alive, both can gain because the child agrees to share consumption resources with the parent.

This view of bequest and consumption arrangements within marriage as an incomplete annuity market becomes intuitive when one contemplates increasing the number of members in the family. To simplify the issue, let ua assume that all individuals within the family have identical survival probabilities and that they enter this multiperson family with identical resources. In the limit as the family (or "tribe") gets large, the consumption path of an individual within the tribe converges to the path a single individual would choose in a complete and actuarially fair annuities market (Kotlikoff and Spivak 1979).

Quantitative Analysis of Family Risk Pooling

In the case of two family members the frontier of efficient marriage contracts is obtained as the solution to the following recursive dynamic programming problem:

$$V_{t-1}(W_{t-1}) = \max_{W_t, C_{t-1}^H, C_{t-1}^S \geqslant 0, t=T,\dots,1} [u^H(C_{t-1}^H) + \theta u^S(C_{t-1}^S)$$

$$+ \alpha P_{t/t-1} Q_{t/t-1} V_t(W_t) + \alpha P_{t/t-1}(1 - Q_{t/t-1})H_t(W_t)$$

$$+ \theta \alpha Q_{t/t-1}(1 - P_{t/t-1})S_t(W_t)], \tag{10}$$

subject to

$$W_t/R + C_{t-1}^H + C_{t-1}^S = W_{t-1}, \tag{11}$$

where

$$V_T(W_t) = \max_{C_T^H, C_T^S} u^H(C_T^H) + \theta u^S(C_T^S).$$

In (10) $V_t(W_t)$ is the period t maximum-weighted expected utility of the two family members with joint wealth W_t. In the expression the letters H and S denote the two family members, C_t^H and C_t^S are the consumptions of the two, u^H and u^S are their utility functions, $P_{t/t-1}$ and $Q_{t/t-1}$ are their respective period t survival probabilities conditional upon surviving through period $t-1$, and $H_t(W_t)$ and $S_t(W_t)$ are the maximum expected utilities for each member if he or she alone survives to period t. These expressions are obtained from equation (7) by replacing W_0 with W_t and applying the appropriate probabilities. The term θ is the differential weight applied to member S's expected utility.

The first two terms on the right-hand side of (10) represent utility from certain period $t-1$ consumption. The third term is the family's expected period t utility multiplied by the probability that both members survive to period t. The last two terms represent expected utilities when one member dies and the other survives.

The appendix presents an algorithm to solve (10). The algorithm for solving the three-family-member maximization problem is available from the authors.[7]

The Gains from Family Annuity Contracts

The solution to (10) permits a comparison of consumption paths and utility levels of married people with those of single persons, assuming throughout that there is no public annuities market. Both spouses are assumed to have identical iso-elastic utility functions in the sense of the same degrees of risk aversion and rates of time preference.

The shape of consumption paths for married couples while they are both alive may differ from that of single individuals for two reasons. First, even if the two spouses have identical survival probabilities, the reduction in risk within the marriage rate acts like a reduction in the price of future consumption. If the relative risk-aversion parameter γ exceeds (is less than) one, the identical survival probabilities marriage profile will start above (below) the single person's profile. For γ equal to unity the profiles are identical. In terms of figure 4.1, the consumption profiles for married persons lie between the no-annuity and complete annuity profiles. The second reason for different consumption profiles for married people relative to single individuals is possible differences in spousal survival probabilities. Higher survival probabilities act like lower rates of time preferences. When an old man marries a young woman the slope of the optimal marriage consumption profile reflects the survival probabilities of both the old husband and the young wife. The two spouses compromise with respect to the rate at which they eat up their joint wealth while they are both alive. The old husband would prefer to eat up the wealth more rapidly, and the young wife would prefer to consume at a slower rate. The formula for each spouse's consumption when married takes both spouses' survival probabilities into account as well as the relative spousal utility weights. To our knowledge empirical studies of consumption and savings at the household level have not considered this point—that the time preference rate for a household may depend on the age-sex composition of the household.

Table 4.2 reports the gains from marriage as well as three-person polygamy among individuals who have identical survival probabilities and identical initial endowments and who are weighted equally in the contract. The marriage and three-person polygamy gains are calculated as the percentage increase in a single person's initial wealth needed to make him as well off as he would be in the marriage or polygamous relationship. The table also reports the dollar gain as a fraction of the table 4.1 total dollar gain from complete and fair annuities. Since utility is concave in wealth, the dollar gain from these family contracts as a fraction of the dollar gain from fair annuities is smaller than the actual utility gain from these contracts as a fraction of the utility gain from fair annuities. Table 4.2 also reports this latter fraction.[8]

The figures in table 4.2 indicate that marriage can offer substantial risk-pooling opportunities. For a 55-year-old man using male survival probabilities, pooling risk through marriage is equivalent to about a 20 percent increase in his wealth had he stayed single. The gains from marriage increase as one becomes older since the risks incurred are much greater as one ages. At age 75 marriage is equivalent to increasing one's wealth by

Table 4.2
Annuity gains from marriage and three-person polygamy[a]

Age	Risk aversion	Marriage			Three-person polygamy		
		Dollar marriage gain (%)	Dollar marriage gain/dollar annuity gain	Utility marriage gain/utility annuity gain	Dollar polygamy gain (%)	Dollar polygamy gain/dollar annuity gain	Utility polygamy gain/utility annuity gain
30	0.75	11.7	0.478	0.499	15.8	0.645	0.665
55	0.75	20.0	0.426	0.461	28.0	0.597	0.632
75	0.75	25.4	0.357	0.405	37.2	0.522	0.571
90	0.75	28.2	0.283	0.339	43.1	0.432	0.496
30	1.25	13.0	0.429	0.470	18.0	0.594	0.635
55	1.25	22.3	0.377	0.446	32.1	0.542	0.612
75	1.25	30.1	0.310	0.419	45.2	0.466	0.571
90	1.25	37.1	0.243	0.367	58.2	0.381	0.524
30	1.75	13.6	0.392	0.456	19.3	0.556	0.619
55	1.75	23.5	0.341	0.451	34.5	0.501	0.613
75	1.75	33.2	0.279	0.449	50.7	0.426	0.596
90	1.75	43.0	0.216	0.420	68.7	0.345	0.579

a. The table uses male mortality probabilities. $R = 1.01$ and $\alpha = 0.99$.

30 percent when risk aversion is 1.25. Death-risk-pooling through marriage can be quite important even at young ages. The table reports gains from 11.7 to 13.6 percent at age 30 using the male probabilities.

Marriage can also close much of the utility gap between no annuities and complete annuities. For example, for a 55-year-old with risk aversion of 0.75, marriage substitutes 46.10 percent for complete and fair annuities. Marriage is a better substitute for fair annuities at younger ages because at younger ages the probability that both spouses will die simultaneously is quite small relative to the probability that one spouse will die before the other. In addition, there appears to be an interaction between age and the degree of risk aversion, making marriage a better substitute for fair annuities at young ages when risk aversion is low and at old ages when risk aversion is high.

Over a wide range of ages and parameter values, three people appear to be capable of capturing about 60 percent of the gains from fair annuities. While the complexity of the calculations precluded considering a four-person arrangement, we can conjecture using table 4.2 how well four people would do together. In the case of a 55-year-old male with risk aversion of 0.75, adding one marriage partner is equivalent to a 20 percent increase in his wealth had he remained single. The marginal dollar gain from adding a third person (table 4.2) is 8.04 percent. If the marginal dollar gain fell at a constant rate in this range, the fourth person would add $8.04 \times (8.04/20.0) = 3.23$ percent.[9] By adding 3.23 to 28.04, we can roughly calculate the extent to which four people can close the utility gap. The procedure suggests that four people can substitute by 70 percent for a fair annuities market.

Diminishing returns to risk pooling appear, then, to set in at a fairly rapid rate. In this example two people substitute by 46 percent, three people by 63 percent, and four people by over 70 percent for full insurance.

Table 4.3 considers incomplete annuity arrangements between two parents and one child and between one parent and two children. In both cases we assume equal consumption by all family members but permit the initial wealth of the child or children to vary. All individuals are assigned the male survival probabilities; the children are age 30 and the parents age 55. In the case of two parents with one child, if the child has an initial wealth of $35,000 and the parents have an initial wealth of $20,000, entering into an equal consumption–will-swapping arrangement is equivalent to a 32 percent increase in wealth for each parent and a 10.6 percent increase for each child. For the parent this arrangement captures 71.2 percent of the utility gain from full annuities; for the child the arrangement

Table 4.3
Gains from incomplete annunity arrangements in the family[a]

Initial wealth of each child ($)	Two parents with one child		Two children with one parent	
	Dollar gain to parent (%)	Dollar gain to child (%)	Dollar gain to parent (%)	Dollar gain to child (%)
25,000	14.4	34.2	2.3	24.8
30,000	23.2	20.4	16.9	18.9
35,000	32.0	10.6	31.5	14.6
40,000	40.8	3.2	46.1	11.5

a. The calculations assume equal consumption by all family members. Initial wealth of parent or parents is $20,000. $R = 1.01$, $\alpha = 0.99$, and $\gamma = 0.75$.

substitutes by 45.4 percent for full annuities. The last two columns of table 4.3 present the case of two children contracting with one parent. When each child contributes $35,000, the gain to the parent is 31.5 percent, while each 30-year-old child enjoys a 14.6 percent gain relative to consuming as a single person. The numerical differences in the table for the two different types of families reflect, on the one hand, different monetary contributions of parents relative to children and, on the other hand, differences in the rate at which resources are consumed when all family members are alive. Resources are consumed at a slower rate in the two-children–one-parent case than in the one-child–two-parent case, since each individual's survival probabilities are given equal weight in determining the optimal rate of consumption.

Is Marrying People of Similar Ages More Efficient?

Suppose one had to decide how to pair up four people, two who are old and two who are young. Is it more efficient to marry the old people together and the young people together than it is to mix ages? Intuitively, marrying two 90-year-olds together and two 20-year-olds together leaves a large chance that both 90-year-olds will die in the immediate future, and resources that they have failed to consume will be lost to the 20-year-olds who, on average, will still be alive.[10] The countervailing argument against mixed-age marriages is that mixing ages involves greater risk to one of the two partners; the utility cost of this greater risk may exceed the utility gain from the increase in expected resources arising in mixed marriages.[11]

We investigated potential efficiency gains from mixed marriages between two 55-year-olds and two 30-year-olds, where each individual was risk averse at the 0.75 level. The 55-year-olds were assigned male survival probabilities, while the 30-year-olds were assigned female survival probabilities. When risk aversion equals 0.75, weights of 1.7 for the old person yield utility levels for both old and young which exceed those in the old-old, young-young marriages of table 4.2. The additional dollar gain to the old person from this weighted marriage with the young person is 3.1 percent; the added gain to the young person is 1.6 percent.

These additional gains from mixed-age marriages require, however, a fairly skewed distribution of consumption within the marriage. For this example the young-old weighting scheme that dominates old-old, young-young coupling involves the older spouse's consuming about 86 percent more than the younger spouse while they are both alive. If it is too costly to negotiate such an arrangement within the marriage or if the type of consumption (e.g., housing) within marriage is nonexcludable, then equal consumption marriages of individuals with similar survival probabilities (of similar ages) will be the rule rather than the exception. Of course, we have been discussing here marriages in which each spouse has the same initial dowry. The old-young marriages can dominate old-old, young-young marriages even under an equal consumption arrangement provided the dowry of the young spouse sufficiently exceeds that of the old spouse.

4.3   Enforcement with and without Altruism

In the absence of altruism would family members voluntarily maintain these implicit contracts as family members age? The answer is that there always are ways of structuring payments to individuals within the family so that each individual at each moment in time has a selfish interest in maintaining the original implicit contract. An equal consumption marriage contract between two individuals with the same survival probabilities and the same initial endowment is a good first example. If each spouse maintains control over his own wealth while both spouses are alive and consumes at the same rate as the other spouse, then each will separately have an incentive to continue the contract at each point in time. A similar type of individual control can be maintained in family arrangements; rather than have the parents use up all their resources before the children begin contributing to their support, the children can contribute each period in return for that period's expected parental bequest. This scenario of parents' maintaining control over their wealth until the very end, as enforcement leverage over their children, may partly explain the limited use of gifts as a tax-saving intergenerational transfer device.

The proof of this proposition is immediate from equation (10). Given their initial endowments at time $t - 1$, W_{t-1}^H and W_{t-1}^S, family members choose a value θ^* such that the contract to consume the contingent plan $[C_{t-1}^H(\theta^*), C_{t-1}^S(\theta^*), C_t^H(\theta^*), C_t^S(\theta^*), \ldots, C_D^H(\theta^*), C_D^S(\theta^*)]$ is in the core at time $t - 1$. The consumption plan at time $t[C_t^H(\theta^*), C_t^S(\theta^*), \ldots, C_D^H(\theta^*), C_D^S(\theta^*)]$ represents the period t Pareto-efficient contract corresponding to the initially chosen utility weight θ^*. This plan is in the core for a set S_t of individual endowments of family members in period t, W_t^H and W_t^S, which satisfy $W_t^H + W_t^S = W_t$. To ensure that the initial contract remains a core allocation for each family member, side payments are made at time $t - 1$ when consumption in period $t - 1$ occurs. The side payments leave the period t individual endowments in set S_t. Since the initial contract $[C_{t-1}^H(\theta^*), C_{t-1}^S(\theta^*), C_t^H(\theta^*), C_t^S(\theta^*), \ldots, C_D^H(\theta^*), C_D^S(\theta^*)]$ is in the core, each selfish family member will have a personal incentive to make or accept these side payments.

There are two additional questions of enforcement to consider. One problem is that a spouse may covertly name a third party as beneficiary in his will in exchange for the same commitment by the third party or in exchange for a particular service. A second type of cheating may occur when one or both spouses covertly consume in excess of the consumption levels dictated by an optimal implicit marriage contract; while each spouse may correctly believe that he or she is the beneficiary in the other spouse's will, each may try to take advantage of the other by increasing his own consumption and thus reducing the potential bequest available to the other spouse.

These two types of cheating will be more problematic for implicit incomplete annuity agreements between friends or relatives who are physically separated. The consumption cheating scenario can be modeled as a Nash equilibrium in which each partner chooses his consumption path by taking the other partner's consumption path and potential bequest path as given. Resources are consumed at a faster rate in the Nash equilibrium as each partner fails to consider how his consumption will diminish his expected bequest and thus the expected utility of his partner.

Using male survival probabilities we calculated for two 55-year-olds the dollar equivalent utility gain from engaging in a Nash consumption-cheating partnership. The gains in the Nash equilibrium proved to be almost identical to those in the more efficient marriage contract. For levels of risk aversion of 0.75, 1.25, and 1.75, the percentage dollar increments are, respectively, 19.9, 22.2, and 23.5. While the rate of consumption is faster in the Nash equilibrium, it is not much faster than in the marriage contract. Intuitively cheating by overconsuming is fine provided one's partner actually dies; but if one's partner survives, the early excessive consumption will require relative deprivation later on. Apparently this latter consideration dominates the former, leaving utility in the cheating equilibrium at essentially the same level as under a marriage contract. These examples suggest that consumption cheating does not represent a substantial impediment to consumption–risk-sharing arrangements.

Another means of enforcing these implicit contracts is simply altruism. All of our calculations have involved maximizing a weighted sum of individual family members' utilities. If, however, each family member is altruistic toward each other and each weights each family member's utility from consumption in the same way, then all family members would unanimously agree on the utility maximand. The calculations we have presented can, therefore, be thought of as resulting from the maximization of an agreed-upon altruistic family utility function. Since all family members agree on the maximand, there is no problem of enforcement.

4.4 Summary and Conclusion

This paper has demonstrated that consumption and bequest-sharing arrangements within marriage and larger families can substitute to a large extent for complete and fair annuity markets. In the absence of such public markets, individuals have strong economic incentives to establish relationships which provide risk-mitigating opportunities. Within marriages and families there is a degree of trust, information, and love which aids in the enforcement of risk-sharing agreements. Our calculations indicate that pooling the risk of death can be an important economic incentive for family formation; the paper also suggests that the current instability in family arrangements may, to some extent, reflect recent growth in pension and social security public annuities. The methodological approach of this paper can be applied to the study of family insurance against other types of risks. Of chief interest are those types of risks that are handled very poorly by anonymous public markets. Disability insurance and insurance against earnings losses are good examples.

Our approach has been to compare family insurance with perfect insurance. It would seem worthwhile to compare family insurance with public market insurance where the market insurance is subject to adverse selection and moral hazard problems and family insurance is not. Realistic specification of the degree of adverse selection and moral hazard may indicate that family insurance dominates public market insurance even in small families.

Finally, the paper suggests the empirical difficulty of determining whether intergenerational transfers reflect altruism or simply risk-mitigating arrangements of essentially selfish individuals in the absence of perfect insurance markets. Distinguishing between the selfish and altruistic models is fundamental to a number of major economic questions, including the impact of the social security system on national saving and the effectiveness of fiscal policy.[12]

Appendix: Computational Algorithm for the Two-Family-Members Dynamic Risk-Pooling Problem

This appendix indicates the algorithm used to solve the two-family-members dynamic programming problem, copied here as equation (A1). The algorithm for the case of three family members is similar to that for two members and is available from the authors. While we consider the iso-elastic family of utility functions, our algorithm can be applied to any homothetic utility function.

$$V_{t-1}(W_{t-1}) = \max_{W_t, C_{t-1}^H, C_{t-1}^S \geq 0, t=T,\ldots,1} [u^H(C_{t-1}^H) + \theta u^S(C_{t-1}^S)$$
$$+ \alpha P_{t/t-1} Q_{t/t-1} V_t(W_t) + \alpha P_{t/t-1}(1 - Q_{t/t-1}) H_t(W_t)$$
$$+ \theta \alpha Q_{t/t-1}(1 - P_{t/t-1}) S_t(W_t)], \tag{A1}$$

subject to

$$W_t/R + C_{t-1}^H + C_{t-1}^S = W_{t-1}. \tag{A2}$$

Again, the letters H and S correspond to the two family members with respective conditional survival probabilities $P_{t/t-1}$ and $Q_{t/t-1}$. The expression W_t is joint family wealth, θ is the weighting factor, and $H_t(W_t)$ and $S_t(W_t)$ are the expected utility levels for each family member if he alone survives to period t.

Optimal values for C_t^H and C_t^S are found recursively starting at period T and proceeding to period 0. We demonstrate that $V_t(W_t)$ may be written in the form

$$V_t(W_t) = v_t \frac{W_t^{1-\gamma}}{1 - \gamma}, \tag{A3}$$

where v_t is a constant. We also show that total family consumption, C_t, is given by

$$C_{t-1} = W_{t-1} \frac{v_T^{1/\gamma}}{v_T^{1/\gamma} + (\alpha K_t R)^{1/\gamma} R^{-1}}, \tag{A4}$$

where K_t is another constant. Given total family consumption, consumption of the two members is

$$C^H_{t-1} = \frac{C_{t-1}}{1 + \theta^{1/\gamma}}, \; C^S_{t-1} = C_{t-1}\frac{\theta^{1/\gamma}}{1 + \theta^{1/\gamma}}. \tag{A5}$$

We demonstrate that K_t is a function of v_t and that v_{t-1} is a function of K_t. Starting then at the initial value for K_t, K_{T+1}, we can compute v_T; v_T in turn gives K_T, which in turn gives v_{T-1}. Proceeding in this fashion to period zero we compute the entire sequence of v_t's and K_t's. These values can then be used in equation (A4) to compute the ratio of consumption to wealth at each period. These ratios together with an initial level of wealth plus (A2) and (A5) generate the optimal path. The homotheticity of the utility function permits us to calculate recursively the shape of the consumption path independently of the initial level of wealth.

Starting with period T the maximization problem for equation (A1) is

$$V_T(W_T) = \max \frac{1}{1 - \gamma}(C^H_T)^{1-\gamma} + \theta\frac{1}{1 - \gamma}(C^S_T)^{1-\gamma}$$

such that $C^H_T + C^S_T \leqslant W_T$, C^H_T, $C^S_T \geqslant 0$.

Solving this maximization and computing the indirect utility function for V_T, we have

$$V_T(W_T) = v_T\frac{1}{1 - \gamma}W_T^{1-\gamma}, \text{ where } v_T = (1 + \theta^{1/\gamma})^\gamma, \tag{A6}$$

$$C^H_T = W_T\frac{1}{1 + \theta^{1/\gamma}}, \; C^S_T = W_T\frac{\theta^{1/\gamma}}{1 + \theta^{1/\gamma}}. \tag{A7}$$

For $t < T$, (A1) for the iso-elastic case is written as

$$V_{t-1}(W_{t-1}) = \max_{C^H_{t-1}, C^S_{t-1}} \frac{1}{1 - \gamma}(C^H_{t-1})^{1-\gamma} + \frac{\theta}{1 - \gamma}(C^S_{t-1})^{1-\gamma}$$

$$+ \alpha\frac{P_t}{P_{t-1}}\frac{Q_t}{Q_{t-1}}v_t\frac{1}{1 - \gamma}W_t^{1-\gamma}$$

$$+ \alpha\frac{P_t}{P_{t-1}}\left(1 - \frac{Q_t}{Q_{t-1}}\right)h_t\frac{1}{1 - \gamma}W_t^{1-\gamma}$$

$$+ \theta\alpha\left(1 - \frac{P_t}{P_{t-1}}\right)\frac{Q_t}{Q_{t-1}}s_t\frac{1}{1 - \gamma}W_t^{1-\gamma}$$

such that $C^H_{t-1} + C^S_{t-1} + \frac{W_t}{R} = W_{t-1}. \tag{A8}$

In going from (A1) to (A8) we use the fact that $H_t(W_t) = h_t[W_t^{1-\gamma}/(1-\gamma)]$ and $S_t(W_t) = s_t[W_t^{1-\gamma}/(1-\gamma)]$ for the iso-elastic utility function. The values for h_t and s_t are implicitly defined as the bracketed term in equation (7) in the text with $j = 0$ corresponding to time t and with each family member's survival probabilities from time t substituting for P_j.

It is easy to see from (A8) that for given total family consumption, C_t, C_t^H and C_t^S will always satisfy (A5). Hence we may rewrite (A8) as

$$V_{t-1}(W_{t-1}) = \max_{C_{t-1}} v_T \frac{1}{1-\gamma} C_{t-1}^{1-\gamma}$$
$$+ \alpha \frac{W_t^{1-\gamma}}{1-\gamma} \left[\frac{P_t}{P_{t-1}} \frac{Q_t}{Q_{t-1}} v_t + \frac{P_t}{P_{t-1}} \left(1 - \frac{Q_t}{Q_{t-1}} \right) h_t \right.$$
$$\left. + \theta \left(1 - \frac{P_t}{P_{t-1}} \right) \frac{Q_t}{Q_{t-1}} s_t \right]. \tag{A9}$$

Denoting the term in brackets by K_t we now have

$$V_{t-1}(W_{t-1}) = \max_{C_{t-1}} v_T \frac{1}{1-\gamma} C_{t-1}^{1-\gamma} + \alpha \frac{1}{1-\gamma} W_t^{1-\gamma} K_t$$

$$\text{such that } C_{t-1} + \frac{W_t}{R} = W_{t-1}. \tag{A10}$$

Maximizing (A10) and computing the indirect utility functions yields

$$v_{t-1} = [v_T^{1/\gamma} + (\alpha R K_t)^{1/\gamma} R^{-1}]^{\gamma}, \tag{A11}$$

$$C_{t-1} = W_{t-1} \frac{v_T^{1/\gamma}}{v_T^{1/\gamma} + (\alpha K_t R)^{1/\gamma} R^{-1}}. \tag{A12}$$

Notes

We are grateful for financial support from the Foundation for Research in Economic Education and the National Bureau of Economic Research. Any opinions expressed here are solely our own. We wish to thank Finis Welch, Joe Ostroy, Bryan Ellickson, John McCall, Steven Shavell, John Riley, Jon Skinner, and Gary Galles for helpful discussions.

1. The transaction costs we have in mind here include the time costs involved in negotiating individual specific annuity contracts. As we demonstrate in the text, each individual's optimal annuity contract depends on his rate of time preference, his degree of risk aversion, and his survival probabilities. Some individuals may prefer a constant annuity stream, others an increasing or decreasing stream of annuity payments.

2. Kotlikoff and Spivak (1979) present a proof that family annuity contracting converges to a complete annuities market as the number of family members increases.

3. Yaari (1965) is the pioneering paper on this subject. Sheshinski and Weiss (1981) provide an illuminating discussion on the interaction of annuities and social insurance. Barro and Friedman (1977) provide an analysis of the risks of the uncertainty of the date of death.

4. The gains from access to an annuities market are greatest when the individual has all his resources up front. This assumption, then, dramatizes the demand for annuities; but dropping this assumption would not alter the theoretical point that families can substitute for annuity markets. For the sake of completeness one can think of the individuals described in this paper as having received all their resource streams prior to their current age. In the no-annuity, no-family world involuntary bequests can be thought of as being collected by the government and redistributed to individuals at their birth.

5. We use the low mortality male and female probabilities reported on pp. 17 and 19 of the Social Security Administration Actuarial Study 62 (see US Department of Health, Education, and Welfare 1966).

6. The ratio of consumption at age 75 to consumption at age 55 is 0.62. When risk aversion equals 0.75, the ratio of consumption at age 85 to consumption at age 55 equals 0.06; it is 0.33 at age 75.

7. In the three-member family we maximize a weighted sum of the three members' expected utility taking all survival contingencies into account. If one of the three dies first, the other two jointly inherit the remaining wealth and consume according to the optimal two-person plan.

8. This fraction is calculated as $[(1 + m)^{1-\gamma} - 1]/[(1 + a)^{1-\gamma} - 1]$, where m is the fractional wealth equivalent gain from marriage, and a is the fractional wealth equivalent gain from fair annuities.

9. This is probably a lower bound estimate for the contribution of the fourth person; the marginal dollar gain cannot fall at a constant 40 percent rate forever, because if it did the total dollar gains would, in the limit, not sum up to 46.9 percent, the full annuity gain of table 4.1. Presumably the marginal dollar gain falls at a decreasing rate, and 3.23 percent probably underestimates the fourth person's marginal contribution.

10. We assume here that any involuntary bequests that arise from the simultaneous death of both marriage partners or from the death of a surviving spouse are not inherited by any of these four individuals. Again the government can be thought of as collecting these residual bequests and distributing them each year to the newborn. We thank Finis Welch for a helpful discussion on this section.

11. To see this consider an old-young marriage in which the young person promises to consume less than the old person in the state of nature in which both

spouses survive. Suppose that this promise to the old person of higher consumption in the "both survive" state is large enough to exactly compensate the old person for the loss in expected utility from the state in which his spouse dies but he survives. The old person's expected utility from this latter "bequest" state is lower when he marries someone young, rather than someone old, because the probability of the young person actually dying is smaller. While the old person is by assumption no worse off in this compensated old-young marriage, the young person could be worse off than if he had married someone young. By entering into the compensated old-young marriage, the young person reduces his payoff in the both survive state while leaving the payoff in the bequest state unchanged. He also increases the probability of the bequest state and lowers the probability of the both survive state. Although expected consumption for the young spouse rises, the spreading of the payoffs may lower expected utility, depending on the young spouse's degree of risk aversion.

12. See Barro (1974).

5

Annuity Insurance, Savings, and Inequality

with John Shoven and
Avia Spivak

5.1 Introduction

While death and taxes may be the two most certain elements in one's life, the date of one's death is surely one of the least certain. Uncertainty concerning the length of life is obviously of great importance to saving decisions; "taking it with you" is not an option, but immediately consuming all resources (less an intended bequest) is no alternative either since with high probability one will still be alive but will be very poor in the immediate future. To avoid the prospect of remaining alive in a state of relative poverty, risk-averse individuals will be cautious about their rate of consumption. The extent of precautionary saving motivated by life-span uncertainty depends on the availability of market and nonmarket annuity insurance. Annuity insurance permits those who live longer than average to share the economic risks of this outcome with those who live shorter than average. This paper examines the amount of precautionary savings arising from life-span uncertainty by comparing saving behavior under perfect insurance arrangements with that arising under imperfect arrangements, namely, when longevity risk can be pooled only with members of one's own family. We consider both intergenerationally altruistic preferences and selfish (zero bequest motive) life-cycle preferences, determining stochastic steady-state wealth levels and wealth distributions in both models.[1]

The central findings of the paper are that (1) perfecting insurance arrangements can sharply lower savings in both intergenerationally altruistic and

This chapter is a combination of "The effect of annuity insurance on savings and inequality" [with J. Shoven and A. Spivak, *Journal of Labor Economics* 4(3), pt. 2, S183–S207 (1986); © 1986 by The University of Chicago] and "Annuity markets, savings, and the capital stock" [with J. Shoven and A. Spivak, in *Issues in Pension Economics*, Z. Bodie, J. B. Shoven, and D. A. Wise, eds. (Chicago, Ill.: University of Chicago Press, 1987), 211–34; © 1987 by the National Bureau of Economic Research]. Reprinted with permission.

life-cycle economies and (2) in intergenerationally altruistic economies perfecting annuity insurance can greatly influence the degree of inequality; indeed, in the long run, switching from imperfect family insurance to perfect insurance can mean the difference between absolute inequality and absolute equality.

In addition to several important analyses of the relation of intergenerational transfers to inequality (Stiglitz 1978, pp. 271–303; Stiglitz and Bevan 1979), there are now several studies that examine the effect of annuity insurance on saving. Sheshinski and Weiss (1981) were the first to point out that a fully funded social security program could alter household saving through its provision of annuity insurance, assuming such insurance is not otherwise available. Hubbard (1983) reaches a similar conclusion in a partial equilibrium life-cycle analysis. Davies (1981) and chapter 4 of this book discuss the size of involuntary bequests in life-cycle models in the complete absence of insurance arrangements. Fuller descriptions of life-cycle economies in the absence of annuity insurance are presented by Abel (1983) and Eckstein, Eichenbaum, and Peled (1983). Both papers consider the stochastic steady-state properties of economies in which agents involuntarily leave bequests to their children.

While each of these papers indicates that improvements in annuity insurance reduces precautionary saving, their specification of bequest behavior in the absence of annuity insurance is either incomplete or rather arbitrary. For example, Eckstein et al. and Abel assume that while parents are selfish and have no interest in their children, they nonetheless involuntarily bequeath all their wealth to precisely their own children, extracting no quid pro quo in exchange. An alternative assumption explored in chapter 4 is that selfish parents and selfish children jointly pool longevity risk in a manner that is mutually beneficial. Kotlikoff and Spivak point out that longevity risks are substantial as measured by the amount of resources that even mildly risk-averse selfish individuals would sacrifice to gain access to fair annuity insurance. In addition they demonstrate that risk sharing among even as few as two relatives can provide a large fraction of the gains available from perfect insurance. Hence, in selfish life-cycle models, longevity risk pooling between parents and children appears well "worth the trouble," with the gains far exceeding any reasonable transactions costs. In contrast to the selfish life-cycle model, in the altruistic model the pooling of otherwise uninsurable longevity risk between parents and children is an immediate implication of utility maximization since the utility of children is an argument in the utility function of parents.

Our model of risk-sharing arrangements between parents and children assumes the smallest possible family risk-sharing pool, namely, at most one parent sharing risk with one child at any point in time. Since family insurance approaches perfect insurance as the number of family members increases, this assumption leads to the largest precautionary motive for saving and provides an upper bound for calculating the potential decline in savings resulting from perfecting annuity insurance arrangements.[2]

While at most two relatives are simultaneously alive, risk sharing in both the altruistic and the selfish models also involves all future generations. In the altruistic model current relatives consciously take into account the effect of their behavior on their descendents' inheritances and, therefore, on their levels of expected welfare. As a consequence, altruistic families automatically share any current adverse shocks with future generations by reducing the bequests they leave to future generations. In the life-cycle model the risk-sharing arrangements between current parents and children is chosen, taking into account that today's adverse shocks will affect the future bargaining position of current children when they strike selfish deals with their children. This future bargaining with the next generation is, in turn, contingent on the nature of subsequent future bargaining with the succeeding generation, and on and on. Hence the solution to the bargaining problem between living family members takes account of the infinite sequence of bargains struck by family descendants.

The next section considers the effect of annuity insurance in an intertemporal altruistic economy in which families can borrow the present value of their certain future labor earnings. Asymptotically, the distribution of resources and consumption in this economy approaches complete inequality, with successively fewer families holding all the economy's resources and engaging in all the economy's consumption. Section 5.3 considers a presumably more realistic financial setting in which altruistic families cannot borrow against the present value of their infinite stream of future earnings. In contrast to the unconstrained borrowing case in which the altruistic economy's savings is infinitely elastic at a particular interest rate, with borrowing constraints aggregate savings is a continuous increasing function of the interest rate. In addition, the reduction in steady-state wealth from introducing perfect annuity insurance is considerably larger if there are borrowing constraints in the altruistic economy. The borrowing constraints also lead to a stationary wealth distribution in contrast to the increasingly unequal, asymptotically degenerate wealth distribution arising in the altruistic economy without borrowing constraints. The fourth section contains our life-cycle model of bargaining in which nonaltruistic agents consider the infinite sequence of selfish bargaining agreements. The calculations in this section suggest a very sizable effect of perfecting annuity insurance on long-run savings.

The models in Sections 5.2 and 5.4 have 4 potential periods of life, while Section 5.3's model has at most 2 periods of life. A minimum of 4 periods is necessary to examine selfish life-cycle bargaining. While Section 5.3's analysis of liquidity-constrained altruistic behavior could be formulated in the 4-period framework, simplifying to 2 periods greatly reduces the computational costs of solving the problem. To facilitate comparisons of the predictions of the three models all illustrative calculations are based on a common utility function, and parameters in the 2-period model of Section 5.3 are calibrated on the basis of the 4-period models' parameterizations. In the final section, 5.7, there is a summary of the paper's findings and suggestions for additional research on issues of precautionary savings.

5.2 The Unconstrained Intergenerationally Altruistic Model

In this model and in that of Section 5.4 there are 4 periods of life. People live with certainty for the first 3 periods and survive to the fourth with probability P. Children are 1 when their parents are 3. Individuals are exogenously endowed with labor earnings, which they receive during the first 3 periods of life. Hence the present value of earning for an altruistic family is certain, and we assume in this section that families can borrow the present value of the infinite stream of earnings.

The family's utility function is taken as separable in consumption of the parent (C_f) and the child (C_s) over time. Throughout the paper we consider the isoelastic form for utility of consumption at a point in time, $U(C)$, that is,

$$U(C) = \frac{C^{1-\gamma}}{1-\gamma}, \tag{1}$$

where γ is the coefficient of relative risk aversion. The utility of children is assumed to enter the family's expected utility function with weight θ, and future utility is assumed to be discounted by the time preference factor α.

Let W_t stand for the family's total human plus nonhuman wealth at time t. The expected utility of a family with a 1-period-old child and a 3-period-old parent at time t is a function of W_t and is denoted $V(W_t)$. Equation (2) expresses $V(W_t)$ in terms of the certain utility of the child's and parent's immediate consumption, the expected utility of their subsequent period consumption, and the expected utility of the family when the next child is born. For notational convenience the time subscript, t, is omitted wherever the time period is implicitly clear. In addition, we set $t = 1$ initially:

$$V(W_1) = \max \left\{ \frac{C_{f3}^{1-\gamma}}{1-\gamma} + \theta \frac{C_{s1}^{1-\gamma}}{1-\gamma} + \alpha P \left[\frac{C_{f4}^{1-\gamma}}{1-\gamma} + \theta \frac{C_{s2,a}^{1-\gamma}}{1-\gamma} + \alpha V(W_{3,a}) \right] \right.$$

$$\left. + \alpha(1-P) \left[\theta \frac{C_{s2,d}^{1-\gamma}}{1-\gamma} + \alpha V(W_{3,d}) \right] \right\}. \tag{2}$$

The first two terms on the right-hand side of (2) are, respectively, the family's utility from the parent's third- and from the child's first-period consumption. The bracketed terms multiplied by αP indicate the family's expected utility in the case the parent lives through the fourth period. The child's second-period consumption in this case is $C_{s2,a}$, and the family's full wealth at the time the initial child is a parent $W_{3,a}$. In the case the parent dies early, the child's second-period consumption and the family's resources when the child becomes a parent are, respectively, $C_{s2,d}$ and $W_{3,d}$. The bracketed terms multiplied by $\alpha(1-P)$ express the family's expected utility if the parent dies early.

The family is constrained in maximizing (2) by

$$W_1 = C_{f3} + C_{s1} + R(C_{f4} + C_{s2,a} + RW_{3,a}),$$
$$W_1 = C_{f3} + C_{s1} + R(C_{s2,d} + RW_{3,d}), \tag{3}$$

where R is one divided by one plus the interest rate. These equations simply relate the ongoing family's full future resources at the time the child becomes a parent ($W_{3,a}$ or $W_{3,d}$) to the appropriately discounted difference between initial family resources and total family consumption during the child's first and second periods. The two constraints correspond to the two possible outcomes, namely, the parent dying early and the parent dying late.

Given the functional form for V, maximization of (2) subject to (3) is straightforward. Consider the following as a possible solution function $V(W)$: $V(W) = k[W^{1-\gamma}/(1-\gamma)]$, where k is a constant. Next replace in (2) $V(W_{3,a})$ by $k[W_{3,a}^{1-\gamma}/(1-\gamma)]$ and $V(W_{3,d})$ by $k[W_{3,d}^{1-\gamma}/(1-\gamma)]$. With this substitution $V(W_1)$ is now a homothetic function of each of the consumption demands plus $W_{3,a}$ and $W_{3,d}$. Hence the solution values for the consumption demands and for $W_{3,a}$ and $W_{3,d}$ are all proportional to W_1. Inserting these solutions into (2) and collecting constants, we have

$$V(W_1) = k \frac{W_1^{1-\gamma}}{1-\gamma} = g(P, \alpha, \theta, R, \gamma, k) \frac{W_1^{1-\gamma}}{1-\gamma}, \tag{4}$$

where $g(P, \alpha, \theta, R, \gamma, k)$ is the sum of constants, multiplying $W_1^{1-\gamma}/(1-\gamma)$ after solution values have been substituted into (2). From (4), $k = g(P, \alpha, \theta, R, \gamma, k)$, and this expression can be used to solve for k.[3] Hence we have a proof by construction that $V(W) = k[W^{1-\gamma}/(1-\gamma)]$ is the form of the value function in (2).

The homotheticity of the value function (2) permits an immediate characterization of the evolution of full resources for each family through time and for the aggregate economy. The solution to (2) implies that

$$W_{3,a} = AW_1 \tag{5}$$

and

$$W_{3,d} = DW_1,$$

where A and D are constants depending on the model's parameters P, α, θ, R, and γ. For each family, expected resources when the current child becomes a parent, EW_3, are related to initial resources by

$$EW_3 = [PA + (1-P)D]W_1. \tag{6}$$

Since this equation holds for all families regardless of their initial value of W_1, per capita wealth in the economy will remain constant (assuming an arbitrary large number of families) if and only if

$$PA + (1-P)D = 1. \tag{7}$$

Now A and D depend on the interest factor R as well as on the fixed survival probability and the fixed preference parameters. Hence, in general, equilibrium R must adjust until the values of A and D satisfy (7). Since A and D are monotonically increasing functions of R, there is a unique value of R that satisfies (7).[4] The economy's long-run supply of savings is clearly infinitely elastic at this value of R since for larger or smaller values of R full resources (human plus nonhuman wealth) in the economy either grow indefinitely or decline to zero.

The term A is less than D, reflecting the additional demand for fourth-period parental consumption in the case the parent lives to consume C_{f4}. Since, by (7), the weighted sum of A and D equals unity, we have $A < 1$ and $D > 1$. Hence, when expected future resources equal current resources, each favorable mortality outcome reduces the family's resources, while each unfavorable mortality outcome increases its resources.

The process governing the family's accumulation and decumulation of wealth through time, with time measured in generations, can be expressed as

$$W_{t+1} = W_t e^{\varepsilon_t},$$ (8)

where ε_t equals $\log A$ with probability P and $\log D$ with probability $1 - P$. Expressing the process in terms of the logarithm of family resources, we have

$$\log W_{t+1} = \log W_t + \varepsilon_t.$$ (9)

The expected value of ε_t is negative since

$$E\varepsilon_t = P \log A + (1 - P) \log D < \log[PA + (1 - P)D] = 0,$$ (10)

using the concavity of the logarithmic function and (7). Hence the logarithm of family resources is a random walk with a negative drift. Since each family's resources follow this process and, by assumption, since all families start out with the same initial resources, the distribution of each family's resources as well as the distribution of any functions of family resources, such as the logarithm, are equivalent to the economy-wide distributions. The fact that the logarithm of resources follows a random walk with drift indicates that there is no stationary distribution of resources in the economy. Although the mean value of family resources is constant, the distribution of family resources becomes increasingly unequal through time.

To see this, rewrite ε_t as $\varepsilon_t = -\rho + \mu_t$, where μ_t is i.i.d. with zero mean and with variance σ^2. The expected logarithm of resources at $t + \tau$ is given by

$$E \log W_{t+\tau} = \log W_t - \tau\rho,$$ (11)

and the variance of the logarithm of resources at $t + \tau$ given $\log W_t$ is

$$\text{var}(\log W_{t+\tau}) = \tau\sigma^2.$$ (12)

Equations (11) and (12) indicate that for each successive generation the distribution of the logarithm of resources has a smaller mean and a larger variance. Not only are successive resource distributions less equal, as indicated by the increasing variance of the logarithm, but they are also increasingly skew. This is suggested by the fact that the mean of the logarithm of resources falls through time at a faster rate than its standard deviation rises. Using Chebyshev's inequality, one can show that the fraction of families whose resources in the future exceed their current values is bounded by a number that declines with each successive generation.[5] Asymptotically, the economy's resource distribution approaches complete inequality, with an infinitesimal fraction of families holding all the economy's resources

Table 5.1
Unconstrained altruistic model: Percentage savings reduction from switching from family insurance to perfect insurance

Percentage savings reduction[a]	Parameter values			
	α	θ	γ	P
−6.9	0.86	1	4	0.6
−48.6	0.10	1	4	0.6
−33.4	0.24	1	4	0.6
−20.0	0.50	1	4	0.6
−3.7	0.99	1	4	0.6
0.0	0.99	1	4	0.6
−6.1	0.86	2	4	0.6
−8.6	0.86	0.5	4	0.6
−13.4	0.86	0.1	4	0.6
−26.2	0.86	1	10	0.6
−0.8	0.86	1	1	0.6
−0.8	0.86	1	0.5	0.6
−4.3	0.86	1	4	0.8
−7.8	0.86	1	4	0.4
−6.1	0.86	1	4	0.2
−75.1	0.24	0.5	10	0.5
−62.8	0.50	0.5	10	0.5

a. Calculations assume a Cobb-Douglas production function with capital's output share equal to 30 percent.

and the rest holding no resources. This increasing inequality should be contrasted with the complete equality that arises in the case of perfect insurance under the same assumption that all families have identical initial resources. While each family consciously plans to pursue a policy that leads to immiserization with essentially 100 percent probability, the process of immiserization can be quite slow.

Table 5.1 presents calculations of the economy's reduction in savings per worker from switching to perfect insurance for a set of illustrative parameter values. Given knowledge of the equilibrium interest rate under imperfect annuity insurance determined in (7), savings per worker is calculated, assuming a Cobb-Douglas production function with a capital share equal to 0.3; that is, the economy's general equilibrium condition is that the marginal product of capital equals the interest rate, which provides an equation for computing the economy's stock of savings (capital) per worker. Under perfect insurance the family's budget constraint is simply that the present expected value of consumption equals the present value of resources. As is well known, in this case R equals α in the steady state, and this equation plus the marginal productivity condition are used to solve for steady-state savings per worker under perfect insurance.[6]

In the base case, α, the time-preference factor equals 0.86, and P, the fourth-period survival probability, equals 0.6. If we think of each period as corresponding to roughly 15 years, then the 0.86 value corresponds to a 1 percent annual time-preference rate, and the 0.6 fourth-period survival probability is roughly equivalent to a life span of 54 years. We view "children" in the model as very young adults who are initially roughly age 20 and who are parents of adult children at roughly age 50. Hence the 54-year life span corresponds to a real-world adult life span starting at 20 and ending, on average, at 74. Base-case values of γ and θ are four and one, respectively.

Adopting the base-case parameters, the altruistic economy's total savings is 7 percent larger with imperfect family annuity insurance than with perfect annuity insurance. This figure is quite sensitive to the time-preference rate. Ceteris paribus, lowering α to 0.5, which corresponds to a 4.1 percent annual time-preference rate, implies a much smaller stock of savings but a 20 percent difference between savings under family and perfect annuity insurance. For α equals 0.24, equivalent to a 10 percent annual time-preference rate, there is a 33 percent savings reduction. The reduction is 49 percent for α equals 0.10. Alternatively, assuming α equals 0.99, there is essentially no difference between savings under family and perfect insurance arrangements.[7]

The sensitivity of savings changes to the weight on the child's utility, θ, is surprisingly small. As θ rises, more weight is placed on the consumption of the child, and, in the limit, as θ approaches infinity, life-span uncertainty does not affect utility since families only care about their children's consumption, which is not subject to life-span risk. Hence as θ rises, R approaches α, and the savings reduction from perfect insurance goes to zero. While table 5.1 indicates larger precautionary savings the smaller the value of θ, lowering the value of θ from 1 to 0.5 raises precautionary savings by less than 2 percent. The precautionary savings response to larger values of γ, the relative risk-aversion coefficient, also has the expected positive sign. The magnitude of the savings difference is quite sensitive to γ. For values of γ below one, precautionary savings is less than 0.5 percent of the total; on the other hand, it is 26 percent for γ equals 10, assuming base-case values of other parameters. Finally, precautionary

Table 5.2
Resource inequality in the unconstrained altruistic model after successive generations

Case	Generation				
	1	10	50	200	∞
Base case					
Resource share of poorest 90%	0.90	0.88	0.83	0.80	0.00
Resource share of poorest 50%	0.50	0.45	0.34	0.30	0.00
Resource share of poorest 30%	0.30	0.26	0.16	0.15	0.00
Resource share of poorest 10%	0.10	0.08	0.06	0.04	0.00
Coefficient of variation of resource distribution	0.00	0.12	0.27	0.57	∞
Base case except $\alpha = 0.5$:					
Poorest share of poorest 90%	0.90	0.81	0.62	0.27	0.00
Poorest share of poorest 50%	0.50	0.33	0.16	0.03	0.00
Poorest share of poorest 30%	0.30	0.17	0.07	0.01	0.00
Poorest share of poorest 10%	0.10	0.04	0.01	0.00	0.00
Coefficient of variation of resource distribution	0.00	0.45	1.23	5.13	∞

savings appears to be maximized for values of P between 0.4 and 0.6. This is also intuitive since uncertainty disappears from the model when P equals zero or unity. The bottom two rows of table 5.1 consider combinations of parameters chosen to raise the level of precautionary savings. For α equals 0.24, γ equals 10, and θ and P both equal to 0.5, there is a 75 percent reduction in the economy's wealth stock associated with switching from family to perfect annuity insurance. This figure declines only slightly, to 63 percent, if α equals 0.5 and the other parameters take these specified values.

Table 5.2 illustrates the transmission of inequality through time. The first generation of families is assumed to have identical resources. The table reports the fraction of resources held by the poorest 10 percent, 30 percent, 50 percent, and 90 percent of families. Since the model's 2 periods between generations correspond to roughly 30 years, the resource distribution after 10 generations corresponds in real time to roughly 300 years. In the base case the increase through time in inequality is extremely slow, with the richest 10 percent holding only 20 percent of total resources after 200 generations. The time-preference factor, α, appears to be the most critical parameter for affecting the rate at which inequality increases through time. The transition to complete inequality is much faster if α equals 0.5 and the other parameters are held at their base-case values. Lowering α to 0.5

produces roughly the same degree of inequality within 10 generations that arises after 200 generations when α equals 0.86. After 200 generations (6,000 years in real time) of the α-equals-0.5 process, the 10 percent richest families own almost three-quarters of all resources. If α equals 0.24 (roughly a 10 percent annual time-preference rate), the 10 percent richest families own close to 30 percent of all resources after 10 generations. This compares with 19 percent for α equals 0.5 and 12 percent for α equals 0.86. A time-preference rate of 10 percent per annum is quite high but is within the range estimated empirically (Hausman 1979). In addition the associated equilibrium interest rate of 8.5 percent computed on a yearly basis, while high, is not implausible.

While risk premiums in uncertainty models are not invariant to the specified number of periods, it may be of some interest to know the welfare gain from perfect insurance in this model. Assuming baseline parameter values, the lack of perfect insurance has a small—less than 1 percent—welfare cost as measured by the percentage increase in resources with family insurance required to obtain the expected utility level under perfect insurance. As expected, this figure is highly sensitive to the degree of risk aversion. Ceteris paribus, raising γ to 10 raises the equivalent variation to almost 16 percent.

To summarize these findings, in the unconstrained intergenerationally altruistic model, switching from family to perfect insurance reduces aggregate savings by either a modest or a significant amount, depending, primarily, on the time-preference rate and the degree of risk aversion. The time-preference rate is critical for determining the rate at which the resource distribution becomes more unequal. If one accepts a relatively high time-preference rate, the model suggests an important potential contribution of imperfect annuity arrangements in increasing inequality.

5.3   The Constrained Altruistic Model

The solution to the unconstrained altruistic model involves, in the long run, essentially all families holding close to zero future resources, meaning they are in debt by an amount equal to the present value of their certain future labor earnings. In contrast, this section examines the behavior of the altruistic economy under the assumption that families cannot borrow against their future earnings. For this problem the state variable corresponding to equation (2) is no longer full future resources; rather, it is current nonhuman wealth, A_t. To simplify the numerical calculations required to solve this problem we considered a 2-period version of the Section 5.2 model. Each child lives for 1 period with certainty and survives with probability P for 2 periods. Hence when children are born their parents may be dead. The family's expected utility in the case the parent is alive, EU_a, is given by

$$EU_a(A_1) = \frac{C_{f2}^{1-\gamma}}{1-\gamma} + \theta \frac{C_{s1,a}^{1-\gamma}}{1-\gamma} + \alpha V(A_{2,a}), \tag{13}$$

where A_1 is the family's initial nonhuman wealth. The term $A_{2,a}$ is the value of such assets at the time the grandchild is born given that the grandfather lives for 2 periods. If the parent is dead when the child is born, the family's expected utility, EU_d, is

$$EU_d(A_1) = \theta \frac{C_{s1,d}^{1-\gamma}}{1-\gamma} + \alpha V(A_{2,d}), \tag{14}$$

where $A_{2,d}$ is the family's assets when the grandchild is born given that the grandfather dies at the end of period 1.

The expected utility function, $V(A)$, is defined by

$$V(A) = PEU_a(W) + (1 - P)EU_d(A). \tag{15}$$

If the initial father (the second child's grandfather) is alive, the family maximizes (13) subject to

$$A_{2,a} = \frac{(A_1 - C_{f2} - C_{s1,a})}{R} + e \tag{16}$$

and

$$C_{f2} + C_{s1,a} \leqslant A_1.$$

In (16), e is the child's first-period earnings. The constraint that $C_{f2} + C_{s1,a}$ not exceed A_1 implies that family assets are never smaller than e. The corresponding constraint in maximizing (14) is

$$A_{2,d} = \frac{(A_1 - C_{s1,d})}{R} + e \tag{17}$$

and

$$C_{s1,d} \leqslant A_1.$$

The value function, $V(A)$, as well as the consumption demands, C_{f2}, $C_{s1,a}$, and $C_{s1,d}$, were computed numerically using the contraction properties of the maximization problem (Denardo 1967). Specifically, we started with a guess of the function $V(A)$ and used this function to solve for

$EU_a(A_1)$ and $EU_d(A_1)$. From (15) these $EU_a(A_1)$ and $EU_d(A_1)$ functions provide a new guess of the $V(A)$ function. This iteration was repeated until the $V(A)$ function converged to its fixed-point solution.

While there is a critical interest rate above which the economy's wealth increases without bound, there is a unique distribution of family assets for each interest rate below this critical value. Corresponding to each of these stochastic steady-state asset distributions is an aggregate stock of assets. Hence the introduction of liquidity constraints in the altruistic model produces (1) a supply schedule of aggregate savings that increases with the interest rate and (2) a nondegenerate wealth distribution. The equilibrium interest rate in this model is no longer determined solely by household preferences; rather, it is determined by equating the household supply of savings to firm's demands for savings (capital).

Assuming a Cobb-Douglas production function with a capital share of 0.3, a time preference factor α of 0.742 (corresponding to a 1 percent annual time-preference rate), and values of θ and γ equal to 1 and 4, respectively, the constrained economy's equilibrium steady-state capital-output ratio is roughly 30 percent larger than it is in the corresponding unconstrained model. For these parameter values the reduction in aggregate savings from switching to perfect insurance is 50 percent. This number should be contrasted with the 7 percent figure in the first row of table 5.1. The percentage reduction in wealth in this model is highly sensitive to the value of α. At α equals 0.25 (a 4.7 percent annual time-preference rate) the percentage reduction is 95 percent. At α equals 0.57 (a 10 percent assumed time-preference rate) the percentage reduction is 99 percent. The per capita wealth stock is much more sensitive to α in the unconstrained perfect insurance version of this model than it is in the constrained family insurance version. This is expected since, for values of α above a critical level, the family is always constrained, and assets in each family equal e, their lower bound [see (16) and (17)].

The lower bound on a family's nonhuman wealth also means a lower equilibrium interest rate than with no borrowing constraints. Since families always save at least as much with liquidity constraints as they do without these constraints, an interest rate equal to or greater than the unconstrained equilibrium value would imply explosive wealth accumulation in the constrained case. The lower equilibrium value of the interest rate in the constrained model reduces the savings incentives of all agents in the economy, particularly those with the greatest wealth, and, therefore, reduces the dispersion in the distribution of wealth. For the baseline parameter values the richest 10 percent of families hold less than 15 percent of economy-wide resources. Inequality in wealth, while limited in all our constrained economy calculations, declines rapidly with increases in α.

5.4   The Selfish Life-Cycle Model

The family insurance model, in which each member acts solely out of self-interest, is more complicated. In this case all transfers that occur are the result of ex ante selfish bargains. A 4-period framework is required here to permit these intergenerational risk-sharing arrangements. When the bargaining takes place, the child is age 1 and the parent is age 3. The parent has 1 period more of certain life followed by 1 period of uncertain life. The agreement reached by parent and child can be thought of as the parent buying an annuity from the child. In return for some money in period 3 the child promises to offer a specified level of support for the parent in period 4 in the event that the parent lives that long. Equivalently, the deal can be arranged such that the child gives the parent some money before period 3 in return for being made beneficiary of the will of the parent. The timing and labeling of payments in these arrangements is not critical; what is critical is that the child share the risk of the parent's life span. Both these arrangements involve such risk sharing. If the parent dies prior to period 4, the child ends up receiving in present value more money than he (she) pays. Alternatively, if the parent dies late, the child pays more money in present value than he (she) receives. There is also no requirement that those risk-pooling arrangements be explicitly stated or written down. Chapter 4 describes mechanisms for enforcing implicit family annuity contracts.

Both the parent and the child can be made better off by striking a bargain. However, there is an indeterminacy as to how the gains from trade should be divided. One can imagine an arrangement under which the parent's utility in the bargain is just the same as if no deal had been struck and, therefore, all the gains from trade go to the child. Alternatively, one can arrange the risk sharing such that all the gains from trade go to the parent. An additional complication is that the child, in striking an arrangement with the parent, considers the third-period bargain he (she) will make with his (her) own child. The expected utility from the future bargain is denoted $\hat{V}$ and depends on the child's level of third-period wealth (human plus nonhuman) W_{s3}, that is, $\hat{V} = \hat{V}(W_{s3})$. Since we assume that successive children all earn identical amounts with certainty in the first 3 periods of their lives, the resources of the grandchild, with whom the child will bargain, is suppressed as an argument of $\hat{V}$.

The frontier of the utility possibilities space with intergenerational bargaining is located by solving the following. Maximize

$$
\frac{C_{f3}^{1-\gamma}}{1-\gamma} + \frac{\alpha P C_{f4}^{1-\gamma}}{1-\gamma} + \frac{\theta C_{s1}^{1-\gamma}}{1-\gamma} + \theta P \left[\frac{\alpha C_{s2,a}^{1-\gamma}}{1-\gamma} + \alpha^2 \hat{V}(W_{s3,a}) \right]
$$

$$
+ \theta(1-P)\left[\frac{\alpha C_{s2,d}^{1-\gamma}}{1-\gamma} + \alpha^2 \hat{V}(W_{s3,d}) \right] \tag{18}
$$

subject to

$$
C_{f3} + C_{s1} + R(C_{f4} + C_{s2,a}) + R^2 W_{s3,a} = W_{s1} + W_{f3} \tag{19}
$$

and

$$
C_{f3} + C_{s1} + RC_{s2,d} + R^2 W_{s3,d} = W_{s1} + W_{f3}. \tag{20}
$$

As in (2), C_{f3} and C_{f4} are the parent's certain and contingent consumption levels in periods 3 and 4, respectively; C_{s1} is the child's first-period consumption, and $C_{s2,a}$ and $C_{s2,d}$ are the child's respective second-period consumption levels contingent on the parent being alive or dead in period 4. Children initially have no nonhuman assets. Each child's certain present value of labor earnings is W_{s1}, and his (her) parent's third-period human plus nonhuman wealth is W_{f3}. Finally, $W_{s3,a}$ and $W_{s3,d}$ are the respective third-period wealth levels of the child, which he or she uses in bargaining with the grandchild, contingent on the parent being alive or dead in period 4.

Problem (18) involves maximizing a weighted sum of the two participants' expected utility where the weight θ, applied to the child's utility, potentially ranges from zero to infinity. The child considers his or her consumption in periods 3 and 4 under two eventualities: either the parent dies early and the child does not have to pay off on the annuity insurance agreement [this is reflected in the final term of (18), which is weighted by the $(1 - P)$ possibility of its occurrence], or the parent dies late and, hence, the child does have to pay off on the annuity insurance [the fourth term in (18)]. As stated, the $\hat{V}(W)$ function gives the expected utility the child experiences from his third- and fourth-period consumption discounted to period 3 of his life as a function of his wealth in period 3.

Problem (18) has two budget constraints; total consumption plus savings for the child's third period equals total initial wealth of the parent and child under both lifetime possibilities for the parent. The weight θ reflects the terms of trade in this bargaining problem. In general one would expect θ to be a function of the resources of both the parent and the child, W_{f3} and

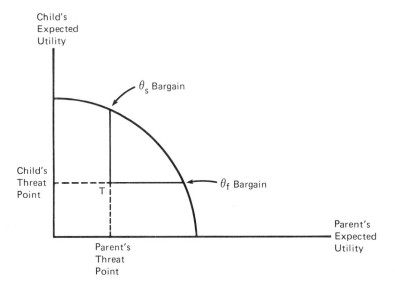

Figure 5.1
Utility possibilities frontier.

W_{s1}, respectively. However, since W_{s1} is constant in our analysis, we express $\theta = \theta(W_{f3})$.

Solving problem (18) for different values of θ traces out the utility possibility frontier for family deals shown in figure 5.1. Obviously, not all values of θ will generate outcomes that are in the core. We have labeled as θ_s the critical value for θ for which the parent receives none of the gains from trade (i.e., the child receives all gains from trade). The term θ_f is defined symmetrically with the parent getting all the surplus. The point T is the threat point, indicating the parent's and child's expected utility levels if they fail to bargain with each other. As is clear from problem (18), figure 5.1 depends on the respective resources of the father and the son, W_{s1} and W_{f3}, and on the function $\hat{V}_s(\cdot)$.

Since we consider a stationary environment in which tastes and endowments of children remain unchanged, we will limit ourselves to stationary bargaining solutions. That is, we assume that the $\hat{V}$ function will be the same for the bargaining of each successive pair of generations. An implication of stationary is that the parent's expected utility in (18), expressed as a function of his wealth, W_{f3}, equals the child's expected utility function, $\hat{V}$, when the child becomes a father. An immediate property of stationarity is that the child reaches the same deal with his child as his parent did with him if respective resources are the same. More formally, a stationary solution is defined as a bargaining function $\theta(W_{f3})$ and an expected utility function $V(W)$ such that if C_{f3}^*, C_{f4}^* are optimal values of consumption derived from solving problem (18), where $V(W_{s3})$ is substituted for $\hat{V}(W_{s3})$, then $V(W_{f3}) = [1/(1 - \gamma)]C_{f3}^{*1-\gamma} + \alpha P[1/(1 - \gamma)]C_{f4}^{*1-\gamma}$.

Solving problem (18) involves searching for a fixed-point function V and an associated $\theta(W_{f3})$ function that produces outcomes that are in the core. We consider and compute three solutions to problem (18). In the first solution, denoted θ_s, the child receives all the gains from trade; furthermore, all successive bargains involve children receiving all gains from trade. In the second solution, denoted θ_f, the initial and all the successive fathers receive all gains from trade. In the third solution the gains from trade are always divided between child and son according to Nash's (1983) two-person bargaining solution.

In the θ_s solution parents receive their threat-point level of expected utility. This is the expected utility received by the parent if he acts on his own and is given by the solution to (21). Maximize

$$\frac{C_{f3}^{1-\gamma}}{1 - \gamma} + \frac{\alpha P C_{f4}^{1-\gamma}}{1 - \gamma} \tag{21}$$

subject to

$$C_{f3} + RC_{f4} = W_{f3}.$$

The structure of the problem is very much like that with perfect annuities, except that providing for C_{f4} costs R instead of only PR. The advantage of annuity markets is precisely this reduced cost of consumption in periods where survival is uncertain.

Denote $V_s(W_{f3})$ as the maximum utility that the parent with wealth W_{f3} can achieve on his own by solving (21). The term $V_s(W_{f3})$ is, thus, the indirect utility function when no deal is struck and is given by

$$V_s(W_{f3}) = k\left(\frac{W_{f3}^{1-\gamma}}{1 - \gamma}\right),$$

where

$$k = R^{\gamma-1}\{[1 + (\alpha P)^{1/\gamma}]R^{(\gamma-1)/\gamma}\}^\gamma.$$

Naturally, $V_s(W_{f3})$ is the minimum the parent is willing to accept in an annuity bargain with his child. The term V_s is also the expected utility function of the child in the θ_s bargain with his own child. Replacing $\hat{V}$ with V_s in (18) and choosing θ_s for each value of W_{f3} such that $V_s(W_{f3}) =$

$C_{f3}^{*1-\gamma}/(1-\gamma) + \alpha[PC_{f4}^{*1-\gamma}/(1-\gamma)]$ provides a proof by construction that V_s is a fixed-point function for the θ_s problem. In addition the computed values of θ_s for different values of W_{f3} determine the function $\theta_s(W_{f3})$. While parents, in this θ_s bargain, receive their threat-point levels of expected utility, their actual pattern of consumption differs from what they would choose on their own; C_{f3}^* is smaller and C_{f4}^* greater than the respective solution values to problem (21).

Although the V_s function was obtained analytically, finding an analytic expression for $\hat{V}$ for other bargaining solutions is generally not possible. For the θ_f and Nash (denoted θ_n) solutions an iterative technique described below is used to find fixed-point functions and their associated θ functions. Both the θ_f and the θ_n solutions require specifying the child's threat point. Given our assumption of a cooperative, efficient solution to parent/child bargaining, the child, if he (she) fails to bargain with the parent, can credibly assert to the parent that he (she) will be able to reach a deal with his child. The child's threat point, EU_s^T, is the solution to problem (22); it involves the child's consuming C_{s1} and C_{s2} in his first 2 periods, respectively, and bargaining with his child in period 3 based on third-period wealth, W_{s3}.

Maximize

$$EU_s^T = \frac{C_{s1}^{1-\gamma}}{1-\gamma} + \frac{\alpha C_{s2}^{1-\gamma}}{1-\gamma} + \alpha^2 \hat{V}(W_{s3}) \tag{22}$$

subject to

$$C_{s1} + RC_{s2} + RW_{s3} = W_{s1}. \tag{23}$$

In the case of $\hat{\theta}_f$ bargaining, $\hat{V}$ is replaced by V_f in (22) as well as in (18). The θ_f solution proceeds by first guessing a function, V_f. Next we solve (22) to determine the son's threat-point utility, EU_s^T. Given the guess of V_f and the derived value of EU_s^T, θ is chosen in (18) such that the son's expected utility in the solution to (18) equals EU_s^T. This last calculation is repeated for different values of W_{f3}, thereby generating a function, $\theta_f(W_{f3})$. In addition to computing a θ_f function on the basis of the initial guess of V_f, the solution to (18) based on $\theta_f(W_{f3})$ determines the father's expected utility in the bargain. The maximizing values of $C_{f3}^{*1-\gamma}/(1-\gamma) + P\alpha[C_{f4}^{*1-\gamma}/(1-\gamma)]$ for different values of W_{f3} provide an expected utility function for the parent in the θ_f bargain with the child. This function is used as the next guess of the V_f function, and the calculations are repeated. The iteration proceeds until the guess of the V_f function equals the parent's expected utility as a function of W_{f3}, that is, until we have found a function, V_f, which is a fixed point of the mapping described.

In the Nash bargaining case a very similar solution technique is applied. The Nash solution involves choosing θ in (18) to maximize the quantity $(EU_f - EU_f^T)(EU_s - EU_s^T)$, where EU_f and EU_s are the expected utilities obtained by the parent and child, respectively, and EU_f^T equals V_s, the parent's threat point. To find V_n, the Nash fixed-point function, we again choose an initial guess of V_n and solve (22) to find EU_s^T. We also solve (21) to find EU_f^T. Next the guessed value of V_n is substituted for $\hat{V}$ in (18), and θ_n is chosen to maximize $(EU_f - EU_t^T)(EU_s - EU_s^T)$. Repeating this last step for alternative values of W_{f3} generates a function, $\theta_n(W_{f3})$, as well as an expected utility function of the father arising from Nash bargaining. This latter function is used as the second guess of the V_n function. The iteration continues until we find a fixed-point function, V_n. In this bargaining solution, as in the previous θ_s solution, the $\theta_f(W_{f3})$ and $\theta_n(W_{f3})$ functions calculated in the last round of the iteration correspond to the correct bargaining functions for the functions V_f and V_n, respectively.

The V_s function is used as the initial guess of the V function for the θ_f and Nash bargaining solutions. In each iteration we computed the solution to (4) for 80 different values of W_{f3}. We then fit a fifth-order polynomial in W_{f3} to these points and used the resulting regression as the guess of V in the next iteration. The iterative procedure for determining V converged roughly by the eighth iteration; 12 iterations each were used for the θ_f and Nash cases. By "rough convergence" we mean that economic choice variables were identical to at least the second digit between iterations. For a range of intermediate values of W_{f3} the calculated consumption terms are identical to five digits between iterations. While we believe more accurate values of the V_s and V_n functions could be obtained, the computation costs of achieving the additional accuracy is considerable; solving (4) for any one of the 80 values of W_{f3} in any one of the 12 iterations requires rather extensive computation.

The Involuntary Bequest Model

The next case we examine is the situation in which there are no insurance arrangements but unintentional bequests are made to children. This case has been examined in 2-period models by Eckstein et al. (1985) and Abel (1985). The solution differs from that of the threat points because the child inherits money unspent by the parent. The child in period 1 of his life can observe the wealth of his parent and can calculate the potential inheritance,

I, he will receive should his parent die young. The child is assumed to solve the following problem.

Maximize

$$\frac{C_{s1}^{1-\gamma}}{1-\gamma} + P\left[\frac{\alpha C_{s2,a}^{1-\gamma}}{1-\gamma} + \alpha^2 V_s(W_{s3,a})\right] + (1-P)\left[\frac{\alpha C_{s2,d}^{1-\gamma}}{1-\gamma} + \alpha^2 V_s(W_{s3,d})\right]$$
(24)

subject to

$$C_{s1} + RC_{s2,a} + R^2 W_{s3,a} = W_{s1}$$

and

$$C_{s1} + RC_{s2,d} + R^2 W_{s3,d} = W_{s1} + I,$$

where

$$I = W_{f3}/R - C_{f3}.$$

The child maximizes his welfare subject to the certain earnings endowment, W_{s1}, and the inheritance I left by the parent if he dies young. The V_s function gives the level of expected utility the child can receive in periods 3 and 4 with no deal with his child.

5.5   The Transmission of Wealth in the Stochastic Steady State

Figure 5.2 graphs the wealth of children in their third period (when they are parents) against their parents' wealth, W_{f3}, for the case of family insurance bargains. The amount of wealth the child brings into his third period depends, of course, on the age at which his parent dies. The curves $W_{s3}^d(W_{f3})$ and $W_{s3}^a(W_{f3})$ indicate the third-period wealth of the child if his own parent lives for 3 periods and 4 periods, respectively. Note that the two curves intersect on the vertical axis, since a child whose parent has no wealth engages in the same consumption regardless of the date of his parent's death.

The exact position and shapes of these curves depend on the specification of the utility function as well as the parent-child bargaining solution. For the examples we describe here, the curves were constructed by fitting fifth-order polynomials to the values of $W_{s3}^d(W_{f3})$ and $W_{s3}^a(W_{f3})$ calculated for 80 different values of W_{f3}. The intercepts in each regression were constrained to equal the amount of resources a child would save for period 3 assuming he engages in no bargain with his parent. In each calculation,

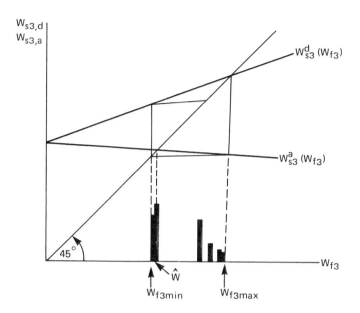

Figure 5.2
Wealth transmission functions and the steady-state distribution of parents' wealth.

the estimated curves were essentially straight lines, with $W_{s3}^d(W_{f3})$ and $W_{a3}^a(W_{f3})$ monotonically increasing and decreasing W_{f3}, respectively.

Intuitively, $W_{s3}^d(W_{f3})$ rises with W_{f3} because a fraction of the parent's increased resources will be allocated to the parent's contingent fourth-period consumption, C_{f4}. If the parent dies after period 3, the additional C_{f4} is passed on to the child. For the child the inheritance is allocated to larger second-period consumption as well as larger third-period savings, $W_{s3}^d(W_{f3})$, that is, used in the bargain with his own child. The decline in $W_{s3}^a(W_{f3})$ as W_{f3} increases is explained as follows: regardless of the bargaining solution between the parent and child, the parent's contingent bequest rises with W_{f3}. Part of the price the child pays for the larger contingent bequest is somewhat lower values of second-period consumption and third-period wealth in the case the parent does not die young. This permits the parent to consume more in period 3 and, potentially, in period 4.

Assuming, as is verified in our actual calculation, that the slope of $W_{s3}^d(W_{f3})$ is everywhere positive and less than unity, $W_{f3\,max}$ is the unique limiting value of a parent's third-period wealth when *all* his forefathers have died early. For values of W_{f3} above $W_{f3\,max}$, successive early deaths of parents lead to smaller values of W_{f3} for each successive parent until the sequence converges to $W_{f3\,max}$. Similarly, starting with a value for W_{f3} below $W_{f3\,max}$ and assuming that all successive parents die early leads to successively larger values of W_{f3} until $W_{f3\,max}$ is reached.

We next turn to the minimum bound on the stochastic steady-state distribution of a parent's wealth. If the slope of $W_{s3}^a(W_{f3})$ is between 0 and -1, which is the case in the examples presented below, then $\hat{W}_{f3}$ is the unique limit of the value of a parent's wealth as successive parents in a family continue to live through period 4. In this case the sequence of W_{f3}s, starting at any particular value, converges as a "Cobb-web" to $\hat{W}_{f3}$; that is, each successive parent with more wealth than $\hat{W}_{f3}$, who lives to period 4, has a child who has less than $\hat{W}_{f3}$ when the child becomes a parent.

In the stochastic steady state $W_{f3\,min}$ is the lower bound on a parent's third-period wealth. Values below $W_{f3\,min}$ cannot arise in the stochastic steady state; any parent with W_{f3} below $W_{f3\,min}$ will have a child whose wealth as a parent is between $W_{f3\,min}$ and $W_{f3\,max}$. Once the W_{f3} for a particular family falls within $W_{f3\,min}$ and $W_{f3\,max}$, no parent in the family will ever appear with wealth outside this range. Values of W_{f3} below $W_{f3\,min}$ and above $W_{f3\,max}$ are nonrecurrent states in the Markov process that maps W_{f3} into $W_{s3}^d(W_{f3})$ with probability $1 - p$ and into $W_{s3}^a(W_{f3})$ with probability p. As can readily be seen by tracing out alternative p and $(1 - p)$ sequences, starting with values of W_f between $W_{f3\,min}$ and $W_{f3\,max}$, the larger the value of W_f in the preceding generation, the smaller will be the W_{f3} in the next generation if the parent dies late. $W_{f3\,min}$, therefore, corresponds to the value of $W_{s3}^a(W_{f3})$ for $W_{f3\,max}$, that is, $W_{f3\,min} = W_{s3}^a(W_{f3\,max})$. Hence, if the richest parent survives to period 4, his child is the poorest parent when he reaches period 3. This extreme "riches to rags" result is quite intuitive. A parent with the largest possible wealth, $W_{f3\,max}$, provides the largest estate if he dies early but no estate if he dies late. In order to "purchase" the right to this largest potential estate the child pays the largest price in terms of reduced consumption and third-period wealth if his parent lives.

Since the Markov process described in figure 5.2. is nonrecurrent, there are large regions between $W_{f3\,min}$ and $W_{f3\,max}$ that have zero mass with respect to the steady state distribution of wealth. The shaded areas in figure 5.2 chart this distribution for the case θ's in which parents receive none of the gains from bargaining with their children. This distribution was constructed by giving 100,000 families the same initial value of W_{f3} and then simulating 25 successive generations using a 0.6 probability of a 4-period lifetime. The distribution of W_{f3} stabilized after roughly eight generations. Since we assume that a new generation is born every period, rather than every other period, there are also orphaned 2-period-old children as well as 2-period-old children with surviving parents who hold wealth at any point in time. Calculating the stochastic steady state's stock of wealth requires simply summing the wealth holdings of all age 3 parents, the wealth of orphaned children, and the wealth of 2-period-old children and their surviving 4-period-old parents. The wealth holdings of these latter two groups are derived from the distribution of wealth holdings of 3-period-old parents; the consumption of each of the 100,000 parents and their children, when these parents are age 3, is subtracted from the income of these families to compute their combined saving. This saving plus each parent's initial wealth represents the next-period wealth holdings of families consisting either of orphaned children or of children with surviving parents. Since this wealth distribution is stationary in the stochastic steady state, next period's wealth holdings of these groups is identical to this period's wealth holdings of such groups. Similar calculations are made for the case in which there are no insurance bargains between parents and children, but children nonetheless inherit their parents' estates.

Parameter values were chosen as follows: the time preference factor, α, and the discount factor, R, both equal 0.86. The coefficient of risk aversion, γ, equals 4, and the fourth-period survival probability, ρ, equals 0.6. If one thinks of each period as consisting of 15 years, then a discount factor of 0.86 corresponds to a 1 percent annual real rate of return. In addition, if we view parents as being age 50 and children age 20 when the bargains are struck, the 0.6 fourth-period survival probability is roughly equivalent to assuming an expected age of death of 74.

Table 5.3 presents the calculated values for a parent's third- and fourth-period consumption at alternative levels of W_{f3} under perfect insurance, the three alternative parent-child bargains [the θ_f, Nash, and θ_s solution to (6)], and the case of no-insurance arrangements. In each of these cases, the parent's consumption increases with his third-period wealth. Access to perfect insurance results, for this parameterization of utility, in higher levels of consumption for the parent in both periods 3 and 4 relative to the other cases of partial or zero insurance. For example, if the parent's wealth is 4.4 at the beginning of period 3, he consumes 2.9 and 2.5 in periods 3 and 4, respectively, with no insurance, and 3.4 in both periods with perfect insurance. The present value difference in these consumption paths is 25%.

A parent-and-child bargain in which successive parents receive all gains from trade with successive children, the θ_f bargain, provides parents with consumption values that are roughly midway between those of perfect and

Table 5.3
Parent's consumption under alternative insurance arrangements[a]

Parent's third-period wealth ($WF3$)	Perfect insurance		θf bargain (parents receive all gains from trade)		Nash bargaining solution		θs bargain (children receive all gains from trade)		No insurance arrangements	
	CF3	CF4	CF3	CF4	CF3	CF4	CF3	CF4	CF3	CF4
9.0	6.9	6.9	6.4	5.8	6.2	5.6	5.9	5.3	5.0	5.3
8.0	6.7	6.7	5.7	5.2	5.5	4.9	5.2	4.7	5.3	4.6
7.0	5.4	5.4	5.0	4.5	4.89	4.3	4.5	4.1	4.6	4.0
6.0	4.6	4.6	4.4	4.0	4.2	3.8	3.9	3.6	4.0	3.5
5.0	3.8	3.8	3.6	3.3	3.5	3.2	3.2	3.0	3.3	2.9
4.4	3.4	3.4	3.2	3.0	3.0	2.8	2.8	2.6	2.9	2.5

a. $\gamma = 4$, $P = 0.6$, $\alpha = R = 0.86$.

zero insurance. Consumption values for the parent under the Nash bargaining solution lie between the θ_f and θ_s deals. This is the expected result since the Nash solution divides the gains from trade between parents and children. The θ_s bargain, in which the parent receives no benefits from dealing with his child, involves slightly less third-period consumption and slightly more fourth-period consumption when old than in the case of zero insurance.

Table 5.4 shows consumption and third-period wealth values of children in different insurance regimes. Under perfect insurance the child's consumption is 3.4 in each period; with no insurance arrangements and no involuntary bequests the child consumes 3.2 during the first 3 periods and 2.8 in the last period. Depending on the parent's wealth and longevity and the bargain struck between the two, the child can potentially consume well in excess of the perfect insurance values. As an example, take the case of a parent with wealth of 6.0 who agrees to a θ_s bargain with his child. The child's first-period consumption is 3.4, the same as under perfect insurance. If the parent dies after his third period, the child consumes 4.5 in period 2 rather than 3.4, the perfect insurance amount. Furthermore, the child's third-period wealth in this case is 7.9, substantially in excess of 4.4, the third-period wealth of a son under perfect insurance. With third-period wealth of 7.9, the child's third- and contingent fourth-period consumption values are, from table 5.3, roughly 5.5 and 4.9. For this child the total potential realized present value of consumption is 14.4, although the present value of his earnings is only 10.

5.6   The Savings Impact of Alternative Insurance Arrangements

Table 5.5 compares steady-state per capita wealth stocks in the different insurance regimes under alternative assumptions about age-earnings profiles. Each of the age-earnings profiles has a present value of 10, which is received with certainty over the course of the first 3 periods. Since the child's resources are identical in each of these cases, the consumption decisions of the child and parent are the same for each of these earnings paths. Hence, the difference in stocks of wealth by row in table 5.5 are simply a function of the timing of the receipt of labor income.

The absolute size of these economies' wealth stocks may appear small in comparison to the level of earnings or income in a particular period. However, such stock-flow ratios must be adjusted for the fact that flows in this model are received over a period that corresponds to roughly 15 years. In the case of the third and probably the most realistic earnings profile in

Table 5.4
Child's consumption under alternative insurance arrangements. Consumption and wealth values: Father-son bargains[a]

Father's wealth	θ_s bargain (children get all gains from trade)					Nash bargaining solution					θ_f bargain (children get no gains from trade)				
	CS1	CS2A	CS2D	WS3, A	WS3, D	CS1	CS2A	CS2D	WS3, A	WS3, D	CS1	CS2A	CS2D	WS3, A	WS3, D
9.0	3.4	3.1	5.2	5.4	9.1	3.4	3.1	5.5	4.6	8.3	3.3	2.9	5.1	4.4	8.5
8.0	3.4	3.1	4.9	5.4	8.7	3.5	3.1	5.2	4.6	7.9	3.3	3.0	4.9	4.4	8.1
7.0	3.4	3.1	4.7	5.4	8.3	3.5	3.1	5.0	4.6	7.5	3.3	3.0	4.7	4.5	7.7
6.0	3.4	3.1	4.5	5.4	7.9	3.5	3.1	5.0	4.6	7.1	3.3	3.0	4.5	4.5	7.3
5.0	3.3	3.1	4.3	5.4	7.5	3.4	3.1	4.5	4.7	6.8	3.2	3.0	4.3	4.5	6.9
4.4	3.3	3.1	4.1	5.4	7.3	3.4	3.2	4.4	4.7	6.6	3.3	3.0	4.2	4.6	6.7

a. $\gamma = 4$, $P = 0.6$, $\alpha = R = 0.86$. Consumption values under perfect insurance: CS1, 3.4; CS2, 3.4; CF3, 3.4; CF4, 3.4. Consumption values with no insurance arrangements and no involuntary bequests: CS1, 3.2; CS2, 3.2; CF3, 3.2; CF4, 2.8.

Table 5.5
Wealth per capita and percentage long-run decline in wealth from switch to perfect insurance[a]

Age-earnings profile	Perfect insurance (Wealth)	θ_f bargain (parents receive all gains from trade)		Nash bargaining solution		θ_s bargain (children receive all gains from trade)		No bargain, involuntary bequests	
		Wealth	Percentage wealth decline	Wealth	Percentage wealth decline	Wealth	Percentage wealth decline	Wealth	Percentage wealth decline
(10, 0, 0, 0)	12.7	13.9	8.6	14.2	10.6	15.9	20.1	15.5	18.1
(5.0, 5.8, 0, 0)	7.7	8.9	13.5	9.2	16.3	10.9	29.4	10.5	26.7
(3.3, 3.9, 4.5, 0)	2.2	3.4	35.3	3.7	40.5	5.4	59.3	5.0	56.0
(3.0, 5.8, 2.7, 0)	3.4	4.6	26.1	4.9	30.6	6.6	48.5	6.2	45.2
(2.0, 5.8, 3.5, 0)	0.7	2.9	171.4	3.2	78.1	3.9	82.0	3.5	80.0

a. $\gamma = 4$, $P = 0.6$, $\alpha = R = 0.86$.

table 5.5, the ratio of wealth to one-fifteenth of a period's labor earnings is 6.9 in the case of the θ_s bargain. A wealth/earnings ratio of 6.9 is somewhat greater than that observed in the United States.

The percentage reductions in wealth from moving to perfect insurance reported in table 5.5 are very large. For the earnings profile in the third row the long-run wealth reduction is 59 percent starting from the θ_s (children take all) stochastic steady state. It is 41 percent in the case of an initial Nash bargaining equilibrium and 35 percent when the initial equilibrium involves θ_f (parents take all) bargain.

The values in table 5.5 are highly sensitive to the shape of the age-earnings profile. The smallest percentage wealth reduction arises when all earnings are received in the first period; in this case wealth falls by 20.1 percent starting from the θ_s bargain and by 13.9 percent starting from the θ_f bargain.

The percentage change in wealth appears relatively insensitive to variations in the degree of relative risk aversion, γ. For example, reducing γ from 4 to 1.5 lowers the percentage decline in wealth under row 3's earnings profile and initial θ_s bargaining from 59.3 percent to 50.7 percent. Raising γ to 8 increases the value to 63.2 percent. Under table 5.3's first age-earnings profile the percentage wealth reductions starting from θ_s economies are 15.1, 20.1, and 22.9 for values of γ equal to 1.5, 4, and 8, respectively.

There is considerably more sensitivity to changes in the fourth-period survival probability P; however, the sensitivity depends on the choice of earnings profile. For example, lower P from 0.6 to 0.3, which reduces the expected age of death from roughly 74 to roughly 69, converts the 59.3 percent θ_s reduction (row 3, table 5.5) to 83.6 percent. The same reduction in P raises table 5.5's row 1, θ_s value from 20.1 percent to only 23.4 percent.

The large differences in wealth stocks between the perfect insurance and family insurance regimes suggests that steady state welfare could actually be lower in the case of perfect insurance. This is indeed possible. Under θ_f (children take all) bargaining and assuming γ equals 1.5, the expected utility of even the child of the poorest parent exceeds the uniform, steady-state expected utility under perfect insurance. Starting from a situation of zero insurance, achieving the perfect insurance expected utility level requires a 7 percent increase in resources; achieving the expected utility of the child with the poorest parent in the θ_s stochastic steady state requires an 8 percent increase in lifetime resources, starting from this benchmark regime. Attaining the level of welfare of the child whose parent in the θ_f steady state has the maximum potential wealth, $W_{f3\,max}$, requires a corresponding 12 percent increase in resources.

The steady-state stocks of wealth in the case of no family arrangements, but involuntary bequests to children, are slightly smaller than those under θ_s bargaining. This is not surprising since in both cases parents receive their threat-point levels of utility and consume roughly similar amounts. In the θ_s deal, however, the child's insurance provision leads to a somewhat lower level of the parent's consumption in period 3 and a somewhat higher level in period 4 (see table 5.3). In addition, given W_{f3}, the child consumes slightly less in period 1 in the θ_s deal than in the involuntary bequest setting. This consumption pattern explains the larger wealth stock in the θ_s insurance regime.

Another question raised by table 5.5 is the extent to which imperfections in annuity markets can fully explain observed intergenerational transfers. Chapter 1 invoked the assumption of perfect insurance arrangements in estimating that roughly 80 percent of private US wealth corresponds to accumulated inheritances of those currently alive. This assumption that annuity insurance is fairly well developed in the United States can be defended by pointing to social security and other government annuities, private pensions, old age labor earnings that are partly contingent on survival, and the potential for family risk sharing involving multiple members. Still, it is interesting to ask how their calculation turns out when it is applied to the two-member family insurance economy described above. Their technique involves subtracting accumulated consumption from accumulated earnings for each cohort and then summing across cohorts to get a total wealth stock. This "life-cycle" wealth is then compared with actual wealth holdings. If agents in the economy are selfish and annuity arrangements are perfect or very close to perfect, computed and actual aggregate wealth will be identical or extremely close to one another.

The two-person family regime is, however, quite far from that of perfect insurance. As described here, this imperfection produces a stochastic steady state in which observed consumption profiles often exceed what could be financed from one's own labor earnings even under perfect insurance. Hence, in this economy, subtracting, for all cohorts, accumulated consumption, part of which is financed by past intergenerational transfers, from accumulated earnings produces an underestimate of the economy's actual wealth. For the θ_s bargain, with γ equals 4 and with table 5.5's row 3 earnings profile, 1.5, the underestimate is close to 90 percent of actual wealth. Since chapter 1's calculation understates United States wealth by 80 percent, imperfections in annuity markets appear potentially capable of fully explaining actual intergenerational transfers in the United States.

5.7   Summary and Conclusions

This paper has explored the effect of perfecting annuity insurance on savings and inequality using two standard neoclassical models—the intergenerationally altruistic model and the nonaltruistic life-cycle model. While the modeling is intentionally structured to produce the maximum precautionary savings, the results are, nonetheless, quite surprising. Partial equilibrium calculations based on the life-cycle model suggest very substantial reductions in national wealth associated with improving annuity insurance. Indeed, in the life-cycle model the reduction in savings from the annuity insurance associated with social security could be larger than the savings reduction arising from social security's "pay as you go" method of finance. In addition, imperfections in annuity insurance appear potentially capable of explaining a sizable fraction of observed intergenerational transfers in the United States.

In the intergenerationally altruistic model, perfecting annuity insurance can also significantly lower national savings, but the results here are much more sensitive to precise parameter values as well as to assumptions about liquidity constraints.

In the presence of family annuity insurance each of the models provides a theory of the distribution of resources. While the life-cycle model suggests a rather limited dispersion in family resources in the stochastic steady state, the altruistic model, absent liquidity constraints, generates increasing inequality through time. Asymptotically, the altruistic model's resource distribution is completely skew. In the long run, virtually all families hold close to zero resources, and an infinitesimal fraction of families hold all the economy's wealth.

The results of this analysis suggest the importance of studying other motives for precautionary savings, such as uncertainty with respect to future earnings and future health status. A variety of government programs, including disability and unemployment insurance, welfare, and progressive taxation, may be greatly affecting the extent of precautionary savings in the economy. To the extent that such savings is highly responsive to government insurance programs, the government may wish to offset their adverse savings effects not by reducing its provision of insurance but by using alternative policy instruments that raise savings without increasing economic uncertainty.

Notes

We thank Zvi Eckstein, Bronwyn Hall, Joe Stiglitz, Truman Bewley, Andy Abel, Ludo Van der Heyden, Linus Yamane, and Steven Galatis for helpful discussions. Steven Galatis and Linus Yamane provided excellent research assistance.

1. Our discussion of behavior in the life-cycle model draws heavily on Kotlikoff, Shoven, and Spivak (1983).

2. See chapter 4. This statement assumes independent morality probabilities across family members.

3. The formula for $g(\cdot)$ is

$$g(P, \alpha, \theta, R, \gamma, k) = \{a^{1/\gamma} + \alpha^{1/\gamma}R^{(\gamma-1)/\gamma}[P(a + \alpha^{1/\gamma}R^{(\gamma-1)/\gamma}k^{1/\gamma})^\gamma$$

$$+ (1 - P)(\theta^{1/\gamma} + \alpha^{1/\gamma}R^{(\gamma-1)/\gamma}k^{1/\gamma})^\gamma]^\gamma\}^{1/\gamma},$$

where $a = (1 + \theta^{1/\gamma})^\gamma$. For each set of particular values considered in the paper there is a unique value k, satisfying $k = g(\cdot)$.

4. A and D are given by

$$A = R^2[1 - (M/a)^{-1/\gamma}][1 - (k/a)^{-1/\gamma}],$$

$$D = R^2[a - (N/\theta)^{-1/\gamma}][1 - (k/a)^{-1/\gamma}],$$

where

$$a = (1 + \theta^{1/\gamma})^\gamma, \qquad M = [a^{1/\gamma} + (\alpha R^{-1}v)^{1/\gamma}R]^\gamma$$

and

$$N = \{[\theta^{1/\gamma} + (\alpha R^{-1}v)^{1/\gamma}]^{1/\gamma}R\}^\gamma.$$

5. Actually, Chebyshev's theorem provides an even stronger statement about changes in the distribution of family resources through time. Let c be an arbitrary constant. Then the probability at time t that $\log W_{t+\tau}$ exceeds c is bounded by a number that declines with τ if $\log W_t$ is less than or equal to c. If $\log W_t$ exceeds c, the bound on the probability that $\log W_{t+\tau}$ exceeds c declines with τ for $\tau \geqslant \log W_t - c/\gamma$. In other words, the bound of $P(\log W_{t+\tau} \geqslant c)$ monotonically declines with τ if the process has already reached c, and, if not, it declines monotonically once the process has had enough time to drift down to c. More formally, from Chebyshev's theorem we have

$$P(\log W_{t+\tau} \geqslant \log W_t - \tau\rho + \lambda\sqrt{\tau\sigma}) \leqslant \frac{1}{\lambda^2},$$

where λ is a positive constant. Choose λ such that $c = \log W_t - \tau\rho + \lambda\sqrt{\tau\sigma}$; then,

$$P(\log W_{t+\tau} \geqslant c) \leqslant \frac{1}{\lambda^2},$$

where

$$\lambda = \frac{c - \log W_t + \tau\rho}{\sqrt{\tau\sigma}}.$$

Since $\tau\rho \geqslant \log W_t - c$, $\partial\lambda/\partial\tau > 0$ and $\partial(1/\lambda^2)/\partial\tau < 0$.

6. The intuitive explanation here is that, as the time-preference factor approaches unity, families become increasingly indifferent between their own welfare and that of their far distant, indeed infinitely distant, descendants. At the limit, when α equals one, current family members are completely indifferent between consuming now and saving everything for the future consumption of their descendants. They are also indifferent with respect to allocating consumption at any point in time between children and parents, i.e., eliminating parental consumption, and, thereby, the entire concern with life-span uncertainty is a matter of indifference to families when α equals one. Since life-span uncertainty becomes an increasingly less important issue as α rises, it is not surprising that, for α equal to .99, savings with imperfect insurance is equal to savings with imperfect insurance.

7. By "rough convergence" we mean that economic choice variables were identical to at least the second digit between iterations. For a range of intermediate values of W_{f3} the calculated consumption terms are identical to five digits between iterations. While we believe that more accurate values of the V_s and V_n functions could be obtained, the computation costs of achieving the additional accuracy is considerable; solving (18) for any one of the 80 values of W_{f3} in any one of the 12 iterations requires rather extensive computation.

6   Health Expenditures and Precautionary Savings

The precautionary motive for saving is an important issue that is receiving increasing attention. Part of the motivation for this interest stems from the postwar coincidence of two trends, one a decline in the US rate of saving and the other an increase in insurance of various types, including unemployment insurance, annuity insurance, disability insurance, and health insurance. The postwar decline in the ratio of US net national product less total US consumption to net national product is quite striking. This ratio averaged 8.8 percent in the 1950s, 8.7 percent in the 1960s, 7.7 percent in the 1970s, but only 5.1 percent since 1980, with values of 3.2 percent, 5.8 percent, and 4.4 percent in the nonrecession years of 1983, 1984, and 1985, respectively. Over this period the provision of insurance, particularly by the government, increased enormously. The Social Security system, including Medicare, now represents the nation's primary source of insurance for length of life, disability, and old age health expenditures. Given these two trends, a natural question to pose is whether improvements in the provision of insurance reduced the demand for precautionary savings and explain the decline in the US saving rate.

In recent years economists have examined precautionary saving arising from life span uncertainty and earnings uncertainty. Less attention has been paid to precautionary saving to meet uncertain, uninsured health expenditures. The lack of research on this topic may reflect the difficulty of precisely quantifying the economic risks of morbidity. Unlike the case of life span uncertainty for which there are published mortality tables that can be easily incorporated in the analysis, there are no corresponding tables specifying the probabilities of particular levels of health expenditures by characteristics such as age and sex. In addition, unlike certain causes of death, such as being hit by a car, the causes of morbidity and health expenditures are not likely to be independent from one year to the next.

What one would really like to have are probabilities of health expenditures conditional on past health expenditures.

An additional problem involved in realistically studying saving for uninsured health expenditures is grappling with the wide array of insurance policies purchased by the public. Many of these policies are employer provided and are not subject to choice by the employee. Empirical analysis of household saving in response to health expenditure uncertainty requires knowledge of the specific medical insurance policies held by households. Unfortunately there do not appear to be available any microeconomic data sets that detail type of health insurance coverage together with information about consumption and saving.

This chapter abandons the difficult goal of attempting to model realistically uncertainty with respect to health expenditures and pursues the simpler task of heuristically considering the question of precautionary saving to meet uncertain health care payments. The heuristic analysis here includes examining theoretical issues in a simple two-period model and illustrating the theoretical points with simulations of a 55-period life cycle model. Several different insurance settings are examined. These are no insurance, actuarially fair insurance, actuarially unfair insurance, and incomplete insurance provided through a government program somewhat similar to the US Medicaid system. Another option that individuals may elect is simply not to receive medical care. While this option eliminates the precautionary motive for saving, it also eliminates consumption of health care services. Hence an economy choosing not to pay for health care may end up with a level of savings similar to that of an economy with significant health expenditures and a significant precautionary saving motive.

The next section discusses briefly some evidence concerning the size of uninsured health expenditures. Section 6.2 looks at precautionary saving for health expenditures and the affect of insurance arrangements on such saving in a simple two-period model. Section 6.3 uses a 55-period simulation model to illustrate how health insurance arrangements can affect the economy's long-run level of savings. The concluding section points out that uncertainty with respect to health expenditures may interact with uncertainty concerning earnings and length of life in influencing precautionary savings and that this interaction merits additional research.

The simulation analysis of section 6.3 is conducted in partial equilibrium since it takes factor prices (wages and interest rates) as given. Partial equilibrium exercises of the kind conducted are likely to overstate the corresponding general equilibrium results (chapter 12). Even so, the simulations give one the impression that precautionary savings for uncertain health expenditures could explain a fairly large amount of aggregate savings. Adding uncertain health expenditures to the base-case economy raises long-run savings by almost one-third, assuming that individuals self-insure. The insurance arrangements available for dealing with uncertain health expenditures also have potentially quite sizable effects on savings. Introducing actuarially fair insurance to the economy with uncertain health expenditures reduces the steady-state level of wealth by 12 percent. Switching from the fair insurance arrangement to a Medicaid-type program with an asset test further reduces steady-state wealth by 75 percent.

6.1   The Size of Uninsured Medical Expenditures

In a recent study of uninsured non–nursing home health expenditures, Rossiter and Wilensky (1982) report quite modest average levels of uninsured health expenditures. Their data come from the 1977–1978 National Medical Care Expenditure Survey of about 14,000 households. Three-quarters of the US population had some out-of-pocket expenses for health services in 1977. The per capita level of such expenses was $275. This figure and all subsequent dollar figures in this section are expressed in 1985 dollars. Among persons with positive expenditures, expenses averaged $364. Average uninsured health expenditures obviously depend importantly on age. For the 83 percent of those 65 and older with positive expenditures, expenditures averaged $579 per person.

Most participants in the survey report quite small out-of-pocket health expenditures. Almost 65 percent of surveyed individuals report either no uninsured health expenditures or expenditures totaling less than $177 (100 1977 dollars). There are, however, some respondents for whom these expenditures are more significant. The percentage of individuals with 1977 expenditures above $888 (500 1977 dollars) is 6.6 percent; the percentage above $1,775 (1,000 1977 dollars) is 2.3 percent. For elderly individuals the percentage with noninsured expenditures above $888 is 12.5 percent, while the percentage with noninsured expenditures above $1,775 is 4.9 percent. For 70 percent of surveyed individuals out-of-pocket expenditures represent less than 3 percent of income; they represent 20 percent or more of income for 4.2 percent of surveyed individuals.

Unfortunately no more detailed information concerning expenditures in excess of $1,775 is provided in the study. Hence one cannot assess the extent of extremely large uninsured health expenditures. It could well be that a quite small fraction of the population incurs extremely large uninsured expenses. A variety of studies documenting the high cost of particular illnesses and particular health episodes are suggestive of this possibility. For example, Long et al. (1984) report that terminal cancer patients averaged $21,219 in Blue Cross and Blue Shield reimbursed expenditures in their terminal year. Lubitz and Prihoda (1984) show that, for 6 percent of 1978 decedents enrolled in Medicare, Medicare expenses exceeded $15,000.

Another consideration in viewing the Rossiter and Wilensky findings is that they only describe uninsured expenditures over a short period of time and do not indicate the cumulative uninsured health expenditures of a prolonged illness such as cancer. Their data also do not include nursing home expenditures. For private pay patients the cost of a year in a reasonably nice nursing home currently appears to range between $25,000 and $50,000. Obviously, nicer nursing homes can be even more expensive.

An extended stay in a reasonably nice nursing home could easily dissipate the assets of the typical middle class household. Venti and Wise (1986b) examine the 1983 Survey of Consumer Finances and report a median level of wealth of those households with household head age 55 to 64 of $55,000; among households with head age 65 +, the median is $40,100. Most of this wealth is tied up in real estate. For both groups the median level of financial assets is less than $3,600.

The uninsured risks of nursing home care and other health expenditures cannot, of course, be assessed without considering the government's role through Medicaid as a residual insurer. Indeed, for most of the 12.6 percent of Americans with no medical insurance the government presumably represents the insurer of first resort. For high-quality nursing homes, middle class individuals seeking to ensure access to such homes may only need to save enough to cover the first year or so of a stay since they can, in many cases, become eligible for Medicaid and remain in the same nursing home under Medicaid. Switching to Medicaid coverage of nursing home stays is not, however, without its drawbacks. Medicaid patients in private pay nursing homes typically have smaller rooms or must share their room with another patient. They also lose some of their autonomy. For example, Medicaid severely restricts the number of days one can be away from the nursing home. Finally, once on Medicaid there is the possibility that the nursing home patient will lose his or her bed because of a prolonged stay in a hospital. In this case the patient may be transferred to a much less desirable nursing facility.

In sum, it appears that for at least most middle income and upper income households future health expenditures represent a major uninsured risk. While most health problems that do not involve prolonged use of hospitals and nursing home facilities appear to be well insured, catastrophic or near-catastrophic health problems may require and induce substantial levels of precautionary savings by middle and upper income households. For lower income households the availability of Medicaid in conjunction with the sizable costs of medical care may make the option of relying on Medicaid preferable to engaging in precautionary savings. Hence, for the better off segment of society, the high costs of medical care in conjunction with the lack of catastrophic insurance may induce substantial additional savings, whereas for the less affluent segment the high cost of medical care in conjunction with the availability of Medicaid may be substantially lowering savings.

6.2   Modeling Precautionary Saving for Health Expenditures

Alternative Regimes

To understand how uncertainty with respect to health expenditures can influence savings, consider a simple two-period life cycle model in which individuals work when young and consume when young and old. There is no population growth. In their first period, when they are young, individuals are healthy; in the second period they become ill with probability P. If they fall ill, it costs an amount e to become well again. Whether or not individuals who become ill choose to spend e and be cured depends on the utility loss of not making the health expenditures and on the availability of insurance to help defray the health expenditures.

Consider first the "live with it" case in which individuals choose not to be cured if they become ill. Letting C_y denote consumption when young and C_o consumption when old, expected utility is given by

$$EU^\alpha = U(C_y) + P\alpha\beta U(C_o) + (1 - P)\beta U(C_o), \tag{1}$$

where β is a time preference factor and α is a parameter whose value lies between 0 and 1 and determines the disutility from being ill. The budget constraint for this problem is simply

$$C_y + RC_o = W, \tag{2}$$

where W is first-period labor earnings and R is 1 divided by $1+$ the interest rate. The first-order condition for utility maximization is

$$U'(C_y^\alpha) = [P\alpha + (1 - P)]\beta U'[(W - C_y^\alpha)/R]/R, \tag{3}$$

where C_y^α is the optimal choice of C_y in this case.

Next consider the case of self-payment in which the individual chooses to be cured but must pay for it herself because there is no private insurance or government assistance. In this case the individual chooses C_y to maximize

$$EU^s = U(C_y) + P\beta U[(W - C_y)/R - e] + (1 - P)\beta U[(W - C_y)/R], \quad (4)$$

and the first-order condition is

$$U'(C_y^s) = P\beta U'[(W - C_y^s)/R - e]/R + (1 - P)\beta U'[(W - C_y^s)/R]/R. \quad (5)$$

The third case to examine is that of private insurance. Assume that for a total premium of vF, paid when young, the individual can purchase medical insurance paying F if the individual falls ill. Expected utility with private insurance is

$$EU^i = U(C_y) + P\beta U[(W - vF - C_y)/R + F - e]$$
$$+ (1 - P)\beta U[(W - vF - C_y)/R]. \quad (6)$$

The first-order condition for choosing C_y is

$$U'(C_y^i) = P\beta U'[(W - vF - C_y^i)/R + F - e]/R$$
$$+ (1 - P)\beta U'[(W - vF - C_y^i)/R]/R. \quad (7)$$

And the first-order condition for the choice of F is

$$(1 - v/R)PU'[(W - vF - C_y^i)/R + F - e]$$
$$= v/R(1 - P)U'[(W - vF - C_y^i)/R]. \quad (8)$$

If the premium per dollar of coverage v is actuarially fair, then

$$v = PR, \quad (9)$$

and from (8) $F = e$; that is, when insurance is fairly priced, the individual fully insures. Equation (7) in this case becomes

$$U'(C_y^i) = \beta U'[(W - PRe - C_y^i)/R]/R. \quad (7')$$

The last case to consider involves a government policy described here as Medicaid. If the individual becomes ill, the government pays for the cure, but also confiscates all of the individual's assets. Medicaid provides the individual with a level of old-age consumption equal to $\bar{C}$. Under Medicaid expected utility is determined by

$$EU^m = U(C_y) + P\beta U(\bar{C}) + (1 - P)\beta U[(W - C_y)/R], \quad (10)$$

and the first-order condition governing the choice of C_y is

$$U'(C_y^m) = (1 - P)\beta U'[(W - C_y^m)/R]/R. \tag{11}$$

Medicaid health care payments and consumption payments for Medicaid recipients are financed from Medicaid's confiscation of assets of its recipients, that is,

$$e + \bar{C} = (W - C_y)/R. \tag{12}$$

In this two-period model the expected utility from self-payment always exceeds that under Medicaid since the individual is effectively required to pay for her own health care plus old-age consumption, but the choice of old-age consumption when ill is predetermined by Medicaid.

While Medicaid provides no risk pooling in this two-period example, it does provide risk pooling in the 55-period simulation model of the next section. In the 55-period model individuals may become ill in any of their last 35 periods. The size of their assets that they surrender to Medicaid will depend on when they become ill. If they become ill early in life, their assets will be small and the value of Medicaid payments for health care and subsequent consumption will exceed the value of the assets that Medicaid confiscates. If they become ill when quite old, assets will again be small and Medicaid will again receive less than it pays out. For those becoming ill in middle age the assets that the assumed compulsory Medicaid program takes will exceed the benefits Medicaid provides. Hence modeling Medicaid as being financed purely from confiscation of the assets of its recipients implies that Medicaid does not pool risk across the healthy and the unhealthy; rather it pools risk, to some extent, among the unhealthy.

Savings Comparisons

Figure 6.1 is convenient for comparing savings in the four regimes. The figure plots the function $H(C_y)$ against C_y, where

$$H(C_y) = RU'(C_y) - (1 - P)\beta U'[(W - C_y)/R], \tag{13}$$

which is clearly decreasing in C_y since $U'' < 0$. From equations (3), (5), (7'), and (11) we have

$$H(C_y^a) = P\alpha\beta U'[(W - C_y^a)/R], \tag{3'}$$

$$H(C_y^s) = P\beta U'[(W - C_y^s)/R - e], \tag{5'}$$

$$H(C_y^i) = -(1 - P)\beta U'[(W - C_y^i)/R] + \beta U'[(W - C_y^i)/R - Pe], \tag{7''}$$

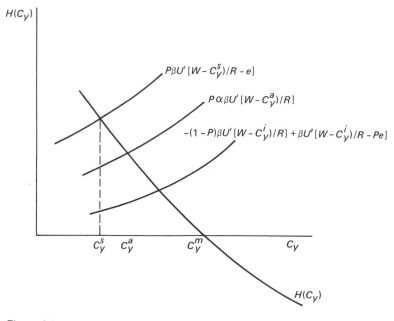

Figure 6.1
Consumption when young under different regimes.

$$H(C_y^m) = 0. \tag{11'}$$

The right-hand sides of (3'), (5'), and (7") are positive. The right-hand sides of (3') and (5') are increasing in C_y. If $U''' > 0$, the right-hand side of (7") is also increasing in C_y. The right-hand sides of these three expressions are also plotted in figure 6.1, adopting the assumption $U''' > 0$. Note that, if $U''' > 0$,

$$
\begin{aligned}
H(C_y^i) &= -(1 - P)\beta U'[(W - C_y^i)/R] + \beta U'[(W - C_y^i)/R - Pe] \\
&< (1 - P)\beta U'[(W - C_y^i)/R] + P\beta U'[(W - C_y^i)/R - e] \\
&\quad + (1 - P)\beta U'[(W - C_y^i)/R] \\
&= P\beta U'[(W - C_y^i)/R - e]. \tag{14}
\end{aligned}
$$

From the figure it is clear that consumption under Medicaid exceeds that under the other three regimes. Two other relationships are also immediate. First, $C_y^a > C_y^s$; that is, consumption when young in the case the individual chooses to "live with it" exceeds consumption when young in the self-insurance (self-payment) regime. Second, $C_y^i > C_y^s$; that is, consumption when young with actuarially fair insurance exceeds that under self-payment. Whether C_y^i is larger or smaller than C_y^α depends on the size of α, the term PRe, and the degree of risk aversion. The figure depicts the case in which $C_y^\alpha > C_y^i$, but the curve representing the right-hand side of (7″) could lie below that representing the right-hand side of (3′).

Aggregate wealth held by individuals in this two-period model equals only the savings of the older generation because the young have not yet accumulated wealth. Since the savings of the elderly equals the saving they did when young, wealth per young person A in the four regimes equals

$$A^\alpha = W - C_y^\alpha,$$

$$A^s = W - C_y^s,$$

$$A^i = W - C_y^i - vF + vF = W - C_y^i,$$

$$A^m = W - C_y^m. \tag{15}$$

With fair insurance the assets of the economy A^i equal the wealth of the elderly $W - C_y^i - vF$ plus the reserves of the insurance company vF.

It is clear from (15) that the larger C_y, the smaller the economy's savings. Hence, if $U''' > 0$, savings is largest in the case of self-payment and smallest under Medicaid and the relative size of savings in the eases of fair insurance and "live with it" depends on the specification of α, PRe, and the degree of risk aversion. If $U''' < 0$, savings is largest in the case of fair insurance, followed by savings under self-payment, savings under "live with it," and savings under Medicaid.

It may seem surprising that consumption when young with self-payment could exceed consumption when young with fair insurance, but there are two offsetting factors involved in determining the extent of precautionary saving. On the one hand the individual with no insurance is motivated to consume less because of the possibility that he or she will become ill and will need to pay for the cure; on the other hand there is the chance that the individual will not become ill and hence will have the money that would otherwise have been spent on the cure to spend on consumption. In this case the individual will feel ex post that he or she has oversaved. By consuming more now, the individual can reduce the extent of ex post oversaving in the case of good health in old age, albeit at the risk of greater ex post undersaving in the case of bad health in old age. If $U''' > 0$, the concern about saving too little outweighs the concern about saving too much and consumption in the absence of insurance is less than consumption with fair insurance.

Another case not yet considered is less than actuarially fair insurance. One can show that, starting at the actuarially fair value of v and rebating insurance company profits in a lump sum fashion, the choice of F will be reduced as v increases. The derivative of C_y^i, however, evaluated at the actuarially fair choice of F and C_y^i equals 0. Hence small departures from actuarial fairness, while inducing less insurance purchase, will not alter C_y and therefore will not alter savings. Larger departures from actuarial fairness will, in contrast, affect C_y^i and savings. However, the direction of this effect cannot be determined even assuming $U''' > 0$. Of course, if v is sufficiently large, the optimal choice of F will be 0, transforming the insurance regime into the self-payment regime. Hence, if v is increased sufficiently, C_y^i will equal C_y^s, which, assuming $U''' > 0$, is smaller than the level of consumption under actuarial fairness. Thus sufficiently large increases in the insurance premium will ultimately raise savings. It also appears possible that more moderate increases in the insurance premium could be associated with savings in excess of that under self-payment. The simulations of unfair insurance in section 6.4 illustrate this possibility.

Choice of Regime

The choice of whether to "live with it," to pay oneself for the cure, to purchase insurance, or to rely on Medicaid obviously depends on which regime provides the greatest expected utility. The insurance regime dominates self-payment because one cannot be worse off with the option of buying health insurance. The self-payment regime in this two-period setting dominates the Medicaid regime because the individual who falls ill is effectively forced to purchase her own cure and is constrained in her choice of consumption after becoming sick. Thus, as modeled here, Medicaid would exist only if it were a compulsory program run by the government.

The choice of regimes depends on which offers the largest value of expected utility, which depends, in turn, on the set of parameter values W, e, α, and P.[1] As these parameter values change, the optimal regime may switch, producing abrupt and potentially significant changes in savings. To see this, take the case in which there are only two possible regimes, no cure and self-payment. Suppose that initially $EU^s > EU^\alpha$, and consider how savings is affected by an increase in e. Provided that EU^s remains above EU^α, C_y^s will fall and savings will rise as e increases. At some point, however, the inequality will switch, and the no cure regime will be preferred to the self-payment regime. At that point savings will drop, potentially quite sharply, since $C_y^\alpha > C_y^s$. A similar discontinuity could arise with increases in α that might arise, for example, because of improvements in pain killers. While EU^s may initially exceed EU^α, as α rises, EU^α will eventually exceed EU^s. When the switch occurs, saving will drop abruptly. Savings may also abruptly increase either because of a fall in e or α or a rise in W starting in a situation in which EU^α exceeds EU^s. Note that, as W increases, EU^s converges to the case of no health expenditure risk. The level of utility in the case of no health expenditure risk obviously exceeds EU^α.

6.3 Simulating the Savings Response to Uncertain Health Expenditures

The Simulation Model

Simulations of a 55-period life cycle model can provide a sense of the savings differences that might arise under the different regimes. The model assumes that individuals work full-time from age 1 (corresponding to a real world age of 20) through age 45 (a real age of 65) earning a constant amount W. Between ages 45 and 55 (a real age of 75), where 55 is the age of death, the individual is retired. During the first 20 years of life there is no possibility of becoming ill. Beyond age 20 there is a P percent chance of becoming ill in a particular year given that one has not already been ill. The illness, once cured, cannot strike again. Illness occurs at the beginning of the period. Once the illness occurs, the sick have the option either to purchase the cure or to remain ill. If they remain ill, their utility from consumption is multiplied, as before, by α, a parameter whose value lies between 0 and 1.

The specific form of utility from consumption in a particular year is

$$U(C) = \frac{C^{1-\gamma}}{1 - \gamma}, \tag{16}$$

and, as before, there is a time preference factor β that discounts future values of utility from consumption. The four regimes considered are "live with it," self-payment, insurance, and Medicaid. For insurance, unfair and fair insurance arrangements are examined, with the premium per dollar of coverage in the unfair insurance case set equal to 1.5 times that in the fair insurance case.

The consumption choice problems in the four regimes can be solved with dynamic programming. Consider first self-payment. At any age above age 20 there are two types of individuals, those who have become ill (either in the past or in the immediate period) and those who have not yet become ill. Those who already have become ill cannot become ill again and therefore face no additional health expenditure risk. Those who have already become ill maximize (17) subject to (18):

$$\hat{U}_k = \sum_{j=0}^{55-k} \beta^j \frac{C_{k+j}^{1-\gamma}}{1-\gamma},$$ (17)

$$M_k = \sum_{j=0}^{55-k} R^j C_{k+j},$$ (18)

where M_k stands for the present value of resources at age k and equals the sum of current assets plus the present value of future labor earnings. Let $\hat{V}(M_k)$ stand for the indirect utility function for this problem. The indirect expected utility function for an individual age k who has not yet become ill is defined by

$$V_k^s(M_k) \equiv \max_{C_k} \frac{C_k^{1-\gamma}}{1-\gamma} + \beta P \hat{V}_{k+1}[(M_k - C_k - e)/R]$$

$$+ \beta(1-P)V_{k+1}[(M_k - C_k)/R].$$ (19)

The indirect utility functions $V_k(M_k)$ can be calculated recursively by using (19) and by noting that

$$V_{55}(M_{55}) = \frac{M_{55}^{1-\gamma}}{1-\gamma}.$$ (20)

The case of no cure is quite similar. The indirect utility function for those who have already become ill is

$$\hat{V}_k^\alpha(M_k) = \alpha \hat{V}_k(M_k).$$ (21)

And for those not yet ill the indirect utility function can be derived from the recursion (22) plus (23):

$$V_k^\alpha(M_k) \equiv \max_{C_k} \frac{C_k^{1-\gamma}}{1-\gamma} + \beta P \hat{V}_{k+1}^\alpha[(M_k - C_k)/R]$$

$$+ \beta(1-P)V_{k+1}^\alpha[(M_k - C_k)/R],$$ (22)

$$V_{55}^\alpha(M_{55}) = \frac{M_{55}^{1-\gamma}}{1-\gamma}.$$ (23)

The case of insurance is slightly more complicated. Given the choice of F, the amount of coverage, the appropriate recursion for indirect utility of those not yet ill is

$$V_k^{iF}(M_k) = \max_{C_k} \frac{C_k^{1-\gamma}}{1-\gamma} + \beta P \hat{V}_{k+1}[(M_k - C_k + F - e)/R]$$

$$+ \beta(1 - P) V_{k+1}^{iF}[(M_k - C_k)/R], \tag{24}$$

$$V_{55}^{iF}(M_{55}) = \frac{M_{55}}{1-\gamma}. \tag{25}$$

The superscript F refers to the fact that the indirect utility functions of those not yet sick is conditional on the level of F. Denoting by v the premium payment made for lifetime coverage of F, regardless of when one becomes ill, the optimal choice of F, F^*, satisfies

$$F^* \equiv \max_F V_0^{iF}(M_0 - vF). \tag{26}$$

Thus, to find the optimal choice of insurance coverage F, one solves the dynamic programming problem for all possible choices of F and chooses that value of F yielding the highest initial ($k = 0$) value of expected utility. With actuarially fair insurance the solution does not require dynamic programming, since F is set equal to e in this case and the consumption path is derived by maximizing U_0 subject to the constraint that the present value of consumption equals $M_0 - v_f F$, where v_f is the actuarially fair premium. Note that v_f equals the present expected value of the payment of \$1 at the time one becomes ill.

This analysis assumes that any profits made by the insurance company if it charges an actuarially unfair premium are retained by the insurance company and not rebated to the insured. This assumption is inappropriate to the macroeconomic model because there are no seperate agents in the model who are owners of the insurance company. A more appropriate assumption, made later, is that the profits of the insurance company are rebated to the insured as lump sum payments. Since individuals view these rebates as lump sum, they will still perceive that at the margin the price of insurance is actuarially unfair. The rebate is calculated as the difference between the actuarially fair and unfair premiums on the coverage purchased. The optimal value of F is no longer determined by (26) but by

$$F^* = \max_F V_0^{iF}(M_0 - vF + r), \tag{26'}$$

where r stands for the rebate and equals $(v - v_f)F^*$. Equation (26') suggests a procedure for finding F^*. For each possible value of F^* one can form r and check using the V_0^{iF} functions whether the candidate value satisfies (26'). If it does, it is the true value of F^*.

The last case to consider is Medicaid. Once one has become ill, one goes onto Medicaid and is forced to consume $\bar{C}$. Utility under Medicaid is given by

$$V_k^m = \sum_{j=0}^{55} \beta^j \frac{\bar{C}^{1-\gamma}}{1-\gamma}. \tag{27}$$

The recursion for indirect utility for those not yet ill is

$$V_k^m(M_k) = \max_{c_k} \frac{C_k^{1-\gamma}}{1-\gamma} + \beta P V_{k+1}^m + \beta(1-P)V_{k+1}^m[(M_k - C_k)/R] \tag{28}$$

and

$$V_{55}^m(m_{55}) = \frac{M_{55}^{1-\gamma}}{1-\gamma}. \tag{29}$$

Calculating Aggregate Savings

In both the cases of no cure and self-payment, aggregate wealth just equals the sum of the private savings of all individuals in the economy. Since the population growth rate is assumed to be 0, at any point in time there is a fixed distribution of individuals of different ages with different medical histories. For an individual of age k, private wealth equals the difference between labor earnings and consumption plus medical expenditures at each age in the past accumulated with interest up through age k. Since individuals at a given age will differ with respect to their medical histories and therefore their past expenditures, one needs to keep track of all possible medical histories and the number of individuals in each cohort with each medical history.

Aggregate wealth in the case of medical insurance equals the sum of private wealth holdings plus the reserves of the stylized insurance company. In this case private wealth is calculated by accumulating earnings plus insurance payments plus the one-time rebate (paid at age 1) less consumption and medical expenditures less the initial payment of the lifetime insurance premium. The reserves of the insurance company equal the sum of reserves on the policies of each individual. Although the sum of reserves is positive, the reserves on any one policy can be positive or negative. The reserves on an individual's policy equals the accumulated value of the initial premium less the initial rebate less any insurance payments.

Adding up for this case, private wealth and the reserves of the insurance company may seem a rather cumbersome calculation. There is, indeed, a much simpler method of arriving at aggregate wealth. One can ignore the transfers to and from the insurance company and simply sum over all individuals in the economy the accumulated difference between earnings and consumption plus medical expenditures at each age. This same method can be used in calculating aggregate wealth in the Medicaid economy. Alternatively, one could calculate the wealth in private hands and add this to the Medicaid trust fund, which in the fully funded system considered here would have assets that equal the sum of accumulated confiscated assets less accumulated Medicaid payments on $\bar{C}$ and medical expenditures. The assumption that the Medicaid trust fund is fully funded provides an equation to determine the value of $\bar{C}$. In a fully funded Medicaid system the present expected value of payments to each individual over his or her lifetime, including payment of the consumption stream $\bar{C}$ and the health expenditure e, equals the present expected value of Medicaid's confiscation of assets from Medicaid participants.

Solution Method and Parameterization of the Model

It should be clear that there are not, in general, closed form solutions to the dynamic programming problems outlined. As a consequence, the solutions to these problems were computed numerically. The technique here is simply to calculate the values of the $V_k(\cdot)$ functions for specific grid values of M_k. Since the calculation of $V_k(\cdot)$ depends on the entire function $V_{k+1}(\cdot)$ and not simply on particular grid values, one needs to interpolate values of $V_{k+1}(\cdot)$ from the calculated grid values.

Given the interpolated function $V_{k+1}(\cdot)$, the value of V_k for a particular grid value of M_k is determined by finding, numerically, the value of C_k that maximizes the relevant expression for $V_k(\cdot)$. Hence, as a by-product of calculating the $V_k(\cdot)$ functions, one obtains optimal values of C_k for the grid values of M_k. Interpolating across these values gives $C_k(M_k)$ functions, indicating approximately the optimal level of consumption. Clearly the finer the grid of values of M_k, the better the approximation. For my purposes here, the fineness of the M_k grid was chosen such that increased fineness would have only a trivial effect on the calculation of total wealth.

The $C_k(\cdot)$ consumption functions are then used in calculating the economy's total savings. This calculation involves starting with a cohort age 1, deriving each possible lifetime consumption and health expenditure path, determining the number of members of the cohort who will experience each path, and then computing accumulated savings as just described.

In the base case economy, γ (the reciprocal of the coefficient of relative risk aversion) equals 4, a value suggested by the empirical literature (Auerbach and Kotlikoff 1987). The base case economy also features a 4 percent interest rate and a 4 percent rate of time preference. Hence both R and β equal $1/1.04$. The value of M_0 is set equal to 100, and W, the yearly wage, is determined by the condition that the present value of earnings equals M_0. The resulting value of W is 4.64.

The value of e, the cost of the cure, is five times W, or 23.2. The probability of becoming ill in any year given that one is healthy, P, equals 0.05. With these assumptions the actuarially fair value of a dollar of health expenditure coverage v_f is 24.8 cents. Hence for fair insurance total initial premium payments equal 5.75, almost 6 percent of the present expected value of total lifetime consumption plus health expenditures. The premium under unfair insurance is set equal to 1.5 times the fair insurance premium. For the "live with it" case the value of α is $\frac{1}{2}$. For the case of Medicaid, the value of $\overline{C}$ that Medicaid can finance from its asset confiscation is 2.25. The calculation of total wealth is based on a population of 1,000 in each cohort.

6.4 Simulation Results

Table 6.1 presents the values of total wealth for the base case economy under the different health expenditure regimes. The table also indicates the separate effects on savings in each of the regimes of reducing e by half and lowering P to 0.01. As suggested by the fact that $U''' > 0$ [in (16)] and by figure 6.1, base case savings for self-payment exceeds that under fair insurance, while base case savings is smallest for the case of Medicaid.

Table 6.1
Aggregate savings under alternative health expenditure regimes

Regime	Parameterization		
	Base case	Base case, $e = 2.5W$	Base case, $P = 0.01$
Self-payment	1,008,670	869,710	1,136,140
Fair insurance	891,521	828,212	822,061
Unfair insurance	1,016,510	915,333	1,173,450
Live with it	527,017	527,017	682,301
Medicaid	222,062	325,871	626,383

Savings under fair insurance also turns out to exceed the amount of savings under the "live with it" regime. Savings under unfair insurance slightly exceeds savings under self-payment. The amount of insurance coverage chosen in this case is 7.00, less than one-third of the cost of the cure.

The savings differences across these regimes are substantial. The introduction of actuarially fair insurance reduces savings by 12 percent if the economy is initially in the self-payment regime. If Medicaid, rather than fair insurance is introduced, savings is reduced by 80 percent! Alternatively, if individuals opt to "live with it," savings would fall by 48 percent relative to the self-payment regime. These numbers would likely be reduced quite a bit if general equilibrium considerations were included in the analysis, but even so they would remain quite large.

Wealth is so small in the Medicaid case because of the significant saving disincentive associated with Medicaid's asset confiscation. Quite simply, this asset confiscation and Medicaid's provision of $\bar{C}$ make assets worthless once an individual becomes ill; hence the individual's need for assets in the future is greatly reduced by Medicaid. This major saving disincentive from asset confiscation would remain even if part of Medicaid's expenditures were financed from general revenues, such as a wage tax.

In the "live with it" regime individuals consume more when young relative to self-payment case because they know that, if they become ill, their marginal utility of consumption will be greatly reduced. Since 83 percent of individuals ultimately become ill in the base case, there is a substantial incentive to consume early in the "live with it" regime. One way of assessing the sensitivity of savings in this regime to its perceived future value is to determine the change in savings associated with lowering α from $\frac{1}{2}$ to $\frac{1}{4}$. Savings in this case falls by 16 percent.

Because earnings are the same in each of the different regimes, any differences in total wealth are due to differences in consumption levels and, in comparing "live with it" with the other regimes, to differences in health expenditures. Table 6.2 presents consumption levels at different ages for individuals who have not yet become ill and for individuals who become ill at specified ages. In the case of fair insurance, consumption always equals 4.10 regardless of age or the occurrence of the illness. This is because the individual is fully insured and because the interest rate equals the time preference rate. The consumption profiles for the other three regimes of table 6.2 are also flat up through age 20, reflecting the $R = \beta$ assumption; for each of these cases the future after age 20 is uncertain, but this uncertainty does not affect the marginal decision between consumption at different ages before age 21.

Table 6.2
Consumption

Age	Not yet ill				Age of onset of illness	Already ill			
	Self-payment	Fair insurance	Live with it	Medicaid		Self-payment	Fair insurance	Live with it	Medicaid
1	4.05	4.10	4.53	4.62	1	NA	NA	NA	NA
5	4.05	4.10	4.53	4.62	5	NA	NA	NA	NA
10	4.05	4.10	4.53	4.62	10	NA	NA	NA	NA
20	4.05	4.10	4.53	4.62	20	NA	NA	NA	NA
21	4.06	4.10	4.52	4.61	21	3.64	4.10	4.07	2.25
30	4.34	4.10	4.20	4.12	30	3.89	4.10	3.97	2.25
40	4.74	4.10	3.87	3.61	40	4.18	4.10	3.87	2.25
50	5.29	4.10	3.52	3.17	50	4.50	4.10	3.45	2.25
54	5.87	4.10	3.46	2.95	54	4.80	4.10	3.40	2.25
55	29.00	4.10	3.34	2.85	55	4.83	4.10	3.34	2.25

NA = Not applicable.

Under the self-payment regime consumption grows after age 20 for those remaining healthy, reflecting the fact that the extra precautionary savings accumulated in case an individual had become ill in the previous year rather than the future did not have to be tapped. In the last year of life, at age 55, the individual who remains healthy is able to consume an additional 23.2, which corresponds to the amount that would otherwise have been spent on the cure if the individual had become ill in his or her last year. If, on the other hand, the individual becomes ill at a particular age after age 20, his or her consumption immediately falls and stays constant at this lower level through age 55 (again reflecting the $R = \beta$ assumption). For example, the individual who is healthy at age 40 in the self-payment case consumes 4.74, while if he had become ill at age 40, his consumption would have been only 3.87.

The consumption profile for those remaining healthy in the "live with it" regime falls after age 20, reflecting the trade-off between the marginal utility of consuming today and the possibly lower marginal utility of consuming tomorrow in the event one is ill. Once an individual becomes ill, however, the consumption profile is flat because $\beta = R$, and there is no further uncertainty.

The Medicaid age consumption profile also declines after age 20, again because of the lower expected marginal utility of saving another dollar relative, for example, to the fair insurance case. Consumption before age 21 is highest under Medicaid, reflecting the lower marginal utility of saving for consumption after age 20 relative to the marginal utility of consuming before age 20.

After the Medicaid regime consumption before age 21 is greatest in the "live with it" regime. This reflects the fact that individuals will never be making health expenditures and hence need not save for them. Note that the present expected value of health expenditures, if they were made, is 5.75.

The level of savings is fairly sensitive to the size of medical costs and to the probability of becoming ill. Reducing by half the cost of medical treatment leads to a 14 percent drop in wealth in the self-payment regime and a 9 percent drop in the fair insurance regime. In these regimes the reduced incentive to save is offset somewhat by the reduction in health expenditures in the determination of the net impact on savings. In the Medicaid regime the reduction in the cost of treatment, rather than reducing savings, raises savings by almost one-third. At the individual level the incentive to save under Medicaid is not affected by the reduced treatment cost; because Medicaid will pay these costs and because $\bar{C}$ is also under

Medicaid's control, the trade-off remains between current consumption when healthy and future consumption when healthy.

Although private wealth is not altered under Medicaid by the reduction in e, the size of Medicaid's trust fund increases because the health expenditure payments it must make are reduced. On the other hand, with a lower e Medicaid can afford to pay a higher $\bar{C}$. For $e = 2.5W$ the value of $\bar{C}$ paid by Medicaid is 3.00, 25 percent larger than its base case value. The reduction in e and the increase in $\bar{C}$, while leaving unchanged Medicaid's receipts from asset confiscations, pushes the timing of its expenditures off into the future. A smaller e and a larger $\bar{C}$ means fewer Medicaid payments at the time the individual becomes ill and more payments later in the individual's life. The consequence of this change in the timing of Medicaid expenditures means that Medicaid will have a larger trust fund.

Returning to table 6.1, there are also some dramatic changes in savings that arise from a reduction in P from 0.05 to 0.01. Wealth under Medicaid almost triples as individuals respond to the reduced probability of experiencing Medicaid's effective asset tax. The private incentive to save is also strengthened in the "live with it" case; in this case the reduction in the likelihood of becoming ill and having greatly diminished marginal utility from consumption prompts a 30 percent increase in aggregate savings. In the self-payment regime the reduction in P reduces the need for precautionary savings. Despite this fact there is a modest increase in wealth. This reflects the reduced health expenditures. Relative to the higher-P self-payment case, total cohort consumption plus health expenditures in the $P = 0.01$ self-payment case is greater before age 21, smaller through age 49, and greater thereafter. Hence the last case has more lifecycle saving among the middle-aged (counting their health expenditures), although less among the young. The increased saving occurring in middle age reflects the reduced health expenditures.

A reduced P also means less health expenditures in the fair insurance regime, but in this case the increased consumption of individuals more than offsets this reduction in health expenditures, leading to a somewhat lower level of wealth. The lower P means a premium of 1.75 rather than 5.75 and finances a higher level of consumption at every age. Hence the reduced saving of the young outweighs the increased saving of the middle-aged (including their reduced health expenditures and total wealth health expenditures) and total wealth falls by 8 percent compared to the $P = 0.05$ case.

One may summarize this table by saying, first, that the changes in savings down any column indicate that insurance arrangements and government intervention in the form of Medicaid can significantly alter the amount of precautionary savings and, second, that the changes along any row indicate that, holding constant the saving regime, changes in the size and riskiness of health expenditures can greatly influence savings.

Before concluding this section it may be useful to consider the level of savings that would arise in this economy if there were zero probability of the illness occurring. The answer is 758,878. This is almost a quarter below base case savings under self-payment and 15 percent below base case savings with fair insurance. Intuitively the introduction of significant health expenditures, whether insured or uninsured, shifts the age consumption (including health expenditures) profile of each cohort toward more consumption at later ages. This change implies more accumulated savings at each age.

Because moving from an economy with zero health expenditures to one depicted in column 2 of table 6.1, in which health expenditures equal roughly 6 percent of total lifetime consumption, could mean anywhere from a 33 percent increase in savings to a 71 percent decrease in savings depending on the chosen regime, it is clear that health expenditures are a potential critically important determinant of savings.

6.5   Conclusion

This chapter has examined some of the theoretical issues involved in precautionary savings for uncertain health expenditures. The highly stylized simulation model gives the strong impression that uncertain health expenditures represent a strong motive for saving, which may, however, be greatly influenced by the availability of private insurance and the presence of government programs such as Medicaid. The model is too stylized to be anything more than suggestive. More realistic modeling will require improved estimates of the riskiness of health expenditures and a better understanding of the extent to which private insurance mitigates that risk.

A more realistic model should also consider the interaction of health expenditure risk and earnings and life span risk. These risks are clearly interdependent. Saving for future health care may become much more important if one's earnings and indeed one's life depend on receiving that care. In this context disability insurance, which represents earnings insurance in particular health episodes, may have a substantial effect on precautionary savings.

Insuring the riskiness of life span, like insuring the riskiness of earnings, appears to require special types of insurance related to health or health expenditures. In the absence of uncertainty with respect to health expenditures, one could purchase annuities that would hedge the risk of living longer than expected and not having sufficient savings. In the presence of health expenditure uncertainty and less than full health insurance coverage, fully annuitizing, the best option if only life span is uncertain and fair indexed annuities are available, becomes highly risky. If one is fully annuitized and cannot borrow against future annuity payments, one will have no resources to meet immediate uninsured health expenditures. Perhaps this is why the private market in annuities in the United States is virtually nonexistent.

Another issue in thinking about health expenditure risk and precautionary savings is the role of the extended family in directly providing health care and financial assistance for the purchase of health care. In other contexts the family appears to constitute an excellent implicit insurance market (chapter 4); presumably the same applies in this context and perhaps more so.

In sum, exploring the interactions of savings, health expenditures, medical insurance, and other types of risks represents a fertile and apparently quite important area for future research.

Notes

I am grateful to Jagadeesh Gokhale for excellent research assistance and to Jack Meyer and Jagadeesh Gokhale for helpful discussions. This research was funded by the American Enterprise Institute through a Commonwealth Fund grant. Additional support was provided by the National Bureau of Economic Research under grant 1PO1A605842-01 from the National Institute of Aging.

1. It is easy to show that the regime that is preferred ex ante is also preferred ex post.

II

Fiscal Policy and Savings

Introduction

The secular decline in the US rate of saving has stimulated research into fiscal policies that might encourage saving. Chapter 7 reviews current knowledge about the saving effects of a variety of different fiscal policies. The chapter draws on the Auerbach-Kotlikoff dynamic life cycle simulation model to illustrate many of these effects. Chapters 8 and 9 use this model to examine two particularly important fiscal policies, deficit financed tax cuts and investment incentives.

The discussion in chapters 7 through 9 illustrates the arbitrary nature of deficit accounting by describing policies that are structurally similar, if not identical, but lead to greatly different time paths of deficits. Chapter 10 directly examines the question of deficit accounting, pointing out that the labeling of government receipts and payments as "taxes," "transfers," "borrowing," or "repayment of loans" is inherently arbitrary. Hence the deficit is an arbitrary accounting construct and provides no systematic basis for assessing the stance of fiscal policy. To assess fiscal policy properly, at least the intergenerational aspects of fiscal policy, one needs to construct generational accounts that detail in present value each generation's expected lifetime net payments to the government.

Thinking about fiscal policy in generational terms raises the question of how generations collectively decide how much each should pay to finance the government's consumption. As chapter 11 points out, if one models generations as bargaining over their obligations to the government, intergenerational transfers either will not arise or will have no effect on savings. Hence debt may be neutral even in the life cycle model.

The central questions of this part are:

1. Are the saving effects of certain fiscal policies unambiguous from a theoretical perspective and how big are these effects?

2. What are the structural relationships between deficit finance, changes in the tax base, changes in investment incentives, and changes in unfunded social security? Is there a common effect of these different policies on savings?

3. Is the deficit a meaningful measure of fiscal policy from the perspective of neoclassical economic models?

4. How do savings incentives differ from investment incentives?

5. How does a noncoercive model of government in which the young bargain with the old differ in its implications concerning the effects of deficit finance and other intergenerational transfer policies on savings?

6. What is the timing of crowding out of savings because of policies such as a deficit financed tax cut?

7. Can short-run policy effects on savings differ from long-run effects?

8. If the deficit is an accounting rather than an economic concept, how should one measure fiscal policy?

The principal lessons of this part are:

1. Fiscal policies can have powerful effects on aggregate savings.

2. Fiscal policies can operate in subtle ways. For example, investment incentives lower consumption and raise saving by causing capital losses on the value of existing assets.

3. The half-lives of fiscal policy effects can be long.

4. Long-run fiscal policy effects may be exactly opposite to short-run effects.

5. The deficit is an arbitrary accounting construct with no necessary relationship to the true stance of fiscal policy.

6. In the absence of coercion of the young by the old, debt is neutral in the life cycle model.

7. Depending on its method of finance, increased government consumption may crowd in rather than crowd out saving and investment.

8. From the perspective of neoclassical economics, proper evaluation of fiscal policy requires specifying generational accounts that indicate in present value the expected lifetime net payment of each generation to the government.

7

Taxation and Savings: A Neoclassical Perspective

7.1 Introduction

The ability of governments to alter an economy's rate of wealth accumulation is a question that has intrigued economists since the inception of the discipline. Recently the issue has received considerable attention from researchers puzzled by historically low US saving rates and dramatic differences in saving rates across industrialized countries. While no consensus on the appropriate model of saving behavior has been reached, investigation of tax policy within a variety of neoclassical models suggests that governments can significantly influence the accumulation of national wealth. This assessment of the current state of knowledge about neoclassical models of savings behavior and government policy differs markedly from a view, still accepted in many circles, that tax policy within the standard economic paradigm has highly ambiguous impacts on wealth accumulation. The ambiguity is associated with allegedly opposing income and substitution effects arising from changes in tax rates, in particular, capital income tax rates. While this allegation is true for a subset of tax changes, neoclassical models admit a host of policies with clear and potentially powerful affects on national savings.

"Structural" tax changes provide an important example of such effective policies. They are defined here as changes in either the tax base or the progressivity of the rate structure holding constant both the time path of receipts and the time path of government consumption. Holding constant the time path of receipts provides a prescription for setting tax rates through time. A key feature of these policies is that they "compensate" the private sector for imposing a new tax by removing an old one. Since these

Journal of Economic Literature 22:1576–1629 (1984). © 1984 by the American Economic Association. Reprinted with permission.

policies involve no changes in the timing and level of the government's direct absorption of resources, they leave unchanged, in the aggregate, the private sector's intertemporal consumption and leisure possibility frontier.[1] If it so chooses, the private sector can consume as much and work as little in the new tax regime as it does in the old. Such a response clearly leaves the private sector in the aggregate with the same collective resources to finance its own as well as the government's unaltered time path of consumption. The private sector will, however, generally respond to new tax regimes by choosing a different point on its budget frontier. The movement along this intertemporal frontier and its associated changes through time in savings and labor supply are determined by unambiguous substitution effects and, potentially, income effects. Although there is no aggregate change in income for the private sector, since its possibility frontier has not changed, structural tax changes typically redistribute resources across and within generations. However, for many structural tax policies the net income effects of this redistribution reinforce the substitution effects in raising or lowering savings.

The distinction between compensated and uncompensated policy changes is clarified by considering the government's intertemporal budget constraint. Excluding the possibility that government debt can grow indefinitely at a faster rate than that of the economy, this constraint requires governments to equate the present value of receipts, inclusive of base money creation, to the present value of expenditures, inclusive of interest and principal payments on net government debt. While restricting the set of policies, including structural tax policies, that can be used over time to alter wealth formation, the government's long-term budget is consistent with a wide range of short- and medium-term policies. In particular, the government can permit debt to grow for a long time at a faster rate than the economy, although indefinite use of this policy is not feasible.[2]

In addition to Structural Tax Policy, the government's intertemporal budget constraint suggests three other classes of policies for organizing a discussion of taxation and saving. These are:

1. Tax-financed changes in government consumption—Changes in the time path of government consumption that are contemporaneously financed by adjustments in tax rates of a particular tax base.

2. Intergenerational tax policy—reduced taxation of particular cohorts financed by increased taxation of other cohorts, holding constant the tax base and the time path of government consumption. In contrast to structural tax policy, this rule for setting tax rates involves changes in the time

path of total annual tax receipts while holding constant the time path of government consumption.

3. Intragenerational tax policy—reduced taxation of particular members of a cohort contemporaneously financed by increased taxation of other members of that cohort. In contrast to broad structural changes in either the tax base or tax progressivity which are not cohort specific and, consequently, redistribute intergenerationally, these cohort-specific policies involve only intragenerational redistribution.

Analysis of these four classes of policies provides insight into the economic impacts of the essentially unlimited broader combination of these and other policies.

This survey is limited to the savings effects of fiscal policy in "full employment" neoclassical models, assuming, in most of the discussion, well-functioning capital markets. The emphasis on "full-employment" neoclassical models may be justified by the secular, rather than cyclical nature of the subject. In addition, the very significant new body of literature based on such models provides more than enough material for a single survey. Finally, much of the popular discussion concerning the behavior of savings and related variables over the cycle invokes these models, although not always correctly.

Section 7.2 provides background information for the subsequent discussion; it describes long-term trends in US saving rates and domestic investment rates. Striking differences in postwar saving behavior among industrialized nations are also documented. This historical and international evidence provides a healthy perspective on the issue of taxation and saving. Few would argue that long-term trends in US saving rates and the current low rate of US saving relative to those of our principal trading partners are due solely, or even primarily, to differences in fiscal environments. Government policy is a significant determinant of national savings, but it is only one of several important forces at play. Other critical factors that jointly influence savings are intertemporal preferences, demographics, existing technology and the rate of technical change, patterns of human capital formation, the extent of market and intrafamily lending, and the degree of market and intrafamily risk-pooling.

Each of the four stylized policies is considered sequentially in Sections 7.4–7.7. An examination of them raises a number of traditional topics including the impact of government debt on national savings, the extent to which government consumption substitutes for private consumption, the distinction between investment and savings incentives, the savings impact of progressive taxation, the relationship between human and physical capital accumulation, the degree to which borrowing constraints alter the analysis, and the welfare implications of alternative tax structures. The discussion in these sections, which takes up a large portion of this article, ignores issues of uncertainty. Many important and interesting insights can be obtained by working with models of certainty. The introduction of uncertainty, in some cases, obscures these insights. In addition, many of the results from certainty models carry over to models with uncertainty. In general, certainty models provide a benchmark against which to examine current policies in more realistic settings in which tastes, technologies, and indeed future government behavior are uncertain.

Analysis of the four classes of policies as constrained by the government's long-term budget makes it clear that the fundamentals of fiscal policy are not aggregate "taxes," "spending," and "deficits," but rather changes in marginal incentives, intramarginal redistribution across and within generations, and direct government consumption. Section 7.3 examines government and private intertemporal budget constraints for purposes of precisely defining the policies considered in Sections 7.4–7.7. The main objective of Section 7.3 is, however, to identify the government's underlying policy instruments and to caution the reader that official accounting definitions of taxes, expenditures, and debt provide little guide to the underlying fiscal structure. On the contrary, our proclivity to discuss such issues as savings and government policy in terms of this conventional nomenclature is symptomatic of widespread fiscal illusion. To drive home this point, Section 7.3 demonstrates how identical fiscal policies can be conducted with the government reporting essentially any level of taxes, spending, and deficits it desires. Describing fiscal policy in terms of its effects on marginal incentives, intramarginal transfers, and direct absorption or resources requires changes in vocabulary and accounting, but a new fiscal language is necessary to discuss consistently the savings impact of our plethora of fiscal policies, all of which ultimately involve these basic elements. A key feature of the new fiscal language should be descriptions of the lifetime budget constraints of a small set of representative households as well as descriptions of the fundamental fiscal instruments that affect these constraints. Household budget constraints depend only on net marginal prices and net intramarginal endowments. Since the calculation of these prices and endowments are free of accounting conventions, a set of representative budget constraints would provide a coherent basis for analyzing the changes in and the consequences of a large variety of fiscal policies.

Section 7.8 addresses the impact of taxation on savings in uncertain environments. A series of contributions (Domar and Musgrave 1944; Tobin 1966; Mossin 1968; Diamond 1977; Mirrlees 1974; Diamond and Mirrlees 1978; Baily 1978; Shavell and Weiss 1979; Varian 1980; Gordon 1981; Auerbach 1981; Bulow and Summers 1982; Eaton and Rosen 1980; Merton 1983) expressly or by implication suggest that a variety of tax/transfer schemes constitute implicit insurance markets. To the extent that private provision of insurance is both available at the margin and is as efficient as government insurance, the government's pooling of risks through the tax/expenditure system will have few or no implications either for risk-pooling or for national saving. At the opposite extreme one could imagine that, in the absence of government insurance, particular risks would be pooled neither in formal private markets nor in informal family settings. In this case the effect of government taxation on savings is analyzed by simply considering the impact of the availability of each particular type of insurance on national savings.

Section 7.8 describes the potential insurance properties of a number of fiscal policies including capital and labor income taxation, and Social Security's unfunded tax/benefit provisions. Unfortunately, there are few studies that directly compare wealth accumulation with and without particular forms of insurance. Section 7.8, as a consequence, draws inferences about taxation, insurance, and savings that are rather speculative in nature. These types of comparisons certainly represent a promising area for future research.

The government as a cause of uncertainty, rather than a source of insurance, is an alternative possibility explored briefly in Section 7.8. In principle, the private sector could self-insure against random government redistribution among current generations. Capricious redistribution between current and future generations is also potentially insurable assuming intergenerational altruism as in Robert Barro (1974). Without such private insurance, the impact on savings of government-imposed uncertainty is again determined by comparing economies with and without the particular risks generated by the government.

The final section plays devil's advocate to Sections 7.4–7.7, by presenting a set of conditions under which government policy, regardless of type, has no effect whatsoever on national saving. The conditions required are extreme and reveal the improbability of such behavior. But the example also illustrates the fact that the underlying effective tax schedules influencing saving may have little or nothing to do with the legislated tax system. The distinction between effective and legislated tax schedules dates at least from Tiebout (1956) and underlies the emerging literature on the "dynamic inconsistency" of government policy (Kydland and Prescott 1977; Calvo 1978; Fischer 1979; Turnovsky and Brock 1980). Dynamic inconsistency refers to the proposition that, as ongoing institutions, governments are likely continually to reoptimize their fiscal choices taking current, but not past circumstances into account. As a result, policies slated today to go into effect in the future will likely be altered by the government in power in the future. In this sense, the government's actual actions may be inconsistent with its previously expressed intention.

Research in this area cautions that rational households look at what governments do, not what governments say. If households understand the government's objective function, they can potentially deduce the course of future tax policy independent of the government's current declarations. The difficulty of ascertaining private beliefs about future government actions presents special problems for studying the savings impact of current tax policy. Such analyses are clearly sensitive to assumptions concerning private beliefs about actual future tax policy.

7.2 US Savings Behavior: Some Stylized Facts

The net national saving rate is one of several important indicators of a nation's savings behavior. It records the fraction of annual net output that will be available to support future consumption and is defined as NNP less private and government consumption, C and G, respectively, divided by NNP. The first column of table 7.1 presents averages of the annual US net national saving rate over the five decades prior to 1980 and the period 1980 through 1982. Values for NNP, C, and G differ somewhat from those reported in the National Income and Product Accounts (NIPA). The major difference is that private spending on consumer durables and government spending on highways, structures, equipment, other durables, and military hardware are treated as saving in the present figures. Private consumption excludes expenditures on durables, but includes imputed rent on the stock of durables. Government consumption excludes purchases of structures and other durables, but includes imputed rent on these tangible assets, including military assets. NNP includes imputed rent on consumer durables and government assets less depreciation of these assets.[3] The figures in column 1 are little affected by the treatment of military durable purchases as investment. For reference column 2 presents the net national saving rate based on NIPA definitions of the relevant variables.

Both sets of figures reveal major variations in the saving rate over the 53-year period. The corrected numbers in column 1 show a 28 percent

Table 7.1
Indices of US saving behavior: 1930–1982 (average annual rate over specified period, %)

Sample period	(1) Net[a] national saving rate	(2) Net national saving rate (NIPA basis)	(3) Household[a] consumption rate (C/NNP)	(4) Government[a] consumption rate (G/NNP)	(5) Rate of[a] household consumption out of disposable NNP (C/NNP-G)
1930–1939	− 1.17	− 2.86	87.66	13.51	101.49
1940–1949	10.23	5.32	68.35	21.42	87.29
1950–1959	15.60	8.79	67.64	17.02	81.60
1960–1969	14.25	8.71	65.35	20.40	82.09
1970–1979	11.90	7.70	67.10	21.00	84.92
1980–1982	7.04	5.07	68.62	24.35	90.71

a. Household consumption C equals NIPA personal nondurables consumption expenditures plus imputed rent on household durables. Government consumption G equals NIPA government nondurables consumption expenditures plus imputed rent on government tangible assets, including military hardware. NNP equals NIPA NNP plus imputed rent on household durables and government tangible assets less depreciation of these assets.

reduction in the average saving rate since 1970 compared with the average rate in the preceding two decades. The comparable reduction is 19 percent based on the NIPA definitions of the relevant variables.

Columns 3 and 4 display rates of household and government consumption out of NNP. At first glance the 7 percentage point increase in the government consumption rate between the 1950s and early 1980s appears responsible for the recent dramatic decline in the rate of US saving; household consumption as a share of NNP increased by only 1 percentage point across these two time intervals. Had this share remained constant, the nation's saving rate would still have fallen by 21 percent.

A neoclassical perspective suggests, however, that private behavior determines most if not all of these historical changes in the nation's saving rate. Consider the following two alternative hypotheses: The first assumes that government consumption substitutes perfectly for household consumption. In this case, since household consumption is a marginal choice, the sum of the figures in columns 3 and 4 indicate that households, on average, collectively chose to consume 85 percent of NNP in the 1950s and 1960s and 89 percent of NNP in the 1970s and early 1980s. NNP, in this case, properly measures annual household disposable income, since the government is simply engaging in consumption the household sector would otherwise do on its own.

The second extreme hypothesis is that government consumption provides no welfare whatsoever to the private sector. As Section 7.3 points out, under reasonable assumptions concerning limitations on deficit finance, the private sector must eventually pay for current government consumption. Hence the amount of net national product remaining after government consumption, NNP-G, provides a measure of the private sector's effective annual disposable income; this is true despite the fact that net tax payments may differ from government consumption in particular years. Column 5 examines the rate of consumption out of this definition of annual household disposable net national product. Note that this consumption rate rose from 82 percent in the 1950s to 91 percent in the early 1980s. Had the post-1969 rate of household consumption out of NNP-G remained at its 1950–1969 average value, the net national savings rate would have fallen by 5 percent rather than 28 percent. This second assumption concerning the substitutability of private and government consumption attributes none of the increased government consumption to private sector decisions. Hence, from this perspective, increased government consumption is directly responsible for at most one-fifth of the post-1969 drop in the net national saving rate.

The figures in table 7.1 showing considerable variations in national and household saving propensities may appear surprising in light of what has been dubbed "Denison's Law." Denison (1958), Hickman (1966), and David and Scadding (1974) document that the US ratio of gross private saving to gross national product has been remarkably stable through time. Without questioning the validity of this proposition, it is well to point out that gross private saving is the difference between gross national saving and the NIPA definition of government deficits. As Section 7.3 emphasizes, the NIPA definition of deficits is an entirely arbitrary accounting choice. If one assumes that economic behavior depends on real variables rather than accounting conventions, then the US gross private saving rate is similarly an entirely arbitrary accounting construct. Had government accountants chosen a quite different definition of deficits, the gross private saving rate would have exhibited substantial variation through time.[4] Unlike measures of "private" saving rates, measurement of the net national saving rate is independent of accounting conventions that arbitrarily label particular variables as "private" or "government"; in addition, assuming no fiscal illusion on the part of economic agents, the actual rate of net national saving responds only to economic variables and not to accounting labels.

Much of the variation in saving rates described in table 7.1 may simply reflect intertemporal consumption smoothing during periods of fluctuating

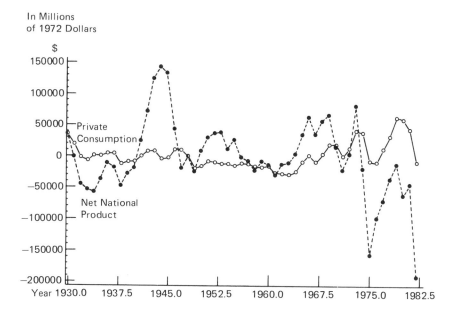

Figure 7.1
Volatility of national aggregates: deviations from trend.

net national product. Figure 7.1 displays deviations from trend in corrected measures of private consumption and net national product. Detrended consumption is clearly a much smoother series than detrended NNP. This well-known fact provides some empirical support for examining neoclassical models that assume reasonably well-functioning capital markets and predict intertemporal consumption smoothing.

International Comparisons of Saving Rates and International Capital Mobility

For the period 1930 to 1982 the correlation coefficient between the US net national saving rate and the net domestic investment rate, defined as the ratio of the net domestic investment to NNP is 0.99. The absolute discrepancy between these two rates exceeds 1.5 percentage points in only 4 of the last 53 years. Studies by Feldstein and Horioka (1980) and Feldstein (1982a) of time series and cross-country correlations between saving and investment rates suggests that policies generating an additional dollar in national saving increase domestic investment by roughly 85 cents. Harberger (1980) and Sachs (1981a, 1981b) reject this view, and present evidence that numerous countries are financing major portions of their domestic investment through foreign sources.

While the debate on the degree of international capital mobility has been joined, the issue has not been resolved. Eaton and Gersowitz (1981) and Dooley and Isard (1980) provide a theoretical foundation for the Feldstein-Horioka findings based on a perception of potential foreign expropriation; their models suggest possibly large gross international capital flows, but quite small net flows. The limited size of net international flows is ascribed to the increasing probability that a country will expropriate foreign equity investments or default on its foreign borrowing as the amount of net foreign claims on its assets increases. An alternative explanation of the Feldstein/Horioka findings, that is consistent with full international capital mobility at the margin, is that factor price equilization eliminates the incentives for international capital flows.[5] Given the unresolved nature of this debate, prudence suggests analyzing the savings impact of domestic fiscal policies in both closed and open economics; In open economies—as originally pointed out by Musgrave (1969) and recently examined by Goulder, Shoven, and Whalley (1983) and Harberger (1983)—policies that stimulate domestic investment can be quite different from policies that stimulate national saving. The concluding subsection in 7.4 briefly points out the nature of these differences.

Whether or not capital is perfectly mobile internationally, cross-country comparisons of saving rates are obvious guides to changes over time in the international distribution of wealth and in relative standards of living. Table 7.2 compares the net national saving rates of US and other OECD countries based on newly available OECD data. The OECD concepts of NNP, C, and G are roughly those used in the US National Income and Product Accounts except that government consumption, G, excludes expenditures on nonmilitary durables and structures.

Table 7.2 provides evidence of persistent and sizable international differences in rates of net national saving and rates of household consumption out of NNP-G. Since 1960, the US net national saving rate has averaged 55 percent of the corresponding rate for the European OECD countries, and 34 percent of the Japanese rate. For this period the average US household consumption rate, C/(NNP-G), exceeds the corresponding European OECD rate by 8 percentage points and the Japanese rate by 18 percentage points.

International differences in rates of domestic capital formation and increases in capital-labor ratios are equally striking. OECD data indicates that the US net domestic capital stock grew at an average annual rate of 3.6

Table 7.2
Saving and consumption rates: International comparisons (average annual rates over specified period, %)

Period	Net national saving rate			Government consumption rate: G/NNP			Household consumption rate: C/(NNP-G) out of disposable NNP		
	United States	OECD Europe	Japan	United States	OECD Europe	Japan	United States	OECD Europe	Japan
1955–1959	9.8	NA	21.5	19.1	NA	10.6	87.9	NA	76.0
1960–1969	10.5	17.3	17.0	20.1	15.7	9.4	86.9	79.8	70.2
1970–1979	8.0	15.1	25.5	20.1	18.5	10.4	89.9	81.5	70.5
1980–1981	5.0	11.0	21.3	20.9	19.9	11.7	93.6	86.3	75.9
1960–1981	8.7	15.7	25.8	20.2	17.3	10.1	88.9	81.0	71.3

Source: OECD (1983); variables are defined according to UN System of National Accounts.
NA = Not available.

percent between 1960 and 1982; the comparable figures for France and Germany are 12.3 percent and 10.4 percent, respectively. Over this period US capital per worker grew on average by 1.5 percent per year compared with 11.6 percent in France and 10.4 percent in Germany.

7.3   Government and Private Budget Constraints: A Description of Fundamental Policy Instruments

The government, as an institution with potentially unlimited life, is in a position to borrow from succeeding new generations to meet its liabilities to existing generations. If the real interest rate paid on such borrowing exceeds the economy's rate of population plus productivity growth, a policy of continually borrowing to meet all interest and principal payments means that government debt continually grows relative to the size of the economy. Such a policy is clearly infeasible; if government creditors demand real resources upon settlement with the government, all current output plus claims to existing assets will eventually be insufficient to meet these demands. In an economy in which the pretax real return paid on government borrowing exceeds the underlying rate of economic growth, deficit-financed spending ultimately requires the government to raise real resources either by explicit taxation or by expropriation through inflation or otherwise of its creditors' nominal assets. In the long run, these revenues must meet government spending plus the excess of interest payments on past borrowing over the expansion of debt that could perpetually be financed by the growth in the economy. The limitation on debt finance implies the following relationship between the course of taxation, base money creation, spending on government consumption plus transfer payments, and the market value of the government's initial net liabilities, D_0:

$$\sum_{t=0}^{\infty} \frac{T_t + \Delta M_t}{1 + r_t} = \sum_{t=0}^{\infty} \frac{E_t}{1 + r_t} + D_0. \tag{1}$$

Equation (1) expresses the government's intertemporal budget constraint in terms of conventional fiscal taxonomy. T_t, ΔM_t, and E_t are, respectively, nominal taxes, base money creation, and nominal expenditures on consumption and transfer payments in year t. These flows are discounted at nominal interest rates, r_t, that are realized between time zero and t. In a world of certainty, the r_ts are given by the term structure of interest rates prevailing at time zero. D_0, the market value of net government liabilities at time zero, can also be written as the discounted value of interest plus principal repayments.

The budget constraint indicates that "printing" of high-powered money is a source of government revenue; in the US and in many other countries government acquisition of real resources by simply "printing" money is effected by the treasury or finance ministry selling bonds to the private sector which the central bank then purchases with newly created money. Equation (1) consolidates the fiscal behavior of these institutions.

The long-run connection between this constraint and the economy's growth and interest rates is evident in equation (2) which expresses the constraint when the economy is in a stationary state in which all real variables are growing at the rate n and the inflation rate is Π:

$$t + \Delta m = e + (r - \Pi - n(1 + \Pi))d. \tag{2}$$

Each of the variables in (2) is measured per effective worker. This expression verifies the proposition that long-run real revenues including base money creation $(t + \Delta m)$ less spending (e) must cover real interest payments on debt $(r - \Pi)d$ less the additions to the stock of debt that can be financed by economic growth alone $n(1 + \Pi)d$.

7.3.1 The Fragility of Government Bookkeeping and the Potential for Fiscal Illusion

Macroeconomists typically discuss fiscal policy in terms of officially reported values of "taxes," "spending," and "deficits." "Taxes" in excess of "spending" is commonly referred to as "tight" fiscal policy, while the converse is described as "loose" fiscal policy. Unfortunately, the accounting definitions of "taxes," "spending," and "deficits" are arbitrary, having no counterparts in economic theory; in full employment equilibrium models with operative capital markets, household budget constraints depend on marginal prices and endowments and are independent of accounting conventions with respect to government policy. From the perspective of these microbudget constraints, fiscal policies that are tight are often mislabeled loose and vice versa. The failure to discuss fiscal policy in terms of household budget constraints raises the potential for fiscal illusion.

The "pay-as-you-go" financing of the US Social Security system provides an excellent example of our propensity to engage in fiscal illusion. The Social Security System represents the federal government's largest program of intergenerational transfers, yet none of what effectively constitutes enormous borrowing from current and future generations was officially recorded as "deficits." Recent estimates by Social Security actuaries suggest an unfunded Social Security liability of $4 to 6 trillion owed to the current adult population. These liabilities, while they are not legally enforceable obligations and have different risk properties than official debt, swamp estimates of the government's current official net liabilities. Indeed, official US net liabilities (D_0 above) measured at market value appear to be slightly negative (the government's official net worth is positive), reflecting considerable federal holdings of financial and tangible assets and sizable capital gains on nominal government liabilities accrued during the 1970s (Eisner and Pieper 1983, *1982 Economic Report of the President*, chs. 4 and 5).

Historically, the government could have made its hidden annual Social Security "deficits" explicit by simply handing each Social Security taxpayer a piece of paper indicating his or her projected claim to additional future benefits "purchased" with his or her annual payment of Social Security "taxes." Had the government recorded Social Security "taxes" as payments for Social Security bonds, the government would have reported deficits, inclusive of these bond issues, in excess of $300 billion dollars in several of the last 20 years, and deficits in excess of $100 billion dollars in most of the last 20 years. One imagines that this alternative tally of government indebtedness would have engendered very different estimates of concepts such as "*the* full employment deficit" and would have led to an array of quite different econometric findings. Economists, insensitive to the problem of fiscal illusion, may well have reached very different conclusions about the degree of fiscal stimulus.

Presumably, such a redefinition of official government liabilities would raise the question of classifying other implicit commitments to future expenditures as government debt.[6] If one is willing to label implicit promises to pay future retirement benefits official liabilities, why not include implicit expenditure commitments to maintain the national parks, to defend the country, or to provide minimum sustenance to the poor?

A heated debate about the appropriate definition of government debt would likely lead some exasperated officials to suggest eliminating deficit financing entirely and simply relying on taxation. These officials might also argue that one could switch from "deficit" to "tax" finance with no effect whatsoever on the economy. Under the assumption of perfect capital markets, they would be quite correct. Rather than raise additional funds by issuing treasury securities, the government could simply levy a head "tax" per adult promising to provide each adult in the following year a tax credit equal to the tax plus interest in the tax. If the adult died during the year, the payment would be made to his or her estate. Those too poor to pay the head tax could borrow against next year's tax credit to obtain the required funds. The equality, in present value, between each household's head tax and its head tax credit, leaves household budgets and, therefore, private behavior unaltered. However, since future tax credits, like future Social Security benefit payments, are not recorded in the current budget, this policy permits the government to report a smaller deficit.

An analysis of (1) indicates more precisely how shrewd accounting can eliminate the reporting of deficits without changing any real policy. Define a sequence of head taxes, $\bar{T}_t$, that may be negative or positive, but that sum in present value for each household and, therefore, for the aggregate economy to zero, by

$$\bar{T}_0 = D_0(1 + r_0) + E_0 - (T_0 + \Delta M_0) \quad \text{and} \quad \bar{T}_t = E_t - (T_t + \Delta M_t) \text{ for } t > 0.$$

(3)

Condition (4) follows immediately from (1) and (3):

$$\sum_{t=0}^{\infty} \frac{\bar{T}_t}{1 + r_t} = 0.$$

(4)

Adding zero as defined by (4) to the left-hand side of (1) and letting $T_t^{**} \equiv T_t + \bar{T}_t$ produces

$$\sum_{t=0}^{\infty} \frac{T_t^{**} + \Delta M_t}{1 + r_t} = \sum_{t=0}^{\infty} \frac{E_t}{1 + r_t},$$

(5)

and for all $t > 0$,

$$T_t^{**} + \Delta M_t = E_t.$$

(6)

According to (6) the government can now report zero debt and zero deficit in every year in the future, while running exactly the same policy. The trick in going from (1) to (6) is simply to have the government label private sector loans to the government positive "taxes" and to classify government loan repayments as negative "taxes."

Starting from (6) the government could further modify its accounting practices and start reporting enormous "surpluses," although it again engages in no real policy change. The game here involves the government imposing additional positive head taxes, $\bar{\bar{T}}_t$, and positive head transfer payments, $\bar{\bar{E}}_{t+1}$, related by

$$\bar{\bar{T}}_t = \bar{\bar{E}}_{t+1} \frac{(1 + r_t)}{(1 + r_{t+1})}.$$

(7)

Provided the "tax" payers at t are the "transfer" recipients at $t + 1$, this policy has no effect on household budget constraints. The official "surplus" (a stock) at time t, S_t, for $t > 0$ is now reported as

$$S_t = S_{t-1} \frac{(1 + r_t)}{(1 + r_{t-1})} + \bar{\bar{T}}_t + T_t^{**} + \Delta M_t - E_t - \bar{\bar{E}}_t = \bar{\bar{T}}_t, \qquad (8)$$

since $\bar{\bar{E}}_t = S_{t-1}[(1 + r_t)/(1 + r_{t-1})]$ by construction, and $T_t^{**} + \Delta M_t - E_t$ equals zero from (6). The government can potentially make $\bar{\bar{T}}_t$ and, therefore, its reported surplus at time t as large as the economy's stock of wealth at time t.[7]

The fact that economic theory does not distinguish positive "taxes" or negative "spending" from government "borrowing" and positive "spending" or negative "taxes" from government "debt service" potentially permits the government to report essentially any level of debt and deficits it wants without affecting the economy. In addition to this freedom to manipulate the reporting of "deficits," the government has essentially unlimited flexibility in altering the size of reported "taxes" and "spending" given the level of "deficits" it chooses to report. The government could, for example, declare a new set of taxes and transfers of equal value. Assuming that households paying these additional "taxes" receive an identical amount back in the form of additional "spending" and that any changes in marginal incentives (prices) associated with the new "taxes" are exactly offset by changes in marginal incentives (prices) associated with the new "spending," economic activity will remain unchanged. Reducing the "size" of government taxes and spending with no real consequences is also in the power of government bookkeepers.

Between 1960 and 1983, US federal spending on transfer payments, including grants-in-aid to state and local governments, rose from 6 percent to 14 percent of GNP, leading many to praise, many to decry, and others to study the "growth" in government. The bulk of federal transfer payments, 75 percent, are direct payments to individuals; most federal transfers to state and local governments are ultimately paid to individuals in the form of medical, housing, and general welfare support.

In principle, the federal government could have incorporated all postwar transfer payments within the tax code in the form of special tax credits and deductions. Had the government embedded this "growth" in spending in the tax code as additional "tax expenditures," a term coined by Surrey (1973), and adopted in the Congressional Budget Act of 1974, reported federal spending would simply have consisted of consumption. Federal consumption, excluding purchases of durable goods, but including imputed rent on government assets, fell as a fraction of NNP in the postwar period from 10 percent in the 1950s to 8 percent in the 1982. One presumes that this manner of displaying economic reality would have led many of those who now praise, decry, and study the growth in government, to decry, praise, and study its decline.

The point here is certainly *not* to claim that there were no economic effects from the postwar rise in reported transfer payments. These policies were associated with significant changes in the intertemporal budget constraints of virtually all American households. The point is that the size and character of the effects of fiscal policy cannot be judged from the size of "taxes," "deficits," etc, because these accounting entries can vary widely without having any affect whatsoever on economic activity. Discussing fiscal policy and savings without engaging in fiscal illusion requires identifying the government's fundamental policy instruments including those that have a direct impact on the economy and those that indirectly affect the economy by altering household budget constraints.

7.3.2   Real versus Illusory Fiscal Policy

Equation (9) represents a final rewriting of equation (1) that conveniently illuminates the government's fundamental policy instruments. This description of the government's budget uses the fact that D_0, the government's initial net liabilities, may be expressed as the present value of net interest plus principal payments on D_0. In (9) all government outlays including interest and principal payments on D_0, but excluding consumption outlays, G_t, are incorporated in a "tax expenditure" tax code denoted by $\hat{}$. The $\hat{}$ tax code treats all such outlays as either refundable tax credits or deductions, specifying, where necessary, the names of particular households in society receiving these payments. All households that are alive or will be alive are referenced by the index j. Obviously, the $\hat{T}_{jt}s$ are zero for years prior to and after the households are in economic existence.

$$\sum_{t=0}^{\infty} \frac{\hat{T}_t + \Delta M_t}{1 + r_t} = \sum_{t=0}^{\infty} \sum_{j=1}^{\infty} \frac{\hat{T}_{jt} + \Delta M_t}{1 + r_t} = \sum_{t=0}^{\infty} \frac{G_t}{1 + r_t}. \tag{9}$$

Transforming all nonconsumption outlays into equivalent "tax expenditures" permits one to focus directly on net lump sum and net marginal taxation of households; i.e., each $\hat{T}_t$ terms equals a net (positive or negative) lump sum tax imposed in year t on households j, plus year t, household j tax schedules applied to corresponding year t, household j tax bases.[8]

In the US, earnings- and incomes-tested welfare and social insurance programs significantly alter marginal incentives to work and save. By adding this implicit net tax schedule to other explicit federal, state, and local tax schedules, the ^ code identifies the ultimate effective tax structure facing each household. Piercing the "welfare veil" of taxation under the tax code reveals that "negative income taxation" is already a reality in the US, although the negative income tax schedules confronting US households differ greatly from those that have been proposed (Friedman 1962); current US negative income tax schedules are categorical, depending on the household's demographic composition, and often exhibit extraordinarily high marginal tax rates on labor supply at low earnings levels. The ^ tax code should also be understood as piercing the "corporate veil," taking account of both corporate and personal taxation and subsidization, (e.g., investment incentives) of the return to capital in describing the government's net influence on the trade-off between current and future consumption and leisure.[9]

The government's fundamental policy instruments are thus its choices of ΔM_t, G_t, its effective net marginal tax schedules, and its net intramarginal taxation. Household preferences and budget constraints are, by assumption, the sole determinants of household consumption and labor supply decisions. Hence, government policy involving feasible [satisfying Eq. (9)] choices of the terms $\hat{T}_{jt}$, ΔM_t, G_t and the net marginal tax rates and the net intramarginal taxes influencing its T_{jt} revenue alters private behavior only by changing the after-tax prices and after-tax endowments appearing in household intertemporal budgets.

7.3.3   Marginal Taxation and Human Capital Formation

The government's effective marginal tax schedules affect household budgets in three ways. First, they change after-tax prices between current and future values of consumption and leisure. Second, they change the present value of households' resource endowments, including their human and nonhuman wealth. Third, they change incentives to accumulate human capital, which, in turn, alters the household's time path of pretax wage rates. Research on fiscal policy and savings has focused most closely on the first two channels by which government marginal taxation affects household behavior. Boskin's (1975) article on taxation and human capital formation is a notable exception. Under the assumption that time spent in training and related activities is the only input into human capital formation, Boskin showed that a proportional labor tax has no distorting affect on the human capital investment decision; the proportional labor tax reduces the opportunity cost of human capital accumulation (i.e., it reduces the size of net foregone earnings) while also reducing the return from the investment paid in the form of future after-tax wages. The additional incentive to invest in human capital is exactly offset (in present value) by the additional disincentive in the case of proportional labor taxation.

Boskin further clarified the net disincentive to human capital formation under progressive taxation of labor income or under proportional taxation, assuming that additional inputs are required for this investment and that expensing of these inputs is not permitted. Subsequent articles by Heckman (1976) and Kotlikoff and Summers (1979) stressed the incentive to human capital formation arising from capital income taxation; higher capital income tax rates mean lower after-tax rates of return and larger discounted values of the future returns from human capital investment.

In neoclassical models with no uncertainty and no borrowing constraints the timing of household consumption decisions is not contingent on the timing of the receipt of labor earnings. Hence, more human capital investment means less current labor supply, less current output, as conventionally measured, and, with household consumption not directly reduced, less conventional saving. In addition, if consumption goods, such as educational services, are used in human capital investment, the expansion of such investment directly increases consumption of this type, further lowering current saving. A corollary to this point is that tax incentives that promote human capital formation typically do so at the cost of less nonhuman capital formation. In the case of capital income taxation, incentives for greater current human capital formation (smaller current labor earnings) reinforce incentives to substitute current for future consumption in discouraging nonhuman wealth accumulation (Kotlikoff and Summers 1979).

While additional investigation of the trade-offs between human and nonhuman capital formation is needed, it appears unlikely that realistic modeling of these interactions would greatly affect many of the findings about taxation and nonhuman capital formation described below.

7.3.4   Structural Tax Policy

Household budget constraints, like those of the government, can be rewritten in multiple ways. In particular, quantities can be multiplied by either before-tax or after-tax prices, with additional terms appearing in the expression that uses before-tax prices. The conventional formulation multiplies quantities by after-tax prices, since households are presumed to consider after-tax prices in making economic choices. In the standard expression the present after-tax prices of current and future consumption incorporate consumption and capital income tax rates, while the present after-tax prices of current and future leisure incorporate labor and capital income tax rates. Structural tax policy involves changes in tax rates and, therefore, changes in relative prices of current and future consumption and leisure. The requirement that the new tax code generate the same time path of receipts as the code it replaces provides a rule for setting net tax rates through time. Such changes in tax bases or the rate structure under a given tax base leave unchanged the private economy's intertemporal possibilities frontier, although they typically induce different choices of points on that frontier.[10]

While each household, acting independently, perceives that its budget has been changed by structural policy, the private sector as a whole ultimately operates with the same budget; i.e., it experiences no aggregate change in income. To see this, consider equation (10), which presents the aggregate (private plus government) economy's intertemporal budget constraint. In (10) Z_{jt} equals expenditures in year t by household j on leisure and consumption goods, including imputed rent on consumer durables and money holdings. H_0 and A_0 are, respectively, human wealth (the present value of labor earnings) and the market value of nonhuman wealth of the economy at time zero. All terms in (10) are measured in pretax nominal units of account discounted at pretax nominal interest rates:

$$\sum_{t=0}^{\infty} \sum_{j=1}^{\infty} \frac{Z_{jt}}{1 + r_t} + \sum_{t=0}^{\infty} \frac{G_t}{1 + r_t} = H_0 + A_0. \tag{10}$$

The right-hand side of (10) indicates the total present value of the economy's current and future resources available to finance the present value of government consumption and private purchases of consumption goods and leisure, the first term on the left side of (10).

For a given time path of G_t, (10) corresponds to the private economy's intertemporal budget, i.e., the resources available for private consumption and leisure are the economy's total resource endowment, $H_0 + A_0$, less the government's claim on that endowment, $\sum_{t=0}^{\infty} [G_t/(1 + r_t)]$.[11] Hence, one feasible response to the government's switching tax bases or altering the rate structures of prevailing tax bases is that private behavior as well as all before-tax prices (including the r_t's) remain unaltered. Changes in the tax structure in the presence of unchanged private behavior and before-tax prices imply, of course, changes in some if not all the $\hat{T}_{ij}$'s, but, according to (9) these new taxes plus base money creation must still equal, in present value, the present value of government consumption. From (10), then, the economy's resources remaining for private expenditures on consumption and leisure are unaltered. Stated differently, if real private sector behavior and the G_t's remain unchanged, the government will be forced to choose tax rates under the new tax structure that are consistent with (9) for unchanged values of both the r_t's, the ΔM_t's and the G_t's.

If the private sector consisted of a single, infinitely lived household, one would expect that household to understand the aggregate economy's budget constraint (10). Such a rational household would know it had to pay for the government's time path of consumption regardless of what tax system was being used to collect the resources; more precisely, it would know that changes in its behavior would automatically lead to changes in tax rates. A single household would, therefore, internalize the government's budget constraint and treat taxes, no matter how they were imposed, as lump sum levies. In such a setting structural tax changes would have no effect whatsoever. However, in the case of a large number of households, none of whom pay more than a trivial fraction of total taxes, the assumption that no single household considers the feedback of its behavior on government tax rates is more appealing. Under this Cournot-Nash assumption each household attempts to "free ride" on the tax payments of other households by altering its behavior in response to changes in tax incentives. In partial equilibrium, i.e., holding constant before tax prices, including the r_t's, (9) and (10) indicate that the new values of private consumption and leisure (summarized by Z_{jt}), after the private sector responds to the new tax structure, lie on the private economy's original budget frontier. Thus, structural tax changes, in partial equilibrium, produce compensated changes in behavior of the type described by Harberger (1964) and Diamond (1970). These compensated changes along the initial budget frontier, like Hicks's (1942) compensation around an initial indifference surface, are unambiguous in sign.

Figure 7.2 illustrates this type of partial equilibrium compensated change for a consumer who chooses consumption over two periods, C_1 and C_2, based on an exogenous initial endowment, E_1. The government taxes the consumer to finance its consumption, which has a present value of G_1. The slopes of lines 1 and 2 equal $1 + r$, where r is the before-tax interest rate. The slope of line 4 is $1 + r(1 - \tau_r)$, where τ_r is the capital income tax rate. Point A is the equilibrium under lump sum taxation, while point B corresponds to the equilibrium under a capital income tax structure. The government collects the same present value, G_1, in taxes under both tax structures, and private consumption occurs along the same budget frontier, line 2;[12] the increase in capital income taxation is compensated by a decline in lump sum taxation permitting the consumer to end up consuming on his initial budget frontier. Assuming smooth convex indifference curves,

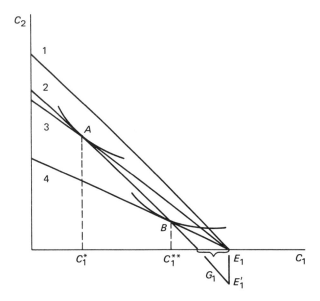

Figure 7.2
The saving effect of a compensated capital income tax.

private consumption in period I unambiguously rises from C_1^* to C_1^{**}. Note that if the private sector had maintained its initial consumption bundle, the government's capital income tax rate would have been lower by the difference in the slopes of lines 3 and 4 divided by r.

Figure 7.2 can be used to describe the impact on national savings of a structural shift from lump sum to capital income taxation. Since structural tax policy, as here defined, leaves unaltered the time path of government revenues, the lump sum tax, like the capital income tax, is assumed to be levied in period 2. The post-tax endowment point in figure 7.2 is thus E_1' under the lump sum tax and E_1 under the capital income tax.

In a simple two-period overlapping generations life cycle model (Modigliani and Brumberg 1954; Ando and Modigliani 1963), each generation lives for exactly two periods. The young generation in this model has no initial wealth and all private wealth is held by the old generation. The wealth of the old generation, in turn, corresponds to the savings accumulated by the old generation when it was young. Letting W_{P1} stand for the private wealth of the old generation accumulated during its first period and letting W_g denote government wealth, the national wealth W is given by $W = W_g + W_{P1}$.[13] In terms of figure 7.2, W_{P1} under lump sum taxation equals $E_1 - C_1^*$, since E_1 is first period income, and C_1^* is first period consumption. The period-to-period change in national wealth, national saving, equals output less government and total private consumption. By assumption government consumption is fixed; hence, current changes in national saving depend only on changes in private consumption.

Consider an announcement at time t that the government will permanently switch to capital income taxation starting at time $t + 1$. Such a policy has no impact on the consumption of the elderly at time t, since they still face the lump sum tax in period t and do not survive to period $t + 1$. The young at time t, however, increase their consumption according to figure 7.2 by $C_1^{**} - C_1^*$, which corresponds precisely to the partial equilibrium reduction in national wealth. This savings reduction is permanent because all successive young generations face the same budget constraint, line 4 in the diagram, and save $E_1 - C_1^{**}$ rather than $E_1 - C_1^*$. In this example, the change in national savings is unambiguous in sign. This compensated tax change involves only substitution effects; the change in income for the private sector in toto and for each age cohort is zero.[14]

An example of a structural tax policy in which income effects also arise is an immediate switch from proportional capital income to consumption taxation. While the government collects the same total revenue each period under the new tax structure, as Summers (1981a) recently emphasized, such a policy typically alters the taxes collected from each cohort. In particular, the tax extracted from the elderly at the time the change is introduced is likely to be substantially in excess of their tax liability under the capital income tax. Since, as implied by (9), the present value of all future taxes remains unchanged, the greater tax burden on the initial elderly implies a smaller lifetime tax burden on young and/or future generations. This redistribution away from the elderly reinforces the substitution effects of the tax policy in lowering current consumption and stimulating current saving; while the larger tax burden imposed on the initial elderly means a smaller burden on the initial young, the elderly, in life cycle models, have larger marginal propensities to consume than the young. In addition, the associated reduction in tax burdens for future generations obviously has no affect on current consumption. The larger consumption propensities of the elderly than the young in a strict life cycle model simply reflect their shorter life expectancies and their absence of a bequest motive.

To summarize, structural tax policies leave the private sector's aggregate income unchanged, but they produce unambiguous substitution effects and, potentially, income effects for specific groups that may, on net, reinforce the substitution effects.

7.3.5   Tax-Financed Changes in Government Consumption

In contrast to structural tax policy, contemporaneous tax-financed changes in government consumption can produce aggregate changes in income for the private sector. Assume government consumption does not enter private utility functions; then permanent increases or reductions in government consumption require permanent increases or reductions in taxes to finance such changes in government consumption.[15] If the government is using distortionary taxation, the required changes in tax rates produce a rotation of the private intertemporal budget reflecting government-induced changes in private after-tax relative prices. As an example, consider how private consumption is altered when both government consumption and the capital income taxation used to finance that consumption are eliminated. For the initial elderly generation alive in the period the new policy is first implemented, the change provides a windfall gain equal to the capital income taxes it would otherwise have paid. Since the old are in the last period of their life and have no bequest motive, they immediately consume the entire amount of the windfall. But since government consumption, by assumption, had exactly equaled capital income tax revenues, the reduction in government consumption in the first period of the policy is exactly offset by an equal increase in the consumption of the initial elderly. Hence, the policy's initial period effect on total national consumption and, therefore, initial period total national saving, depends on the consumption of the young in the initial period. The impact on the consumption of the young at the time the policy is implemented is ambiguous. For the young, the elimination of capital income taxation serves to rotate their lifetime budget from line 4 to line 1 in figure 7.2. The initial period change in national consumption (which equals the change in national saving) has, in this case, the opposite sign as the uncompensated elasticity of first period consumption (consumption of the current period young) with respect to the interest rate. Thus, this is a question about tax policy and saving to which a particular "interest elasticity" by itself provides useful information, but this is a very special type of policy experiment embedded in one very simple neoclassical model.

Unfortunately, much research effort (Harberger 1964; Feldstein 1978; Wright 1969; Weber 1970, 1975; Blinder 1975; Boskin 1978; Howrey and Hymans 1978; Summers 1981a, 1982; Evans 1983; Starrett 1983) has focused on defining and measuring "*the* interest elasticity of saving" suggesting that a single number could provide a summary statistic for the effects of a wide range of government policies. Such is not the case.

According to the government's budget constraint, exogenous changes in the return to saving arising from changes in capital income tax rates necessarily require some offsetting adjustment in current and/or future fiscal instruments. Changes in the course of government consumption is only one of many possible adjustments to changes in capital income taxation that would restore balance to the government's intertemporal budget. Suppose, for example, that the cut in capital income tax rates is temporary; in this case the fiscal adjustment might take the form of higher future capital income tax rates. Exactly which policy instrument or set of instruments is used to satisfy (9) and the timing of their use is critically important for determining the response of current national saving to a current reduction in capital income taxation. Thus "the interest elasticity" of current saving will be one number if the tax cut is expected to last one year, it will be a different number if the tax cut is expected to last 10 years, and it will be a still different number if the tax cut is expected to last 20 years. Furthermore, the percentage response of national saving to a tax cut depends on whether the tax cut is financed by reduced government consumption, concomitant increases in other tax rates, or future increases in other tax rates. Neither the sign nor the absolute magnitude of the change in saving can be determined without specifying precisely what policies will accommodate a current reduction in capital income tax rates.

The time series regression analyses of private consumption decisions referenced above do not include variables capturing the future time path of accommodating fiscal policy. In particular they do not distinguish current from future capital income tax rates, nor do they include estimates of the future values of wage or consumption tax rates. As a consequence the estimated coefficients are of dubious value in describing the potential saving impact of changes in fiscal policy. Other studies (Summers 1981a, 1982; Evans 1983; Starrett 1983) purport to simulate *the* interest elasticity of savings by examining the impact on wealth accumulation of a permanent cut in capital income taxation. Since they alter no other tax rates in this analysis of interest elasticities, they are implicitly assuming, according to (9), that government consumption will be permanently reduced. These elasticities have, therefore, as much to do with the savings response to reduced government consumption as they do with private responses to capital income taxation. Indeed, since the bulk of government consumption is financed by wage taxes it is surprising that attention has focused on "the interest elasticity of saving" as opposed to "the wage elasticity of saving."

Other research has been more sensitive to the multiplicity of future after-tax prices determining current consumption and saving. Boskin and

Lau (1977) estimate aggregate demands for consumption and leisure taking account of several current and future cross price effects. Unfortunately, while they report sizable elasticities of current consumption both with respect to the current wage and the price of future consumption, they do not trace out the implications of these findings for feasible, concomitant changes in the time paths of fiscal instruments. A different approach to determining potential household responses to government policies is direct estimation of household intertemporal preferences. Hall (1978) is the first of a series of articles (Grossman and Shiller 1981; Hansen and Singleton 1983; Hall 1981; Mankiw, Rothenberg, and Summers 1982) to directly test some of the implications of intertemporal optimization under uncertainty. These tests, the results of which are rather mixed, require specifying explicit functional forms for household utility. A by-product of these tests is estimates of key preference parameters, knowledge of which is sufficient to determine household responses to virtually all hypothetical policy changes. Several of the utility functions estimated in the empirical literature have been used in simulation studies discussed below.

The effects on national saving of contemporaneous tax-financed changes in government consumption depend not only on concomitant adjustments in particular tax instruments but also on private valuation of government consumption. If government consumption is a perfect substitute for private consumption and is always intramarginal with respect to private consumption decisions (i.e., the private sector always consumes more of each good than the government directly provides) then (10) may be re-expressed as

$$\sum_{t=0}^{\infty} \sum_{j=1}^{\infty} \frac{\hat{Z}_{jt}}{1 + r_t} = H_0 + A_0, \tag{10'}$$

where $\hat{Z}_{jt}$ equals consumption by household j inclusive of its imputed consumption of government purchases of consumption goods and services in year t.

Intramarginal changes in the level and/or timing of government consumption as well as concurrent changes in its finance through the tax system need not, according to (10'), necessitate any changes in the $\hat{Z}_{jt}$'s. As in the case of structural tax changes, such alterations in government policy leave the private sector with sufficient resources to maintain its prior behavior. Here again there is no change in aggregate income for the private economy; from a partial equilibrium perspective, i.e., holding before-tax factor returns constant, tax-financed increases in government consumption simply alter after-tax relative prices and produce compensated movements along the private sector's pretax budget frontier. Assuming changes in particular households' imputed government consumption are not exactly matched by intramarginal changes in their net tax burden, there will be offsetting income effects across households. In this case one must account not only for the impact of tax changes on the after-tax relative prices confronting particular households, but also for the net income effects on those households arising from the government's revised pattern of consumption.

7.3.6   Intergenerational Tax Policy

Intergenerational tax policy, as defined here, involves reduced taxation of particular cohorts paid for (in present value) by increased taxation of other cohorts. The time path of government consumption is held constant under this policy. As in the case of structural tax policy, in partial equilibrium this intergenerational redistribution leaves unaltered the intertemporal consumption and leisure frontier of the private sector. To simplify the analysis, assume for the moment that all taxes are lump sum. If the private economy consists of a single household that, because of concern for its progeny, is effectively "infinitely lived" (Barro 1974), its budget constraint, from (10), is

$$\sum_{t=0}^{\infty} \frac{Z_t}{1 + r_t} = H_0 + A_0 - \sum_{t=0}^{\infty} \frac{G_t}{1 + r_t}. \tag{11}$$

Since intergenerational tax policy, by definition, generates zero revenue in present value and, under the assumption of nondistortionary (lump sum) taxation, also alters no marginal prices, the private sector's budget constraint (11) is completely unaffected by such a policy. Consequently, intergenerational redistribution will have no impact whatsoever on the economy. This argument, originating with Ricardo (1951) and rigorously demonstrated by Barro (1974), can obviously be extended to the case of multiple infinitely lived households each of which experiences intergenerational net lump sum taxation that sums to zero in present value.

In contrast to "infinitely lived" households, for "finite lived" life cycle households who, at least after their children are adults, are concerned only with their own welfare, government intergenerational, nondistortionary transfers alter private sector behavior. According to the strict, nonaltruistic life cycle paradigm household heads and their spouses selfishly spend their resources over the remainder of their own lives. The age of the household is, thus, a critical variable in determining its marginal propensity to consume; elderly households with only a few remaining years exhaust additional resources at a much faster rate than younger households, who spread incremental resources over more periods. These age-related differences in marginal propensities to consume goods and leisure explain why intergenerational transfers to older generations lead to increased aggregate consumption and reduced aggregate labor supply.

To procure the resources to redistribute towards early generations, the government either draws down its own stock of assets, "borrows" from the private sector, or "taxes" the private sector. As indicated above, whether the government acquires current resources under the heading "borrowing" as opposed to "taxes" may be of little or no economic consequence. Increased taxation (resource payments to the government) of younger (including future) generations which is not offset in present value by increased transfers (resource receipts from the government) to such generations is necessary either to restore the government's own net asset position, or, at a minimum, to offset the reduction in the government's net capital income. Such higher net lifetime taxes are likely to fall most heavily on young or yet unborn generations. Thus the economic as opposed to accounting definition of "deficit finance" is any policy resulting in an intergenerational redistribution of resources (Atkinson and Stiglitz 1980).

Assuming those households experiencing positive increases in net lifetime resources predate those experiencing the losses, the policy will increase the consumption and leisure of early generations and decrease the consumption and leisure of later generations assuming consumption and leisure are both normal goods and that net taxation is lump sum. In real terms the additional consumption accorded early generations is financed not by additional current output, since early generations presumably work less not more, but by reductions in the economy's stock of wealth. This "crowding out" of the economy's real assets leaves future generations with less capital to combine with their labor in production and implies, except for small open economies, general equilibrium changes in factor returns. Each future generation may associate their reduced standard of living resulting from economic deficits with higher net lifetime taxation; but equation (11), which holds from each point in time forward, indicates that, under lump sum taxation, it is ultimately a lower value of A_0, relative to what would otherwise have occurred that limits the private sector's future consumption and leisure possibilities. A necessary and sufficient condition for intergenerational redistribution under lump sum taxation is a change in the time path of the economy's holding of real wealth (i.e., values of A_0 in successive years).

While income effects are the primary focus of intergenerational tax policy, redistribution across generations is typically conducted by changing the timing and level of distortionary taxes. Hence, substitution as well as income effects play a role in determining the full economic consequences of many intergenerational tax policies.

7.3.7 Intragenerational Tax Policy

This policy is defined as contemporaneous redistribution among members of a given cohort. Assuming these members belong to different households, such a policy will produce offsetting income effects, with the net impact on aggregate private consumption and saving depending on household differences in marginal propensities to consume and to work. Intragenerational tax policy encompasses redistribution potentially cross-classified by a very large set of socio-economic characteristics including sex, race, education, marital status, number of children, earnings, and accumulated wealth. Unfortunately, empirical evidence on differences in marginal propensities to consume and work by such characteristics is exceeding scarce.

The commonplace notion that "redistribution from the rich to the poor reduces saving" is probably the central concern surrounding intragenerational tax policy. This concern seems based, to a large extent, not on a detailed comparison of differences in consumption propensities, but rather on the simple observation that the rich have wealth and the poor do not. There are at least four immediate reasons why the level of current assets could be unrelated to underlying differences in preferences, and, therefore, differences in consumption propensities. First, current wealth may reflect receipt of intergenerational transfers from wealthy parents and ancestors (Kuznets 1961). Second, current wealth may reflect random high returns to past investments (Friedman 1957). Third, current wealth may simply reflect differences in the timing of receipt of labor earnings for a given present value (Modigliani and Brumberg 1945; Ando and Modigliani 1963). Fourth, household differences in earnings abilities will produce differences in levels of accumulated wealth when household intertemporal preferences and marginal consumption propensities are identical.

Of course, the current rich at a given age may be rich because of differences in intertemporal preferences. Alternatively, the rich may differ from the poor with respect to marginal consumption propensities because the poor are liquidity constrained at the margin. Section 7.7 briefly examines the available evidence concerning intragenerational transfers in the presence of differences in intertemporal preferences and liquidity constraints.

7.4   Savings and the Quantitative Impact of Structural Tax Policy

Neoclassical models of economic growth posit utility maximizing consumption and leisure decisions over either a finite or infinite horizon. Modigliani and Brumberg (1954) and Ando and Modigliani (1963) invoke the former assumption in their seminal development of the life cycle model, while the later assumption is an implication of Barro's (1974) equally seminal article on intergenerational altruism. Structural tax policies as well as the three other fiscal policies defined above can have markedly different transitional and long-term effects depending on which of these two sets of preferences is considered.

The extent to which altruistic as opposed to selfish behavior best characterizes actual intertemporal preferences is a matter of considerable controversy. Articles by Ando and Modigliani (1963), Tobin (1967), Davies (1981), King and Dicks-Mireaux (1982), and Modigliani (1983) provide evidence in support of the strict, nonaltruistic life cycle model. In contrast, White (1978), Mirer (1979), Darby (1979), chapter 1, Danziger, van der Gaag, Smolensky, and Taussig (1982), Bernheim (1982), Kurz (1984b), and Boskin and Lau (1984) report results contrary to the life cycle model, suggesting an important, if not predominant, role for private intergenerational transfers in explaining the current stock of US wealth. Chapter 1 stresses that the shapes of age-earnings and age-consumption profiles are far from those required under the strict life cycle model to produce significant hump saving. This finding does not, however, preclude the possibility that the majority of households conform to the selfish life cycle model. The majority of households could have such preferences, but simply have very little "hump" savings. As stressed by Kurz (1984a) and suggested by Boskin and Lau's (1984) findings, we may well live in a mixed society consisting of a minority of quite wealthy, altruistic households, and a majority of rather poor, life cycle households. While life cycle households may hold little, if any, of the current stock of wealth, their response to new structural as well as intergenerational tax policies could well dictate the economy's saving behavior over several decades, even if not the indefinite future.

Another explanation of the evidence for significant intergenerational transfers that is consistent with life cycle behavior involves imperfections in the market for annuity insurance. In the absence of a well-functioning annuity market, elderly households may share the risk of their uncertain longevity with their children in a manner that involves intergenerational transfers (chapter 4). Alternatively, in the face of uncertainty about their own life spans and needs, or if wealth exceeds the satiation level of consumption, the elderly may simply involuntarily bequeath wealth to their children extracting either nothing or nonmonetary services in exchange (Kuznets 1961; Davies 1981; Bernheim, Shleifer, and Summers 1983).

Section 7.6 describes the failure of econometric research based on the limited available data to clarify the degree of marginal altruism in the US economy. Given our state of ignorance concerning the distribution of intertemporal preferences, exploring the implications of tax policy within each of the two alternative models is important; indeed, analysis of models with heterogeneous preferences is an obvious area for additional research.

7.4.1   Structural Tax Policy in a Life Cycle Model

In the life cycle model each household makes independent choices, but the combined behavior of more than 60 contemporaneously living adult age cohorts enters into the determination of the general equilibrium transition path of a life cycle economy. The economy's transition path also depends on the future decisions of generations not yet in existence; today's generations base current economic choices partly on information about future wages and interest rates. These future prices are determined not only by the saving and labor supply decisions of those currently alive, but also by the saving and labor supply behavior of succeeding generations; the expectations about wage rates for today's twenty-year-olds, when they reach thirty, are partly influenced by their expectations of the labor supply of twenty-year-olds, ten years from now, whose labor supply, in turn, depends on expectations of the labor supply of twenty-year-olds, twenty years from now, and on and on.

The complexity of the multi-cohort life cycle model as well as its extensive, if not unlimited data requirements, has led many economists to simulate rather than empirically estimate the effects of government policy in nonaltruistic neoclassical environments. Simulation analysis of steady (or stationary) state predictions of life cycle economies dates from Ando and Modigliani (1963), Tobin (1967), and Atkinson (1971). Papers by Tobin and Dolde (1971, 1981), Sheshinski (1978), and chapter 12 of this book simulate the impact of social security on steady-state labor supply and savings. Summers (1981a) presents a steady-state simulation analysis of other government fiscal policies, in particular, structural tax policy. Miller and Upton (1974) and Summers (1981a) simulate effects of selected government policies on the growth path of life cycle economies under the assumption of myopic expectations.

Summers' 1981 article represents a very important contribution to the analysis of taxation and savings. His comparison of equal (annual) revenue wage and consumption tax regimes illustrates the intergenerational redistribution underlying many structural tax policies; the paper stresses that lowering capital income tax rates reduces current private consumption not only through substitution effects associated with the higher price of current relative to future consumption, but also through income affects associated with the reduced present value of a household's human capital endowment.

In a series of articles Auerbach and Kotlikoff (1983a–d) and Auerbach, Kotlikoff, and Skinner (1983) extended this research by developing a perfect foresight general equilibrium life cycle simulation model. "Perfect foresight" in this context means that households make economic choices based on common projections of future wages, interest rates, and tax rates, and these decisions, in the aggregate, produce equilibrium time paths of these variables equal to those projected. In the life cycle version of the model considered here agents live for 55 periods, corresponding to adult ages of 21 to 75, and are concerned only with their own welfare, i.e., they have no bequest motive. The model incorporates variable labor supply, including endogenous retirement, and a wide range of fiscal instruments, including investment incentives, progressive taxes, and social security. Its chief contribution is determining the equilibrium transition path generated by fiscal policies. "Equilibrium transition path" corresponds to the course of the economy as it moves from one stationary equilibrium to another. During this transition there is market clearing for all goods, factors, and assets. While the model solves for the course of all economic variables over a 150-year period, convergence to the new stationary state in the simulations described here typically occurs within 70 years.

The extended focus on this particular model's results in the succeeding discussion may appear excessive, but the intention is to illustrate potential differences in the quantitative affects of the four policies considered; obviously, isolating these differences requires holding the model constant while changing the experiment. The computer simulation model used here incorporates CES utility and production functions, which are frequently posited in empirical studies. In addition, the parameterization of these functions is based on empirical findings. We are able to display the (usually limited) sensitivity of the results to variation in the values of key parameters. Other models incorporating utility or production functions of other types would doubtless yield different results. The apparent impacts of changes in tax policy would certainly be quantitatively different—in some instances, perhaps qualitatively different than those that emerge in the simulations reported below. Those we do report, however, have the virtue of illustrating the operation of alternative tax policies in a model that incorporates commonly employed and widely studied functional forms. Moreover, this analysis permits one to obtain an understanding of the factors which control the impact of a change in tax policy on saving.

In addition to their pedagogic value, simulation studies can be viewed as a second stage of empirical analysis, i.e., as ways to display the implications of parameter estimates and assumptions about particular function forms. From this perspective they are also useful tools for designing empirical studies. Empirical work proceeds by assuming functional relations and testing their validity; simulating the affects of these functional relations for different parameter values in advance of empirical testing permits the researcher to trace out the full implications of his/her assumptions and to distinguish critically important from less important parameter values. Such knowledge will likely lead the econometrician to "spend" more of his/her limited data on estimating parameters to which the simulation results are most sensitive.

One may also question the emphasis on simulation results rather than empirical findings. Simulation analysis is certainly no substitute for empirical research; rather, it provides a methodology for exploring the full implications of empirical findings. Unfortunately there is no large-scale neoclassical econometric model that can be simulated to estimate the general equilibrium savings impact of policy. While one may be dubious about the absolute magnitude of changes in economic variables arising in simulation models, the models are likely to permit more reliable inferences concerning the relative effects of alternative policies. Thus one may find through simulation analysis that one tax structure is virtually always more conducive to saving than another within a large class of economic models. For certain policy choices a qualitative ranking of alternatives may be all that is needed.

Equation (12) presents the CES utility function of consumption, C, and leisure, l, underlying the life cycle policy simulations described below:

$$U = \sum_{\alpha=1}^{55} \left(\frac{1}{1+\delta}\right)^{a-1} [\mu C_a^{(1-1/\rho)} + (1-\mu)l_a^{(1-1/\rho)}]^{(1-\gamma)/(1-1/\rho)}. \qquad (12)$$

In (12) δ in the time preference rate, ρ is the "static" elasticity of substitution between consumption and leisure at each age a, and γ is the intertemporal elasticity of substitution between consumption and leisure at different ages. The reciprocal of γ equals the coefficient of relative risk aversion.

Baseline parameter values for δ, γ, ρ, and σ, the elasticity of substitution of capital for labor in the production function, are 0.015, 0.25, 0.8, and 1. These figures are mid-range estimates based on a variety of empirical studies, many of which are cited in Auerbach, Kotlikoff, and Skinner (1983).

Table 7.3 contains simulation results for three structural tax policies involving changes in the tax base from proportional income taxation to either proportional consumption, wage, or capital income taxation with each designed to yield equal revenues. The simulated economy has an initial steady-state capital-output ratio of 3.7, a capital-labor ratio of 5, a pretax wage normalized to 1, a 6.7 percent pretax real interest rate, a 3.7 percent net national saving rate, and a 15 percent proportional tax on all income. Since there are no transfer programs conducted either through "official" or "unofficial" mechanisms, receipts from the 15 percent income tax are solely used to finance government consumption. In each of table 7.3's simulations government consumption per capita is held fixed, and the tax rate of the specified tax base is adjusted to produce revenues equal, on an annual basis, to the exogenous path of government consumption.

Table 7.3 displays the primarily large impact structural tax policies can have on an economy's saving rate and related variables. Relative to the initial income tax regime, long-run saving rates are 19 percent larger under a consumption tax, 8 percent larger under a wage tax, and 32 percent smaller under a capital income tax. Changes in the economy's saving rate during the transition period are even more dramatic; in the first year after the switch to consumption taxation, the saving rate rises to 9.3 percent from an initial value of 3.7. In the case of the capital income tax, there is a negative 2.9 percent saving rate in the first year of the transition, and saving rates remain negative for over a decade. As table 7.1 indicates such swings in saving rates are within the range of US historical experience, although US saving experience is certainly neither solely nor primarily a reflection of historical changes in fiscal policy. The figures in table 7.3 would, of course, all be magnified in absolute value if one started with a larger initial steady-state income tax. For example, a structural shift to consumption taxation starting from a 30 percent income tax ultimately increases the capital-labor ratio by 63 percent, rather than the 24 percent increase of table 7.3.

The capital deepening associated with switching from the 15 percent income tax to consumption and wage taxation generates long-run pretax wage rates that are respectively 6 percent and 2 percent larger than their

Table 7.3
Structural tax change[a] (switch from 15% proportional income tax to specified proportional tax regimes)

Initial steady state: Year of transition	Capital-labor ratio, tax base			Wage rate (pretax), tax base			Real interest rate (pretax), tax base			Net national saving rate, tax base		
	Consumption	Wage	Capital income	Consumption	Wage	Capital income	Consumption (%)	Wage (%)	Capital income (%)	Consumption (%)	Wage (%)	Capital income (%)
	5.0	5.0	5.0	1.00	1.00	1.00	6.7	6.7	6.7	3.7	3.7	3.7
1	4.8	5.1	4.8	0.99	1.00	0.99	6.9	6.6	6.8	9.3	5.3	−2.9
5	5.1	5.1	4.4	1.01	1.01	0.97	6.5	6.5	7.3	8.2	5.0	−1.9
10	5.4	5.2	4.1	1.02	1.01	0.95	6.3	6.4	7.7	7.2	4.7	−1.0
50	6.2	5.4	3.0	1.05	1.02	0.88	5.7	6.3	9.7	4.5	4.0	2.0
150	6.2	5.4	2.9	1.06	1.02	0.87	5.7	6.3	10.1	4.4	4.0	2.5

a. Simulations assume a population growth rate of 1.5 percent, a time preference rate of 1.5 percent, "static" and intertemporal elasticities of substitution in consumption and leisure of 0.8 and 0.25, respectively, and a Cobb-Douglas production function.

initial values. In the case of capital income taxation, the long-run wage rate is 13 percent smaller than in the initial equilibrium. The long-run pretax real interest rate declines by 1 percent or less under consumption or wage taxation, while it rises 3.4 percentage points under capital income taxation. Long-run tax rates are 17.6 percent under a consumption tax, 20.1 percent under a wage tax, and 62.7 percent under a capital income tax. The much larger rate required under capital income taxation obviously reflects the fact that capital income is a much smaller tax base than total income, labor income, or consumption.

These changes in after-tax prices of factors and goods obviously alter the utility levels of each cohort alive at the time of the tax change or born thereafter. One measure of these utility differences is the equivalent per-centage increase in full lifetime resources needed in the original income tax regime to produce each cohort's realized level of utility under the specified alternative tax regimes. For cohorts living in the new long-run equilibrium under consumption, wage, and capital income tax regimes the equivalent variations are 2.32 percent, -0.89 percent, and -1.14 percent. These figures are smaller than the long-run changes in wage rates indicated in table 7.3, because they encompass the additional amount of both lifetime leisure and consumption that could hypothetically be afforded in the old steady state. Stated differently, since 65 percent of lifetime resources are spent on leisure in the initial steady state, a 2.32 percent increase in full-time resources would permit a 6.63 (2.32/0.35) percent increase in lifetime consumption, holding leisure constant.

One perhaps surprising feature of these numbers is that steady-state utility is lower under wage taxation than under income taxation despite an 8 percent increase in capital intensity. While the before-tax wage rises to 1.02 from an initial value of 1, the after-tax wage is 0.80 in the wage tax steady state compared with 0.85 under the income tax. In addition, the long-run after-tax interest rate, which determines prices of future consump-tion and leisure is only 0.61 percentage points greater in the wage taxation steady state. These numbers are indicative of, rather than the reason for, the lower level of steady-state welfare under wage versus income taxation. Despite the 21 percent greater capital stock in the wage tax steady state, aggregate steady-state consumption is lower reflecting the smaller aggre-gate supply of labor induced by the increased wage tax. While the new steady state has sufficient resources to sustain a higher level of welfare, the choice between consumption and leisure is suboptimally skewed toward leisure by the new post-tax intertemporal price structure imposed by a wage tax. Auerbach, Kotlikoff, and Skinner (1983) demonstrate that for the

CES utility function given in (12) wage taxation is Pareto inefficient relative to income taxation over a wide range of parameter values partly because it places all the tax distortion on the static choice between consumption and leisure, while leaving intertemporal decisions free of marginal distortions; i.e., it does not directly alter the after-tax rate of return, a key determinant of relative prices of goods and leisure at different dates. The income tax, in contrast, spreads the tax distortions over both margins of choice and the larger tax base permits lower tax rates.[16] The situation here is similar to that pictured in figure 7.2, where utility at B is less than at A, although the resource endowment (line 2) is unchanged.

The consumption tax affords a higher steady-state level of welfare than the income, wage, or capital income taxes, because it derives a part of its portion revenue from an implicit lump sum levy, which implies less dead weight loss from distortionary taxation. Intuitively, consumption taxation is, in part, effectively equivalent to a capital levy, because household wealth is indirectly taxed when it is ultimately surrendered in exchange for consumption goods. The capital levy represents a lump sum tax, since at the time the consumption tax is imposed, current wealth is given (i.e., is in perfectly inelastic supply). Chamley (1981) and Black (1981) emphasize the equivalence, for time invariant tax rates, of consumption taxation to wage taxation plus a one-time capital levy. In the case of time varying tax rates a consumption tax is structurally equivalent to a capital levy, plus taxation of wage and capital income at different rates over time.

The second reason for the long-run utility gain under consumption taxation as opposed to income taxation is the shift in the tax burden from later to earlier generations, a point stressed by Summers (1981a) and Bradford (1980). Take the age 55 life cycle agent as an example. In his last year in the 15 percent income tax steady state he consumes the principal plus 85 percent of the capital income earned from his terminal period assets. Since the after-tax interest rate in the initial steady state is 5.7 percent, terminal consumption is 1.057 times terminal assets plus any after-tax labor income. If the economy switches abruptly to a consumption tax, the first year consumption tax rate is 19.2 percent, and the 55-year-old's terminal assets will purchase only 0.839 unit of consumption times the amount of these assets. While the equivalent negative variation in *lifetime* utility for the 55-year-old in the consumption tax simulation is less than one-third of a percent, the equivalent variation is −15.2 percent if one considers only the remaining life span of the 55-year-old. The loss in welfare to these early generations plus the use of a more efficient tax structure are what pays for the higher level of welfare of later generations, including those in the new steady state, under consumption taxation.

7.4.2   Simulated Structural Tax Policy: Sensitivity Analysis

The sensitivity of the table 7.3 results to assumed parameter values and functional form for preferences and production is of obvious importance for their evaluation. The empirical literature suggests extreme values for γ, the intertemporal elasticity of substitution, of between 0.1 and 0.5, and values for ρ, the static elasticity of substitution of between 0.1 and 1.5. Holding all other parameter values constant, combinations of these values generate percentage increases in the long-run capital-labor ratio under the structural shift from income to consumption taxation ranging from 22.6 to 26.9. The baseline ($\gamma = 0.25$, $\rho = 0.8$) simulation generated a 24.0 percent increase.

There is more sensitivity to these parameter values in the case of structural wage tax policy. Here the baseline increase in capital intensity is 8.0 percent with extreme values of 3.8 percent and 11.1 percent over the specified range of values for γ and ρ. The third structural tax policy described in table 7.3, a shift from income to capital income taxation, produces a 42.0 percent drop in the capital-labor ratio for baseline values of γ and ρ and a sensitivity range of 28.6 to 51.5 percent.

Evans's 1983 article suggests that life cycle simulation results may be highly sensitive to assumptions concerning the rate of time preference. This appears not to be the case for a structural change from income to consumption taxation. The baseline simulation that incorporates a 1.5 percent rate of time preference, yields a 24.0 percent change in capital intensivity. Lowering the time preference rate to -3 percent produces a 24.8 percent increase, while raising it to 4 percent yields a 24.6 percent increase. Similar experiments for shifting to wage taxation led to respective changes in capital-labor ratios of 2.23 percent and 12.9 percent compared with the 8 percent baseline change. In the case of a structural shift to capital income taxation, the sensitivity to time preference rates is quite substantial. The percentage decrease in capital intensity is 12.5 percent when the time preference rate, δ, is -0.03, it is 42.0 percent when δ is 0.015, and it is 56.5 percent when δ is 0.04.

A final parameter value to consider in the context of this model is the elasticity of substitution in the production function. Lowering this rate in the CES production function from 1 to 0.8 led to 19.8 percent, 9.6 percent, and 50.7 percent long-run changes in capital-labor ratios, respectively, from consumption, wage, and capital income structural tax changes. These numbers can be compared with 24.0 percent, 8.0 percent, and 42.0 percent in the baseline case.

The following points summarize these results concerning structural changes in proportional tax bases in the standard CES life cycle model. First, for a set of plausible parameter values a shift from income to consumption taxation generates significant increases in long-run savings, wage rates, and economic welfare. The opposite is true for capital income taxation. Structural wage tax policy, on the other hand, while it stimulates some additional savings, can lower long-run economic welfare. Second, long-run gains or losses in economic welfare are paid for, in part, by opposite changes in the welfare of certain generations alive during the transition induced by the new tax structure. Third, the impact of a shift to consumption taxation is quite insensitive to reasonable variations in parameter values. The effects of these structural wage and capital income tax policies are more sensitive to deviations in baseline parameter values, but such deviations do not alter the sign of their impact on long-run savings. Finally, substitution effects appear to dominate offsetting cross-cohort income effects in altering long-run savings rates. The move to capital income taxation provides a good example. Here the negative income effects of an increased tax burden faced by the elderly and the corresponding positive income effects of decreased taxation experienced by young and middle-aged cohorts, which serve to stimulate saving (because of generational differences in marginal propensities to consume goods and leisure), and outweighed by the negative substitution effects that induce more current and less future consumption and leisure. These substitution effects are determined not only by preferences, but also by the household's time path of full-time earnings capacity; i.e., as stressed by Summers (1981a), a given change in after-tax interest rates will produce different revaluation of the worker's endowment of full-time earnings if these full-time earnings arrive more in the future than in the present. Summers' "human-wealth effect" plays a role in determining both income and substitution effects of changes in discount rates.

A final issue of sensitivity analysis involves choice of functional form. Presently there appear to be no studies comparing structural tax changes in life cycle models using different general functional forms for preferences and technologies. Such a study would be quite informative. Starrett (1983) uses the Stone-Geary generalization of the CES utility function in a study of tax-financed changes in government consumption. He finds smaller increases in national wealth arising from reductions in government consumption that are financed by cuts in capital income taxation than does Summers (1981a) who employs the standard CES functional form. Whether Starrett's nonhomothetic preferences are more plausible than those considered here is obviously an issue to be determined empirically.

7.4.3 Structural Tax Policy: Increasing the Progressivity of the Rate Structure in a Life Cycle Model

The impact of progressive tax schedules on savings is illustrated, in part, by considering an equal revenue switch from proportional to progressive taxation. There is obviously no unique progressive tax schedule to compare with proportional taxation, but consideration of the linear marginal tax schedule given in (13) provides a sense of potential affects.

$$\tau_m = \alpha_1 + \alpha_2 B. \tag{13}$$

In (13) B stands for the tax base, and α_1 and α_2 are two coefficients that are chosen each year subject to the constraint that the new tax schedule produces the same annual revenue as the proportional tax structure.

The baseline life cycle simulation model outlined above was used to examine the consequences of switching from 30 percent proportional taxation to a progressive tax schedule featuring a marginal rate of 20 percent (i.e., $\alpha_1 = 0.2$) at zero income. Pegging α_1 at 0.2 leaves the annual revenue constraint to determine α_2 in (13). Households in the model fully incorporate the time path of changes in progressive tax schedules (annual changes in α_2 occurring during the transition) in making their intertemporal consumption and leisure decisions. With the exception of the income tax, this type of progressive structural tax change produces rather small changes in capital-labor ratios and savings rates. The percentage change in capital intensity (saving rates) is -36 (-46) percent in the case of income taxation, it is -10 (-7) percent under capital income taxation, and -6 (-4) percent under wage taxation. There is a positive 3.7 (2.8) percentage change in capital intensity (the net national saving rate) in the case of the switch from proportional to progressive consumption taxation. Since the reduction in capital intensity and, therefore, the reduction in the tax base per capita is greatest under the progressive income tax, the level of α_2 needed to generate the requisite per capita revenues is substantially larger (over 3 times) under progressive income taxation than under wage or consumption taxation, and almost twice as large as the α_2 obtained in the case of progressive capital income taxation. Marginal tax rates peak at 82 percent, 51 percent, 45 percent, and 33 percent, respectively, under the progressive income, wage, capital income, and consumption tax regimes.

The increase in savings in the progressive consumption tax simulation reflects, in large part, the intergenerational transfer from the initial elderly implied by this policy. Since consumption rises with age in the initial steady state, the first generation of aged faces a larger tax burden under the equal revenue progressive consumption tax than under the proportional consumption tax; i.e., the initial elderly find themselves in higher marginal consumption tax brackets than younger cohorts. In contrast, the shift from proportional income to progressive income taxation reduces the tax burden of the initial elderly, since their income (capital plus wage) is low relative to that of middle-aged workers, although their capital income is relatively high. Hence the intergenerational income effects reinforce the substitution effects of lowering savings under progressive income taxation. Similar income effects do not arise in the case of increasing the progressivity of either a wage tax or a capital income tax.

7.4.4   Structural Tax Policies: Proportional Taxation in an Infinite Horizon Model

Barro's 1974 article describes how overlapping intergenerational altruism generates a utility function in which each household effectively acts as if it were infinitely lived. The argument is clarified in (14) which assumes that generation t's utility, U_t, depends on its own consumption and leisure and the utility of its immediate offspring, U_{t+1}. For simplicity, generations are assumed to live for only one period.

$$U_t = U(C_t, l_t, U_{t+1}(C_{t+1}, l_{t+1}, U_{t+2}(C_{t+2}, l_{t+2}, \ldots)$$

$$= V(C_t, l_t, C_{t+1}, l_{t+1}, \ldots). \tag{14}$$

The utility linkage of generation t to generation $t + 1$ effectively connects generation t to all future generations, and (14) collapses into a function of the entire future time path of consumption and leisure of the current household and its descendants. If this utility function is homothetic, then the marginal rate of substitution $(\partial V_t/\partial C_{t+1})/(\partial V_t/\partial C_t)$ is independent of the stationary state levels of C_t and l_t. Utility maximization requires an equality between this rate of substitution and 1 plus the after-tax real rate of return, denoted here as $r(1 - \tau_r)$, where τ_r is the marginal tax rate on capital income. Hence the long-run after-tax rate of return is equal to the time preference rate, $(\partial V_t/\partial C_{t+1})/(\partial V_t/\partial C_t) - 1$, a constant for a homothetic utility function that is independent of the levels of consumption and leisure. The term r, however, is determined in general equilibrium by the marginal product of capital. Assuming constant returns to scale in production, it is easy to show that the long-run capital-labor ratio is independent of marginal wage or consumption taxes, but depends simply on the capital income tax rate, the constant steady-state rate of time preference and parameters of the production function. For example, if the production function is Cobb-Douglas with a capital share of 0.25, a switch from a 15 percent income tax to either a wage or consumption tax increases long-run capital intensity in general equilibrium by 24 percent; starting with a 30 percent income tax, the long-run percentage increase is 61 percent. A switch to capital income taxation from a 10 percent income tax steady state lowers long-run capital intensity by 47 percent; structural shifts to capital income taxation starting with a larger initial income tax are not feasible long-run policies for this model. The reason for the reduction in capital intensity in the case of a structural shift to capital income taxation is the higher tax on capital income, 44 percent instead of 10 percent required to satisfy the revenue constraint. Using a 0.8 elasticity of substitution in production, σ, reduces these changes in capital intensity by about 30 percent; the sensitivity of tax policy to this parameter value is discussed in Chamley (1981). The fact that a lower value of σ reduces the impact of structural tax policy is intuitive, at least in the limit; when σ equals zero, capital and labor are used in fixed proportions, and the distinction between capital and labor income taxes disappears.

In the case of progressive taxation, homothetic preferences of the form given in (14) still imply a steady-state equality between the after (marginal) tax return to capital and the time preference rate. If the progressive tax structure exhibits monotone increasing tax rates, marginal tax rates will exceed average tax rates, and the steady-state marginal tax rate under the progressive tax structure must differ from that in the initial proportional tax steady state due to the equal revenue requirement. While it seems likely that a switch from proportional to progressive taxation of all income, or simply capital income, will be associated with higher marginal taxation of capital income and, therefore, smaller values of capital per worker, this remains an area for future investigation. A related set of apparently unexplored structural tax questions is the consequence of switching from proportional to progressive wage or consumption taxation. The results in each of these cases will depend on assumptions concerning legal restrictions and additional tax obligations confronting altruistic households in shifting taxable income to family members in lower marginal tax brackets.

7.4.5   Structural Tax Policy in a Small Open Economy

The foregoing discussion applies to closed economies or to a world economy consisting of countries that are identical up to a scale factor and that simultaneously engage in the same fiscal policy. To see how strikingly different the impact of particular structural tax policies can be in an open economy, consider switching from wage to capital income taxation under the following four simplifying assumptions. First, the economy in question is small and places no restrictions on imports or exports of perfectly mobile financial and physical capital. Second, there are only two factors of production, capital and labor. Third, labor is mobile domestically, but not internationally. Fourth, foreign governments do not engage in any fiscal policy whatsoever.

Under these circumstances the foreign pretax rate of return is given and domestic residents will change their mix of foreign and domestic investment to maximize their after-tax return. If the home country taxes the capital income of domestic residents regardless of where that income is earned, the switch from wage to capital income taxation will have the type of effects on savings just described, except that general equilibrium changes in before-tax factor prices will be trivial because the home country is small. If, on the other hand, the home country taxes both its own residents and foreigners at the same rate on income earned only on domestic capital, capital will flow out of the home country until after-tax rates of return are equalized internationally. The domestic pretax wage will fall in response to a reduction in the capital-labor ratio. If labor is supplied inelastically, the pretax wage will decline until the fall in pretax labor income exactly equals the government's tax revenue; i.e., labor bears the entire burden (incidence) of the capital income tax. Hence, "the shift to capital income taxation" in this case simply replaces an explicit wage tax with an implicit wage tax. If labor is elastically supplied, the wage will differ somewhat across the two tax regimes, but the basic point holds that the economy effectively ends up with a wage tax despite the reported change in tax structure.

The degree of international capital mobility at the margin is particularly important for determining whether to try to stimulate savings through changes in corporate or personal capital income taxation. If the personal capital income tax is levied on such income regardless of where it is earned, while the corporate income tax is levied only on capital income earned domestically, a switch from wage to corporate profits taxation may simply replace an explicit wage tax with an implicit one. Switching to personal taxation on capital income earned either at home or abroad, on the other

hand, could have major impacts on intertemporal prices confronting domestic households, and, therefore, major impacts on household consumption and national savings.

7.5 The Impact of Contemporaneous Tax-Financed Increases in Government Consumption

7.5.1 Results for the Life Cycle Model

This section considers changes in government consumption under the
assumption that such consumption either is not an argument of private
utility functions or that the utility of government consumption is separable
from that of private consumption and leisure. In either case the choice of
government consumption does not directly affect private marginal rates of
substitution between current and future consumption and leisure. Hence,
changes in government consumption affect private choices of these variables only indirectly by altering variables (e.g., tax rates) entering private
budget constraints. In life cycle economies increases in the level of government consumption, financed on a contemporaneous basis by increases in
tax rates have quite different impacts on national savings depending on the
tax base in place. For example, using the baseline parameter values of
Section 7.4, a permanent doubling of the level of government consumption
per capita (from an initial level equal to 15 percent of the specified tax base)
leads to respective reductions between initial and final steady states in
capital-labor ratios and national savings rates of 26.2 percent and 20.4
percent under the income tax, 12.3 percent and 9.7 percent under the wage
tax, 14.5 percent and 11.0 percent under the capital income tax, but only
1.2 percent and 0.01 percent under the consumption tax. Long-run crowding out of capital per dollar increase in government consumption is 5.9
dollars under income tax finance, 4.8 dollars under wage tax finance, 6.5
dollars under capital income tax finance, but -3 cents under consumption
tax finance.[17]

Different income and substitution effects experienced by particular
cohorts are important for understanding these results. Compare, for example, the consumption and wage tax results. In the consumption tax case
initial elderly generations, with high marginal propensities to consume,
share immediately and significantly in the burden of the higher taxes and
reduce their consumption and leisure accordingly. Younger cohorts also
lower their current consumption and leisure in response to their lower
effective lifetime resources; however, they spread this lifetime loss over

the future as well as the present. These private changes significantly offset the increased rate of government consumption; in the first year of the economic transition each dollar increase in government consumption is offset by 89 cents less in private consumption.

In contrast, the contemporaneous wage tax-financed increase in government consumption has little impact on the elderly who are largely out of the workforce; while younger cohorts do reduce their current consumption and leisure in response to the increased lifetime tax burden, their immediate response is limited because of their ability and desire to smooth these reductions over the remainder of their lives. In addition, the substitution effects leading to reduced labor by the young and middle-aged are significantly greater under wage taxation than under consumption taxation; the reason is the higher effective tax on labor earnings and lower effective net wage, when the net wage is measured in terms of additional consumption that can be attained by working an additional hour. The fact that initial elderly generations pay for little if any of the additional government consumption means higher effective marginal taxation of labor supply for younger and future generations.

In the first year of the wage tax transition there is over a 3 percent reduction in the simulated economy's labor supply. This implies, of course, less current output, and less current saving even holding aggregate consumption constant. These initial effects are not transitory; they are part of an equilibrium shift to a permanently different economy. The reduction in current saving means lower capital-labor ratios in subsequent periods, lower pretax wages, and higher wage tax rates given the prespecified revenue requirement of the government.

Substitution effects also play a major role in the simulation of income tax and capital income tax financed increases in government consumption. The higher capital income taxes here lead households to substitute current consumption and leisure for future consumption and leisure. In the income tax case, each dollar of increased government consumption in year 1 of the transition is offset by only 73 cents of reduced private consumption; in addition there is a 1.5 percent reduction in employment. Under a pure capital income tax regime the private consumption offset is only 10 cents on the dollar; however, the initial change in employment is minimal.

These results are presented to illustrate rather than exhaustively examine the savings impact of contemporaneous tax-financed increases in government consumption. As in the case of structural tax policy some of these results are sensitive to certain parameter values and the functional form of the utility function (Starrett 1983).

7.5.2   Tax-Financed Increases in Government Consumption:
The Infinite Horizon Model

Under the assumption of a homothetic, infinite horizon utility function and constant returns to scale in production the discussion in Section 7.4 indicated that steady-state capital intensity is independent of wage or consumption income taxes since neither tax structure directly alters the marginal return to saving in the steady state. Hence, an immediate permanent increase in government consumption will have no long-run affects on capital-labor ratios to the extent this consumption is financed by wage or consumption taxation. The absolute levels, however, of capital and labor supply may change both in the short and long run in response to the increased taxation. This clearly depends on variability in labor supply. If labor supply is exogenous and the utility function is time separable, the private sector immediately reduces its own consumption by an amount exactly equal to the increase in government consumption and the capital stock, a closed economy's wealth in a one good model, remains unchanged.[18] When labor supply is variable or the increase in government consumption is financed, at least partially, by capital income taxation, there will be short- as well as long-run effects on the absolute amount of savings.

Illustrative simulations of steady-state changes in levels of government consumption for the infinite horizon version of the CES utility function in (12), assuming Section 7.4's baseline parameter values and government consumption initially financed by a 15 percent tax rate, produce the following results. Doubling government consumption decreases the economy's long-run per capita wealth by 22 percent if financed by income taxation, by 0.5 percent if financed by wage taxation, by 22 percent if financed by capital income taxation, and by −2 percent if financed by consumption taxation.

7.6   The Savings Impact of Intergenerational Tax Policy

7.6.1   Major Themes in the Literature

Feldstein's (1974b) article on social security and savings sparked an intensive empirical and theoretical analysis of the savings impact of intergenerational transfers. Much of this research has focused on the particular effects of unfunded social security on savings (Munnell 1974; Feldstein and Pellechio 1979; 1979b; Barro 1978; Darby 1979; Kurz 1981; Lesnoy and Leimer 1981; Feldstein 1980, 1982a; Blinder, Gordon, and Wise 1981; Kurz 1982; Diamond and Hausman 1983; Auerbach and Kotlikoff 1983d; and see chapter 15 of this book). But this research also stimulated economists to search for other subtle, but potentially quite powerful mechanisms by which the government transfers resources across generations. In his second seminal contribution to this literature Feldstein (1977) demonstrates how tax-induced revaluation of land transfers resources intramarginally across generations. While such asset revaluations have no effect in infinite horizon economies (Barro 1974; Calvo, Kotlikoff, and Rodriguez 1979), they are important in the life cycle model; for middle-aged and elderly cohorts who are the principal owners of land and other assets, government-induced capital losses lower the value of nonhuman wealth measured in terms of consumption goods. It is important to realize that these capital losses can far exceed the current explicit tax payments which induce such revaluations. In the case of a land rent tax, the price of land falls by the present value of the infinite stream of current and future tax payments. For young and unborn generations the reduced land price is equivalent to a lump sum subsidy, since they now purchase this fixed productive asset by surrendering fewer consumption goods to their predecessors.[19] As mentioned in Section 7.3, such intergenerational redistribution in life cycle models alters current saving because of cross-cohort differences in marginal propensities to consume goods and leisure.

Just as unfunded social security constitutes a hidden way for governments to run *economic* deficits, tax-induced asset revaluation constitutes a hidden way for governments to run *economic* surpluses. If they so chose, governments could explicitly report very sizable official surpluses without changing any real economic policy: Rather than covertly taxing the wealth of older generations and indirectly handing the receipts to young and future generations, they could explicitly levy a one-time wealth tax, collecting proceeds that exactly equal each household's capital loss under the corresponding implicit policy, and distribute the funds over time in a lump sum fashion to young and future generations. While this change in accounting procedures, if properly enacted, alters no one's intertemporal budget constraint, including the government's, the increase in current period receipts from the wealth tax would be reported as a surplus.

Feldstein's (1977) essay was followed by analyses by King (1977), Auerbach (1979), and Bradford (1980, 1981) demonstrating that if corporations are prohibited from repurchasing their shares, one may still observe corporations paying dividends despite the fact that personal income taxation favors capital gains relative to dividend income. The advantage to capital gains is arbitraged away, in equilibrium, by equity values that rise by less than a dollar for every dollar of retained earnings. That is, shareholders are indifferent at the margin between receiving dividends, or having corporations retain earnings. Dividends are taxed at higher rates, while retained earnings lead to less than dollar-for-dollar capital gains, but are taxed at a lower rate when realized. In such economies where dividends are being paid, equity values always adjust to provide the same effective rate of return on investments yielding dividends as on investments yielding capital gains. In these models the marginal after-tax return to capital income is a direct function solely of the tax rate on capital gains. The tax rate on capital gains is the rate that influences marginal capital income taxation because it is lower than the dividend tax rate; i.e., the return on dividends is forced to adjust to the return on retained earnings via equity valuation. A corollary of this result is that increasing the dividend tax rate has no direct impact on the after-tax return to capital. Increasing dividend taxation does, however, lead to a fall in stock market values and an associated intergenerational redistribution of resources that simulates life cycle savings.

This surprising result in which increasing a particular capital income tax instrument unambiguously stimulates savings in a life cycle model is characteristic of a much broader class of policies than simply increases in dividend taxation. Summers (1981c) describes the implications for asset valuation of a variety of fiscal policies, pointing out that the price of old capital declines in response to investment incentives that discriminate in favor of new capital. Chapter 9 demonstrates in a general equilibrium context that investment incentives, such as accelerated depreciation or investment tax credits, stimulate saving (investment in a closed economy) through implicit one-time wealth taxation of preexisting capital; in addition, in the presence of significant investment incentives, such as those now in place in the United States, raising either corporate or personal tax rates on capital income also lowers stock market values, thereby redistributingresources intergenerationally and stimulating savings in life cycle economies.

The example of introducing 100 percent expensing of new capital in an economy with a τ percent proportional income tax permits an intuitive explanation of these results. Assume, for simplicity, that there is a single homogeneous form of capital that does not physically depreciate. Then the legislated and effective marginal tax rate on capital income is τ prior to the introduction of expensing. Introducing full expensing completely eliminates the effective marginal tax on capital income; for new capital, the immediate subsidy of τ cents per dollar invested offsets in present value the stream of taxes that are paid on the return to this marginal infinitely lived investment.[20]

By assumption, preexisting capital is either ineligible for expensing, or is effectively ineligible because of recapture taxes. Hence, in order to provide the same after-tax return to investors as new capital, the market value of old capital must fall by τ cents on the dollar; i.e., the value of capital relative to its replacement cost, "Tobin's q," is given by $q = 1 - \tau$. If 100 percent expensing is initially in place, raising τ has no impact on the marginal return to capital, since investing in new capital provides a larger initial subsidy to offset the now larger future taxes on the investment's return. On the other hand, raising τ induces additional capital losses to old capital according to the formula for q. This covert redistribution from older to young and future generations reduces current national consumption and increases savings in the life cycle model because of cross-cohort differences in marginal consumption propensities.

Hidden *economic* surpluses of this type can be quite sizable relative to officially reported deficits. Auerbach and Kotlikoff (chapter 9) estimate that the 1981 US Tax Act imposed an implicit tax, in the form of a 1981 capital loss to holders of the US capital stock of roughly $260 billion. Had the government explicitly imposed this wealth tax, reported tax receipts would have risen by approximately $260 billion, and the government would have reported a $202 billion surplus for 1981. Such a change in the reported 1981 deficit notwithstanding, real policy would have remained unchanged had the government also redistributed the $260 billion tax on stockholders in a nondistorting fashion to young and future generations according to the benefits that would otherwise have accrued to them under the implicit surplus policy.

The estimated $260 billion capital loss assumes zero marginal costs of adjusting the economy's capital stock, i.e., zero costs to physically installing new capital or training workers to use new capital. The assumption of substantial adjustment costs is likely to reduce this $260 billion figure by roughly one quarter (chapter 9). The relationship between investment and stock market valuation dates from the "q" theory of Tobin (1969). Papers by Abel (1979) and Hayashi (1982) analyze the firm's optimal investment strategy in the presence of adjustment costs, producing a simple linear relationship between a firm's investment rate and q when adjustment costs are quadratic. Poterba's (1980) study of housing investment appears to be the first inclusion of taxation in the q investment model. Summers (1981b) and Salinger and Summers (1983) employ this partial equilibrium model to study the impact of corporate and personal taxation on investment in plant and equipment.

The general equilibrium implication of this research is that, apart from policies such as investment incentives that have a direct depressing affect on stock values, fiscal policies that increase (decrease) national capital formation will likely be associated with temporary increases (decreases) in stock market values; such capital revaluations arise because capital that has already been installed is a quasi-fixed factor that earns intramarginal rents on its ability to aid in the installation of additional capital. As indicated, even in the case of investment incentives, the presence of adjustment costs can significantly mitigate the fall in stock values associated with tax policies which discriminate against old capital. In a life cycle model the income effects of asset revaluation arising from adjustment costs appear to lengthen fiscal policy transitions as well as reduce the size of short-run changes in most economic variables; however, their impact on long-run outcomes appears minor (chapter 9). The slower transitions reflect not only the adjustment costs of varying capital stocks over a short period of time, but also the intergenerational income effects of the capital gains and losses associated with the short-term asset revaluation.

7.6.2   Empirical Research on Savings and Intergenerational Transfers

Time series analysis of the effect of intergenerational transfers on aggregate consumption has proved inconclusive. Estimates of the impact of unfunded social security on consumption vary from very large positive effects (Feldstein 1974b) to negative effects (Lesnoy and Leimer 1981).

If one takes the life cycle model as the maintained hypothesis of these studies, the econometrics is plagued by special problems of aggregation, simultaneity, misspecification, and errors in measuring indices of intergenerational transfers, such as Social Security wealth (Williamson and Jones 1983). The standard procedure ignores differences by cohort in marginal consumption propensities, producing coefficients of the resulting aggregated equation that are a weighted average of cohort-specific coefficients. There is no reason to suspect the weights will be constant through time. The simultaneity problem arises from the inclusion of aggregate disposable income as an explanatory variable that is presumed exogenous from current consumption. Misspecification arises from using disposable total income, rather than the after-tax present value of future labor earnings as an explanatory variable. In addition, even at the cohort level, the specified coefficients are not, in general, constant; rather they are variables that depend on the anticipated time paths of future tax rates and benefit levels, and such anticipations change through time.

Chapter 9 demonstrates the problem of the time series statistical approach for the life cycle model by running the standard time series specification on simulated data that conform perfectly to this theory's predictions concerning the impact of unfunded social security on savings. The coefficients on the critical social security wealth variable as well as many other variables are extraordinarily sensitive to the choice of sample period as well as the speed with which unfunded social security is phased into the economy; the social security coefficients ranged from 10.8 to -11.4. This exercise suggests that the conventional time series approach has very little power with respect to rejecting the strict (no altruism) life cycle model of saving. In addition, even if one improved the econometric specification and estimated the equation with instrumental variables, the absence of cohort-specific time series data appears to preclude resolving problems of aggregation.

Surprisingly, there seems to have been no attempts to use time series data to reject the alternative hypothesis, namely that of intergenerational altruism. This model, which in its simplest formulation reduces to the case of a single infinitely lived household, is more suited to aggregate data and has the following testable implications. First, the economy's stocks of human and nonhuman wealth (discounted at pretax rates of return) should have identical predicated effects on aggregate consumption (assuming human wealth can be properly measured, which is particularly difficult given the potential degree of uncertainty concerning earnings), and the present value of the stream of future government consumption should have an equal negative effect: see equation (11). Second, the distribution of resource ownership by age should have no impact on aggregate consumption;[21] Boskin and Lau (1984) have recently constructed time series data on the distribution of resource ownership by age which should permit tests of this type.

Cross-section analyses have also been hampered by limited data; in addition, many studies (including those of the author) proceed without clearly formulating rejectable hypotheses concerning altruism. These particular studies involve regressions of household private wealth on social security tax and transfer variables. The central question posed in much of this literature is whether households reduce their private asset accumulation when young because of the anticipation of receiving net windfall transfers when old. The evidence here is mixed, but even if each of these studies had strongly confirmed the proposition that expected future windfalls lead to higher current consumption and, therefore, less private wealth accumulation, the results would still leave unresolved the issue of intergenerational altruism; the altruistic hypothesis like the life cycle hypothesis, suggests that increases in the future resources of a particular household should raise that household's consumption and lower its own savings.[22] In the altruistic case, however, the future windfall to the household in question would presumably also raise the consumption of all other altruistically linked households in the extended family. Unfortunately, this latter proposition is not tested in the existing literature, nor does it appear capable of being tested given current data sources. If one had data on the consumption and resources of potentially altruistically linked households, one could test for such linkages by examining whether the consumption of one household depended on the resources of the other.

To summarize, the empirical literature on intergenerational transfers has focused very narrowly on the predicted impact of particular policies, primarily Social Security. Many of the broader implications of selfish, finite horizon behavior of altruistic, infinite horizon models have not yet been directly tested. Blinder, Gordon, and Wise (1981) and Boskin and Lau (1984) are notable exceptions. Their papers consider the fundamental prediction of the life cycle model that the elderly have larger marginal propensities to consume goods and leisure than the young. The evidence presented by Blinder et al. is weakly supportive of this proposition, while that of Boskin and Lau provides stronger support.

7.6.3 Intergenerational Tax Policy: Simulation Analyses

Presumably as a consequence of standard accounting conventions much of the concern about intergenerational transfers has focused on the impact of "official deficits" on investment, economic growth, and interest rates. As stressed in Section 7.3, whether officially reported current deficits are associated in life cycle models with actual intergenerational redistribution requires close scrutiny of changes in household lifetime budget constraints. Conventionally reported deficits can certainly coincide with real economic deficits, where economic deficits are defined as net intergenerational transfers from younger to older generations. Holding other fiscal policies constant, short-run tax cuts, leading to the accumulation of debt, the interest on which is paid for by higher future taxes (rather than reduced government consumption) provide one example in which a higher reported official deficit is associated with a real redistribution of resources across generations; for the current elderly the short-term tax cut expands their lifetime budgets because they will either not be alive when taxes are increased or they will be alive for a relatively short period of time after the tax increases.

The simulation model outlined in Section 7.4 produces the following effects of temporary tax cuts followed by a policy of maintaining constant the government's resulting accumulated per capita stock of official debt. The baseline tax regime involves a 15 percent proportional income tax. A one-year cut in the income tax rate from 15 to 10 percent (a 5 percent of GNP deficit) has no significant impact on the economy in the long run. This debt policy lowers the long-run capital stock by slightly less than 2 percent and reduces the before-tax wage by close to 0.5 percent. The long-run income tax rate is 15.3 percent, the rate needed to finance the interest payments on the endogenously accumulated stock of debt as well as pay for government consumption. Interestingly, the long-run path to a "crowded out" capital stock involves short-run "crowding in" of capital. In year 1 of the transition when the income tax rate is 10 percent, labor supply increases by 3.7 percent while consumption rises by only 1.7 percent. The increase in income exceeds the increase in consumption, producing a 32 percent increase in the saving rate in year one relative to the initial steady state. In year 2 of the transition the income tax rate is raised to 15.2 percent to avoid a further increase in the stock of per capita debt; labor supply now falls below its initial steady-state value as does the saving rate. In comparison with the long-run effects of this policy, the immediate effects are quite striking. Sizable short-run saving effects from temporary life cycle wage appear consistent with several of MaCurdy's (1981) longitudinal findings. This example, in which the saving rate first rises, then falls, indicates that short-run "supply side" responses may be quite poor predictors of long-run supplies of capital and labor and of the size of the long-run tax base.

A twenty-year income tax cut from 15 to 10 percent has much more dramatic long-run effects; the decline in capital across steady states in this case is 49 percent, with every dollar of long-run debt associated with 1.2 dollars less in long-run capital. The pretax wage ultimately declines by 14 percent in the simulation, while the after-tax falls by 30 percent reflecting, in part, the 30 percent income tax rate required for long-run budget balance. The long-run real interest rate rises by 4 percentage points in this experiment.

The year 1 response in the twenty-year tax cut simulation involves a 2.5 percent increase in labor supply, but a 2.6 percent rise in private consumption. Consequently national saving per worker falls and crowding out begins in year 1. The crowding out process is, however, quite slow; in the first ten years the per capita capital stock falls by less than 2 percent; it falls by an additional 4 percent between years 10 and 20. In the subsequent decade after the income tax is raised, which induces a substitution away from labor supply and saving, there is an additional 14 percent decline in per capita capital relative to its initial value. Thus less than one-half of the total drop in capital per person occurs during the first 30 years of the perfect foresight economic transition. By year 60 about four-fifths of the transition is complete.

The short-run differences in these two tax cut simulations clearly reflect the predominance of substitution over income effects in the case of the short period tax cuts and the converse for the twenty-year tax cut; in the case of the one-year tax cut, all but the oldest generation alive in the first year will face higher tax rates through the rest of their lives. Young generations will face the higher tax rates for such a long period of time that their budget possibilities and levels of welfare are actually reduced. While the income effects experienced by most current age groups from the change in the time path of tax rates in the one-year tax cut are trivial, if not negative, the substitution effect leading to less current consumption and more current labor supply at the time of the tax cut are nontrivial. A key lesson of these two simulations is that policies that inevitably crowd out saving and investment can look quite effective in promoting capital formation if one evaluates such policies using only the first few years of information.

It is instructive to compare these results arising from presumably explicitly reported deficits with those arising from the unreported deficits embedded in unfunded Social Security. Starting out from the same initial equilibrium, introducing a "pay as you go" Social Security system with a 40 percent replacement rate and financed by payroll taxes leads to a 19 percent long-run decline in capital per person and a 5 percent drop in the pretax wage. Hence, in its ability to crowd out capital in this life cycle model, introducing an unfunded Social Security system with a substantial benefit replacement rate can have as deleterious an impact on capital formation as officially reported economic deficit policies arising from multi-year tax cuts.

The importance of considering unreported intergenerational transfers is further highlighted by a final simulation experiment. Suppose the economy's initial fiscal policy is a 15 percent income tax with 100 percent expensing of new capital. As argued above, this tax structure involves no marginal taxation of capital income, and increases in the capital income tax simply produce capital losses for elderly owners of capital, with large marginal consumption propensities, thus transferring resources to young and future generations, with low or zero current marginal consumption propensities. Consider a permanent increase in the tax rate on capital income from 15 to 50 percent coupled with a 20-year cut in the wage tax rate from 15 to 10 percent. While the government reports official deficits in the first few years of the economic transition in excess of 4 percent of GNP, the unreported economic surplus associated with the asset revaluation crowds in more capital than the wage tax cut crowds out. By the twentieth year of the transition the increase in the government's tax base has sufficed to retire the official debt issued in the early years of this policy, and the government finds itself running a very sizable surplus. To balance its budget after 20 years the wage tax rate must be cut; the new long-run wage tax rate is only 2 percent. The long-run per capita capital stock is 70 percent larger than its initial steady-state value, and the government (stock) surplus equals close to 7 percent of private wealth.

These results illustrate the variety of outcomes, many of which are quite surprising, that the standard CES life cycle model can produce in response to intergenerational tax policies. They should, however, be viewed cautiously; augmenting this type of model with liquidity constraints on unsecured borrowing, as in Dolde and Tobin (1981) can significantly diminish the simulated response to such policies in life cycle economies.

7.7   The Savings Impact of Intragenerational Tax Policy

Recent papers by Heckman (1981), Hausman (1979, 1981), and Diamond and Hausman (1983) suggest a great deal of heterogeneity in household preferences. While these and other articles carefully model taste differences, virtually all applied microeconometric studies successfully employ demographic and related variables to "control" for differences in household behavior. This evidence, as well as casual observation, suggests a within-cohort distribution of time preference rates and, therefore, of differences in marginal propensities to consume goods and leisure. For the issue of savings and intragenerational redistribution, the important empirical question is whether transfer recipients within an age group have, on average greater marginal propensities to dissave out ot transfers than their contemporaries who are the source of such transfers. Since the intent of intragenerational transfers is presumably to improve the lot of the poor, attention has naturally focused on the correlation of spending propensities with levels of economic resources. Blinder (1975), using aggregate time series data finds that equalizing incomes is more likely to stimulate than retard savings. On the other hand, Menchik and David's (1983) study as well as that of Diamond and Hausman (1983) supports a view that marginal spending propensities decline with economic resources.

Even if the poor do not systematically differ from the rich in their intertemporal preferences, the poor may be liquidity constrained at the margin; i.e., they may face different shadow prices for intertemporal consumption than the rich. Other within-cohort differences in intertemporal relative prices could, however, be offsetting. For example, under a progressive income tax the poor face lower marginal taxes on capital income and, through this channel, lower relative prices of future consumption and leisure.

There is mounting evidence that liquidity constraints are binding for lower income households. Diamond (1977) and Diamond and Hausman (1983) stress the low levels of liquid wealth held by a significant fraction of the middle and low income population. Chapter 17 demonstrates that the timing of the receipt of lifetime resources significantly influences patterns of lifetime wealth accumulation. Hurd and Boskin (1984) present evidence that retirement probabilities depend on the level of tangible wealth. Hall and Mishkin (1982) test the Euler conditions of unconstrained intertemporal maximization and conclude that such a model is inappropriate for roughly 20 percent of US households. King and Dicks-Mireaux (1982) reach a similar conclusion using Canadian data. Hayashi (1982) focuses directly on the issue of liquidity constraints. His novel approach is to see whether the consumption function of presumably unconstrained households systematically differs from that of constrained households. Hayashi's answer is strongly in the affirmative. Over half of the households in his sample of the 1963–1964 Federal Reserve Survey of Financial Characteristics meet his definition of potentially liquidity constrained; this group reported receiving close to 40 percent less in disposable income than the unconstrained group. While this group as a whole appears to be consuming only about 3 percent less than they would in the absence of such constraints, for the 18- to 33-year-old constrained households, actual consumption is close to 10 percent less than predicted unconstrained consumption.

Lawrence (1983) examines the long-run general equilibrium savings impact of intragenerational transfers in a 55 period life cycle model with exogenous labor supply, a utility function that is additively separable and isoelastic in consumption, and a Cobb-Douglas production function. The model contains two sets of agents, low earners and high earners. The populations of each group are identical. The high earners have time preference rates of 1.5 percent while the low earners have rates of 6 percent. Thus low earners have larger marginal consumption propensities than high earners. In examining the impact of within-cohort transfers, Gilde considers cases in which the poor both are and are not liquidity constrained. Gilde finds that very significant levels of intragenerational redistribution have rather minor impacts on her economy's long-run stock of wealth. For example, a uniform lump sum transfer to each poor worker during each working year that raises that worker's lifetime resources by close to 25 percent and which is financed by a uniform lump sum tax on rich workers of the same generation during each working year reduces the stock of wealth by less than 4 percent in the case of no liquidity constraints and less than 7 percent when liquidity constraints are binding. The finding of rather small savings effects of redistributing to the poor appear to be quite robust in the face of reasonable variations in the intertemporal elasticity of substitution in consumption, but they are rather sensitive to the ratio of rich to poor workers.

The explanation for these small changes in the case of no liquidity constraints is simply that neither the differences in marginal consumption propensities across the two groups nor the size of the transfers are sufficiently large to have much impact on the economy's total wealth accumulation. In the case the poor are liquidity constrained, their marginal consumption propensities are unity, but the resource increment multiplying their unitary propensities is only the current year's transfers. For rich, unconstrained young workers making the transfers, their reduction in current consumption equals their much smaller marginal propensity to consume multiplied by the present value of the annual transfers, typically a much larger number than simply the current year payment.

7.8 Fiscal Policy and the Government's Implicit Provision of Insurance

Governments explicitly provide a variety of forms of insurance including unemployment insurance, disaster insurance, disability insurance, health insurance, etc. But they may also provide insurance in more subtle, unreported ways. The interpretation of a variety of fiscal policies as potentially implicit provision of insurance is illustrated by the following simple example. Imagine an economy in which each identical risk average agent owns a home worth $10,000 and faces an exogenous 10 percent probability of losing his home through fire. Assume the probability of having a fire is independent across households and that exactly 10 percent of all houses in the economy burn down each year. In such a setting a competitive insurance market, absent transaction costs, would fully insure each home-owner, and the fire insurance premium would be $1,000. Now suppose the government passes a law taxing each household $1,000. At the same time the government announces a relief program for households hit by fire which pays $10,000 to each affected household. Obviously, this fiscal policy replicates and would replace private provision of fire insurance. If the government tax is set at $500 rather than $1,000, and the relief payment is $5,000 rather than $10,000, private insurers would find a ready market for $5,000 of additional fire insurance at a competitive premium of $500. Rather than underinsuring the private sector, the government might overinsure by placing a $2,000 tax on each household and providing $20,000 in housing relief payments. In this case the private market would respond by selling insurance against *not* having a fire; i.e., the original full insurance equilibrium is restored by having each household pay a premium of $9,000 for a policy that pays zero in case of fire and $10,000 in case of no fire.

This example illustrates two points. First, fiscal policies could, except for their accounting labels, constitute insurance markets. Second, such implicit insurance provision may have no impact whatsoever on the economy because equivalent private insurance is available at the margin.

This result does not hinge on the assumption of no risk in the aggregate economy. Assume for example that with equal probability either 10 per-cent or 20 percent of all homes will burn. In this case the competitive market premium for $10,000 of fire protection is $1,500 with a $500 surcharge is 20 percent of the houses ignite and a $500 rebate if only 10 percent catch fire. The government could obviously replicate this outcome by imposing a $2,000 head tax in a bad year (20 percent of houses catch fire) and a $1,000 head tax in a good year (10 percent of houses catch fire). These funds would, of course, be used to finance the $10,000 relief pay-ments to fire victims. As in the case of no economy-wide risk, over or under provision of insurance by the government in these two states of nature will be fully offset by perfect private insurance markets to the extent such markets exist. It should be noted, of course, that while the govern-ment, like the private insurance market, can efficiently pool aggregate risks across the populace, neither it nor the private market can provide complete insurance against economy-wide risks.

In providing insurance in this example, the government need not even mention the word "fire" in its fiscal operations. Indeed, capital income taxation (with full loss offset) can potentially provide the type of fire insurance just described. To see the connection between this example and capital income taxation, think of this same economy as having two assets, A and B. A pays $10,000 if 20 percent of the houses, including one's own, burn down and nothing if only 10 percent of the houses burn down. B pays $11,000 if 10 percent of the houses burn, including one's own, and zero if 20 percent are destroyed. If the price of both assets is $1,000, then an agent who purchases each of these assets will end up with the same fire protection previously described.

Now assume the government places a 50 percent tax on the gross return to each asset. Hence, if 20 percent of the houses, including one's own, catch fire the government collects $5,000 from each affected agent on his return of asset A. Similarly, the government's receipts per affected agent when only 10 percent of the houses burn down, including one's own, equals $5,500. Next assume that these receipts are returned to each affected agent in the two states of nature in the form of a lump sum subsidy. If each agent responds to this fiscal policy by simply continuing to purchase the two assets, he will end up in exactly the same situation as if the government had not imposed the capital income tax cum lump sum subsidy; i.e., if 20 percent of the houses catch fire, each agent whose house burns is left with $8,000, corresponding to an after-tax return of $5,000, on asset A, plus the government subsidy of $5,000, less the $2,000 initial investment. If only 10 percent of the houses burn down, each agent whose house burns ends up with $9,000, representing $5,000 earned after tax on asset B plus a $5,500 government subsidy, less the $2,000 investment.

Obviously, there is nothing intrinsic in this example of capital income taxation as implicit insurance that necessarily relates to the number of fires. One could just as well consider assets A and B as paying off contingent upon some other event or set of events, such as the weather, changes in demand conditions, etc., that adversely affect some agents and benefit others. As Gordon (1981) emphasizes the assumption that the government's revenue is handed back to the agents in a lump sum is also not critical to the result that capital income taxation could effectively represent superfluous government risk pooling in capital and insurance markets that has no independent effect on the economy. Rather than returning the capital income tax revenues to the private sector, suppose the government spends these receipts on consumption. One can, for convenience, think of the government as handing the revenues out as a lump sum subsidy and then retrieving them through a separate lump sum tax to pay for its consumption. In this case the replacement of capital income taxation by lump sum taxation leaves the economy unaffected, since the private market, by assumption, steps in to provide the risk pooling that was previously arising under the capital income tax.

Varian (1980) and Eaton and Rosen (1980) demonstrate that wage taxation and subsidization, in the presence of earnings uncertainty, can analogously be viewed as government provision of human capital insurance. Social Security's provision of annuity, disability, and life insurance through its benefit structure is fairly obvious, and Social Security "taxes" could easily be relabeled insurance premia for the purchase of these policies. At first glance, however, many of Social Security's provisions appear at odds with efficient insurance provision. Social Security's earnings test for receipt of benefits is one example. Diamond and Mirrlees (1978), on the other hand, argue that this provision is plausibly a component of optimally configured government insurance against the risk of old age disability in cases where disability is very difficult to verify. Just as fire insurance pays off only to those experiencing a fire, the earnings test makes sure that only those who are not working (or are not working much), presumably the disabled, are the only elderly to receive benefits. Merton (1981) develops one of the more ingenious of these arguments that fiscal policy is a veil for government insurance. In his model the government combines both unfunded social security and a consumption tax to pool human capital risk and nonhuman capital risk optimally across young and old generations.[23]

In assessing the savings impact of these potential forms of government insurance provisions, the key question appears to be the extent to which the private market would otherwise provide each particular form of insurance. Since capital markets, at least in developed countries, appear to offer substantial risk sharing opportunities, it appears unlikely that eliminating capital income taxation would significantly alter the pooling of risky returns to nonhuman capital. This conclusion seems much less plausible in the case of human capital risk. Ignoring possible risk pooling within families and firms, there are no private markets in which one can sell off a portion of his or her future earnings and purchase that of others.

Assuming that the government is the sole effective insurer of human capital, the savings impact of this insurance is assessed by considering an alternative hypothetical state of nonhuman capital insurance. Articles by Leland (1968), Sandmo (1970), Miller (1974, 1976), Skinner (1983a, 1983b), and Barsky, Makiw, and Zeldes (1984) suggest that increased earnings uncertainty is likely to lead risk averse agents to reduce their current consumption and leisure holding the expected level of earnings constant.

In addition, earnings risk that is specifically related to the returns from training may inhibit human capital formation, leading to less training and more labor supply when young. This implies a steeper age consumption profile and flatter age earnings profile, on average, in the economy than would occur with earnings insurance. This suggests more savings in the form of nonhuman capital in the no insurance stochastic steady state. Estimates of the extent of such differences in long-run wealth stocks would contribute both to understanding how potential government earnings insurance as well as government-generated earnings uncertainty associated with random taxation (Weiss 1976; Stiglitz 1982; Eaton 1981; Skinner 1983b) affects savings.

There are now a number of articles dealing with saving behavior in the absence of private annuity insurance. Sheshinski and Weiss (1981) is the first analysis of the pure insurance effects of government pensions on national saving. They demonstrate that when private arrangements for pooling the uncertainty of longevity are unavailable, the government's provision of fully funded old age annuities alters household consumption possibilities. In their model in which agents have a bequest motive, the short-run saving impact of such provision is ambiguous. Hubbard (1983) points out that this provision will likely reduce national saving if agents have no bequest motive. The insurance provision reduces the precautionary demand for saving, inducing a higher rate of consumption. A fuller description of life cycle (zero bequest motive) economies, in the absence of annuity insurance, is presented in Eckstein, Eichenbaum, and Peled (1983) and Abel (1983). Both papers independently derived the stochastic steady-state properties of economies in which agents involuntarily leave bequests to their children. Abel also considers the effects of introducing a fully funded social security system in such an economy, his chief finding being that such a policy reduces savings. A related article by Kotlikoff, Shoven, and Spivak (chapter 5) compares the long-run stock of wealth prevailing in economies with and without perfect annuity insurance. In the latter type of economies there is partial insurance provided by family members; older family members selfishly trade title to their equally selfish children for support if they live longer than average. In contrast to the perfect insurance steady state, these authors find that wealth in the stochastic steady state can be significantly higher in an economy with imperfect family annuity insurance. Their estimates suggest that social security's provision of annuity insurance is potentially as important as its method of finance in reducing wealth accumulation.

7.9   Policy Announcements and Policy Perceptions: The Problem of Dynamic Inconsistency

Section 7.4 through 7.7 analyzed the impact of new tax policies assuming such policies take "rational" agents by surprise and that the public fully believes these policies will be implemented through time. The proposition that "rational" agents can systematically be "taken by surprise" sounds, and is, a contradiction in terms. Fischer (1979) nicely illustrates the problem of intertemporal change in government policy; he points out that rational agents who are cognizant of the government's future objectives will be able to predict future policy changes. Thus an announced program to stimulate saving may have the opposite effect on private behavior if the public conjectures that once additional wealth has been accumulated the government in power will find this a convenient source of explicit or implicit revenues. Stated differently, a current wealth tax would depress current consumption and leisure and raise saving if households believe such a tax will not be imposed again in the future. The alternative perception of continued future wealth taxes translates into very high implicit present prices of future consumption and leisure and leads household to substitute toward current consumption and leisure.

Of course the private sector may be incapable of accurately predicting future fiscal policy. If such were the case, one would expect (especially in a neoclassical setting with well-functioning capital markets) the private sector to take steps to self-insure against changes in government fiscal policy, in particular against inter and intragenerational redistribution.

Indeed, if the economy consisted of a large number of households with Barro-type intertemporal preferences, equation (14), these families could conceivably write binding contracts to hedge themselves through eternity against intramarginal redistribution. If one further assumed that all such families were interlinked through marital ties, they could conceivably share the same altruistic objective function. In this case they would fully inter-nalize the government's budget constraint and treat all government taxes as lump sum levies no matter how they were levied. Thus the government would be powerless to alter the set of marginal prices entering household budgets. Finally, if this household sector viewed government consumption as a perfect substitute for private consumption, changes in government consumption would also have no impact on the economy. In such a hypo-thetical economy the government's fiscal policy has no influence what-soever on national saving.

This example and the prior discussion is obviously extreme, but it highlights the fact that most neoclassical studies of savings and taxation appear implicitly to assume away the existence of particular insurance markets and/or the ability of otherwise rational agents to learn from the past in considering the government's impact on their future.

7.10   Concluding Comments

Economics is most exciting when it challenges conventional views; it is ultimately most persuasive in relating theory to fact when the theory is based on fundamental notions of optimization, and it is most important when it addresses macro-relationships. Recent neoclassical analyses of taxation and earnings are exciting, persuasive, and important. In contrast to conventional notions, properly designed fiscal policy can have clear and powerful savings affects in most neoclassical models. Efficacious application of such policies appears as much a question of choice and timing of changes in fiscal instruments as it is a question of exact values of preference parameters. In addition, the extent of market and family credit and insurance arrangements is critical for determining the savings impact of policy; fiscal instruments may, themselves, constitute government insurance provision. Alternatively, frequent, unexpected changes in these instruments may be a major source of private uncertainty.

The findings of recent research provide important lessons for the conduct of fiscal policy. First, this research warns that official reporting of fiscal policy can be highly misleading, with economic deficits reported as surpluses and effective marginal subsidization officially reported as positive taxation. Second, in the presence of certain policy instruments, changes in other instruments can have effects exactly the opposite to that intended and normally presumed (e.g., raising capital income tax rates might stimulate savings in the presence of 100 percent expensing). Third, short-run impacts of fiscal policy may be exactly the opposite of long-run impacts, suggesting that policy assessment based only on current outcomes may be highly misleading. Fourth, although the precise amount of "crowding out" associated with economic deficits remains unresolved, the potential major reductions in national wealth associated with explicit and implicit economic deficits make such policies very risky gambles for future generations. Fifth, from the perspective of neoclassical models, frequent changes in policy instruments appear undesirable; once the private sector begins to anticipate fiscal revisions, it will attempt to insure against such changes, reducing the effectiveness of policy, if not reversing the direction of its intended impact. Finally, both the insurance and risk-generating properties of fiscal policy are important, if not primary considerations in policy design.

As in other fields of economics, theoretical advances in the analysis of taxation and savings have outpaced the acquisition of data of sufficient detail to discriminate among theories. Resolution of questions as basic as the burden of the debt turns on quite subtle types of behavior, such as the extent of mutual caring within families, that will require new data to fully discern. Private beliefs about precise future government policies, while difficult to ascertain, are crucial determinants of current incentives to work and save. Such beliefs need to be identified as part of any empirical assessment of the impact of particular fiscal measures. There are other deeper questions that will make savings and taxation an exciting field for years to come. The most fundamental question is surely the applicability of the neoclassical paradigm to actual household savings behavior. There is as yet no convincing empirical evidence and certainly no professional consensus that households make saving decisions in accordance with the dictates of neoclassical optimization. The assumption of continuous equilibrium, particularly in labor markets, and the extensive information processing requirements of certainty as well as uncertainty models are two characteristics of neoclassical models that raise frequent objections. These and other concerns about the neoclassical framework recommend caution both in assessing the extensive recent research in neoclassical savings and in relying on these findings in the actual setting of fiscal policy.

Notes

The editors provided extensive and extremely valuable comments on each of several drafts of this article. I am also indebted to Stanley Fischer, Alan Auerbach, Micheal Boskin, David Bradford, Christophe Chamley, Mervyn King. Thorsten Persson, James Poterba, John Shoven, and Lawrence Summers for their very careful reviews and helpful comments. John Musgrave provided revised data from the BEA for which I am most grateful. Andrew Myers and Linus Yamane provided excellent research assistance.

1. This is strictly true only in partial equilibrium, i.e., holding pretax factor returns and producer prices constant.

2. MaCallum (1984) demonstrates that the government's budget constraint holds under a weaker condition than that assumed here. In particular the constraint holds even if debt indefinitely grows at a faster rate than the economy, provided that rate is less than the long-run real return to capital.

3. John Musgrave provided the BEA data used in these calculations. Imputed rent is defined here as depreciation (estimated by the BEA) plus beginning of year

assets, measured in current dollars, times the average annualized three month treasury bill rate less the annual percentage change in the Consumer Price Index.

4. David and Scadding (1974) suggest that the private sector may use "taxes," as defined and reported by the National Income and Product account, to measure current government consumption. In this case the gross private saving rate equals the perceived gross national saving rate, and its constancy, assuming a roughly stable economic environment as well as stable preferences, suggests that perceived government consumption substitutes perfectly and intramarginally for private consumption. As Boskin (1978) points out, however, "ultrarational" households presumably take account of the depreciation of the economy's physical capital in making economic choices. Table 7.1 indicates that the net national saving rate, which accounts for depreciation, has been anything but constant since 1950.

5. This requires that each trading country have positive net wealth. David Bradford made this observation in a conversation with the author.

6. The decision to label prospective expenditures "official liabilities" has real effects to the extent that it alters the probability that such expenditures will be made. While the default risk may be smaller for official than for unofficial, implicit liabilities, the real return to official liabilities may still be highly risky. In the United States, for example, official commitments to future nominal expenditures do not correspond to commitments to future real expenditures. During the 1970s the US federal government accrued $365.5 billion, measured in 1980 dollars, in real capital gains on its official liabilities while never missing a nominal principal or interest payment. This default on the real value of official liabilities through inflation is documented in the *1982 Economic Report of the President*, ch. 5.

7. The government, in this case, "owns" all wealth and invests its wealth in the private sector each period either directly through government firms or indirectly through government loans to private firms and individuals. For neutrality, the allocation of government direct and indirect investment must correspond to what would otherwise have arisen in the absence of the "surplus." In this example the government effectively acts like the private sector's bank, since private sector wealth is simply funneled through the government's hands and invested back in the economy. The "taxes," $\bar{\bar{T}}_t$, are, in effect, loans to the government, and the "spending," E_t, represents repayment of principal plus interest. Just as positive "taxes" may constitute private loans to the government, negative "taxes" may be equivalent to government loans to the private sector. For example, accelerated depreciation allowances and other investment incentives at the early stages of an investment prospect, coupled with positive taxation of investment returns at later stages, can, apart from their impact on marginal incentives, be viewed as government loans to the private sector. The repayment of these "loans" is paid in the form of "capital income taxes."

8. For example, a household's welfare and Social Security benefit payments, before any reduction for earnings, are treated as lump sum tax credits; and the schedule of potential losses of these benefits because of labor earnings is added to other marginal labor tax and subsidy schedules facing the household (more precisely

specific household members) in year t to produce a total net labor earnings tax schedule. This schedule is applied to household j's actual earnings to calculate total taxes on labor earnings in year t by household j. Similarly, the government's year t payments of interest and principal on net official debt held by household j are subtracted from other net intramarginal taxes to determine household j's total net lump sum tax in year t. Effective (net) capital income tax rate schedules confronting each household in each future year are determined by comparing before-tax returns earned on a household's marginal investment with the after-tax (including corporate and personal tax) return received by that household (Auerbach and Jorgenson 1980).

9. For most fiscal programs the relationship between their provisions and these fundamental policy instruments is easily discerned. For other policies the connection is extremely subtle. Section 7.6, for example, describes how government investment incentives redistribute resources from older to younger cohorts not through the explicit collection and transfer of resources but by lowering stock market values. Another example, pointed out by Boskin (1982), are government regulations governing the characteristics of particular commodities; a rule that mandates automobile seat belts in new cars can effectively be equivalent to the government's levying a tax on the purchase of each automobile and spending (consuming) these revenues on safety belts for each new automobile.

10. This statement and the subsequent discussion ignore differential rates of taxation of the same factor across industries and assume constant pretax factor returns and producer prices.

11. Substituting for $\sum_{t=0}^{\infty} [G_t/(1 + r_t)]$ from (9) into (10) gives the private sector's budget constraint with quantities multiplied by before-tax prices.

12. Note that in the case of a capital income tax, τ_r, the present value of revenues is $\tau_r r(E_1 - C_1)/(1 + r)$, where $E_1 - C_1$ is first period saving, and $r(E_1 - C_1)$ is capital income in period 2. The household budget constraint, $C_1^{**} = C_2^{**}/1 + r$. In figure 7.2, C_2^{**} equals the vertical distance BC_1^{**}, and the slope of line 2, $1 + r$, divided into the length BC_1^{**} equals the horizontal distance $E_1 - G_1 - C_1^{**}$, i.e., $E_1 - G_1 - C_1^{**} = C_2^{**}/1 + r$. Hence the distance G_1 in the diagram measures the present value of tax receipts under either lump sum or capital income taxation.

13. This equation for national wealth is unaffected by manipulation in government accounting; for example, if the government chooses "to run a larger surplus" by levying a lump sum tax of L_1, in period 1, which is returned with interest as a lump sum rebate, L_2, in period 2, then W_g and W_{p1}, will respectively increase and decrease by L_1, leaving national wealth, W, unchanged.

14. The assumption that the policy is enacted at time $t + 1$ rather than t is made to simplify the discussion. If the policy change is enacted at time t, the outcome is the same except the government must raise its capital income tax rate after t to reflect the reduced accumulation of the period t young.

15. According to (11), in partial equilibrium (i.e., holding the r_t's constant), the government can finance a temporary increase (decrease) in its consumption by a

future decrease (increase) in its consumption with no necessary change in private consumption or leisure.

16. The capital income tax component of the income tax also involves an element of lump sum taxation since it taxes, in part, the immediate return on existing wealth, which is obviously predetermined (Chamley 1981).

17. Section 7.5. This crowding in of capital in the consumption tax case is consistent with a reduced capital-labor ratio because labor supply rises by a larger percentage than capital.

18. To see this, note that under the stated assumptions and ignoring, for simplicity, productivity growth, steady-state private consumption, C, is proportional to the present value of resources over the infinite horizon, R. Thus we can write $C = \theta R$. The proportional factor θ equals $r/1 + r$, where r is the steady-state interest rate. This follows from the infinite horizon budget constraint $\sum_{t=0}^{\infty} C(1 + r)^{-t} = \sum_{t=0}^{\infty} \theta R(1 + r)^{-t} = R$, where C is not indexed by time because of the assumed steady state. Let ΔG be the permanent increase in government consumption. Then, since consumption or wage taxation is equivalent to lump sum taxation in this steady state, the change in private consumption, ΔC, equals $-\theta T$, where T is the equivalent present value lump sum tax needed to finance the permanent stream ΔG, i.e.:

$$T = \sum_{t=0}^{\infty} \Delta G(1 + r)^{-t} = \Delta G(1 + r)/r.$$

Hence, $\Delta C = -\theta T = -r/(1 + r)T = \Delta G$, as asserted.

19. A more precise explanation of the redistribution to young and future generations is that they gain the government's disbursement through time of the land rent tax revenues (since government consumption is assumed fixed) and the higher pretax wages that would arise in a closed economy from the increased capital accumulation induced by the land rent tax.

20. The government can be thought of as lending the investor τ dollars today, which is returned with interest in the future in the form of positive capital income taxes.

21. Lawrence Weiss suggested using this variable in a discussion with the author.

22. Robert Barro pointed this out in a 1979 conversation with the author.

23. In Merton's model elderly generations pay for their receipts of positive, but variable Social Security benefits by paying positive, but variable amounts of consumption tax. Since Social Security's benefits are proportional to earnings in Merton's model and variations in consumption tax receipts depend, in part, on the random return to capital, these fiscal instruments provide the elderly with a share of the economy's human capital risk and the young with a share of the economy's physical capital risk.

8   Economic Impact of Deficit Financing

The combination of large budget deficits among industrial countries and exceptionally high short-term real interest rates has rekindled interest in crowding out and its potential effects on saving, capital formation, and financial variables. This chapter describes how fiscal policies that result in economic deficits alter an economy's saving behavior. Depending on the economy's size and degree of openness, the changes in domestic savings arising from deficit financing can produce major changes in domestic investment, real interest rates, and real wage rates. Even if pretax returns to capital and labor are unaltered by deficits, because of international capital mobility and the equalizing of factor prices through trade, economic deficits can dramatically lower an economy's long-run welfare. This paper provides a quantitative sense of how burdensome the "burden of the debt" may be.

Section 8.1 briefly summarizes the basic neoclassical life cycle model that underlies most discussions of crowding out. This model provides a framework for defining economic deficits as a redistribution of resources across generations. A serious shortcoming in the deficit debate is the failure of many to distinguish economic deficits from what are recorded as deficits by government accountants. One objective of this paper is to clarify just how poorly conventional measures of deficits describe a government's underlying fiscal policy. This point is emphasized in various sections of the paper in three different ways. First, the actual operational steps taken by the government in transferring resources across generations are described without reference to such terms as "taxes," "spending," and "bond finance," since these labels have been applied quite arbitrarily to particular government receipts and payments. Describing economic deficit policy in

International Monetary Fund Staff Papers 31(3):549–80 (September 1984). © Reprinted with permission.

accounting-free terms suggests immediately that the critical operations—the receipts from and payments to particular generations—involved in economic deficit financing can, in many circumstances, be equally well conducted by the government under the titles "taxation," "spending," and "net sale of bonds." Second, it is shown how a government, armed with a clever accountant, could radically change the reporting of official government debt with potentially no change whatsoever in real economic debt policy. Third, it is illustrated that the quantitative impacts of unreported economic deficits can far exceed those that eventuate in very large reported official deficits.

Section 8.2 discusses crowding out as a dynamic process whose dimensions cannot be reliably inferred from short-run responses to policy changes. While crowding out, as defined here, refers to a reduction in national wealth accumulation, a second concept, typically referred to as "financial crowding out," is often advanced as the causal link between current US deficits and high short-run interest rates. Much of the concern with financial crowding out ultimately appears to revolve around the actual transaction of selling bonds as opposed to concern with the government's underlying real policy. Surely, the argument goes, a government's sale of bonds, regardless of its use of the proceeds, raises the total supply of bonds on the market. The greater supply of bonds, according to this view, means a lower bond price, that is, a higher interest rate, which reduces (crowds out) the private supply of bonds (private borrowing).

This line of argument ignores the fact that if the course of government policy, including monetary policy, is held fixed, the demand for government bonds by the private sector is, over the range being considered, likely to be highly elastic; in the United States alone, private holdings of real wealth exceed $12 trillion. Suppose the US government sought to borrow $12 trillion tomorrow and could promise to its lenders *with absolute certainty* the return of this principal plus the capital income that would otherwise have been earned. For the private sector, this purchase of bonds simply represents swapping one portfolio of assets for an identical portfolio. Ignoring transactions costs, the private sector should be perfectly indifferent to such a policy and be perfectly elastic with respect to swapping its real assets for identical real government claims. The point here is that the magnitude of a government's gross financial transactions may have nothing at all to do with its real policy, and it is the real policy of government that should ultimately influence market clearing prices, including interest rates. Economic deficits that ultimately crowd out a significant fraction of an economy's real wealth may involve little or no increase in short-term real interest rates, although they produce potentially sizable increases in long-term interest rates. While there are channels by which economic deficit policies can raise short rates, such channels have nothing to do with the volume of government transactions per se in bond markets.

Section 8.3 provides the reader with a sense of the potential quantitative impact of policies that crowd out saving and capital formation. The presentation here draws on simulation findings from a dynamic neoclassical life cycle model developed by Auerbach and Kotlikoff (1983b) and Auerbach, Kotlikoff, and Skinner (1983). The policies considered include economic deficits arising from short-term, medium-term, and longer-term tax cuts, economic deficits associated with unfunded government retirement programs, structural tax policy, and changes in investment incentives. The general message of this research is that economic deficits, if sufficiently large and maintained for a sufficient period of time, can greatly reduce a life cycle economy's long-run stock of wealth and level of welfare.

The discussion of investment incentives indicates that governments can generate major economic deficits and surpluses in very subtle and unreported ways. For investment incentives, economic deficits and surpluses are generated by altering equity values on the stock market. Recent public discussions of official deficits have totally ignored these and most other unofficial intergenerational transfer programs. For many countries, including the United States, unofficial and unreported postwar economic deficit policies appear to swamp policies that were reported as producing deficits when such policies are measured by their ability to crowd out savings and capital formation. The excessive focus on accounting deficits suggests that fiscal illusion, defined here as the misreading of fiscal policy, is widespread. Section 8.4 dramatizes the potential problem of fiscal illusion by describing what is ultimately an accounting policy that entirely eliminates official debt without necessarily altering real economic policy in the slightest.

The proper response to the problem of fiscal illusion is not to construct more elaborate accounting definitions of government liabilities. Revised bookkeeping of the type advocated by Buiter (1983) and Eisner and Pieper (1983) is open to the same type of manipulation and misreading as the current bookkeeping. The proper response involves describing fiscal policy in terms of its impact on underlying household intertemporal budget constraints. Since household budgets depend only on marginal prices and inframarginal endowments, describing fiscal policy in terms of its effects on these variables leaves policy descriptions and discussions free of accounting conventions. Obviously, characterizing the lifetime budgets of each household in an economy is infeasible; but for many policies, such as economic deficits, examination of a quite small subset of budget constraints is sufficient. For the analysis of economic deficits, which redistribute resources across generations, the household's age is central. The major features of a government's economic deficit policy could be illustrated by describing changes in the budgets of as few as three representative households, one young, one middle aged, and one elderly.

Section 8.5 discusses empirical attempts to test whether the life cycle assumptions needed to produce crowding out actually hold. For reasons that will become clear as the discussion proceeds, distinguishing life cycle from alternative forms of economic behavior is a subtle enterprise. Direct tests of the hypothesis requires either cohort-specific time-series data or particular types of cross-sectional data covering extended families. No such data, at least for the industrial countries, are available; in its absence, economists have used the available data to conduct indirect tests of life cycle behavior, the results of which are best described as inconclusive.

Much of this paper adopts the neoclassical assumption that households optimally choose consumption and leisure over their lifetimes and have access to capital markets that permit both borrowing and lending. Section 8.6 discusses how certain conclusions about deficit financing are altered by dropping the assumption that all households can freely borrow at the margin. Under the assumption that the great majority of young and middle-aged households are liquidity constrained at the margin, traditional accounting definitions of deficits represent somewhat better indicators of underlying economic deficits. The assumption of widespread liquidity constraints appears, however, at odds with some broad features of at least US time-series data. In addition, empirical analysis of US consumption and income data suggest that, at most, a small minority of US households faces such constraints.

The final section summarizes the paper and emphasizes the very considerable downside risks of running sizable economic deficits.

8.1   The Life Cycle Model

Standard Neoclassical Framework for Analysis of Deficit Policy

Resources are generally scarce both at a point in time and over time; hence, any positive (negative) net transfer made to older generations must typically be paid for by negative (positive) net transfers from younger or future generations. Economic deficits, as defined here, are government policies that redistribute resources from younger to older generations. This definition of economic deficits, as intergenerational transfer policies, may seem odd to those accustomed to viewing deficits as the excess of "spending" over "taxes." However, as is spelled out below, official definitions of "spending," "taxes," and "deficits" are quite arbitrary and provide little basis for a systematic discussion of government policy. To the extent that officially reported deficits raise concerns about crowding out of saving and investment, such official deficits must be associated with fundamental government policy changes. While redistribution among generations is only one of several fiscal policies, such redistribution has historically been the basis for concerns about deficit financing, and properly provides the focus for this discussion.

The life cycle model, developed by Modigliani and Brumberg (1954) and Ando and Modigliani (1963), provides strong predictions about the saving impact of intergenerational transfers. The life cycle model describes the behavior of economies in which households optimally choose how much to save and how much to work over their lifetimes. These decisions are constrained by lifetime budgets that restrict households from spending more (in present value) on consumption goods than they earn (in present value) in the labor market. In the strict version of the model considered here, households are assumed neither to make net transfers to nor to receive net transfers from an older or younger relative, with the exception of supporting young children. This feature of intergenerational selfishness is critically important for the proposition that economic deficits alter national saving.

Since each generation in the selfish life cycle model is basically out for itself, each generation consumes any net transfers that come its way, even if these resources are extracted by the government from their own (adult) children. The fact that net government transfers are consumed by generations receiving them does not, by itself imply any change in national saving. Consider, for example, a net transfer from the current young to the current old. In principle, the increased consumption of the old arising from this transfer could be matched dollar for dollar by the reduced consumption of the young; that is, the marginal propensities to consume of the young and the old could be the same. Such equivalence of marginal consumption propensities across age groups is not, however, consistent with optimizing life cycle saving behavior. According to the life cycle model, the marginal propensity to consume is an increasing function of age. To understand this key proposition, take the case of selfish life cycle individuals with one remaining year of life. Such individuals will exhaust all their remaining resources in their final year of life and, hence, have a marginal propensity to consume (calibrated on an annual basis) that equals unity. Next, consider the second oldest age group with two remaining years of life. Since this age group is concerned with next year's consumption, as well as this year's, it will allocate a fraction of any additional resources to increasing next year's consumption and consume the remaining fraction this year. Hence, its marginal propensity to consume is less than unity. In the simplest version of the life cycle model, the marginal consumption propensity equals one divided by the number of remaining years of life. For the second oldest generation, the marginal consumption propensity, in this case, is one-half.

In the life cycle model, the fact that older generations consume, in the current period, a greater fraction of transfers than do younger generations means that redistribution from younger to older age groups increases total current private consumption and reduces national saving. Stated differently, a dollar transferred from a younger to an older household increases the older household's consumption by an amount that exceeds, in absolute value, the reduction in consumption of the younger household. If the policy of transferring from the current young to the current old is permanent, that is, it occurs each period, the economy's consumption level each period will be greater relative to that which would occur if the policy were immediately halted. As a consequence, a permanent policy of transferring from the young to the old has a permanent depressing effect on saving. Note that a real-world policy of permanently shifting from taxes levied primarily on the elderly to taxes levied primarily on the young constitutes exactly this type of economic deficit.

Intergenerational Transfers to the Living from the Unborn

Intergenerational transfers need not occur only among the living. If it so chooses, the government can redistribute resources to all living generations at the expense of future generations. Since generations that are not yet born have marginal propensities to consume that equal zero, while all living life cycle generations have positive propensities, such a policy obviously raises current consumption and lowers current saving.

At first glance it might appear impossible to redistribute in the current period from future generations to current generations, since future generations are not yet alive. Operationally, this redistribution is conducted in the following manner. First, the government acquires resources from current generations in a manner that does not alter their consumption or welfare. Next, the government turns around and hands these resources back to the same current generations, leading them to increase their current consumption. This leaves current generations better off and, as will be immediately apparent, future generations worse off. Ignoring for the moment incentive effects and liquidity constraints, the government can acquire some, and potentially all, of the economy's real wealth without altering any living household's current consumption if it promises to return these resources in the future with interest. Such a policy leaves private intertemporal budgets unchanged, giving households no reason, under the stated assumptions, to alter their current consumption. In the real world, governments can gain access to real resources by issuing what they call "official bonds," by levying what they call "taxes," by cutting what they call "spending," and/or by creating base money that is used to purchase real resources. The government's future return (inclusive of interest) of the resources it currently acquires from the private sector can take the form of households receiving payments labeled by the government "return of interest plus principal on official government debt," "government transfer payments," or "tax reductions." Reducing future levels of money creation is another mechanism by which the return of the initial resource receipt can be effected. In this case, the lower rate of money creation means higher private real money balances that can be traded for more real resources.

Once the government gets possession of current real resources, it can immediately distribute them to current generations, thus expanding their lifetime budgets and, accordingly, raising their current consumption. As described thus far, the transaction involves (1) the government's taking from the private sector resources which it promises to return and does return (with interest) in the future, and (2) immediately transferring to the private sector these current resources, which it treats as a net addition to lifetime income. The impact of this policy is thus greater current consumption and less current national saving. In addition, since the real resources needed by the government to adhere to its future repayment commitments to initial generations are taken (in the future) from future generations, the policy just described involves a real resource transfer from future to current generations.

The description of this economic deficit policy is not yet complete; one needs to specify precisely which future generations will pay the bill for the welfare improvement of current generations. The government can delay, up to a limit, imposing an added burden on future generations by rolling over repayment commitments. It collects resources to meet its previous repayment commitments while simultaneously promising additional future repayments to compensate households who are surrendering these current resources. While such a policy is feasible in the short run, it cannot be sustained indefinitely. Ultimately, the government has to start extracting, in present value, net resources from successive generations to meet at least the interest component (adjusted for growth) of the repayment commitments.

One option before the government is to extract from a subset of future generations sufficient resources to retire completely its repayment commitments. The economy will, after a transition period, return to the same steady-state growth path and level of real wealth that it would have experienced in the absence of the transitory economic deficit. Alternatively, the government may choose to maintain a constant (adjusted for growth) stock of outstanding promises to future repayments through a rollover policy and simply cover interest payments (adjusted for growth). In this case, the economy's growth path and level of wealth are permanently altered. Each future generation living under this long-run fiscal regime is forced by the government to give up resources to meet these interest payments; that is, since the principal component of the stock of promises is never retired, there will always be an interest burden on future generations and a corresponding reduction in their consumption that represents part of the payment for the increased consumption of initial-recipient generations. Since a part of the burden of the initial resource transfer will always be paid by generations as yet unborn, in the form of reduced consumption, at any time the initial positive increase in consumption of early-recipient generations will not yet have been fully offset by reduced consumption of ensuing generations. As a consequence, a transfer policy that involves perpetual outstanding government repayment promises means a perpetually smaller stock of real wealth. In closed economies where investment equals domestic saving, this implies a smaller capital stock as well as a smaller capital-labor ratio than would otherwise have prevailed. Reductions in capital-labor ratios, in turn, imply lower (pretax) real wage rates and higher (pretax) real returns to capital. Such general equilibrium changes in factor returns means reductions in the standards of living of future generations. These reductions are in addition to their welfare loss from the burden of meeting interest payments.

Intergenerational Altruism: The Competing Neoclassical Model

The implications of intergenerational transfers are very different in altruistic models in which each generation cares about the welfare of its children. As Barro (1974) points out, if such redistribution is already being conducted within families, economic deficits may simply substitute for private intergenerational redistribution, with no net impact on the economy. Ignoring the incentive effects of economic deficits and assuming identical families, Barro's intergenerational altruistic households respond to the receipt of net government resource transfers by maintaining their level of consumption and passing the full amount of these receipts to successive generations of descendants. These additional private transfers provide future relatives with the resources needed to meet the government's eventual offsetting of net transfers. Private behavior can also offset negative government transfers to older generations. The generations making these payments maintain their consumption levels and pass fewer resources to future generations. This leaves the position of future generations unchanged, since the initial negative government transfers imply eventual positive government transfers to future generations. Since the behavior of altruistic families completely offsets public redistribution, economic deficits per se have no impact in such economies; in particular, apart from possibly altering household saving and work incentives and redistributing among altruistic households, there is no change in the consumption or labor supply of any generation and, therefore, no change in the economy's level of output or its accumulation of wealth over time.

8.2 The Crowding-Out Process

The standard neoclassical definition of crowding out is a reduction in national (private plus public) wealth accumulation that arises from government policies. Accumulated national wealth is simply the sum of past levels of net national saving, which, in turn, corresponds to the difference between net national product and national consumption. If government policy succeeds in reducing national wealth, it must also reduce net national saving in some, if not all, periods during which the policy is in place. A decline in net national saving in any particular year requires an increase in national consumption, holding national product fixed; a decline in national product, holding national consumption fixed; or a simultaneous change in national product and consumption that lowers their difference.

A government-induced reduction in saving in a particular year will automatically lower the amount of national wealth available in the following year. Since national product includes capital income earned on national wealth, a decline in national saving this year means less capital income next year. The decline in next year's capital income implies a change in next year's national saving unless labor income or national consumption changes by precisely the amounts required to leave national saving unchanged. The direct link between current saving and future output and the influence of future output on future saving indicates that crowding out is a dynamic process whose impact cannot be fully discerned by considering only short-term changes in saving.

Another aspect of the dynamics of crowding out is that short-term policy changes almost invariably require adjustments in future policies. The connection between current and future policies arises from the requirement that the government's short-run, medium-run, and long-run policies be mutually compatible. An example of incompatible policy is permanently cutting tax rates and, thereby, reducing the government's acquisition of real resources from the private sector, while significantly and permanently raising government consumption. Such a policy involves the government's increasing its absorption of resources through time with no corresponding reduction in the absorption of resources by the private sector. Since the economy's possibility frontier is limited both at a point in time and through time, such a policy is generally infeasible. Current cuts in tax rates require future increases in tax rates, changes in the time path of government consumption, or changes in the government's creation of base money (its use of "printing press" financing).

The extent of crowding out associated with any short-term policy depends critically on the nature and timing of future policy adjustments. Thus, the time path of crowding out from a temporary cut in income tax rates will be quite different if the tax cut lasts 1 year, 5 years, or 20 years; it will be different still if these changes are accompanied by changes in the time path of government consumption, changes in the time path of money creation, or changes in the time path of other tax rates. This sensitivity to the precise path of accommodating policy applies to the entire time path of crowding out, that is, the short and medium run as well as the long run. As described below, policies that produce long-run crowding out may involve short-run crowding in. "Short run," in this case, usually means several years, but could exceed a decade. The fact that a policy that ultimately lowers savings could increase saving in the short run suggests the need for considerable caution in assessing policies based on short-run outcomes.

Since the limitations on feasible intertemporal government policies necessarily require adjusting future policy instruments in response to changes in current instruments, one cannot meaningfully discuss the impact of deficits per se. Rather, one is obliged to compare the effects of fully specified alternative time paths of mutually feasible policies. Given this restriction, one is, however, free to concentrate on those sets of feasible policy paths that involve significant intergenerational redistribution. To isolate crowding out resulting from economic deficits from crowding out associated with changes in the time path of government consumption, the following discussion is restricted to feasible intertemporal policies that hold constant the time path of government consumption. Since the central concern of this analysis of deficits is saving as opposed to inflation, the discussion ignores the use of money creation as a fiscal instrument for redistribution across generations.

8.3 Simulation Analysis of Economic Deficits

In the life cycle model, each household makes independent choices, but the combined behavior of more than 70 contemporaneous, living adult cohorts enters into the determination of the general equilibrium transition path of a life cycle economy. The economy's transition path also depends on the future decisions of generations not yet in existence; today's generations base current economic choices partly on information about future wages and interest rates. These future prices are determined not only by the saving and labor supply decisions of those currently alive but also by the saving and labor supply behavior of succeeding generations; the expectations of today's 20-year-olds about wage rates when they reach 30 are partly influenced by their expectations of the labor supply of 20-year-olds 10 years from now whose labor supply, in turn, depends on expectations of the labor supply of 20-year-olds 20 years from now, and on and on.

The complexity of the multicohort life cycle model, as well as its extensive, if not unlimited, data requirements, has led many economists to simulate rather than empirically estimate the effects of government policy in nonaltruistic neoclassical environments. Simulation analysis of steady- (or stationary-) state predictions of life cycle economies dates from Ando and Modigliani (1963), Tobin (1967), and Atkinson (1971). Papers by Tobin and Dolde (1971, 1983), Sheshinski (1978), and chapter 12 of this book simulate the impact of social security on steady-state labor supply and savings. Summers (1981b) presents a steady-state simulation analysis of other government fiscal policies, in particular, structural tax policy. Miller and Upton (1974) and Summers (1981a) simulate effects of selected government policies on the growth path of life cycle economies under the assumption of myopic expectations.

In a series of articles, Auerbach and Kotlikoff (1982, 1983a, 1983b) and Auerbach, Kotlikoff, and Skinner (1983) extended this research by developing a perfect foresight, general equilibrium life cycle simulation model. "Perfect foresight" in this context means that households make economic choices based on common projections of future wages, interest rates, and tax rates, and these decisions, in the aggregate, produce equilibrium time paths of these variables equal to those projected. The model incorporates variable labor supply and a wide range of fiscal instruments, including investment incentives, progressive taxes, and social security. Its chief contribution, however, is determining the equilibrium transition path generated by fiscal policies.

Simulation analysis is certainly no substitute for empirical research; rather, it provides a methodology for exploring the full implications of empirical findings. Unfortunately, there is no large-scale neoclassical econometric model that can be simulated to estimate the general equilibrium savings impact of policy. The computer simulation model used here incorporates constant elasticity of substitution (CES) utility and production functions, which are frequently posited in empirical studies. In addition, the parameterization of the model is based on empirical findings.

The CES utility function of consumption, C, and leisure, l, underlying the life cycle simulation results is presented as

$$U = \sum_{a=1}^{55} [1/(1 + \delta)]^{a-1}[\mu C_a^{(1-1/\rho)} + (1 - \mu)l_a^{(1-1/\rho)}]^{(1-\gamma)/(1-1/\rho)}.$$

In the equation, δ is the time preference rate, ρ is the "static" elasticity of substitution between consumption and leisure at each age a, and γ is the intertemporal elasticity of substitution between consumption and leisure at different ages. The reciprocal of γ equals the coefficient of relative risk aversion. Baseline parameter values for δ, γ, ρ, and σ, the elasticity of substitution of capital for labor in the production function, are 0.015, 0.25, 0.8, and 1. These figures are midrange estimates based on a variety of empirical studies; see, for example, Auerbach, Kotlikoff, and Skinner (1983).

The simulated economy has an initial steady-state capital-output ratio of 3.7, a capital-labor ratio of 5, a pretax wage normalized to 1, a 6.7 percent pretax real interest rate, a 3.7 percent net national saving rate, and a 15 percent proportional tax on all income. Since, in the initial steady state there are no transfer programs conducted either through official or unofficial mechanisms, receipts from the 15 percent income tax are used solely to finance government consumption.

Simulations of three economic deficit policies that would produce increases in officially recorded liabilities according to conventional accounting procedures are presented in table 8.1. In each simulation, the time path of government consumption per capita is held fixed, and the income tax rate is temporarily reduced from 15 percent to 10 percent. The three

Table 8.1

Crowding out under alternative deficit policies

Year	S/Y[a]	τ_y[d]	W[c]	r[d]	L[e]	K[f]
Initial steady state	0.037	0.150	1.000	0.067	19.10	95.1
One-year income tax reduction						
1	0.049	0.100	0.991	0.069	19.80	95.1
2	0.034	0.152	1.002	0.067	19.04	95.4
3	0.034	0.152	1.001	0.067	19.04	95.3
4	0.035	0.152	1.001	0.067	19.04	95.3
5	0.035	0.152	1.001	0.067	19.04	95.3
10	0.036	0.153	1.000	0.067	19.05	94.9
30	0.037[g]	0.153	0.998	0.067	19.07	94.2
60	0.037[g]	0.153	0.997	0.068	19.08	93.9
90	0.037[g]	0.153	0.997	0.068	19.08	93.9
Final steady state	0.037[g]	0.153	0.997	0.068	19.08	93.9
Five-year income tax reduction						
1	0.046	0.100	0.992	0.069	19.76	95.1
2	0.045	0.100	0.992	0.068	19.74	95.3
3	0.044	0.100	0.993	0.068	19.73	95.6
4	0.043	0.100	0.994	0.068	19.71	95.8
5	0.026	0.161	1.006	0.066	18.83	95.9
10	0.028	0.161	1.002	0.067	18.87	94.6
30	0.032	0.162	0.992	0.069	18.96	91.3
60	0.036	0.163	0.987	0.070	19.02	89.9
90	0.036	0.163	0.987	0.070	19.02	89.7
Final steady state	0.036	0.163	0.987	0.070	19.02	89.7
Twenty-year income tax reduction						
1	0.034	0.100	0.994	0.068	19.58	95.1
2	0.033	0.100	0.994	0.068	19.56	95.0
3	0.031	0.100	0.994	0.068	19.55	94.9
4	0.030	0.100	0.994	0.068	19.53	94.8
5	0.029	0.100	0.993	0.068	19.51	94.6
10	0.023	0.100	0.991	0.068	19.45	93.3
30	−0.014	0.246	0.964	0.075	17.72	76.1
60	0.011	0.284	0.888	0.096	18.08	56.0
90	0.020	0.297	0.867	0.103	18.11	50.8
Final steady state	0.023	0.304	0.856	0.107	18.13	48.5

a. S = net saving rate; Y = net national product.

b. τ_y = income tax rate.

c. W = wage rate.

d. r = interest rate.

e. L = aggregate labor supply.

f. K = capital stock.

g. This saving rate is below that in the initial steady state to the fourth decimal.

simulations involve tax cuts lasting 1, 5, and 20 years. During the period that rates are lowered, the government's official debt is endogenous; in these years the government issues precisely the amount of debt needed to maintain its consumption, given the loss in receipts from the income tax, as well as to meet interest payments on previously issued debt. After the tax cut is terminated, the income tax rate becomes endogenous, while the per capita stock of official liabilities is held fixed. The income tax rate is chosen annually to provide the government with sufficient receipts to purchase its fixed level of per capita consumption and to meet interest payments adjusted for the amount of new debt that can be financed by population growth.

As indicated in table 8.1, the long-run income tax rates, τ_y, resulting from reducing income tax rates by one-third for 1, 5, and 20 years, are 15.3 percent, 16.3 percent, and 30.4 percent, respectively. The long-run reduction in per capita capital, K, is 1.3 percent for the 1-year tax cut, 5.7 percent for the 5-year tax cut, and 49.1 percent for the 20-year tax cut. Per capita labor supply, L, falls by a trivial amount in the 1-year and 5-year tax cuts, but by 5.1 percent for the 20-year tax cut.

The transition paths displayed in table 8.1 reveal a number of surprising and important features of crowding-out processes. First, the 1-year and 5-year tax cut policies exhibit *crowding in* prior to the year tax rates are increased. In the 1-year tax reduction, the simulated economy's saving rate rises by 32 percent in the first year of the transition. However, in the second year of this simulation, after taxes have been raised, the saving rate is 8 percent lower than its initial steady-state value. In contrast to the two shorter-term tax cuts, the 20-year tax cut exhibits immediate crowding out. The short-run differences in these simulations clearly reflect the predominance of substitution over income effects in the short-period tax cuts and the converse for the 20-year tax cut; in the 1-year tax cut, all but the oldest generation alive in the first year will face higher tax rates through the rest of their lives. Young generations will face the higher tax rate for such a long period that their budget possibilities and levels of welfare are actually reduced. While the income effects experienced by most current age groups from the change in the time path of tax rates are trivial, each age group has strong incentives to substitute future for current consumption and leisure in response to the very short-term rise in after-tax wage rates and returns to capital. The key lesson of these short tax cut simulations is that policies that inevitably crowd out saving and investment can look quite effective in promoting capital formation if one evaluates such policies using only the first few years of information.

A second point illustrated by table 8.1 is that crowding out is typically a slow and gradual process. While the 20-year tax cut reduces the capital stock (per capita) by almost half its initial value, the reduction during the first 10 years of the policy is only 1.9 percent. Indeed, most of the reduction in capital formation occurs after the first 30 years of the policy's enactment. The crowding-out process, once it begins, is also slow for the shorter-duration tax cuts. For economies of the type described in the simulation model, economic deficits can have a barely discernable impact on the economy in any particular year, although their cumulative impact is quite dramatic. A reasonable analogy is a slowly growing tumor that initially can barely be detected, and, once detected, may be misdiagnosed as benign. Indeed, the very dangerous tumor might conceivably be beneficial, in the short run, in mitigating other ailments.

Unlike a malignant tumor for which there are possible cures, there is no way to escape the long-run costs of short-run deficit financing. This is the third important lesson of these simulations and the standard life cycle intertemporal theory on which they are based. While one might wishfully think that, having crowded in capital through short-term tax cuts, one could adopt a painless policy for eliminating the accumulated debt (meeting repayment commitments), such is not the case. One cannot postpone indefinitely raising tax rates, and once these rates are raised, the stimulus to saving through substitution effects is reversed; in addition, the cross-generational income effects that are at the heart of the crowding-out process ultimately play a decisive role in reducing national saving. Consider those older initial households, who, in large part, escape (through death) the eventual tax increases; that is, they face higher taxes for a relatively short period. These elderly may delay consuming their increases in lifetime resources until tax rates are raised, but once these rates are raised, their planned increase in consumption from their expanded after-tax lifetime budgets proceeds pari passu.

It is also indicated in table 8.1 that the extent of crowding out is a nonlinear function of the duration of the tax cuts. The reduction in capital in the 20-year tax cut is 8.6 times that in the 5-year tax cut. This nonlinearity is not surprising given other well-understood nonlinear features of such economies. One example is the long-established proposition that tax distortions rise as the square of the tax rate. Note that the increase in the income tax rate under the 20-year deficit policy is 11.8 times that under the 5-year deficit policy. Hence, the inefficiency in the former economy's final steady state is considerably greater than that of the latter, and much of the response to the much greater tax distortion appears to take the form of considerably less saving.

The long-run welfare reduction associated with the 20-year tax cut policy is quite significant. Generations born in the new steady state experience a level of welfare that is 12 percent below that of generations in the initial steady state; the welfare reduction is measured as the fraction of lifetime resources one would need to take from a generation in the initial steady state to leave that generation with the new (lower) steady-state level of welfare. The size of the welfare loss inflicted on future generations is, perhaps, more easily understood by observing that the long-run after-tax wage falls by 14 percent, while the after-tax return to capital rises by less than 1 percent.

Note that the before-tax return to capital rises considerably, from 6.7 percent to 10.7 percent, but also quite slowly; the policy raises 30-year yields by less than 1 percentage point. Intuitively, the slow change in pretax yields, in this standard neoclassical growth model, arises because interest rates are set by pretax marginal returns to capital, which, in turn, depend on the ratio of the stock of capital to the economy's labor supply. While there is some short-term variation in labor supply, the capital stock is fixed in the immediate period of a policy change and, as is expected of stock variables, changes rather slowly through time.

Introducing costs of adjusting the representative firm's level of capital input (e.g., time and monetary costs of installing new equipment or putting up a new plant) breaks the tight connection between short-term interest rates and the marginal product of capital. If one models capital adjustment costs by positing that a firm's currently installed capital is useful in installing additional capital, then the amount of installed capital at a point in time is a quasi-fixed factor that earns inframarginal rents on its ability to install new capital. These inframarginal rents are reflected in the price of installed capital. If a firm is undergoing a policy of expanding its capital input, the market price (the stock market value for listed firms) of its installed capital will be high. Over time, as the installation proceeds, the market price will fall because less installation is required in the future, meaning smaller prospective rents from capital installation. If the firm is engaged in reducing its capital stock, the opposite circumstances hold with respect to the price of the firm's existing capital. In this case the price of its capital is low, but rises through time, reflecting the fact that there are fewer periods in the future during which a part of the firm's capital must be removed. In models with adjustment costs of this type (Lipton and Sachs 1980; Summers 1981a; Abel 1982; Auerbach and Kotlikoff 1982), initial-period interest rates equal that period's marginal product of capital plus the expected end-of-period capital gain or loss. Hence, this model frees up the tight linkage between interest rates and marginal products of capital. In the case of an economic deficit policy in which firms are reducing their capital intensity, these neoclassical adjustment-cost models produce short rates in excess of the short-term marginal productivity of capital, with the difference equal to expected end-of-period capital gains. Introducing very sizable adjustment costs within the Auerbach-Kotlikoff life cycle simulation model does indeed produce immediate increases in short rates in response to economic deficits; but the simulated short-rate increases, even with very sizable economic deficits, such as the 20-year tax cut policy shown in table 8.1, are less than a single percentage point. Based on these conventional models of neoclassical growth, it appears quite difficult to argue that even enormous economic deficits would be associated with dramatic increases in short rates.

Economic Deficits Arising from Unfunded Retirement Programs

A 20-year tax cut of the dimensions indicated may appear unrealistic and perhaps not worth worrying about. It is important, therefore, to know that an economy could arrive at the final steady state generated by the 20-year tax cut through a sequence of economic deficits; that is, one could envision a succession of governments enacting temporary tax cuts which, in toto, would produce the long-term reduction in capital and welfare illustrated in the 20-year tax cut simulation.

Another aspect of the 20-year tax cut simulation that might, at first glance, appear unrealistic is that over half of final steady-state tax revenues are used to service interest on the government's accumulated debt. While for most industrial countries the ratio of official interest payments to official government revenues is much smaller than one-half, there is nothing in the model that distinguishes official from unofficial debt. For most developed countries, unfunded retirement policies potentially represent their largest form of economic debt. If one chooses the "right" accounting procedures, one could easily arrive at an expanded definition of interest payments, such that redefined interest payments would total over half of reported tax revenues in most industrial nations.

Consider, as an example, the unfunded US social security system. While the US government chooses to label a worker's contributions to social security "taxes," it could just as well label such payments "loans." Similarly, the US government could label social security benefit payments "return of principal plus interest." Note that from the worker's point of view, social security "tax" payments and "benefit" receipts involve payments to the government when young and receipt of payments back when old. But making payments now and receiving payments back in the future is exactly what the worker experiences when he or she purchases a US treasury bill or bond. Hence, from the worker's point of view, social security "tax" contributions are, in most respects, equivalent to the purchase of a government liability. While the mean return and risk properties of invisible social security bonds may differ from those of official government bonds, such differences in risk properties provide no basis for labeling one set of payments "taxes" and the other set of payments "loans." [1] If the US government were to drop its current arbitrary definition of deficits and arbitrarily broaden it to include social security payroll "taxes," the government's 1983 deficit would increase by over $200 billion. If we also arbitrarily labeled benefit payments "principal plus interest," rather than "spending," the US budget would appear quite bloated with interest payments.

The next section explores more fully concerns about fiscal illusion arising under any particular arbitrary accounting definition of "taxes," "spending," and "deficits." Labeling particular payments or receipts one thing or another does not, of course, demonstrate anything; in particular, relabeling the receipts and payments of unfunded retirement programs does not indicate how such programs could alter the intergenerational distribution of resources. The assertion that unfunded retirement programs produce economic deficits, that is, redistribute toward early generations, rests on the following line of argument. Holding other government policies fixed, introducing an unfunded retirement program means there is an initial set of elderly and middle-aged generations who receive retirement benefits in excess of their own contributions plus interest. This increase in the welfare of initial old generations comes at the cost of lower welfare of young and future generations. In an unfunded retirement program, the rate of return paid on contributions into the system eventually equals the economy's growth rate. If the growth rate is less than the pretax market return to private saving, successive generations of workers end up paying contributions that exceed, in present value, their receipt of retirement benefits. Future generations are worse off as a consequence of being forced to participate in such a program, just as future generations are worse off under the conventional deficit policies described in table 8.1 as a consequence of being forced to meet interest payments on accumulated official debt. In addition, if factor returns are altered as a consequence of crowding out associated with unfunded retirement programs, these changes imply even further reductions in long-run welfare.

The simulation model can also be used to study economic debt arising from unfunded retirement programs. Starting from the initial steady state indicated in table 8.1, introducing an unfunded social security system that replaces 60 percent of lifetime earnings produces a 15.1 percent reduction in the long-run (per capita) capital stock, a 4.2 percent decline in the pretax wage, and an 11.8 percent rise in the pretax return to capital.

Note that the long-run crowding out of capital in this simulation of an unofficial economic debt policy is 2.7 times that arising under the 5-year tax cut policy shown in the table. Hence, in terms of its economic impact, unofficial and unreported economic deficits appear as important as, if not important than, many officially reported economic deficit policies.

Subtle Ways of Running Economic Deficits and Surpluses

Structural tax change provides another means by which governments can redistribute toward early generations. One example is a policy of switching from consumption to wage taxation. Such a policy shifts the tax burden from the current elderly, who are largely retired, to young and middle-aged workers as well as future generations. While these latter generations escape consumption taxation, the present value of the wage taxes exceeds the present value of the consumption tax payments they would otherwise have paid. Hence, their lifetime tax burden is increased by the policy. Except for the nature and timing of tax distortions, structural tax changes of this kind are quite similar to economic deficits arising from short-term tax cuts or those arising from unfunded government retirement programs. Each of these policies makes an initial set of generations better off at the expense of later generations.

The switch from consumption to wage taxation leads to a 13 percent long-run decline in the simulated economy's (per capita) capital stock for the time paths of government consumption assumed in table 8.1. This is well over twice the reduction in capital formation that arose from cutting income tax rates for 5 years by one-third.

Another subtle method by which governments run economic deficits and surpluses is by altering investment incentives. Investment incentives are defined here as tax provisions that discriminate in favor of newly produced capital. An example of such a policy is permitting the expensing of newly produced capital, while, at the same time, denying expensing for capital that was produced in the past. Expensing permits the purchaser of a new capital good to immediately deduct its acquisition cost. In the United States, investment incentives, including expensing and depreciation allowances but excluding the investment tax credit, are, in principle, available to previously produced (old) as well as newly produced (new) capital; effectively, however, old capital is, in large part, excluded by provisions that require a change in ownership of old capital for it to be offered the same depreciation and expensing tax treatment as new capital. In addition, a recapture tax must be paid on the difference between the sale price of the old capital and its adjusted tax basis. The US recapture tax for equipment is sufficiently steep to render turnover of old equipment unprofitable (Auerbach and Kotlikoff 1983). For plant, the gain in turning over old capital and taking advantage of investment incentives available to new capital is quite small; that is, old plant, like old equipment, is essentially excluded from new investment incentives.

The connection between these issues and economic deficits revolves around the pricing of old capital. Since each unit of old capital is at a tax disadvantage relative to a unit of new capital (for which investment incentives are available), its price must be less than that of a new unit of capital by exactly the present value difference in tax treatment. For example, if expensing is the investment incentive available to new capital, and the rate at which new capital can be expensed (immediately written off) is τ, then the price of old capital equals $(1 - \tau)$ times the price of new capital. If τ is 0.3, the price per unit of old capital is 70 percent of the per unit price of new capital. As τ increases, the tax advantage of expensing rises, and the relative price of old capital falls. A decline in the relative value of old capital implies capital losses and an equivalent reduction in real resources for the owners of such capital. While increases in capital income tax rates in the presence of investment incentives constitute an implicit tax on the owners of old capital, for individuals seeking to accumulate capital there is a corresponding gain; savers are now able to purchase new or old capital either directly or by buying stocks at a lower net price. The lower net acquisition price implies a higher effective after-tax rate of return. This ignores, however, the higher taxes that must be paid on the capital's future stream of returns. As described below, even if effective capital income tax rates remain unchanged or even rise, there are other channels through which the capital losses to early generations redound to the benefit of latter generations.

The capital losses incurred by owners of old capital, coupled with the gains to those acquiring additional capital, constitute intergenerational redistribution, in this case, from older to younger and future generations— that is, an economic surplus; in the life cycle model, older and middle-aged generations are primary holders of old capital at any point in time. Younger generations, as well as unborn generations, represent the principal current and future purchasers of capital. Hence, raising capital income tax rates in the presence of investment incentives redistributes from the old and from a large fraction of the middle-aged to their descendants. Alternatively, lowering capital income tax rates in the presence of investment incentives or reducing investment incentives in the presence of significant capital income tax rates constitutes a subtle mechanism for running sizable economic deficits.

Simulating the elimination of investment incentives in the model described above provides a sense of the potential impact of these unreported intergenerational transfers and of their importance relative to other economic debt policies. Starting in a steady state with the level of per capita government consumption shown in table 8.1, a proportional uniform tax on capital and labor income, and full expensing, the elimination of expensing leads to a 19 percent long-run decline in the economy's (per capita) capital stock. If only half of the purchases of new capital are initially permitted expensing, the elimination of the partial expensing provision lowers long-run (per capita) capital by 9.8 percent. These figures are quite sizable relative to the crowding out associated with the "official" debt policies of the table.

Investment incentives, like temporary tax cuts, involve changes in marginal saving and labor supply incentives. For certain changes in investment incentives, however, it is clear that intergenerational income effects are driving the results. Consider starting in a steady state with a 15 percent proportional income tax and full expensing. The marginal effective tax on capital income in such an economy is zero. While investors in capital must pay taxes at rate τ as its return, they receive an immediate subsidy of τ percent per dollar invested. This subsidy is received either directly in the form of the government's expensing subsidy or indirectly in the form of purchasing old capital at a cheaper price. This marginal subsidy exactly offsets in present value the marginal taxes paid on the return to the investment, leaving the effective tax on capital income equal to zero. Now, increasing the tax rate on the capital income component of total income raises both the initial investment subsidy and the future stream of tax payments. In present value, the subsidy and the taxes remain exactly offsetting, and the effective tax on capital income stays equal to zero. While leaving unaltered the direct incentive to saving, the higher capital income tax generates capital losses for elderly and middle-aged owners of capital. Their increased tax payments, as well as the expansion of the tax base associated with their reduced consumption and the consequent crowding in of capital, produces more tax revenue through time for the government.

To maintain a feasible policy in which the claim of the government on the economy's real resources does not become indefinitely large, an adjustment must be made in some other tax instrument that lowers the tax burden on the young and future generations. A natural candidate here is lowering the tax rate on labor income. A simulation of this kind was conducted involving an increase in the capital income tax rate from 15 percent to 50 percent under full expensing; the wage tax rate was adjusted downward annually such that government tax receipts exactly equaled government consumption. This policy resulted in more than a 70 percent increase in the long-run (per capita) capital stock. Obviously, reversing the policy (running an economic deficit) by cutting capital income tax rates from 50 percent to 15 percent leads to an equivalent absolute decline in per capita capital. The results of this economic deficit policy far exceed anything reported in table 8.1 and certainly do not rest on increased disincentives for saving, since nominal capital income tax rates are cut by over two-thirds, while effective capital income tax rates remain equal to zero.

8.4   Economic Deficits and the Potential for Fiscal Illusion

The fact that the sizable economic deficits underlying a large set of fiscal policies receive such little notice while the difference between arbitrarily defined "taxes" and arbitrarily defined "spending" receives such concentrated attention suggests endemic misreading of fiscal affairs. While the current unprecedented peacetime official US deficits are rightfully raising major concerns, no similar concerns were voiced in nonacademic circles during the 1960s and 1970s when the United States enormously expanded its unfunded social security, civil service, and military retirement programs. Another example of partial, if not inconsistent, discussions of deficits is the failure of most analysts of the current US deficits to recognize either the significant economic surplus embedded in the 1981 legislated investment incentives or those arising from the recent US shift away from income taxation toward a hybrid wage/consumption tax structure.

The concern with fiscal illusion is further heightened by understanding that even the economic deficits arising from the type of tax cuts shown in table 8.1 could go unreported. To see this point, assume that the government, in the simulated economy of the table, can impose lump-sum head taxes and also make lump-sum per capita transfers. Suppose, during the period the tax cuts of the table are in place, the government levies lump-sum head "taxes," rather than issuing official "bonds," in order to "balance the budget." If it simultaneously promises to make lump-sum per capita transfer payments in the future to each taxpayer (or his heir/estate) in an amount exactly equal to the lump-sum head tax plus interest, the budget constraints of households in the model would be unaffected. For each household the future lump-sum transfers would exactly offset the new lump-sum tax in present value; under the assumption of no liquidity constraints, these current lump-sum taxes and future lump-sum subsidies leave household budgets and household behavior unaffected. They do, however, permit the government to report zero deficits; that is, each year that the government would otherwise sell what it calls "bonds" to collect receipts, it instead levies an equal volume of lump-sum "taxes," promising with absolute certainty future repayment in the form of lump-sum "subsidies." To the household, the purchase of a bond is equivalent to the payment of lump-sum taxes, combined with the assurance of future repayment with interest in the form of lump-sum transfers. For the government, however, labeling the receipts from the lump-sum taxes "taxes" rather than "bonds" permits it to report zero official deficits and zero official debt through eternity, despite running potentially enormous economic deficits.

The point of describing this alternative method of conducting the same real policy is to illustrate that a government could, in principle, run any feasible economic deficit policy, generating a corresponding path of eventual crowding out (crowding in), and yet always report official budget balance. While governments do not appear to have such lump-sum fiscal instruments at their disposal, the example raises the question of whether governments, intentionally or unintentionally, use distortionary taxes and transfer payments, in a similar manner, to obscure fundamental economic deficits.

A different set of concerns about fiscal illusion and economic deficits involves the propensity to consider various economic policies in isolation, ignoring the potential simultaneous determination of policies. For example, the introduction of an unfunded government retirement program may be accompanied by, and indeed explain, increases in tax rates that leave the economy's economic deficit little altered. In such circumstances, one would observe actual simultaneous changes in retirement programs and tax rates and would, presumably, be able to evaluate their joint effect relative to no change in policy, that is, the status quo. It should, however, be further recognized that the status quo is a quite arbitrary benchmark for evaluating individual or comprehensive policy changes. Rather than take current policy—for example, constant tax rates and no government unfunded retirement programs—as the benchmark for considering changes in policy, one could argue that a path of rising tax rates and no unfunded retirement programs was the actual course of policy from which the government had deviated. Alternatively, one might argue that, in the absence of establishing unfunded retirement programs, the government would have reduced taxes, particularly on the elderly, and that the unofficial economic debt arising from such programs simply substituted for officially reported debt policies that would otherwise have been enacted. Since the choice of a benchmark set of conditions is quite arbitrary, calculating "the" economic deficit and crowding out arising from any particular policy is predicated on subjective judgments about the counterfactual policies that would otherwise have been undertaken.

While these considerations may appear esoteric relative to what appear to be pressing concerns, such as reducing the current sizable US economic deficits, they are of direct relevance when one considers precisely which taxes might be varied to reduce these deficits. If the source of additional tax revenues is increased business taxation, and such increased taxation takes the form of rolling back the recently enacted investment incentives, much of the reduction in the official US deficit will have been achieved by increasing unofficial economic debt. Recall that reducing investment incentives raises the relative price of old versus new capital, and thus redistributes toward older generations. If the trade-off is only between running essentially equivalent explicit (officially reported) or implicit (not officially reported) economic deficits, then economic deficit policy is, for practical purposes, predetermined. In such an environment, where, for practical or other reasons, the intergenerational distribution of resources cannot be significantly altered, advocates of changing that distribution presumably suffer from delusions that such changes are feasible, or illusions that officially reported deficits are reliable measures of economic deficit policy.

Two points summarize this section. First, officially reported deficits may have little or nothing to do with underlying economic deficits, and reliance on the former to estimate the latter is symptomatic of fiscal illusion. Second, policies are not formulated in isolation, and labeling any particular policy the cause of economic deficits presupposes knowledge of what other policies would have been in its absence. Since suppositions about what policy would otherwise have been are inherently subjective, estimating "the" impact of economic deficits ultimately appears to be a normative enterprise. Although the examination of alternative counterfactual policies is of no practical importance if the intergenerational distribution of resources is fundamentally predetermined, such analyses do provide important guides to successfully reducing economic debt when comprehensive changes in the intergenerational distribution of resources are feasible.

8.5 Empirical Analysis of Economic Deficits

Much of the recent empirical research relating to the effects of economic deficits falls into three categories: time-series analysis of the savings impact of intergenerational transfers, cross-sectional analysis of social security's impact on household wealth accumulation, and estimates of the extent of intergenerational transfers in the economy.

The time-series analysis (Feldstein 1974c, 1982; Barro 1978; Darby 1979, Leimer and Lesnoy 1981; and numerous others) has proved inconclusive; the econometrics here is plagued by problems of aggregation, simultaneity, and errors in defining variables such as social security wealth. Auerbach and Kotlikoff (chapter 19) demonstrate the problem of the time-series statistical approach by running the standard time-series specification on simulated data that conformed perfectly to the nonaltruistic life cycle hypothesis. The coefficient on the critical social security wealth variable, as well as on many other variables, proved extraordinarily sensitive to the choice of sample period. Auerbach and Kotlikoff concluded that the standard time-series approach could easily accept the altruistic hypothesis even if it were false; that is, the standard time-series approach has very little power to reject the strict life cycle, nonaltruistic hypothesis. While it would be useful to improve the time-series specifications, what is ultimately needed for sharp time-series tests is cohort-specific time-series data on consumption and human and nonhuman wealth. Such data could be used to test whether the intergenerational distribution of resources determines the intergenerational distribution of consumption, which is a direct implication of the life cycle model.

The cross-sectional analysis has been plagued by data problems as well as by conceptual errors in formulating rejectable hypotheses concerning altruism. A variety of studies, including those of Feldstein and Pellechio (1979) and chapter 15 of this book, involve regressions of household private wealth on social security tax and transfer variables. The central question posed in much of this literature is whether households reduce their private asset accumulation when young because of the anticipation of receiving net windfall transfers when old. The evidence here is mixed, but even if each of these studies had strongly confirmed the proposition that expected future windfalls lead to higher current consumption and, therefore, less private wealth accumulation, the results would still leave unresolved the issue of altruism; the altruistic hypothesis, like the life cycle hypothesis, suggests that increases in the future resources of a particular household should raise that household's consumption and lower its own savings. In the altruistic case, however, the future windfall to the household in question would presumably also raise the consumption of all other altruistically linked households in the extended family. A central proposition of the altruistic hypothesis is that the consumption of particular family members depends on the resources of other extended family members. Unfortunately, this latter proposition is not tested in the empirical literature dealing with developed countries, nor does it appear capable of being tested for these countries, given current data sources.

The third source of evidence bearing on the issue of altruism is provided by estimates of the extent of intergenerational transfers in the US economy. Recent studies by White (1978), Darby (1979), and chapter 1 of this book suggest that over two-thirds of US private wealth holdings can be traced to intergenerational transfers; longitudinal age-earnings and age-consumption profiles are far from consistent with predictions of the strict, nonaltruistic life cycle model (Modigliani and Brumberg 1954). This finding does not, however, preclude the possibility that the majority of households conform to the selfish life cycle model. The majority of households could have such preferences, but simply have very little "hump" savings. The distribution of wealth in the United States and many other Western countries is highly concentrated, and the distribution of bequests and other transfers is accordingly highly concentrated. It may well be that ours is a mixed society consisting of a minority of quite wealthy, altruistic households and a majority of rather poor, life cycle households. While life cycle households may currently own little, if any, of the stock of wealth, their response to new government policies, in particular, intergenerational transfers, could dictate the economy's short-run saving behavior, where "short run" here corresponds to several decades. Hence, for the issue of deficits and saving, it is important to assess the degree of intergenerational altruism among the masses of middle-income and lower-income households.

8.6 Deficit Financing Under Liquidity Constraints

An extremely simplified two-period, closed economy model of deficit financing under liquidity constraints has the following elements: (1) life cycle labor supply is exogenous; (2) young individuals, because of liquidity constraints, consume precisely their after-tax labor earnings plus any government transfers; (3) older individuals also consume precisely their disposable income. Both the young and the old, in such a model, have unitary marginal propensities to consume; since the old are in their last period, they fully consume any net additions to their resources. For the young, their desire to transfer consumption from the future to the present, a desire that is thwarted by market restrictions on borrowing against future resources, implies a unitary consumption propensity.

Since both the young and the old have unitary consumption propensities, redistribution between them has no effect on national consumption or saving, and, therefore, implies no crowding out of investment. Since redistribution among the living implies no crowding out, any intergenerational redistribution that alters national saving must, therefore, be between the living and the unborn. As mentioned, the unborn have zero current marginal consumption propensities; hence, if the government can engineer net transfers to those currently alive and finance such transfers with net taxation on further generations, it will succeed in crowding out saving. In the model described, however, the private sector holds no real wealth whatsoever, since it never engages in any saving. Hence, if there is any wealth in the economy it must be owned by the government. If the government owns no wealth, there is no way it can alter the economy's consumption, since all of national output is already being consumed, and the economy has no wealth to consume. Clearly, the government, in such a setting, cannot cut taxes and sell bonds to the young generation; assuming the young remain liquidity constrained, they consume all income flows and have no funds left over for bond purchases.

For the government to reduce national wealth in this setting, it must initially own some wealth. In this case, the government can finance increased private sector consumption by allocating some or all of its initial wealth to those currently alive. Future generations are worse off because they have to finance the reduction in the government's capital income. In addition, the reduced stock of national wealth, all of which is owned by the government, means general equilibrium changes in factor returns that are also detrimental to future generations.

In this economy, only officially reported debt policies, involving declines in the government's official surplus, would generate crowding out. Policies such as unfunded retirement programs or structural tax policies that involve transferring resources between the current young and old would have no crowding-out effects. Economies of this type would, however, exhibit zero or very small holdings of private wealth relative to variables such as income or consumption. For the United States, in contrast, ratios of private wealth to income range between 3 and 4, while ratios of wealth to consumption range between 4 and 5.

A less extreme model involving liquidity constraints results from relaxing the assumption that all first-period young are constrained. Suppose, instead, that a small minority of the young do save positive amounts. In this case, the government could sell bonds to this minority of the young and distribute the proceeds from the sale of these instruments to current young and old in the form of transfer payments or tax cuts. Since the interest on this debt would be paid for through higher net taxes levied on future generations, officially reported policies of this type would produce crowding out. On the other hand, redistribution from the masses of current liquidity-constrained young to the masses of elderly through unfunded retirement programs, structural tax changes, or changes in investment incentives will have negligible effects on aggregate private consumption, implying rather minor crowding-out effects.

While models in which the large majority of young and middle-aged households are liquidity constrained place conventional reporting of economic deficits in a better light, the empirical relevance of such models appears quite doubtful. Studies by Hall and Mishkin (1982), King and Dicks-Mireaux (1982), and Diamond and Hausman (1983) suggest that less than one-fourth of US households face liquidity constraints. Since these are among the poorest of US households, one would expect such households to account for a much smaller fraction of total US consumption and, depending on the particular policy, for a much smaller fraction of changes in US consumption.

Other stylized facts about US saving behavior cast doubt on liquidity constraints as a dominating factor influencing the effects of policy toward savings. First, US private wealth is quite large relative to annual consumption, and very large relative to the increase in consumption that would arise from unofficial economic deficit policies. Second, the time series on US net national product is considerably more variable than that of US national consumption, particularly when consumption of durables is properly measured; that is, there is considerable consumption smoothing in the US time-series data, a finding that is at odds with a view of widespread liquidity constraints.

8.7 Summary and Conclusion

This paper has taken a close look at the cause and consequences of economic deficits from the perspective of neoclassical models of saving. Analysis of the crowding-out mechanism led immediately to defining economic deficits as redistribution of resources toward older generations. Once one observes that such intergenerational redistribution underlies arguments about deficits, crowding out, and saving, it becomes apparent that numerous fiscal policies, none of which lead to officially reported deficits, also constitute economic deficits. Conventional accounting of US deficits appears to have missed most of the significant US economic deficits of the postwar period, with the exception of those currently underway. The failure of conventional accounting to provide sensible indicators of intergenerational redistribution, coupled with the intense public focus on these figures, suggests that fiscal illusion is widespread. There is a clear and compelling need to develop alternative ways of describing fiscal policy that are not sensitive to accounting conventions. Ultimately, this appears to require describing the underlying budget constraints facing representative households in the economy.

While empirical research has failed to distinguish among neoclassical models with respect to the concerns of crowding out, as well as between neoclassical and nonneoclassical models in general, the fault primarily lies with the data, not with the quality of the analyses. Discriminating among neoclassical models requires probing fairly subtle issues of household preferences, and sharply differentiating tests of these preferences require types of data quite different from what are now available. While empirical resolution of the crowding-out hypothesis appears off in the future, the simulation analyses provide strong warnings about the potential long-term detrimental consequences of economic deficits. The simulations also indicate that crowding out is a slow and surprisingly complex dynamic process whose full dimensions cannot be discerned by consideration of short-term policy effects.

Notes

Professor Kotlikoff was a visiting scholar in the Fiscal Affairs Department when this paper was prepared. He is currently with Boston University and the National Bureau of Economic Research. He is a graduate of the University of Pennsylvania and Harvard University.

1. The decision to label particular government prospective expenditures "official liabilities" has real effects to the extent that it alters the probability that such expenditures will be made. While the default risk may be smaller for official than for implicit liabilities, the real return to official liabilities may still be highly risky. In the United States, for example, official commitments to future nominal expenditures do not correspond to commitments to future real expenditures. During the

1970s, the US government accrued $365.5 billion, measured in 1980 dollars, in real capital gains on its official liabilities while never missing a nominal principal or interest payment. This default on the real value of official liabilities through inflation is documented in "Tax Policy and Economic Growth," chapter 5 of *Economic Report of the President, Transmitted to the Congress February 1982* (Washington, D.C.: US Government Printing Office, 1982), 109–33.

9

Investment versus Savings Incentives: The Size of the Bang for the Buck and the Potential for Self-Financing Business Tax Cuts

with Alan J. Auerbach

In closed economies, saving and investment represent, respectively, the supply of and demand for new domestic capital. Saving incentives shift the supply curve for new domestic capital, while investment incentives shift the demand curve. The basic public finance equivalence theorem—the real effects of a tax (subsidy) are independent of who nominally pays the tax (receives the subsidy)—applies equally well to the market for new capital. Hence, in closed economies, saving and investment incentives do not represent conceptually distinct policies, and the real effects of taxes or subsidies applied to the supply of new capital, saving, can be replicated by taxes or subsidies applied to the demand for new capital, investment.

While economically meaningful distinctions between saving and investment incentives do not arise, there are meaningful distinctions between policies that affect savings, the sum of past and current saving, and those that directly affect only current saving, or, in equilibrium, current investment.

This chapter examines the closed economy effects of government policies that vary with respect to whether they treat newly produced capital differently from old capital. Policies that distinguish new capital from old are denoted investment policies, while those that do not are labeled savings policies. While both types of policies alter marginal incentives to accumulate new capital, investment incentives can generate significant inframarginal redistribution from current holders of wealth to those with small or zero claims on the existing stock of capital. In the context of a neoclassical growth model, this redistribution runs, in large part, from the elderly to young and future generations. The direction of this intergenera-

*In *The Economic Consequences of Government Deficits*, L. H. Meyer, ed. (Norwell, Mass.: Kluwer-Nijhoff, 1983), 121–49. © 1983 by Kluwer Academic Publishers. Reprinted with permission.

tional transfer is opposite to that associated with the "burden of government debt;" in the case of debt, the government passes the tax bill for current expenditures on to future generations.

Intergenerational transfers can have important effects on national saving and capital formation in the life cycle model that posits zero or limited intergenerational altruism. The process by which these transfers affect capital formation is often referred to as the crowding out of investment. A natural question to pose in a life cycle model is whether the crowding in of new capital formation arising from investment incentives exceeds the crowding out produced by deficits potentially associated with these incentives. This question has particular relevance to present economic affairs since current and projected US deficits reflect, in large part, business tax cuts.

In addition to analyzing the net impact on capital formation of deficit-financed business tax cuts, this chapter considers the potential for self-financing business tax cuts. A self-financing business tax cut is defined here as a deficit-financed investment incentive that produces an increase in the economy's long-run tax base sufficient to permit the government to reach long-run budget balance without ever raising tax rates.

A third issue of considerable relevance to current economic policy is whether gradual increases in investment incentives delay investment until the incentives have been fully phased in. The 1981 Economic Recovery Tax Act (ERTA) provided for even greater investment incentives after 1984 than between 1981 and 1984. The 1982 Economic Report of the President indicated a potential decline in the effective tax rate on equity financed new investment in general industrial equipment from 21 percent in 1982 to −54 percent in 1986. In part, these figures reflect steadily declining projected inflation rates interacting with historic cost depreciation provisions. In addition, ERTA authorized more favorable depreciation schedules starting in 1985. While the 1982 tax act reduced future increases in the acceleration of depreciation, the 1981 act may, in part, be responsible for the historically low investment rate in 1982.

The principal findings of this paper with respect to these three issues are:

1. Investment incentives, even those financed by short-run increases in the stock of debt, significantly increase capital formation in life cycle economies.

2. Deficit-financed savings incentives, in contrast, typically reduce the economy's rate of capital formation in the long run.

3. Deficit-financed investment incentives can be self-financing for particular, but not unreasonable, parameterizations of neoclassical life-cycle growth models.

4. Gradual phasing in of investment incentives can actually reduce rather than stimulate short-term investment.

5. The underlying explanation for the relative efficacy of investment as opposed to savings incentives in stimulating capital formation in life cycle models is that investment incentives redistribute from the old to the young. Since the old in life cycle models have higher marginal propensities to consume out of lifetime resources than the young, this transfer reduces current consumption, permitting the crowding in of current investment.

The analysis of investment incentives is based on the Auerbach and Kotlikoff (1983) life cycle computer simulation model. The model describes the perfect foresight growth path of life cycle economies in response to a wide variety of fiscal policies. For purposes of this study the model has been expanded to include full or partial expensing of new capital as a policy option. Expensing is only one of several types of currently legislated investment incentives; its use is limited to a small subset of total US investment. However, expensing is a convenient device for analyzing a variety of other investment incentives including the investment tax credit (ITC) and the acceleration of depreciation; rates of fractional expensing can be chosen that produce effective tax rates on new investment equal to those arising from these other policies. In addition, if deficit policy is chosen appropriately, expensing policies can produce a time path of cash flows to the government similar to those that would arise from changes in the ITC or depreciation schedules.

The second substantive addition to the model is the inclusion of cost of quickly adjusting the economy's capital stock. As described by many authors [including Abel (1979), Hayashi (1981), and Summers (1981)], such increasing marginal costs of investment generate inframarginal rents to existing capital. As a consequence, the market valuation of the economy's existing capital stock can differ from its replacement cost. The assumption of quadratic adjustment costs leads to a theory of investment in which the rate of investment is a linear function of Tobin's q (Tobin 1969), the ratio of the stock market value of capital to its replacement cost. Tobin's q is also an important variable in determining household consumption and labor supply decisions. These decisions are based on the current and future wages and rates of return households foresee, but also on the household's initial wealth, including the market value of its claims to existing capital.

Since the elderly are the primary owners of capital in a life cycle model, consideration of adjustment costs, with their associated implications for changes in the wealth of the elderly, can be quite important in assessing the redistributive impact of numerous fiscal policies. One example is a switch from an income to an equal revenue consumption tax. Such a policy suggests a significant loss in welfare to the elderly, whose wealth holdings must now be spent, in part, to meet taxes on the purchase of consumption goods. With capital adjustment costs, however, there is a countervailing effect serving to increase the wealth and welfare of the elderly. The stimulus to capital formation associated with the consumption tax produces an immediate increase in stock market values, reflecting increased inframarginal rents to the existing capital stock. The higher initial stock market values obviously redound to the advantage of the elderly.

In addition to mitigating the intergenerational redistribution from the old to the young in the case of a switch to a consumption tax, the inclusion of adjustment costs in the model cushions the fall in stock market values associated with investment incentives that discriminate against old capital. Permitting expensing of new capital at higher rates than were previously allowed and restricting this expensing solely to new capital is an example of a policy injurious to the elderly, since it places existing capital at a financial disadvantage relative to new capital. But the welfare loss to the elderly is mitigated to the extent that the economy's desire for an ultimately greater level of capital per worker raises inframarginal rents on previously installed, i.e., existing, capital.

The next section of this paper ignores the issue of adjustment costs in order to clarify, in a simple framework, differences between investment and savings incentives. The discussion points out equivalence relationships between investment incentives and other fiscal policies. In particular, permitting 100 percent expensing of new capital in the presence of a capital income tax (levied either on individuals or on businesses, in the form of a profits tax) is equivalent to imposing a one-time wealth tax at a rate equal to that of the capital income tax. If the economy also taxes labor income at this same rate, introducing 100 percent expensing taxes wages and initial wealth at the same rate. This tax structure, in turn, is equivalent to a proportional consumption tax.

With the exception of the investment tax credit, new US business investment incentives are available to old as well as new capital; the old capital must, however, be sold to qualify for the new incentives. The sale of old capital requires payment of recapture taxes calculated on the difference between the asset's new sale price and its adjusted basis. If the taxes incurred in turning over old assets exceed the present value gain in investment incentives from such a transaction, turnover will not be stimulated; in this case the economic outcome of new investment provisions that do not explicitly exclude old capital will be identical to that which would have occurred had the new incentives been restricted solely to new capital.

The third section considers the potential for turning over old capital under the 1981 Tax Act; for much of US capital produced prior to 1981 the costs of turnover exceed the benefits. For the remaining assets, however, turnover, in the absence of transaction costs, is profitable, but turnover taxes still recapture most of the gains from these transactions. Hence, with respect to recent tax legislation, the effective, if not the nominal, tax treatment of new and old capital is quite different, and the new law primarily provides investment as opposed to savings incentives.

The fourth describes the version of the Auerbach-Kotlikoff simulation model used to compare savings and investment incentives in both the presence and absence of capital adjustment costs. The following section presents simulations of these policies and examines the extent of short-run and long-run crowding out.

The sixth section considers three alternatives to the deficit-financing of investment incentives. One involves a delay in the introduction of expensing. A second involves actually increasing the tax on capital income in conjunction with full expensing, while a third involves a reduction in the extent to which expensing is permitted.

The first simulation shows that a time path of increasingly generous investment incentives can be associated with simultaneous declines in stock market values, quite low and, possibly, negative short-term interest rates and fairly large, positive long-term interest rates. Such a policy actually suppresses short-run investment. The second simulation demonstrates the somewhat paradoxical result that, given a structure of investment incentives, increases in capital income tax rates (e.g., corporate or dividend tax rates) will generally stimulate, rather than retard, capital formation, while requiring an immediate decline in wage taxes to avoid running surpluses. Finally, our third simulation shows that the government, through a policy of partial expensing, can raise investment and generate a surplus without ever raising either the capital income tax or the labor income tax.

The last section of the paper summarizes major findings and relates these results to recent economic events.

9.1   Investment Incentives: Structural Relationship to Other Fiscal Policies

A simple two-period life cycle model of economic growth provides a convenient framework for examining the underlying nature of investment incentives. Consider such an economy with a tax $\tau_{w,t}$ on labor income, a tax $\tau_{r,t}$ on business profits, and an expensing rate for new capital of e_t. The subscript t denotes the period in which the three instruments are applied. To simplify the analysis further, assume individuals work only when young and that the depreciation rate, the rate of population growth, and the rate of technological change are zero.

Equations (1) and (2) characterize the economy's process of capital formation:

$$K_t = [W_{y,t-1}(1 - \tau_{w,t-1}) - C_{y,t-1}]/q_{t-1}, \tag{1}$$

$$C_{0,t} = q_{t-1}K_t(1 + r_t). \tag{2}$$

In equation (1), $W_{y,t-1}(1 - \tau_{w,t-1}) - C_{y,t-1}$ is the saving of the young in period $t - 1$, their after tax wages in period $t - 1$ less their consumption in period in $t - 1$. The net price of a unit of capital in period $t - 1$ is given by q_{t-1}. Dividing the financial saving of the young by q_{t-1} determines their purchase of physical capital. The physical capital acquired by the young at the end of period $t - 1$ equals the economy's capital stock at the beginning of period t, K_t; the old generation in period t (those young in $t - 1$) hold claims to all the economy's capital, since the young in period t have no beginning of period assets.

For the old in period t, consumption, $C_{0,t}$, equals the return of principal, $q_{t-1}K_t$, plus the after tax return on the investment, $q_{t-1}K_tr_t$. The after-tax return, r_t, includes capital gains and losses:

$$r_t = \frac{F_{K,t}(1 - \tau_{r,t}) + q_t - q_{t-1}}{q_{t-1}}. \tag{3}$$

In equation (3) $F_{K,t}(1 - \tau_{r,t})$ equals marginal after tax profits per unit of capital. In combination, (2) and (3) imply

$$C_{0,t} = q_tK_t + K_tF_{K,t}(1 - \tau_{r,t}). \tag{4}$$

This new expression is also intuitive: the consumption of the old in period t (the young of period $t - 1$) equals after tax business profits plus the value of the sale of their capital at the prevailing asset price q_t.

Equation (5) expresses q_t, the net price of purchasing a unit of capital, in terms of $\tau_{r,t}e_t$:

$$q_t = 1 - \tau_{r,t}e_t. \tag{5}$$

For new capital the net acquisition cost is 1, the price of new capital, less the tax rebate from expensing, $\tau_{r,t}e_t$. Equation (5) also determines the price of old capital. Since old capital and new capital are perfect substitutes in production, their net acquisition costs must be identical in equilibrium; hence, old capital sells for $\tau_{r,t}e_t$ less than new capital because the purchaser of new capital receives $\tau_{r,t}e_t$ from the government, while the purchaser of old capital receives no tax rebate. Since the value of old capital depends on the product of $\tau_{r,t}e_t$, the price of old capital falls not only when expensing is increased (and $\tau_{r,t}$ is positive), but also when the rate of business profits taxation rises, given an expensing policy.

Equations (1), (4), and (5) may now be combined to indicate the lifetime budget constraint of the young in period $t - 1$,

$$C_{y,t-1} + C_{0,t}\frac{(1 - \tau_{r,t-1}e_{t-1})}{(1 - \tau_{r,t}e_t) + F_{K,t}(1 - \tau_{r,t})} = W_{y,t-1}(1 - \tau_{w,t-1}), \tag{6}$$

and the old in period $t - 1$:

$$C_{0,t} = K_{t-1}(1 - \tau_{r,t-1}e_{t-1}) + K_{t-1}F_{K_{t-1}}(1 - \tau_{r,t-1}). \tag{7}$$

These equations suffice to describe the relationship of savings and investment incentives to other tax structures. First, consider the case of zero expensing ($e_{t-1} = e_t = 0$). This assumption produces an economy with period t capital income and wage tax rates of $\tau_{r,t}$ and $\tau_{w,t}$, respectively. In such an economy, the return to new capital, capital produced in period $t - 1$ and old capital, capital produced prior to period $t - 1$, are taxed at the same effective rates in period t and beyond. With zero expensing, there is no discrimination in favor of newly produced capital; the relative price of new and old capital is always unity. Changes in the time path of $\tau_{r,t}$ and $\tau_{w,t}$ that satisfy the government's long-term budget constraint [see Auerbach and Kotlikoff (1983)] are classified, in our taxonomy, as savings incentives. The fifth section indicates that lowering capital income tax rates will typically depress rather than stimulate long-term capital formation if such savings incentives are deficit-financed.

The essential feature of investment incentives can be illustrated most simply by assuming zero wage taxation, permanent capital income taxation at rate τ_r, zero expensing prior to period $t - 1$, and a permanent move to 100 percent expensing starting at time $t - 1$. Under these assumptions, all tax terms drop out of equation (6); the young of period $t - 1$ and all future generations face zero effective taxation over their lifetimes. While the young and future generations nominally pay business profits taxes in their old age, the reduced cost of purchasing capital when they are young exactly offsets the present value cost of this taxation. Stated differently, new generations starting in year $t - 1$ are subsidized when young to purchase capital and taxed when old on its return. The subsidy and tax cancel in present value and the young face no net taxation on their capital investments.

While this new tax structure effectively exempts the young of period $t - 1$ and all future generations from paying any taxes over their lifetime, elderly individuals at time $t - 1$ suffer a capital loss on their assets equal to $K_{t-1}\tau_r$. According to equation (7), the consumption of the elderly falls by this amount; the $K_{t-1}\tau_r$ capital loss constitutes a one-time wealth tax on the old of period $t - 1$. Considering the tax treatment of the young and old together, this new tax system is equivalent to the government's collecting $K_{t-1}(1 + F_{k_{t-1}})\tau_r$ in taxes from the old period in $t - 1$ and abolishing taxation thereafter.[1]

This example highlights the special feature of investment incentives, namely that they tax initial holdings of wealth. A second important feature is that they lower the effective tax on the return to saving of young and future generations. With 100 percent expensing the effective capital income tax rate is reduced to zero.

The presence of wage taxation alters the analysis somewhat. Let us now assume positive and permanently fixed values of τ_r and τ_w. In this case moving to full expensing leaves young individuals facing a lifetime wage tax, or equivalently a lifetime consumption tax, since equation (6) can now be rewritten as

$$C_{y,t-1}(1 + \tau_C) + C_{0,t}\left(\frac{1 + \tau_C}{1 + F_{K_t}}\right) = w_y, \tag{6'}$$

where

$$1 + \tau_C \equiv \frac{1}{1 - \tau_w}.$$

The elderly in period $t - 1$ again face an additional wealth tax of $K_{t-1}\tau_r$ in addition to business profits taxes of $K_{t-1}F_{K_{t-1}}\tau_r$. If τ_r equals τ_w, the case of a proportional income tax, equation (7) becomes

$$C_{0,t-1}(1 + \tau_C) = K_{t-1}(1 + F_{K_{t-1}}). \tag{7'}$$

Equations (6′) and (7′) demonstrate that the movement to full expensing in the presence of a proportional income tax produces a consumption tax, or equivalently, a wage tax plus a one time wealth tax on the elderly where the wage and one-time wealth tax rates are identical. Other proposals, which are billed as "providing consumption tax treatment" of income flows, such as unlimited use of IRAs and abolition of the corporate income tax, produce wage tax rather than consumption tax structures. In the case of unlimited IRAs, the initial owners of capital can place all their holdings of capital into IRAs, receiving tax deductions that equal in present value the taxes on withdrawals of principal plus interest from the IRA. Thus the owners of existing capital face no effective taxation on the conversion of their capital into consumption expenditures; a policy of unlimited IRAs effectively eliminates the capital income tax component of the income tax with no effective wealth tax on existing assets. For those with no initial assets, wage taxation and consumption taxation are structurally equivalent. Hence, a policy of unlimited IRAs and a zero corporate income tax replicates a wage tax. It does not replicate a consumption tax.

Another complication of the foregoing analysis is that the actual US tax law permits existing assets to qualify for new tax incentives, if they are sold by the existing owner. For example, the 1981 Accelerated Cost Recovery System (ACRS) does not explicitly exclude old capital, though application of ACRS to old capital requires a change in the capital's ownership. It is important to distinguish here between direct capital ownership and indirect ownership through firms. One normally thinks of life cycle transfers of assets as being accomplished by the sale of shares in firms owning capital goods. This is not considered to be a change in the ownership of the capital goods themselves, which would require the sale of the actual goods by one firm to another. Thus, we may imagine that in selling off their assets the elderly can choose whether to transfer ownership of assets or ownership of firms, with the only resulting difference being whether sale of the capital goods themselves is recognized for tax purposes. We refer to the former case as turnover of assets.

If old capital is eligible for new investment incentives (expensing) subject to recapture taxation, the budget constraint facing the elderly is no longer equation (7), but rather

$$C_{0,t-1} = K_{t-1}(1 - R_{t-1}) + K_{t-1}F_{K_{t-1}}(1 + T_{r,t-1}), \tag{7''}$$

where R_{t-1} is the recapture tax per unit capital.

A comparison of equations (7) and (7″) implies that the sale of old capital to acquire eligibility for current investment incentives available to new capital will only occur if $\tau_{r,t-1}e_{t-1}$ exceeds R_{t-1}. If these two terms are equal, the elderly are indifferent between selling their capital as old capital, e.g., selling equity title to previously expensed capital, or selling the actual capital at its replacement cost of unity and paying recapture taxes.

If turnover is advantageous, equation (7″) indicates that recapture taxes are equivalent to lump sum taxes of equal size on the initial generation of elderly. For the young in period $t-1$, the lifetime budget constraint is no longer equation (6) but

$$C_{y,t-1} + \frac{C_{0,t}(1 - \tau_{t-1}e_{t-1})}{1 - R_t + F_{K_t}(1 - \tau_{r,t})} = W_{y,t-1}(1 - \tau_{w,t-1}). \tag{6″}$$

For given values of F_{K_t}, $\tau_{r,t-1}$, $\tau_{r,t}$, and e_{t-1}, values of R_t that make turnover profitable imply a larger effective after tax return on the saving of the young. In the case of a zero recapture tax, expensing implies no additional taxation of the elderly, and an effective subsidy on capital income to the young.

9.2 Recapture Taxes and the Exclusion of Old Capital from the Accelerated Cost Recovery System

The extent to which recapture taxation inhibits turnover is an empirical question that depends on the size of changes in investment incentives. The set of new incentives considered here are those provided by the Accelerated Cost Recovery System. Though the business tax provisions have again been altered by the Tax Equity and Fiscal Responsibility Act of 1982, the more recent legislation represents a small change from previous law, and introduces no additional incentives to turn over old assets to obtain the tax treatment accorded new assets. This is because the 1982 act maintains current depreciation allowances indefinitely.

The 1981 act introduced a sharp increase in the present value of depreciation allowances for a new asset purchased under pre-1981 law, we increase in the expensing fraction restricted to newly produced capital, accelerated depreciation can lower the value of existing assets. While the new ACRS provisions are available to owners of old assets provided they sell (turn over) their old assets, the sale of these assets generates recapture taxes that may exceed the net increase in depreciation allowances. To the extent that such a sale is attractive, the fraction of the loss in value that the seller recoups represents a leakage to old capital of the investment incentive embodied in ACRS.

The recapture treatment of structures and equipment differs and they must be considered separately. For structures, the seller must pay a tax on the difference between the sale price and the depreciated basis, with the difference between sale price and hypothetical straight line basis taxed as a capital gain, and the additional difference between straight line basis and actual basis (positive if a more accelerated depreciation method has been used), taxed as ordinary income. Thus, the total tax due on an asset with a one dollar sale price is

$$R = c(1 - B_{SL}) + \tau(B_{SL} - B),\tag{8}$$

where c is the capital gains tax rate (equal to 0.28 for corporations) and τ is the income tax rate (0.46 for corporations). The basis B and hypothetical straight line basis B_{SL} depend on the age of the asset, which determines the extent to which depreciation allowances have been taken, and the asset's initial purchase price. If a t-year-old asset physically depreciates at a constant exponential rate δ, and the inflation rate is π, then its initial purchase price was $e^{(\delta - \pi)t}$. Thus, letting b_{SL}^t and b^t be the straight line basis and actual basis for an asset aged t per initial cost, we have from equation (8)

$$R_t = c(1 - b_{SL}^t e^{(\delta - \pi)t}) + \tau e^{(\delta - \pi)t}(b_{SL}^t - b^t).\tag{9}$$

In return for this recapture tax, the potential seller receives one dollar times the number of units of capital (at replacement cost) for his asset rather than the value it would command with its old depreciation allowances. Since investors must be indifferent between old and new capital, the price of an asset not turned over must reflect the differences in depreciation allowances afforded new capital and those available to old capital:

$$q^t = 1 - r[Z_{ACRS} - Z_0^t e^{(\delta - \pi)t}],\tag{10}$$

where Z_0^t is the present value of remaining depreciation allowances for an asset of age t initially purchased for a dollar and Z_{ACRS} is the present value of allowance per dollar of new capital under ACRS. Equation (10) corresponds to the earlier equation (5) derived for the case of expensing. Here, the expensing fraction e is replaced by the more general expression of the difference between the values of prospective depreciation allowances on new and old assets.

Using equations (9) and (10), we may now ask whether the turnover tax R_t exceeds the increase in sale price $(1 - q^t)$ that the seller can obtain by opting for recapture. In addition, letting Z_0 be the present value of depreciation allowances for a new asset purchased under pre-1981 law, we may calculate what fraction of the capital loss generated by ACRS is avoided when turnover is profitable. Since the price of an asset of age t would have been

$$q_0^t = 1 - \tau[Z_0 - Z_0^t e^{(\delta - \pi)t}] \tag{11}$$

had there been no change in tax regime, the capital loss caused by ACRS for existing assets not turned over is

$$q_0^t - q^t = \tau(Z_{ACRS} - Z_0) \tag{12}$$

per dollar of age t capital.

Our calculations require parameter values for δ and π, the depreciation and inflation rates, and prior depreciation provisions. For purposes of illustration, we set $\delta = 0.03$ and $\pi = 0.08$. We assume an after tax nominal discount rate of 0.10 and that prior tax depreciation followed the 150 percent declining balance formula with optimal straight line switchover, based on a tax lifeline of 35 years. These estimates of both actual and tax depreciation are meant to correspond roughly to a typical structures investment [see Jorgenson and Sullivan (1982)]. We assume assets are purchased six months into the tax year and that payments are made annually, midway through the tax year as well. Post-1981 tax depreciation follows the 175 percent declining balance formula with optimal straight line switchover, based on a tax lifetime of 15 years, as dictated by ACRS.

Table 9.1 shows the results of calculations of q^t and R^t for structures purchased t years before the enactment of ACRS. The last column shows the fraction of the capital loss caused by ACRS (equal to 12.1 cents per dollar of capital) that could be recouped by turnover. Though turnover would not be useful for structures already completely written off, it appears advantageous for the bulk of structures. Because of growth and depreciation, a large fraction of the structure's capital stock is represented by assets purchased in recent years. For those assets, recoupment is substantial. For structures purchased within four years of the 1981 tax change, turnover allows a recoupment of over half the capital loss caused by ACRS. This figure is 85 percent for assets only one year old. Overall, if we assume a constant real rate of annual investment growth of three percent, this recoupment from turnover amounts to about one-third of the capital loss on structures, given our parameterization. This result also suggests that, absent transaction costs, a large fraction of the structures capital stock ought to have been turned over upon the enactment of ACRS. However, such costs are clearly substantial for certain assets, such as factories and build-

Table 9.1
Incentive to resell assets (structures)

Age (t)	Per dollar of age t capital			Fraction of capital loss Recovered
	Recapture tax $- R^t$	Value without resale $- q^t$	Gain from resale $(1 - q^t - R^t)$	
1	0.021	0.876	0.103	0.85
2	0.046	0.864	0.090	0.74
3	0.069	0.853	0.078	0.64
4	0.090	0.843	0.067	0.55
5	0.107	0.834	0.059	0.49
6	0.124	0.825	0.051	0.42
7	0.139	0.818	0.043	0.36
8	0.153	0.811	0.036	0.30
9[a]	0.164	0.805	0.031	0.26
10[a]	0.174	0.800	0.026	0.21
⋮	⋮	⋮	⋮	
> 35	0.280	0.727	−0.007	—

a. Once an asset is 100 months old, the fraction of $(B_{SL} - B)$ subject to ordinary income taxation declines by 1 percent per month until it reaches 0 at 200 months. This is accounted for in these calculations.

ings, complementary to other productive factors in a company's production process. However, one would expect to see a greater turnover activity in commercial structures, such as apartment buildings and office buildings.

We turn next to the recapture treatment of equipment. Here, the analysis is complicated by the fact that most equipment qualifies for the investment tax credit, but only if the asset is new. The law greatly restricts the ability of an investor in used property to obtain the ITC. Moreover, the credit obtained by the original purchaser is also subject to recapture if the number of years the asset has been held is less than the minimum number of years required to qualify for such a credit. For example, equipment purchased before 1981 needed a tax lifetime of at least seven years to qualify for the full 10 percent credit. Assets with lifetimes of between 5 and 7 years received only a $6\frac{2}{3}$ percent credit, and those with lifetimes between 3 and 5 years received a $3\frac{1}{3}$ percent credit. If an asset with a lifetime exceeding seven years were sold after, say, six years, the seller would have to repay one-third of the original credit received; if the sale were after four years, two-thirds of the original credit would be repaid, and so on.

A second difference in recapture treatment of equipment is that the entire differential between sale price and basis is taxed as ordinary income, unless sale price exceeds initial purchase price, in which case the gain on purchase price is taxed as a capital gain. These two differences in the recapture treatment of equipment make turnover less attractive than in the case of structures.

As long as the sale price of the asset is less than original purchase price, the total recapture tax on one dollar of equipment aged t is

$$R_t = \tau[P - b^t e^{(\delta - \pi)t}] + (k - k^t)e^{(\delta - \pi)t}, \tag{13}$$

where b^t, δ, π, and T are defined as before, k is the investment tax credit claimed originally, and k^t the credit that, ex post, the asset lifetime t would have dictated for the asset. P, less than unity, is the sale price. It accounts for the fact that, unlike a dollar of new capital, this asset will only receive the ACRS depreciation deductions and not the investment tax credit. Thus[2]

$$P = 1 - (k + \tau Z_{ACRS} - \tau P Z_{ACRS}) \tag{14}$$

or

$$P = \frac{1 - k - \tau Z_{ACRS}}{1 - \tau Z_{ACRS}}.$$

If the asset is not sold, then the value of the t-year-old capital per dollar of replacement cost is

$$q^t = 1 - [k + \tau Z_{ACRS} - \tau Z_0^t e^{(\delta - \pi)t}], \tag{15}$$

which differs from the equation for structures (10) only in the inclusion of the investment tax credit.

The seller of an asset will gain from turning the asset over if $P - q^t$ exceeds R^t. However, for representative parameters for equipment, this will not occur. Table 9.2 shows the values of R^t and q^t for an asset that depreciates at a rate of 0.12 and under old law was written off over a tax lifetime of ten years using the double declining balance method with a switchover to straight line. The value of P is 0.839, and the inflation rate and discount rates are, as above, set at 0.08 and 0.10. As the results show, the prospective seller would always lose by turning assets over on resale. Thus, owners of equipment can escape none of the capital loss induced by the liberalization of depreciation allowances for new capital goods. This loss is described by equation (12) and equals 10.5 cents of capital (measured at replacement cost).

Table 9.2
Incentive to resell assets (equipment)

Age (t)	Per dollar of age t capital		
	Recapture tax — R^t	Value without resale — q^t	Gain from resale $(P - q^t - R^t)$
1	0.054	0.847	−0.062
2	0.135	0.796	−0.092
3	0.167	0.753	−0.081
4	0.215	0.718	−0.103
5	0.220	0.690	−0.071
6	0.255	0.667	−0.083
7	0.246	0.645	−0.052
⋮	⋮	⋮	⋮
> 10	0.386	0.521	−0.068

Thus no equipment, but a substantial fraction of structures, could gain by being brought under ACRS. In the case of structures, a large fraction of the capital loss induced by ACRS could be avoided in this way. However, the presence of transaction costs of unknown magnitude makes it difficult to know how much of this turnover would take place. We may place upper and lower bounds on the size of the capital loss induced by the introduction of ACRS. With no turnover, the loss equals approximately 10.5 cents per dollar of existing equipment and 12.1 cents per dollar of existing structures. With the maximum gain from turnover, about one-third of the loss on structures is recouped. Using estimates of the equipment/structures breakdown of 44.4 percent and 55.6 percent, respectively, obtained from data for 1975,[3] and with an estimate of 2.56 trillion for the value in 1980 of the replacement cost of the business capital[4] stock, we obtain a range of $233 to $292 billion as the effective wealth tax induced by the introduction of ACRS.

The result is only a rough calculation and ignores the actual heterogeneity of the capital stock. Moreover, in the presence of adjustment costs (see below), the prices of all capital goods, including old ones, may rise with a surge in demand induced by an investment incentive such as ACRS. This would act to offset part of the capital loss induced by the more generous tax treatment of new capital versus old. However, the losses just calculated still are meaningful in that they represent the drop in value of existing capital relative to the value such capital would have had, had the additional tax benefits of ACRS applied to all capital.

9.3   The Simulation Model and Its Parameters

The Auerbach-Kotlikoff simulation model calculates the equilibrium growth path of an economy consisting of government, household, and production sectors. The life cycle version of the model used in this study incorporates expensing of new capital and costs of adjusting the level of the capital stock. In addition to expensing, the government's policy instruments include capital income, consumption, and wage taxes, the level of government consumption, and the choice of a deficit policy.

The household sector consists of fifty-five overlapping generations, with the total population growing at a constant rate. The fifty-five period life span corresponds roughly to the life span of an adult. In each generation there is a single, representative individual, and generations differ only with respect to their opportunity sets. The production sector is characterized by firms maximizing the present value of their profits by choosing both annual levels of labor input and annual rates of investment.

Each household chooses life cycle labor supply and consumption by maximizing an intertemporally separable CES utility function (Auerbach, Kotlikoff, and Skinner 1983) with a constant static elasticity of substitution between consumption and leisure at a point in time and a constant intertemporal elasticity of substitution between consumption at different points in time, leisure at different points in time, and consumption and leisure at different points in time. The simulation presented below incorporates a 1 percent population growth rate, a static elasticity of substitution of 0.8, and an intertemporal elasticity of substitution of 0.25. These elasticities are suggested by recent empirical studies of saving and labor supply.[5]

The production function used here is Cobb-Douglas, with capital's income share equal to 25 percent. The costs associated with investment are quadratic as in the simulation model of Kotlikoff, Leamer, and Sachs (1981); that is, the marginal cost of a new dollar of capital, including installation costs, is

$$\varnothing(I) = 1 + b\left(\frac{I}{K}\right), \tag{16}$$

where I is investment and K is existing capital. The term b is the adjustment cost coefficient. Larger values of b imply greater marginal costs of new capital goods for a given rate of investment.

The government choice of policy instruments is constrained by an intertemporal budget that holds over infinite time. This budget constraint requires that the present value of government capital income, wage, and consumption tax receipts be sufficient to pay for the present value of government consumption, the present value of expensing deductions, and the value of existing government net debt. The assumption that government debt (surplus) per capita cannot grow infinitely large is sufficient to generate this constraint on the time path of government policies.

The constraint implies that government policies are necessarily interdependent. A corollary is that certain deficit policies are not feasible. For example, the government cannot permanently change its expensing policy and permanently meet the consequent change in its receipts by simply altering its issue of debt. Such a policy would lead, over the long term, to either an infinite debt or an infinite surplus per capita. The probability that the change in the present value of tax receipts exactly equals the present value loss in revenues from changes in expensing is zero. Hence, to meet its budget constraints, the government must eventually raise or lower a tax instrument or its level of consumption in response to changes in its expensing policy. The next section indicates that, for certain expensing policies, the government need never raise any tax rate and, indeed, must lower tax rates at some point in the future to bring government finances into long-term balance. Investment incentives that require no increases in current or future tax rates or reductions in current or future government consumption are described here as self-financing.

9.4   Investment versus Savings Incentives: Illustrative Simulations

No single comparison of policies that do and do not discriminate against old capital can meaningfully summarize all differences in economic growth paths associated with investment versus savings incentives; the government's intertemporal budget constraint requires adjusting other government policies in response to these incentives in order to maintain a present value equality between its receipts and expenditures (including interest and principal repayments on debt). The differences in capital formation arising from the implementation of investment rather than savings incentives depends on the choice and timing of these other necessary policy adjustments.

Contrast, for example, two policies that begin with a proportional income tax, one introducing permanent, 100 percent expensing, and the other permanently removing the tax on capital income. The reduction or possible increase in revenues from either of these policies could be financed by immediate or future changes in the tax rate on labor income, current or future changes in government consumption, or some combination of changes in these and/or other available instruments. Given the range of possible concomitant adjustments in other policies, statements such as "investment incentives stimulate more capital formation than savings incentives" are meaningless. Comparisons of investment and savings incentives for explicitly specified policies of adjusting to the associated revenue changes do, however, permit meaningful conditional comparisons of investment and savings incentives.

The first simulation we present involves a permanent removal of capital income taxes, with debt policy used to maintain the wage tax rate at 30 percent for 5 years, and wage taxes adjusted thereafter to maintain a constant level of debt per capita. This simulation also assumes that there are no adjustment costs involved in changing the capital stock.

The initial steady state is characterized by a capital output ratio of 3.04 and a gross interest rate of 8.22 percent. The specified policy leads to a 7.35 percent reduction in capital per capita, and a greater reduction in labor supply, with the resulting drop of 8.90 percent in output per capita. The wage tax rises to 47.8 percent in the long run. The path of per capita capital stocks over the transition period is shown by the solid line in figure 9.1.

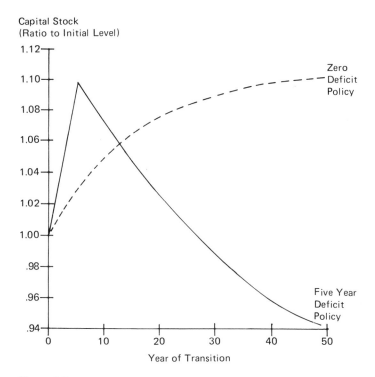

Figure 9.1
Capital paths (per capita): capital income tax removal.

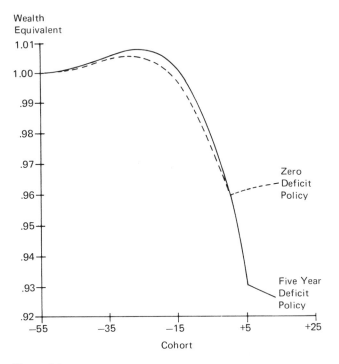

Figure 9.2
Wealth equivalents: capital income tax removal.

The solid line in figure 9.2 shows the welfare effects on transition cohorts of this deficit financed elimination of capital income taxation; the horizontal axis indexes the cohort's year of birth (relative to the first transition year, 1), and the vertical axis measures the amount by which the cohort's labor endowment vector would need to be increased (or decreased) under the old regime to allow the achievement of the same utility level as that attained under the new regime. The long-run welfare loss is 8.7 percent, but, in the short run, older generations gain relative to their ex ante prospects. This pattern of gains and losses is similar to that occurring under a policy [examined in Auerbach et al (1983)] of switching immediately to wage taxation without running deficits, represented by the dotted line in figure 9.2. However, both the short-run gains and the long-run losses are larger when debt policy is used, because of the further shifting of tax liabilities onto future generations. The impact on capital formation is another difference associated with the use of deficits to finance savings incentives; the dotted line in figure 9.1 shows the path of capital

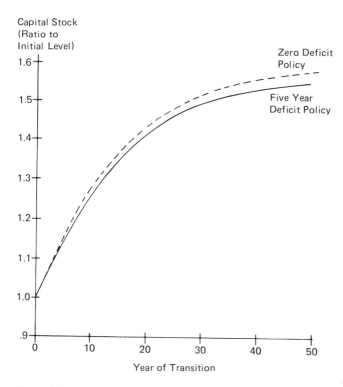

Figure 9.3
Capital paths (per capita): full investment expensing.

per capita arising from a balanced budget switch from income to wage taxation. Rather than falling, the capital stock rises in the long run.

The next policy we consider is a move to immediate expensing of all investment, with the income tax held at 30 percent for 5 years and deficits used to finance the loss in revenue. After five years, income taxes rise to maintain a constant level of debt per capita. The capital stock and welfare transitions are shown by the solid lines in figures 9.3 and 9.4, with corresponding paths under immediate balanced budget expensing [as discussed in Auerbach et al. (1983), shown by the dotted lines. The effects of the implicit wealth tax on the original owners of capital is evident in both diagrams. The utility of older transition cohorts is decreased, and capital accumulation enhanced by the reduction in their consumption.

The five-year delay in allowing tax rates to rise again leads to a lower long-run capital stock, but to a much smaller degree. The reason for this is that the deficits created by the policy during its first five years are much

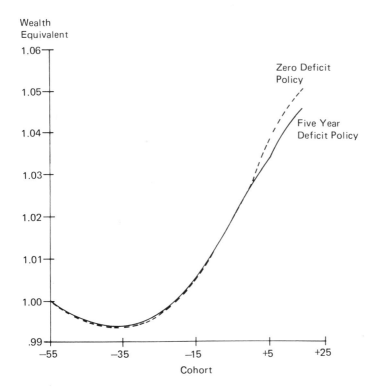

Wealth
Equivalent

Figure 9.4
Wealth equivalents: full investment expensing.

smaller. The long-run level of debt to capital is just 2.13 percent, compared to 13.8 percent in the case of the first simulation. In fact, the long-run rate of income taxation is 28.9 percent—lower than the value that obtained before the creation of the debt.

Thus far in our simulations, we have ignored the possibility that the short-run supply curve for capital goods may slope upward. That is, attempts to increase quickly the amount of capital in response to an increased investment or savings incentive may result in a higher price of capital goods relative to consumption goods. If this is true, then our results may overstate the capital loss borne by holders of existing capital arising from an investment incentive such as expensing.

Setting the adjustment parameter b [see equation (16)] equal to the empirically plausible value of five for the simulation of a transition to expensing with a five-year deficit policy yields the following results. First, the drop in capital stock values by the full value of expensing is not

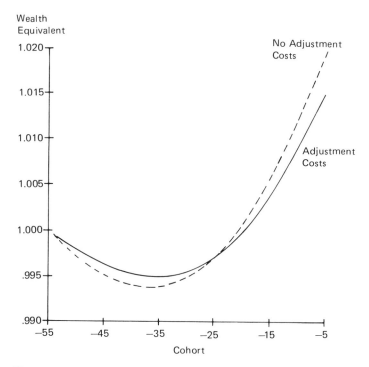

Figure 9.5
Wealth equivalents: The impact of adjustment costs (switch to expensing under five-year deficit policy).

immediate, because of the offsetting effect of the increasing supply price of new capital goods. The price drops by 22.5 percent in the first year of the transition rather than 30 percent. Second, the welfare loss of older transition cohorts is smaller and the long-run gain also smaller (5.92 percent) than in the simulation without adjustment costs (6.29 percent). The welfare paths are compared in figure 9.5. Finally, the capital stock grows by a smaller amount, because not all of the demand induced by the investment incentives translates into increased output of capital.

9.5   Dealing with Deficits

Various strategies have been offered to reduce short-run deficits associated with tax cut policies. In this section, we present three simulations that bear on the feasibility and advisability of avoiding short-run deficits while increasing the incentive to invest.

A typical solution to short-run revenue losses is a phase-in of investment incentives. This characterized the Economic Recovery Tax Act of 1981, which called for the acceleration of depreciation allowances to increase in 1981 and again in 1985 and 1986.[6] The problem with policies of this kind is that they induce capital losses gradually over the phase-in period. The awareness of potential investors of such future losses discourages investment in the short run, defeating the entire purpose of the legislation. This can be seen in the next simulation, which measures the effects of a five year phase-in of expensing without deficits, with the expensing fraction rising linearly from 0.2 in the first transition year to 1 in the fifth. Deficits are avoided by the adjustment of the income tax.

Though investment eventually expands under this policy, the short-run impact is to discourage investment. Figure 9.6 compares per capita capital stocks for the first twenty years of this policy with those arising from an

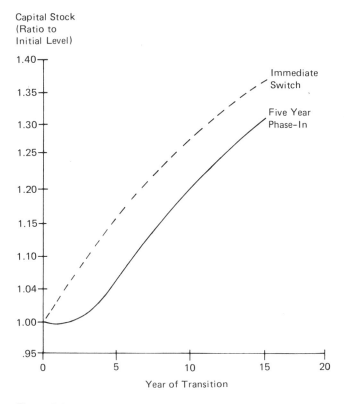

Figure 9.6
Capital paths: expensing without deficits.

immediate balanced budget switch to full expensing. The short-run disincentive to invest is also reflected by the drop in interest rates. The initial steady-state interest rate is 8.22 percent. Under the investment phase-in policy, the gross interest rate (the yield that bonds would have to offer to provide the same after tax return as capital, inclusive of capital gains and losses) is negative until the phase-in is completed, and then jumps to over 12 percent. Thus, such a policy would sharply increase the slope of the yield curve.

A more successful way of avoiding deficits recognizes that investment incentives can often be achieved by raising rather than lowering capital income taxes. Recall that, under a policy of full expensing that is effectively restricted to new capital, the effective tax rate on capital income is zero. While the return on savings is not taxed at the margin, the increase in the statutory capital income tax rate increases the implicit wealth tax on existing capital. This reduces the consumption of wealth holders, permitting an expansion of national saving and investment. In addition, the extra revenue from the capital income tax allows the government to lower other taxes. Starting from an initial steady state with full expensing and a 30 percent income tax, raising the capital income tax rate to 50 percent allows an immediate drop in the wage tax rate to 26.5 percent (falling eventually to 21.6 percent) and an eventual increase in capital per person of 34.6 percent.

Finally, investment incentives may be self-financing in the long run, requiring no current or future increase in statutory tax rates to achieve a more capital intensive long-run steady state with no debt. As an example, from an initial steady state with no expensing consider a policy of moving directly to 50 percent fractional expensing, with the income tax held constant at 30 percent for 20 years; while there are short-run deficits, the expansion of the income tax base over time raises revenue sufficient to retire this debt. Indeed, in the twentieth year the debt-capital ratio is −0.36 percent. This surplus permits a slight decrease in the income tax thereafter (to avoid an expanding surplus), to 29.2 percent in the twenty-first year and 29.0 percent in the long run. The per capita capital stock increases by 25.9 percent in the long run.

Part of the explanation of this result is that, while taxes on capital income and, eventually, labor income decline, existing capital owners face increased implicit wealth taxation under this same policy. Their welfare declines, thus distinguishing this policy from those offered by the "free lunch" theorists. A second aspect of this policy is that the economy has shifted to a more efficient tax structure, substituting lump sum taxes on initial wealth holders for distortionary income taxes on current and future generations. These efficiency gains also provide economic resources to "cut taxes and raise revenues."

While this policy of fractional expensing eventually leads to surpluses and tax rate reductions, a policy of full expensing (discussed at the beginning of section 9.4) does not have this feature, indicating the presence of nonlinearities in the functions determining the economy's behavior. One such nonlinearity is associated with the well-known result that the excess burden of a tax rises at a rate proportional to the square of the tax rate itself. Thus, the initial reduction in the effective tax rate on saving induced by a policy of 50 percent expensing does proportionally more to reduce the distortion of savings behavior than does a policy of moving from 50 percent to full expensing.

9.6 Summary

The key difference between savings and investment incentives in closed economies is the applicability of these incentives to old as well as new capital. Investment incentives discriminate against old capital; savings incentives do not. This discrimination reduces the market value of old capital and, therefore, the economic resources of owners of the existing capital stock. The reductions in the resources and welfare of initial wealth holders under investment policies are essentially identical to those arising from a one-time wealth tax.

In life cycle economies, the remaining resources of the elderly are held primarily in form of nonhuman as opposed to human wealth. The effective wealth tax generated by investment incentives falls, therefore, most heavily on the elderly. For a given time path of government consumption and given characteristics of tastes and technology, extra taxes on the currently elderly imply offsetting receipts of resources of young and future generations. In life cycle economies, the elderly have a greater marginal propensity to consume than the young because of their shorter life expectancies; future generations obviously have zero current marginal propensities to consume. Hence, the intergenerational redistribution of resources away from the elderly, arising from investment incentives, leads to a major reduction in the economy's current consumption. The reduction in the consumption of the elderly effectively finances the crowding in of investment.

For certain ranges of investment policy instruments, the long-term tax revenues arising from the increase in capital intensity are sufficient to finance the short-run loss in revenue from these incentives. Hence, there is a range of investment incentives that are self-financing. In general, deficits associated with investment incentives are less injurious to capital formation than those associated with savings incentives.

In contrast to investment incentives, savings incentives such as permanent reductions in the taxation of profits at the corporate level typically redistribute toward rather than away from the elderly. The impetus to current consumption arising from this redistribution—the income effect—is offset to some extent by the greater marginal incentive to save—the substitution effect of a higher after tax rate of return. The net impact of savings incentives on capital formation depends on the use of deficits to finance these incentives. As demonstrated here, deficit-financed reductions in capital income tax rates can sharply lower national capital formation.

The policy most conducive to capital accumulation involves simultaneously increasing investment incentives and capital income tax rates. Such a policy could eliminate deficits, raise the after tax return to marginal saving, and produce income and substitution effects that both operate in the direction of stimulating capital formation.

Notes

We are grateful to the National Bureau of Economic Research and the National Science Foundation for financial support. Andrew Myers provided excellent research assistance. The views expressed are solely those of the authors.

1. For the government to maintain long-term budget balance, it needs to choose a path of government consumption that equals $K_{t-1}(1 + F_{K-1})\tau$, in present value.

2. After the effective date of the 1982 act, this result would be altered by the application of a 50 percent basis adjustment for new credits taken.

3. US Department of Commerce, Bureau of Economic Analysis, "Fixed Non-Residential Business and Residential Capital in the US, 1925–1975," PB 253 725, 1976.

4. *Flow of Funds*, "Balance Sheets for the US Economy, 1945–1980," Board of Governors of the Federal Reserve System, Washington, D.C., 1981.

5. Auerbach, Kotlikoff, and Skinner (1983) survey this literature.

6. The 1985 and 1986 changes have been repealed by the Tax Equity and Fiscal Responsibility Act of 1982.

10   Deficit Delusion

The last five years have witnessed an enormous hue and cry over federal government deficits. No wonder. Since 1981 government debt held by the public has more than doubled. The current $1.7 trillion debt corresponds to over $7,000 for each man, woman, and child in the country. The interest alone on this debt will total roughly $600 per person this year.

The government has not blithely accumulated this debt. Rather, it has done so with considerable and sincere hand-wringing culminating in the unprecedented Gramm-Rudman legislation. This law mandates automatic spending cuts over the next five years if deficits exceed specified levels. The deficits have also captured the attention of the media and the American public to the point where deficits are now widely viewed as the country's number one economic problem.

Given the strength of concern over recent deficits, it is surprising that so much has been made of the numbers and so little attention has been devoted to asking what exactly these numbers measure—and whether they should be causing so much alarm. Indeed, the notion that these deficit numbers are meaningful indices of economic difficulties is so instilled in our collective perceptions that the thesis of this article will surely disturb many readers.

This thesis is that the deficit is an inherently arbitrary accounting construct that provides no real guide to fiscal policy. The fact that the definition of deficits is so arbitrary means that even adjusting the official numbers for inflation, the increase in government assets, full employment, etc. will still leave an arbitrarily defined number that has no necessary relationship to the fundamentals of the government's fiscal behavior.

Such improved deficit accounting has recently been espoused by Eisner and Pieper (1985). In their view, there are right and wrong ways to

Public Interest 84 : 53–65 (1986). © Reprinted with permission.

measure deficits, and the government has simply chosen the wrong way. Their analysis usefully illustrates the variety of deficits one can define, based on officially defined assets and liabilities alone. But their discussion misses the more fundamental point that the official labeling of something as an asset or a liability is an arbitrary choice that has no general basis in economic theory, and certainly not in the economic theory that underlies the concern about deficit finance.

Part of the problem in recognizing and discussing the arbitrariness of the government's language is that this language is all we have. Using words like "deficits," "taxes," and "spending" presupposes that these are well-defined concepts, which they are not. Hence, one has to use more neutral terms, such as "receipts" and "payments," to avoid the circularity inherent in using ill-defined terms and to emphasize their lack of definition.

10.1   Labeling Receipts and Payments

The government can be described in terms of this more neutral language as simply an institution that, over time, takes in receipts and makes payments. The only real constraint facing the government is that its receipts (including those from printing money) be sufficient to cover its payments. In the most basic terms we can view the government as consisting of a single individual, called the Treasurer, who is in charge of the government's interest-bearing checking account. All monies deposited in the account, including accrued interest, are receipts, while all checks written correspond to payments. The Treasurer decides how much money to take in as receipts and how much to pay out. But the Treasurer isn't free to bounce checks.

The Treasurer's choice of labeling specific receipts as "taxes," "borrowing," "receipts from sale of assets," "receipts from printing money," or "interest received" is entirely arbitrary. Equally arbitrary is his choice to label specific government payments as "consumption," "purchase of assets," "transfer payments," and "interest and principal payments." The particular labels chosen by the Treasurer should be of complete indifference to the citizens, who are concerned not with what receipts and payments are called, but rather with the difference over their lifetimes in their payments to the government and their receipts from the government.

To see how arbitrary is the choice of labeling, consider the following example. Suppose that the Treasurer has chosen labels for all current and future receipts and payments with the exception of those involving Mr. X in the two years when Mr. X is age forty and age fifty. At age forty Mr. X pays the government $1,000, and at age fifty Mr. X receives $1,500 back from the government. Assume that the $500 equals ten years accumulated interest on the $1,000.

The Treasurer might label the $1,000 receipt "taxes" from Mr. X and the $1,500 repayment "transfer payments" to Mr. X. Alternatively, he could label the $1,000 receipt "borrowing" from Mr. X and call $500 of the $1,500 payment "interest payments" and the rest "repayment of principal." A third possibility is to label $500 of the initial $1,000 "taxes" and the other $500 "borrowing." Half of the $1,500 subsequent payment from the government could then be labeled "transfers" and the other half "repayment of principal plus interest." A fourth possibility is the Treasurer's labeling the $1,000 net receipt as "borrowing" of $2,000 less "transfer payments" of $1,000, and the net payment of $1,500 could be labeled "interest plus principal payments" of $3,000 less "taxes" of $1,500. All of these possibilities have a significant impact on that which we call the "deficit," as is shown in table 10.1.

Since the net receipts and net payments of the government are identical in each of the four cases, the real behavior of the economy will be the same in each case. However, the reported deficit will differ. In Case 1 the labeling leads to a $1,000 smaller deficit when Mr. X is forty and a $1,500 larger deficit when Mr. X is fifty. Case 2 is the base case in which the reported deficit is unchanged. Case 3, like Case 1, involves an initially smaller reported deficit and a subsequently larger reported deficit. Case 4 produces the opposite result; with this labeling the government reports a $1,000 larger deficit when Mr. X is forty and a $1,500 smaller deficit when Mr. X is fifty.

Table 10.1
Government "deficit": Four cases

Case	Labeling		Impact on "deficit"	
	Mr. X's $1,000 net payment	Mr. X's $1,500 net receipt	When Mr. X is age 40	When Mr. X is age 50
1	"Taxes	"Transfers"	−$1,000	+$1,500
2	"Borrowing"	"Interest + Principal"	No change	No change
3	$500 "Borrowing"	$750 "Interest + Principal"	−$500	+$750
	$500 "Taxes"	$750 "Transfers"		
4	$2,000 "Borrowing"	$3,000 "Interest + Principal"	+$1,000	−$1,500
	$1,000 "Transfers"	$1,500 "Taxes"		

It is important to understand that the example doesn't hinge on the $1,500 equalling $1,000 plus ten years of interest. Suppose Mr. X's receipt at age fifty equals $2,000. If $500 of this $2,000 is labeled "transfers," then we are left with the same question of how to label a $1,000 payment of Mr. X at age forty and the remaining $1,500 receipt at age fifty.

These examples, by the way, have nothing to do with the issues of measurement raised by Eisner and Pieper. The same problems of arbitrary labels would arise if one made all their recommended measurement adjustments.

Of course, the Treasurer in this economy is free to play the receipt-and-payment-labeling games with all the country's citizens. It should thus be clear that the Treasurer is able to engage in exactly the same economic policy while reporting essentially whatever amount of debt or surplus he prefers. It should also be clear that, since the economy is not affected one iota by the change in labels, economics per se will provide no guide to the choice of labels.

Stated differently, from the perspective of economics the choice of labels is totally arbitrary, as is the reported level of government debt. The logical conclusion to draw from this is that one cannot learn anything about the underlying economy by considering only the size of its officially reported debt.

10.2   The Social Security "Tax"

Lest one view the prior discussion as purely academic and somehow irrelevant to the United States, consider the labeling of the US Social Security system, and, more specifically, the use of the word "taxes" to describe the FICA payments you and your employer make to the government. Why is the word "taxes" used? It is used because the government arbitrarily chose that word back in 1936 or thereabouts. But suppose we label these payments to the government differently. Let's label them "loans" from you to the government. Let's also label Social Security benefit payments "return of principal plus interest."

Note that, from your point of view, the new terminology is not completely foreign. With the new jargon you can now think of yourselves as lending money to the government (in the form of Social Security contributions) during your working years and receiving principal plus interest (in the form of Social Security benefit payments) during your retirement.

Surely this sequence of payments and receipts is very similar to those associated with purchasing a Treasury bond. When you purchase a Treasury bond or other security you make payments to the government now in exchange for receipts from the government later. Hence, from your point of view, your payment of what is called Social Security "taxes" is, in most respects, equivalent to your purchase of a government liability. While the return and risk properties of your invisible Social Security bonds differ from those of official government bonds (which, by the way, are subject to considerable revaluation risk), such a difference provides no basis for labeling one set of payments to the government "taxes" and the other set of payments "loans."

Let's now make the invisible Social Security bonds visible by supposing that the federal government, starting at the inception of the Social Security system, had also adopted the language of lending and borrowing to describe its flows of payments from and to the public sector—and, indeed, had issued explicit Social Security bonds to the public in exchange for Social Security contributions. We are supposing then that the Social Security system sends a piece of paper marked Social Security Bond to each worker in exchange for his or her Social Security contributions.

These pieces of paper would give the worker formal title to the return of his taxes plus interest as determined by the government. The interest paid on these Social Security bonds would not necessarily correspond to a market rate of return. Nor would the amount of interest be guaranteed; rather it would depend on Social Security's financial condition, in just the same way that, under current language, what are called Social Security "benefits" are not guaranteed and may be adjusted by Congress in light of Social Security's financial projections. The value of a worker's or retiree's Social Security bonds, like the value of Treasury bonds, would correspond to the risk-adjusted expected present value of the future return of principal and interest.

Consider now the impact on the government's measure of official debt of switching from the "tax"/"transfer" language to the language of "lending" and "repayment." Table 10.2 reproduces a table from the *1982 Economic Report of the President*, except that all figures are in billions of 1985 dollars. The first column shows the book value of gross federal debt. If we make one of the adjustments advocated by Eisner and Pieper and measure debt at market rather than book value, we arrive at column 2. Subtracting column 4, which gives the government's tangible assets, from column 3, which gives its net financial liabilities, indicates the government's official net debt (or, in the case of a surplus, official net worth). It is this figure that Eisner and Pieper view as the correct series for government debt.

The fifth column in the table presents estimates of the value of invisible

Table 10.2
Federal net liabilities and Social Security debt (billions of 1985 dollars)[a]

Year	Gross financial liabilities		(3) Net financial liabilities,	(4) Tangible assets,	(5) Social security debt	(6) Total net debt[a]
	(1) Book value	(2) Market value	Market value	Replace- ment cost		
1950	1,053	1,060	864	494	319	750
1955	1,000	986	772	730	1,401	1,529
1960	944	936	712	711	1,742	1,812
1965	998	970	691	759	1,889	1,880
1966	1,002	981	686	758	1,984	1,975
1967	1,021	984	692	770	1,803	1,798
1968	1,032	989	680	775	2,225	2,205
1969	998	933	617	787	2,096	2,008
1970	1,010	992	653	776	2,675	2,636
1971	1,032	1,028	683	768	3,146	3,144
1972	1,044	1,028	672	771	3,330	3,315
1973	1,053	1,025	618	798	4,104	4,007
1974	1,040	1,014	553	825	4,528	4,333
1975	1,131	1,119	679	815	4,826	4,761
1976	1,224	1,240	772	827	4,986	4,996
1977	1,278	1,262	780	860	5,343	5,320
1978	1,335	1,280	734	889		
1979	1,344	1,279	606	938		
1980	1,391	1,304	598	966		

Source: 1982 Economic Report of the President, table 4.5.
a. This column equals the sum of columns 3 and 5 less column 4 and less the social security Trust Fund.

Social Security bonds. In 1977, the last year for which the data is available, the estimated value of Social Security debt was $5.34 trillion. In contrast, the value of official net debt (net financial liabilities less tangible assets) as reckoned by Eisner and Pieper was actually negative $80 billion in 1977—that is, on its official account the government had an $80 billion surplus in 1977. But including Social Security debt less Social Security's trust fund along with net official debt would enormously alter one's notion of the correct figure for government debt, changing the 1977 debt from negative $80 billion to the $5.32 trillion figure in column 6. With this change in bookkeeping, the government would have reported official deficits, measured in 1986 dollars, in the respective years 1969 and 1970, of $628 billion and $508 billion! During the period 1971 through 1977, official deficits would have averaged $363 billion.

Presumably, had the nation become accustomed to living with such large deficits in the 1970s, there would have been considerably less anxiety about policies that increased reported deficits by only $200 billion in the 1980s.

10.3   A Payment by Any Other Name

One response to the Social Security illustration is that, unlike the purchase of official government bonds, the purchase of Social Security bonds is not voluntary. While this is true, the fact that payments to Social Security are mandated by law is likely to have either minor economic implications or none at all. Consider first the case in which there is no such legal mandate and in which Social Security bonds pay the same return as long-term official government bonds. For those households that have enough liquid assets on hand (or can borrow against their illiquid assets) to purchase the Social Security bonds, such a purchase will not affect their economic opportunities or their economic choices. A number of recent studies indicate that the overwhelming majority of American households are not liquidity constrained and could afford to make such a purchase.

Next consider the case in which Social Security pays less, after adjusting for risk, than the market rate of interest on official government bonds. In this case we can simply relabel Social Security's receipts and payments on its bonds as constituting the sum of (1) "the purchase of Social Security bonds"; (2) "the repayment of principal plus market interest"; and (3) a "tax" equal to the difference between the market rate of interest on official bonds and the rate of interest Social Security can afford to pay. While all Social Security participants will be unhappy because of the "tax" component of the system's return, the economic situation of nonliquidity-constrained participants will not be affected.

In sum, while the voluntary nature of a government's receipts might provide a basis for distinguishing "borrowing" from "taxes" in a liquidity-constrained economy—that is, one in which most people could not afford such a voluntary purchase—the American economy is very far from being liquidity constrained. Indeed, the stock of US private wealth currently exceeds $12 trillion, while Social Security taxes are only $265 billion. Hence, the private sector has in assets more than forty-five times the amount of funds needed to purchase this year's Social Security bonds.

Perhaps the reason current labeling practices are viewed as meaningful by most economists and other students of economics is that most such individuals alive today were brought up on the very simple, if not simplistic, short-run Keynesian model. In this model, it is current income that is the driving determinant of the decision to consume and save, and household assets as well as future income play a quite negligible role. The Keynesian model thus effectively assumes that households are either partially or completely liquidity constrained.

The irony is that the Keynesian model generally suggests that "deficits" are good things—indeed the more the better. Despite this, most economists along with the rest of the country view current federal "deficits" with considerable trepidation.

The model underlying the concern with labeling is quite different from the Keynesian model. It is the life cycle model of saving put forward by Nobel laureate Franco Modigliani, Robert Brumberg, and Albert Ando. In the life cycle model, assets and lifetime earnings, not current income, play the key role, and agents are therefore not liquidity constrained. Unfortunately, this model (or any other neoclassical model) provides no guidance whatsoever as to the proper labeling of government receipts and expenditures. Stated differently, the life cycle model predicts the exact same economic events regardless of the choice of labels, and one can infer nothing about the stance of fiscal policy based simply on information about the amount of official debt.

10.4 "Debt" Policy in the Life Cycle Model

In the life cycle model, fiscal policies have real effects on the economy not because they are labeled one thing or another, but because they either (1) alter economic incentives, (2) redistribute within generations, or (3) redistribute across generations. It is this third issue, intergenerational redistribution, that underlies the concern about "deficits" from the perspective of the life cycle model.

Intergenerational redistribution occurs whenever a government policy increases the present values of payments-less-receipts it makes to some generations at the expense of reducing the present value of payments-less-receipts to other generations.

Consider, for different generations, what happens to the present value of lifetime payments-less-receipts when the government runs a policy it describes as a "tax cut," financed in the short run by what it calls a "deficit" and in the long run by what it calls a "tax increase" to pay the interest on the accumulated "debt."

Older generations are made better off by this policy. In the short run they have to pay less to the government, and at the time the tax increase occurs they may be dead, or if they are still alive they will only have to make the larger payments for a relatively short period of time. Hence, the present value of their lifetime receipts from the government less payments to the government increases.

Middle-age generations may also be better off. If, for example, the tax is assessed on earnings, middle-age generations make smaller payments to the government during the tax cut period, but may escape through retirement most or all of the subsequent larger payments arising from the tax increase.

Younger generations will, in contrast, be worse off because paying the higher amount of taxes for most of one's life will more than outweigh (in present value) the temporarily lower payments. Future generations will also be worse off because they will face higher net payments throughout their lives.

Thus the "tax cut" policy redistributes income from young and future generations to the currently middle-age and older generations. But note that the same fundamental policy could have been achieved with the government announcing a "surplus," rather than a "deficit" at the beginning of the policy. Rather than cutting taxes, the government could have increased transfer payments to middle-age and older generations to leave them in the same position as under the tax cut. For younger generations, the government could have announced a very major tax increase in the current period, coupled with future transfers to these generations that would have left the present value of their receipts-less-payments unchanged. Since future transfer payments don't show up on the government's current books, the government would announce a "surplus" with this change in labels. Hence, the "tax cut" policy could be relabeled a "tax increase" policy with no impact whatsoever on the policy's intergenerational redistribution.

However, intergenerational redistribution from younger and future generations to older generations does lower national saving because older generations will increase their consumption by more than younger generations lower their consumption. The reason is that older generations have fewer years left to live and consequently have fewer years over which to consume the additional resources. Younger generations, on the other hand, spread their reduction in lifetime resources over more years; hence their response to a decline in the present value of net lifetime receipts is to lower their consumption this year somewhat, knowing they will also lower their consumption for many years in the future. In the jargon of economists, older generations have larger marginal propensities to consume than younger generations.

Economists and others in the United States should indeed be concerned about this "crowding out" process. Since 1980 we have been saving only 5.1 percent of our net national product (NNP). In contrast we saved 7.7 percent of NNP in the 1970s, 8.7 percent in the 1960s, and 8.8 percent in the 1950s. Last year's saving rate of 4.4 percent is 50 percent lower than the saving rate of the 1950s.

10.5   Passing the Intergenerational Buck

Once one becomes attuned to thinking about debt policy in terms of intergenerational redistribution, it becomes clear that a variety of government policies, many of which have no direct effect on reported government "deficits," transfer resources from later to earlier generations. One somewhat subtle mechanism is running an unfunded "pay as you go" Social Security system.

In this Ponzi scheme younger working generations pay money to Social Security, which then hands the money over to older, retired generations in the form of "retirement benefits." Every generation pays for the retirement benefits of the previous generation—with one exception: At the initiation of the program, the first generation receives benefits without having had to finance the retirement of its immediate predecessors. This generation receives a windfall at the expense of younger and future generations who receive, on average, a lower rate of return on their Social Security contributions than they would if they had invested these funds privately.

While many of the big winners from Social Security are already deceased, there is still significant intergenerational redistribution underway.

Middle-income household heads who were born in 1930 are predicted roughly to break even from the system. In contrast, middle-income household heads in the cohort to be born in 1990 are projected over their lifetimes to lose, on net, roughly $60,000 in present value as a consequence of participating in Social Security.

Another subtle intergenerational transfer mechanism is a change in the tax base that shifts the burden of taxation from older to younger generations. An example here is switching from an income tax that taxes the capital income of the elderly as well as the labor earnings of the young and middle-aged to a wage tax that hits only the young and middle-aged. Increases in the progressivity of the income tax represent a variant of this type of fundamental debt policy. Switching from a less to a more progressive tax on earned income shifts more of the tax burden onto middle-aged and younger workers whose annual incomes are larger than those of retired elderly for whom taxable income consists primarily of the return on savings.

Perhaps the most subtle mechanism of intergenerational redistribution is government policy that lowers the market value of financial assets. Since older generations are the primary owners of assets, a reduction in asset values reduces the consumption opportunities of the elderly; at the same time it expands the consumption opportunities of younger generations who, through time, can purchase these assets from older generations at a lower price.

An example of such a policy is reducing investment incentives, which, by the way, is part of the president's tax reform proposal. Since investment incentives in the United States are effectively restricted to new investment, old capital—capital that has been fully or partially written off—sells at a discount reflecting the preferential tax treatment available to new capital. A reduction in investment incentives means a smaller discount on old capital, that is, a capital gain to owners of old capital. This capital gain accrues to older generations, and young and middle-aged generations are worse off because they must pay a higher price to acquire claims to the economy's capital stock.

10.6   What Numbers Should We Look At?

If our official debt numbers are inherently arbitrary and provide no real guide to the extent and nature of fiscal policy's intergenerational redistribution, what numbers should one consider in assessing the government's fundamental debt policy? The answer is that we need to examine directly the lifetime budget constraints of different generations and ask whether government policies have expanded the lifetime consumption opportunities of older generations at the price of reduced lifetime consumption opportunities of younger and future generations. The answer to this question bears no relation to how we label particular receipts and payments between the private economy and the government. Accounting doesn't matter when looking at a generation's budget constraint, because the bottom line is how much the generation can afford to consume; this depends on the generation's lifetime receipts from the government net of payments to the government, not on how particular receipts and payments are labeled.

Describing changes in the lifetime budget constraints of all current and successive generations is not easy. First, there are an infinite number of generations to think about. Second, there is great diversity within a generation. Presumably, one could address these concerns by presenting projected lifetime budget constraints for several representative generations and family types within each generation.

A third and much more difficult problem is accurately assessing the expected values of future receipts and payments of current and future generations. In forming such expected values one needs to take into account the likelihood that the government's policy will change in the future. Eisner and Pieper argue that such calculations would be subject to "huge uncertainty" since they involve future receipts and payments that are, in the words of the US Treasury, "highly speculative." While it is easy simply to ignore numbers that are difficult to estimate, ignoring these numbers in considering fiscal policy is akin to navigating in Los Angeles using a highly detailed map of New York rather than a poorly detailed map of Los Angeles.

10.7   Reagan's "Debt" Policy

Having outlined these various mechanisms for running true economic debt policies and having argued that one cannot gauge these policies by looking at official debt numbers, it is time to look at the reality of recent economic debt (intergenerational transfer) policy. The Reagan personal income tax cuts have certainly enhanced the lifetime budgets of older generations at the expense of younger generations. But, up to the present, the magnitude of this intergenerational redistribution appears small when set against the massive intergenerational redistribution in the 1960s and 1970s associated with Social Security.

A second feature of Reagan's fiscal policy is the sizable investment incentives passed in 1981. As just argued, this policy generates capital losses to owners of existing (old) capital and constitutes an economic surplus policy. The magnitude of this redistribution, when set against the redistribution from the tax cuts, appears to correspond to having postponed the tax cuts by roughly one year.

The reform in 1983 of the Social Security system constitutes a third significant fiscal policy altering the intergenerational resource distribution. As late as 1977, Social Security's long-run finances seemed fairly secure. But the ensuing recessions and other economic and demographic events changed the long-run as well as short-run picture. The 1983 reforms made very substantial cuts in the future benefits of all current young generations. The new Social Security law gradually raises the retirement age to sixty-seven and envisions, through the process of bracket creep, the eventual income taxation of Social Security benefits of all retirees, not simply high-income retirees as is now the case.

For current young generations these legislated long-term cuts in Social Security benefits are sizable when compared, for example, with the tax savings they have enjoyed to date from the Reagan tax cut. Hence, this policy also represents a significant economic surplus policy, since it is reducing the welfare of current young generations while helping ensure that future generations will not have their Social Security contributions substantially raised.

My rough assessment is that the Reagan fiscal policy has to date generated, on net, a small economic surplus, although this assessment could change in the near future depending on policy decisions still to be made. However, whether one views the policy in toto as transferring to older or to younger generations, it is clear that the national hysteria concerning "deficits" has been predicated on a set of numbers that have little or no relationship to the issue of fundamental concern. Asserting that the deficit numbers "have no clothes" is not the same as asserting that all is fine in our economic house. On the contrary, it appears clear that the country is experiencing a long-term decline in saving which may well be the result of the unreported but enormous economic deficits associated with Social Security and other unfunded federal government retirement programs in the last three decades.

Given the nation's extremely low saving rate, the current concern about deficit policy is welcome, albeit, as it appears, about ten years too late. However, since our current fixation is on the official budget deficit and not on the fundamental course of intergenerational transfer policy, the concern is not likely to last, for once the official deficit number is fixed, through either a real or an accounting policy, the public and government will lose interest in the question of debt, and indeed may return to more of the kinds of *hidden* debt policies of the last thirty years. It is high time to remove the blinders. Fiscal illusion is a very real problem; it not only blinds us to current fiscal reality, it also leaves us little perspective on the real alternatives for improving our economic future.

11   Is Debt Neutral in the Life Cycle Model?

This paper questions the widely accepted view that deficits have real effects in the life cycle model. The standard analysis of deficit policies within life cycle models treats the government as a dictatorial entity that can effect any intergenerational redistribution it desires. In contrast, if one drops the assumption of compulsion and models the government as a coalition of self-interested parties whose bargaining determines government decisions, then redistribution per se among these parties will not arise and any transfers between these parties will simply represent payment for particular goods or services.

The self-interested parties comprising the government in the present analysis are the young and the old. The young and old share a common interest in a public good, and their representatives bargain over the amount of financing to be provided by each generation. Given this decision, the method by which these funds are raised, whether by issuing debt or levying (lump sum) taxes, is immaterial, since each generation is responsible for its own obligations. In addition, while one selfish generation may absorb the debt of another, such absorption will always be quid pro quo for another payment received or relieved.

The fact that each generation must pay its obligations either immediately or in the future means that a current cut in taxes paid by a particular generation will trigger a future increase in that generation's taxes of equal present value. As in Barro's (1974) altruism model, in which the timing of taxes of effectively infinitely lived households does not matter, the timing per se of the taxes paid by specific generations has no real effects.

The next section presents a two-period life cycle overlapping generations model in which debt is neutral. Section 11.2 discusses the model's implications. Section 11.3 considers whether the paper's economic view of government is consistent with existing political institutions. The fourth section briefly summarizes and concludes the paper.

11.1 A Life Cycle Model with Debt Neutrality

In this two-period model, as in Kotlikoff, Perrson, and Svensson (1986), the members of each generation are identical and each generation elects a single representative. The ratio of the young population to the old population is $1 + \eta$, and the size of the old population is normalized to unity. The technology determining the production of the model's single good is linear. Hence, if the two generations did not share a desire to consume a public good, they would be economically independent.

Let C_{yt} and C_{ot} stand for consumption of the young and old at time t, respectively. Assuming utility is separable at a point in time and over time in consumption and public goods, utility of the young at time t, U_{yt}, and utility of the old, U_{ot}, are given by

$$U_{yt} = U(C_{yt}) + U(G_t) + \beta U(C_{ot+1}) + \beta U(G_{t+1}), \tag{1}$$

$$U_{ot} = U(C_{ot}) + U(G_t), \tag{2}$$

where G_t stands for consumption of the public good at time t and β is 1 divided by $1 +$ the rate of time preference.

The lifetime budget constraint confronting the young at time t is

$$C_{yt} + RC_{ot+1} = E_y + RE_o - T_{yt} - RT_{ot+1}, \tag{3}$$

where R is 1 divided by $1 +$ the rate of interest, E_y and E_o are full-time earnings when young and old, and T_{yt} and T_{ot+1} are lump sum taxes imposed on generation t when young and old. The budget constraint of the elderly at time t is

$$C_{ot} = A_t/R + E_o - T_{ot}, \tag{4}$$

where A_t stands for assets of the elderly at time t and T_{ot} is the lump sum tax on the elderly at time t.

The time t indirect utilities of the young, V_{yt}, and the old, V_{ot}, are given by

$$V_{yt} = V_y(E_y + RE_o - T_{yt} - RT_{ot+1}) + U(G_t) + \beta U(G_{t+1}), \tag{5}$$

$$V_{ot} = V_o(A_t/R + E_o - T_{ot}) + U(G_t). \tag{6}$$

The government at any time t consists of a representative of the young and a representative of the old. They bargain over the level of G_t, the amount of G_t to be financed by the young (F_{yt}), and the amount of G_t to be financed by the old (F_{ot}). The budget constraining their negotiation is

$$G_t = (1 + \eta)F_{yt} + F_{ot}. \tag{7}$$

In addition to financing the amount F_{yt} of G_t, the young at time t can anticipate providing financing of F_{ot+1} at time $t + 1$ to help pay for G_{t+1}. These financing commitments must be paid, in present value, with taxes. Hence

$$T_{yt} + RT_{ot+1} = F_{yt} + RF_{ot+1}. \tag{8}$$

Generation t's commitment to pay F_{yt} can be met either with tax receipts or receipts from the sale of bonds. Denoting by D_t the debt issued by generation t, we have

$$D_t = F_{yt} - T_{yt}. \tag{9}$$

For the old at time t taxes must be sufficient to cover both the payment F_{ot} for G_t and the retirement with interest of their period $t - 1$ issue of debt. Thus

$$T_{ot} = F_{ot} + D_{t-1}/R. \tag{10}$$

Using (8) and (9), one can eliminate the tax terms appearing in the budget constraints of the young and old:

$$C_{yt} + RC_{ot+1} = H - F_{yt} - RF_{ot+1}, \tag{3'}$$

$$C_{ot} = W_t/R + E_o - F_{ot}, \tag{4'}$$

where H stands for the present value of full-time labor earnings and W_t, the real wealth of the old at time t, is given by

$$W_t = E_y - C_{yt-1} - F_{yt-1}. \tag{11}$$

The indirect utilities of the young and the old at time t can be rewritten using (3'), (4'), and (7):

$$V_{yt}(F_{yt}, F_{ot+1}, F_{ot}, F_{yt+1}) = V_y(H - F_{yt} - RF_{ot+1}) + U[(1 + \eta)F_{yt} + F_{ot}]$$
$$+ \beta U[(1 + \eta)F_{yt+1} + F_{ot+1}], \tag{5'}$$

$$V_{ot}(F_{ot}, F_{yt}, W_t) = V_o(W_t/R + E_o - F_{ot}) + U[(1 + \eta)F_{yt} + F_{ot}]. \tag{6'}$$

Note that, given W_t, the sequence of F_{ys} and F_{os} for $s \geq t$ fully determines the evolution of the economy.

Next consider unique stationary solutions to this sequential bargaining problem arising under different bargaining processes. Given the bargaining process and a unique stationary bargaining solution, the economy can differ from one period to the next only in terms of the level of W_t. Hence each unique stationary solution can be characterized by two single-valued functions:

$$F_{yt} = f_y(W_t), \tag{12}$$

$$F_{ot} = f_o(W_t), \tag{13}$$

where the forms of $f_y(\cdot)$ and $f_o(\cdot)$ depend on the bargaining process.

To clarify the determination of $f_y(\cdot)$ and $f_o(\cdot)$ take as an example a cooperative bargaining solution in which the two representatives maximize a weighted average of the utility of the young and the utility of the old, where the weight Φ applied to the utility of the young and the weight $1 - \Phi$ applied to the utility of the old depend on the level of W_t; that is, $\Phi = \Phi(W_t)$. Letting J_t given in (14) stand for this weighted average, the bargaining solution involves the maximization at time t of J_t with respect to F_{yt} and F_{ot}:

$$J_t = \Phi(W_t)(1 + \eta) V_{yt}(F_{yt}, f_o(W_{t+1}(F_{yt})), F_{ot}, f_y(W_{t+1}(F_{yt})))$$

$$+ [1 - \Phi(W_t)] V_{ot}(F_{ot}, F_{yt}, W_t). \tag{14}$$

Note that the representative of the young at time t will anticipate the impact of the choice of F_{yt} on W_{t+1} and, according to (12) and (13), on F_{ot+1} and F_{yt+1}. Hence $f_o(W_{t+1}(F_{yt}))$ and $f_y(W_{t+1}(F_{yt}))$ are substituted for F_{ot+1} and F_{yt+1}, respectively, in V_{yt}.

Expressing the optimal choices of F_{yt} and F_{ot} as functions $m_y(W_t)$ and $m_o(W_t)$, these functions must satisfy the fixed-point mappings

$$m_y(\psi) = f_y(\psi), \tag{15}$$

$$m_o(\psi) = f_o(\psi). \tag{16}$$

Clearly, noncooperative stationary bargaining solutions will also feature fixed-point mappings. Current decisions about F_{yt} and F_{ot} given W_t are always made with the knowledge that future bargaining outcomes depend on W_{t+1}, and stationarity requires that the choices of F_{yt} and F_{ot} when $W_t = \psi$ be identical with the period $t + 1$ choices of F_{yt+1} and F_{ot+1} when $W_{t+1} = \psi$.

11.2   Implications of the Model

The neutrality of debt is implied by the fact that the sequence of F_{yt} and F_{ot} depends only on W_t and is independent of the sequence of D_t. Stated differently, since the solutions to F_{yt} and F_{ot} can be determined before knowing the sequence of T_{yt} and T_{ot}, any reduction in T_{yt}, according to (8), necessitates an increase in T_{ot+1} of equal present value. Deficits may arise, but they are not associated with intergenerational redistribution. In this model, since the young at time t pay F_{yt} regardless of the size of D_t, the choice of D_t is essentially an accounting decision to label a portion of F_{yt} "taxes" and a portion "borrowing."

In chapters 8 and 10 I argue that in neoclassical models the labeling of government receipts and payments as "taxes," "spending," "borrowing," and "debt repayment" is arbitrary and that with judicious relabeling governments can maintain their same real policies while reporting essentially any size deficit or surplus to the public. The point of those discussions was to stress that one may mistake deficit accounting policies for real intergenerational redistribution. The current model has the property that deficits always reflect accounting policies and are never associated with intergenerational redistribution.

Since each generation is responsible for its own debt, one might wonder whether any generation would voluntarily absorb (pay off) the debt of another. The answer is that, given F_{yt} and F_{ot}, the young at time t are equally well off if all or part of their payment of F_{yt} is spent to retire D_{t-1}, provided that the old at time t reciprocate and spend on G_t the funds they would otherwise have spent retiring D_{t-1}. In other words, (7) can be rewritten as

$$G_t = [(1 + \eta)F_{yt} - D_{t-1}/R] + (F_{ot} + D_{t-1}/R), \tag{7'}$$

where the first term on the right-hand side represents the payment of the young spend on G_t and the second term represents the payment of the old spent on G_t.

A related question is whether this model admits long-term debt that is not retired over a large number of time periods. Again the answer is yes. Take the case of consuls. Suppose that each old generation sells its consuls to the young generation on the private market and that the representative of the old transfers to the representative of the young an amount equal to the value of these consuls including interest.

11.3 Is This Economic Model of Government Consistent with Observed Political Institutions?

In the model of government offered here, government decisions are determined by economic rather than political factors, with each group's power emanating from its option to operate independently. Provided that power is not circumscribed, it appears that a wide range of political institutions could be established that would affirm and conduct policies determined by economic fundamentals.

Even if political institutions that simply ratify economic bargains are not established, economic factors may still underlie political decisions. Suppose, for example, that the government in power, be it a collection of individuals or a single individual, is interested in selling political decisions to the highest bidder. Also assume that the government has the power to choose any values of F_{yt} and F_{ot}, provided that the utility levels of the young and old are not reduced below some minimum threat point values. Each age group will, if necessary, bid up to the point that it is indifferent between winning the bidding and receiving its minimum utility value. The age group winning the bidding will instruct the government to choose those levels of F_{yt} and F_{ot} that will maximize the group's own utility subject to the other age group receiving its threat point utility. Hence the rent-seeking activity of the government leads to efficient provision of the public good and determines precisely the shares of the public good to be financed by the young and old. As argued, given these shares, deficits are neutral.

Of course we do not commonly observe political parties or politicians representing distinct age groups. In addition to age differences there are a large number of other differentiating factors that provide a basis for political groupings. Nevertheless, in making decisions affecting the interests of the young as a group and the old as a group, governments may either effectively act as if they consist of young and old representatives who bargain with each other or sell their decisions to the age group offering to pay the highest price.

In contrast to positing an economic view of government, the standard life cycle model appears to assume that the government is free to engage in any intergenerational policy that it desires, including, in the limit, totally impoverishing one generation to the benefit of another. Or, stated differently, the standard model of government assumes that the economic positions of old and young generations place no constraints whatsoever on intergenerational redistribution. Although a purely economic model of government may not be fully realistic, it may more closely approximate reality than a purely political model in which economic decisions are made irrespective of economic circumstances and economic desires.

11.4 Conclusion

Given the critical assumption of generation selfishness in the life cycle model, no generation will accept the debts of another unless it is compensated in one form or another or unless it is coerced. If coercion is ruled out, the issue of government debt is neutral with each generation having to pay off in one form or another its own liabilities. Thus the issue of debt causes a change in the timing (labeling) of tax payments but no change in their present value.

Acknowledgment

I thank Jim Poterba for helpful comments. The research reported here is part of the NBER's research program in taxation. Any opinions expressed are those of the author and not those of the National Bureau of Economic Research.

III

Social Security,
Demographics, and
Savings

Introduction

In the United States, as in other countries, the postwar period has witnessed enormous demographic changes. The United States has experienced a major baby boom followed by a major baby bust, a rapid increase in divorce rates, an increase in life expectancy, a significant lengthening of the retirement period primarily because of early retirement, remarkable changes in the living arrangements of the elderly, an increase in the age of first birth, and a dramatic increase in female labor force participation rates. Each of these demographic changes has had an impact on the US Social Security system, and the US Social Security system may, in turn, be responsible for some of the demographic changes.

This part discusses the impact of Social Security on savings, the impact of baby booms and baby busts on savings, and the interaction effects on savings of Social Security and fertility changes. This part also examines how changes in life spans and work spans can alter savings. Chapter 12 shows how unfunded Social Security can lower savings in life cycle models. It then presents a simulation analysis of unfunded Social Security's impact on savings, demonstrating how general equilibrium effects can modify conclusions based on partial equilibrium analyses. Chapter 13 begins by discussing problems confronting the US Social Security system in light of the demographic transition underway in the United States. Next the chapter uses the Auerbach-Kotlikoff dynamic life cycle simulation model to assess how demographic change over a 250-year period can alter an economy's time path of savings. Finally, the discussion combines Social Security and demographic change and uses the simulation model to look at savings interactions.

The last chapter, chapter 14, discusses why increases in life expectancy and decreases in retirement age are likely to increase savings in life cycle models. The chapter points out that changes in work spans have implications for human capital accumulation and thus age-earnings profiles of young adults. Work and life span changes also have implications for the finances of unfunded Social Security, and these are discussed as well. The main contribution of this chapter, however, is to provide a quantitative sense of the importance of changes in work span and life span to aggregate savings and capital labor ratios.

The main questions addressed in this part are:

1. Why does unfunded Social Security lower savings in life cycle models?

2. How large is the likely effect of unfunded Social Security on aggregate savings?

3. How do partial and general equilibrium savings effects of Social Security differ?

4. If unfunded Social Security encourages early retirement, can the increased saving from a shorter work span offset the decreased saving from unfunded Social Security?

5. How do baby booms and baby busts affect savings in the short, medium, and long runs?

6. What are the implications of baby booms and baby busts on the finances of unfunded Social Security in the short, medium, and long runs?

7. How do baby booms and baby busts affect the rest of the government's fiscal programs?

8. If a baby bust is bad for Social Security, is it nonetheless good for the economy?

9. Does a decrease in the work span because of earlier retirement increase or decrease capital labor ratios?

10. Are there important nonlinearities of changes in the work span and life span on savings?

Some of the principal findings of this part are:

1. A stylized life cycle model suggests that unfunded Social Security has reduced US savings by at most 25 percent in general equilibrium.

2. The offsetting saving stimulus from Social Security–induced early retirement is likely to be small relative to the main effect of unfunded Social Security in reducing saving.

3. Changes in fertility rates can have sizable short- and long-run effects on savings.

4. A prolonged baby bust is likely to improve long-run welfare even if Social Security policy is unaltered. The reason is that the capital deepening associated with the demographic change raises real wages.

5. A baby bust, while increasing the ratio of retirees to workers, reduces the ratio of children to workers and lowers the overall dependency ratio.

6. Because of the decline in the dependency ratio and the capital deepening, income tax rates are likely to decline as a consequence of the baby bust.

7. Equal proportional increases in work span and life span are likely to increase capital per worker by roughly the same percentage.

8. Life span extension can significantly raise total savings.

12

Social Security and Equilibrium Capital Intensity

The past few years have witnessed a growing concern over an aggregate capital shortage. The debate has identified the unfunded social security system as a major factor in reducing aggregate savings and the capital stock since its introduction in 1935. The unfunded financing of the social insurance program is central to the discussion. While the original 1935 legislation authorized the accumulation of a large trust fund, this goal was essentially abandoned with the 1939 amendments. These and other amendments severely weakened the link between taxes paid in and benefits received permitting, it is argued, a time path of aggregate consumption in excess of what would have occurred in the absence of social security.

Recent empirical work at the macro level suggests a substantial reduction in the capital stock generated by social security. One initial estimate put forth by Feldstein (1974c) entails a 38 percent decrease in the capital stock in the long run. Obviously a 38 percent reduction in the capital stock has enormous implications for the steady state level of welfare and factor rewards. This paper investigates the impact of social security on the steady state capital stock of an idealized economy. The purpose of this analysis is to determine whether a simplified economy would exhibit reductions in the capital stock of the 40 percent order of magnitude. The model permits a comparison of general equilibrium steady state effects in which factor returns respond to the fall in the capital stock with the partial equilibrium reduction in the capital stock when factor rewards are held constant. Our analysis considers growth in population and productivity and permits the age of retirement to respond to social security. As Feldstein and others have pointed out, social security may induce early retirement due to an implicit tax on post-sixty-five earnings.[1] The savings response of the young

Quarterly Journal of Economics 43(2):233–54 (1979). © 1979 by the President and Fellows of Harvard College. Reprinted by permission of John Wiley & Sons, Inc.

to a planned earlier retirement is likely to be positive; hence, earlier retirement may lead to more aggregate savings and thus dampen the reduction in the capital stock due to the introduction of an unfunded social security system. We are particularly interested here in determining whether more savings induced by reasonable retirement responses could substantially offset or even reverse social security's otherwise potential reduction in the capital stock.

The paper is organized in the following manner. The first section reviews the theory of social security and life cycle savings. We analyze here the "one for one" replacement of private savings by social security taxes, the retirement effect, and the effect of changes in lifetime wealth due to the yield of the social security system. In sections 12.2 through 12.4 we present our comparative static steady state results for an economy characterized by life cycle savers. Calculations are presented for a range of initial growth rates, interest rates, and retirement ages. The replacement, retirement, and yield effects of unfunded social security on the steady state capital stock are each analyzed in turn. Section 12.5 considers some issues not captured in our life cycle model and raises some doubts at the macro level about the extent of social security's reduction in the capital stock. Section 12.6 summarizes the findings of this paper.

12.1   The Theory of Social Security and Life Cycle Savings[2]

The different effects of social security on life cycle savings are easily understood with the help of figure. 12.1. In the diagram a representative life cycler with fixed life span D faces, in the absence of social security, an earnings stream such as $W(t)$ and chooses a consumption stream such as $C(t)$ and an age of retirement R. The choice of consumption at every age as well as the age of retirement arises from the maximization of an intertemporal utility function subject to the lifetime budget constraint (assuming no bequests) LTW:

$$\int_0^D C(t)e^{-rt}\,dt = LTW = \int_0^R W(t)e^{-rt}\,dt, \tag{1}$$

where $r = $ the rate of interest.

At the micro level the introduction of social security reduces the earnings profile by the amount of the social security tax $\theta \cdot W(t)$ prior to retirement and provides a social security benefit stream $B(t)$ thereafter. The new budget constraint facing the individual is

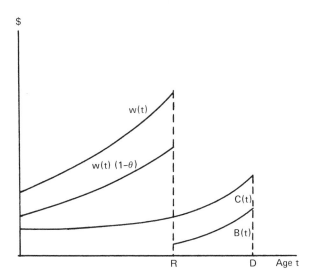

Figure 12.1
Lifetime income and consumption profiles under social security.

$$LTW' = \int_0^{R'} W(t)(1 - \theta)e^{-rt}\, dt + \int_{R'}^{D} B(t)e^{-rt}\, dt. \qquad (2)$$

If retirement does not change ($R' = R$), and the social security system offers an implicit yield on paid-in taxes equal to the market rate of interest r, then lifetime wealth is not affected ($LTW' = LTW$) by the social security system, and the consumption profile is unaltered. Under these assumptions, social security taxes simply replace private savings out of earnings one dollar for one dollar prior to retirement age R. This will be referred to below as the replacement effect.

The assumption of a social security yield equal to the rate of interest requires that

$$\int_0^R W(t)\theta e^{-rt}\, dt = \int_R^D B(t)e^{-rt}\, dt. \qquad (3)$$

Equation (3) states that the present value of lifetime taxes paid in must equal the present value of lifetime benefits received for the system to be actuarially fair. Assuming a stable population with growth rate n and identical individuals, we can write the social security budget constraint as

$$B(t) = \theta W(t)L/M, \qquad (4)$$

where L stands for the labor force and M for the number of retirees. Equation (4) simply equates benefits received to taxes paid in. Using the assumption of a stable population, L/M we may express as

$$\frac{L}{M} = \frac{\int_0^R e^{-na}\, da}{\int_R^D e^{-na}\, da}.$$

(5)

In (5) we integrate over age cohorts. Letting real wages grow at a rate g and combining (3), (4), and (5), we see that when $r = n + g$, social security yields the market rate of interest, and there is no change in lifetime wealth from the yield on social security taxes.

A lifetime wealth increment (the yield effect) arising from growth rates of population plus productivity in excess of the market interest rate would mean a higher LTW and an upward shift in the consumption profile.[3] This lifetime wealth increment would reduce savings at every age implying a greater than one for one reduction in private savings. The yield effect would, correspondingly, be opposite in sign if the interest rate exceeded the growth rates of population plus productivity. A reduction in the age of retirement (the retirement effect) will reduce lifetime wealth by shortening the earnings stream. This will shift the consumption profile downward increasing savings at young ages.[4]

So far the analysis has been partial equilibrium; we have not yet taken into account the general equilibrium shifts in $W(t) \cdot (1 - \theta)$ and $C(t, LTW)$ arising from changes in the steady state capital stock and age of retirement. A reduction in the steady state capital stock may be associated with higher or lower wage earnings and interest rates due to the simultaneous reduction in labor input arising from earlier retirement. In the most likely case where the wage falls and the interest rate rises, both $W(t)(1 - \theta)$ and $C(t, LTW)$ will shift downward. LTW will decline not only because earnings at every age are lower, but also because the interest rate at which future earnings are discounted is higher. The shape of the consumption profile is also likely to change as the discrepancy between the rate of time preference and the interest rate changes.

Each one of the three effects mentioned above—replacement, yield, and retirement—plays a role in determining the final steady state capital stock; the three effects are examined within the life cycle model of Section 12.2. While social security's wealth replacement and lifetime yield have unambiguous impacts on the steady state capital stock, the theoretical effect on the capital stock of induced early retirement is ambiguous. While it is true that the young will accumulate more, the earlier retirement age may leave older cohorts with less accumulated wealth at a given age. Since the steady state capital stock is simply the summation over age cohorts of private wealth holdings, early retirement may increase or decrease the capital stock.

While our purpose here is to determine the quantitative importance of these three effects of social security within an idealized life cycle economy, we realize that social security may alter the capital stock through other channels. For example, if capital markets are imperfect and one cannot borrow against future social security benefits, fixed savings goals (e.g., for a down payment on a house or for children's education) prior to retirement age may lead to a one for one reduction in consumption up to a certain age, and an increase in consumption compared to previous levels thereafter. In other words, the consumption profile could rotate counterclockwise at a given age. By not considering other mechanisms through which social security affects savings, we feel we have, in net, biased our results toward a larger reduction in the capital stock. We shall return to this question of alternative specifications in Section 12.5.

12.2   Social Security and the Steady State Capital Stock in a Life Cycle Economy

In this section we derive the formula for the steady state capital stock in a simplified life cycle economy and consider changes in the steady state capital intensity induced by the introduction of an unfunded social security system. While there is more than one way in which a social security system can become unfunded, for the United States the unfunding resulted from paying out benefits to retirees who had paid little or nothing into the system. The scenario of a historical reduction in US savings relative to consumption entails increased consumption by retirees receiving unanticipated social security benefits without a concomitant reduction in consumption by young taxpayers (the replacement effect predominates). After a transition period the economy arrives at a new steady state with a smaller capital intensity. The extent of the steady state changes will, in general equilibrium, depend on preferences. We specify below preferences exhibiting a constant elasticity of marginal utility l and a time preference parameter ρ. While we shall consider variations in these taste parameters, we stress that our results may be sensitive to the general choice of utility function as well as the assumption of a fixed age of death. Unfortunately, more realistic considerations of family structure and increasing probabilities of death preclude obtaining differentiable formulas of the sort developed here.[5]

Consider, then, an economy characterized by identical individuals, a constant population growth rate n, constant labor augmenting productivity growth g, a fixed life span of D years, and a retirement age R. We assume an intertemporal utility function of the form

$$U = \int_0^D e^{-\rho t} \frac{C_t^{1-l}}{1-l} dt, \tag{6}$$

where ρ is the rate of time preference and l is the elasticity of marginal utility. Letting I stand for the present value of lifetime wealth, we can write the consumption profile as

$$C(t) = \lambda I e^{(r-\rho)t/l}, \tag{7}$$

$$\lambda = \frac{[r(1-l)-\rho]/l}{e^{[r(1-l)-\rho]D/l}-1}, \tag{8}$$

and the lifetime budget constraint is

$$I = \int_0^R W(1-\theta)e^{-(r-g)t} dt + \int_R^D Be^{-(r-g)t} dt. \tag{9}$$

In (4) W and B are, respectively, the wage and benefit prevailing at age zero and are assumed to grow at the rage g. To make our calculations as realistic as possible, we shall consider wage and interest income taxes. Hence in (4), W and r are the net (of wage tax) wage and the net interest rate. Throughout the analysis we assume no government savings; i.e., expenditures on current government consumption equal wage and interest tax payments. In addition, as the social security budget constraint dictates, all social security tax contributions are immediately paid out as benefits.

The steady state capital stock of this economy is simply the aggregate of individual private wealth holdings. To find private holdings at each age, we solve the two differential equations for workers and retirees given in (10) and (11), respectively:[6]

$$\frac{dK_L(t)}{dt} = W(1-\theta)e^{gt} - C(t, I) + rK_L(t), \tag{10}$$

$$\frac{dK_m(t)}{dt} = Be^{gt} - C(t, I) + rKm(t). \tag{11}$$

The solution of (11), using the initial condition that $K_L(0) = 0$, gives the capital stock owned by workers at each age, $K_L(t)$. Similarly, from the terminal condition $K_m(D) = 0$ and (11), we obtain an equation for the capital stock of retirees at each age, $K_m(t)$. Integrating piecewise the capital owned by workers and retirees over age cohorts gives the formula for the aggregate steady state capital stock K per age zero worker measured in efficiency units. In this formula (12) (see Appendix A), the absence of capital owned by the government incorporates our assumption of zero social security funding. The terms H_1, H_2, H_3, H_4 are defined in Appendix A:

$$K = \frac{W}{r - g}(H_1 - \theta H_2 + H_3 H_4). \tag{12}$$

Equation (12) indicates that the steady state capital stock depends on net factor returns, growth rates, the ages of retirement and death, preference parameters, and the social security tax rate θ. Using equation (12), we now consider the effect on the capital stock of changes in θ evaluated at an initial θ equal to zero. The numbers presented below are calculated assuming a 10 percent differential change in the social security tax rate, a 30 percent wage tax (tw), and a 50 percent interest income tax (tr).

12.3   Partial Equilibrium Effect

In this section we consider the reduction in the stock of capital resulting from unfunded social security holding, for the movement, W and r constant. Taking W and r as fixed ignores the disequilibrium that would arise in a closed economy in the factor market for capital. The demand by firms for capital at the initial levels of W and r would exceed the now lower household supply of capital. If we also hold the age of retirement R constant and consider initial conditions given by $r = n + g$, the partial equilibrium effect of social security on the capital stock is independent of preferences. A comparison of general with partial equilibrium effects is interesting in the following sense. If a simple life cycle model indicates that the general equilibrium effects differ little from the partial equilibrium effect, one would have more confidence in using the easily calculable partial equilibrium effect as an estimate of the total effect. In addition, the partial and general equilibrium changes are identical in the case of a small open economy whose interest rate is pegged from abroad. In this case of internationally mobile capital, the introduction of social security will reduce domestic ownership of the world capital stock, but not necessarily the capital in place in the home country, since foreign owned capital can flow in.

From (12), the term $-W\theta H_2/(r-g)$ is the partial equilibrium effect of social security on K holding W, r, and R constant. Evaluating $-H_2$ under the assumption $r = n + g$,[7] we see that the partial equilibrium effect is

$$\frac{-W\theta H_2}{n} = \frac{-W\theta}{n}\left[R + (R - D)\frac{L}{M}e^{-nD}\right]. \tag{13}$$

From (13) it is clear that for this case of $r = n + g$ the partial equilibrium effect is independent of tastes; by assumption nothing has happened to change lifetime wealth; hence the consumption profile remains unaltered, and the change in accumulated capital depends only on the changes in the (net of social security tax) earnings and benefit streams, i.e., the replacement effect. To obtain empirical estimates of the magnitude of this partial equilibrium change, we convert (13) into a capital stock percentage change. For the Cobb-Douglas production function, $K = W_g L/r_b \alpha/1 - \alpha$, where w_g and r_g are labor and capital gross factor returns, and α is capital's share. Dividing this expression into (13) yields the equation in table 12.1; table 12.1 calculates partial equilibrium capital stock changes for different values of R and $D - R$.

The parameter values in table 12.1 were chosen to approximate roughly the US situation. The working period and life spans should be considered as measured from the age at which work begins. If age 20 is taken as the average age at which young people enter the labor force, a retirement age of 45 in the table corresponds to a real world retirement age of 65.

Table 12.1 reports extremely large partial equilibrium changes in the capital stock. Even if we reduce these numbers by the ratio of capital to total assets in the public's portfolio, a number about 0.8, the partial equilibrium effects are still substantial.[8]

Table 12.1
Partial equilibrium change in the capital stock[a]

Retirement age	Age of death		
	50 (%)	55 (%)	60 (%)
40	−35.90	−38.87	−41.78
45	−36.93	−40.07	−43.06
50	−38.03	−41.39	−44.37

a. $r = 0.04$, $d\theta = 0.10$, $n = 0.02$, $tr = 0.5$, $tw = 0.3$, $\alpha = 0.3$, $g = 0.02$.

$$\frac{dK}{K/W, r, R, r = n + g} = -d\theta\left[\frac{R}{L} + \left(\frac{R - D}{M}\right)e^{-nD}\right]\frac{(1 - \alpha)r}{\alpha n}\frac{(1 - tw)}{(1 - tr)}$$

The temptation to invoke the partial equilibrium results becomes apparent when one observes that the partial equilibrium effect reported above is equivalent to the ratio of the unfunded social security deficit to the initial capital stock (see Appendix B). The deficit of the social security system is defined as the present value difference between future benefits and future tax obligations of the current living population. In this partial equilibrium analysis, a fully funded trust fund would have assets exactly covering that differential. Hence the partial equilibrium effects of table 12.1 are equivalent to the reduction in the capital stock from a one time eating up of a fully funded social security trust fund.

Equation (13) indicates that for values of $R = 45$, $L = 55$, and $r - g = 0.02$ a fully funded trust fund would have assets equivalent to about thirty times annual tax contributions. In addition, an examination of (13) reveals that the fully funded trust fund is larger the longer the working period for a fixed life span. It is also larger the longer the life span for a fixed working period. A longer working period for a fixed length of life implies higher yearly benefits after retirement (holding θ fixed). The higher benefits are financed partly out of greater tax revenue due to more older workers and partly out of a larger trust fund. A longer life span, holding retirement fixed, raises the social security wealth of the aged despite a reduction in yearly benefits. Since the present value of tax revenues is fixed, this increase in social security wealth must be financed by a larger trust fund.

Kaplan (1976) calculated that for the United States the current social security deficit was about $1.4 trillion.[9] In 1976 NNP equaled $1,511.8 trillion. Assuming a capital-output ratio of 3 gives us a more direct estimate of the partial equilibrium effect, simply the deficit divided by the capital stock. This figure equals 30.87 percent, somewhat smaller than those presented in table 12.1 (Assuming a 2.5 capital-output ratio yields 37.04 percent.)

The appeal of this partial equilibrium calculation lies in the fact that it does not require specifying tastes. However, as will be made clear below, the general equilibrium effects may be substantially smaller than the partial equilibrium impact. The computational findings for our particular utility functions caution against relying too heavily on partial equilibrium results.[10]

12.4   General Equilibrium Changes in Capital Intensity

In general equilibrium, changes in the wage, interest rate, and age of retirement feed back to affect earnings, benefits, and consumption profiles.

Ignoring issues of retirement and social security yield for the moment, we see that changes in factor returns will have both income and substitution effects on consumption. On the one hand, the lower net wage and higher net rate of interest reduce lifetime wealth and presumably savings when young; on the other hand, the higher rate of interest reduces the price of old age consumption and induces more savings by the young. In a life cycle model where the young substantially outnumber the old, their savings behavior is, of course, crucial to the final outcome. It appears, then, that the general equilibrium changes can be either larger or smaller than those in partial equilibrium.

Turning to the general equilibrium calculation, we differentiate (12) totally with respect to the security tax rate θ (see Appendix A). Again we evaluate the percentage response of the capital stock to a 10 percent social security tax starting from an initial zero social security equilibrium. The final formula for the percentage change in the capital stock assumes a constant returns to scale production function; the actual calculations assume a Cobb-Douglas technology. Equation (12) gives the capital stock supplied by life cyclers as a function of factor returns, growth and taste parameters, and retirement and death ages. Given factor returns, growth parameters, and the age of retirement, there is a corresponding demand by firms for capital based on their production function. In equilibrium, the supply of capital by households equals the demand for capital by firms at the prevailing factor returns. To ensure an initial equilibrium, we select ρ, the time preference parameter, such that the capital stock supplied by life cyclers facing the corresponding net interest rate (the net wage is normalized to 1), retirement age, and other parameters equals the capital stock demanded by firms assuming the Cobb-Douglas technology. Specifically, we choose a value for the net interest rate and a set of values for all of the parameters of the model except ρ. We then calculate the demand for capital by firms and adjust the supply of capital by households to that demand by altering the value of ρ.

In the differentiation, R, the retirement age, is taken to be a function of W_N, defined as the net wage W, less social security taxes and benefits, i.e., the wage facing the worker for post-age R labor effort; $W_N = W(1 - \theta) - \beta$. A retirement elasticity with respect to W_N is developed in the final formula:

$$\frac{dK}{K} = \left[\frac{Q\gamma(ESF_1 + RF_2 + F_3 LSCr) + H_2 G}{(g - r)KG/W + \Psi(F_1 + RQF_2) + F_3 \lambda r} \right] d\theta. \tag{14}$$

Despite the large number of terms, (14) permits some insight into the general equilibrium response. First, note that Q is the retirement elasticity and Ψ and λ are, respectively, the elasticities of the wage and interest rate with respect to capital. When all these terms are zero; i.e., when retirement and factor rewards are invariant to changes in the capital stock, (14) is identical to the partial equilibrium effect described above. E and C are, respectively, elasticities of the wage and interest rate with respect to the labor force. From the bracketed term in the numerator of (14), it is clear that earlier retirement affects the capital stock, in part, by raising the wage rate and lowering the interest rate. Examination of the denominator of (14) for fixed retirement ($Q = 0$) shows that general equilibrium changes in the wage will magnify rather than dampen the partial equilibrium capital stock reduction. The term ΨF_1 captures this magnification; its sign is opposite to that of the other terms in the denominator.

In the calculations presented below we consider, in turn, replacement, retirement, and yield effects as well as variations in tastes. The calculations assume a life span of 55 years and equal rates of population and productivity growth. A retirement elasticity of 0.1 is assumed throughout. The rationale for this figure is the following: A two- to three-year reduction in a forty-five-year working period in response to a 50 percent reduction in the post-retirement wage (assuming a benefit-wage replacement ratio of 40 percent and a 10 percent social security tax) yields elasticities ranging from 0.089 to 0.133. Hence, 0.1 appears to be a historically plausible figure. The reader is of course free to apply his own subjective retirement elasticity to the formula.

Table 12.2 reports replacement and retirement effects for economies initially at an $r = n + g$ steady state. In this calculation the elasticity of marginal utility l equals 1, the logarithmic case. Other values for l will be explored below. The values of the rate of time preference that equate demands and supplies for capital in the initial equilibrium are also indicated. Changes in the capital stock are presented only for those economies that satisfy the initial equilibrium condition for a positive time preference parameter. For calculating the pure replacement effect the elasticity of retirement Q in (14) is set to zero; similarly in measuring the retirement effect by itself, H_2 is set to zero. Table 12.3 gives the initial level of capital as well as its distribution among the working and retired population for different parameter values. Table 12.4 presents savings profiles for a life cycler prior to and after the introduction of social security for selected parameters values. Throughout the tables the initial age zero net wage is normalized to one.

Table 12.2
Effects of Social Security on the steady-state capital stock[a]

Net rate of interest	Age of retirement	Rate of time preference	Retirement effect	Replacement effect	Total effect
0.04	42	0.0070	0.043	−0.260	−0.210
	45	0.0028	0.063	−0.258	−0.189
0.05	42	0.0160	0.047	−0.267	−0.213
	45	0.0120	0.066	−0.263	−0.190
	50	0.0058	0.147	−0.258	−0.104
0.06	42	0.0232	0.048	−0.267	−0.212
	45	0.0196	0.068	−0.263	−0.189
	50	0.0138	0.148	−0.256	−0.102

a. Elasticity of marginal utility, 1. Age of death, 55. Elasticity of retirement, 0.1. Interest income tax rate, 0.5. Wage income tax rate, 0.3. Social Security tax rate, 0.1. $r = n + g$. $n = g$

Table 12.3
Stock of capital[a]

Rate of interest	Age of retirement	Rate time preference	Capital stock of pre-retirees	Capital stock of retirees	Total stock of capital
0.04	42	0.0070	180.35	36.90	217.25
	45	0.0028	201.05	25.18	226.23
0.05	42	0.0160	132.58	26.74	159.32
	45	0.0120	147.52	18.05	165.57
	50	0.0058	169.05	5.56	174.61
0.06	42	0.0232	101.73	20.10	121.83
	45	0.0196	111.79	13.34	125.13
	50	0.0138	127.37	4.02	131.59

a. $n + g = r$. $n = g$. Age of death, 55. Interest income tax, 0.5. Wage income tax, 0.3. Elasticity of marginal utility, 1.

Table 12.4
Patterns of life cycle savings[a]

Age	No social security	Social security in partial equilibrium	Social security in general equilibrium
0	0.329	0.229	0.304
5	0.414	0.263	0.374
10	0.511	0.302	0.444
15	0.618	0.335	0.502
20	0.732	0.353	0.532
25	0.849	0.337	0.511
30	0.961	0.276	0.400
35	1.056	0.145	0.141
40	1.117	-0.089	-0.347
45 $-$[b]	1.118	-0.471	-1.187
45 $+$[b]	-1.962	-0.347	-0.613
50	-3.398	-0.886	-1.765
55	-5.424	-1.705	-3.621

a. Rate of interest, 0.04. Age of retirement, 45. Rate of time preference, 0.012. $r = n + g$. $n = g$. Elasticity of marginal utility, 1.
b. 45 $-$ and 45 $+$ correspond to instants prior to and after age of retirement.

The results of table 12.2 suggest a general equilibrium reduction in the steady state capital stock ranging from 10 to 21 percent. The retirement effects can be quite important, offsetting by over half the replacement effects of social security for certain parameter values. The theoretical conjecture that the retirement effect may be negative is not confirmed in table 12.2; all retirement effects are positive. Assuming no retirement response at all, we see that the replacement effect is at most 27 percent; 27 percent, though smaller than Feldstein's 38 percent figure, is still quite a large change. The figures for a forty-five-year working period are quite similar, independent of the initial rates of interest and time preference. If we take these numbers as the most reliable, the steady state reduction in the capital stock is about 19 percent with the retirement effect offsetting the replacement effect by about 7 percent.

In contrast to the partial equilibrium findings of table 12.1, table 12.2 indicates that the reduction in the steady state capital stock is smaller the larger the initial age of retirement. However, different initial interest rates

Table 12.5
Yield effect of social security on the steady-state capital stock[a]

Growth rate of population plus produc- tivity $(n + g)$	Rate of time preference	Yield effect	Retirement effect	Replacement effect	Total effect
0.03	0.0234	0.106	0.043	−0.312	−0.158
0.04	0.0178	0.053	0.054	−0.286	−0.172
0.05	0.0120	0.000	0.066	−0.263	−0.190
0.06	0.0064	−0.056	0.081	−0.246	−0.213

a. Net rate of interest, 0.05. Age of retirement, 45. Elasticity of marginal utility, 1. $n = g$. Social security tax, 0.10.

and the associated time preference parameters appear to have little effect on the results. Table 12.3 reveals that the initial levels of the capital stock are much more sensitive to starting parameter values than are the percentage change calculations of table 12.2.

So far we have reported only results that assume a social security tax yield equal to the net rate of interest. Table 12.5 considers non- (private) golden rule assumptions. The yield effect is computed as the change in the replacement effect when the term $-H_3 H_5$ is included in forming H_2; when $r = n + g$, $H_3 \cdot H_5$ equals zero.

The numbers presented indicate that even a small (1 percent) differential in yields can have a substantial influence on the final steady state outcome. All yield effects have the theoretically indicated sign. Higher than interest yields on social security tax contributions lead to more consumption and reduce accumulation while lower yields promote savings. A 1 percent yield differential appears to have about a 5 percent impact on the final steady state capital stock. However, table 12.5 also indicates that higher social security yields are associated with larger retirement and smaller replacement effects, leaving the general equilibrium changes still in the neighborhood of 19 percent.

Comparing the replacement effects of tables 12.2 and 12.5 with the partial equilibrium changes in table 12.1, we see that in general equilibrium the response of saving to a higher interest rate plays a major role in dampening the partial equilibrium impact. In table 12.4 this saving response is depicted for a typical life cycler. The table presents saving patterns for three situations: zero social security, social security assuming only partial equilibrium changes in the capital stock and social security

Table 12.6
Steady-state capital reductions under various preference structures[a]

Elasticity of marginal utility	Rate of time preference	Retirement effect	Replacement effect	Total effect
0.50	0.0310	0.016	−0.154	−0.135
0.75	0.0216	0.043	−0.213	−0.165
1.00	0.0120	0.066	−0.263	−0.190
1.25	0.0026	0.086	−0.307	−0.212

a. Net rate of interest, 0.05. Age of retirement, 45. $r = n + g$. $n = g$.

allowing for general equilibrium changes in factor returns but no retirement or yield effects. The table indicates a strong response of savings to changes in factor returns for this particular set of preferences. For the utility function under consideration the reaction of savings to the interest rate is neatly parameterized by l, the elasticity of marginal utility. High elasticities of marginal utility flatten out consumption profiles and produce a smaller savings response to higher interest rates. Low elasticities of marginal utility imply the opposite characteristics. Table 12.6 presents capital stock changes that assume different elasticities of marginal utility. For an elasticity of 1.25 the replacement effect is 31 percent, while an elasticity of 0.5 entails only a 15 percent replacement impact in general equilibrium.

12.5 Alternative Specifications and Some Macro Issues

The analysis above has highlighted some aspects of social security's impact on savings to the exclusion of others. First, as mentioned above, capital market imperfections may imply a substantially different savings response by the young from that posited above. Second, social security may reduce the uncertainty of old age consumption and retirement savings by providing an indexed real annuity.[11] A third important issue raised by Barro is the extent to which the intergenerational transfers associated with unfunded social security led to offsetting private transfers with no reduction in aggregate savings.[12] The argument here is that transfers from the young to the old through social security simply replace private transfer from young to old. Alternatively, forced social security transfers from young to old may result in offsetting transfers from the old to the young in the form of bequests. Unfortunately, there is little empirical evidence to resolve this question. By ignoring private intergenerational transfers in our analysis, we do not mean to belittle this issue; rather, we have attempted here to provide an upper bound for social security's impact on the steady state capital stock.

At the macro level the notion that the US experience under social security can be understood as a movement across steady states with a concomitant decline in the capital stock begs a number of issues. Chief among these is the historical ability of the economy to transform the consumption expenditures that were generated by the unfunded social insurance system into savings while maintaining full employment. In other words, in the absence of social security would the federal deficit have stayed the same or risen to match the historic rise in the social security deficit? Much of the historic depletion of the social security trust fund was due to redistributional considerations. The early dissolution of the link between tax payments and benefits came about because of a desire to aid elderly citizens who had never paid into the system as well as dependent wives and widows who had never worked. Hence, it is appropriate to inquire whether this type of redistribution would not have taken place in any case with similar consequences for the historic level of aggregate savings.

Finally, even if agreement could be reached on the statement that social security has depleted US wealth holdings, the openness of the US economy argues against assigning the entire depletion to the capital stock in place in the United States.

12.6   Summary and Conclusion

These caveats are important for viewing our results in proper perspective. We have provided evidence above that supports the proposition that social security *could* have caused a *major* reduction in the capital stock. The life cycle model with its retirement effects suggests a 20 percent steady state reduction in general equilibrium, although a substantially greater partial equilibrium reduction. While we caution that our results may be sensitive to the particular preference structure considered, it appears that reasonable retirement responses can only partially offset the replacement effect of social security on the capital stock. In addition, the analysis has suggested how general equilibrium changes in factor returns can magnify or dampen the partial equilibrium effects presented above.

To conclude, we feel that the final resolution of social security's effect on capital accumulation will require additional empirical work at both the micro and macro levels. The results for our simplified life cycle economy indicate that the impact of unfunded social security on capital intensity can be quite large and, hence, deserve to be taken seriously.

Appendix A

Solution of differential equations (5) and (6) in the text are given by

$$K_L(t) = W(1 - \theta)\left(\frac{e^{rt} - e^{gt}}{r - g}\right) + vI[e^{(r-\rho)t/l} - e^{rt}] \tag{A1}$$

and

$$K_M(t) = \frac{-B[e^{gt} - e^{gL+r(t-L)}]}{r - g} - vI[e^{xD+rt} - e^{(r-\rho)/lt}], \tag{A2}$$

where

$$x = [r(1 - l) - \rho]/l$$

and

$$v = \frac{1}{1 - e^{xD}}.$$

Integrating $K_L(t)$ and $K_M(t)$ over age cohorts yields (A3) [expression (7) in the text]:

$$K = \frac{W}{r - g}(H_1 - \theta H_2 + H_3 H_4), \tag{A3}$$

where

$$H_1 = \left(\frac{1 - e^{(r-u)R}}{u - r}\right) - \left(\frac{1 - e^{-nR}}{n}\right),$$

$$H_2 = \frac{L}{M}\left[\left(\frac{e^{-nR} - e^{-nD}}{n}\right) - \left(\frac{e^{(r-u)R} - e^{(r-u)D}}{u - r}\right)e^{(g-r)D}\right] + H_1 - H_3 \cdot H_5,$$

$$H_3 = \left[\frac{e^{zD} - 1}{z} - \left(\frac{1 - e^{(r-u)R}}{u - r}\right) - \left(\frac{e^{(r-u)R} - e^{(r-u)D}}{u - r}\right)e^{xD}\right],$$

$$H_4 = \frac{1 - e^{(g-r)R}}{1 - e^{xD}},$$

$$H_5 = -H_4 + \frac{L}{M}\left(\frac{e^{(g-r)R} - e^{(g-r)D}}{1 - e^{xD}}\right),$$

$u = n + g,$

$z = [(r - u)l - \rho]l.$

Differentiating (A3) with respect to θ yields

$$\frac{dr}{d\theta}K + (r - g)\frac{dK}{d\theta} = \frac{dW}{d\theta}F_1 + W\frac{dH_2}{d\theta} - WH_2 + WH_3\frac{dH_4}{d\theta} + H_4\frac{dH_3}{d\theta},$$

(A4)

where

$F_1 = H_1 + H_4 H_3$ (see text for definition of symbols) (A5)

$$\frac{dH_1}{d\theta} = [e^{(r-u)R} - e^{-nR}]\frac{dR}{d\theta} + \left[\frac{(r - u)(R - 1)e^{(r-u)R} + 1}{(r - u)^2}\right]\frac{dr}{d\theta},$$

(A6)

$$\frac{dH_3}{d\theta} = (e^{xD} - 1)\frac{dR}{d\theta}e^{(r-u)R} + J\frac{dr}{d\theta},$$

(A7)

$$\frac{dH_4}{d\theta} = (r - g)ve^{(g-r)R}\frac{dR}{d\theta} + \left[Re^{(g-r)}v + v^2\frac{(1 - l)D}{l}(1 - e^{(g-r)R})e^{xD}\right]\frac{dr}{d\theta}.$$

(A8)

Let $f(L, K)$ stand for the production function

$W_g = f_L(L, K),$ (A9)

$$\frac{dW_g}{d\theta} = f_{LL}\frac{dL}{dR}\frac{dR}{dWn}\frac{dWn}{d\theta} + f_{LL}\frac{dK}{d\theta}.$$

(A10)

Taking R as a function of $Wn = W(1 - \theta) - B$ and setting $\gamma = (M + L)/M$ implies that

$$\frac{dWn}{d\theta} = \frac{dW}{d\theta} - W\gamma.$$

(A11)

(A10) and (A11) give

$$\frac{dW}{d\theta} = \frac{-W\gamma EQS}{1 - EQS} + \frac{(1 - tw)f_{LK}}{1 - EQS}\frac{dK}{d\theta},$$

(A12)

where

$$S = \frac{dL}{dR}\frac{R}{L},$$

$$E = \frac{f_{LL}L}{W},$$

$$Q = \frac{dR}{dWn}\frac{Wn}{R}.$$

Similarly we can find that

$$\frac{dr}{d\theta} = \frac{-rCQS\gamma}{1 - EQS} + H_6\frac{dK}{d\theta},$$ (A13)

where

$$H_6 = \frac{rCQS}{W}\frac{(1 - tw)f_{LK}}{(1 - EQS)} + (1 - tr)f_{KK},$$

$$C = \frac{f_{LK}L}{r}.$$

Substituting the above expressions into (A4), using the additional terms defined below, and dividing by K we obtain (a) in the text. Additional terms entering equation (19) are

$$\Psi = f_{KL}L/W,$$

$$\lambda = F_{LK}L/r,$$

$$F_2 = \frac{H_3(r - g)e^{-(r-g)R}}{1 - e^{xD}},$$

$$F_3 = \frac{-K}{W} + \frac{R}{r - g}F_2 + H_4J + F_4 + \frac{H_4H_3D}{e^{-xD} - 1}\frac{(1 - l)}{l},$$

$$F_4 = \frac{[(r - u)R - 1]e^{(r-u)R} + 1}{(r - u)^2},$$

$$G = 1 - EQS,$$

$$J = \frac{[(zD - 1)e^{zD} + 1]}{lz^2} - F_4$$

$$+ \frac{[(R(r - u) - 1)e^{(r-u)R} - (D(r - u) - 1)e^{(r-u)D}]}{(r - u)^2}e^{xD}$$

$$+ \left[\frac{e^{(r-u)R} - e^{(r-u)D}}{(r - u)}\right]e^{xD}\frac{(1 - l)D}{l}.$$

Appendix B

The deficit (DEF) of an unfunded social security system is defined as the present value of future benefits less future taxes for the living population:

$$DEF = \int_0^D PVB(a)e^{-na}\, da - \int_0^R PVT(a)e^{-na}\, da, \tag{B1}$$

where $PVB(a)$ and $PVT(a)$ are the present value of benefits and taxes for an individual age a.

Prior to retirement

$$PVB(a) = \int_R^D Be^{(g-r)(t-a)}\, dt = B\left[\frac{e^{(g-r)R} - e^{(g-r)D}}{r - g}\right]e^{(r-g)a}, \tag{B2}$$

and after retirement

$$PVB(a) = \int_a^D Be^{(g-r)(t-a)} = B\left(\frac{e^{(g-r)a} - e^{(g-r)D}}{r - g}\right)e^{(r-g)a}. \tag{B3}$$

$PVT(a)$ is given by

$$PVT(a) = \int_a^R We^{(g-r)(t-a)} = \theta W\left(\frac{e^{(g-r)a} - e^{(g-r)R}}{r - g}\right)e^{(r-g)a}. \tag{B4}$$

Using (B1)–(B4), setting $r = n + g$, and recalling that

$$B = \frac{1 - e^{-nR}}{e^{-nR} - e^{-nD}} = \frac{L}{M}, \tag{B5}$$

we obtain

$$DEF = \frac{\theta W}{n}\left(R + (R - D)\frac{L}{M}e^{-nD}\right), \tag{B6}$$

the partial equilibrium effect discussed in the text.

Notes

The author has benefited greatly from discussions with Martin Feldstein, Laurence Weiss, and Lawrence Summers, but especially Christophe Chamley. I gratefully acknowledge financial support from the Hoover Institution.

1. For a comprehensive review of the growing literature on social security and retirement see Cambell and Cambell (1976) and Pellechio (1978).

2. Feldstein (1976) is the pioneering work in this area and contains a survey of the literature. We consider here the pure life cycle model without intergenerational transfers in order to indicate the maximum possible reduction in the capital stock from unfunded social security.

3. Assuming consumption at every age is a normal good.

4. Kotlikoff (1979) presents a micro econometric study of the replacement, yield, and retirement effects.

5. See, for example, Tobin (1967).

6. See Appendix A.

7. This is a private golden rule condition, not a social golden rule, since r is the net, not the gross, rate of return. The current US situation appears to approximate $r = n + g$.

8. See Tobin (1967), p. 255.

9. See Kaplan (1976).

10. Indeed, once general equilibrium changes occur, a partial equilibrium computation (such as that just performed for the United States), which uses current values of r, R, L, and M, may be substantially biased away from the true partial equilibrium effect.

11. See Diamond (1967).

12. See Barro (1974).

13

Simulating Alternative Social Security Responses to the Demographic Transition

with Alan J. Auerbach

The 1983 amendments to the Social Security Act contain a number of significant changes in the system's current and projected fiscal operations. These include federal income taxation of half of social security benefits of high-income recipients starting in 1984, gradual increases in the normal retirement age from 65 to 67 starting in 2000, and the expansion of coverage to new government workers and to employees of nonprofit organizations. If fully implemented these provisions are projected (under intermediate IIB assumptions) to close social security's OASDI, 75-year, open-group deficit, with little or no need for additional payroll tax increases beyond those currently stipulated in law.

While the new legislation has greatly alleviated if not eliminated OASDI's short-term cash flow problems, the longer-term financial picture remains very much in doubt. There are four important reasons for continued concern with and analysis of the system's long-term finances. First, even if all aspects of the new law are actually implemented, economic and demographic conditions close to the social security actuaries' pessimistic assumptions may prevail. In this case the OASDI deficit, expressed as a fraction of taxable payroll, equals 10.0 percent over the period 2034 to 2058.

The second reason for continued concern about social security's long-term finances is that most of the long-run financial savings from the new legislation arise from measures that are scheduled to be implemented. These measures include increases in the retirement age and the gradual rise, through inflationary bracket creep, in the fraction of social security recipients whose benefits are taxed under the federal income tax. If future administrations and congresses periodically legislate away this bracket

National Tax Journal 38(2): 153–68 (1985). © 1985 by the National Tax Association–Tax Institute of America. Reprinted with permission.

creep, or if they delay or eliminate raising the retirement age, the nation will again face, under intermediate assumptions, significantly higher OASDI tax rates in the early part of the next century.

The third concern about the new legislation is closely tied to the second. During the period 2000 to 2015, the ratio of the OASDI trust fund's cummulative projected surplus to annual benefit payments rises from 2.3 to 5.4. To put this figure in perspective, the current ratio of gross US debt to current social security benefits is roughly 4.5. Since the OASDI trust fund holds its reserves in the form of government securities, the 1983 amendments implicitly project social security's holding of a significant fraction, if not all, of official government liabilities. While such an OASDI investment policy raises questions of its own, there is the logically prior question of whether future politicians will have the will to preserve a trust fund for future generations that would represent over 5.4 years of benefits by 2015 (7.0 years under the IIA assumptions). Such a surplus is unprecedented in the history of the program; the current OASDI reserve can cover less than 3 months of benefit payments. Rather than accumulate a large trust fund, future politicians may dissipate the projected social security surplus by legislating larger benefit payments, or by indexing federal income taxation of social security benefits, or by reversing the scheduled retirement age increases. Another, more subtle way in which this trust fund could be dissipated involves the government running larger official deficits over this period because they find the Social Security Trust Fund a ready purchaser of these securities. From the perspective of the government's overall deficit policy, such a program, in the extreme, simply transforms an implicit liability into an explicit liability and transfers concerns about major increases in payroll tax rates into concerns about major increases in income tax rates.

The fourth concern about social security's long-run finances involves the very sizable long-term Medicare (HI) deficit projected by the Senate Finance Committee. Under current law and using the actuaries' intermediate IIB assumptions, the HI deficit reaches 7.9 percent of taxable payroll by 2030 and rises to 8.3 percent of taxable payroll by 2055.

The unsettled nature of social security's long-term finances certainly provides ample rationale for analyzing social security and the demographic transition. A second motivation for the paper is the rather limited understanding of the general equilibrium effects of demographic change per se on numerous macroeconomic variables, including savings, interest rates, wage rates, and non–social security tax rates. While the US is engaged in a very dramatic demographic swing, the potential impact of the baby boom's baby bust on general economic performance has received surprisingly little attention. The dearth of research in this area probably reflects the difficulty in deriving analytic expressions for the time paths of economies experiencing complex demographic change. This paper addresses the issue using a dynamic life cycle simulation model that simultaneously considers a large variety of economic choices and relationships.

The simulation model is highly stylized. As a result, its social security cost estimates cannot be directly compared with those of the social security actuaries. While the model does not contain much of the detail entering the actuaries' calculations, it provides insight into certain issues that cannot be addressed by the Social Security Administration's actuarial model. These issues include (1) general equilibrium changes in capital formation, labor supply, wage rates, and interest rates arising from demographic change as well as social security policy, (2) changes in living standards associated with demographic swings that are independent of social security, (3) general equilibrium changes in the lifetime budget opportunities of different generations associated with alternative social security policies, and (4) the impact of social security policy on other elements of the government's fiscal policy, e.g., income tax rates.

In contrast to the government's studies the results presented here are heuristic and should not be construed as empirical estimates. The simulation methodology used here is probably most useful for assessing the relative effects of alternative policies and the changes through time generated by such policies. Simulation studies of this kind are certainly not substitutes for empirical work, but they can provide general insight into how demographic swings influence economic variables, how different social security and other fiscal policies interact, into the timing and duration of policy impacts, and into the relative importance of particular policies in altering social security finances and economic variables.

Section 13.1 summarizes several key findings of our previous modeling of social security that ignored demographics. This discussion is helpful in understanding the contribution of demographic change to the economy's dynamic equilibrium. Section 13.2 describes the model's general characteristics and its method of solution. The particular version of the model developed for this analysis has a number of unique features, in particular the inclusion of demographic factors in household saving behavior.

The third section presents two different types of demographic transitions for economies both with and without social security systems. The two demographic changes considered are (1) a baby bust involving an immediate and sustained decline in birth rates and (2) a bust-boom-bust cycle of birth rate changes that appears more closely to resemble the past 60 years of US fertility experience.

Section 13.4 examines four different policy alternatives to simply raising social security payroll taxes in response to the long-term reduction in the fertility rate. These policy options are (1) reductions in social security's replacement rate, (2) increases in social security's retirement age, (3) taxation of social security benefits under the income tax, and (4) accumulation of a trust fund through general revenue finance, interest on which is used to help finance future social security benefit payments. Each of these policies constitutes part of the government's current response to social security's financial problems.

The simulations presented here, with a more elaborate general equilibrium life cycle model, confirm several general conclusions reached in Auerbach and Kotlikoff (1984). First, demographic changes of the type now projected require very major adjustments in social security's finances. Second, while future young generations face a significant burden of supporting parents, they also face a greatly reduced financial burden with respect to child support. On balance, future young workers in the simulation model enjoy higher standards of living than initial young generations under each of the social security policy responses considered as well as the response of annually adjusting social security payroll taxes to meet prespecified benefit payments.

The impact of demographic change on the simulated economy's time path of economic variables is quite sizable. A major baby bust or cycles of baby booms and busts and both capable of producing sharp increases and declines in saving rates long before the demographic transition is complete. In our base case simulation of a baby bust, the economy's saving rate falls by 20 percent in the first year of the transition. It then rises over the next 20 years to a value in excess of that in the initial steady state. By year 50 the saving rate drops to less than two-fifths of its initial value. A second general finding concerning demographic transitions is that fertility cycles are capable of producing major economic cycles in wages and interest rates. A third feature of the simulations is that many of the more important changes in economic variables coincide with the appearance in the workforce of baby boom or baby bust generations.

13.1   General Equilibrium Modeling of the Impact of Social Security

The impact of social security on the economy is complicated, because it involves so many aspects of individual behavior. General equilibrium simulation models can be extremely helpful in assessing these effects. In two previous papers (Auerbach and Kotlikoff 1983, 1984), we have used such models to evaluate particular effects of an unfunded social security system. These models, as well as the one used in the present paper, extend in various ways the basic model presented in Auerbach and Kotlikoff (1983a). The basic model consists of three sectors: household, government, and production. Most of the model's complexity lies in its characterization of household decisions as being made, at any time, by 55 overlapping generations of adults, each saving to accumulate resources according to an optimal, life-cycle consumption plan. Household behavior is characterized by perfect foresight; i.e., the future wages, interest rates, and tax rates anticipated by each household at each date are those that actually occur. Labor supply, including the retirement decision, is endogenous. The family structure is modeled as follows. Children spend their first 20 years being supported by adults 20 years older. At age 21 children start their own families. Children are, therefore, included in each family's consumption decision for that family's first 20 years of existence.

In order to simulate the demographic transition, we have had to simplify the previous Auerbach-Kotlikoff (1984) model by dropping the assumption of heterogeneous intertemporal preferences and considering only life-cycle families. We hope this restriction can be relaxed in the future, though the solution of the heterogeneous model with fluctuating cohort size assuming perfect foresight is a considerable and apparently very computer-expensive challenge. In the next section we review the version of the Auerbach-Kotlikoff simulation model used in this chapter.

13.2   The Model and Its Solution

The basic model with variable labor supply is described in detail in Auerbach, et al. (1983). The inclusion of children and social security is described in Auerbach and Kotlikoff (1984). The reader is referred to these papers for the relevant equations describing the behavior of households, firms, the government in general, and the social security system in particular. We will summarize these relations briefly before describing how the model is solved and how we have introduced changing fertility rates to the simulations.

Households maximize a lifetime utility function based on the consumption and leisure of adults from age 21 to 75 and their children from the parents' age 21 to 40. The utility of parent and child is described by a nested, constant elasticity of substitution utility function, with an intertemporal elasticity of substitution (between present and future consumption) of 0.25 and a static elasticity of substitution between current consumption and leisure of 0.8. The pure rate of time preference in the function is equal to 1.5 percent. Children's consumption and leisure has a weight that increases over time in their parent's objective function. As the child grows this modeling leads to more consumption. The wage paid to particular age groups follows a profile that rises steeply during childhood, continues to rise less steeply until middle age, and then falls off gradually. This typically leads to a commencement of part-time work during the late teens and retirement during the late 60s. Households have perfect foresight, in that the relevant future parameters entering into their decisions are those that, in general equilibrium, will actually prevail.

Firms in the model are represented by a single, competitive firm producing with a constant-returns-to-scale, Cobb-Douglas production function in labor and capital. The social share in output is set at 0.25. Aside from social security, the government's fiscal policy involves financing a predetermined path of government consumption with a proportional income tax under the constraint of annual budget balance. When population structure changes, we keep constant the level of government consumption expenditures per capita.

The social security system is financed by a flat rate payroll tax; this tax pays for benefits received after the date of initial benefit receipt based on a formula similar to the one actually used to calculate average indexed monthly earnings (AIME). The model's calculated values of AIME are multiplied by a replacement rate to arrive at the benefit level. Our baseline assumptions are that benefits begin at age 65 and that the replacement rate is 60 percent. Because of their complexity, we ignore the ceiling on the payroll tax base (now quite high, anyway), the earnings test that currently prevails between the ages of 65 and 72, and the early retirement provision available between 62 and 65. We also assume that the payroll taxes themselves have no work disincentive effects, i.e., are viewed as lump-sum taxes by the worker.

The model is solved using a Gauss-Seidel procedure that begins with guesses about aggregate stocks of capital and labor and uses these and the production function to generate wage and interest rates. These factor price paths plus tax rate paths provide time paths of net prices that households use in determining their annual saving and labor supply. Aggregating household saving and labor supply provides new estimates of the economy's capital stock and labor force. Household factor supply, given the government's fiscal constraints, also generates new guesses of the levels of income tax rates, social security benefits, and social security system payroll tax rates. In each iteration of the model these guesses about tax rates and benefits are incorporated into the households' plans. Hence, when convergence is reached (i.e., the guessed values of variables equal those computed based on these guesses), households have taken account of the tax rates and benefits levels that actually prevail in the perfect foresight equilibrium.

This general method of solution is applied first to the economy's initial steady state, then to the final one to which the economy will converge. Finally, we solve for the years of transition *simultaneously*, assuming the transition is completed within 250 years. This simultaneous solution is necessary because, with perfect foresight, future variables, such as the interest rate, affect current decisions. We assume that the policy change that led to the disturbance of the initial steady state was unanticipated, but that perfect foresight is immediately reestablished.

Fertility change is introduced into the model in the following way. For a certain period after the beginning of the transition, we exogenously specify the number of births per adult. Thereafter, a procedure is needed to make the population's age structure converge to that of the new steady state. Constancy of the birth rate will not suffice, since the perfect regularity in the birth cycle would perpetuate cohort size differences through an infinite series of "echo effects." In the "real world," this happens to a very much smaller extent because births are distributed over parents of different ages, but such a solution would be infeasible for a simulation model. Instead, we assume that, after a specified period time, typically 50 years, births equal the number born the previous year times the annual population growth rate of the final steady state. The impact of this modeling is that after at most 75 additional years the population age distribution stabilizes. This procedure makes the fertility rates themselves endogenous for a period, and they may fluctuate somewhat unrealistically for a time. However, experiments varying the critical date at which fertility rates become endogenous suggest that, as long as it is well after the posited demographic transition has occurred, this date has no important influence on the basic nature of the results.

13.3   Baseline Simulations: The Economic Effects of a Demographic Transition

In this section, we present simulation results for two types of demographic transitions: a sudden and permanent reduction in the birth rate (bust) and a cycle of decline and increase in the birth rate followed by a permanent drop ("bust-boom-bust"). In the simulations of the bust transition, the fertility rate drops from one involving a 3 percent rate of annual population growth to one yielding a stationary population. In the second set of simulations, containing the "bust-boom-bust" (BBB) fertility behavior, the birth rate drops to one child per parent over a 5-year period. For the next 10 years the rate stays constant, after which it gradually rises reaching its original level twenty years into the transition. Between years 20 and 35 the birth rate remains at this high value. It then gradually falls again to the zero population growth fertility rate between years 35 and 45. The birth rate remains at this level until year 50, after which birth rates are endogenously determined according to the requirement that a flat ZPG (zero population growth) age structure is achieved by year 125 and thereafter. The model is given an additional 125 years (a total of 250 years) to reach a new steady state.

In all of our simulations we have had to introduce the assumption of a positive government capital stock to generate plausible values for the economy's capital-output ratio. This was not necessary in our previous life-cycle modeling work because of the absence of children. With the consumption needs of nonproductive children added to the population, life-cycle behavior based on plausible preference parameters yields extremely small capital stocks. The inability of the life-cycle model, by itself, to explain US wealth is a point that has been made by several authors [e.g., chapter 1 of this book]. This model provides further indication of the inadequacy of the pure life-cycle model without bequests to explain observed rates of capital accumulation. While the current model excludes bequests, the assumption of a net positive government capital stock yields plausible magnitudes for observed macroeconomic variables. While our modeling of private saving ignores the significant intergenerational transfer behavior that appears to arise in the US, it provides an important benchmark for considering such models. In addition, it should be stressed that large masses of US households could have the types of preferences assumed here, but simply hold small or zero amounts of wealth because of the particular shape of their age-wage profile.

We begin our analysis by examining how the composition of the population changes over time for each of these transitions. Table 13.1 presents the fraction of the population at different ages during the demographic transition. The top panel presents data for the bust transition, while the bottom panel considers the BBB transition. In the bust transition the age structure flattens smoothly over time until, in year 50, it is essentially flat,

Table 13.1
Population age structure in transition

Year/Cohort	1–20	21–40	41–60	61–75
Bust transition				
0	0.50	0.28	0.15	0.07
20	0.37	0.36	0.20	0.09
50	0.28	0.28	0.28	0.16
70	0.26	0.27	0.27	0.20
110	0.27	0.27	0.27	0.21
150	0.27	0.27	0.27	0.20
Bust-boom-bust transition				
0	0.50	0.28	0.15	0.07
20	0.41	0.33	0.18	0.08
50	0.40	0.30	0.19	0.11
70	0.27	0.34	0.26	0.13
110	0.25	0.25	0.25	0.25
150	0.27	0.27	0.27	0.20

and equal to its long-run structure. The bust-boom-bust transition has a more complicated picture, starting out similar to the straight bust, but maintaining through year 50 a fairly steep age structure because of the rebound in the birth rate. The boom cohort is clearly evident in year 70's bulge in the fraction of young adults between 20 and 40 and, again in year 110, in the fraction of the population age 61 to 75. The different time patterns in age structures in these two cases suggest that the BBB transition will take longer to evidence large changes in macroeconomic variables, but will generate larger swings in these variables as the boom cohort moves through the population.

This intuition is supported by the results of the basic simulations of the economy without social security, summarized in table 13.2. In these simulations we normalize the initial wage rate to unity and set the government surplus (capital stock) so that the gross interest rate is approximately ten percent. The stock of government capital per capita is held constant throughout each simulation.

In the bust simulation wages rise and interest rates gradually fall throughout the transition reflecting the increase in capital per worker as the fraction of young workers, who own relatively little wealth, decreases. The association of capital deepening with lower population growth rates dates at least from Solow's (1956) growth model with its Keynesian saving

Table 13.2
Characteristics of demographic transitions (no social security)

Year	Saving rate	Wage rate	Interest rate	Marginal tax rate
Bust transition				
0	7.6	1.00	9.9	15.0
1	6.1	1.00	9.9	13.0
5	6.6	1.00	10.0	12.4
10	7.4	1.00	10.0	11.8
20	7.9	1.02	7.4	11.6
50	3.0	1.10	7.3	10.6
70	−0.01	1.11	7.1	10.3
110	−1.5	1.11	7.1	10.5
130	0	1.11	7.1	10.6
150	0	1.11	7.1	10.6
Bust-boom-bust transition				
0	7.6	1.00	9.9	15.0
1	6.2	1.00	9.8	14.7
5	6.7	1.00	9.9	12.7
10	7.7	1.00	10.0	12.1
20	8.7	1.02	9.3	14.1
50	4.3	1.04	8.9	11.8
70	6.2	1.06	8.3	9.9
110	−5.0	1.13	6.9	10.9
130	0	1.11	7.1	10.7
150	0	1.11	7.1	10.6

behavior. The decline in marginal income tax rates arises because government consumption per capita is held fixed, but the fraction of the population with no taxable income, in this case, children, falls through time. Once the transition has begun, saving rates immediately fall. They then rise through year 20 to a value above that in the initial steady state. There follows a decline in saving rates, which reach negative values in year 110. Between 110 and 150 the saving rate rises to its ultimate steady state value of zero. The initial drop in the saving rate is unrelated to concurrent demographic changes, which in period 1 are still unimportant, but to *anticipated*, general equilibrium increases in future after tax wages. These projected increases in budget opportunities produce higher current consumption and lower current saving. Between years 1 and 20 the drop in fertility reduces the number of children and the importance of their dissaving, i.e., consumption; by year 20 the fraction of the population between 20 and 60 has increased from 45 percent to 56 percent, and this group is doing more saving because of the reduced number of mouths they must feed. By year 70, however, the decline in birth rates has affected the size of the young and middle age adult saving population, so that the only boom group remaining are the aged dissavers. This leads, temporarily, to a slightly negative saving rate.

The BBB transition as suggested, occurs more slowly and is then characterized by erratic swings in macroeconomic activity as the bulge cohort ages. The wage rate rises gradually to 1.06 by year 70, rather than the 1.11 of the bust transition. It then overshoots its long-run level as the boom cohort, with its large accumulated savings of capital, retires. Likewise, marginal tax rates take longer to fall and undershoot their long-run value. Saving rates remain positive and quite high through year 70; they then fall precipitously to -5.0 percent of income in year 110 before converging to zero.

The well-being of individuals alive during either of these transitions can be compared to that of cohorts who die before there is any change in fertility. The method we use is to ask what additional fraction of lifetime resources an individual in the initial steady state would have to receive to be as well off as a member of a particular transition cohort. Normally a well-defined measure, this approach has some ambiguity in the current context, because the parent's utility function depends on the consumption and number of children. Our model does not, however, provide reasons for specified changes in fertility. Hence, equating a decline in the number of children with a decline in parental welfare seems rather arbitrary. In a more elaborate model that fully described the fertility decision, a decline in the number of children could be associated with both negative and positive changes in parental welfare. For example, if children provide pleasure to their parents, but changes in social customs make childbearing more difficult, this would imply a loss in welfare not present if reduced fertility came about due to, say, an income effect associated with increased living standards. We side-step this problem by focusing on the welfare adults receive directly from their own consumption and leisure. That is, our measure of welfare changes of transition adult cohorts is the increase or decrease in resources (spent on own adult consumption and leisure) that adults in the initial steady state would receive to be left with the level of utility from adult consumption and leisure enjoyed by particular transition cohorts during their adulthoods. This is essentially the equivalent variation measure of the change in economic circumstances faced by a transition cohort.

In Table 13.3 we express these welfare effects as a percentage of the lifetime resources of initial steady state cohorts. The cohort born in year − 75 (75 years prior to the date the transition begins) is the last generation not affected by the transition. The first part of the table, labeled "bust," shows the welfare effects of the transition under various fiscal regimes. The first column corresponds to the basic transition without social security discussed above. The drop in birth rates causes a large long-run welfare gain of 12.57 percent, about three-fourths of which is realized by those born in year − 10. The primary reason for this upward shift in welfare is the reduction in children per adult. As we are considering welfare measured in terms of adult expenditure on consumption and leisure, such as demographic shift permits a higher level of welfare since adults now shift a greater fraction of their resources toward their own consumption and leisure. The corresponding BBB transition, represented in the first column of the second part of table 13.3, evidences the same jump in welfare as birth rate declines, but also displays a temporary welfare drop associated with the temporary rise in fertility.

We now consider the inclusion of unfunded social security in each of these transitions. The baseline model of social security assumes a 60 percent replacement rate and an initial age of benefit receipt of 65. The choice of a 60 percent replacement rate may seem odd given that actual US replacement rates are currently about 40 percent. A 60 percent rate is used to account for several types of social security benefits not explicitly modeled in our analysis. These include dependent and survivor benefits, medical benefits, and disability benefits. The simulated payroll tax rate associated with the 60 percent replacement rate assumption is 5.2 percent, which is still quite low relative to the current combined employer-employee OASDHI payroll tax. Hence, from the perspective of approximating a realistic payroll tax rate our replacement rate assumption is too low. As mentioned above, however, one aim here is not to provide empirical estimates, rather to provide a qualitative sense of the relative impact of various demographic swings and alternative social security policies. Such qualitative findings are quite similar whether one uses a 40, 60, or 80 percent replacement rate for a baseline value.

Summary statistics for the bust and the bust-boom-bust simulations are given in table 13.4. As expected, saving rates are generally lower and interest rates higher in the presence of social security. Chapter 12 discusses why unfunded social security in a life cycle model leads to a permanently lower long-run level of savings and welfare. A brief explanation is that an unfunded social security program is able, in the long run, to

Table 13.3
Welfare effects of demographic transition, equivalent variations as percent of adult resources

Generation born in year	No social security	With social security	Immediate cut in benefits	Immediate increase in retirement age	Trust fund policy	Taxation of social security benefits
Bust						
−75	0.00	0.00	0.00	0.00	0.00	0.00
−65	0.02	0.01	−0.16	0.01	0.01	−0.05
−50	0.16	0.12	−0.02	−0.00	0.06	0.08
−25	0.95	0.99	1.50	1.26	0.53	1.18
−10	9.23	9.50	10.61	10.22	10.46	9.88
0	10.33	9.95	11.35	10.87	13.06	10.41
10	11.32	9.87	11.67	11.03	12.81	10.42
25	12.36	8.70	11.29	10.37	11.97	9.54
50	12.76	7.29	10.46	9.24	11.07	8.29
75	12.66	6.72	10.09	8.82	10.56	7.79
100	12.57	6.94	10.23	8.93	10.77	7.97
125	12.57	6.94	10.21	8.93	10.78	7.98
150	12.57	6.95	10.21	8.94	10.79	7.99
Bust-boom-bust						
−75	0.00	0.00	0.00	0.00	0.00	0.00
−65	0.01	0.01	−0.16	0.01	0.00	−0.05
−50	0.11	0.08	−0.06	−0.04	0.03	0.03
−25	0.63	0.66	1.17	0.92	0.14	0.87
−10	8.54	8.80	9.89	9.51	9.49	9.23
0	2.09	1.46	2.85	2.39	4.37	2.03
10	2.43	1.40	2.99	2.47	4.51	2.03
25	9.91	9.02	10.60	10.06	12.30	9.55
50	12.09	9.54	11.67	10.90	12.58	10.23
75	13.03	6.66	10.17	8.88	10.20	7.79
100	12.57	6.84	10.09	8.82	10.42	7.87
125	12.57	6.84	10.12	8.84	10.44	7.89
150	12.57	6.95	10.15	8.88	10.48	7.93

Table 13.4
Characteristics of demographic transitions (with social security)

Year	Savings rate	Wage rate	Interest rate	Marginal tax rate	Payroll tax rate
Bust transition					
0	6.8	1.00	11.1	15.0	5.2
1	5.5	1.00	11.1	12.9	5.2
5	5.9	1.00	11.2	12.3	5.3
10	6.7	1.00	11.2	11.7	5.4
20	7.0	1.02	10.6	11.6	5.6
50	1.7	1.09	8.5	10.8	10.1
70	− 1.3	1.08	8.8	10.1	14.0
110	− 1.5	1.07	9.1	10.1	15.0
130	0	1.07	9.0	10.3	13.9
150	0	1.07	9.0	10.3	13.9
Bust-boom-bust transition					
0	6.8	1.00	11.1	15.0	5.2
1	5.5	1.00	11.0	14.7	5.3
5	5.9	1.00	11.2	12.6	5.2
10	6.8	1.00	11.2	12.0	5.3
20	7.8	1.02	10.5	14.1	5.5
50	3.6	1.03	10.1	11.8	7.5
70	5.1	1.05	9.6	9.9	8.6
110	− 5.6	1.08	8.7	10.5	18.7
130	0	1.07	9.1	10.3	13.8
150	0	1.07	9.0	10.3	13.9

pay only the economy's growth rate as the rate of return on social security contributions rather than the marginal return to capital. Since the return to capital exceeds the growth rate in the simulated economy, in the long-run steady state every dollar contributed by the agents in the model to social security is repaid with benefits that equal less than a dollar in present value. This feature would, by itself, make those living in the long run under unfunded social security worse off. In addition the introduction of unfunded social security permanently lowers capital per worker and, therefore, workers' wages. The reason for the decline in saving and capital per worker is that "start up" elderly generations who experience windfalls at the initiation of unfunded social security consume more and, thereby, generate a reduction in total national saving. The increased consumption of this initial start up generation of elderly is partially offset by the decreased consumption of younger generations who find they are receiving a lower rate of return than the market can offer on their social security contributions. However, this reduced consumption is never large enough to restore the economy's stock of capital; part of the burden of paying for the initial start up elderly generation's increased consumption always lies in the future in the form of reduced consumption of future generations. At any point in time then, the initial increased consumption of the start up elderly has not been fully offset by reduced consumption of generations ensuing up to that point in time. As a consequence, the stock of savings is permanently reduced.

Aside from the payroll tax, the two simulations with social security behave rather similarly to their counterparts without social security presented in table 13.2. The presence of the payroll tax means that, as fertility declines, part of the adult welfare gain previously discussed will be offset by the increased ratio of beneficiaries to workers associated with rising payroll taxes. This is evident if one compares the second column of the two parts of table 13.3, corresponding to the welfare effects under the two transitions in the presence of social security. While the qualitative patterns of welfare change are the same, cohorts gain uniformly less. About 45 percent of the long-run gain is lost. The effect is smaller in the short run, since the earlier generations escape the burden of higher social security taxes.

Payroll tax rates are quite different in the bust and the bust-boom-bust transitions. In the first, the number of retirees per worker increases fairly smoothly, with the rise in the payroll tax similarly behaved. In the second, the population bulge represented by the baby boomers holds down payroll tax increases while they are working, and causes them to jump sharply once this cohort retires. In year 110 the payroll tax rate is 18.7 percent, almost 3.5 times the initial steady state value.

13.4 Social Security Policy Responses to the Demographic Transition

Table 13.5 shows saving, wage, interest, and tax rates arising under the two demographic transitions if social security's replacement rate is cut in year zero from 60 to 40 percent. These benefit cuts apply to all cohorts receiving benefits at the time they are implemented. The table also presents comparable figures for a gradual reduction in the replacement rate to 40 percent starting in year zero and ending in year 20. Table 13.4 indicates the

Table 13.5
Immediate cut in replacement rate from 60% to 40%

Year	Baby bust					Bust-boom-bust				
	S/Y	w	r	τ_y	τSS	S/Y	w	r	τ_y	τSS
0	6.8	1.00	11.1	15.0	5.2	6.8	1.00	11.1	15.0	5.2
1	6.6	1.00	11.2	12.7	3.5	6.7	1.00	11.1	14.5	3.5
5	6.8	1.00	11.1	12.3	3.5	6.8	1.00	11.1	12.6	3.5
10	7.2	1.01	10.9	11.9	3.6	7.4	1.01	10.9	12.1	3.5
20	7.3	1.03	10.2	11.8	3.8	8.1	1.03	10.5	14.3	3.7
50	3.0	1.12	10.2	10.9	6.7	4.5	1.05	9.6	12.0	5.0
70	−1.1	1.11	8.0	10.4	9.4	5.4	1.06	9.2	10.1	5.8
100	−0.3	1.11	8.2	10.9	9.4	−1.4	1.17	7.7	11.2	8.9
110	−1.5	1.10	8.2	10.5	10.0	−5.5	1.11	8.1	10.9	12.5
130	0.0	1.10	8.4	10.6	9.2	−0.1	1.10	8.4	10.7	9.2
150	0.0	1.10	8.4	10.6	9.2	−0.01	1.10	8.4	10.7	9.2

time paths of these variables when the replacement rate is held fixed. A quick comparison of these two tables indicates that the social security tax rate is quite sensitive to the benefit cut policy, while the impact on other variables is relatively minor. Rather than rising to 13.9 percent, as in table 13.4, the long-run social security tax rate in table 13.5 increases from 5.2 percent to 9.2 percent. The social security tax rate is significantly lower throughout the transition under the policy of immediately cutting the replacement rate than in the transitions of table 13.4.

The benefit cuts, by reducing the scale of unfunded social security, generates a 3 percent larger pretax wage rate than would otherwise occur. The additional capital deepening associated with this larger long-run wage rate explains the slightly larger saving rates in table 13.5 compared with those of table 13.4. The effect of phasing in the replacement rate cut rather than implementing it immediately is to leave the economy with roughly 20 percent higher payroll tax rates during the first ten years of the transition. The welfare effects of these benefit cuts are predictable. For both demographic transitions, the immediate cut in benefits causes a welfare loss to older generations alive in year zero (table 13.3), but a welfare improvement for younger cohorts, even for those who are age twenty-five, and hence already working, at the time of the change. In the long run, such a policy leads to substantially greater welfare then under the policy of simply passively adjusting social security tax rates to meet the benefits associated with a 60 percent replacement rate.

An alternative to the explicit reduction in benefit levels would be an increase in the retirement age. Table 13.6 presents the characteristics of the demographic transition for two such policies, an immediate increase in the retirement age from 65 to 67, and the same rise occurring in year 20, after being announced in year zero. The welfare effects of the first of these policies is shown in the fifth column of table 13.3. Both in terms of macroeconomic and welfare effects, an immediate increase in the retirement age by two years has a similar but smaller impact than the immediate 40 percent benefit cut. In the long run, the payroll tax rate rises to 11.0 percent, higher than the 9.2 percent in the former case. Likewise, the long-run welfare gain of 8.94 percent is smaller than the previous gain of 10.21 percent. If one extrapolates from our results, they suggest that maintenance of the original payroll tax rate would require a benefit cut of close to 75 percent, and/or an increase in the retirement age by 6 years.

Another alternative that has been suggested to reduce the growth in payroll taxes is the taxation of social security benefits. Indeed, starting with the Tax Equity and Fiscal Responsibility Act of 1982, higher income families will face regular income taxation on half their social security benefits. In table 13.7 and the last column of table 13.3, we show the effects of taxing all social security benefits beginning at the start of the demographic transition, with the receipts kept within the social security system to reduce payroll taxes. Such a policy leads initially to reductions in social security taxes, but in the long run has a smaller impact than any of the policies previously examined, because of the relatively low rate of income taxation. As this suggests, the long-run welfare impact of this policy is smaller than the others, but generations reaching adulthood early in the transition actually do almost as well as under the other policies.

Finally, we consider in table 13.8 a policy that some have advocated as a long-run solution to the long-run social security deficit: the accumulation of a trust fund. The simulated policy involves a one-third surcharge on the payroll tax for the first twenty years of the transition, proceeds of which are contributed to the trust fund, i.e.; in the initial twenty year period this policy raises revenues by one-third more than is necessary, in equilibrium, to pay for current benefits. After year 20 the accumulated trust fund is held constant per capita, and the income and principal beyond that needed to maintain a constant per capita trust fund is used to help pay for benefits. Under this policy the social security tax rate drops to essentially zero in year 20 of both transitions and, as the retiree/worker ratio rises, significantly limits the rise in the payrolls tax. In each simulation, the long-run payroll tax (8.4 percent for the bust case, 8.8 percent for the BBB case) is

Table 13.6
Immediate and gradual increase in retirement age from 65 to 67

	Baby bust					Bust-boom-bust				
Year	S/Y	w	r	τ_y	τSS	S/Y	w	r	τ_y	τSS
Immediate										
0	6.8	1.00	11.1	15.0	5.2	6.8	1.00	11.1	15.0	5.2
1	5.9	1.00	11.2	12.8	5.2	6.0	1.00	11.1	14.6	5.2
5	6.4	1.00	11.2	13.3	4.2	6.3	1.00	11.2	12.6	4.1
10	7.0	1.00	11.1	11.8	4.1	7.2	1.00	11.1	12.0	4.1
20	7.3	1.02	10.3	11.7	4.3	8.0	1.03	10.3	14.3	4.2
50	2.4	1.11	8.2	10.9	7.7	4.1	1.04	9.8	11.9	5.8
70	−1.2	1.10	8.4	10.3	11.6	5.3	1.06	9.4	10.0	7.2
100	−0.4	1.10	8.4	10.8	10.9	−1.5	1.12	7.8	11.1	10.1
110	−1.5	1.08	8.7	10.3	12.3	−5.6	1.10	8.3	10.7	15.9
130	0	1.09	8.6	10.5	11.0	0.1	1.09	8.7	10.5	11.1
150	0	1.09	8.6	10.5	11.0	0	1.09	8.6	10.6	11.0
Gradual										
0	6.8	1.00	11.1	15.0	5.2	6.8	1.00	11.1	15.0	5.2
1	5.6	1.00	11.1	12.9	5.2	5.7	1.00	11.0	14.6	5.2
5	6.1	1.00	11.2	12.3	5.3	6.1	1.00	11.2	12.6	5.2
10	6.8	1.00	11.1	11.8	5.3	7.0	1.00	11.1	12.0	5.3
20	7.3	1.02	10.5	11.6	5.0	8.0	1.02	10.4	14.2	4.9
50	2.1	1.10	8.2	11.9	7.9	3.8	1.04	9.9	11.9	5.8
70	−0.2	1.10	8.4	10.3	11.6	5.3	1.06	9.4	10.0	7.2
100	−0.3	1.10	8.4	10.8	10.9	−1.5	1.12	7.8	11.1	10.1
110	−1.5	1.08	8.7	10.3	12.3	−5.6	1.10	8.3	10.8	15.9
130	0.0	1.09	8.6	10.5	11.0	1.2	1.09	8.7	10.5	11.0
150	0.0	1.09	8.6	10.5	11.0	0	1.09	8.6	10.6	11.0

Table 13.7
Immediate taxation of Social Security benefits

	Baby bust					Bust-boom-bust				
Year	S/Y	w	r	τ_y	τSS	S/Y	w	r	τ_y	τSS
0	6.8	1.00	11.1	15.0	6.0	6.8	1.00	11.1	15.0	6.0
1	5.8	1.00	11.1	12.8	4.5	6.0	1.00	11.1	14.6	4.5
5	6.2	1.00	11.2	12.3	4.6	6.2	1.00	11.2	12.6	4.6
10	6.8	1.00	11.1	11.8	4.7	7.0	1.00	11.1	12.1	4.7
20	7.1	1.02	10.4	11.7	5.0	7.9	1.02	10.4	14.2	4.7
50	2.2	1.10	8.3	10.9	9.0	3.9	1.04	9.9	11.9	6.6
70	−1.3	1.09	8.6	10.2	12.6	5.2	1.05	9.5	9.9	7.8
100	−0.4	1.09	8.6	10.7	12.6	−1.6	1.12	8.0	11.0	11.8
110	−1.5	1.08	8.9	10.2	13.5	−5.6	1.09	8.5	10.7	16.7
130	0.0	1.08	8.8	10.4	12.5	0.1	1.08	8.9	10.4	12.4
150	0.0	1.08	8.8	10.4	12.5	0.0	1.08	8.8	10.5	12.5

Table 13.8
Accumulation of a Social Security trust fund

	Baby bust					Bust-boom-bust				
Year	S/Y	w	r	τ_y	τSS	S/Y	w	r	τ_y	τSS
0	6.8	1.00	11.1	15.0	6.0	6.8	1.00	11.1	15.0	6.0
1	5.9	1.00	11.2	12.8	7.0	6.0	1.00	11.1	14.6	7.0
5	6.4	1.00	11.2	12.4	7.0	6.4	1.00	11.2	12.7	7.0
10	7.2	1.00	11.1	12.0	7.1	7.5	1.00	11.1	12.3	7.1
20	7.5	1.03	10.2	12.5	−0.0	8.5	1.03	10.1	15.2	0.9
50	2.1	1.11	8.0	11.4	5.3	3.4	1.05	9.5	12.9	1.8
70	−1.4	1.11	8.1	10.9	8.3	5.3	1.07	9.0	10.7	3.6
100	−0.0	1.11	8.1	11.4	8.8	−1.6	1.13	7.6	11.7	8.7
110	−1.5	1.10	8.3	11.0	9.2	−5.6	1.11	8.1	11.4	13.2
130	0.0	1.10	8.3	11.2	8.4	0.2	1.10	8.4	11.2	8.6
150	0.0	1.10	8.3	11.2	8.4	0.1	1.10	8.3	11.2	8.8

the lowest of any of the simulations presented. As one would expect, the trust fund transitions produce the highest long-run welfare gains of any of the social security transitions considered (table 13.3). At the same time, they are the only policy simulations, excluding simply passively adjusting payroll tax rates, under which each generation gains from the changes in fertility.

13.5 Summary and Conclusion

A central lesson of the simulations presented here is that demographic conditions are potentially very significant determinants of economic performance and welfare. Indeed, the time path of demographic change dominates the outcomes of each of the five social security policy transitions, despite the fact that these five simulations involve significantly different and quite substantive social security policy responses. The simulated demographic transitions suggest that the swings in US fertility currently underway can have very major impacts on factor returns over the long run and produce quite precipitous changes in saving rates in the short run. To place our findings on demographic change in perspective, it should be noted that the simulated long-run changes in factor returns and capital-labor ratios from major fertility declines are of the same order of magnitude as the simulated effect of entirely abolishing unfunded social security. In comparison with the very considerable research that has been conducted concerning the saving impact of this and other government fiscal policies, the effect of demographic change on saving is a little studied phenomenon.

The presence of a social security system does have important effects on the economic transition associated with either baby busts or cycles of baby booms and busts; but the attendant financial squeeze placed on social security in these transitions is of secondary importance with respect to the long-run level of economic welfare. While payroll tax rates may rise dramatically, long-run welfare is nonetheless substantially higher, as measured in terms of equivalent increases in levels of adult consumption and leisure. This reflects, in part, the fact that each adult parent has "fewer mouths to feed" and, therefore, can enjoy a higher individual standard of living. In addition, while the replacement fertility rate prevailing in the long run leaves more elderly per capita in society, the sharp drop in children per capita means an overall decline in the ratio of dependents to prime age workers in the economy. For the government these changes potentially imply smaller demands on its regular fiscal operations (e.g., educational expenditures) which we model here as involving a fixed level of government consumption expenditure per capita. In our model the marginal income tax rate used to finance this spending falls from 15 percent to roughly 10.5 percent in each of the simulations in response to the lower overall dependency ratio. Hence, while the typical worker must support more elderly through social security, he (she) supports fewer children, both directly as a parent and indirectly as an income taxpayer. A glance at table 13.4 indicates that under a passive policy of adjusting social security payroll taxes, combined income and payroll tax rates rise from an initial 20.2 percent to a long-run value of 24.2 percent. Had the income tax rate not dropped to 10.3 percent, the combined long-run tax rate would have equaled 28.9 percent.

While the combined long-run tax rate is 4.2 percentage points higher in this simulation, the pretax wage rises by 7 percent reflecting the significant increase in capital intensity associated with the long-run decline in fertility rates. It is this general equilibrium impact on factor returns that is primarily responsible for the higher long-run level of welfare.

Although reasonable alterations in social security policy appear incapable of significantly altering the basic economic impact of substantial demographic swings, the particular choice of social security policy is nonetheless quite important. In comparison with simply allowing payroll taxes to adjust upward to meet required benefit payments, major reductions in replacement rates, major increases in the retirement age, or the accumulation of a significant trust fund are all policies that can raise the long-run level of welfare by an amount equivalent to almost 4 percent of lifetime expenditure on consumption and leisure. A 4 percent long-run welfare increase is a large number when compared with the simulated long-run welfare effects of a variety of major fiscal policy changes. The potential long-run welfare gain is not, however, freely obtained; rather, such long-run welfare gains come at the price of reductions in the welfare of transition cohorts, typically those alive at the time of the demographic change as well as those born within 25 years of the initial date of the change. Hence the choice of social security policy in the midst of the demographic transition is of considerable importance to the intergenerational distribution of welfare.

Acknowledgment

We thank Andrew Myers for outstanding research assistance. This paper is part of the Brookings Institution project on retirement and aging which is funded by Brookings and the Department of Health and Human Services.

14 Some Economic Implications of Life-Span Extension

This chapter is concerned with the question: What would the economy look like if we suddenly discovered the fountain of youth? Though this question may seem fanciful, a growing number of contemporary Ponce de Leons with impressive scientific credentials would argue that there is a significant chance of unraveling the mystery of aging in the near future. The search for the famed fountain of youth has moved from the swamps of Florida to the laboratories of biologists, chemists, and physicians. These gerontologists are not, however, searching for some magical elixir; they are instead exploring the biochemical nature of aging with the goal of ultimately stopping, if not reversing, the aging process.

The scientific community appears to differ about the near-term likelihood of discovering a drug that would prevent or at least retard aging. While the probability of quickly finding such a youth drug may be small, the socioeconomic consequences of such a discovery could be enormous. The expected value of social science research on this type of life-span extension may be very large from the perspective of a cost-benefit calculation. Until some very basic social science research is done on the subject, however, it will be difficult to judge how much of the nation's scientific as well as social science research support should be devoted to life-span extension.

I concentrate here on the implication of life-span extension for aggregate factor supply and economic welfare. While this is the major focus, I also consider the impact of life-span extension on the economy's skill composition and on existing economic institutions, particularly the social security system.

The major conclusion I draw from my analysis is that the expansion of work-span and total life-span should significantly increase economic

In *Aging: Biology and Behavior*, J. March and J. McGaugh, eds. (New York: Academic Press, 1981), 97–114. © 1981 by Academic Press, Inc. Reprinted with permission.

welfare, which is measured as average consumption per year over an individual's lifetime; increasing the length of life, including productive life, appears to permit a higher level of consumption in every year that an individual is alive.

Life-span extension is taken to mean keeping people young for longer periods of time. This is quite different from what one conventionally means by life-span extension—keeping old people alive for longer periods.

The youthful extension of life with which I am here concerned represents a true expansion of the lifetime leisure and consumption opportunities of individuals. Assuming that both consumption and leisure are normal goods, this increase in individuals' life-spans permit them to purchase more commodities as well as to enjoy more leisure during their elongated lives. The purchase of additional commodities does require, however, additional earnings. Hence, at least some fraction of the increased number of years resulting from the youth drug will be devoted to additional work

In the stylized economic models examined below, I consider equal increases in the age at retirement and the age at death as well as proportionate increases in age at retirement and age at death. Since the potency of the youth drug is as much in doubt as the availability of the drug itself, I attempt to distinguish the economic consequences of short extensions of life from those of long extensions.

In the first section I investigate how life-span extension affects our per capita output and economic welfare, assuming a fixed stock of capital in the economy. The section demonstrates that even if output per worker falls due to diminishing returns to increases in the labor force, output per capita and economic welfare may still rise.

The second section considers the impact of longer lives on aggregate capital accumulation and the economy's capital-labor ratio. This analysis indicates that capital intensity is likely to rise or at least not to fall as life-spans and work-spans are extended. This in turn implies that output per worker and wages per worker will not be adversely affected by longer life-spans. Combining the results of these two sections I arrive at a fairly optimistic assessment of the economic welfare consequences of the extension of life.

The third section explores how the skill composition of the labor force and the relative wages of skilled and unskilled workers are likely to change as a result of the youth drug; the fourth section is concerned with the impact of life-span extension on the social security system and other economic institutions.

14.1 Per Capita Output and Economic Welfare Assuming a Fixed Stock of Capital

Assuming that total annual births remain unchanged and that after a transition period total annual deaths are also unchanged, life-span extension will be associated with an increase in total population. While the total stock of people who are alive will rise, assumptions about births and deaths indicate that the long-run growth rate of population is unaffected by life-span extension. The discovery of the youth drug will lead initially to a decline in total deaths as the number of physically old people declines. Assuming the drug is potent for only a fixed period of time, the number of physically old people will eventually return to its former level, as the early users of the drug reach the limits of its effectiveness. During this transition period, the population growth rate will exceed its long-term rate and the total population will rise.

Practitioners of the "dismal science" have long been concerned with population increases. Population increases arising from life-span extension have quite a different impact on per capita output and economic welfare from that of population growth arising from, for example, higher birth rates.

Population growth due to life-span extension involves an increase in the ratio of productive persons to dependent persons. The change in this dependence ratio can potentially reverse the dismal Malthusian prescription that population growth is immiserating. The Malthusian argument that population growth reduces economic welfare relies on the law of diminishing returns. For a fixed stock of nonlabor inputs, output as a function of labor input is subject to diminishing returns, that is, the level of output per worker will decline as the number of workers increases.

An interesting feature of life-span and work-span extension is that although output per worker could fall as the total work force rises, output per person in the economy may still rise because the ratio of workers to total population increases.

Per capita output seems to be a good measure of economic well-being because it indicates the level of consumption that each member of society could enjoy for each year of his or her life if output were uniformly distributed. While total lifetime utility would surely rise from the introduction of the drug (this would be evidence simply by the voluntary purchase of the drug), it seems interesting to inquire whether this lifetime utility increase represents a higher or lower yearly level of economic well-being. Per capita income seems to be a good measure of potential yearly economic welfare.

To examine precisely the changes in per capita income, let us consider a very simple economy in which each person lives D years, is unproductive for C years (reflecting, for example, childhood, schooling, and retirement years), and works for $(D - C)$ years. Let us further assume that conventional population growth is zero and that the number of people at each age equals N. The total population of this economy is then DN, and the work force is $(D - C)N$.

Per capita output, y, may be written as

$$y = \frac{F[(D - C)N]}{DN},\tag{1}$$

where F is the economy's production function that relates output to labor input. The assumption of positive but diminishing marginal productivity means that $F' > 0$ and $F'' < 0$. Differentiating y with respect to D yields

$$\frac{\delta y}{\delta D} = \frac{F'N}{DN} - \frac{F}{D^2N} = \frac{F'DN - F}{D^2N}.\tag{2}$$

Equation (2) allows us to consider how per capita output responds to equal increases in life-span and work-span. The technological assumptions that $F' > 0$ and $F'' < 0$ imply that

$$F > F'(D - C)N \quad \text{or} \quad F + F'CN > F'DN.\tag{3}$$

Condition (3) does not suffice to determine the sign of Eq. (2), that is, whether life-span extension increases or decreases per capita output. While nothing definitive can be said about the impact of small increases in life-span and work-span on per capita output, for very large increases in life-span the force of diminishing returns holds sway, and per capita output definitely declines. To see this, consider the inequality

$$\frac{F}{F'} > DN.\tag{4}$$

While inequality (4) may not hold for small values of D, as D increases the inequality must hold; the right side of (4) increases at a rate N as D increases, while the left side increases at rate

$$\frac{\delta F/F'}{\delta D} = N - \frac{FF''N}{F'^2},$$

which exceeds N since $F'' < 0$.

For our economy, the sign of Eq. (2) seems clearly to be positive. Using the conventional Cobb-Douglas description of United States' production,

$$F = [(D - C)N]^{\alpha},\tag{5}$$

where α is labor's share in total output equal to about 0.7. Using Eq. (5) and expressing Eq. (2) in terms of the percentage change in per capita output due to a percentage change in life-span, I arrive at

$$\frac{\delta y}{\delta D}\frac{D}{y} = \left(\frac{\alpha D}{D - C} - 1\right).\tag{6}$$

In our economy, a working-span $(D - C)$ of 45 years, from age 20 to age 65, and a life-span (D) of 75 years seems to be the norm.

Applying these numbers to Eq. (6) yields a value of 0.17, suggesting that a 10 percent increase in life-span gives rise to a 1.7 percent increase in per capita output. The increase in per capita income would, of course, be much greater if output per worker did not fall. In this case, a 10 percent increase in life-span would give rise to a 6.7 percent increase in per capita output. One should keep this fact in mind when reading the next section, which indicates that output per worker could easily rise when capital accumulation is considered.

The prognosis for per capita output is less sanguine if, instead of assuming that the total increase in life-span is devoted to work, we assume that a constant fraction of the total life-span is spent working as longevity is extended. Per capita output in this case definitely falls. The change in per capita output for this case is given in Eq. (7), which from Eq. (3) is negative:

$$\frac{\delta y}{\delta D} = \frac{F'(D - C)N - F}{D^2 N} < 0.\tag{7}$$

Which type of labor supply response seems most likely to occur—a year-for-year increase in the work-span, or a smaller, proportionate increase in working lives? A year-for-year increase in work-span as total life-span rises means that there is no desire for additional lifetime leisure as income rises. Evidence about retirement patterns in this century seems to rule out the year-to-year increase in work-span. As real wages have risen, there has been a dramatic increase in early retirement of men. In 1920, 60.1 percent of men over age 65 were in the labor force. The comparable number in 1977 was 20.1 percent. If the real wage were the only thing that had changed during this period, we could unambiguously conclude that life-time leisure was a normal good; since the substitution effect of a higher wage leads to a larger labor supply, the reduction in labor supply must reflect a positive income effect for lifetime leisure. The counterargument is that much of the increase in early retirement may reflect social security's implicit taxation of the labor supply of older workers [see Kotlikoff (1978)]. Another potentially important consideration is that this historic increase in lifetime leisure has occurred only for ages at which physical stamina and general health are poorest. If the youth drug permits individuals to remain highly energetic for years and years, desired lifetime leisure could actually fall; the preference for leisure appears to be strongly dependent on one's state of physical well-being, even for individuals who are adjudged to be medically healthy relative to their age cohort.

Another factor involved in thinking about changes in $(D - C)$ is that much of C reflects childhood and old age, periods during which work is physically impossible. The fraction of the lifetime that represents non-discretionary leisure will certainly fall with the advent of the youth drug. Hence, even if the period of discretionary leisure increases proportionately with the period of work, the work-span as a fraction of total life-span will rise.

Population growth due to life-span extension is special in that it increases the ratio of productive to nonproductive people in society (i.e., it increases the fraction of each person's life that is productive). For a fixed stock of capital, population increases lead to a reduction in output per worker because of diminishing returns. Output per capita can, however, still rise if the ratio of productive to nonproductive years increases, an event that I perceive as highly likely.

14.2   Capital Stock, Capital Intensity, and Output per Worker

The capital-labor ratio determines output per worker; if the capital-labor ratio does not fall as a consequence of life-span extension, output per worker will not decline. If the capital-labor ratio rises, output per worker will rise as well. The message of this section is that diminishing returns to additional labor input need not occur, provided there are concomitant increases in the capital stock arising from life-span extension.

To make the analysis as intuitive as possible, I first present a very simplified life-cycle model of capital accumulation that ignores inter-temporal discounting, conventional population growth, and various types of economic uncertainties. Consider then, an economy in which individuals live for D years and work for the first R years. Letting e stand for the earnings per year of work, lifetime earnings equal eR. I assume equal consumption per year over one's life; consumption per year is then eR/D.

Conventional population growth is zero. There are N individuals at each age. The total capital stock for this economy consists of the capital (wealth) owned by workers plus the capital owned by retirees (i.e., those older than R). Each person saves $e(1 - R/D)$ per year until retirement; thereafter, he or she dissaves an amount eR/D each year until death at age D. A pre-retirement worker of age x has saved $e(1 - R/D)$ for x years and thus has a net worth of $e(1 - R/D)x$. The total assets of workers, Aw, is given by the integral over workers from age zero to age R of assets held at age x times N, the population at each age:

$$Aw = \int_0^R e\left(1 - \frac{R}{D}\right)Nx\,dx = e\left(1 - \frac{R}{D}\right)N\frac{R^2}{2}. \tag{8}$$

Assets for retirees equal their net worth at retirement age, $e(1 - R/D)R$, less their accumulated dissaving from age R to their current age x. Assets for a retiree age x can thus be written as $e(1 - R/D)R - eR/D(x - R)$, or $eR - (eR/D)x$. Total assets of retirees, A_R, equal the integral over ages R to D of retiree's assets at age x:

$$A_R = \int_R^D \left(eR - \frac{eR}{D}x\right)N\,dx = eR(D - R)N - \frac{eR}{D}\left(\frac{D^2 - R^2}{2}\right)N. \tag{9}$$

Adding Eqs. (8) and (9) gives the total capital stock, K, in this economy:

$$K = Ne\frac{(D - R)R}{2}. \tag{10}$$

Let us now consider equal increases in life-span D and retirement age R, that is, the differential $D - R$ is constant. The change in the capital stock is thus $Ne(D - R)/2$, which is clearly positive. There appear to be two opposing forces involved here. On one hand, simultaneously increasing D and R reduces the relative length of the retirement period. This reduces the annual savings of each worker, $e(1 - R/D)$, and increases the annual dissaving of each retired person, eR/D. On the other hand, there is an absolute increase in the number of workers, while the number of retirees stays constant. Although each worker saves less, there are so many additional workers that total savings of workers as well as the capital stock rise. To obtain some notion of the magnitude of these capital stock increases, I present the elasticity of the capital stock with respect to this type of life-span and work-span extension:

$$\frac{\delta K}{\delta D}\left(\frac{D}{K}\right) = \frac{D}{R}. \tag{11}$$

Since D exceeds R, this elasticity exceeds unity. Values of D of 55 and R of 45 give an elasticity of 1.22. In our model, a value of 55 corresponds to a real-world age of death of 75, since the age at which work begins (e.g., 20) is normalized to zero. An elasticity of 1.22 implies that a 10 percent increase in life-span would increase the capital stock by 12.2 percent.

If, rather than assuming that $D - R$ stays constant, we assume that $(D - R)/R$ stays constant as D increases, the elasticity of capital to D equals 2.

Since the labor force equals NR, the capital labor ratio, K/L, is easily computed:

$$\frac{K}{L} = \frac{Ne(D - R)R/2}{NR} = e\frac{(D - R)}{2}. \tag{12}$$

Note that equal increases in life-span and work-span leave the capital-labor ratio unaltered, while equal proportionate increases in D and R increase the capital-labor ratio by the same percentage.

Proportionate increases in retirement and death ages that increase the absolute length of retirement lead to more capital per worker, while changes in life-span that leave the length of retirement unaltered do not alter capital intensity. Equation (12) paints a rosy picture of the impact of life-span extension on per capita output independent of whether the work-span increases year-for-year with life-span or increases proportionally. If work-span increases pari passus with life-span, output per worker will remain fixed, but per capita output will rise due to the increase in workers per person in the economy. If the extension of the work-span is proportionate, per capita output will rise because output per worker increases, although the ratio of workers to the population remains fixed.[1] Since the real wage, e, is also an increasing function of capital intensity, the same story can be told for yearly consumption, which is eR/D. When R/D rises, e remains fixed; then R/D is fixed, e rises. Yearly consumption rises in either case.

The analysis to this point has assumed that each worker is fully employed for each year prior to retirement. I now permit the quantity of labor supplied each year to be chosen by the individual and ask whether this type of labor supply response to life-span extension will alter the economy's capital intensity. To begin, let us assume that each person works for the same fraction of each year. As life-span is extended, the increases in potential lifetime resources discussed above might lead individuals to reduce their labor supply, l, during each working year, as well as alter the total number of years, R, spent working. This type of labor supply reduction, by reducing earnings, will reduce savings and the capital stock. Although the capital stock falls, the capital-labor ratio is unaffected.[2]

To see this, let $e = wl$, where w is the wage per year. The economy's labor supply, L, in this case is NRl. Rewriting the capital-labor equation (12) for this situation of variable labor supply gives

$$\frac{K}{L} = \frac{Nwl(D - R)R/2}{NRl} = \frac{w(D - R)}{2}. \tag{13}$$

In Eq. (13) it is clear that the capital-labor ratio is independent of annual labor supply l. Intuitively one knows that the yearly labor supply falls by the same percentage as the capital stock falls, leaving the capital-labor ratio unaltered. Even if labor supply differs from one period to the next, as long as the percentage reduction in the labor supply in each period is the same, the capital-labor ratio will be unaltered. To the extent that labor supply when young falls (rises) by a greater (lesser) percentage than labor supply when old, the capital-labor will fall (rise).

The conclusion that emerges from this very simplified model is that the economy's capital intensity is likely to rise or at least remain constant in response to life-span extension.

It is important to determine whether those results hold for a more realistic and correspondingly more complex model of economic growth. I therefore constructed a more detailed steady-state life-cycle model that takes into account interest rates, population and productivity growth, and intertemporal optimal consumption choice. Rather than consuming at a constant level each year, individuals choose a consumption path that maximizes an intertemporal utility function, U, of the form

$$U = \int_0^D \log C_t e^{-\rho t}. \tag{14}$$

In Eq. (14), ρ is the rate-of-time preference that indicates the consumer's relative preference for consumption today rather than consumption tomorrow. C_t is consumption at time t. Individuals choose the path of C_t that maximizes Eq. (14) subject to the lifetime budget constraint

$$\int_0^D C_t e^{-rt} \, dt \leqslant \int_0^R w_t e^{-rt} \, dt. \tag{15}$$

Equation (15) indicates that the present value of the consumption path chosen must not exceed the present value of lifetime earnings. The interest rate at which dollar values are discounted back to time zero is r; R and D are, respectively, ages of retirement and death; and w is the real wage in year t. The real wage is assumed to grow at a constant rate, g, due to labor augmenting technological change. To make the model somewhat more realistic, I incorporate a 30 percent tax on wage income and a 50 percent tax on interest income in the analysis.

Given the optimal consumption and earnings paths, one can compute savings and wealth holdings at each age for a representative individual in this economy. Aggregating the wealth holdings of each person at each age, I arrive at Eq. (15) which indicates the total supply of capital at time t in the economy, K_t^s, corresponding to different parameter values of the model:

$$K_t^s = \frac{w_t}{rg}(H_1 + H_3 H_4),$$

where

$$H_1 = \left(\frac{1 - e^{(r-u)R}}{u - r}\right) - \left(\frac{1 - e^{-nR}}{n}\right),$$

$$H_3 = \left[\left(\frac{e^{zD} - 1}{z} - \frac{1 - e^{(r-u)R}}{u - r}\right) - \left(\frac{e^{(r-u)R} - e^{(r-u)D}}{u - r}\right)e^{-\rho D}\right], \quad (16)$$

$$H_4 = \frac{1 - e^{(g-r)R}}{1 - e^{-\rho D}},$$

$$u = n + g,$$

$$z = (r - u) - \rho.$$

In Eq. (16), n and g are respectively rates of population and productivity growth.

The demand for capital by firms corresponding to given after-tax factor prices, w_t and r, is derived from the Cobb-Douglas production function

$$K_t^D = \frac{\alpha w_t (1 - tr)}{(1 - \alpha)r(1 - tw)} \frac{1 - e^{-nR}}{n}, \quad (17)$$

where α is capital's share in total income (taken here to be 0.3), tr is the tax rate on interest income (0.5), and tw is the tax rate on wage income (0.3).

To investigate how changes in life-span D and work-span R influence the capital stock in general equilibrium, I first solve for the equilibrium value of K, which equates capital supply and demand for initial values of D and R. I then change D and R and compute the new equilibrium value of K. To find equilibrium solutions for Eqs. (16) and (17), I eliminate K_t/w_t from both equations, leaving an equation in r. This equation was solved using a

Table 14.1
General equilibrium capital-labor ratios and wage rates for various life spans and work spans[a]

Age of retirement	Age of death										
	50	60	70	80	90	100	110	120	130	150	200
40	6.89	10.25	13.29	15.99	18.32	20.46	22.16	23.95	25.12	27.19	30.90
	1	1.15	1.28	1.37	1.50	1.59	1.66	1.74	1.79	1.88	2.04
50		7.42	10.23	11.27	14.92	17.02	18.86	20.43	21.89	24.47	27.80
		1.02	1.14	1.19	1.35	1.44	1.52	1.59	1.65	1.76	1.91
60			8.02	10.13	12.27	14.22	15.86	17.49	19.06	21.30	25.09
			1.05	1.14	1.23	1.32	1.39	1.46	1.53	1.63	1.79
70				8.36	10.23	11.85	13.59	15.00	16.56	18.73	22.66
				1.05	1.14	1.22	1.29	1.35	1.42	1.51	1.69
80					8.80	10.15	11.60	13.27	14.16	16.40	19.93
					1.08	1.14	1.20	1.28	1.32	1.41	1.57
90						9.00	10.33	11.57	12.62	14.47	18.30
						1.09	1.15	1.20	1.25	1.33	1.50
100							9.23	10.23	11.39	13.56	16.12
							1.10	1.14	1.20	1.29	1.40

a. Top number in each cell is capital-labor ratio; bottom number is the wage rate. The wage rate for a retirement age of 40 and a death age of 50 is normalized to 1. The table assumes 1% growth in population, 2% growth in productivity, and a 1% rate of time preference.

computer. The solution is unique because in Eq. (16) K_t/w_t is a decreasing function of r, while in Eq. (17) K_t/w_t is an increasing function of r. Given the equilibrium value of r, Eq. (15) or (16) may be used to solve for the equilibrium value of K_t/w_t.

Table 14.1 reports general equilibrium capital-labor ratios for a range of different retirement ages and death ages. By general equilibrium I mean that all changes in the optimal consumption path that arise due to changes in wages and interest rates are taken into account. Since age zero in this model corresponds to the age of entrance into the labor force, an age of death of 50 and a retirement age of 40 should be thought of as corresponding to real-world ages of 70 and 60. The table also reports real net wage rates corresponding to the different capital-labor ratios, for which the net wage for a death age of 50 and a retirement age of 40 is normalized to 1.

The numerical values in table 14.1 support the finding from the more simplified model that proportionate growth in retirement and death ages will raise capital intensity. An increase in retirement age from 40 to 80 concomitant with an increase in the age of death from 50 to 100 raises capital intensity from 6.89 to 10.15, or 47.3 percent. At the same time the real wage rises by 14 percent and per capita output rises by 18 percent. An interesting feature underlying these proportionate changes is that although the ratio of the retirement age to the death age stays constant, the ratio of productive to nonproductive workers rises. This reflects the positive rate of population growth, that is, there are few people aged 80–100 relative to people under 80 due to population growth. Even at a low 1 percent rate of population growth there are only 0.37 100-year-olds for every 1-year-old in the population.

The table indicates some nonlinearities with respect to equal increases in retirement and death ages. Holding the retirement period at 10 years, increases in life-span from 50 to 100 raises capital intensity from 6.89 to 9.00, the real wage by 9 percent, and per capita output by 21 percent. On the other hand, for a 20-year retirement period, raising the age of death from 60 to 110 leads to very little change in capital intensity; it rises from 10.25 to 10.33. Per capita output rises, however, by 22 percent primarily because of the increase in the ratio of productive to nonproductive citizens.

14.3 The Skill Composition of the Labor Force

The extension of the age of retirement will affect career choices and human capital investment (training) decisions. Increases in the age of retirement will make careers that require an initial period of training relatively more attractive than careers that involve no initial training because the length-ened work-span permits a longer period of amortization on the initial training investment. If there is no change in the length of training received in these careers, an increased number of workers will choose skilled careers; the growth in skilled workers relative to unskilled workers in the economy will continue until skilled wages are depressed relative to unskilled wages to the point that marginal workers are again indifferent to a choice between unskilled and skilled careers.

This increase in the skill composition of the labor force and fall in the relative wages of skilled and unskilled workers need not, however, occur. The increase in the retirement period makes additional training desirable. If each skilled worker engages in additional training, the returns to the career paths can be realigned with the same proportion of skilled to unskilled workers in the economy, although with an increase in the ratio of effective skilled workers to unskilled workers. By effective skilled workers I mean the number of skilled workers adjusted for their degree of training. In this scenario, the wage per unit of skilled human capital falls, although annual earnings of skilled workers could actually rise because of the greater amount of human capital per skilled worker.

These points are illustrated in the following simple model. I assume that the economy's output, F, can be described by a Cobb-Douglas production function in effective skilled labor, S^*, and unskilled labor, U:

$$F(S^*, U) = S^{*\alpha} U^{1-\alpha}, \tag{18}$$

where α is the share of effective skilled labor in total income. I let W_S denote yearly earnings per skilled worker and W_U yearly earnings per unskilled worker; competitive choice of career paths will ensure an equali-zation of lifetime earnings in both careers:

$$W_S(R - E) = W_U R. \tag{19}$$

The effective stock of skilled labor is related to the number of skilled workers, S, by

$$S^* = SH(E). \tag{20}$$

In Eq. (20), $H(E)$ is the human capital production function that indicates the number of effective skill units of labor provided by a worker with E years of training. I assume that $H'(E) > 0$ and $H''(E) < 0$; W_S and W_U are determined in competition factor markets and equal, respectively, the mar-ginal products of skilled and unskilled workers:

$$W_S = \frac{\alpha F}{S}, \qquad W_U = (1 - \alpha)\frac{F}{U}. \tag{21}$$

Equations (19) and (21) imply

$$\frac{\alpha}{1 - \alpha}\frac{R - E}{E} = \frac{S}{U}. \tag{22}$$

If one holds E, the length of training, constant, then increases in R definitely raise the economy's skill composition. However, this need not occur because E will increase with R.

The length of training is chosen to maximize lifetime earnings in a career as a skilled worker:

$$W_S(R - E) = W_{S^*}H(E)(R - E). \tag{23}$$

In Eq. (23) W_{S^*} is the wage per unit of skilled human capital. Individuals take W_{S^*} as given by the market when they determine their optimal amount of training, E. Optimal choice of E satisfies

$$H'(E)(R - E) = H(E). \tag{24}$$

It is also clear that

$$\frac{dE}{dR} = -\frac{H'(E)}{H''(R - E) - 2H'(E)} > 0. \tag{25}$$

Equation (25) indicates that the length of training unambiguously rises with increases in the age of retirement, R. The greater the age of retirement, the longer the period of time that a skilled worker can amortize his or her training investment. Hence, increases in the retirement age make additional training more desirable. The skill composition, S/U, determined in Eq. (22), may, however, remain unchanged. If the elasticity of the training period, E, with respect to the retirement age, R, is unity, E will rise in the same proportion as R, and S/U will be unaltered. In every case, the wage per unit of skilled human capital, W_{S^*}, falls relative to the unskilled wage, W_U:

$$\frac{W_{S^*}}{W_U} = \frac{R}{H(E)(R - E)} \tag{26}$$

and

$$\frac{dW_{S^*}/W_U}{dR} = -\frac{H(E)E}{H(E)^2(R - E)^2} < 0. \tag{27}$$

In the case of zero population growth, the ratio of trainees, T, to skilled workers, S, is

$$\frac{T}{S} = \frac{E}{R - E}.$$ (28)

Taking N to be the population at each age, the total labor force, RN, is divided between trainees, skilled workers, and unskilled workers:

$$RN = S + U + T.$$ (29)

If E and R move in equal proportions, Eqs. (22), (28), and (29) dictate a proportionate growth in the number of skilled workers, unskilled workers, and trainees. If E rises less than in proportion to R, the skilled work force will rise relative to the unskilled work force, and the number of trainees will fall relative to the number of skilled workers.

While I know of no empirical study that has investigated the elasticity of the training period with respect to the age of retirement, my own impression is that this elasticity is likely to be less than unity. This impression is based on the observation that in many areas there is a fixed body of knowledge that can be digested in a few years, and that additional training time will be subject to severe diminishing returns.

Although it will influence the skill mix, the length of training, and relative wages of skilled and unskilled workers, life-span extension will not necessarily increase the number of people choosing to have multiple careers during their lifetimes. Leaving aside the issue of boredom, the decision to pursue a single career over one's lifetime rather than to pursue multiple careers will always generate greater lifetime earnings. To see this, consider an individual who at the beginning of his or her working life must choose between careers A, B, and C. Let us assume that each of these careers requires some period of training and that each career provides the same present value of lifetime earnings. Suppose the individual chooses career A. Is it ever optimal in the sense of income maximizing for the individual to switch careers at some time during his or her working life after he or she has received training in career A? The answer is no; while each career offers the same present value of earnings for an individual who has received no training, once the individual has received training in career A, remaining in career A will always generate a higher present value of earnings because no additional training is required to remain in A, while training would be required in careers B or C. Except for the increase in boredom for remaining in a single career over an extended period I would not expect to see a marked increase in the percentage of the work force that engages in multiple careers.

14.4   The Social Security System and Other Economic Institutions

The past two decades have witnessed an enormous growth in the social security system and old-age health insurance. During this period, the number of social security recipients has more than doubled, and benefits— including retirement, disability, and old-age health insurance payments— have almost quadrupled in real terms. Since 1960 the combined employee and employer social security tax rate has doubled from 6 percent to 12.1 percent. The 1977 legislation calls for even higher social security taxes in the near future; between 1978 and 1982, social security taxes for a middle-income worker will rise in real terms by about 52 percent, about $1,000 1978 dollars. Even these massive tax increases may prove quite insufficient to finance the program through the first half of the twenty-first century. Robertson (1978), Chief Actuary of the Social Security Administration, projects that if the current law is maintained up to the year 2025, tax rates will have to increase by more than 8 percent to meet scheduled benefit payments. Projecting far into the future is, of course, a hazardous business; still, forecasts of a 23 percent or greater social security tax in 2025 do not augur well for the future of the social security's system.

A large part of recent increases in the tax burden reflects healthy legislated increases in real social security benefits for the elderly. Much of the problem down the road reflects the enormous recent reductions in fertility rates; in 1957, the fertility rate reached a postwar high of 3.7 children born per woman; in 1976, the figure was 1.8. The lower fertility rates imply that the ratio of workers to retired beneficiaries will fall from a current level of 3.2 to about 2 by the middle of the next century.

Increases in life-span and work-span could greatly relieve our social security problems. Our system is set up on a pay as you go basis, in which young workers pay taxes that are handed over to old people as retirement benefits. If, through life-span extension, we can markedly increase the ratio of workers to retired people, the tax burden per worker will be greatly alleviated.

Certain features of the social security program will have to be changed to permit the extension of life to improve the financial status of the system; if structural changes in the program are not implemented, life-span extension could greatly exacerbate our funding problems. The main change that would need to be made is to eliminate implicit taxation of the work efforts of the elderly. Prior to age 72 (age 70 after 1981, under the new law), the social security earnings test reduces or eliminates benefits for many working aged people. Not only do aged workers lose their benefits by working, but they also receive, in most instances, little return on the social security taxes they continue to pay. The earnings test represents an implicit 50 percent tax rate on the labor earnings of the elderly over a wide range of potential earnings.

If we maintain the earnings test in its current form in the face of extended life-spans, we could quickly create a situation in which most physically young people were induced by social security to retire because they were old in calendar time and ran into the social security tax bite. Surely we will want to either eliminate the earnings test altogether or raise the minimum age at which benefits can be received. If we are responsive to the need for institutional change in the social security system when the youth drug is discovered, the extension of life will undoubtedly greatly relieve our social security problems.

There are other economic institutions that would be dramatically affected by life-span extension. Certainly the medical profession and health delivery system would suffer a relative if not an absolute decline as the percentage of physically old people declines. Insurance companies and pension funds with annuity obligations would face severe financial problems if their beneficiaries suddenly stopped dying, perhaps for 40 years. The economy would presumably become much more youth oriented with corresponding increases in the demand for physical recreational activities.

The list of potential changes in the structure of the economy is indeed a long one. I have focused on just a few important economic issues involved in life-span extension. My analysis leads me to be highly optimistic about the economic gains from life-span extension; life-span extension is likely to raise per capita income and the economic welfare of a vast majority of people. In addition, life-span extension can greatly relieve the financial crunch of our social security and old-age health insurance programs.

Note

1. It can be demonstrated that these per capita output results hold in a model in which there is an initial nonproductive period of B years, followed by $(R - B)$ years of work and $(D - R)$ years of retirement.

IV

**Empirical Studies
of Saving**

Introduction

This part contains five empirical studies of savings. The first, chapter 15, uses microeconomic data to test the life cycle model's prediction that unfunded Social Security reduces household wealth accumulation. This analysis shows what coefficients are predicted by the life cycle model on Social Security variables in a regression explaining household wealth, then uses the Parnes data to estimate the regression. The second section, chapter 16, uses microeconomic data to study the elasticity of bequests with respect to life time resources. This study uses a new technique for addressing this question. Rather than examine the bequests of those who have already died, this study considers the bequests that survey respondents would leave if they died at the time of the survey. The Retirement History Survey provides a rich source of data for this study. Chapter 17 examines the adequacy of savings by implicitly comparing old-age levels of consumption with consumption when young. Chapter 18 formulates a structural Barro model and tests the model using time series data. And chapter 19 presents a critique of reduced-form time series studies that attempt to test the savings effects of Social Security. The method of chapter 19 is to estimate standard reduced-form time series consumption functions with data taken from the Auerbach-Kotlikoff life cycle simulation model. Since these data are perfect life cycle data, it is interesting to determine whether the standard time series regressions using these data will reject or accept the life cycle model.

A common thread in four of the five analyses is concern with proper model specification. The main point of chapter 19 is that, because of aggregation issues, reduced-form time series consumption functions are badly misspecified and are likely to reject the life cycle model even if the data conform perfectly to the model being tested. Chapters 15 and 18 are careful to specify structural models that conform to the theories being tested. The precision demanded in testing structural models leads one, however, to the realization that tests of such models often involve tests of joint hypotheses. For example, chapter 18 assumes a specific form of the Barro utility function and a bivariate distribution of uncertain labor earnings and rates of return. The reported rejection of this model may reflect the failure of the Barro model to hold; alternatively, it may reflect a misspecification of preferences or subjective probability distributions. Unfortunately, as chapter 19 points out, reduced-form coefficient estimates provide no reliable basis for inferences, leaving structural tests, even if they involve joint hypotheses, as the only sensible empirical approach. The chapter also suggests the need for data that detail consumer expectations. In the first three studies expectations of the future play a key role in the determination of central explanatory variables.

In contrast to the other studies, chapter 17 examines savings from a broader, less model-oriented perspective. The goal here is to test in a general sense whether saving for old age is rational. A finding that the level of old-age consumption is dramatically smaller for a large fraction of households than their consumption when young suggests widespread failure to save adequately. A similar methodology has been applied in subsequent studies of the adequacy of life insurance. The methodology of chapter 18 may also have wider applications. This chapter stresses the important testable implication of the Barro model and, indeed, all models of altruism—that consumption depends on the collective resources of altruistically linked individuals and not on the distribution of resources. Chapter 18 directly tests this proposition of altruism by asking whether the age distribution of resources helps predict consumption after one controls for the level of consumption predicted by the Barro model.

The central questions of this part are:

1. Does unfunded Social Security reduce household wealth accumulation in the amount predicted by the life cycle model?

2. Do the lifetime rich save more than the lifetime poor? That is, is the elasticity of bequests with respect to lifetime resources greater than, less than, or equal to unity?

3. Is saving for old age adequate for the vast majority of American households?

4. If Social Security was not available, would private old-age savings still be adequate?

5. How well does the US consumption time series conform to the predictions of a stylized Barro model?

6. Does the age distribution of resources help predict consumption after controlling for the level of consumption predicted by a stylized Barro model?

7. Are reduced-form time series consumption functions reliable means for testing the effects of Social Security on savings?

8. How do aggregation problems affect reduced-form time series consumption function coefficients?

9. Are reduced-form time series consumption function coefficients stable with respect to the choice of sample period?

The key findings of this part are:

1. The microeconomic data provide mixed support for the life cycle model's predicted impact of Social Security on household savings.

2. Although Social Security does significantly reduce household savings, the estimated coefficients do not rule out the Keynesian model in favor of the life cycle model.

3. Surprisingly, the elasticity of bequests with respect to lifetime resources appears to be less than unity. This result implies that redistribution from the lifetime rich to the lifetime poor would increase savings.

4. An elasticity of bequests with respect to lifetime resources that is less than unity also implies that wealth to income ratios will decline as countries grow.

5. There is little evidence of inadequate levels of old-age savings for elderly American households.

6. The adequacy of old-age savings appears in larger part to reflect compulsory saving through private pensions and Social Security. In the absence of these institutions savings in old age for a significant minority of Americans would be inadequate, not in absolute terms but relative to the savings that purdent accumulation would have produced.

7. Although a stylized Barro model fits the time series data fairly well, the age distribution of income remains a significant predictor of aggregate consumption in contradiction to the stylized Barro model.

8. Aggregation and other econometric problems mean that the standard reduced-form time series consumption functions are essentially content free. The misspecification involved in these regressions can easily lead to highly unstable coefficients and to rejection of the hypothesis that Social Security reduces savings, when this is in fact true.

15

Testing the Theory of Social Security and Life Cycle Accumulation

Since its inception the Social Security system has engaged in resource transfers of three kinds, intergenerational, intragenerational, and intertemporal. Transfer of resources across generations, the consumption loan feature of the system, began in 1939 with the payment of benefits to elderly citizens who had paid little or nothing into the system. The 1939 and subsequent amendments to the Social Security Act also weakened the link between taxes paid and benefits received within generations. Within a generation, dependent and surviving widow and widower benefits lead to resource transfers from single to married households and from two-earner households to single-earner households. The third resource transfer, the intertemporal transfer, involves simply a reduction in resources when young due to Social Security taxation and an increase in resources when old, the receipt of Social Security benefits.

The impact of these three transfers on the historic level of aggregate savings and hence the size of the current capital stock has been the subject of much recent debate. The unfunded financing of the social insurance program is central to the discussion. While the original 1935 legislation authorized the accumulation of a large trust fund, this goal was essentially abandoned with the 1939 amendments. The failure to accumulate a trust fund, the pay-as-you-go feature of the system is, of course, equivalent to the intergenerational resource transfer. It is argued that this transfer is responsible for a historic reduction in savings relative to consumption.

The theoretical impact of these three types of resource transfers is, however, quite model dependent. For example, a simple Keynesian consumption function with a constant and identical marginal propensity to save out of disposable income for all age groups predicts no change in

American Economic Review 69(3):396–410 (1979). © 1979 by the American Economic Association. Reprinted with permission.

aggregate savings arising from Social Security resource transfers. A life cycle model of accumulation has, on the other hand, quite different implications. Within a simple life cycle model the introduction of an unfunded Social Security system characterized by a 10 percent tax rate reduces the steady-state capital stock by about 20 percent in general equilibrium and 40 percent in partial equilibrium (see the author). One prerequisite to the resolution of Social Security's historic impact on capital accumulation is, therefore, the empirical verification of microeconomic behavioral responses to Social Security.

This paper presents new micro evidence on the accumulation response of households to Social Security. It is organized in the following manner: Section 15.1 reviews the theory of Social Security and life cycle savings: considered here will be the one-for-one replacement of accumulated Social Security taxes for accumulated private savings, the retirement effect, and the effect of changes in lifetime wealth due to the yield of the Social Security system. In Section 15.2 econometric specification is used to test the theory. Section 15.3 discusses the sample selected from the National Longitudinal Survey (NLS) of men aged 45–59, and Section 15.4 presents the empirical findings.

15.1 The Theory of Social Security and Life Cycle Savings[1]

The different effects of Social Security on life cycle accumulation are easily understood with the help of figure 15.1. In the diagram a representative life cycler with (for simplicity) a fixed life span D faces, in the absence of Social Security, an earnings stream such as $W(t)$ and chooses a consumption stream such as $C(t)$ and an age of retirement such as R. The choice of consumption at every age t as well as the age of retirement arises from the maximization of an intertemporal utility function of consumption and leisure subject to the following budget constraint (assuming no bequests):

$$\int_0^D C(t)e^{-rt}\,dt = \int_0^R W(t)e^{-rt}\,dt, \tag{1}$$

where $r =$ the rate of interest.

At the micro level the introduction of Social Security reduces the earnings profile by the amount of the Social Security tax $\theta \cdot W(t)$ prior to retirement and provides a Social Security benefit stream $B(t)$ thereafter. The term $\theta \cdot W(t)$ refers to the combined tax on employers and employees. The new budget constraint facing the individual is

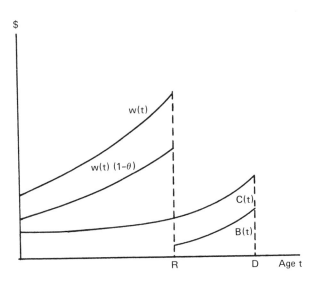

Figure 15.1
Lifetime income and consumption profiles under social security.

$$\int_0^D C(t)e^{-rt}\,dt = \int_0^{R'} W(t)(1-\theta)e^{-rt}\,dt + \int_{R'}^D B(t)e^{-rt}\,dt \tag{2}$$

If retirement does not change $(R = R')$ and the Social Security system offers an implicit yield on paid taxes equal to the market rate of interest r, then lifetime wealth is not affected by the Social Security system and the consumption profile is unaltered. Under these assumptions accumulated Social Security taxes simply replace accumulated private savings dollar-for-dollar prior to retirement age R.[2] This will be referred to below as the replacement effect.

The assumption of a Social Security yield equal to the rate of interest requires

$$\int_0^R W(t)\theta e^{-rt}\,dt = \int_R^D B(t)e^{-rt}\,dt. \tag{3}$$

Equation (3) states that the present value of lifetime taxes paid in must equal the present value of lifetime benefits received for the system to be actuarially fair. The failure of this equation to hold implies either lifetime wealth increments or decrements due to the Social Security system. Certainly the vast majority of Social Security beneficiaries up to the present have enjoyed positive lifetime wealth increments from the system due on the one hand to high real benefit levels and, on the other hand, to their escape from taxation when young; so far no cohort has paid Social Security taxes for more than forty years. The life cycle model predicts an upward shift in the consumption profile in responses to a positive lifetime wealth increment, assuming consumption at every age is a normal good. This lifetime wealth increment would reduce savings at every age implying a greater than one for one reduction in private accumulation. The magnitude of this departure from the one-for-one replacement of private net worth by accumulated Social Security taxes is limited at any age to some fraction of the lifetime wealth increment evaluated at age zero (LWI_0). For example, if the increase in consumption financed by the LWI_0 was a constant ΔC at every age, then

$$\int_0^D \Delta C e^{-rt} \, dt = LWI_0 \tag{4}$$

or

$$\Delta C = \frac{r}{1 - e^{-rD}} LWI_0.$$

In terms of the diagram, the consumption profile would shift upward by an amount $rLWI_0/(1 - e^{-rD})$ at every age. By age x the fraction of LWI_0 consumed equals $(1 - e^{-rx})/(1 - e^{-rD})$. The effect of this additional consumption on wealth holdings at age x is found by accumulating forward up to age x the reduction in savings due to the LWI_0 and may be expressed as

$$\int_0^x \Delta S e^{rt} \, dt = \frac{-(1 - e^{-rx})}{(1 - e^{-rD})} e^{rx} LWI_0$$

$$= \frac{-(1 - e^{-rx})}{(1 - e^{-rD})} LWI_x. \tag{5}$$

LWI_x is the value at age x of the lifetime wealth increment receivable at age zero. Economic theory suggests then that the inclusion of the variable LWI_x in an accumulation regression should yield a coefficient ranging between 0 and -1 depending on the age of the respondent. For example, in the case of constant incremental consumption at every age x, the term $(1 - e^{-rt})/(1 - e^{-rD})$ takes the value 0.68 for an age of death of 55, x equal to 30, and an interest rate of 0.02. Since age zero in the life cycle model corresponds not to birth but rather to the beginning of one's productive life, say age 20, 0.68 is the fraction of LWI_x a 50-year old would have consumed who expected to live until age 75.[3]

Both the intergenerational and intragenerational resource transfers are captured by the LWI_x variable. The intertemporal transfer, holding LWI_x constant, is neatly summarized by the amount of accumulated Social Security taxes ($ASST$). Again the intertemporal transfer refers to the payment of taxes when young and the transfer back of these taxes when old in the form of benefits with an implied return equal to the market rate of interest. Ceteris paribus, the predicted coefficient of $ASST$ in an accumulation regression should equal -1. The life cycle model predicts explicit signs and magnitudes of coefficients for resource transfer variables within an annual savings regression as well. In an annual regression of savings every dollar of Social Security taxes should reduce annual private savings by more than one dollar holding LWI_x fixed, since disposable income is reduced by the amount of interest on accumulated Social Security tax payments. Holding LWI_x fixed, the annual reduction in savings for the preretirement age group should equal the annual amount of taxes plus the interest on accumulated Social Security taxes. A dollar increase in LWI_x should reduce annual savings by a fraction of a dollar depending on the age of the respondent.

Thus far I have not considered the impact of Social Security on the age of retirement and through retirement age on accumulation. As Martin Feldstein has pointed out, Social Security may induce early retirement due to an implicit tax on post-62 earnings;[4] the savings response of the young to a planned earlier retirement is likely to be positive. A reduction in the age of retirement will reduce lifetime wealth by shortening the earnings stream. Under reasonable assumptions this will shift the consumption profile downward increasing savings at young ages. The magnitude of the retirement effect is critical in determining Social Security's net impact on accumulation. The argument for a historical reduction in aggregate US savings relative to consumption rests on an increase in consumption due to intergenerational transfers (the lifetime wealth increment effect) by the initial older generation without a completely offsetting reduction in consumption because of earlier anticipated retirement by the young. Note that the intertemporal transfer, the replacement effect, implies by itself no change in aggregate consumption according to the life cycle model since it involves no change in anyone's lifetime budget constraint.[5]

The above discussion concerning the lifetime wealth increment and replacement characteristics of Social Security is subject to qualification in the case of imperfect capital markets. If capital markets are imperfect and one cannot borrow against future Social Security benefits, fixed savings goals (for example, a downpayment on a house) prior to retirement may lead to a one-for-one reduction in consumption up to a certain age and an increase in consumption compared to previous levels thereafter. In other words the consumption profile could rotate counterclockwise at a given age. Variables to test for this capital market imperfection will be suggested below.

15.2   Econometric Specification

To test empirically the micro response to Social Security I specify two linear regressions, one for household wealth accumulation prior to age of retirement and one for the expected age of retirement. The basic framework for the accumulation equation is given by

$$Net\ Worth = B_1 + B_2 ASST + B_3 LWI_x + B_4 RETAGE$$

$$+ B_6 LTLABI + \gamma' Z + E, \tag{6}$$

where $Net\ Worth$ = assets less liabilities of the household. $ASST$ = the value to the present of household accumulated Social Security taxes; that is, paid in employee plus employer Social Security taxes are accumulated up to the present at the market rate of interest. Households here are taken to be the husband and wife if married, otherwise the single household head. Social Security taxes and benefits of other family members are not considered.

   LWI_x = the absolute dollar yield of the Social Security system to the individual household in current dollars and is equal to the present expected value of future Social Security benefits less the present expected value of future Social Security taxes less the value of past paid in Social Security taxes accumulated up to the present. Letting $PVFB$ and $PVFT$ stand for the present value of future benefits and taxes, respectively,

$$LWI_x = PVFB - PVFT - ASST.$$

If LWI_x is positive, the household has received a higher yield on its taxes from the Social Security system than the market rate of return.

   $RETAGE$ = the expected age of retirement of head. $LTLABI$ = the current dollar value of household lifetime gross labor income; where gross refers to gross of employer plus employee Social Security taxes although net of income taxes. $\gamma' Z$ = the vector sum of additional exogenous variables. E = the error of the regression.

   Recall that the expected coefficient on the term $ASST$ is -1: to see this most clearly, compare two families. Family A is insured by Social Security and family B is not insured. Both families have identical streams of gross labor income. Assume all other characteristics of the two families are identical and that the family with Social Security has an LWI_x equal to zero. Assuming either no capital market constraints to borrowing against future Social Security benefits or that such borrowing is not desired, the consumption streams of the two families are identical since they are both based on the same lifetime wealth. Hence, the sum of accumulated savings in both private (*Net Worth*) and Social Security forms (*ASST*) will be identical for both families and the coefficient on *ASST* should equal -1. (The predicted partial coefficient for *ASST* is -1 regardless of the value of LWI_x.)[6] Let us now make the assumption that family A has a positive value of LWI_x. Family A has therefore a higher lifetime wealth than does family B. Family A will consume more at any point in time than family B assuming non-inferiority of consumption at any point in time. Prior to retirement family A will have less private plus Social Security accumulation (*Net Worth* plus *ASST*) than family B since they have consumed more each year for identical gross labor incomes. The coefficient in LWI_x should therefore be negative. In addition this coefficient should be less than 1 in absolute value since only a portion of this lifetime wealth increment will have been consumed by family A each year up to the current period. A significant negative coefficient on the lifetime wealth increment variable is critical to the argument that Social Security has reduced aggregate savings. A negative coefficient on *ASST* for our preretirement sample would not by itself imply a reduction in aggregate savings since even a simple Keynesian savings function of the form $S = a + bY_d$ (where S is savings, Y_d is disposable income, and a, b are coefficients) would predict a reduction in preretirement savings because of the reduction in disposable income from the Social Security tax.

Ideally equation (6) should include the expected retirement age of the spouse as well as that of the head, *RETAGE*. Unfortunately the *NLS* data reports this information only for the head. In addition the data does not report information about earnings histories. Hence in our regression we use a proxy for *LTLABI* a two-year average of disposable labor income adding in the employer's tax contribution to Social Security based on the two-year earnings average and deducting an estimate of income taxes paid on that labor income.[7] To capture rising accumulation for bequests as lifetime resources increase the square of this constructed average gross labor income (henceforth *ALY* and *ALY2*) is included in the regression. Since this proxy presumably measures *LTLABI* with error the education of the head is included as an explanatory variable. An additional bequest variable *IHER* was coded 1 for respondents indicating a desire to leave an inheritance.

The savings behavior of two-earner families may differ from that of single-earner families for at least two reasons. First two-earner families have greater work-related expenses; hence for a given level of *ALY* the disposable labor income of two-earner families is less than that of single-earner households. Second the riskiness of the future labor earnings stream from death, disability, or loss of work is smaller when the labor income is divided among two earners rather than one. Hence two-earner families will have a smaller precautionary motive for savings. To allow for the possibility that two-earner families save less, we include the variables *ALYT* and *ALY2T* which equal *ALY* and *ALY2* multiplied by a dummy variable for two-earner households.

Other variables included in the regression are dummies for marriage (*MAR*), race (*RACE*), and heads who are separated, widowed, or divorced (*SWD*). In addition the head and wife's ages and the square of their ages (*AGEH, AGEH2, AGEW, AGEW2*) as well as the number of family members (*SIZE*) are exogenous variables. Ideally one would like to treat pension contributions in an identical manner as Social Security taxes, accumulating them up at the market rate of interest and testing for a coefficient of -1. Unfortunately the data do not provide reliable information for current, let alone past, pension contributions. Hence two dummy variables are introduced to capture the average effects of pensions on the accumulation of wealth: *PEN* takes the value 1 if the respondent reported participation in a pension plan; since government workers have more generous and secure pensions, *GPEN* was coded 1 if in addition the respondent was a government worker.

So far I have presented variables to capture three of the four theoretical points in Section 15.1, viz., replacement, lifetime wealth increment, and retirement. The fourth issue pertains to capital market constraints on borrowing against future Social Security benefits. Families with fixed accumulation goals such as downpayment for a house may be forced to reduced consumption in response to the Social Security tax if these taxes constitute a large fraction of their pre–Social Security savings. For such families the coefficient of the Social Security variables *ASST* and LWI_x may be zero. To test for this possibility, two additional variables are used in separate regressions below. They are *HASST* and $HLTW_x$, dummy variables for home ownership multiplied by *ASST* and LTW_x. The coefficients of *HASST* and *ASST* should be $+1$ and -1, respectively. The coefficients on $HLTW_x$ and LTW_x should also be of opposite sign, equal, and less than one in absolute value. Hence, when homeownership is indicated the two sets of variables will cancel implying zero effect of Social Security on accumulation.[8]

Social Security and Retirement Intentions

The *NLS* data provide an excellent opportunity to test whether the Social Security system does indeed reduce the intended age of retirement. The decision to retire rests on a comparison of the shadow price of leisure at a given age with the wage. A number of factors enter the calculations of the shadow price of leisure including health, work attitudes, marital status, and age. Certainly a key to the decision is the level of Social Security benefits available when working compared to the available benefits when retired. For workers between the ages 65 and 72 the Social Security earnings test represents an implicit tax on labor supply (see Michael Boskin). Currently, benefits for this age group are reduced by 50 cents for every dollar earned over $4,000. Beyond the age of 72 all workers are entitled to full benefits independent of retirement. Between the ages 62 and 65 the same earnings test applies; however, available benefits are "actuarially" reduced $\frac{5}{9}$ of 1 percent for each month that benefits are received before age 65. Thus a worker retiring at age 62 receives a benefit which is permanently 20 percent lower than the benefit he would receive if he first retires at age 65. The "actuarial" reduction, if it is truly actuarially fair, implies that the Social Security earnings test does not represent an implicit tax on work effort between 62 and 65; foregoing benefits at these ages will result in higher benefits in later years when actual retirement occurs, leaving the present expected value of benefits as of age 62 the same independent of age of retirement between 62 and 65. Given the extent of early retirement between 62 and 65, the possibility that workers either do not have knowledge of or do not understand actuarial reduction must be strongly entertained.[9] Our econometric analysis will consider each possibility, perception of actuarial reduction and nonperception of actuarial reduction in turn.

The nonlinear Social Security earnings test schedule implies that the implicit marginal tax on an additional hour of work depends itself on the extent of earnings as well as the age. If our data on expected future work effort were sufficiently rich, a maximum likelihood technique could be employed assessing the probability of a worker's locating on a given branch of his budget frontier at a given age. Given the data limitations the econometric path chosen was to specify a Social Security tax variable (*SBENL*) defined as the ratio of Social Security benefits lost at full-time work to full-time earnings. While this tax variable obviously does not capture the full complexity of the kinky budget frontier, it distinguishes quite well workers facing high implicit taxes in the neighborhood of full-time work. Since the dependent variable to be explained is the expected age of retirement, that is, the expected age at which full-time work will cease, this tax variable seems quite appropriate. The basic framework for the expected retirement age regression can now be written as

$$RETAGE = \alpha_1 + \alpha_2 SBENL + \alpha_3 LWI_x + \alpha_4 LTLABI + \delta'H + u, \qquad (7)$$

where $\delta'H$ is a vector of additional exogenous variables and u is the regression error. The specification of (7) is suggested by the life cycle theory which relates the endogenous decisions of accumulation and work effort to the exogenous variables of lifetime wealth and provisions of the Social Security system. Indeed since the error term in (7) may be correlated with E in (6) we shall consider a two-stage estimation of (6) as well as simple OLS. Even under the assumption of nonperception of actuarial reduction, (7) is inappropriately specified for the entire sample. Prior to age 62 there is no implicit Social Security tax on work effort. Hence, OLS estimation of (7) over the entire sample will yield an estimate of the tax rate coefficient α_2 biased toward zero; given the decision to retire prior to age 62, the choice of the exact age to retire before 62 is independent of the tax rate one would face after age 62. In the case that actuarial reduction is perceived, the decision to retire prior to age 65 is independent of the tax rate one would face after age 65. To test this possible bias on α_2 equation (7) was run for samples with expected retirement ages greater than 62 and 65 correcting for the sample selection bias introduced from truncating the sample on the dependent variable.[10]

The exogenous variables of the expected retirement age regression not yet identified include dummies for race, marriage, and separated, widowed, or divorced heads; age and education of the head; two pension dummies mentioned above; and number of family members. In addition there are three health dummies HG, HF, and HP, corresponding to the respondent's assessment of his health as good, fair, or poor, the excluded category being excellent health. Finally, three dummy variables are included to capture work attitudes and attachment: $PROF$ takes the value 1 for respondents reporting professional or managerial occupations; $ATDJ$ corresponds to attitude toward current job and is coded 1 for people who indicated disliking their job either somewhat or very much: $ATDW$ takes the value 1 for respondents answering no to the question, "If you could live comfortably without working, would you still work?"

15.3   The National Longitudinal Sample

Beginning in 1966 the Bureau of Census conducted a series of surveys of male household heads age 45–59. While the surveys deal primarily with labor market questions, a rich amount of information was collected concerning financial status, retirement plans, and eligibility for private pensions and Social Security. The data used in this study come almost exclusively from the 1966 survey. The 1966 survey also asks extensive questions about earnings in 1965. The dependent variable, household accumulated wealth, is one of the key variables recreated by statisticians in the US Department of Labor. This variable falls short of the economist's definition of net worth since it fails to include the cash value of equity in life insurance and the value of consumer durables.

Information detailing the expected age of retirement is of two kinds. Either the respondent stated an actual age, or he indicated the intention never to retire (this group represents 14 percent of respondents in our sample). In the accumulation regression in $RETAGE$ variable is replaced by RET, the actual retirement age when indicated or by $NORET$, a dummy taking the value 1 when the respondent stated he would never retire. For purpose of the expected retirement age regressions, an expected age of retirement of 70 was assigned to this second group.

Since the construction of the Social Security variables (see the Appendix) is based in large part on estimates of labor income, only those observations reporting positive labor income for working heads in both 1965 and 1966 were included; self-employed heads were excluded since their reported wage income may include a return to capital. After several additional consistency checks the final sample totaled 2,124.

In table 15.1, I present the distribution of computed household lifetime wealth increments (LTW_x) by age of head, marital status, and average household labor income (ALY). The table is based on 2,587 observations; both households with covered and uncovered heads are included; the distribution excluding uncovered heads is quite similar.

The intergenerational transfers in table 15.1 are quite large when compared with either the mean value of average household labor income $7,000, or the mean value of household net worth, $15,000. Perhaps the most striking feature of table 15.1 is the unequal treatment of married and single households. The average married lifetime wealth increment of $10,431 is 3.7 times the average for single heads, $2,802. If we divide the married figure by 2, it is clear that for some cells the gain in becoming married is as much as $4,000 per person.

Table 15.1
Mean household lifetime wealth increments[a]

Household average labor income	45–50		51–54		55–59		Total	
	M	S	M	S	M	S	M	S
0–3,000	8997	2647	9998	3838	11310	4652	10023	3668
	(1632)	(664)	(2364)	(542)	(3193)	(921)	(2418)	(718)
3–6,000	9880	1046	12048	3049	15588	5542	11910	3032
	(2364)	(852)	(3120)	(904)	(3133)	(1315)	(2783)	(1028)
6–10,000	8599	−273	11441	1748	14720	4968	10821	1671
	(2541)	(796)	(2558)	(965)	(3282)	(1457)	(2725)	(1036)
10–15,000	6705	−458[b]	9578	−	13018	−	8677	1071[b]
	(3358)	(729)	(3180)		(3593)		(3352)	(1179)
15–25,000	6447	−	9068	−	13378	−	8948	−
	(3779)		(3475)		(3375)		(3583)	
25,000+	8036[b]	−	10845[b]	−	13744[b]	−	10385	−
	(3952)		(3732)		(3920)		(3744)	
Total	8330	1058	10954	2929	14098	5102	10431	2802
	(2768)	(763)	(2844)	(779)	(3290)	(1249)	(2919)	(936)

a. Standard deviations are in parentheses. Dashes indicate fewer than five observations. M and S stand for married and single, respectively.
b. Fewer than fifteen observations.

The lifetime wealth increments increase by age for two reasons. The older the cohorts, the fewer the number of years exposed to the Social Security tax; 59-year-olds in the sample were age 30 at the initiation of the Social Security system and thus escaped ten years of tax payments. The second reason for the sharp increase in LWI_x with age is that for a given age-zero lifetime wealth increment (LTW_0), the older the cohort, the longer the accrued interest on the LTW_0; i.e., $LWI_x = e^{rx}LWI_0$. For example, if a 50-year-old and a 40-year-old both had a lifetime wealth increment of $10,000 evaluated in present dollars as of age zero, the value of the $10,000 evaluated in present dollars as of age 50 must exceed the $10,000 evaluated in present dollars as of age 40. To make the figures for the older 55–59 age group more comparable to those of the 45–50, we can ask what the value of the former group's increment was ten years earlier when the cohort was 45–49. Discounting $14,098 at 3 percent for ten years yields a figure of $10,432, $2,102 greater than the $8,330 figure for the 45–50 group. This differential is now solely a function of the number of years of exposure to the Social Security tax. Table 15.1 indicates that as a fraction of labor income the lifetime wealth increments arising from Social Security are progressive. The standard deviations are substantial and point to sizable within cell inequalities.

15.4   The Empirical Findings

Table 15.2 reports the regression results for the accumulation regression specified above as equation (6). The regression is highly significant with an R^2 of 0.332. The coefficient of accumulated Social Security taxes is -0.666 with a standard error of 0.305. This coefficient is significantly different from zero and lies within 1.3 standard deviations of -1, the prediction of the life cycle theory. The coefficient for LWI_x, 0.237, on the other hand, differs significantly from a predicted negative fraction of about -0.68. One interpretation of this insignificant coefficient for LWI_x is simply that households fail to accurately foresee their future benefits prior to age of retirement. Accurate projection of Social Security benefits requires detailed knowledge of the dependent and surviving spouse benefit provisions, an assessment of husband and wife survival probabilities at different ages, an understanding of current benefit levels, and some notion of the future growth rate of these benefits. In the absence of such knowledge, households may simply assume they will receive the market yield on their tax contributions, that is, that LWI_x is zero. This, of course, casts doubt on the validity of life cycle model in general, since the life cycle model requires a great deal of foresight if it is to be valid. Objections may be raised to including uncovered respondents in the regression since they account for a large part of the variance in the Social Security variables and are primarily government employees who may become eligible for Social Security in the future. Excluding this group leads to coefficient values of -0.902 ($t = 1.977$) for $ASST$ and 0.189 ($t = 0.065$) for LWI_x.

Turning to the retirement variables, the coefficients for RET and $NORET$ are each significantly negative as predicted by the life cycle theory. The expectation of a year's earlier retirement increases accumulation by about \$428. Multiplying \$428 by 63.8, the average expected age of retirement for those stating an explicit expectation, yields \$27,306. This figure is \$149 less than the coefficient for $NORET$, a dummy for respondents who state they will never retire. These respondents appear, then, to accumulate only \$149 less than respondents expecting to retire at age 63.8.[11] The \$428 figure appears small when compared to the mean value of the heads average labor income, \$6,034. Four factors are pertinent to the evaluation of this figure. First the average head's age in the sample is 51.1 (12.7 years

Table 15.2
Regression coefficients from accumulation equation[a]

Variable	Mean	Coefficient	Standard error
ASST	6629	-0.666	0.305
LWIx	9591	0.237	0.202
ALY	6994	1.25	0.598
ALY2	$0.621\ D + 8$	$0.158\ D - 3$	$0.250\ D - 4$
ALYT	3799	0.004	0.327
ALY2T	$0.351\ D + 8$	$-0.684\ D - 4$	$0.256\ D - 4$
AGEH	51.1	$-2756.$	3059.
AGEH2	2633.	30.6	29.7
AGEW	42.1	105.3	363.
AGEW2	2016.	1.72	4.25
PEN	0.647	$-1054.$	1221.
GPEN	0.147	141.	1500.
RET	55.0	$-428.$	150.
NORET	0.138	$-27455.$	9714.
MAR	0.894	$-7997.$	8747.
EDH	9.46	489.	163.
RACE	0.686	3482.	1190.
SWD	0.075	$-2801.$	3263.
IHER	0.595	1325.	983.
SIZE	4.67	$-370.$	-1.71
Constant	1.00	82609.	79027.

$R^2 = 0.330$

$F(20,2104) = 51.687$

Mean of Dependent Variable $= 15098$

a. Variables are defined in the text. The notation $D + a$ means the coefficient is multiplied by 10^a.

less than the average expected age of retirement for those with retirement expectations). Hence a typical respondent has an additional thirteen years to save for his retirement period.[12] Second, Social Security benefits will replace foregone earnings for retirement ages greater than 65 beyond which actuarial reduction does not occur. Third, the stated intention to retire does not necessarily mean the respondent plans to stop working altogether. Forty percent of new male and 34 percent of new female Social Security beneficiaries reported some employment in a 1968 survey (see Lauriat and Rabin 1970, p. 8). Finally, these retirement expectations are formed under considerable uncertainty about future health and family needs. Indeed the correlation between retirement intentions and actual retirement is not high.

The NLS data permits a comparison of expected with actual retirement behavior. The expected retirement age stated in 1966 was compared with 1973 retirement expectations and 1973 employment status for 1,787 respondents who appeared in both the 1966 and 1973 surveys. Of the 1,787 observations, 369 (21 percent) exhibited employment behavior at variance with their stated 1966 expectation. An additional 570 observations (32 percent) changed their expected age of retirement by at least one year. The figures for the 56–59 age group are more revealing since a larger percentage of this group had the opportunity to demonstrate employment behavior at odds with their 1966 expectations. For this group 38 percent exhibited inconsistent behavior and another 8.6 percent changed their expectations about retirement. The change in expected retirement age averaged 4.0 years for those who revised upward their retirement expectation and 3.7 years for those who revised downward (after excluding those expecting never to retire either 1966 or 1973). These figures suggest that the expectations formed in 1966 are best characterized as guesses rather than firm plans. Serious planning and saving for retirement may occur only a few years prior to the actual reduction in work effort. Given the uncertainty with which these retirement expectations appear to be held, the small coefficient on RET is not surprising.

The size of the RET coefficient rules out the possibility that increased savings due to induced earlier retirement substantially offsets the replacement of private savings by Social Security taxes. Taking the point estimate of the ASST coefficient, -0.666, the average reduction in private accumulation from this variable was $4,415. To offset this reduction expected retirement age must fall by an implausible $10.32 = \$4,415/\$428$ years.

The coefficient of the labor income variables ALY, and its square ALY2, and those of ALYT and ALY2T (the ALY and ALY2 variables times a dummy for two-earner households) exhibit predicted signs and reasonable magnitudes. At the mean level of ALY an additional dollar of average labor income raises accumulation by \$3.46 for single-earner families and \$2.51 for two-earner families. The point elasticities of accumulation with respect to ALY are 1.59 for single-earner and 1.15 for two-earner households and accord well with wealth elasticities of bequest estimated in Adams (1975). While the inclusion of $ALYT$ and $ALY2T$ seems justified on theoretical grounds we caution that the coefficients of $ASST$ and LWI_x are highly sensitive to these variables. Omitting these variables leads to coefficients of 0.686 ($t = 3.88$) for LWI_x and -1.270 ($t = -4.71$) for $ASST$.

The effects of both the head's education and race on accumulation are measured quite precisely. Whether these variables independently influence life cycle accumulation or are simply correlated with the error in the proxy for lifetime earnings ALY is impossible to say. The coefficient on household size, -370 ($t = 1.71$), probably reflects offsetting consumption expenditures for children and increased savings for their education.

Surprisingly, neither the pension dummy PEN nor its interaction with a dummy for government workers is significantly negative. Allowing for interaction of these variables with ALY failed to yield significantly negative coefficients. These findings differ from those of Munnell (1976) who used the same data set to run an annual savings regression. Rather than examine Munnell's specification in detail, I report findings on a savings regression of my own derived from differentiating the accumulation equation with respect to time. The dependent savings variable is defined as in Munnell by the difference in net worth in 1969 and 1966 divided by 3. In the savings equation $ASST$ is replaced by $SSTX$, household Social Security tax contributions. The coefficient for $SSTX$ is -2.42 but is measured very imprecisely; the standard error is 2.53. The LWI_x coefficient again displays the wrong sign (0.203 with a standard of 0.099). In addition neither of the pension dummies is significantly negative; indeed $GPEN$ is significantly positive. The overall explanatory power of the exogenous variables is quite low, $R^2 = 0.046$. The coefficient of LWI_x suggests that my savings equation provides no support for a reduction in aggregate savings due to the introduction of unfunded Social Security.

Returning to the accumulation regression, the capital market constraint variables await discussion. Recall, to test capital market constraints against borrowing, we add two variables $HASST$ and $HLWI_x$, defined as $ASST$ and LWI_x, multiplied by a dummy for home ownership. The results here are quite supportive of the borrowing constraint hypothesis. The coefficients are -1.500 for $ASST$ and 1.173 for $HASST$ with respective t-values of

-4.029 and 3.842. The LWI_x coefficient is 0.080 ($t = 0.322$), and the $HLWI_x$ coefficient is 0.139 ($t = 0.859$). These findings imply essentially a dollar-for-dollar replacement of savings by tax contributions for non-homeowners and a zero reduction in savings for homeowners. Since homeowners constitute a large proportion of this sample (70 percent) and of household heads in general, this finding greatly narrows the scope for an aggregate reduction in savings due to Social Security. However, the potential endogeneity of the homeownership dummy as well as its unproven ability to proxy for households with fixed savings goals facing borrowing constraints cautions against relying too strongly on these results.

One final accumulation regression requires reporting. Since RET and $NORET$ are potentially endogenous, I estimated the accumulation equation with two-stage least squares. In the second stage the coefficient for the predicted retirement age is a positive 2028.5 ($t = 3.342$). The coefficient of $ASST$ increased to -0.773 and that of LWI_x decreased to 0.093. Other coefficients were essentially unaffected with the exception of the PEN variable. This coefficient is now 1915.9 although still insignificant. The R^2 for the first stage retirement age prediction equation is only 0.131 and presumably accounts for these poor second stage findings.

Expected Retirement Age Regressions

The coefficients for the expected retirement age regression appear in table 15.3. In this regression I ignore the issue of bias in the coefficient of $SBENL$ and run over the entire sample. The coefficient of the key Social Security tax rate variable $SBENL$, 0.626, is insignificant and the wrong sign. Eliminating respondents who reported compulsory retirement ages and those not covered by Social Security produced a negative, although still insignificant -0.488 ($t = -0.475$) $SBENL$ coefficient. Since the wife can collect dependent benefits only if the husband collects some benefits, $SBENL$ was changed to include the wife's dependent benefit less her own benefit for wives no more than five years younger than their husbands. This second lost benefit variable yielded a -0.260 coefficient but still insignificant ($t = 0.448$). Table 15.3 indicates that positive lifetime wealth increments captured by LWI_x also do not lead to earlier expected retirement.

In contrast with the Social Security variables the pension dummies are important predictors of expected retirement age. Coverage under a private pension plan entails a 1.2-year earlier expected retirement; for government pension coverage the impact is 1.8 years.

Table 15.3
Expected age of retirement regressions[a]

Variable	Coefficient	Standard error
SBENL	0.626	0.847
LWIx	$0.570 \, D - 4$	$0.330 \, D - 4$
ALY	$-0.320 \, D - 3$	$0.838 \, D - 4$
ALY2	$0.921 \, D - 8$	$0.374 \, D - 8$
ALYT	$0.733 \, D - 4$	$0.535 \, D - 4$
ALY2T	$-0.238 \, D - 8$	$0.428 \, D - 8$
AGEH	0.097	0.028
AGEW	-0.026	0.015
PEN	-1.236	0.197
GPEN	-0.601	0.245
SIZE	0.006	0.036
MAR	0.092	0.896
EDH	$-0.541 \, D - 2$	0.029
RACE	-0.044	0.198
SWD	-0.880	0.539
HG	-0.036	0.175
HF	-0.235	0.252
HP	-0.229	0.642
ATDJ	-0.823	0.311
ATDW	-1.595	0.190
PROF	0.758	0.251
Constant	62.834	1.575

$R^2 = 0.128$

$F(21,2102) = 14.708$

Mean of Dependent Variable = 64.64

a. Variables defined in the text. The notation $D + a$ means the coefficient is multiplied by 10^a.

The coefficient on the age of the head is significant and quite interesting. A ten-year increase in age means an 11.6-month later expected date of retirement. Since my comparison of retirement intentions with actual practices indicates that both the young and the old tend to overproject their additional working span, this coefficient probably reflects the general trend among the young to retire earlier (see *Manpower Report of the President*). The health and employment attitudinal variables all display the anticipated negative signs, although none of the health dummies is significant. Professionals and managers expect to retire about nine months later than other respondents, indicating a lower disutility to work for this group.

Correction for Bias in the Social Security Tax Variable

The regression in table 15.3 is a reduced form even when actuarial reduction is perceived; however, the coefficient on *SBENL* is likely to be biased toward zero as discussed in Section 15.2. Including the term to correct for sample selection bias, and estimating the regression for the sample with expected retirement age greater than 62 failed to yield a significantly negative coefficient for *SBENL*; the estimated coefficient is -1.061 ($t = -1.458$). Checking for a remaining bias due to actuarial reduction by sampling over the post-65 expected retirement age group also failed to yield a significantly negative coefficient for *SBENL*. For this sample the estimated coefficient is -0.069 ($t = -0.067$). At this stage we tentatively conclude that Social Security does not significantly influence the intended age of retirement for our sample of 45–59-year-olds. Taking the largest coefficient found for *SBENL*, -1.0612, implies only one-third of a year earlier intended retirement when this tax rate falls from its mean of about 0.3 to 0. Finally, since one may object to the arbitrary assignment of age 70 to respondents intending never to retire, a simple probit regression was run explaining the choice of intended retirement age—between those who would choose to retire at or before 65, and those who would retire later. Here the variable *SBENL* was introduced independently and yielded a coefficient of -0.155 ($t = 0.475$).

15.5   Summary and Conclusion

This paper has examined the theoretical savings response to Social Security implied by the life cycle theory of accumulation. The life cycle theory predicts explicit signs and magnitudes of coefficients for Social Security variables in both accumulated savings and annual savings regressions. In addition, the theory predicts that savings is responsive to retirement plans; these retirement plans may, in turn, be influenced by the availability of Social Security benefits.

The econometric results give mixed support to the notion that the microeconomic mechanisms of the life cycle model are at work. Social Security appears to significantly reduce accumulated savings of this 45–59-year old sample. Whether they view Social Security taxes as equivalent to other taxes or as a significant replacement for private savings remains unclear, however. The point estimate of this replacement ($ASST$) is -0.666 which is neither significantly different from the -1 predicted by the life cycle theory or the -0.2 to -0.3 predicted by a simple Keynesian consumption function. The finding of a positive and insignificant coefficient for LWI_x for this age group runs counter to the life cycle theory. While there is evidence that Social Security tax contributions have reduced private savings of the young, there is no evidence that aggregate saving has been reduced. The poor findings on the lifetime wealth increment imply that the savings of the old may have increased to offset the reduced savings of the young leaving zero net impact on aggregate savings. Since the argument for an historic aggregate reduction in savings invokes the life cycle theory and the wealth increment effect, the findings lend little support to the notion that Social Security has reduced the capital stock. The results cast doubt on the ability of people to accurately project their Social Security benefits and their age of retirement; large differences in lifetime wealth generated by the Social Security systems do not appear to influence savings. The expected age of retirement coefficient does, on the other hand, provide some support for the life cycle theory as opposed to a simple Keynesian consumption out of disposable income theory. The magnitude of the retirement coefficient is small; its size rules out the possibility that increased savings due to induced early retirement substantially offset the reduction in accumulation due to Social Security taxation ($ASST$). Indeed our parameterization of Social Security's implicit tax on post-62 work effort indicates that Social Security does not significantly influence the expected retirement decision.

In conclusion I feel that the final resolution of Social Security's effect on capital accumulation will require additional empirical work at both the micro and macro levels. Of particular interest at the micro level is determining the savings behavior of the post-65 age group. If every dollar of taxes reduces savings of the young by $0.666, what does a dollar of benefits imply for the savings of the elderly? At the opposite end of the age distribution, the savings response of the very young to Social Security deserves attention, this age group is both more likely to face borrowing constraints and less likely to think about retirement when deciding how much to save. Additional empirical work as well as improved data detailing earnings histories and pension contributions will hopefully resolve the question of Social Security's effect on capital accumulation.

Appendix: Construction of Social Security Variables

Feldstein (1974a−e) has presented concepts of gross and net Social Security wealth. The Social Security variables $ASST$ and LWI_x presented here are closely related to his 1976 Social Security wealth variables, and the methodology used to construct these variables follows his. All computations to form $ASST$ and LWI_x are based on separate information for the head and wife. For example, $ASST$ is the sum of the head's accumulated taxes and that of the wife's where the head's accumulated taxes are based on his average (1965 and 1966) labor income and the wife's accumulated taxes are based on her average (1965 and 1966) labor income. Since earnings histories are not available, $ASST$ was generated by applying historic growth rates of nominal wages to the two-year average of labor income (here gross of income taxes) as well as historic tax rates and tax ceilings. The estimated paid in taxes were accumulated forward at a 6 percent nominal rate of interest.

The starting date for tax accumulation was 1937 or later. For respondents indicating they were in college beyond 1937, accumulation began the year they finished college. Other respondents indicated they had begun full-time work before age 20. In this case the year such work began or 1937 was used depending on which occurred latter. In all other cases the larger of 1937 and the year the respondent reached age 20 was the starting date. For wives, accumulation started the last year of college, the year they reached 20, or 1937 depending on which year was latest. The tax ceilings, starting age, marital status, employment of wife, income tax rate, and ages of the head and wife all contribute to variation in $ASST$ independent of the household average labor income (ALY).

Turning to the LWI_x variable, the 1937 starting date for the Social Security system means that for the majority of heads and wives in my sample, a substantial number of their early working years were years of no Social Security tax payments. Since benefits are only loosely related to tax contributions LTW_x is a positive and large number for almost all households (see table 15.1). The higher than interest yield on Social Security is due here not to a rate of labor force plus productivity growth in excess of the rate of interest, rather it is due to a truncation of the age-tax profile at the early end, that is, the intergenerational transfer.

In computing LWI_x, the present expected value of future taxes and future benefits are needed. To obtain the former of these magnitudes, I project a real growth of current Social Security taxes at 2 percent up to age 65 and discount them back at a 3 percent real rate of interest applying survival probabilities at each age for the husband and wife separately.[13] The computation of present expected future benefits is much more involved. First basic benefits were assigned to the head and wife based on their individual current average labor income (again gross of income taxes). Next these basic benefits were assumed to grow at a 2 percent rate into the future and to become available for the head or wife the year the head or wife attains age 65.[14] Beyond the age 65 both the husband and the wife may be eligible for dependent or widow (widower) benefits. For each year the maximum possible benefit under each household survival contingency is used, the probability of each contingency occurring is applied to this benefit, and the expected benefit is discounted back. Thus, for example, if the wife can collect more as a dependent than she can collect based on her own tax contributions, this higher benefit is used for the contingencies that both spouses are alive. This assignment of highest possible benefits is the Social Security procedure.

Two methods of allocating basic benefits were tried. The first method treats individuals as if they could retire immediately and collect benefits based on their computed average monthly wage. The second method applies replacement ratios to current average labor income where the replacement ratios are based on the individual's position in the distribution of labor income. These replacement ratios are derived from looking at the distribution of benefits of new retirees. Since the results proved quite insensitive to which benefit allocation method was used, I report only results using the first method.

Finally, as mentioned above, the NLS data reports on Social Security eligibility. For heads reporting they would never be eligible for Social Security, all head components of household Social Security variables were set to zero and the wife was permitted no dependent or widow benefits.

Notes

I have benefited greatly from discussions with Martin Feldstein, Gary Chamberlain, Steven Marglin, Christophe Chamley, Anthony Pellechio, George von Furstenburg, and Peter Diamond. I wish to thank George Borts and an anonymous referee for helpful suggestions.

1. The pioneering work on this subject is by Feldstein (1974).

2. To see this let A_T be the value of private assets at time T, then

$$A_T + \int_R^D B(t)e^{-r(t-T)}\,dt + \int_T^R W(t)(1-\theta)e^{-r(t-T)}\,dt = \int_T^D C(t)e^{-r(t-T)}\,dt.$$

Future consumption is financed out of current private assets, future Social Security benefits, and net future earnings. Using equation (3) we may rewrite the expression as

$$A_T + \int_0^T \theta W(t)e^{r(T-t)}\,dt = \int_T^D C(t)e^{-r(t-T)}\,dt - \int_T^R W(t)e^{-r(t-T)}\,dt.$$

Since the right-hand side is independent of Social Security, private assets are offset dollar-for-dollar by accumulation Social Security taxes.

3. The presence of inflation does not alter any of these conclusions since all the variables in the preceding equations may be taken as real, including the rate of interest. In this empirical work all variables are measured in real 1966 dollars.

4. The "actuarial" reduction of benefits for those choosing early retirement may imply a zero implicit tax between the ages 62 and 65 to the extent that the actuarial reduction is truly fair. To be truly fair, benefits levels must rise to compensate for the postponement, the higher risks of mortality, as well as the additional tax contributions paid in during these years. For a comprehensive review of the growing literature on Social Security and retirement, see Cambell and Cambell (1976).

5. The intertemporal transfer would occur whether or not the system was funded. For example, under a fully funded system we would still observe people paying in taxes when young and drawing out benefits when old. Under a fully funded system, however, the benefits drawn out would equal one's own contribution plus interest, while under an unfunded system the benefits drawn out would correspond to the tax contribution of the succeeding generation.

6. To see this, alter (3) to let the lifetime wealth increment equal the difference between present benefits and present taxes and proceed as note 2.

7. Presumably, reported labor income is gross of the employee's Social Security tax contribution but net of the employer's; hence we need add in only the employer's half to obtain gross labor income.

8. This assumes that savings for fixed savings goals occurs up to the current age of the respondent.

9. Another explanation for Social Security induced retirement between 62 and 65 is the inability to borrow against Social Security benefits. Note, there is a trivial 1 percent annual reduction in benefits for retirement prior to age 72 but after age 65.

10. See James Heckman (1977). The procedure is simply to take account of the fact that the error u in (7) has a nonzero mean given the sample selection rule. An

additional variable $E(u/$sample selection) is added to the list of exogenous variables (written compactly here as $\lambda'Z$) to form the regression: $RETAGE = \lambda'Z + E(u/$sample selection$) + v$. Since $v = u - E(u/$sample selection) the expectation of v over the selected sample is zero and the above equation may be estimated by least squares, yielding consistent estimates for the coefficients in λ. In forming the term $E(u/$sample selection), let us follow the labor leisure choice literature. It is assumed that the expectation of full-time work beyond the attainment of age 65 is based on a comparison of the shadow price of leisure expected to prevail at age 65, S^e_{65}, with the expected age 65 net wage W^{en}_{65}. The decision to retire implies that the shadow price of leisure at forty hours of work exceeds the wage. This comparison gives rise to a probit regression from which $E(u/$sample selection), which is called a mills ratio, is estimated up to a constant; that is, the coefficients obtained in the probit regression are used in forming the mills ratio.

11. This comparison simply uses the regression equation to determine the difference in predicted net worth for two respondents, identical in all respects, except that one expects to retire at age 63.8 and the other expects never to retire.

12. This is confirmed by respecifying RET as RET times three dummies for age 45–50, 51–55, and 56–59. The coefficients obtained are -406, -449, and -466, respectively.

13. In this and other computations separate male and female survival probabilities were constructed from information provided in Social Security Administration (1966a).

14. The early retirement provisions of Social Security permit the receipt of these benefits as of age 62 but on an actuarially reduced basis. This actuarial reduction makes our computation independent of whether age 62, 63, 64, or 65 is used as the starting age.

16

Estimating the Wealth Elasticity of Bequests from a Sample of Potential Decedents

The elasticity of lifetime bequests with respect to lifetime resources is an important determinant of the transmission of inequality across generations, the aggregate savings rate, the factor income distribution, and the incidence of factor taxation. If this elasticity exceeds 1, the rich will leave proportionately more to their heirs than the poor, tending to enhance the degree of lifetime resource inequality.[1] An elasticity of bequests in excess of unity means a growing economy will exhibit increasing savings rates leading to higher capital-labor ratios with concomitant changes in factor returns and factor shares depending on the elasticity of substitution. A higher than unity elasticity also implies that progressive taxation on labor income reduces savings and hence shifts the long-run burden of the tax onto labor.

Although these are obviously important economic issues, the size of this key elasticity has received only limited empirical attention. Estate tax data exist that detail actual bequests, and panel data provide earnings histories; however, no data set exists that reports both actual bequests and earnings histories. This fact has precluded any direct estimation of actual bequests with respect to lifetime resources.[2]

This paper presents a direct estimation of the bequest elasticity by exploiting information on potential decedents. The discussion in much of the empirical and theoretical literature has ignored the issue of uncertainty as to date of death and has treated the demand for bequests as the demand for a certain, although quite special, commodity. This paper reemphasizes the fundamental uncertainty of the date of death; the uncertainty of death provides the opportunity to estimate directly the elasticity of bequests with respect to lifetime resources. The idea is quite simple; since death may occur at any time, people arrange their affairs to make a bequest contingent upon dying at each point in time. This contingent bequest may differ over time depending on the age of the potential decedent, the number, ages, and incomes of other surviving family members, changes in estate tax laws, etc. Life insurance and annuities are important mechanisms that permit the contingent bequest to differ from accumulated savings and free up the consumption decision from the contingent bequest decision. At any point in time the contingent bequest equals the face value of life insurance plus the potential decedent's current net worth.

The Retirement History Survey (RHS) of the Social Security Administration is a reliable panel of data detailing the two components of the contingent bequest, net worth and the face value of life insurance. In addition, the RHS provides substantial information about earnings histories, permitting the calculation of lifetime earnings. This chapter presents estimates of the elasticity of contingent bequests with respect to lifetime earnings. While stressing that contingent bequests are not actual bequests but potential bequests if the respondents die at the time the information is gathered, the elasticity of contingent bequests with respect to lifetime resources should equal the elasticity of actual bequests with respect to lifetime resources if data existed to estimate one.[3]

Given the uncertainty of date of death and the fact that contingent bequests may differ with the age of the respondent, the elasticity one would really like to know is not the contingent or actual bequest elasticity at a particular age but the elasticity of the present expected value of bequests with respect to the present expected value of lifetime resources. Given ample data, one could calculate the contingent bequest elasticity at each age and then compute the present expected value elasticity. Unfortunately, to date, the RHS sample covers only household heads in the narrow age range of 58–65; hence there is only limited scope to consider changes in the elasticity with age.[4] However, as is demonstrated later, for a widely used family of utility functions, the elasticity of contingent bequests is invariant with respect to age; hence our estimated elasticity may prove to be identical with the preferred expected present value elasticity.

This paper proceeds in the following manner. In section 16.1 we review the theory of bequests, life insurance, and annuities within a simple two-period life cycle model.[5] We demonstrate Yaari's separation theorem and indicate its testable propositions. Section 16.2 describes the data and the calculation of lifetime earnings. Section 16.3 reports the results of our contingent bequest regression, and section 16.4 discusses some implications of the findings and concludes the paper.

16.1   The Theory of Bequests, Life Insurance, and Annuities

Consider a two-period model in which individuals die with probability p at the end of period 1 and die with probability $(1 - p)$ at the end of period 2. Individuals receive expected utility from consumption in periods 1 and 2 as well as bequests potentially realized at the ends of periods 1 or 2. Let W stand for lifetime expected utility, and assume for simplicity separability of the expected utility function with respect to bequests and consumption in the different periods; then we write W as

$$W = U_1(C_1) + pV_1(B_1) + (1 - p)[U_2(C_2) + V_2(B_2)]. \tag{1}$$

Here the time periods are denoted by subscripts 1 and 2, and C and B stand for consumption and bequest. The first time period bequest function V_1 may differ from V_2, and U_1 may differ from U_2. Let A stand for the expenditure on annuities at the beginning of period 1 and Y_1 for first-period earnings; B_1 may be expressed as first-period savings $(Y_1 - C_1)$ less expenditures on annuities times 1 plus the interest rate r that is paid at the end of each period, that is,

$$B_1 = (Y_1 - C_1 - A)(1 + r). \tag{2}$$

For each dollar invested in annuities, individuals receive $1 + ra$ dollars in return if they survive to period 2. A may be negative or positive; negative A means the individual has purchased life insurance at a premium $1 + ra$ that is paid in period 2 if the individual survives. Life insurance and annuities are thus opposite transactions. Life insurance represents a promise to pay money (premium) contingent on survival in the future in exchange for receipt of money today.[6] Annuities represent a promise to receive money contingent on survival in the future in exchange for the payment of money today. The purchase of life insurance is thus equivalent to the sale of an annuity and vice versa.

Take Y_2 as second-period earnings; then the contingent second-period bequest is

$$B_2 = B_1(1 + r) + [Y_2 + A(1 + ra) - C_2](1 + r). \tag{3}$$

The individual surviving to period 2 enters the period with B_1, receives income Y_2 and annuity payments $A(1 + ra)$, and consumes C_2. The difference between these former quantities and C_2 times $1 + r$ is the second-period contingent bequest.

Substituting expressions (2) and (3) into (1) and maximizing expected utility over C_1, C_2, and A yields the first-order conditions:

$$U_1' = pV_1'(1 + r) + (1 - p)V_2'(1 + r)^2, \tag{4}$$

$$U_2' = V_2'(1 + r), \tag{5}$$

$$V' = \frac{(1 - p)V_2'}{p}(ra - r). \tag{6}$$

If annuities (life insurance) are actuarially fair, the present expected value of the return on a dollar invested in annuities must equal a dollar, that is,

$$1 = (1 - p)\frac{(1 + ra)}{1 + r}. \tag{7}$$

Using (7), we may rewrite expressions (4) to (6) as

$$U_1' = V_1'(1 + r), \tag{8}$$

$$U_1' = U_2'(1 + r), \tag{9}$$

$$V_1' = V_2'(1 + r). \tag{10}$$

Equations (8) to (10) represent three equations in the choice variables C_1, C_2, and A and may be solved for the expected utility maximizing values C_1^* C_2^*, and A^*. Starting at the optimum, consider now changes in the stream of lifetime earnings that leave the present expected value of lifetime resources unchanged. Present expected lifetime resources are

$$ER = Y_1 + \frac{Y_2(1 - p)}{1 + r}, \tag{11}$$

and changes in Y_1 and Y_2 holding ER fixed satisfy

$$dY_1 = -dY_2\frac{(1 - p)}{1 + r} = \frac{-dY_2}{1 + ra}. \tag{12}$$

Examine expressions (2) and (3) and let Y_1 increase by a dollar and Y_2 fall by $(1 + ra)$ to satisfy (12). If A also increases by one dollar, B_2 and B_1 and C_1 and C_2 remain at their former optimum levels. Since the individual expected utility maximizer chose $Y_1 - A$ and $Y_2 + A(1 + ra)$ optimally before the change in the Y_1, Y_2 stream, changes in annuities simply offset changes in the stream to maintain the optimum values of $Y_1 - A$ and $Y_2 + A(1 + ra)$. This is Yaari's separation theorem; when annuity markets are actuarially fair, bequests are constrained globally by the value of expected lifetime resources, but they are not affected by the pattern of lifetime resources. This implies, of course, that the contingent bequest B_1, for example, does not depend on the level of savings $(Y_1 - C_1)$ given the value of ER. In addition, differences in individuals' holdings of life insurance and annuities for fixed ER can be explained by the pattern of the lifetime earnings stream. Ceteris paribus, people with more future relative to current and past earnings will hold more life insurance.[7] Essentially, life insurance allows people to borrow against their contingent future earnings.

Present expected lifetime bequests are

$$EB = p\frac{B_1}{1 + r} + B_2\frac{(1 - p)}{(1 + r)^2}. \tag{13}$$

Using (7), we may rewrite (13) as

$$EB = p(Y_1 - C_1) + \frac{(Y_2 - C_2)(1 - p)}{1 + r}. \tag{14}$$

From (14) it is clear that life insurance and annuities affect expected lifetime bequests only insofar as they permit C_1 and C_2 to differ from the no-life-insurance no-annuity-optimum solution. Expected bequests equals the present expected value of net worth holdings over the life cycle. The use of net worth at a given age as a proxy for either the contingent bequest at that age or expected lifetime bequests may be seriously misleading; as was demonstrated, two individuals can have identical contingent bequests at every age and thus the same expected bequest but have markedly different net worth holdings if the timing of their expected resource streams differ.[8] The contingent bequests B_1 and B_2 rather than net worth are the focus of this study. Although B_1 and B_2 may differ in level, there seems no compelling argument for differences in their elasticities with respect to lifetime resources. Indeed, the often used isoelastic utility function of the general form given in (15) exhibits identical elasticities (over age) of contingent bequests with respect to expected lifetime resources:

$$W = \frac{\lambda c_1 C_1}{(1 - \gamma)} + \frac{(1 - p)\lambda c_2 C_2^{1-\gamma}}{(1 - \gamma)(1 + \alpha)}$$

$$+ \frac{p\lambda b_2 B_1^{1-\theta}}{(1 - \theta)(1 + \alpha)} + \frac{(1 - p)\lambda b_2 B_2^{1-\theta}}{(1 - \theta)(1 + \alpha)^2}, \tag{15}$$

where α is the rate of time preference and the λ are other constants. From expression (10) we have

$$B_2 = \left[\frac{(1 + r)\lambda b_2}{(1 + \alpha)\lambda b_1}\right]^{1/\theta} B_1. \tag{16}$$

For the family of utility functions represented in (15), B_2 is proportional to B_1; hence they have identical elasticities with respect to lifetime resources. Furthermore, since the elasticity of expected bequests with respect to expected lifetime resources is just a weighted average of the two contingent elasticities, the contingent bequest elasticity at a given age equals the expected bequest elasticity.

So far the discussion has assumed the existence of perfect insurance markets. If such markets do not exist, contingent bequests and the path of consumption depend on the pattern of the earnings stream. The relevant first-order conditions are now (4) and (5). Holding expected resources ER constant, we can easily show

$$\frac{dC_1}{dY_2/ER} < 0, \qquad \frac{dB}{dY_2/ER} ? 0,$$

$$\frac{dC_2}{dY_2/ER} > 0, \qquad \frac{dB_3}{dY_2/ER} > 0. \tag{17}$$

The reduction in current earnings Y_1 needed to maintain ER as Y_2 rises leads to a fall in C_1 to offset the decline in B_1, which now equals $Y_1 - C_1$; second-period consumption and bequests unambiguously increase. The impact on present expected bequests is ambiguous.

Figure 16.1 summarizes these points about bequest and asset choice with and without life insurance. In the absence of life insurance and annuities, the two shaded regions of figure 16.1 indicate the feasible choice set. The line rising from Y_1 with slope $1 + r$ depicts the first-period consumption bequest trade-off. The choice of a pair such as C_1^0 and B_1^0 determines the second-period budget line $Y_2 + B_1^0$. The introduction of life insurance and annuities broadens the choice set to include the nonshaded regions to the left of $Y_1(1 + ra) + Y_2$. A point such as H indicates first-period purchase of annuities, whereas K corresponds to the purchase of life insurance. Using (13), one can easily obtain the second-period budget line corresponding to first-period choices such as K or H. The algebra and figure indicate that, when annuities and life insurance are available and actuarially fair, the relevant determinant of the contingent bequest is the level of expected lifetime resources; otherwise the timing of these resources is also important. We consider both the level and timing of expected resources in the empirical analysis. There seems little question as to the availability of life insurance and annuities. About 85 percent of married men and 67 percent of nonmarried persons interviewed in the RHS had life insurance (Sherman 1973). Given the theory, one would expect the corresponding percentage

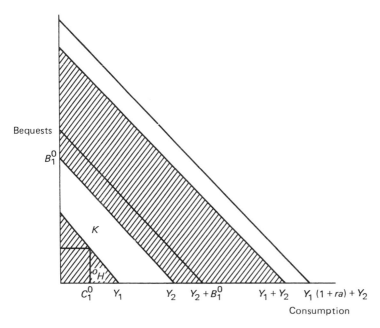

Figure 16.1
Choice of bequests and assets with and without life insurance.

holding annuities to be much smaller. Only 3 percent of all respondents reported holding annuities. However, if one takes into account the enormous annuity represented by future Social Security and pension benefits, then almost all respondents hold annuities. Indeed, life insurance may be purchased in part to offset the government-forced purchase of the Social Security annuity.

16.2   The RHS Data and the Calculation of Lifetime Earnings

The Retirement History Survey of the Social Security Administration is an ongoing ten-year longitudinal study of the retirement process. Data is currently available for the survey years 1969 and 1971. These surveys consitute the data body for this paper. In the 1969 survey 11,153 married and single males and single females between the ages of 58 and 63 were interviewed. Of these respondents 9,924 were reinterviewed in 1971; the remainder either refused the reinterview, had died in the interim, or could not be located. The two surveys ask a wide range of questions covering current assets, past, current, and expected future earnings, retirement plans, current and expected pension and Social Security benefits, and current medical expenditures. Components of net worth and life insurance information is available for both 1969 and 1971.

The two questionnaires are highly complementary in terms of detailing lifetime earnings histories. The 1969 survey reports current earnings, earnings in 1968, and age and earnings at last job. The 1971 survey reports 1971 earnings, 1970 earnings, and the age and earnings at the beginning of the respondent's first full-time job. In addition, the 1971 questionnaire asked the respondent the ages at which he or she earned $\frac{1}{3}$ and $\frac{1}{2}$ of current earnings of earnings at his or her last full-time job if the respondent was not currently working. All together, then, there are eight potential age-earnings observations reported per respondent. For married respondents identical information was gathered for the spouse as well. Years of schooling are also available for both respondent and spouse. Finally, the surveys give extensive information detailing respondents' and spouses' occupational histories; they also detail the type of worker (self-employed, private, and government) he or she was at the various ages for which the occupational information is available. From the surveys we know age, occupation, and type of worker in 1969 and 1971, at the beginning of the 1969 job, and at both the beginning and end of the last job. The age at which the respondent (spouse) experienced a big change in his occupation and the occupation and type of worker before and after the big change is available. The initial and terminal ages of the respondents' (spouses') longest duration job and the occupation and type of worker at that job is stated. Finally, the surveys tell us whether the respondent has ever changed jobs.

This information permitted the calculation of twelve potential age, occupation, and type of worker observations per respondent. Some of these ages corresponded to the ages for which earnings were reported; others did not. The age-earnings information and the age–occupation–type of worker information was jointly sorted to yield eight potential age-earnings observations per respondent (spouse) with codes indicating either the exact occupation and type of worker at that age if it was known or a new code indicating the closest available age adjacent occupations and type of worker codes if the exact information was not known. Thus, if the respondent reported earnings of $4,000 at age 27 in 1936 and his occupation in 1936 is unknown but his occupations in 1939 and 1928 are known and they are different, we specify a code that denotes the two occupations the respondent is between. If the two closest age adjacent occupations or type of worker codes are identical, we assume that the respondent had that occupation or was that type of worker at the interviewing age.

The Calculation of Lifetime Earnings

The strategy followed in calculating lifetime earnings was to use the described data to estimate an age-earnings regression; from this regression we predict the individual's earnings at every age between his first and last or current job and accumulate these predicted earnings up to either 1969 or 1971 at an interest rate. Following some recent findings by Lillard (1977), the specification of the earnings equation includes an individual constant term. Letting LE_{it} stand for the logarithm of earnings of individual i in year t, LAWAGE$_t$ for the logarithm of the national average wage and salary earnings in year t, and X for a matrix of other exogenous variables, including schooling, experience, occupation, and type of worker dummies, the earnings regression is

$$LE_{it} = \gamma_1 + \gamma_2 \text{LAWAGE}_t + XB + \alpha_i + E_{it}. \tag{18}$$

γ and B are coefficients; the error is decomposed into an individual constant α_i and a transitory independently and identically distributed error E_{it}. The α_i are assumed to be uncorrelated with the exogenous variables and uncorrelated across individuals. The coefficients of (18) are estimated by first pooling ordinary least squares, ignoring the error structure, and then computing each individuals' average residual to obtain an unbiased estimate of α_i. The assumption that the L_i are independent of the exogenous variables may be invalid, in which case simple pooled OLS ignoring individual constants will produce biased coefficients. However, since we use the pooled OLS coefficients for prediction and include a potentially biased individual constant, the resulting predicted earnings are unbiased, which is all we require. Armed with the OLS coefficients and the individual constants, we predict earnings at each age including each individuals' constant in the prediction.

Separate earnings regressions are run for males and females. The LAWAGE variable is included to capture inflation and non-experience-related growth in earnings, such as a rise in productivity from capital deepening. The fifteen original occupational categories were combined to obtain a more managable set of 4.[9] In the tables to be presented OCC1, OCC2, OCC3, and OCC4 are dummies indicating the respondent's occupation was unambiguously 1, 2, 3, or 4 in the year of the observation. Dummies such as OCC103 mean the individual was between occupations 1 and 3 at the age of the observation but exactly which occupation, 1 or 3, he actually had is unknown. Dummies such as OCC200 mean the individual's earlier and current occupation are unknown but that his next reported occupation is 2. Dummies such as OCC200 were used primarily for the age-earning observation for the first full-time job for which we often know only the earliest future occupation but not the current or past occupation. A similar notation for type of worker was used. Here CW1 corresponds to private workers, CW2 are government workers and CW3 are self-employed. To preclude singularity, dummies CW1 and OCC4 are excluded from the regressions. In addition, some of the potential occupational and class of worker dummies had no variance (i.e., were zero for all observations) and were omitted.

Besides the occupation and class of worker dummies, there is a dummy, MAR, for respondents who never married, a dummy RACE for whites, and two urban dummies UR1 and UR2. UR1 takes the value 1 when the age-earnings observation occurs in 1969 and the respondent lives in an urbanized area. UR2 is coded 1 for non-1969 observations when the respondent stated in 1969 that he did live in an urbanized area; UR2 is thus similar to the less than full information occupation and class of worker variables. Finally, since the age of retirement was reported, RET is coded 1 when the age of the observation equals or exceeds the stated age of retirement. Since only observations with positive earnings are included in this regression, RET signals a decline in full-time work. In the prediction of earnings the appropriate occupation, class of worker, retirement, and urban dummies depend on the age in question. Thus, for ages for which occupations or worker types are known exactly, the dummies OCC1–OCC3 or CW2–CW3 are used; otherwise the between occupation and type of worker dummies are used.

Turning to the continuous exogenous variables, experience (EXP), its square (EXP2) and its cube (EXP3) are included. Experience is measured as the age of observation less the age at first job. Age at first job, (AGEFJ), years of schooling (S), schooling squared (S2), schooling times experience (EXPS), experience squared times schooling (EXP2S) and experience times schooling squared (EXP2) complete the list of exogenous variables in the earnings regression.

Given the extensive computations required to predict lifetime earnings, only the first 3,500 of the 11,153 RHS observations were used. From these 3,500 records, 2,013 males and 1,310 females (including wives) with satisfactory information were used in the separate age-earnings regressions. For each male there are, on average, 6.07 age-earning observations, leading to a sample size of 12,217 for the pooled male OLS regression. The corresponding female figures are 4.95 and 6,541.

Table 16.1 reports coefficients for the two pooled OLS regressions. The R^2 for the males regression is 0.593; for the females it is 0.496. The

Table 16.1
Pooled OLS age earning regression coefficients[a]

	Males		Females	
Variable	Mean	Coefficient	Mean	Coefficient
RACE	0.958	0.118 (0.032)	0.935	0.042 (0.038)
MAR	0.048	−0.251 (0.029)	0.131	0.154 (0.028)
LAWAGE	8.290	0.129 (0.051)	8.360	0.505 (0.045)
AGEFJ	18.339	0.030 (0.003)	21.297	0.013 (0.002)
UR1	0.109	0.162 (0.024)	0.116	0.293 (0.036)
UR2	0.690	0.103 (0.016)	0.735	0.150 (0.026)
RET	0.025	−0.532 (0.040)	0.033	−0.598 (0.051)
S	11.561	$-0.161E-3$ (0.019)	11.542	−0.032 (0.020)
S2	145.360	$0.394E-3$ $(0.772E-3)$	143.38	$0.347E-2$ $(0.899E-3)$
EXP	28.927	0.069 (0.008)	25.618	0.064 (0.010)
EXP2	1117.600	$-0.158E-2$ $(0.294E-3)$	945.45	$-0.185E-2$ $(0.349E-3)$
EXP3	45651.0	$0.206E-4$ $(0.340E-5)$	37275.0	$0.168E-4$ $(0.407E-5)$
EXPS	332.31	$0.142E-2$ $(0.742E-3)$	297.26	$-0.127E-2$ $(0.961E-3)$
EXPS2	4150.0	$0.567E-4$ $(0.230E-4)$	3705.3	$-0.185E-5$ $(0.288E-4)$
EXP2S	12744.0	$-0.419E-4$ $(0.100E-4)$	10933.0	$0.320E-4$ $(0.153E-4)$
OCC1	0.206	0.408 (0.026)	0.131	0.639 (0.041)
OCC2	0.100	0.176 (0.028)	0.304	0.400 (0.030)
OCC3	0.345	0.171 (0.022)	0.219	0.440 (0.031)
OCC100	0.033	0.227 (0.065)	0.024	0.465 (0.081)

Table 16.1 (continued)

| Variable | Males | | Females | |
	Mean	Coefficient	Mean	Coefficient
OCC102	0.016	0.449	0.008	0.665
		(0.054)		(0.105)
OCC103	0.009	0.449	0.917E − 3	1.047
		(0.068)		(0.302)
OCC104	0.003	0.281	0.003	0.455
		(0.122)		(0.164)
OCC200	0.020	0.136	0.054	0.382
		(0.071)		(0.065)
OCC201	0.003	0.376	0.002	0.399
		(0.117)		(0.210)
OCC203	0.004	0.143	0.002	0.105
		(0.099)		(0.202)
OCC204	0.002	− 0.050	0.002	0.397
		(0.127)		(0.195)
OCC300	0.081	0.071	0.055	0.374
		(0.059)		(0.065)
OCC301	0.003	0.259	0.001	0.820
		(0.124)		(0.275)
OCC302	0.006	0.200	0.001	0.457
		(0.086)		(0.249)
OCC304	0.017	0.176	0.002	− 0.110
		(0.051)		(0.202)
OCC400	0.028	− 0.007	0.031	0.229
		(0.067)		(0.072)
OCC401	0.001	− 0.161	0.002	0.610
		(0.175)		(0.046)
OCC402	0.002	0.221	0.002	0.610
		(0.159)		(0.257)
OCC403	0.007	− 0.082	0.003	0.094
		(0.079)		(0.154)
CW2	0.087	− 0.052	0.020	0.079
		(0.023)		(0.339)
CW100	0.144	0.011	0.168	− 0.095
		(0.055)		(0.054)
CW102	0.009	0.050	0.017	0.201
		(0.067)		(0.072)
CW103	0.001	− 0.100	0.306E − 3	0.404
		(0.160)		(0.526)

Table 16.1 (continued)

Variable	Males		Females	
	Mean	Coefficient	Mean	Coefficient
CW 200	0.015	−0.049	0.021	−0.046
		(0.073)		(0.080)
CW 201	0.001	−0.029	0.001	0.075
		(0.257)		(0.234)
CW 203	0.245 − 3	−0.200		
		(0.406)		
CW 300	0.017	−0.085	0.008	−0.234
		(0.068)		(0.111)
CW 301	0.003	0.159	0.001	−0.247
		(0.118)		(0.261)
CW 302	0.327E − 3	−0.293		
		(0.348)		
CW 3	0.079	−0.188	0.020	−0.176
		(0.025)		(0.324)
Constant		4.929		2.075
		(0.365)		(0.324)

a. Standard errors in parentheses.

residual variance can be decomposed into the part resulting from individual constants and the part resulting from random error. Individual constants explain 36.7 percent of residual male variance and 35.7 percent of residual female variance.[10] Correspondingly, 78.4 percent of the total male earnings variation and 74.9 percent of total female earnings variation is explained by the exogenous variables and the individual constants.

The effects of experience and schooling on earnings is described in table 16.2, where we present the returns to an additional year of schooling or an additional year of experience at given levels of schooling and experience. Holding years of experience constant, table 16.2 reveals increasing return to additional years of schooling for both males and females. For males the returns to schooling are greater the greater the years of experience. Female returns to schooling exceed male return at high initial levels of schooling and early years of experience. Rather than increasing returns we see declining returns to experience for both sexes at all levels of schooling. Again, the positive interaction between experience and schooling in earnings leads to greater return to experience the greater the level of schooling.

Although females' return to schooling generally exceeds that of males', the opposite is true for the return to experience. The inference that one can

Table 16.2
Returns to additional years of schooling and experience at initial levels of schooling and experience

Years of experience	Years of schooling				Return to:	Sex
	5	10	15	18		
1	0.006	0.011	0.015	0.018	Schooling	Male
	0.005	0.040	0.075	0.095		Female
	0.072	0.083	0.096	0.106	Experience	Male
	0.065	0.072	0.079	0.083		Female
5	0.013	0.020	0.027	0.031	Schooling	Male
	0.000	0.035	0.070	0.091		Female
	0.059	0.069	0.081	0.089	Experience	Male
	0.047	0.049	0.051	0.051		Female
10	0.020	0.031	0.040	0.046	Schooling	Male
	−0.003	0.031	0.066	0.086		Female
	0.047	0.054	0.064	0.070	Experience	Male
	0.034	0.038	0.041	0.042		Female
20	0.028	0.044	0.059	0.069	Schooling	Male
	−0.007	0.028	0.062	0.082		Female
	0.030	0.033	0.039	0.043	Experience	Male
	0.026	0.023	0.028	0.033		Female
30	0.028	0.048	0.069	0.083	Schooling	Male
	−0.004	0.030	0.065	0.085		Female
	0.025	0.024	0.025	0.028	Experience	Male
	0.008	0.018	0.027	0.033		Female
40	0.019	0.046	0.072	0.088	Schooling	Male
	0.006	0.040	0.074	0.094		Female
	0.032	0.027	0.025	0.024	Experience	Male
	0.009	0.021	0.034	0.041		Female

draw from this is that females should invest more than males in human capital; that is, they should remain in school longer. For a male with fifteen years of schooling, an additional year of schooling will increase his wages by an average of about 4 percent. In addition, table 16.1 indicates that postponing work by one year raises earnings by 3 percent because of the vintage effect of AGEFJ. Hence 7 percent is the figure one should compare with the 9.6 percent opportunity cost of forgoing the first year of work. For females with fifteen years of schooling, an additional year adds an average of about 6.5 percent to future wages; the vintage effect is 1.3 percent for females; hence 7.8 represents the gain to remaining in school, and 7.9 is the opportunity cost. The optional length of school thus appears longer for females than males, although the similarity in the average male and female years of schooling, 11.561 and 11.542, respectively, does not support this. One should also bear in mind that the schooling and experience effects of table 16.2 are obtained holding occupation and type of worker constant. It seems likely that schooling and experience indirectly influence occupation; table 16.2 reports only the direct effects of schooling and experience and ignores the indirect effects.

16.3   Estimates of the Elasticity of Bequests with Respect to Lifetime Earnings

In this section we present regressions of 1969 and 1971 contingent bequests on lifetime earnings and other exogenous variables. Lifetime earnings are calculated at both a 3 and a 6 percent rate of interest. Exactly what interest rate to use is unclear. From 1926 to 1970 the rate of return on common stock averaged 9.6 percent (Ibbotson 1976, pp. 20–34). During this period the long-term US bond yield averaged 2.9 percent, and the long-term corporate bond yield averaged 3.6 percent. The yield on short-term claims including cash, time deposits, and short-term bonds presumably was below the long-term bond yield. However, only about 15 percent of the middle class portfolio is invested in corporate stock (Lebergott 1976, p. 244). Another 20–30 percent is invested in short-term claims and long-term bonds. A major chunk, 40–50 percent, is invested in home and other real estate and business equity, and about 12 percent is invested in consumer durables. The historic return on homeownership is uncertain because reliable data are not available on the capital gains component of the yield on housing, even ignoring the problem of imputing rent. Finally, tax contributions to Social Security yielded far in excess of 6 percent (Kotlikoff 1977b, pp. 21–22). On the basis of these figures we feel that a rate of interest close to 6 percent is most reasonable, but present results assuming a 3 percent rate of interest can also be used to test for the sensitivity of the elasticity with respect to the interest rate.

The data include all major components of net worth except the market value of automobiles. Automobile debt is recorded, however, and is used in constructing net worth. In 1971 the value of the wife's stocks, bonds, and savings and checking accounts were reported separately from that of the husband; for 1969 there is no breakdown of net worth by ownership. The face value of life insurance in 1969 and 1971 is reported separately for the husband and wife. Bequests cannot be negative; hence we define the contingent bequest to be zero if the value of net worth plus life insurance is less than zero.[11]

The regressions of contingent bequests of married males are presented in tables 16.3 and 16.4; CB69, CB71, and RB71 are the three dependent variables. CB69 and CB71 are the contingent bequests in 1969 and 1971, defined using the combined husband and wife net worth plus the husband's life insurance. RB71 uses only the husband's net worth when a breakdown is given. For 1969 the sample size is 370; for 1971 it is 347. The small sample sizes at this stage of the analysis reflect the nonreporting of the age at first job for many wives. This question was posed to the wife only if she was home at the time of the interview. In addition, about 25 percent of the records give incomplete asset information.

In the 1969 regression the exogenous variables include a dummy for race, age of the husband (AGEM), age of the wife, (AGEF), schooling of the husband (MYSCH), schooling of the wife (FYSCH), and a dummy for the respondent's health reported to be worse than average (HEALTH69). LIFEM693, LIFEM696, LIFEF693, LIFEF696 are lifetime earnings of the husband and wife computed at 3 and 6 percent interest rates (To be more precise, they are lifetime earnings up to 1969 or 1971.) CKIDSUP, PKIDSUP, and NKIDSUP are the number of children completely, partially, and not at all supported by the parents. PAR is a dummy for couples who indicate they support their parents. For nonretired husbands and wives who give an expected retirement age, FUTERNM and FUTERNF are current earnings multiplied by the number of years the husband or wife expects to work in the future. NEURETM and NEURETF are dummy variables for husbands and wives stating they will never retire multiplied by current earnings. Last, ORETM and ORETF equal current earnings for husbands and wives when the other measures of future earnings are both zero. The group with positive ORETM and ORETF is primarily retirees.

The major finding of table 16.3 and this paper is that the contingent bequest elasticity is less than unity. For the 6 percent accumulated life-time earnings variable, the 1969 elasticity at mean values of LIFEM696 and B69 is 0.520. The coefficient of LIFEM696 is 0.059 with a standard error of 0.027. Adding the standard error to the coefficient would raise the elasticity to 0.760. For the 3 percent definition of lifetime earnings the 1969 elasticity is 0.815. Adding in the standard error here would, however, raise this value to 1.08. Although we discuss the 1971 results in detail later, we mention here that they confirm the finding of a smaller than unity elasticity of bequests.

This finding is strengthened by considering the coefficient on the wife's lifetime earnings. Table 16.3 reports significantly negative coefficients. Presumably, the husband's bequest is intended in part to support the wife. High levels of the wife's lifetime earnings reflect a high earnings capacity and hence diminish the need for a wife-supporting bequest. To calculate an elasticity of bequests with respect to the husband and wife's joint lifetime earnings, we think it is reasonable to consider changes in bequests resulting from a dollar increase in the husband's lifetime earnings and a fraction of a dollar increase in lifetime earnings of the wife, where the fraction is given by the ratio of the average wife's lifetime earnings to that of the husband. Such a procedure yields an elasticity of 0.222 at mean value of LIFEM696 plus LIFEF696 and B69. The corresponding 3 percent elasticity is 0.576.

It is important to know whether the estimate of the elasticity is sensitive to the functional form imposed. Inclusion of the square of the husband and wife's lifetime earnings did not yield significant coefficients. With the squared terms the LIFEM696 elasticity is 0.354 and the LIFEM693 elasticity is 0.567 at the means. Since the magnitude of the other exogenous coefficients may not be scale free, we regressed B69 divided by LIFEM696 against the exogenous variables of table 16.3. Again, the estimated elasticity is far below unity, namely, 0.401. Finally, to check for a significantly higher elasticity at higher lifetime earnings, we truncated the sample to include the mean. For this sample the estimated elasticity is 0.571 at 6 percent and 1.04 at 3 percent.

Returning to table 16.3 we find that the wife's age and the husband's schooling significantly influence bequests in the positive direction. There is a significant difference, about $4,000, in bequests to completely supported children and bequests to nonsupported children. More children per se appear to reduce rather than increase bequests. This is not surprising since the effective resources available to the husband and wife are diminished by the presence of children. If we divide the lifetime earnings variables of table 16.3 by family size, the number of children plus 2, and reestimate, the coefficient on number of children entered separately is insignificant and

Table 16.3
Contingent bequest regression (B69) coefficients (standard errors)[a]

Variable	Mean	Coefficient	Coefficient
LIFEM693	161460	0.169 (0.055)	
LIFEM696	297070		0.059 (0.027)
LIFEF693	80621	−0.180 (0.050)	
LIFEF696	142410		−0.088 (0.026)
AGEM	60.235	440.80 (1317.7)	634.55 (1371.3)
AGEF	55.841	853.66 (423.63)	973.25 (442.72)
MYSCH	11.016	3454.0 (854.64)	4030.5 (816.49)
FYSCH	11.473	427.04 (785.75)	214.63 (786.64)
RACE	0.957	11500 (9824.6)	12017 (9896.3)
HEALTH69	0.159	−4207.9 (5422.1)	−4221.8 (5482.6)
CKIDSUP	0.346	1164.0 (2830.0)	1136.6 (2853.7)
PKIDSUP	0.062	−338.34 (5808.9)	−441.68 (5856.1)
NKIDSUP	2.127	−2945.8 (1209.6)	−2920.5 (1219.7)
PAR	0.022	−8375.2 (13392)	−110.14 (3113.6)
FUTERNM	18691	0.012 (0.027)	0.259E − 3 (0.006)
FUTERNF	4035.6	−0.045 (0.140)	−0.035 (0.033)
NEVRETM	291.02	−0.817 (1.446)	0.814 (1.458)
NEVRETF	132.28	−1.495 (2.658)	−1.707 (2.679)
ORETM	2997.0	1.474 (0.457)	1.603 (0.458)
ORETF	2374.5	1.393 (0.664)	1.324 (0.663)
Constant		−0.108E6 (76235)	−0.123E6 (79129)
R^2		0.278	0.265

a. Mean of B69 = 33594. STD deviation of B69 = 42025.

small, -769 ($t = -0.483$). The future earnings variables are all insignificant with the exception of ORETM and ORETF.

In table 16.4 we report regression results for the 1971 contingent bequest. Data was not available to create the NEVRETF variable, so this group is combined in ORETF. ACTROH71 replaces the parental contribution dummy PAR. ACTROH71 is the dollar amount of contributions made to relatives outside the household in 1971. In 1971 the survey reports the net worth of children under age 18. This variable is KNW71 in the regression.

At 3 percent the elasticity of CB71, total net worth plus the respondent's life insurance, is 0.677; at 6 percent the elasticity is 0.367. For the RB71 bequest definition, the husband's net worth plus his life insurance, the 3 percent elasticity is 0.693, and the 6 percent elasticity is 0.357. As with the 1969 regression, entering squared values of the lifetime earnings variables reduces the estimated elasticities. In addition, the elasticities for the 1971 bequests when bequests are deflated by earnings are also smaller than the elasticities when the absolute value of bequests is the dependent variable. For 1971 truncating the sample to include only observations with greater than the average lifetime earnings leads to a 1.387 elasticity at 3 percent and a 0.818 elasticity at 6 percent. The corresponding RB71 elasticities are 1.528 and 0.909. In the 1971 regressions the age of the husband enters negatively and is significant in the CB71 3 percent equation. To test whether the elasticity depends on the age of the respondent, we introduced an interaction between the husband's age and his lifetime earnings. The interaction term proved significantly negative, indicating a 0.798 elasticity at mean value of AGEM, CB71, and LIFEM713 and 0.436 at mean values of AGEM, CB71 and LIFEM716. Hence, to the extent that the elasticity of contingent bequests depends on age, it appears that the elasticity declines with age.

There are other differences between the 1969 and 1971 results besides the AGEM coefficient. The wife's lifetime earnings coefficient is insignificant and small, and none of the future earnings variables is significant. The difference between the children's coefficients is not significant. On the other hand, as with 1969, the schooling of the husband and the age of the wife contributes significantly to the contingent bequest. The amount contributed to relatives outside the household enters with the expected positive sign and is significant. The coefficient of KNW71, although of the expected sign, is insignificant.

The theory suggests that future earnings should be a key determinant of the fraction of the bequest that consists of life insurance. Unfortunately,

Table 16.4
1971 Contingent bequest regression coefficients (standard errors)

Variable	Mean	CB71	CB71	RB71
LIFEM713	175990	0.112 (0.004)		
LIFEM716	334750		0.032 (0.020)	0.026 (0.019)
LIFEF713	88035	−0.017 (0.042)		
LIFEF716	159610		0.001 (0.022)	−0.005 (0.021)
AGEM	62.266	−2282.8 (1146.4)	−1968.9 (1190.6)	−1685.0 (1136.3)
AGEF	57.934	1033.1 (371.24)	981.19 (389.40)	965.68 (371.62)
MYSCH	11.012	2132.3 (676.97)	2591.1 (638.17)	2147.9 (609.01)
FYSCH	11.546	429.97 (636.47)	362.85 (630.88)	522.58 (602.06)
RACE	0.965	11805 (8718.3)	12709 (8769.1)	10257 (8368.6)
HEALTH71	0.165	−5026.0 (4341.8)	−5481.9 (4365.6)	−3369.0 (4166.2)
CKIDSUP	0.260	1040.2 (2639.2)	1133.0 (2655.6)	1207.0 (2534.3)
PKIDSUP	0.121	−2061.1 (3586.4)	−2389.1 (3605.3)	−1418.8 (3440.6)
NKIDSUP	2.136	−653.62 (970.18)	−643.39 (982.07)	−801.93 (937.22)
ACTROH71	36.827	17.787 (7.050)	17.247 (7.090)	17.764 (6.766)
KNW71	62.384	−3.854 (3.379)	−3.965 (3.398)	−3.218 (3.243)
FUTERNM	12434	−0.102 (0.061)	−0.081 (0.061)	−0.045 (0.058)
FUTERNF	8939.4	0.144 (0.080)	0.136 (0.080)	0.028 (0.076)
NEVRETM	1445.9	−0.518 (0.497)	−0.368 (0.495)	−0.398 (0.472)
ORETM	1000.7	0.030 (0.414)	0.067 (0.416)	0.057 (0.397)
ORETF	1172.5	0.005 (0.491)	0.001 (0.491)	0.014 (0.469)
Constant		55706 (70199)	41019 (72611)	28654 (69295)
R^2		0.197	0.188	0.158
Mean of dependent variable		29006		24803

regressions of the fraction of the bequests composed of life insurance yield very low R's (0.02–0.07); neither the absolute levels of future earnings nor the ratio of future earnings to the past earnings significantly influences this dependent variable. One obvious explanation for this poor performance is that much of the life insurance (about two-thirds) held by respondents is whole life rather than term. The decision to purchase whole life life insurance was presumably made when the respondents were substantially younger, based on what they perceived then to be future earnings. Hence our own future earnings variable may have little to do with the relevant future earnings at the time the life insurance was actually purchased.

Joint Bequests of Husbands and Wives

In addition to investigating the bequest contingent on the husband's dying, we can inquire as to the joint bequest contingent on both spouses dying at the same time. This involves simply adding in the face value of the wife's life insurance to the previous bequest definition CB71. The elasticities for the joint contingent bequests proved almost identical with those excluding the wife's life insurance. The other coefficients of the equations changed little from their values in tables 16.3 and 16.4.

Elasticities for Never Married Respondents

The less than unity finding holds for the contingent bequests of both male and female respondents who report they never married. In 1969 at 3 percent the male elasticity with respect to LIFEM693 is 0.866, and the female elasticity is 0.220. In 1969 at 6 percent the elasticities are quite similar, 0.857 for the males and 0.219 for females. Turning to 1971 we find an elasticity for males of 0.922 at 3 percent and 0.726 at 6 percent and for females 0.100 at 3 percent and 0.075 at 6 percent. The sample size in 1969 for never married respondents is 205; in 1971 it is 165. In both years the male's lifetime earnings enter significantly and the female's insignificantly. In these regressions, the education of both males and females are significant positive influences on contingent bequests; in addition, for older males bequests are significantly smaller. Interestingly, even for this group of single individuals, the proportion holding life insurance is quite high, 80.0 percent in 1969 and 75.1 percent in 1971. The mean value of life insurance is, however, about 50 percent smaller for single respondents.

16.4   Caveats, Implications of the Findings, and Conclusions

Throughout this paper we have discussed bequests, financial transfers made at death, as if they comprised the only form of lifetime transfers. This is obviously untrue. Transfers may be made to children in the form of expenditures on education and direct gifts while the transferor is still alive. The true elasticity of lifetime transfers with respect to lifetime resources is a weighted average of the elasticities of the components. Hence, even if the contingent financial bequest elasticity is less than unity, the lifetime transfers elasticity may exceed unity if the other components are elastic. Ishikawa (1974) has put forward one theoretical argument that suggests that the financial bequest elasticity should exceed the elasticity of transfer in the form of schooling for children. Effectively, Becker's (1974) argument is that additional dollars transferred in terms of schooling expenditures will eventually be subject to diminishing returns in terms of producing more earnings for the child. On the other hand, each dollar given in the form of gifts and bequests will yield a dollar to the child. Hence parents whose children are in the diminishing return to schooling expenditure range will tend to leave greater fractions of their incremental transfers in financial form. Hopefully future empirical work will enlighten us on the elasticity of this important transfer component.

The elasticity of gifts with respect to lifetime resources is also quite unknown. Certainly the presence of the estate tax would argue for a elasticity in excess of unity. However, at least for the sample of married households considered in this study, the amount of gift giving is likely to be small. Our sample covers essentially the middle class. We have no observations on millionaires, and fewer than 2 percent of the observations have net worth in excess of $100,000. Few if any of the respondents in our sample would be subject to the estate tax and hence would have little incentive for lifetime gift giving. In any case, determining the size of the total transfer elasticity will require learning more about the other components.

The financial contingent bequest elasticity for the wealthy may differ from that of the middle class. The estate tax is one reason; differences in tastes is another. Hence we caution against facile imputation to the rich of our general findings of inelastic bequests. Indeed, our segmentation of the sample by lifetime earnings indicates higher elasticities for those with higher lifetime resources.

An additional caveat is that the computed lifetime earnings may measure true lifetime earnings with error. Since we have no information on out of labor force and unemployment spells, it was assumed that both men and women worked each year from the age of their first job to the age of their last job. This is probably more problematic for the lifetime earnings of the wives than the husbands. Indeed, we experimented with an interaction of the wife's calculated lifetime earnings and the number of children expecting to find a negative coefficient. The coefficient was positive and significant. In males the error involved in ignoring spells of unemployment is probably greater for the lower earners. This suggests running the regression only on the high lifetime earners; as described, this regression yielded higher elasticities, although they are still below unity at 6 percent.

Another issue not yet addressed is the extent to which bequests are in some sense involuntary. Lack of information and poor terms resulting from adverse selection may partly explain the limited experience of the middle class with annuities. Certainly, private pensions and Social Security are other important reasons. Whatever the reason, individuals who desire not to leave bequests but who fail to purchase annuities may leave a bequest involuntarily. The large fraction of respondents with life insurance (86.7 percent of husbands and 74.6 percent of wives in 1971 and 92.2 percent of husbands and 80 percent of wives in 1969) argues against the notion of involuntary bequests.[12] Surely those people purchasing life insurance were concerned about their bequest at least at some point in their life. Restricting our sample to those holding positive life insurance leads to even less elastic bequests. Furthermore, even assuming all bequests were unintended and involuntary, the elasticity of unintended bequests would still be of interest as an important determinant of lifetime resource inequality over time.

Our analysis has omitted one important component of contingent financial bequests, namely, the life insurance component of the future stream of Social Security benefits. When the husband is alive and the wife is older than age 62, the wife may collect dependent Social Security benefits, which total 50 percent of the husband's benefit. On the death of the husband, the widow may collect surviving wife benefits, which amount to 81.25 percent of the husband's benefits (the current figure is 100 percent, but it was 81.25 percent in 1969 and 1971). Hence the present expected value of 31.25 percent of the husband's benefit, where the expectation is taken, over the probability that the wife survives and the husband dies represents the life insurance component of Social Security. If, however, the wife could collect more than 81.25 percent of her husband's benefit by receiving benefits based on her own work record, then the life insurance component of Social Security would be zero. Although future work will include this Social Security life insurance, we remark that its inclusion is likely to reduce the estimated elasticities since the husband's bequest is a concave function of his lifetime earnings.

Finally, we must admit that, from the evidence presented, one can only weakly infer who the actual recipients of these contingent bequests will be. For the issue of intergenerational resource inequality the elasticity of lifetime transfers to children is crucial.

While the inequality transmission process is only partially clarified here because our sample lacks the super rich, the lifetime consumption behavior of the numerous middle class is crucial to an understanding of the aggregate saving rate and tax incidence. Our findings suggest that progressive labor income taxation will increase rather than diminish aggregate savings. In addition, real growth in the economy may occur at slower rates in the future; the inelastic bequests mean greater shares of consumption out of the economy's real output as the economy grows.

In conclusion, we believe that the evidence presented here strongly supports the notion that the elasticity of contingent bequests with respect to lifetime resource is less than unity for the broad middle class. Since the contingent bequest elasticity appears, if anything, to decline with age, the expected financial bequest elasticity with respect to expected resources is surely less than unity as well.

Notes

I wish to thank Martin Feldstein, Gary Chamberlain, and Lawrence Summers for helpful comments.

1. See Atkinson (1971) for a discussion of the bequest elasticity and the dynamics of lifetime resource inequality.

2. See Blinder (1976) for a survey of some indirect evidence.

3. One would have to control for age of the respondent in both estimations.

4. The RHS is an ongoing ten-year longitudinal survey initiated in 1969 surveying household heads age 58–63. The 1969 data and the 1971 data are now available.

5. Yaari (1965) represents the pioneering work on bequests, life insurance and annuities; our model simply elaborates his results.

6. The fact that one does not actually receive money when one purchases life insurance is immaterial and does not represent a capital market imperfection.

7. The automatic conversion of some life insurance policies into annuities at retirement is thus easily explicable by the theory.

8. Adams (1977) was constrained by his data set, the Federal Reserve Survey of Consumer Finances, to use current net worth as a proxy for bequests and current income as a proxy for lifetime resources. He reports an elasticity in excess of 1; however, this elasticity may simply reflect his proxy problem. Suppose that all members of his sample had identical expected lifetime resources, then the elasticity

$$\frac{d(Y_1 - C_1)}{dY_1} \frac{Y_1}{Y_1 - C_1}$$

would equal $Y_1/Y_1 - C_1$ because dC_1/dY_1 would equal 0. Presumably $Y_1/Y_1 - C_1$ exceeds unity; hence Adams's greater than unity elasticity may have little to do with the true expected bequest elasticity.

9. The average wage series comes from *Historical Statistics*, p. 169. Occupation category 1 includes professional, technical, and kindred co-workers, farmers and farm managers, managers, officials, and proprietors. Category 2 includes clerical and kindred workers and sales workers. The third category is composed of operatives and kindred workers and craftsmen, foremen, and kindred workers. The fourth group is private household workers, service workers, farm laborers and foremen, and other laborers.

10. We use individual residual variation around the mean individual residual to obtain an unbiased estimate of σ_ε^2, the variance of the E_{it}'s. Subtracting this from the square of the standard error of estimate yields an unbiased estimate of σ_α^2, the variance of the individual constants. Lillard (1977) finds a higher ratio of $\sigma_\alpha^2/\sigma_\alpha^2 + \sigma_\varepsilon^2$ and probably reflects the bunching of most of his data between 1955 and 1968. On the other hand, our initial OLS R^2's are higher and, hence we explain a greater fraction of total variation than Lillard.

11. The husband's life insurance may be owned by the wife, in which case the face value of the life insurance cannot be used to pay debts of the estate. Defining the bequest as the face value of the husband's life insurance plus net worth, if net worth is positive or zero otherwise, led to virtually identical results as those reported in the text.

12. Although some of this life insurance may be "forced" on the respondents by their employers at work.

17

The Adequacy of
Savings

with Avia Spivak and
Lawrence H. Summers

Central to the formulation of public policy toward Social Security and
private pensions is the question: how adequately do people save for their
old age? The widely accepted life cycle and permanent income hypotheses
of savings presume that individuals plan their consumption path over their
lifetimes in a way that maximizes their satisfaction. Public policy regarding
the financing of old age consumption is based on a very different view. The
essential premise underlying the Social Security system, as well as government tax breaks for private pensions, is that left to their own devices, a
large number of people would fail to save adequately and find themselves
destitute in their old age. While our Social Security and private pension
systems perform a number of functions in the area of income redistribution
and insurance, their primary function is to force individuals to save for their
old age. This, potentially, prevents personal suffering and reduces the
demand for general welfare.

To date, very little empirical work has directly addressed the question of
the adequacy of accumulation. In the first systematic study of this problem,
Peter Diamond (1977) concluded that in the absence of Social Security, a
substantial fraction of the population would be inadequately prepared for
retirement. The Interim Report of the President's Commission on Pension
Policy (1979) reached a similar conclusion.

This paper uses newly available data from the Social Security Administration's *Retirement History Survey* to examine the adequacy of saving. This
data source is particularly rich; survey data for respondents covering the
years 1969, 1971, and 1973 have been matched with Social Security earnings records covering the years dating back to 1951. In addition to information on the path of lifetime earnings, the survey contains extensive data

American Economic Review 72(5):1056–69 (1982). © 1982 by the American Economic
Association. Reprinted with permission.

on individual asset holdings. The evidence indicates that surprisingly few couples currently suffer significant reductions in their standard of living in their old age. This appears due, in large part, to our compulsory savings institutions, the Social Security and private pension systems. These institutions have succeeded in redistributing the lifetime consumption of private individuals from their youth to their old age.

Section 17.1 examines potential causes of undersaving and considers the scope for public policies. The data and methods of analysis used are described in Section 17.2 Section 17.3 discusses the results regarding the current adequacy of retirement savings. Section 17.4 seeks to explain differences in the adequacy of preparation for retirement. Section 17.5 presents conclusions and discusses some implications for future research.

17.1   Undersaving and Public Policy

Market economies traditionally respect consumer sovereignty. Economists typically do not attempt to examine the wisdom of consumers' choice between good x and good y, work and leisure, or risk and return. Nor do public policies typically seek to affect these decisions. Why then should choices regarding the intertemporal allocation of consumption be subject to special scrutiny?

There are several possible rationales for public intervention in private saving decisions. Paternalism may be appropriate in this context even if not in other, static situations. Decisions about retirement saving are unique in their irreversibility. An individual cannot retrospectively enjoy his wealth, nor can he undo his previous consumption. This problem of irreversibility is heightened by the likelihood of changing tastes. The saver may well have very different goals, tastes, and desires when he retires than at the time the saving decision is made.

Costs of information processing and decision making provide a second possible justification for paternalistic policies. Individuals may find it difficult or unpleasant to confront the possibility of forced early retirement or disability. If these contingencies are sufficiently unlikely or remote, the utility costs of making choices may exceed the expected utility gain from ensuring against unpleasant, remote events. Welfare might then be increased by public planning for these contingencies. A third case for paternalism emphasizes the difficulty of rational decision making. Because of the long lag between action and consequences, and the large number of uncertainties involving low probability events, intertemporal consumption decisions are likely to be particularly difficult.

Even if paternalistic arguments are rejected out of hand, there is a second potential justification for forced savings. By requiring individuals to save, society avoids the negative externality that the ex post improvident might otherwise generate. A precondition for this argument is obviously interdependent utility; under this assumption, forcing individuals to save eliminates the ability of a few to "free ride" on the generosity of many.

Even if one grants a rationale for government intervention in private savings decisions, the question remains whether such intervention can succeed. This depends on the type of "deficiency" in individual decision making as well as the constraints against borrowing in capital markets.

First, consider the length of the savings horizon in the presence of perfect capital markets. If individuals have lifelong, or because of a concern for the welfare of their descendants, infinitely long, savings horizons, they will consider future resources in determining current and future consumption. After consulting their current intertemporal consumption preferences, some or many nonmyopic individuals could plan to consume at a significantly higher level during their youth than during their old age. Other individuals, in general, and public officials, in particular, may view this intertemporal choice as perverse, if not stupid. They may suspect that it will be regretted subsequently. Indeed, policymakers may be sufficiently disturbed to attempt to force these "irrational, but nonmyopic" undersavers to save more for their old age. If this attempt to require additional savings takes the form of our current Social Security system (i.e., of forced contributions when young in return for retirement benefits when old), public policy will fail to achieve its desired goal. This is simply because of the existence of perfect capital markets. In the presence of perfect capital markets, private irrational, but nonmyopic savers will undo a forced government savings plan of the Social Security variety by reducing their own savings out of disposable income and maintaining the original intertemporal consumption allocation plan. Note that if mandatory Social Security tax contributions are sufficiently large, these irrational, but nonmyopic savers will borrow against their future Social Security benefits. Borrowing against future Social Security benefits would presumably occur, however, only after the individual's private net worth was depleted.

Myopic savers, in contrast to irrational but nonmyopic savers, may simply not think about the future in deciding how much to consume today. In the extreme, they may consume all their disposable income as well as inherited assets in each period that they receive these streams. A less-severe form of myopia might entail a rule-of-thumb method of determining how much to consume and how much to save, such as "save 5 percent of all received flows." In this case of myopia, a forced Social Security saving program can indeed change the intertemporal allocation of consumption. Since myopic individuals do not foresee future Social Security benefits, they will lower their current consumption in response to the Social Security tax or pension contribution rather than simply reduce their own private saving.

When capital markets are imperfect, forced saving policies may be effective even in the case of irrational, but nonmyopic savers. The capital market imperfection we have in mind here is an inability to borrow against future streams. Forced contributions to saving plans may lead to a reduction in consumption when young to the extent that the constraint against borrowing against future streams is binding. This constraint may become binding even for individuals who have positive net worth; it may be impossible, or at least very difficult, to consume illiquid assets, such as the equity in one's house. In addition, irrational, but nonmyopic savers may have short-term savings goals, such as the education of their children, that preclude a reduction in their net worth below a certain level. This discussion suggests that individuals with the greatest level of net worth and earnings relative to the size of the involuntary saving contribution will be the least constrained by imperfect capital markets and would provide a better test for irrational, but nonmyopic saving in a world with imperfect capital markets.

For myopic savers, public policy will be effective whether or not capital markets are imperfect; myopic savers, by definition, do not foresee or think about future resource streams and, hence, will never attempt to borrow against those streams. As in the case of nonmyopic, but possibly borrowing-constrained, savers, the strongest test for myopic undersaving will be among that group of savers who have been least affected by forced saving policies. These points about the effectiveness of forced saving policies are summarized in figure 17.1.

17.2   Testing for Undersaving

Tests of myopia or irrationality on the part of consumers must be somewhat arbitrary. Any consumption path can be justified as optimal using some utility function. Our test is based on the premise that rational consumers would be unlikely to plan ahead for significant reductions in consumption levels in their later years.

The test for significant undersaving involves a comparison of the constant level of old-age consumption that can be financed by the elderly

	Unconstrained Savers	Constrained Savers
Nonmyopic Savers	Ineffective	Effective
Myopic Savers	Effective	Effective

Figure 17.1
Effectiveness of forced saving policies.

based on their resources in old age with the constant level of lifetime consumption they could have financed based on the lifetime resources available at the start of their lives. This analysis is based on the actual realized pattern of voluntary and involuntary saving. The comparison of these consumption levels provides an entirely valid test for significant undersaving only in the case of nonmyopic, unconstrained savers. For this group, public forced saving policy will not alter the intertemporal allocation of consumption. As mentioned above, focusing on that group of savers for whom forced saving is a small fraction of lifetime earning will increase the power of the test. For myopic savers as well, the group with the smallest ratio of forced saving to earning will be the group with the greatest potential for exhibiting substantial undersaving.

There is another, but more extreme, way to examine the evidence concerning the current adequacy of savings. This is simply to assume that all forced saving would otherwise have been consumed, and to compare the level of old-age consumption resources with lifetime consumption resources, ignoring those forced saving assets. In addition to presenting results based on total old-age assets, Section 17.4 examines the data under the counterfactual assumption that Social Security had never existed; that is, both Social Security taxes and benefits are ignored in computing the levels of lifetime and old-age consumption. This obviously biases the results toward a finding of undersaving for those nonmyopic as well as myopic savers who would have saved some fraction, if not all, of their Social Security taxes.

So far, our discussion has carefully avoided questions of uncertainty. One major risk that affects intertemporal consumption decisions is the uncertainty of the date of death. Economic theory suggests that this risk can be completely hedged by the purchase of actuarially fair annuities. In the United States, private markets do not appear to provide actuarially fair, or, indeed even indexed, annuities. Private purchase of annuities is rare.

Less than 3 percent of respondents in the *Retirement History Survey* report ownership of annuities. On the other hand, virtually everyone owns annuities in the form of Social Security benefits, pension benefits, and old-age labor earnings. In addition, chapter 4 (1981) suggests that a sizable fraction of the risk of death can be hedged by risk pooling within families. Even very small families can substitute to a significant degree for an actuarially fair annuities market. For example, two-member families, such as a husband and a wife, or a father and son, can capture close to 50 percent of the insurance gains from perfect markets; three-member families can capture close to 70 percent. Furthermore, this family risk pooling does not depend on altruism; complete selfishness is perfectly compatible with family risk pooling of this kind. Given the significant risk-pooling opportunities among family and friends, and given the significant level of Social Security and pension annuities as well as survival contingent labor earnings, most nonmyopic individuals may well formulate their intertemporal consumption plans as if they were purchasing perfectly fair, real annuities.

If one grants that selfish, implicit family annuity contracting may account for a substantial amount of the annuity insurance acquired by the elderly, one needs to ask how this family contracting alters reported old-age resources relative to what one would observe if the elderly acquired all their annuity insurance in the public market. There is reason to believe that in the case of family annuity contracting, the reported old-age resource position of the elderly measures the extent of their potential old-age consumption, and that these reported old-age resources are not encumbered by substantial amounts of implicit debt to children. Indeed, if reported old-age resources do not reflect true potential future consumption, it is more likely that they understate rather than overstate true old-age resources; that is, it seems more likely that children would have outstanding contingent liabilities to their parents in the form, for example, of paying for old-age nursing care, than that the parents would owe money to their children in return for prior payments from their children. Hence, if there is a bias in our comparison of potential old-age consumption relative to potential lifetime consumption, the comparison is likely to be biased toward a finding of inadequate old-age resources.

Since the extent to which consumption choices are subject to the risk of death is in doubt, we present our comparisons of old-age consumption with lifetime consumption for the two polar cases of perfect annuity markets and no annuity markets. For the case of perfect annuity markets, we compute the ratio R_A, where

$$R_A = C_A^0 / C_A^L. \tag{1}$$

In (1), C_A^0 is the level annuity that can be purchased when old given the present expected value of old-age resources PER^0; C_A^L is the level annuity that can be purchased when young based on the present expected value of lifetime resources PER^L. The annuities C_A^0 and C_A^L are in turn calculated as

$$C_A^0 = \frac{PER^0}{PEF^0}, \qquad C_A^L = \frac{PER^L}{PEF^L}. \tag{2}$$

The terms PEF^0 and PEF^L are, respectively, presented expected value factors when old and young. They equal the sum from the initial age a^* of the probabilities of surviving to age a, divided by the discount factor $(1 + r)^{a-a^*}$, where r is the market rate of interest.

When annuities are not available, expected utility maximizers will not equate the present expected value of consumption to the present expected value of lifetime resources; rather, they will equate the present value of planned consumption over the lifetime to the present value of resources. For this case, we compute the ratio R, where

$$R = C^0 / C^L. \tag{3}$$

The terms C^0 and C^L are, respectively, the constant levels of planned consumption based on the present value of old-age resources and the present value of lifetime resources that can be financed over all the possible remaining years of one's life. In this study, 88 is taken to be the maximum age of death. The formulate for C^0 and C^L are simply the ratio of present resources from the age in question to the present value factor from the age in question through age 88.

In the case of married couples, the terms C_A^0, C_A^L, C^0, and C^L refer to the constant streams that each spouse could consume based on the combined lifetime and old-age resources of the two spouses. The present and present expected value factors used to compute C^0, C^L, C_A^0, and C_A^L are the sum of the husband's and wife's present and present expected value factors.

17.3 Data and Sample Selection

The Social Security Administration's *Retirement History Survey* (RHS) was initiated in 1969. Since that time, four additional panels of data have been collected in the years 1971, 1973, 1975, and 1977 from the initial respondents. This paper uses data from the 1969, 1971, and 1973 surveys. The initial 1969 RHS sampled 11,152 respondents between the ages of 58 and

63. The sampling procedures, etc., are described in Irelan et al. Both the 1969 and 1971 surveys provide data that are used to calculate household net worth, including equity in residential and nonresidential real estate.

In each of the years, the survey respondents were asked numerous questions concerning current or expected pension benefits. The respondents also indicated their working status and expected age of retirement. This information was processed to calculate the present expected value of pension wealth (PENW) as of the respondent's age in 1969. Pension benefits were taken to begin in the first year the respondent reports receiving benefits, or in the year the respondent indicated he or she will retire, whichever is earliest. We assume that the reported pension benefit remains fixed in nominal value over time. Survival probabilities are taken from a 1966 Social Security Administration Actuarial Study.

Feldstein's (1974) and Kotlikoff's (chapter 15) procedures are followed to calculate the present expected value of gross Social Security wealth (SSW). The basic benefit for each respondent and his or her spouse is computed using the 1969 Social Security Benefit Schedules. Across-the-board increases in real Social Security benefits after 1969 are not included in the calculations. The Social Security Primary Insurance Amount (PIA) is calculated from the respondent's reported earnings history. The SSW calculation takes into account dependent and survivor benefits as well as basic retirement benefits. Benefits are taken to begin at the age of retirement. An individual's age of retirement was determined, if possible, from the Social Security earnings file. If a respondent was still working in 1974, his or her retirement age was taken to be the 1973 expected retirement age. Respondents who said they would never retire were assumed to retire at age 70.

The procedure of using actual outcomes in calculating the present expected value of pension and Social Security streams in 1969 was also followed in computing the present expected value of future labor earnings (FUTW). The actual value of earnings was estimated from the Social Security earnings records up to 1974. If a respondent indicated in 1973 that he or she expected to work after 1974, we assumed that the respondent continued to earn at the 1974 real earnings level until retirement.[1] Earnings between 1951 and 1969 were obtained from the Social Security earnings records. Earnings prior to 1951 are not reported in the data. Each respondent's earnings back to age 30 are estimated by taking the average earnings between 1953 and 1956 and extrapolating this figure backward starting in 1950 and applying the economy-wide growth rates of real earnings. Since the typical respondent was age 41 in 1950, this imputation procedure was used for about eleven years of earnings.

In the computations, all earnings and benefit streams are first converted into real 1969 dollars. A 2 percent real interest rate was assumed in the calculations. Tabulations were also constructed using a 4 percent real interest rate, and the results proved quite similar. The earnings stream from age 30 to the age of retirement is reduced by 15 percent to allow for income taxes and work related expenses. In addition, Social Security tax contributions made by employees are subtracted out.[2]

The Social Security earnings data report annual earnings up to the covered maximum. They also indicate the quarter in which the respondent exceeded the maximum, if such was the case. A procedure developed by Fox (1976) was used to estimate earnings above the maximum for individuals who hit the ceilings in a particular year.

While the *Retirement History Survey* asks detailed net worth questions, two important components of the net worth of the elderly are not reported, consumer durables and the cash value of life insurance. The exclusion of these data from the net worth calculation biases the calculated values of R_A and R downward.

These estimates of pension wealth, Social Security wealth, and lifetime net labor earnings from age 30 to retirement are used to calculate the present expected value of all lifetime resources as of age 30. The computation of the present expected value of old-age resources is based on the 1969 values of net worth (NW), future net labor earnings ($FUTW$), Social Security wealth (SSW), and pension wealth ($PRNW$). The present-value calculations used to generate R are based on the same flows described above, with the exception that Social Security survivor benefits are ignored in the calculation.

These two measures of lifetime and old-age resources are both potentially biased because they fail to account for inheritance as well as contributions from children, items that are quite poorly reported in the surveys. To the extent that these inheritances and contributions from children have occurred prior to 1969, the estimate of lifetime resources will be undermeasured, while the estimate of future resources is correct. If, on the other hand, such family transfers primarily arrive in the future, both future and lifetime resources will be undermeasured. The former case is the more problematic for our estimate of the ratio of old-age to lifetime sustainable consumption, since the omission of preretirement transfers in the lifetime resources calculation will bias upward the computed ratio of sustainable old-age consumption to sustainable lifetime consumption. However, the potential bias here seems benign; social policy toward savings is presumably concerned not with the intertemporal consumption allocation of family transfers, rather the intertemporal allocation of lifetime earnings and other lifetime resources, for example, pensions and Social Security that individuals can rely on receiving. In this context, systematic family net transfer payments can be thought of as a bonus. For purposes of this study, the appropriate lifetime resources base to consider can be thought of as excluding family transfers since social planners are presumably unconcerned whether a high ratio of old-age to lifetime consumption out of nonfamily transfer resources results from good planning, forced government Social Security, forced pension savings, or family transfers; their main concern is that this ratio be sufficiently high.

Sample Selection

Federal government employees and many state and local government employees are not covered by Social Security, and, hence, have no earnings records to use in the computation. These individuals were excluded from the analysis. A second group that was excluded is the self-employed. Many of the self-employed were first covered by Social Security starting in the late 1950s. For these individuals, the earnings records are obviously incomplete. In addition, quarters-of-coverage information is much more limited for the self-employed than for employees. This fact precludes estimating earnings above the covered ceiling for the self-employed.

This paper focuses on married couples. Surviving widows, in many cases, worked only a limited amount during their lifetimes; since the decedent husband's earnings record is not available, there is no way of determining the widow's pre-1969 standard of living. Respondents were excluded from the basic sample if they failed to report a particular component of net worth or if they indicated receiving a pension benefit, but failed to state the level.[3] The ultimate sample numbers over 1,900 married couples. There are small variations in sample size across the following tables because of differing data requirements.

Tables 17.1 and 17.2 report the distributions of old-age to lifetime consumption ratios, cross tabulated by the average earnings level (in 1969 dollars) of the couple between 1951 and 1969. Both tables indicate that over 90 percent of married couples can afford an old-age level of consumption that exceeds 80 percent of their affordable lifetime consumption level; 85 percent of the couples can afford to purchase a larger annuity in their old age than they could afford to purchase at age 30; and 73 percent of elderly couples in the absence of annuity markets could afford to consume until age 88 at a constant higher level than the constant level of consump-

Table 17.1
R-Ratio of old-age consumption stream to lifetime consumption stream, no-annuity case

Couple's average earnings	0–0.39	0.40–0.49	0.50–0.59	0.60–0.69	0.70–0.79	0.80–0.89	0.90–0.99	1.00–1.09	1.10–1.19	1.20–1.29	1.30 +	Total
$0–2999												
Number	0	0	4	4	6	8	15	20	18	9	98	182
Row percent	0.00	0.00	2.20	2.20	3.30	4.40	8.24	10.99	9.89	4.95	53.85	100
$3000–3999												
Number	0	3	2	2	11	10	13	12	15	15	60	143
Row percent	0.00	2.10	1.40	1.40	7.69	6.99	9.09	8.39	10.49	10.49	41.96	100
$4000–4999												
Number	0	0	1	5	6	12	22	19	27	19	59	170
Row percent	0.00	0.00	0.59	2.94	3.53	7.06	12.94	11.18	15.88	11.18	34.71	100
$5000–5999												
Number	0	0	1	4	11	20	26	30	20	26	77	215
Row percent	0.00	0.00	0.47	1.86	5.12	9.30	12.09	13.95	9.30	12.09	35.81	100
$6000–6999												
Number	0	0	3	3	10	23	31	32	38	29	71	240
Row percent	0.00	0.00	1.25	1.25	4.17	9.58	12.92	13.33	15.83	12.08	29.58	100
$7000–7999												
Number	0	0	2	3	15	17	29	42	52	33	61	253
Row percent	0.00	0.00	0.79	1.19	5.93	6.72	11.07	16.60	20.55	13.04	24.11	100
$8000–8999												
Number	0	0	0	5	15	20	25	26	23	27	67	208
Row percent	0.00	0.00	0.00	2.40	7.21	9.62	12.02	12.50	11.06	12.98	32.21	100

Table 17.1 (continued)

Couple's average earnings	0–0.39	0.40–0.49	0.50–0.59	0.60–0.69	0.70–0.79	0.80–0.89	0.90–0.99	1.00–1.09	1.10–1.19	1.20–1.29	1.30+	Total
$9000–9999												
Number	0	1	1	7	6	10	12	21	29	28	50	165
Row percent	0.00	0.61	0.61	4.24	3.64	6.06	7.27	12.73	17.58	16.97	30.30	100
$10000–11999												
Number	0	0	1	1	6	13	15	18	12	15	30	111
Row percent	0.00	0.00	0.90	0.90	5.41	11.71	13.51	16.22	10.81	13.51	27.03	100
$12000+												
Number	1	0	5	8	17	18	31	38	29	39	91	277
Row percent	0.36	0.00	1.81	2.89	6.14	6.50	11.19	13.72	10.47	14.08	32.85	100
Total												
Number	1	4	20	42	103	151	218	258	263	240	664	1964
Row percent	0.05	0.20	1.02	2.14	5.24	7.69	11.10	13.14	13.39	12.22	33.81	100

Table 17.2
R_A-Ratio of old-age annuity to lifetime annuity

Couple's average earnings	0–0.39	0.40–0.49	0.50–0.59	0.60–0.69	0.70–0.79	0.80–0.89	0.90–0.99	1.00–1.09	1.10–1.19	1.20–1.29	1.30+	Total
$0–2999												
Number	0	0	4	4	4	7	6	13	15	11	118	182
Row percent	0.00	0.00	2.20	2.20	2.20	3.85	3.30	7.14	8.24	6.04	64.84	100
$3000–3999												
Number	1	2	2	2	1	12	4	14	6	12	87	143
Row percent	0.70	1.40	1.40	1.40	0.70	8.39	2.80	9.79	4.20	8.89	60.84	100
$4000–4999												
Number	0	0	1	3	3	10	8	8	20	12	105	170
Row percent	0.00	0.00	0.59	1.76	1.76	5.88	4.71	4.71	11.76	7.06	61.76	100
$5000–5999												
Number	0	0	0	3	3	13	13	15	23	23	122	215
Row percent	0.00	0.00	0.00	1.40	1.40	6.05	6.05	6.98	10.70	10.70	56.74	100
$6000–6999												
Number	0	0	1	2	4	12	14	25	21	20	141	240
Row percent	0.00	0.00	0.42	0.83	1.67	5.00	5.83	10.42	8.75	8.33	58.75	100
$7000–7999												
Number	0	0	2	2	6	9	12	20	26	24	152	253
Row percent	0.00	0.00	0.79	0.79	2.37	3.56	4.74	7.91	10.28	9.49	60.08	100
$8000–8999												
Number	0	0	0	3	4	10	16	19	19	17	120	208
Row percent	0.00	0.00	0.00	1.44	1.92	4.81	7.69	9.13	9.13	8.17	57.69	100

Table 17.2 (continued)

Couple's average earnings	0–0.39	0.40–0.49	0.50–0.59	0.60–0.69	0.70–0.79	0.80–0.89	0.90–0.99	1.00–1.09	1.10–1.19	1.20–1.29	1.30+	Total
$9000–9999												
Number	0	1	1	1	8	6	5	9	10	13	111	165
Row percent	0.00	0.61	0.61	0.61	4.85	3.64	3.30	5.45	6.06	7.88	67.27	100
$10000–11999												
Number	0	0	0	1	3	1	14	10	8	17	57	111
Row percent	0.00	0.00	0.00	0.90	2.70	0.90	12.61	9.01	7.21	15.32	51.35	100
12000+												
Number	0	1	1	4	9	14	16	10	25	30	167	277
Row percent	0.00	0.36	0.36	1.44	3.25	5.05	5.78	3.61	9.03	10.83	60.29	100
Total												
Number	1	4	12	25	45	94	108	143	173	179	1180	1964
Row percent	0.05	0.20	0.61	1.27	2.29	4.79	5.50	7.28	8.81	9.11	60.08	100

tion they could have financed at age 30. The lower tails of the distribution are also of interest. According to table 17.2, fewer than 1 percent of elderly respondents in 1969 faced implied reductions in their standard of living of more than 40 percent. Only 5 couples out of the 1,964 couples in this sample had computed sustainable consumption ratios below 0.5. While these tables are based on an assumed 2 percent real interest rate, tables based on a 4 percent interest rate yielded virtually identical distributions.

The distribution of R_A is shifted to the right relative to the distribution of R. The ability to purchase an annuity enhances consumption opportunities the most when the ratio of current net worth to total present expected resources is the greatest. Hence, the ratio of C_A^0 to C^0 exceeds the ratio of C_A^L to C^L, and R_A exceeds R. The tables do not indicate any obvious correlation between these sustainable consumption ratios and the level of average earnings.

Table 17.3 presents the distribution of R, the consumption ratio under the no-annuities assumption for those couples with retired household heads. These couples appear somewhat less well prepared for their old age than couples whose head is still working in 1969. For 13 percent of the couples, with retire household heads, retirement assets are insufficient to finance old-age consumption streams greater than 80 percent of the lifetime sustainable stream. The comparable percent for the entire sample is 9 percent. Under the annuity concept, 11 percent of retired respondents exhibit a ratio of old-age to lifetime sustainable consumption under 0.8; the overall sample percentage in this case is less than 5 percent.

For those couples with no private pensions, the distributions of the R_A and R ratios suggest somewhat less adequacy in old-age resources than for the overall sample. Under the no-annuity consumption concept, 12 percent of the couples without pensions had a ratio less than 0.8, while 7 percent had an annuity ratio less than 0.8. For the two subsamples of retired couples and couples with no pension, fewer than 1 percent of respondents indicate R and R_A ratios that are less than 0.5.

While readers should draw their own conclusions from the tables, the sustainable consumption ratios are high relative to our priors. Assuming unconstrained and nonmyopic stress, there is no evidence of significant undersaving. In viewing these numbers, it should be recalled that some individuals, even in the presence of perfect annuity markets, may prefer to consume at a lower rate in their old age than in their youth, while some couples may prefer the opposite. In the absence of perfect annuity markets, there is a fairly strong argument for rational, expected utility-maximizing individuals to plan to consume at significantly lower levels in their old age

Table 17.3
R-Ratio of old-age consumption stream to lifetime consumption stream, no-annuity case

Retired couple's average earnings	0–0.49	0.50–0.59	0.60–0.69	0.70–0.79	0.80–0.89	0.90–0.99	1.00–1.09	1.10–1.19	1.20–1.29	1.30+	Total
$0–2999											
Number	0	2	7	8	14	20	15	14	8	25	113
Row percent	0.00	0.00	6.19	7.08	12.39	17.70	13.27	12.39	7.08	22.10	100
$3000–3999											
Number	0	1	3	4	8	5	4	5	6	10	46
Row percent	0.00	2.17	6.52	8.70	17.39	10.87	8.70	10.87	13.04	21.74	100
$4000–4999											
Number	0	2	1	5	8	6	8	10	6	3	49
Row percent	0.00	4.08	2.04	10.20	16.33	12.24	16.33	20.41	12.24	6.12	100
$5000–5999											
Number	0	0	1	4	12	3	5	2	4	6	37
Row percent	0.00	0.00	2.70	10.81	32.43	8.11	13.51	5.41	10.81	16.22	100
$6000–6999											
Number	0	0	0	0	2	7	9	5	6	9	38
Row percent	0.00	0.00	0.00	0.00	5.26	18.42	23.68	13.16	15.79	23.68	100
$7000–7999											
Number	0	0	0	0	2	4	5	5	3	6	25
Row percent	0.00	0.00	0.00	0.00	8.00	16.00	20.00	20.00	12.00	24.00	100
$8000–8999											
Number	1	0	1	3	6	2	1	2	1	0	17
Row percent	5.88	0.00	5.88	17.65	35.29	11.76	5.88	11.76	5.88	0.00	100

Table 17.3 (continued)

Retired couple's average earnings	0–0.49	0.50–0.59	0.60–0.69	0.70–0.79	0.80–0.89	0.90–0.99	1.00–1.09	1.10–1.19	1.20–1.29	1.30+	Total
$9000–9999											
Number	0	0	1	0	1	0	1	2	1	2	8
Row percent	0.00	0.00	12.50	0.00	12.50	0.00	12.50	25.00	12.50	25.00	100
$10000–11999											
Number	0	1	0	0	1	0	3	2	1	1	9
Row percent	0.00	11.11	0.00	0.00	11.11	0.00	33.33	22.22	11.11	11.11	100
$12000+											
Number	0	0	0	0	0	3	4	3	0	4	14
Row percent	0.00	0.00	0.00	0.00	0.00	21.43	28.57	21.43	0.00	28.57	100
Total											
Number	1	6	14	24	54	50	55	50	36	66	356
Row percent	0.28	1.69	3.93	6.74	17.17	14.04	14.45	14.04	10.11	18.54	100

Table 17.4
Age consumption and age wealth paths for single male with no annuities[a]

Age	Risk aversion	Consumption	Wealth
55	0.75	6825	$100,000
65	0.75	4720	47,415
75	0.75	2250	13,830
85	0.75	395	1,420
95	0.75	10	30
55	1.25	5465	100,000
65	1.25	4395	57,200
75	1.25	2810	23,675
85	1.25	990	5,165
95	1.25	110	475
55	1.75	4795	100,000
65	1.75	4100	52,680
75	1.75	2980	30,680
85	1.75	1415	9,505
95	1.75	295	1,690

a. Interest rate is 1 percent. Rate of time preference is 1 percent.

than in their youth. When annuity markets, or good substitutes, are not available, a consumer's probability of death will enter into his intertemporal optimization problem exactly like a higher rate of time preference. Real-world mortality probabilities would suggest a fairly steep decline in consumption with age when annuities are not available. Table 17.4 uses the CES utility function,

$$EU = \sum_{t=0}^{D} P_t \frac{C_t^{1-\gamma}}{1-\gamma} \alpha^t,$$

to calculate the optimal decline in consumption for a single individual with no access to an annuities market. The variable P_t is the probability of surviving to period t; D is the latest date at which the individual can remain alive. The term α is the time preference parameter, and γ is the degree of risk aversion. The table indicates that a single male with a risk-aversion parameter of 1.75 would optimally consume at 65 only 85 percent of his age 55 consumption level. For risk average of 0.75, age 65 consumption is only 70 percent of age 55 consumption.

There are, of course, arguments for rising levels of consumption as one ages. There appear to be particular types of risks (such as the need for nursing home care) that are poorly insured by private markets. In addition, many elderly people appear to have a strong fear of becoming a burden to their children.

How do these numbers square with the standard findings from national surveys of the elderly that large fractions of the elderly have little or no net wealth, and a larger fraction has no positive liquid wealth? The figures presented here are consistent with these facts. While fewer than 5 percent of married couples exhibit values of R_A that are less than 0.8, slightly more than one-third of couples reported levels of net worth that represent less than 10 percent of their total future resources. In addition, 67 percent of married couples held less than 10 percent of their future resources in liquid wealth. Of these couples, 21 percent had no liquid wealth whatsoever. Despite the fact that a significant fraction of the elderly have little or no liquid or illiquid wealth, their Social Security, pension, and earnings stream are sufficient to finance a level of old-age consumption that is as large or larger than they enjoyed in their youth.

Analysis of the rate at which the elderly consume their retirement resources provides another test of the ability of the elderly to cogently plan their old age consumption. Table 17.5 presents the ratio of the annuity that elderly couples could have financed in 1971 to the annuity they could have financed in 1969. A ratio close to unity suggests that couples are managing to provide a level consumption stream as they age. The table indicates that roughly 60 percent of couples have ratios of the 1971 affordable annuity that is within 10 percent of the 1969 affordable annuity. In 1971, 16 percent of couples could have financed an annuity that was more than 10 percent larger than they could have financed in 1969. On the other hand, almost 25 percent of 1971 couples could not have financed an annuity as large as 90 percent of the 1969 annuity; 6 percent of couples could not afford an annuity that was 70 percent of the 1969 annuity.

Our data provide no overwhelming prima facie support for the existing massive forced savings programs; they also provide no strong support for expansion of the Social Security and private pension systems. While this evidence provides little positive justification for forced savings, does it provide any compelling evidence against forced savings? To consider this question, the distributions of R and R_A were recomputed under the extreme assumption that in the absence of Social Security, all individuals would have fully consumed their tax contributions. The effect of setting all Social

Table 17.5
Ratio of annuity in 1971 to annuity in 1969

Couple's average earnings	0–0.29	0.30–0.39	0.40–0.49	0.50–0.59	0.60–0.69	0.70–0.79	0.80–0.89	0.90–0.99	1.00–1.09	1.10–1.19	1.20–1.29	1.30 +	Total
$0–2999													
Number	1	2	2	3	5	4	13	61	53	34	26	17	221
Row percent	0.00	0.90	1.36	2.26	1.18	5.88	27.60	23.98	15.38	11.76	7.89	7.69	100
$3000–3999													
Number	0	0	1	1	5	3	24	64	41	32	9	10	190
Row percent	0.00	0.00	0.53	0.53	2.63	1.58	12.63	33.68	21.58	16.84	4.74	5.26	100
$4000–4999													
Number	0	1	2	1	3	9	26	78	48	29	12	9	218
Row percent	0.00	0.46	0.92	0.46	1.38	4.13	11.93	35.78	22.02	13.30	5.50	4.13	100
$5000–5999													
Number	2	0	1	7	3	6	37	116	72	25	8	11	288
Row percent	0.69	0.00	0.35	2.43	1.04	2.08	12.85	40.28	25.00	8.68	2.78	3.82	100
$6000–6999													
Number	0	0	0	5	8	13	39	134	79	24	4	11	317
Row percent	0.00	0.00	0.00	1.58	2.52	4.10	12.30	42.27	24.92	7.57	1.26	3.47	100
$7000–7999													
Number	0	0	3	5	14	14	43	152	63	23	12	11	340
Row percent	0.00	0.00	0.88	1.47	4.12	4.12	12.65	44.71	18.53	6.76	3.53	3.24	100
$8000–8999													
Number	0	1	0	4	10	15	37	111	61	17	7	7	270
Row percent	0.00	0.37	0.00	1.48	3.70	5.56	13.70	41.11	22.59	6.30	2.69	2.59	100
$9000–9999													
Number	1	1	1	4	5	17	39	94	42	10	3	4	221
Row percent	0.45	0.45	0.45	1.81	2.26	7.69	17.65	42.53	19.00	4.52	1.36	1.81	100

Table 17.5 (continued)

Couple's average earnings	0–0.29	0.30–0.39	0.40–0.49	0.50–0.59	0.60–0.69	0.70–0.79	0.80–0.89	0.90–0.99	1.00–1.09	1.10–1.19	1.20–1.29	1.30+	Total
$10000–11999													
Number	2	0	0	4	8	9	20	58	21	11	5	4	142
Row percent	1.41	0.00	0.00	2.82	5.63	6.34	14.08	40.85	14.79	7.75	3.52	2.82	100
$12000+													
Number	2	3	12	19	11	34	92	124	40	12	12	14	375
Row percent	0.53	0.80	3.20	5.07	2.93	9.07	24.53	33.07	10.67	3.20	3.20	3.73	100
Total													
Number	8	8	22	53	72	124	370	992	520	217	98	98	2,582
Row percent	0.31	0.31	0.85	2.05	2.79	4.80	14.33	38.42	20.14	8.40	3.80	3.80	100

Security taxes and benefits to zero has a dramatic effect on the distribution of the ratios of old-age to lifetime consumption. In the case of the annuity ratios, over 40 percent of the sample would suffer at least a 20 percent reduction in their consumption levels in a world in which Social Security had no effect on private savings. Of this 40 percent, 20 percent would suffer over a 50 percent reduction in consumption, and 9 percent would suffer over a 70 percent reduction in consumption.

The results are even more impressive if one considers the subset of the population that is retired and that has no pension benefits. For this group, eliminating Social Security from the calculation and assuming no offsetting private savings response leaves 32 percent of the sample with a retirement annuity lower than one-third of their lifetime annuity. In the no-annuity framework, 65 percent of the sample would face a 50 percent or greater reduction in their standard of living.

These numbers are sufficiently dramatic to conclude that no strong case could be made for or against Social Security and other forced saving program, based on the adequacy of resources available during retirement, unless and until one pins down the exact saving response to these programs.

17.4   Explaining Individual Differences in the Adequacy of Savings

In this section, we study the determinants of individual savings adequacy. Two broad classes of variables are examined. First, the relation of savings adequacy to demographic characteristics is studied. Second, resource adequacy at retirement is related to the pattern of lifetime income receipts. Under the strict life cycle hypothesis with no capital market constraints or myopia, the level of wealth should be independent of the form and timing of lifetime income. If individuals do not foresee income streams such as Social Security or pensions, which come later in life, or if they do foresee them, but are unable to borrow against them, then persons receiving relatively more income in these forms should have more adequate resources available for retirement consumption.

Table 17.6 presents regressions relating the ratios R_A and R, old-age to lifetime consumption, to demographic variables and variables reflecting the form and timing of lifetime resources. HOME is a dummy variable which equals one if the family owns a home and zero otherwise. The variable SSRAT is the ratio of Social Security wealth to the present value of lifetime resources from all sources—Social Security, labor income and pension benefits. PRAT is a similar ratio constructed using pension wealth (PENW),

Table 17.6
Explaining the intertemporal allocation of consumption[a]

Independent variables	Dependent variables			
	Equation (1), R_A	Equation (2), R	Equation (3), R_A	Equation (4), R
Constant	−2.134	−0.581	−1.813	−0.279
	(5.523)	(2.323)	(4.716)	(1.135)
Age	0.042	0.018	0.044	0.020
	(6.833)	(4.563)	(7.307)	(5.209)
ED 1	−0.063	0.036	−0.088	−0.053
	(3.259)	(2.669)	(4.255)	(3.989)
ED 3	0.085	0.045	0.079	0.047
	(2.734)	(2.281)	(2.586)	(2.435)
RACE	−0.087	−0.052	−0.113	−0.071
	(2.907)	(2.695)	(3.847)	(3.790)
HOME	0.102	0.064	0.120	0.078
	(4.525)	(4.404)	(5.462)	(5.534)
SSRAT	2.517	1.571	2.509	1.372
	(18.611)	(17.962)	(10.375)	(8.878)
PRAT	2.258	1.713	2.315	1.576
	(13.686)	(16.051)	(5.490)	(5.848)
FRAT	2.027	1.243	2.191	1.357
	(23.863)	(22.632)	(11.271)	(10.918)
LTR	−	−	1.5×10^{-7}	-2.3×10^{-7}
			(0.376)	(0.891)
LSSRAT	−	−	-1.2×10^{-5}	-8.1×10^{-6}
			(7.686)	(8.276)
LPRAT	−	−	9.0×10^{-7}	1.6×10^{-6}
			(0.505)	(1.402)
LFAT	−	−	2.3×10^{-7}	2.5×10^{-7}
			(0.247)	(0.409)
$\bar{R}^2$	0.3673	0.3595	0.4030	0.4009

a. Absolute value of t-statistics are shown in parentheses.

and *FRAT* is constructed in the same way using the present value of future labor income (*FUTW*). Equations (3) and (4) include the level of lifetime resources, *LTR*, and the product of *LTR* and *SSPRAT*, *PRAT*, and *FRAT*, respectively designated *LSSRAT*, *LPRAT*, and *LFRAT*.

The results for the demographic variables are quite consistent with a prior expectations. The adequacy of wealth accumulation rises sharply with education and is lower for minority groups. The magnitude of the coefficient implies that the consumption profile of nonwhites is 9 percent lower relative to that of whites during the retirement period. Education has an even greater effect; a 15 percent difference separates persons without a high school degree from those with a college education. As one would expect, home owners, ceteris paribus, have a higher level of retirement assets. Comparison of equations (1) and (2), or (3) and (4), shows that these results do not depend significantly on whether or not feasible consumption is calculated on an annuity basis.

The three variables reflecting the form and timing of lifetime income are all highly significant in all of our regressions. The equations based on the annuity concept imply that an increase of 0.1 in the fraction of lifetime income coming in the form of Social Security (the sample mean is 0.279) raises the ratio of sustainable old-age consumption relative to sustainable lifetime consumption by 0.25. Hence, for couples who would otherwise have a value of R_A equal to unity, the 0.1 increase in *SSRAT* would raise their value of R_A to 1.25.

The impact of private pensions and future labor income is similar. The coefficients imply that in the absence of Social Security and private pensions, consumption in old age relative to lifetime consumption would be about 40 percent lower for the average person. This finding suggests that, because of either capital market constraints or myopia, Social Security significantly raises the level of retirement consumption. Likewise, it implies that the crowing out of private savings is substantially less than dollar for dollar.

It was hypothesized above that if capital markets constraints are an important reason for the positive relationship between Social Security and savings, the relationship should be relatively more attenuated for more affluent persons who have higher lifetime incomes and more access to the capital markets. This suggestion is supported, in part, by equations (3) and (4), which reveal a significant negative interaction between the Social Security fraction of lifetime income, and lifetime income itself. However, a similar effect is not found for private pensions or future labor income.

17.5 Summary and Conclusion

The results in this paper suggest that there is currently no systematic problem of undersaving among the elderly population. The vast majority of the aged population can sustain a higher level of consumption than they could have financed at earlier ages based on their lifetime resources. While these data came from the early 1970s, the substantial increases in real Social Security benefits and real home prices that have occurred over the last decade suggest our conclusion would be strengthened if current data were available.

To a large extent, Social Security contributed to the sound financial position of the aged population. If Social Security were removed, and not replaced by private accumulation, a large fraction of the aged population would face very sharp declines in living standards. Our econometric evidence indicates that persons receiving more Social Security benefits have relatively higher levels of sustainable consumption at retirement. This finding suggests that Social Security may have made a substantial contribution to the economic welfare of the elderly.

While regressions suggest that government forced savings is successful in redistributing lifetime consumption from one's youth to one's old age, we urge some caution in viewing these results. To some extent the observed correlation between sustainable consumption ratios and the variables of table 17.6 may simply reflect the fact that these future resource streams were unanticipated. For example, elderly couples who continue working may be couples who ex post turned out to be healthier than they had expected. Their private savings may have been predicated on the expectation of earlier retirement, but their unexpected good health permitted them to continue working. For these couples the positive correlations between the sustainable consumption ratios and the fraction of lifetime resources earned in old age could well reflect economic uncertainty rather than myopic or nonmyopic, but capital market constrained forced savings. Sorting out the issue of uncertainty versus the efficiency of forced savings is an important topic for further research.

Our research could also usefully be extended by considering more recent data, and by more fully exploiting the longitudinal character of the data. It might also be desirable to examine the economic situation of single persons, particularly widows, who are thought to suffer the most economic deprivation in old age. More fundamentally, our results underscore the need for a fuller understanding of the motivations for and determinants of individual saving.

Notes

We wish to thank Peter Diamond and Jon Skinner for helpful discussions, and Paul Dorosh, David Reitman, and Skinner for excellent research assistance. Research support was provided by the US Department of Health, Education and Welfare and the National Bureau of Economic Research. The research reported here is part of the NBER's research project in Capital Formation and Pensions. All opinions and conclusions expressed herein are solely our own, and not those of either the US Department of Health, Education and Welfare or the National Bureau of Economic Research.

1. In 1969, 18 percent of the couples included in our analysis were retired.

2. The earnings data are already net of the employer's contribution to Social Security.

3. The consumption ratios do not appear to be biased upward because of the omission of those respondents who fail to report either their value of their expected pension benefits or components of their wealth. Marking the extreme assumption that all unreported components of wealth were zero and including respondents with unreported wealth in the analysis generated virtually no change in the distribution of R and R_A. The inclusion of those couples who have pensions but who do not indicate their value in the analysis has a trivial impact on the distributions even under the assumption that these couples will receive no pension whatsoever.

18

Public Debt and United States Saving: A New Test of the Neutrality Hypothesis

with Michael J. Boskin

The significant postwar decline in the United States saving rate is a startling stylized fact that invites explanation. Since 1980 the United States has been saving 4.7 percent of its net national product. This figure contrasts with the 7.8 percent average rate of the 1970s, the 8.7 percent average rate of the 1960s, and the 8.8 percent average rate of the 1950s.[1] The United States saving rate is quite low not only relative to its own recent past level but also relative to the saving rates of its principal trading partners. Since 1960 the United States net national saving rate has averaged only 55 percent of the European OECD rate and 34 percent of the Japanese rate.[2] Over the postwar period the United States economy has experienced remarkable changes in fertility rates, the median age of retirement, and the rate of female labor-force participation; but each of these changes appears more likely to have raised rather than lowered the rate of saving.

The search for a culprit in explaining the saving reduction has led naturally to the federal government's doorstep. This paper examines the government's potential role in influencing postwar United States saving. As argued in the next section, a "smoking gun" in this mystery, if one is to be found, is most likely hiding amid the government's intergenerational transfer policies. Intergenerational transfer policies are referred to here as debt policies; they may be explicit, in the sense of altering the government's official measure of its liabilities, or implicit, in which case cross-generational transfers arise but have no direct impact on accounting deficits.

Resolving the impact of debt policy on saving is no easy task. There are only a few, rather subtle, testable differences between, for example, the life-cycle model (Modigliani and Brumberg 1954) that predicts crowding

Carnegie-Rochester Conference Series on Public Policy 23:55–86 (1985). © 1985 Elsevier Science Publishers B.V. (North-Holland). Reprinted with permission.

out from debt policies and the infinite-horizon Barro (1974) model that predicts no crowding out. Section 18.1 contains a short discussion of this point and a description of tests that can potentially discriminate between these models. The main contribution of this paper is to examine empirically Barro's model of intergenerational altruism. A restatement of the proposition that intergenerational transfers do not influence saving is that saving is invariant to the age distribution of resources.[3] This proposition is directly tested by measuring the excess influence of the age distribution of personal income and components of personal income on aggregate consumption given the level of consumption predicted by our formulation of the Barro model.

This model, which is described in Section 18.2, differs from that underlying the traditional time series consumption regression [e.g., Feldstein (1974), Barro (1978), Munnell (1974), and Darby (1979)] by explicitly incorporating earnings uncertainty, rate of return uncertainty, and demographic change into the optimal consumption decision. From the perspective of uncertainty models, the standard consumption specification seems quite naive; indeed, the failure explicitly to model uncertainty produces major conundrums over squeezing data from an uncertain world into a certainty model (Leimer and Lesnoy 1981). Our approach to including uncertainty in the analysis involves estimating simple stochastic processes for earnings and the return to savings and explicitly solving for the optimal consumption path of the infinitely lived Barro-type family. We then test whether, given the optimal predicted consumption program, the age distribution of resources has an impact on actual aggregate consumption. Since the age distribution of resources is obviously influenced by changes in the population age structure, the model controls for such changes by taking explicit account of variations in the size and age distribution of the population.

Section 18.3 contains a description of the data and the specification of earnings and return uncertainty. The empirical findings are discussed in Section 18.4, and concluding comments appear in Section 18.5.

18.1 Government Fiscal Policy and National Saving

In considering the government's potential impact on saving, one might ask whether postwar growth in total (federal, state, and local) government consumption relative to NNP could be a key factor. The ratio of government consumption to NNP has increased, but the increase has been modest. Government consumption averaged 21.4 percent of net national product in the 1950s, 23.0 percent in the 1960s, 23.5 percent in the 1970s, and 23.1 percent in the period 1980–1984. If, during the last 5 years, government consumption had been 21.4 percent rather than 23.1 percent of NNP and if private consumption as a share of NNP had not changed, the net national saving rate would have averaged 6.5 percent rather than 4.7 percent. Assuming that private consumption is invariant to changes in government consumption seems, however, highly unrealistic. At one extreme, government consumption may substitute perfectly for private consumption (David and Scadding 1974). In this case the 1.7 percentage point increase in the ratio of government consumption to NNP between the 1950s and early 1980s, abstracting from issues of tax distortions and redistributions, would have been completely offset by a 1.7 percentage point decrease in the ratio of private consumption to NNP, leaving the net national saving rate unchanged. With government consumption a prefect substitute for private consumption, the private sector's ultimate disposable income is simply NNP; and the private saving rate would coincide with the net national saving rate. From this perspective, the key question is why the private sector's saving behavior changed such that total consumption, private plus government, rose as a share of NNP.

At the other extreme, government consumption might not enter private utility functions at all, or might enter separately. One would expect the private sector in this case, in choosing its consumption level to view NNP-G, where G is government consumption, as its ultimate disposable income, since current government consumption must ultimately be financed by the private sector.[4] In the 1950s the private sector saved 10.9 percent of this definition of disposable income. In the 1980s the corresponding saving rate has been only 6.1 percent. Had the private sector maintained its 1950s 10.9 percent rate of saving out of NNP-G, the rise in the ratio of government's consumption to NNP would have generated only a 4.5 percent decline in the net national saving rate between the 1950s and 1980s, rather than the 46.6 percent drop actually observed. From this perspective the increase in the government's rate of consumption out of NNP contributed, at most, a small amount to the decline in the net national saving rate. Again, the real question is why an appropriately defined private saving rate fell during this period.

A second accusation that could be leveled at government policy is that the use of distortionary taxes to finance both its consumption and transfer expenditures has reduced incentives to work and save. While there was some increase in average marginal taxes on labor earnings, the increase was modest and seems unlikely to account for the decline in the United States saving rate. A recent article by Barro and Sahasakul (1983) suggests that the average marginal tax on labor income was 22 percent in the 1950s, 22 percent in the 1960s, and 27 percent in the 1970s.[5]

These marginal tax figures exclude Social Security's payroll tax. However, there is reason to believe that inclusion of Social Security's tax and benefit provisions in the analysis would reduce rather than raise estimated marginal labor taxes, particularly in the 1970s. Blinder and Gordon's (1981) analysis suggests that Social Security's tax and benefit provisions constitute a sizable subsidy to labor earnings of married males and others, leaving net effective marginal taxes on labor earnings for these groups quite low. Boskin and Hurd (1984) confirm the significant size of the Gordon effect. Crediting the public with the perspicacity and knowledge required to assess correctly the marginal social security return on the marginal tax contribution may be unrealistic; but the opposite assumption, that workers believe they receive no return at the margin for marginal social security tax payments, seems equally implausible. If one takes an intermediate view that workers view marginal social security taxes as providing marginal social security benefits of equal present value, then the post-1950 rise in the average marginal tax on labor income is adequately captured by Barro and Sahasakul's estimates.

Marginal saving incentives are also determined by capital income taxes. Several studies argue that effective capital income taxes, at least on corporate source income, rose substantially in the 1970s [e.g., Feldstein and Summers (1979)]. But in contrast to this popular belief that such taxes rose between 1950 and 1980, extensive calculations contained in King and Fullerton (1984) suggest a small decline in effective marginal taxes on capital income over this period. The 1981 tax act lowered effective marginal capital income taxes more significantly. Based on a 10 percent pretax return to capital and the prevailing inflation rate, King and Fullerton calculate that the overall effective marginal capital income tax rate was 48 percent in 1960, 37 percent in 1980, 26 percent in 1981, and 32 percent in 1982. In combination with the figures just cited for marginal taxes on labor income, these findings suggest that the distorting effects of government fiscal policy cannot explain the drop in the United States saving rate over the last 35 years.

Another type of policy that could potentially be blamed for the saving decline is intragenerational redistribution from the rich to the poor. The poor may have a higher rate of time preference than the rich. Alternatively, the poor may be liquidity constrained. In either case the poor within any age group will have larger marginal propensities to consume than their better-endowed contemporaries; and intragenerational transfers from the rich to the poor will lower saving. Lawrence (1983) recently examined the potential effect of intragenerational redistribution on saving, using a life-cycle simulation model. Lawrence considered substantial differences in time preference rates between the rich and poor as well as liquidity-constrained consumption by the poor. She found that even significant intragenerational redistribution, such as that characterizing United States welfare programs, has only minor effects on saving in life cycle models.

The explanation for these small changes in the case of differences in time preference rates is simply that neither the associated differences in marginal consumption propensities across the two groups nor the size of the simulated transfers are sufficiently large to have much impact on the economy's total wealth accumulation. Those poor who are liquidity constrained have marginal consumption propensities of unity; but the change in disposable income multiplying their unitary propensities is only the amount of current transfers. For rich, unconstrained transferors, the reduction in current consumption equals their much smaller marginal propensity to consume multiplied by the present value of transfers, which is typically considerably larger than simply the current payment. The reduced consumption of the rich offsets to a significant extent the increased consumption of the liquidity-constrained poor, producing only a small reduction in national saving despite a substantial program of intragenerational transfers. We conclude from this and related models that intragenerational redistribution is probably not a major determinant of the decline in the United States saving rate since 1950.

A fourth channel by which government policy may have reduced saving is by transferring resources from younger and future generations to older generations. Intergenerational transfers toward older generations, which is referred to here as debt policy, can be and have been conducted in subtle ways. The unfunded financing of the United States Social Security System is by now a well-understood, if nonetheless quite subtle, debt policy (Feldstein 1974). Less well-understood debt policies are changes in the tax structure that shift the burden of taxation from older to younger age groups (Summers 1981a; Auerbach and Kotlikoff 1983a) and changes in tax provisions that raise market values of financial assets and, thereby, transfer resources to older age groups who are the primary owners of such assets (Feldstein 1977; Summers 1981b). An example of the former type of policy is switching from income taxation to wage taxation. An example of the latter policy is reducing investment incentives (chapter 9). Since investment incentives in the United States are effectively provided only to new investment, old capital, capital that has been fully or partially written off, sells at a discount reflecting the differential tax treatment. A reduction in investment incentives means a smaller discount and a capital gain to owners of old capital. Younger and future generations are worse off as a result of such policies because they must now pay a higher price to acquire claims to the economy's capital stock.

In addition to these more subtle mechanisms of transferring to older generations, governments can engage in debt policies by reducing taxes levied on current generations and raising taxes levied on future generations. Intergenerational redistribution of this variety may eventuate in large officially reported deficits. An example in which even this more obvious form of redistribution does not necessarily alter official debt calculations is when such tax cuts and tax increases are coincident, respectively, with equivalent reductions and increases in the level of government consumption.

The fact that significant intergenerational redistribution can be run without its ever showing up on government books suggests that officially reported deficits are at best a poor indicator of underlying economic debt policies.[6] This proposition notwithstanding, there has been an enormous public interest, especially in recent years, in officially reported deficits. Curiously, public attention has focused only on a subset of official liabilities of the federal government and has essentially ignored both the official assets of the federal government and the official assets and liabilities of state and local governments. As discussed by Boskin (1982, 1985), Eisner and Pieper (1984), and the 1982 *Economic Report of the President*, the market value of the United States federal government's official assets may currently equal if not exceed the market value of its official liabilities.

In light of the quite significant if not overwhelming difficulties of gauging the extent of true debt policies from official reports, it seems safer to assess postwar United States debt policy by asking the following question: Were the lifetime budget constraints of older generations expanded significantly in the postwar period as a consequence of government policy at the expense of contracted budget constraints for young and future generations? One might point, in this context, to the enormous expansion of the Social Security System which greatly increased the budget opportunities of the elderly. The problem, however, with considering any one component of government policy is that it may have been instituted to offset another component; i.e., the postwar redistribution through social security to the elderly may simply represent the government's way of compensating the elderly for higher income taxes over their lifetimes or for their contribution to the nation during World War II. Just as there is no single correct way to measure official deficits, there is no single correct way of posing counter-factuals about observed government transfer policies. To put this point differently, intergenerational redistribution must always be assessed rela-tive to some benchmark, and the choice of a benchmark seems inherently subjective. The implication of this point is that any calculation of the magnitude of postwar intergenerational transfers will be arbitrary.[7]

Having conceded this point, we believe that at least one interesting, if arbitrary, counterfactual to pose with respect to postwar United States debt policy is an economy with either a very small unfunded Social Security program targeted toward the elderly poor or a larger, but fully funded, Social Security System. There is little need to review here the well-known facts about the magnitude of the United States Social Security System whose unfunded liabilities appear to range between 4 and 6 times the size of the United States government's official liabilities.[8] The growth of this program was coincident with the decline in the net national saving rate. The Social Security System appears to represent the only (potentially) discrete postwar intergenerational transfer policy capable of producing a major drop in the national saving rate. Simulation studies of the poten-tial savings impact of an unfunded Social Security System suggest a pos-sible reduction in long-run savings of 20 to 25 percent (chapters 12 and 13).

To summarize this section, we have identified four stylized features of fiscal policy, viz., government consumption, the extent of distortionary taxation, intragenerational transfers, and intergenerational transfers, each of which can affect a nation's saving behavior. We have tried to argue, although hardly exhaustively, that of these four features of fiscal policy, intergenerational transfers are the most likely to have generated a decline in the United States saving rate over the last three-and-a-half decades.

We turn next to a brief discussion of recent empirical attempts to resolve the impact of debt policies on saving. In the course of reviewing this literature, we indicate that there have been surprisingly few tests designed to distinguish sharply among broad models of saving. Rather than testing more fundamental propositions of particular saving models, most of the research has concentrated on the empirical impact of particular policy variables on consumption and savings. This focus has been excessive; indeed, in many studies the predicted impact of policy variables on depen-dent variables is the same under models with quite different implications about the affect of debt policies on national saving.

18.2   Empirical Analysis of Debt Policies

Much of the recent empirical research relating to the effects of economic deficits falls into two categories: cross-sectional analysis of Social Security's impact on household wealth accumulation and time series analysis of the consumption impact of government policy variables, such as Social Security wealth. Many cross-sectional studies have proceeded without clearly formulating rejectable hypotheses concerning Barro's (1974) conjecture of intergenerational altruism. These studies, including those of Feldstein and Pallechio (1979) and Kotlikoff (chapter 15), involve regressions of household private wealth on Social Security tax and transfer variables. The central question posed in much of this literature is whether households reduce their private asset accumulation when young because of the antici-pation of receiving net windfall transfers when old. The evidence here is mixed, but even if each of these studies had strongly confirmed the prop-osition that expected future windfalls lead to higher current consumption and, therefore, less private wealth accumulation, the results would still leave unresolved the issue of altruism. The altruistic hypothesis, like the life cycle hypothesis, suggests that increases in the future resources of a particular household should raise that household's consumption and lower its own savings. In the altruistic case, however, the future windfall to the household in question would also raise the consumption of all other altruistically linked households in the extended family. Indeed, a central proposition of the altruism hypothesis is that the consumption of particular extended family members depends on the resources of other extended family members. Unfortunately, this latter proposition is not tested in the cross-sectional empirical literature, nor does it appear capable of being tested, at least for the United States, given available micro data sources [although Kurz (1982) indirectly examines altruistic behavior using data on transfers].

While this distinguishing implication of the altruism model has not been tested, a distinctive implication of the pure life cycle model, that the elderly have larger marginal consumption propensities, has been directly tested by Blinder, Gordon, and Wise (1981). Their findings are weakly supportive of this proposition. Other implications of the life cycle model have also been analyzed. For example, chapter 1 finds that life cycle saving cannot explain the bulk of United States savings. Several studies addressing dissaving after retirement by Darby (1979), Mirer (1979), David and Menchik (1980), and Bernheim (1984) find either no dissaving or too little to be consistent with the strict life cycle model.

The time series analyses of Feldstein (1974, 1982), Munnell (1974), Barro (1978), Darby (1979), Leimer and Lesnoy (1981), and numerous others have proved inconclusive. The econometrics here is plagued by problems of aggregation, simultaneity, and errors in defining variables such as Social Security wealth. Auerbach and Kotlikoff (chapter 19) demonstrate the problem of the time series statistical approach by running the standard time series specification on simulated data that conformed perfectly to the non-altruistic, life cycle hypothesis. The coefficients on the critical Social Security wealth variable as well as many other variables proved extraordinarily sensitive to the choice of sample period. Auerbach and Kotlikoff concluded that the standard time series approach could easily reject the strict life cycle, no-altruism hypothesis even if it were true.

Curiously, the time series studies have been vague with respect to which of several (e.g., life-cycle, Keynesian, or altruistic) saving models is being tested. As a consequence a variety of ad hoc specifications have been employed. In a time series context, taking the life-cycle model as the null hypothesis immediately runs afoul of the paucity of cohort specific time series data. When these data are absent, key parameters cannot be identified and one cannot test two basic propositions of the life cycle models alluded to above: first, that consumption of a particular cohort depends only on its own resources and not on collective societal resources; and second, that older cohorts have larger marginal consumption propensities.

The Barro model is much more suited to analysis with time series data since only collective, rather than cohort specific, resources are predicted to influence aggregate consumption. This proposition is particularly useful in incorporating government policy in the model. In a certainty model the private Barro economy's budget can be written as the economy's total human plus nonhuman resources (including those owned by the government), less the present value of government consumption. As described below an analogous private budget constraint, involving only government consumption, i.e., requiring no information about taxes, arises with uncertainty.

As mentioned earlier, the key proposition of the Barro model, that consumption depends on collective resources and does not depend on the age distribution of resources, is the focus of our empirical work. To test this proposition, we specify the Barro model under earnings and rate of return uncertainty and determine whether, given the consumption predicted by this model, variables measuring the age distribution of resources significantly influence actual consumption. Data obtained from annual Current Population Surveys on the age distribution of income, including wages and salaries, property income, and government transfer payments, are used for this test. In addition, we use data compiled by Leimer and Lesnoy (1981) on the distribution of net Social Security wealth by age.

18.3   The Barro Model with Demographics and Uncertain Earnings and Returns

The expected utility of the "infinite horizon" Barro family at time t, U_t, is written in equation (1):

$$U_t = E_t \sum_{\tau=0}^{\infty} \sum_{a=0}^{D} \alpha^\tau P_{t+\tau,a} \theta_a U(C_{t+\tau,a}). \tag{1}$$

The function $U(\cdot)$ when multiplied by θ_a indicates the family's period $t + \tau$ utility associated with the consumption of a member age a at $t + \tau$, $C_{t+\tau,a}$. In this formulation of the utility from particular family members' consumption, the θ_a parameters can be thought of as age-specific utility weights. They determine the relative consumption of different family members at a point in time; i.e., they determine the shape of the cross-sectional age-consumption profile. $P_{t+\tau,a}$ is the number of family members age a (with maximum longevity of D) at time $t + \tau$, and α is a discount factor. Since we are applying this model to the entire United States economy, $P_{t+\tau,a}$ corresponds to the United States population age a at $t + \tau$. The function $U(\cdot)$ is assumed to be of the iso-elastic form, i.e.:

$$U(C) = \frac{C^{1-\gamma}}{1 - \gamma}. \tag{2}$$

Let A_t^p stand for the private sector's net worth at time t, G_t for government consumption at time t, $\tilde{r}_t$ for the stochastic pretax return to savings received at the end of period t, $\tilde{e}_t$ for the stochastic pretax labor earnings of the economy received at the end of period t, and $\tilde{T}_t$ for net taxes paid by the private sector at the end of period t. Private sector net worth evolves according to

$$A_{t+1}^p = \left(A_t^p - \sum_{a=0}^{D} P_{t,a} C_{t,a} \right)(1 + \tilde{r}_t) + \tilde{e}_t - \tilde{T}_t. \tag{3}$$

The Euler equation associated with optimal choice of $C_{t,a}$ is

$$E_t C_{t+1,a+1}^{-\gamma}[1 + \tilde{r}_t(1 - \delta_t)] = \left(\frac{1}{\alpha} \frac{\theta_a}{\theta_{a+1}} \right) C_{t,a}^{-\gamma}. \tag{4}$$

In (4) δ_t is the marginal effective capital income tax, which is assumed here to be nonstochastic.

At any point in time the relationship between consumption of different age groups is given by

$$\frac{C_{t,a}}{C_{t,a+1}} = \left(\frac{\theta_a}{\theta_{a+1}}\right)^{1/\gamma}. \tag{5}$$

Turning to the government's budget constraint, let A_t^g and G_t stand, respectively, for government net worth and consumption at time t; then A_t^g grows according to

$$A_{t+1}^g = (A_t^g - G_t)(1 + \tilde{r}_t) + \tilde{T}_t. \tag{6}$$

Adding (6) to (3) gives the following expression for the evolution of total net worth in the economy, A_t:

$$A_{t+1} = \left(A_t - \sum_{a=0}^{D} P_{t,a}C_{t,a} - G_t\right)(1 + \tilde{r}_t) + \tilde{e}_t. \tag{7}$$

In this model the distribution of tax burdens either at a point in time or over time has no impact on consumption choice; hence government policy is fully described by the evolution of G_t and the marginal effective capital income tax, δ_t. Given the time paths of these policy variables as well as earnings and return distributions, equations (4), (5), and (7) can be used in solving for the optimal choice of consumption at any point in time. In contrast to other analyses such as Feldstein (1974) and Barro (1978), this formulation avoids the difficulties of defining and measuring government debt policy variables such as Social Security wealth.

In this one good model all net worth terms, A_t^g, A_t^p, and A_t, are measured at replacement cost rather than market value. This method of expressing the private and government budget constraints plus the fact that $\tilde{r}_t$ is the pretax rate of return implies that $\tilde{T}_t$ includes taxes levied both on households and on businesses. To illustrate the point, consider an economy with a single tax levied on the profiles of businesses at rate μ. Also assume the government permits full expensing of new investment. For simplicity assume private assets consist only of holdings of capital, K_t, and official government debt, D_t. As described in chapter 9, the market value of private capital is $(1 - \mu)K_t$, where K_t is the replacement value of capital at t. Since the return on capital paid by businesses with full expensing is the pretax return, the private-sector budget constraint with assets values at market prices is

$$(1 - \mu)K_{t+1} + D_{t+1} = \left[(1 - \mu)K_t + D_t - \sum_{a=0}^{D} P_{t,a} C_{t,a} \right] (1 + \tilde{r}_t) + \tilde{e}_t.$$

(8)

Rewriting (8) yields

$$A_{t+1}^P = K_{t+1} + D_{t+1} = (K_t + D_t)(1 + \tilde{r}_t) + \mu(K_{t+1} - K_t) - \mu \tilde{r}_t K_t. \qquad (8')$$

Note the $\mu(K_{t+1} - K_t)$ corresponds to expensing rebates obtained from the government, and $\mu \tilde{r}_t K_t$ corresponds to business profiles taxes. The corresponding government equation is

$$D_{t+1} = (D_t + G_t)(1 + \tilde{r}_t) - \mu \tilde{r}_t K_t + \mu(K_{t+1} - K_t). \qquad (9)$$

Subtracting (9) from (8') yields (7).

The three equations (4), (5), and (7) that are used to solve for the optimal consumption program can be further simplified by using (5) to express (4) and (7) in terms of the consumption of a Barro family member age a^*:

$$E_t C_{t+1,a^*}^{-\gamma} [1 + \tilde{r}_t(1 - \delta_t)] = \frac{1}{\alpha} C_{t,a^*}^{-\gamma}, \qquad (4')$$

$$A_{t+1} = \left[A_t - \sum_{a=0}^{D} P_{t,a} \left(\frac{\theta_a}{\theta_{a^*}} \right)^{1/\gamma} C_{t,a^*} - G_t \right] (1 + \tilde{r}_t) + \tilde{e}_t. \qquad (7')$$

Solving for the Optimal Consumption Program

Our method of determining the optimal consumption plan is to solve the finite period analogue to the infinite horizon model for a time horizon sufficiently large so that extending it would make no difference to our results. Specifically we solve the finite period model for successively larger values of $\bar{\tau}$, where $\bar{\tau}$ is the number of periods, until the consumption programs for each of the first 50 periods converge. Our data cover 1946 through 1984; we choose 2060 as the terminal year. The optimal consumption values for the years 1946 to 1984 based on a terminal year of 2059 were less than a half percent different from those derived using 2060 as the terminal year.

The finite period problem is solved using dynamic programming. At time $t + \bar{\tau}$ the consumption function $\hat{C}_{t+\bar{\tau},a^*}$ is given by

$$\hat{C}_{t+\bar{\tau},a^*}(A_{t+\tau}) = A_{t+\bar{\tau}} - G_{t+\bar{\tau}}. \qquad (10)$$

Substituting this expression into the Euler relationship (4') for period $t + \tau + 1$ yields

$$\frac{1}{\alpha} C_{t+\bar{\tau}-1,a^*}^{-\gamma} = E_{t+\bar{\tau}-1} \hat{C}_{t+\bar{\tau},a^*} (A_{t+\bar{\tau}})^{-\gamma} [1 + \tilde{r}_{t+\bar{\tau}-1}(1 - \delta_{t+\bar{\tau}-1})]. \tag{11}$$

The accumulation equation (7′) for $A_{t+\bar{\tau}}$ can now be plugged into (11):

$$\frac{1}{\alpha} C_{t+\bar{\tau}-1,a^*}^{-\gamma} = E_{t+\bar{\tau}-1} \hat{C}_{t+\tau,a^*} \{ (A_{t+\bar{\tau}-1} - h_{t-1} C_{t+\tau-1,a^*} - G_{t+\bar{\tau}-1})$$

$$\times [1 + \tilde{r}_{t+\bar{\tau}-1}(1 - \delta_{t+\bar{\tau}-1})] + \tilde{e}_{t+\bar{\tau}-1} \}^{-\gamma}$$

$$\times [1 + \tilde{r}_{t+\bar{\tau}-1}(1 - \delta_{t+\bar{\tau}-1})], \tag{11′}$$

where

$$h_{t-1} = \sum_{a=0}^{D} P_{t-1,a} \left(\frac{\theta a}{\theta a^*} \right)^{1/\gamma}.$$

From (11′) and the implicit function theorem, we have that $C_{t+\bar{\tau}-1}$ is monotonic increasing function of $A_{t+\bar{\tau}-1}$, i.e.,

$$C_{t+\bar{\tau}-1,a^*} = \hat{C}_{t+\bar{\tau}-1,a^*}(A_{t+\bar{\tau}-1}; S_{t+\bar{\tau}-1}). \tag{12}$$

In (12) $S_{t+\bar{\tau}-1}$ is a vector of state variables conditioning the distributions of $\tilde{r}_{t+\bar{\tau}-1}$ and $\tilde{e}_{t+\bar{\tau}-1}$. The function $\hat{C}_{t+\bar{\tau}-1}(\cdot)$ can now be used to solve for $C_{t+\bar{\tau}-2}(A_{t+\bar{\tau}-2}; S_{t+\bar{\tau}-2})$. Proceeding in this manner, one can calculate each consumption function $\hat{C}_{t+\tau}(A_{t+\tau}; S_{t+\tau})$ for $0 \leqslant \tau \leqslant \bar{\tau} - 3$.

In general there are no simple closed-form solutions for the $\hat{C}_{t+\tau}(\cdot)$ functions, and these functions must be derived numerically. The numerical method we employ is to select a grid of potential values of $A_{t+\tau}$ and $S_{t+\tau}$. Next, we take random draws from the bivariate distribution of $\tilde{r}_{t+\tau}$ and $\tilde{e}_{t+\tau}$ conditional on the particular grid value of $S_{t+\tau}$. These draws are then used to evaluate (conditional on alternative values of $A_{t+\tau}$) the expectation of $\hat{C}_{t+\tau-1,a^*}(\cdot)^{-\gamma}[1 + \tilde{r}_{t+\tau}(1 - \delta_{t+\tau})]$ for alternative values of $C_{t+\tau,a^*}$. The value of $C_{t+\tau,a^*}$ producing an equality between this expectation and $(1/\alpha) C_{t+\tau,a^*}^{-\gamma}$, i.e., satisfying (4′), is stored as the function $\hat{C}_{t+\tau,a^*}(A_{t+\tau}, S_{t+\tau})$. The number of grid points and random draws chosen are sufficiently large that our empirical results are invariant to further increases in their values.

18.4 Specification of Return and Earnings Uncertainty and Description of the Data

The model outlined in Section 18.3 assumes that current and future population age distributions are known with certainty. To be consistent in modeling earnings uncertainty, we also assume that Barro family planners understand the impact of projected demographic change on future total labor earnings distributions. More generally, we assume that the age distribution of earnings is known with certainty. What is uncertain then is the level of earnings at future dates for a representative worker. Let $\tilde{w}_{t+\tau,a^*}$ be the random annual earnings of the benchmark worker age a^* at time $t + \tau$. Then total earnings at $t + \tau$, $\tilde{e}_{t+\tau}$, can be expressed as

$$\tilde{e}_{t+\tau} = \tilde{w}_{t+\tau,a^*} \sum_{a=0}^{D} \lambda_{t+\tau,a} \psi_{t+\tau,a} P_{t+\tau,a}, \tag{13}$$

where $\lambda_{t+\tau,a}$ is the nonstochastic ratio of earnings of a worker age a at $t + \tau$ to that of a worker age a^* at $t + \tau$, and $\psi_{t+\tau,a}$ is the nonstochastic work experience rate for the population age a at $t + \tau$.

We assume the following fairly simple bivariate process for $\tilde{w}_{t+\tau,a^*}$ and $\tilde{r}_{t+\tau}$:

$$\log \tilde{w}_{t+\tau,a^*} = c_0 + c_1 \log w_{t+\tau-1,a^*} + c_2 r_{t+\tau-1} + \varepsilon_w,$$

$$\tilde{r}_{t+\tau} = c_3 + c_4 r_{t+\tau-1} + c_5 \log w_{t+\tau-1,a^*} + \varepsilon_r, \tag{14}$$

where ε_w and ε_r are mean zero, bivariately distributed normal errors with variances σ_ε^2, σ_r^2, and covariance $\sigma_{\varepsilon r}$. Since the distributions of $\tilde{w}_{t+\tau,a^*}$ and $\tilde{r}_{t+\tau}$ depend on their lagged values, these lagged variables represent the additional state variables $(S_{t+\tau})$ entering the $\hat{C}_{t+\tau,a^*}(\cdot)$ functions.[9]

Values of $w_{t+\tau,a^*}$ are calculated for the years 1946 through 1984 by dividing total annual earnings by the multiplicand of $w_{t+\tau,a^*}$ in (13). Total annual earnings equals NIA wage and salary compensation plus an updated version of Kotlikoff and Summers's (1981) estimate of labor earnings of the self-employed. Values for the relative earnings profile $\lambda_{t+\tau,a}$ come from Social Security data on median earnings by age and sex.[10] There is very little variation in this profile between 1946 and 1984. For years after 1984 the projected profile of relative earnings is set equal to the 1984 relative earnings profile. Work experience rates by age and sex are reported starting in 1959 in the *Employment and Training Report of the President*, although labor force participation rates are available for the entire period.[11] For the period 1946 through 1958 work experience rates are imputed based on a regression of work experience rates on labor force participation rates for the years 1959 through 1984. Work experience rates projected beyond 1984 are assumed to equal the 1984 rates.

Private consumption is measured here as NIA consumer expenditures on nondurables and services plus imputed rent on durables. The BEA consumer durables series was used in this calculation. The rate of imputation equals the annual average three-month Treasury Bill rate less the annual percentage increase in the PCE durables deflator plus an assumed 20 percent depreciation rate. Government consumption is also corrected for durables consumption. The stock of government durables, both military and nonmilitary, was divided into equipment and structures. A 20 percent rate of depreciation was assumed for government equipment, and a 3 percent depreciation rate was assumed for government structures. Like demographics and the age distribution of earnings, we assume that the future course of government consumption is known with certainty. Future government consumption is determined by assuming that government consumption per capita after 1984 equals the 1984 level of government consumption per capita. Besides government consumption, the marginal tax on capital income is the only policy variable influencing the optimal consumption plan. A 30 percent marginal tax on capital income is used in calculating each of the consumption functions for the years 1946 through 2060.

Economy-wide net worth is measured as the sum of private plus government reproducible tangible wealth measured at replacement cost estimated by the BEA, plus the value of private land estimated by the Federal Reserve. These and other series are deflated to 1972 dollars. Given wealth in years t and $t + 1$, and year t earnings, private consumption, and government consumption, equation (7) can be used to solve for $r_{t+\tau}$. This procedure was used to determine the pretax rate of return series for the period 1946 through 1984.

Data for the age distribution of resources, which, according to the Barro model, are irrelevant for aggregate consumption, were obtained from the annual Current Population Surveys (CPS) for the years 1968 through 1984. While the CPS data do not provide information about asset holdings, they do include property income, wage and salary income, and government transfers including welfare, food stamps, unemployment compensation, veterans' benefits, and Social Security retirement and disability benefits. These data and the CPS population weights are used to construct shares of total income as well as shares of labor income, property income, and Social Security income of households with heads whose ages fall in particular age categories.

18.5 Testing the Intergenerational Altruism Model

Equation (15) indicates the nonlinear regression model used to test intergenerational altruism:

$$C_t = \beta_1 + \beta_2 \hat{C}_t(A_t, \log w_{t-1,a^*}, r_{t-1}; \theta_0, \ldots, \theta_D, \gamma, \rho) + \lambda_1 s_{1t}$$

$$+ \cdots + \lambda_m s_{mt} + \varepsilon_{Ct}. \tag{15}$$

In (15) C_t is actual consumption, $\hat{C}_t(\cdot)$ is the level of total consumption predicted by our model and depends on the age-utility weights $\theta_0, \ldots, \theta_D$, the relative risk aversion coefficient γ, and the time preference rate ρ, where $\rho = (1 - \alpha)/\alpha$. The variables s_{1t} through s_{mt} are year t shares of personal income or components of personal income of m different age groups. The error ε_{ct} is assumed to be normally distributed with mean zero and variance σ^2. A test of the altruism model is that all the λ's are zero, conditional, of course, on both our specification of intergenerational altruism and our functional forms for utility, as well as earnings and return uncertainty. Note that the alternative hypothesis includes most other consumption theories such as the life cycle model.

Before presenting the results of this regression, it is useful to describe values of the $\hat{C}_t(\cdot)$ series and changes through time in the share of personal income and its components received by different age groups. Table 18.1 presents actual consumption and consumption predicted by our model ($\hat{C}_t(\cdot)$) for selected years for alternative values of α and γ. Consumption is measured in 1972 dollars. The age-utility weights in this table are set such

Table 18.1
Comparison of actual with predicted consumption for alternative values of ρ and γ[a]

Year	Actual consumption	Consumption predicted by altruism model			
		$\gamma = 1.5$, $\rho = 0.05$, $\theta = 0.3$	$\gamma = 2$, $\rho = 0.04$, $\theta = 0.5$	$\gamma = 2$, $\rho = 0.03$, $\theta = 0.5$	$\gamma = 4$, $\rho = 0.04$, $\theta = 0.3$
1947	298	262	273	260	322
1950	342	250	259	247	296
1955	399	318	335	318	400
1960	479	395	405	388	462
1965	581	465	488	465	565
1970	700	562	663	629	762
1975	785	809	831	798	938
1980	947	1006	1019	972	1132
1984	1087	1044	1032	964	1136
Root-mean square error, 1946–1984		69.7	58.3	75.6	78.6

a. All consumption values are measured in billions of 1972 dollars.

that θ_a equals 0.5 for age a less than 16, or age a greater than 80. At age 40 θ_a is set equal to 1. For ages between 15 and 40, θ_a rises linearly from 0.5 to 1, and θ_a declines linearly from 1 to 0.5 between ages 40 and 80. Quite similar results arise for other choices of the values of θ_a at ages 15 and 80.

From the preliminary examination of alternative parameters values described in table 18.1, it appears that for certain sets of parameter values the model presented in section 18.3 does fairly well in predicting actual consumption. Of the parameter combinations examined in the table, a value of γ equal to 2, ρ equal to 0.04, and θ equal to 0.5 produce the smallest root-mean squared error for consumption. These parameter values are within the middle range of those that have been estimated.

Table 18.2 contains, for selected years, various income shares of households whose heads are in particular age groups. The table also indicates the fraction of all households with heads in particular age intervals; and it displays the ratio of the average income of households with heads in a particular age category to the average income of all households. Table 18.2 indicates sizable changes in income shares of particular age groups between 1968 and 1984. For example, the share of total income of households with heads age 25 to 34 rose from 18.6 percent to 22.5 percent over the period. For the 45–54 age group the income share fell during this period from 25.0 percent to 19.3 percent. Many of these changes are explained by changes in the age distribution of households; the first column of the table is clearly highly correlated with the second. But there were also changes in income shares over the period that are not directly related to demographic change. The figures in column 3 indicate that in 1968 households with heads age 45 to 54 had average incomes that were 1.30 times the overall average household income. In 1984 such households had average incomes that were 1.40 times the overall average. During this 17-year period the ratio of the average income of households with 45–55-year-old heads to that of households with 25–34-year-old heads rose by 22 percent. Shares of property income also changed significantly for certain age groups; the 45–54-year-old group experienced a 35 percent drop in its share of property income between 1968 and 1984. Similar sizable changes in income shares and income ratios are indicated in table 18.2 for labor income and transfer income.

Table 18.3 reports maximum likelihood estimates of equation (15) excluding income shares, including income shares of all age groups, and including only the income share of households age 65 and older. Maximum likelihood estimates were derived by searching over a grid of values of γ,

Table 18.2
Age distribution of income and related variables

Age of head	Year	(1) Fraction of all households	(2) Share of total income	(3) Total income ratio	(4) Share of labor income	(5) Labor income ratio	(6) Share of property income	(7) Property income ratio	(8) Share of transfers	(9) Transfer income ratio
15–24	1968	0.079	0.050	0.633	0.060	0.759	0.009	0.114	0.005	0.006
	1975	0.102	0.058	0.568	0.069	0.676	0.009	0.088	0.006	0.006
	1984	0.092	0.043	0.465	0.051	0.554	0.011	0.120	0.003	0.033
25–34	1968	0.177	0.186	1.048	0.214	1.209	0.049	0.277	0.023	0.130
	1975	0.213	0.219	1.029	0.257	1.207	0.062	0.291	0.017	0.080
	1984	0.243	0.225	0.927	0.273	1.123	0.063	0.259	0.016	0.066
35–44	1968	0.193	0.240	1.243	0.257	1.332	0.105	0.544	0.055	0.285
	1975	0.164	0.207	1.269	0.227	1.384	0.092	0.561	0.042	0.256
	1984	0.188	0.240	1.274	0.275	1.463	0.113	0.601	0.035	0.186
45–54	1968	0.193	0.250	1.296	0.258	1.337	0.193	1.000	0.081	0.420
	1975	0.175	0.236	1.350	0.250	1.429	0.176	1.006	0.074	0.423
	1984	0.138	0.193	1.403	0.214	1.551	0.125	0.906	0.038	0.275
55–64	1968	0.167	0.172	1.033	0.165	0.988	0.243	1.455	0.121	0.724
	1975	0.154	0.167	1.085	0.159	1.032	0.246	1.597	0.138	0.896
	1984	0.144	0.166	1.154	0.153	1.063	0.238	1.660	0.134	0.931
65+	1968	0.191	0.102	0.534	0.046	0.241	0.400	2.094	0.714	3.738
	1975	0.193	0.112	0.583	0.037	0.192	0.416	2.155	0.723	3.746
	1984	0.196	0.134	0.682	0.034	0.173	0.450	2.296	0.774	3.949

Table 18.3
Excess sensitivity of consumption to income shares, 1968–1984, maximum likelihood estimates (standard errors)

Variable	Model		
	(1)	(2)	(3)
γ	1.5	2.0	2.0
	(0.195)	(0.164)	(0.826)
ρ	0.05	0.03	0.04
	(0.017)	(0.031)	(0.016)
θ	0.3	0.5	0.5
	(0.291)	(0.250)	(0.294)
β_1	203.9	292.5	-7358.1
	(45.6)	(72.0)	(4825.3)
β_2	0.772	0.526	0.993
	(0.130)	(0.071)	(0.418)
Income shares			
S_{65+}		62.9	86.8
		(26.0)	(40.7)
S_{55-65}			104.5
			(60.1)
S_{45-54}			80.4
			(59.2)
S_{35-44}			66.1
			(43.6)
S_{25-33}			61.7
			(52.2)
R^2	0.958	0.975	0.992
DW	1.12	0.91	2.18
SSR	12083.6	7293.0	2334.6
SEE	28.4	22.8	15.3
Mean of dependent variable: 845.5			

ρ, and θ. For each combination of these parameters, (15) was estimated by OLS. The maximum likelihood estimates are those producing the smallest residual sum of squares. Following Amemiya (1983), standard errors were computed by replacing $\hat{C}_t(\cdot)$ in (15) with a first-order Taylor's approximation taken around the maximum likelihood estimates and estimating the resulting equation by OLS. The coefficients on the first derivatives of $\hat{C}_t(\cdot)$ with respect to γ, ρ, and first θ are approximately equal to the maximum likelihood estimates, and the standard errors of these and other right-hand-side estimated coefficients are consistent and asymptotically efficient if ε_{ct} is i.i.d. normal.

The first column of table 18.3 confirms the point made above, that our model tracks actual consumption fairly well. The R^2 is 0.958, and the estimated values of γ and ρ are both significant and reasonable. The coefficient on $\hat{C}_t(\cdot)$ is 0.772 and is significantly different from 1 at the 5 percent level. In addition, the intercept is significantly different from zero. Both of these results are at odds with the prediction of our model. Also at odds with our model is the significance of the 65 + income share in column 2 and the five total income shares included in column 3. The critical $F(5, 7)$ for the inclusion of all the shares at the 5 percent level is 3.97, which is below the F of 5.85 calculated for the inclusion of the five shares. The sign and, to some extent, pattern of the income share coefficients accord with the prediction of the life cycle model that redistribution from younger to older age groups raises consumption. According to these estimates a redistribution of 10 percent of income from the youngest to the oldest age group would raise United States consumption by 0.7 percent, evaluated at the mean value of consumption. With prevailing saving rates, a 0.7 percent increase in consumption would lower the net national saving rate by over 10 percent.

The significance of age-resource distribution variables does not apply to the three components of income for which we have separate data: labor income, property income, and Social Security income. To reduce computation costs we constrained γ, ρ, and θ in this analysis to equal their maximum likelihood estimates from column 1 of table 18.3. The $F(5, 10)$ values for the inclusion of the shares of labor income, property income, and Social Security income are 1.87, 2.08, and 1.51, respectively. While these values are each below the critical F of 3.33, if one constrains β_1 to equal 0 and β_2 to equal 1, the respective $F(5, 12)$ values are 12.2 for total income shares, 14.8 for labor income shares, 9.9 for property income shares, and 5.6 for Social Security income shares. The critical $F(5, 12)$ for this test is 3.11. Hence the data reject the hypothesis that age-resource shares are irrelevant given the model's predicted values of β_1 and β_2.

To examine whether the significance of the age-resource variables is robust to choices of γ, ρ, and θ that differ from the maximum likelihood estimates, we tested the significance of the total income shares for several different constrained choices of these three parameters. The critical F value for these tests is $F(5, 10) = 3.33$. For $\gamma = 10$, $\rho = 0.01$, and $\theta = 0.5$ the F statistic is 16.75; for $\gamma = 1.1$, $\rho = 0.04$, and $\theta = 0.5$ the F statistic is 1.59; for $\gamma = 2$, $\rho = 0.15$, and $\theta = 0.5$ the F statistic is 3.78; and for $\rho = 0.05$, $\gamma = 1.5$, and $\theta = 0.8$ the F statistic is 4.75. Hence, for a range of a priori choices of γ, ρ, and θ, most, but not all, of the test statistics for the inclusion of income shares are significant.

Table 18.4 presents maximum likelihood estimates of (15) for the period 1947 to 1977 using levels of net Social Security wealth of different age groups. For this 31-year sample period, the maximum likelihood estimates of γ, ρ, and θ are close to those reported in table 18.3. While β_2 is not significantly different from unity, as predicted by the theory, β_1 is significantly different from zero. In addition, the Social Security wealth levels of different age groups are significant explanatory variables. The $F(6, 20)$ statistic for their inclusion is 16.2, which exceeds the 5 percent critical value of 2.60.

18.6   Conclusion

The results presented here clearly reject our formulation of the altruism model. However, it should be restressed that the model embeds strong assumptions not only about preferences but also about the extent and nature of uncertainty. Rather than a rejection of altruism, the significance of the age-resource shares may reflect misspecification of the altruism model that is correlated with age-resource shares. For example, the age-resource shares might conceivably enter in the processes determining earnings and rates of return. In this case, the state variables, S_t, in $\hat{C}_t(\cdot)$ should include the age-resource information, and the exclusion of this information would bias the results. Alternatively, there may be a large number of discrete altruistic families with different age structures. In this case, changes in the age distribution of resources will typically be associated with changes in the interfamily distribution of resources, and such changes would be expected to alter aggregate consumption.[12]

The paper's contribution is, hopefully, not only to test a particular formulation of the Barro proposition, but also to stimulate additional research that directly tests central implications of life cycle and altruistic saving models.

Table 18.4
Excess sensitivity of consumption to social security wealth shares, 1947–1977, maximum
likelihood estimates (standard errors)

Variable	Model		
	(1)	(2)	(3)
γ	2.0	1.5	1.5
	(0.783)	(0.227)	(0.092)
ρ	0.03	0.05	0.03
	(0.014)	(0.009)	(0.010)
θ	0.5	0.3	0.3
	(0.157)	(0.204)	(0.083)
β_1	114.1	23.1	155.4
	(16.7)	(28.8)	(41.9)
β_2	0.915	1.237	0.764
	(0.149)	(0.159)	(0.195)
Social security wealth levels			
L_{65+}		0.377	0.014
		(0.098)	(0.359)
L_{55-65}			0.644
			(0.570)
L_{45-54}			-0.966
			(0.528)
L_{35-44}			2.022
			(0.338)
L_{25-34}			-1.526
			(0.564)
L_{14-24}			-0.220
			(0.548)
R^2	0.979	0.986	0.996
DW	0.5	0.9	1.6
SSR	18242.1	11796.2	3113.1
SEE	25.1	20.5	11.6
Mean of dependent variable: 540.8			

Notes

We have benefited greatly from conversations with Lawrence Weiss, Takeshi Amemiya, Joseph Stiglitz, Jose Sheinkman, Jim Poterba, Karl Brunner, and John Roberts and from participants of the Carnegie-Rochester Conference and Public Finance Seminars at Stanford and Harvard. We thank John Roberts and Mike Knetter for excellent research assistance and the Center for Economic Policy Research, Stanford University, and the National Bureau of Economic Research for financial support.

1. These average annual net national saving rates are based on NIA data. The 1984 saving rate is 5.2 percent, a lower value than observed in any year in the 1950s. The saving rate over the past 15 years has averaged only slightly more than three-quarters of the average rate of the previous two decades.

2. Chapter 7, Table 2.

3. Lawrence Weiss stressed this point and its implications for empirical tests in a conversation with one of the authors several years ago.

4. This assumes the economy is below the golden rule growth path.

5. Barro and Sahasakul (1983), Table 2, post 1980, column 2.

6. Boskin (1982, 1985) and chapters 7–10 of this book provide extensive discussions of the failure of officially recorded debt to measure underlying redistribution to older generations.

7. One might argue that zero intergenerational transfers is an objective benchmark. There are at least two problems with such a benchmark. First, distinguishing negative intergenerational transfers from taxes required to finance government consumption is completely arbitrary. Second, past intergenerational transfers imply (require) offsetting current or future intergeneration transfers. Hence, taking zero intergenerational transfers as the benchmark requires considering a world in which intergenerational transfers in the past had always been zero.

8. *1982 Economic Report of the President*, Appendix to Chapter 4.

9. Estimation results of this bivariate process are:

Dependent variable	Constant	$\log \tilde{w}_{t+\tau-1,a^*}$	$r_{t+\tau-1}$	R^2
$\log \tilde{w}_{t+\tau,a^*}$	0.028	0.989	0.00111	0.992
	(0.042)	(0.015)	(0.00094)	
$\tilde{r}_{t+\tau}$	17.11	0.435	-3.57	0.302
	(6.66)	(0.149)	(2.38)	

The estimated covariance matrix of ε_w and ε_r is $\begin{pmatrix} \sigma_\varepsilon^2 & \\ \sigma_r^2 & \sigma_{\varepsilon r} \end{pmatrix} = \begin{pmatrix} 5.403 \cdot 10^{-4} & \\ 13.37 & 0.05 \end{pmatrix}$

10. Social Security Administration, *Annual Statistical Supplement.*

11. *Employment and Training Report of the President*, 1982, Table B18, p. 234, and Table A3, p. 122; and Ibid, 1977, Table B15, p. 257.

12. There may be fewer distinct altruistic Barro families than one might think. Chapter 3 and Bernheim (1984) independently demonstrate that marital ties can generate altruistic linkages across families, producing, effectively, extremely large Barro families.

19

An Examination of Empirical Tests of Social Security and Savings

with Alan Auerbach

The effect of social security and other forms of government debt on national savings is perhaps the most widely debated policy question in economics today.[1] The issue has intrigued economists since David Ricardo, but is receiving increasing attention as US economists seek explanations for low rates of capital formation and productivity growth. The numbers at stake in the social security debate are quite large. Martin Feldstein has pioneered theoretical and empirical research on this subject over the last decade. His estimates (Feldstein 1974c) suggest that social security has reduced US savings by almost 40 percent. General equilibrium simulations of the long-run effects of unfunded social security on capital formation (chapter 12) confirm a potentially large effect. Over the years the issue has been joined at both the theoretical and empirical levels (Barro 1974, 1978; Darby 1979; Leimer and Lesnoy 1980).

This chapter examines recent cross-section and time-series empirical tests of the social security savings question and argues that given current data, neither type of test has must potential for settling the controversy. It focuses in particular detail on the specification of social security time series regressions. There are a number of problems of specification that can easily lead to highly unstable coefficients, and to rejection of the hypothesis that social security reduces savings, when this is in fact true. These points are demonstrated by running regressions on hypothetical data simulated from a perfect-foresight life-cycle growth model (Auerbach and Kotlikoff 1987). Although the data are obtained from a model in which social security reduces the nation's capital stock by almost 20 percent, time-series social security regression coefficients vary enormously depending on the specified level of the program, the preferences of hypothetical households, the

In *Social Policy Evaluation: An Economic Perspective*, E. Helpman, ed. (New York: Academic Press, 1983), 161–74. © 1983 by Academic Press, Inc. Reprinted with permission.

level and type of concomitant government policies, and the time interval of the data. Indeed, social security coefficients for certain regressions are negative, despite the significant burden of the social security debt.

The first section discusses theoretical problems, with cross-section and time series tests of the social security savings hypothesis. The second section points out significant errors of specification in time-series social security regressions. The third section describes dynamic simulations of the effect of unfunded social security in a perfect-foresight life-cycle growth model. The fourth section uses data simulated from this model to examine the predictions of the life-cycle model for the sign, magnitude, and stability of social security time series regression coefficients. The time series coefficients obtained from this simplest of life-cycle models are sufficiently unstable to cast major doubt on the value of the entire exercise.

19.1   Empirical Tests of Social Security and Savings: Theoretical Difficulties

The life-cycle (Modigliani and Brumberg 1954) and infinite-horizon (Barro 1974) models of intertemporal consumption choice provide the theoretical underpinning of most tests of the effect of social security on savings. Both models posit rational utility-maximizing behavior; the life-cycle model assumes that economic agents are selfish and care only about their own current and future consumption. The infinite-horizon model assumes that agents are altruistic and care about their descendant's consumption as well. In a life-cycle model, since individuals care only about consumption over their remaining expected lifetimes, their marginal propensities to consume out of full available resources will depend crucially on their age. Intergenerational redistribution of resources in a life-cycle model will affect aggregate consumption, and thus national savings. In a Barro-type infinitely lived family model, consumption of family members of a particular age depends not on their own resources but rather on total family resources. In a Barro model, cohort consumption and thus aggregate consumption is independent of the cross-cohort distribution of resources.

The theory of unfunded social security is identical to the general theory of deficit policy; holding the path of government expenditure constant, any reduction in the net tax liabilities of one generation that are associated with a deficit must be made up by a higher net tax liability on some other generation. Thus, social security, as well as any other government deficit, constitutes an intergenerational transfer. This transfer will have a real effect on aggregate consumption and national savings if different cohorts have different marginal propensities to consume out of transferred resources. Ideally, one would think that the best way to test the Feldstein-Barro government-deficit question is to regress a cohort's consumption on that cohort's own resources as well as on the resources of other cohorts. If resources of other cohorts significantly affect the consumption of a particular cohort, the Barro view would seem to be supported. If the resources of other cohorts did *not* affect a particular cohort's consumption, Feldstein's view would seem to be supported. We use the word *seem* because a finding that resources of other cohorts did not affect the consumption of a particular cohort could be consistent with the Barro view according to the following scenario: Suppose that the family head at each moment in time allocates total resources to the various family members and tells them to consume just like life-cycle consumers. The Barro family head could, then, always redistribute family assets in such a way that each family member at each age appeared to be behaving independently from the others. Such an exact year-by-year reshuffling of family resources seems unlikely, but is nonetheless a theoretical possibility.

It is also possible to provide theoretical arguments consistent with both the Feldstein life-cycle view of savings and an empirical finding that the consumption of one cohort depends on the resources of other cohorts. Imagine a life-cycle world in which unexpected changes in government tax-transfer policies, as well as periodic macroeconomic fluctuations can, ex ante, be expected to significantly alter the cohort distribution of lifetime resources and utility. In such a world, completely selfish but nonetheless risk-averse life-cycle savers might seek to pool these risks with members of other cohorts. In the limit, perfect insurance arrangements between different cohorts alive concurrently will link the consumption of one cohort to the consumption of other cohorts, and the resources of one cohort to the resources of other cohorts. Consider the following simple example of intercohort risk pooling: Suppose life-cycle agents live for two periods, and suppose the government indicates at the beginning of one period that it will announce with probability P a lump-sum transfer from the young to the old at the end of the period, and with probability $1 - P$ a lump-sum transfer from the old to the young at the end of the period. At the beginning of the period, risk-averse old and young cohort members will seek to pool this risk among themselves. Since, by assumption, there is no social risk to be absorbed collectively by the young and the old, insurance arrangements permitting, these cohorts will arrange to consume exactly the same amount independent of the eventual government transfer. Each cohort's consumption will depend on aggregate resources rather than on the cohort distribution of resources after the government enacts its policy.

Although it is hard to point to explicit real-world insurance markets that are in the business of pooling these types of risks across cohorts, implicit cohort risk-sharing arrangements may be operative within real world institutions, such as firms and families. Hall (1980) presents evidence that a sizable fraction of American workers experience a more-or-less permanent relationship with a single firm over their working lives. If one thinks of firms as competing for new young workers by offering implicit lifetime contracts that offer the highest level of expected utility, then firms will certainly have an incentive to provide implicit contracts that pool cohort risks between the firm's current old workers and its new employees. Firms could, for example, offset government tax-transfer policies that redistribute across selfish, but risk-averse, cohorts by adjusting their age-compensation profile. Presumably, selfish old and young family members can also devise acceptable cohort risk-sharing schemes, since such an implicit contract could improve the situation of each member.

We do not mean to suggest here that perfect insurance arrangements between living members of different cohorts would completely undo the long-run effects of social security on savings. Such an argument for debt neutrality would only be valid if all current and future cohorts could come together ex ante and sign an insurance contract protecting themselves against redistributive government behavior. Our point here is that existing cohorts can collectively hedge themselves against government redistribution among themselves, and that this behavior could make them act as if only total resources mattered. Introduction of social security in such a world would raise the consumption of all currently living cohorts, since the program would still constitute redistribution against cohorts not yet born.

Although this discussion suggests that both the life-cycle and infinite horizon models can rationalize a wide range of cohort-specific consumption behavior, actual knowledge of such behavior would greatly narrow the range of theories that are consistent with the facts. Unfortunately, time-series data on cohort consumption and after-tax future resources are not available. In their absence, Feldstein and others have used time-series data on aggregate consumption. The next section examines a host of difficulties with conventional time-series tests of social security and savings.

If time-series data on cohort consumption are not available and aggregate time series consumption data are insufficient, is there hope that cross-sectional microevidence could resolve the controversy? A key problem with using cross-section data is that they are based on households rather than families, and again certain results that might at first glance be thought to verify the life-cycle theory are also perfectly consistent with the Barro theory, and vise versa. In this case, problems arise because the cross-section data do not distinguish transfers across generations from transfers across families.[2]

To give an example, suppose a cross-section regression showed that social security wealth had a positive and significant effect on household consumption. Such a finding is predicted by the life-cycle theory, but it is also consistent with Barro's view for the following reason: Those households with greater than average social security wealth are presumably members of families that receive greater than average social security wealth; thus the social security variable is contaminated with interfamily transfers, and these interfamily transfers will increase the consumption of Barro-type family members in those families receiving these greater than average transfers.

Although a social security wealth coefficient would not help resolve the issue, other cross-section regression experiments might help. Under the life-cycle theory, for example, the marginal propensity to consume this period out of future resources increases with age. This prediction holds for conventional specification of preferences independent of whether the date of death is taken to be uncertain, and independent of whether annuity insurance is available. In a Barro model, the marginal propensity to consume out of total family resources could increase or decrease by age. Hence, given the problem that greater household resources may proxy for greater family resources, the Barro model could not be refuted by a finding that the marginal propensity to consume increased with age. But suppose one found that the marginal propensity declined with age. Such a finding would, we believe, be hard to reconcile with the Feldstein life-cycle view. This is an example of a test that could possibly refute the life-cycle theory, but that could not support the strict life-cycle theory over the Barro view.

Unfortunately the paucity of US consumption data is not confined to the macro level; there exists no US micro data set that simultaneously reports household consumption and household resources in sufficient detail to conduct the experiment described here.

In the absence of micro consumption data, economists have naturally turned to data on net worth and bequests. Net worth partly reflects consumption, but in addition to accumulated past flows of consumption, current net worth reflects accumulated flows of net intergenerational transfers as well as patterns of earnings and rates of return that are not directly related to consumption.

Insofar as net-worth data reflect past patterns of consumption, regression coefficients of net worth on social security variables face the same problems of interpretation as regression coefficients of consumption on social security variables. Thus, a finding that social security wealth depresses private household net-worth accumulation is consistent with both the life-cycle and the infinitely lived family theories of consumption. Again, cross-family transfers could make families with greater than average social security wealth accumulate less private assets than would otherwise be the case.

Cross-section bequest regressions may provide refutable tests of at least the life-cycle theory, but caution is advised here as well. At first glance, the Feldstein view would seem to be refutable by finding that the elasticity of bequests with respect to full future resources was significantly greater than zero both in the statistical sense and in the sense of a large number, and that this large elasticity held true at all levels of resources; that is, for the rich and poor. If bequests represented the only form of intergenerational transfers from the old to the young, and if there were no transfers from the young to the old, the issue would be settled. One could simply take this elasticity, find the percentage change in full resources of the aged represented by social security intergenerational transfers, and compute how much they transferred back.

One might think that simply the real world observation that the elderly at all lifetime income levels leave bequests by itself refutes the life-cycle theory. This is not necessarily so. First of all, the theory is about net transfer flows. Our data generally detail gross bequests, and these gross bequests represent only one component of the gross flow of transfers from the old to the young. Very little information is available concerning transfers from the young to the old. These transfers need not, by the way, be pecuniary. Care of elderly parents in terms of housing and assistance in chores and the like constitutes a transfer of resources from the young to the old.

In general, resource transfers from the old to the young and from the young to the old need not reflect altruism; these transfers can occur and still be perfectly consistent with the selfishness assumed in the life-cycle model. Chapter 4 demonstrates that family risk-pooling behavior, where the risk is the uncertainty of the data of death, could give rise to bequests as well as transfers from the young to the old. These transfers can occur even though family members are completely selfish. Indeed, family members could hate each other and still bequeath and transfer resources to each other simply because of the desire to mitigate the risks associated with the date of death. The way these implicit family annuity contracts work is that old family members use their promise to bequeath in the event that they die to extract consumption support from their children as they continue to live. If the government now comes to this selfish but risk-pooling family and uses social security to transfer a dollar from the young members to the old members, the family risk-sharing deal may be renegotiated with the old extracting more support from the young in exchange for their now-larger promised bequest.[3] The fact that social security comes in the form of an annuity is not fundamental, since old family members can purchase life insurance to, in effect, transfer those future streams into a current contingent bequest. In such a Feldstein world, one could find a positive cross-sectional coefficient of social security on bequests despite the fact that the old people end up consuming more than they would otherwise have consumed. The old may thus increase their gross transfers to the young in response to social security, while expected net transfers from the old to the young decline.

To summarize these general comments, one must be cautious of any macro or micro findings that purport to support one theory and refute the other because both theories are quite flexible in terms of the savings and transfer behavior they can explain and the regression coefficients they can rationalize. In addition, in our preoccupation with social security coefficients, we may be overlooking some more fundamental tests of the life-cycle theory.

19.2 Specification Bias in Social Security Time-Series Regressions

The major difficulty in evaluating time-series results suggesting that social security does or does not reduce private saving is that the regression specifications do not correspond very closely to the life-cycle model of consumer choice. Though this criticism may also be applied to standard attempts at estimating the basic life-cycle model using aggregate time-series data (Ando and Modigliani 1963), it is more serious problem in the "extended" life-cycle model because the particular phenomenon of interest, social security, introduces new difficulties to the interpretation of regression results.

To begin our discussion, we derive the expression for optimal consumption behavior by life-cycle consumers who have no bequest motive or labor supply decision. Lifetime utility is assumed to take the form

$$
U = \begin{cases} \displaystyle\sum_{t=1}^{T} (1 + \rho)^{-(t-1)} \frac{C_t^{1-\gamma}}{1 - \gamma} & \gamma > 0, \quad \gamma \neq 1 \\[2em] \displaystyle\sum_{t=1}^{T} (1 + \rho)^{-(t-1)} \log C_t & \gamma = 1, \end{cases} \tag{1}
$$

where C_t is the household's consumption age t, T is the age at death, and ρ and γ are taste parameters characterizing, respectively, the pure rate of time preference and the inverse of the partial elasticity of substitution between any two years' consumption.

For a household of age i, the appropriate objective function is

$$
U(i) = \begin{cases} \displaystyle\sum_{t=i}^{T} (1 + \rho)^{-(t-i)} \frac{C_t^{1-\gamma}}{1 - \gamma} & \gamma > 0, \quad \gamma \neq 1 \\[2em] \displaystyle\sum_{t=i}^{T} (1 + \rho)^{-(t-i)} \log C_t & \gamma = 1, \end{cases} \tag{2}
$$

Under a regime with a proportional income tax and a social security system supported by payroll taxes, the budget constraint facing a household of age i is

$$
W_i + HW_i + SSW_i \geq PVC_i, \tag{3}
$$

where W_i, HW_i, SSW_i, and PVC_i are, respectively, real assets, human wealth, social security wealth, and the present value of current and future consumption of the household. Real wealth is directly observable. Human wealth equals the present discounted value of labor income, net of income *and* social security taxes. Social security wealth is the discounted value of future benefits.

Solving for the optimal consumption path yields the following expression for current consumption for such a household:

$$
C_i = \alpha_i (W_i + HW_i + SSW_i), \tag{4}
$$

where

$$
\alpha_i = \sum_{t=1}^{T-i} (1 + \rho)^{-(t-1)/\gamma} \left\{ \prod_{s=2}^{t} [1 + r_s(1 - \tau_s)]^{-(1-1/\gamma)} \right\}^{-1} \tag{5}
$$

and r_s and τ_s are the gross interest rate and rate of income tax that prevail when the household is age s.

From (4) and (5), it is apparent that unless γ equals 1, each household's behavior will depend on future interest and tax rates, given the correct computation of HW_i and SSW_i. Thus, even at the individual level, the life-cycle expression (4) will not, in general, exhibit stable coefficients, as interest tax rates vary over time. This problem is particularly acute when one considers as important a change in policy as the introduction of unfunded social security. If the hypothesis that social security drastically reduces savings is correct, it will obviously lead to changes in interest rates and income tax rates along the transition path to the economy's new steady-state equilibrium. Moreover, the presence of active fiscal policy will also make interpretation of regression results difficult, because various deficit and tax policies that need have nothing to do with social security will also change tax rates and rates of return, and hence the estimated time-series coefficients. This is the Lucas (1976) critique.

Even assuming that $\gamma = 1$, in which case α_i is a constant that depends only on ρ and i, aggregation of (4) into an estimable equation is not straightforward. Aggregation of these consumption relations over all households yields the expression

$$C = \bar{\alpha}W + \tilde{\alpha}HW + \hat{\alpha}SSW, \tag{6}$$

where $\bar{\alpha}$, $\tilde{\alpha}$, and $\hat{\alpha}$ are the average values of α in the sample weighted by each cohort's real wealth, human wealth, and social security wealth, respectively, and C, W, HW, and SSW are aggregate measures. At any point in time, the three coefficients will differ because the three forms of wealth are distributed differently across age cohorts in the population. Among young individuals, for example, real wealth will be small (perhaps negative) relative to human wealth. The opposite is true for retirees. Thus, the aggregate coefficient on real wealth should be higher than that on human wealth, since α_i increases with i.

This relationship would not pose a problem in itself if it were fairly stable over time, that is, if there were no important demographic shifts or other changes in the age distribution of these variables. However, such can hardly be claimed for a period during which social security is introduced; the age distribution of human and nonhuman wealth will change, and the aggregate coefficients $\bar{\alpha}$ and $\tilde{\alpha}$, and, as a result, the social security wealth coefficient $\hat{\alpha}$ should be unstable.

Further difficulties arise in actual estimation attempts because the values of HW and SSW are represented by inexact proxies. Human wealth is typically replaced by some measure of disposable income. This involves several problems. First, the appropriate income measure would not include capital income, for this constitutes double counting. Second, the relationship between net labor income and human wealth changes by age, with the ratio of the latter to the former decreasing over time. Again, these ratios will depend on the interest and tax rates expected to prevail in the future, and these surely cannot be assumed constant.

Finally, social security wealth as it appears in (4) and (6) should be calculated using the actual path of future net interest rates; standard empirical analyses assume constant discount rates to estimate social security wealth. Since rates of return will change during the economy's transition response to social security, this procedure obviously introduces an errors-in-variables bias.

In summary there appear to be severe difficulties in estimating a stable relationship between aggregate consumption and the various forms of aggregate wealth when variations in the data reflect changes in tax rates or saving incentives that disturb net rates of return and the age distribution of different forms of wealth. The theory of unfunded social security in a life-cycle model unequivocally predicts significant changes in the time path of interest rates and the distribution of resources by age.

19.3   Simulation of a Life-Cycle Economy with Social Security

The previous section detailed several problems of specification that make the interpretation of social security time-series regression results difficult, if not impossible. Since the specification errors interact in a complex way, it is hard to know a priori what social security regression coefficient one should expect to find under the hypothesis that the data were actually obtained from a life-cycle world. To investigate how serious this problem is in practice requires data for which the social security life-cycle savings hypothesis is actually true. The purpose of this section is to describe simulation experiments that were run, in effect, to manufacture hypothetical life-cycle social security data. These data are used in the next section in time-series regressions to investigate the actual predictions of the life-cycle model for standard time-series regression coefficients.

The simulation model is based on the assumption of perfect foresight or, equivalently, since there is no uncertainty in the model, rational expectations. The interrelated supplies of capital of all cohorts living during the transition from the economy's initial steady state to the new steady state are solved simultaneously with firms' demands for capital along the transition path to compute the economy's equilibrium growth path. We next present additional equations of the model, and then describe the algorithm used to solve for the economy's equilibrium growth path.

To the household behavior already described, we add a single production sector characterized by the Cobb-Douglas production function

$$Y_t = AK_t^\varepsilon[(1 + g)^t L_t]^{1-\varepsilon}, \tag{7}$$

where Y_t, K_t, and L_t are output, capital, and labor at time t, A is a scaling constant, g is an exogenous productivity growth rate that is set equal to 0.02, and ε is the capital share of output that is assumed to equal 0.25. L_t is simply equal to the sum of labor endowments of all individuals in the work force. In our analysis we assume that each individual's endowment of human capital grows at an annual rate of 0.007, and that general population growth is 1 percent per year. K_t is generated by a recursive equation that dictates that the change in the capital stock equals private plus public savings. Competitive behavior on the part of producers ensures that the gross factor returns, r_t and w_t, are equated to the marginal products of capital and labor at time t:

$$r_t = \varepsilon A[K_t/(1 + g)^t L_t]^{-(1-\varepsilon)}, \tag{8a}$$

$$w_t = (1 - \varepsilon)A(1 + g)^t[K_t/(1 + g)^t L_t]^\varepsilon. \tag{8b}$$

The assumption that the return to capital equals its marginal product implies that the market value of capital goods always equals their reproduction cost; that is, adjustment of capital to desired levels is instantaneous.

Leaving aside social security, the government in our model is assumed to have a stream of consumption expenditures G_t that it must finance using income tax and one-period debt. Debt is a perfect substitute for capital in household portfolios and enables the government to save (run surpluses) and dissave (run deficits). If Ag_t is defined as the value of government assets (taking a negative value if there is a national debt), government tax revenue at the end of period t is

$$R_t = \tau_t[W_tL_t + r_t(K_t - Ag_t)], \tag{9}$$

where τ_t and r_t are the rates of income tax and interest at time t. Given the government's ability to issue and retire debt, its budget constraint relates the present value of its expenditures to the present value of its tax receipts plus the value of its initial assets:

$$Ag_0 + \sum_{t=0}^{\infty}\left[\prod_{s=0}^{t}(1 + r_s)\right]^{-1} R_t = \sum_{t=0}^{\infty}\left[\prod_{s=0}^{t}(1 + r_s)\right]^{-1} G_t. \tag{10}$$

(Note that G_t corresponds to a different concept from that reported in the national income accounts, which includes government purchase of capital goods.) Eq. (10) is required to hold in all our simulations.

Social Security is added to this government sector by introducing an announced path of social security benefits. The path of social security benefits is calculated by assuming retired individuals receive a certain replacement rate of average lifetime wages, adjusted for productivity growth. Our procedure corresponds to the lifetime wage-indexing formula of the US social security system. The replacement rate chosen, in combination with the path of wages for each cohort, yields a pattern of liabilities of the social security system, SSB_t. To pay for those benefits, the government uses strict "pay as you go" financing, assessing a payroll tax at rate ϕ_t in year t to yield receipts equal to SSB_t.

The actual solution for the economy's behavior over time always begins with a characterization of the initial steady state, given initial tax structure and government debt. We assume that individuals of different generations alive during this steady state correctly perceive the tax schedule and factor prices they will face over time, and behave optimally with respect to these conditions. We utilize a Gauss-Seidel iteration technique to solve for this equilibrium: We start with an initial guess of the capital-labor ratio (K/L), derive in each iteration a new estimate to update our guess, and continue the procedure until a fixed point is reached. Given the method of deriving new estimates of K/L, such a fixed point corresponds to a steady-state rational expectations equilibrium.

The following is a description of how the iteration technique proceeds. A schematic representation is provided in figure 19.1. In the first stage, a guess is made of the capital-labor ratio (equivalent to a guess of the capital stock, since labor supply is fixed). Given the marginal productivity equations (8a) and (8b), this yields values for the wage w and interest rate r. By using the estimate of w, we may then solve for the steady-state level of benefits SSB as well as the payroll tax ϕ necessary to support those benefits. Since income and required government revenues are given, a first

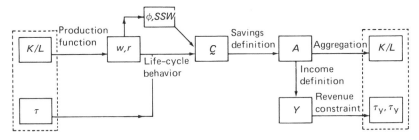

Figure 19.1
Iteration procedure for a progressive income tax.

guess of τ is obtained. From the values of r and τ, we then calculate the present values of social security benefits SSW as well as future earnings HW. Assuming initial assets to be zero, we then apply Eqs. (4) and (5) to obtain the life-cycle consumption path of the representative individual, **C**. From the definition of savings, this yields the age-asset profile A which may be aggregated (subtracting any national debt assumed to exist) to provide a new value of the capital stock and capital-labor ratio. When the initial and final values of K/L and the tax rate are the same, this implies that the steady state has been reached.

Solution for the final steady state proceeds in a similar manner. The transition is solved for in the following way. We assume the transition to the new steady state takes 150 years, then solve simultaneously for equilibrium in each of the 150 years of the transition period under the assumption that everyone believes the new steady state will obtain. This solution method is necessary because each household is assumed to take the path of future prices into account in determining its behavior. Hence, the equilibrium that results in later years will affect the equilibrium in earlier years. Specifically, we assume that individuals born after the transition begins know the transition path immediately and that those born before the beginning of the transition behaved up to the time of the change in government policy as if the old steady state would continue forever. At the time of the announcement of a new policy, existing cohorts are "born again": They behave like members of the new generation except that their horizon is less than 55 years, and they possess initial assets as a result of prior accumulation. An iteration technique is used again, but here we must begin with *vectors* of capital stocks and tax rates (one pair for each year). Further, we cannot simply solve for the behavior of a representative cohort but rather must calculate the behavior of each cohort alive during the transition. This procedure, although conceptually no more difficult than that used to find the steady states, requires considerably more computation. Since the ultimate paths converge to the final steady state well before year 150, the assumption about conditions after year 150 does not influence our results.

The solution technique just described was used to simulate the introduction of an unfunded social security system similar in size and character to that currently in force in the United States. A number of different types of simulations are considered. In each simulation exercise, we assume that there is no social security program in the economy's initial steady state; social security is introduced unexepctedly; and there is no prior announcement of the system before benefits start being paid.

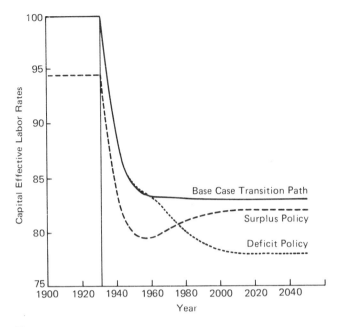

Figure 19.2
Transition of the capital stock under various conditions; a 40 percent replacement rate is assumed.

In our basic simulation the utility taste parameters ρ and γ are set equal to 0.02 and 1, respectively. There is no national debt aside from that implicit in the social security system; the income tax rate is set initially at 0.30, and the replacement rate is immediately set at its long run value of 0.45.

In the initial steady state without social security, the capital-output ratio is 3.11, and the gross interest rate is 8.04 percent. The introduction of social security ultimately leads to a new steady state where the capital stock is lowered by 17 percent, with the gross interest rate rising to 9.24 percent. Because of the lower output levels, the income tax rate must rise to 31.4 percent to raise the required revenue. The solid black line in figure 19.2 describes the transition path of the economy's capital-effective labor ratio. Year 1930 is the hypothetical year of enactment. The value of 100 indicates the capital effective labor ratio that would have prevailed with no social security. Surprisingly, the transition to this final steady state occurs quite rapidly; it is virtually complete only 30 years after social security is first introduced.

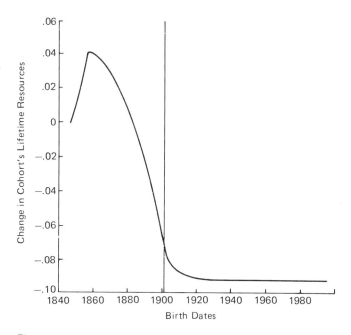

Figure 19.3
Path of welfare changes by the birth date of particular cohorts. The year of enactment is
taken to be 1900.

As expected, the introduction of pay as you go social security is beneficial to initial retirees under the new system since they receive benefits and
are required to pay no payroll taxes. However, ultimate crowding out of
capital lowers the welfare of individuals in the long run. Figure 19.3 depicts
the path of welfare changes by the birth date of particular cohorts; the
vertical line in the diagram marks the year of birth of the cohort born
in the year of enactment. The year 1900 is taken as the hypothetical year
of enactment. The numbers on the vertical axis measure the percentage
increase (decrease) in each cohort's lifetime resources that would leave
them with the same lifetime level of utility in the absence of social security
as they receive under social security. Thus, a cohort born in 1900 at the
time of enactment suffers a loss in welfare due to social security that
corresponds to a 7 percent reduction in lifetime resources in a world of no
social security.

All retirees at the time of enactment gain; those retiring just at the time
of the enactment gain the most—the equivalent of a 4 percent increase in
lifetime resources; these retirees receive benefits for their entire retirement

period, but pay no taxes whatsoever. The gain to initial middle-age generations is smaller, since they must pay payroll taxes, and continues to decline for successive younger cohorts because of the gradual crowding out of capital and reduction in wages. The eventual loss in welfare for generations in the new steady state is quite large—about 9 percent. Moreover, this loss comes on quite rapidly. Even cohorts 15 years old when social security is introduced are net losers, and individuals born in the year of enactment lose close to the full long-run amount.

A more generous social security system would be expected to amplify the results just described. This is indeed the case. In fact, the basic characteristics of the transition are virtually unchanged. Adoption of a 60 percent replacement rate, rather than the 45 percent rate used in the baseline simulation, leads to greater gains and losses by those generations already in these respective categories. The long-run welfare loss is now 12 percent; those just retiring at the time of enactment gain about 55 percent, and again, cohorts aged 15 at the time of enactment approximately break even. The capital stock declines by 22 percent, and the transition is again quite rapid.

Just as a simple increase in replacement rates has little qualitative effect on the pattern of economic consequences of social security, this is also true of a change in preferences. Simulations carried out for values of γ ranging between 0.5 and 2 indicated that both the speed of convergence to the new steady state and the ultimate size of the capital stock reduction were comparable to those of the baseline simulation.

In reality, we are never able to observe the effect of a single isolated fiscal policy change. Many policy shocks may be at work at once, and this fact not only confounds our understanding of how any one of these policies affects the economy but may also influence the coefficients of a time-series regression attempting to hold constant the effects of all but one policy change, such as social security. This latter problem is present because, as discussed earlier, such regressions are misspecified and hence are not invariant to policy.

One major government fiscal policy lever other than social security is the national debt.[4] Figure 19.2 shows the additional effects on the capital stock of an active debt policy during the period of transition to social security. The light dotted line shows what happens when a national debt equal to 10 percent of long-run wealth is introduced over a 10-year period, beginning 20 years into the social security transition, through a temporary cut in income taxes. This leads to a further decline in the capital stock equal to about 70 percent of the debt introduced. An alternative debt policy, shown by the darker dashed line, assumes an initial steady-state debt level equal to 20 percent of wealth; in this simulation, one-fourth of this debt is retired over a 10-year period commencing 20 years after the introduction of social security. Here, of course, there is an offsetting increase in the capital stock that comes from the debt retirement.

19.4 Time Series Regressions Using Simulated Data

The data generated by the various simulations described in the previous section are much "cleaner" than any aggregate data we could hope to collect from actual observation. There is no measurement error, and the multitude of other shocks to the system have been assumed away. Thus, it is not possible to state with confidence that our modeling of the effects of social security is or is not realistic. However, these data may be used to estimate what the time-series regressions coefficients would be for a Feldstein-type consumption function if indeed the "extended" life-cycle model were exactly correct and social security had a major impact on national saving. If the coefficients of such a controlled regression prove to be highly unstable, this should cast doubt on the assumed stability of time-series coefficients in more complicated dynamic economies.

Table 19.1 presents results of regressions on data obtained from the baseline simulation in which an unfunded social security system with a 45 percent replacement rate is enacted at time zero. The dependent variable in the estimated equation is per capita consumption. The independent vari-

Table 19.1
Social security regressions for different sample periods: base case

Independent variable	Interval		
	-10 to $+60$	0 to $+60$	$+10$ to $+60$
Constant	0.247	-0.742	0.029
	(3.23)[a]	(10.43)	(3.43)
YD	0.443	-4.401	-10.026
	(9.00)	(14.53)	(66.43)
$YD - 1$	-0.239	-0.132	11.466
	(4.00)	(4.71)	(57.16)
W	0.146	0.205	-0.036
	(29.71)	(47.21)	(8.27)
SSW	0.281	10.863	-0.523
	(77.33)	(16.47)	(4.64)

a. t-statistics are in parentheses.

ables are disposable income YD, disposable income lagged YD_{-1}, real wealth W, and social security wealth SSW, all measured per capita. The three regressions in table 19.1 differ only with respect to sample period; the first regression is based on 70 years' data starting 10 years prior to enactment. Regression 2 covers 60 years' data, but begins with data from the first year of enactment. The third regression is based on data from year 10 to year 60. The results for the sample period that begins 10 years prior to enactment do not correspond exactly to previous estimates, but are of the appropriate sign and order of magnitude. The coefficients on disposable income and wealth are of the "correct" sign; the wealth coefficient is much larger than that obtained in standard time series regressions, whereas the social security wealth coefficient is about 10 times larger than that presented by Feldstein (1974).

Shifting the sample period wreaks havoc with these results. For the remaining two intervals, the coefficients are nonsensical. The social security wealth coefficient for the middle period suggests that an additional dollar of SSW will increase concurrent consumption by most $11. Yet this same coefficient becomes significantly negative with the next shift in sample period.

One might argue that this is an unfair test because the history of US social security is one of a gradual increase in benefits, whereas the data underlying table 19.1 assume an immediate shift for a social security system with a 40 percent replacement rate. An additional simulation was run that involved a smooth increase in the replacement rate over 40 years from 0 to 60 percent. Table 19.2 provides some regression coefficients based on this simulated data. The coefficients for the -10 to $+40$ sample for the non-social-security variables are in closer compliance with the real-world results, but the SSW coefficient is negative and insignificant. The stability problem is even worse for this simulation as one changes sample periods. Social Security coefficients for 0 to $+50$ and $+10$ to $+60$ regressions are large negative numbers and are highly significant.

Table 19.3 depicts the results of other experiments. Here, the sample period is fixed at -10 to $+60$, as in the first column of table 19.1, and differences in debt policy, social security policy, and preferences are posited to generate simulated data. Reading from left to right, the first two columns of estimated coefficients correspond to cases where the social security policy follows the baseline simulation, but γ is set at 0.5 and then to 1.5, rather than 1. The next two columns present results for the simulations described in the previous section of a phase-in and phase-out of national debt, again with the basic social security policy. The last two columns correspond to simulations of a higher level of the social security

Table 19.2
Social security regressions: Forty-year gradual phase into a 60% replacement rate

Independent variable	Interval		
	−10 to +40	0 to +50	+10 to +60
Constant	−9.609	−23.001	−33.896
	(30.82)[a]	(−19.67)	(−9.976)
YD	0.766	0.147	0.506
	(1.293)	(1.137)	(1.908)
YD − 1	−0.089	−0.172	−0.487
	(−0.185)	(−1.369)	(−2.074)
W	0.102	0.909	1.428
	(1.896)	(15.37)	(9.375)
SSW	−0.00136	−6.277	−11.408
	(−0.077)	(−11.01)	(−7.082)

a. *t*-statistics are in parentheses.

Table 19.3
Social security regressions for different regimes and preferences (sample period = −10 to +60)

Independent variable	Preferences		Debt policy		Social security	
	$\gamma = 0.5$	$\gamma = 1.5$	Phase-in	Phase-out	$rr = 0.6$	$rr = 0.6$[a]
Constant	0.291	0.193	2.642	0.063	0.337	−0.357
	(4.35)[b]	(2.31)	(10.44)	(0.48)	(3.31)	(3.50)
YD	0.150	0.592	0.439	0.434	0.425	0.613
	(3.64)	(10.52)	(2.62)	(8.88)	(8.94)	(13.85)
YD − 1	−0.223	−0.239	−0.206	−0.091	−0.231	0.030
	(4.44)	(3.52)	(1.06)	(1.56)	(−3.98)	(0.561)
W	0.145	0.149	0.121	0.107	0.148	0.052
	(35.05)	(23.56)	(9.99)	(20.07)	(28.14)	(8.52)
SSW	0.165	0.386	0.222	0.280	0.379	0.303
	(75.74)	(67.91)	(19.07)	(59.72)	(82.15)	(89.06)

a. Gradual adoption.
b. *t*-statistics are in parentheses.

replacement rate, 0.6, enacted either immediately or in three stages over a 20-year period.

The most interesting general characteristic of these results is their stability relative to those in the previous table. However, there is still substantial variation in the coefficients where naive theory would not predict any. For example, an increase in the level of social security from a replacement rate of 0.45 to one of 0.6 increases the social security coefficient by over 30 percent. However, this instability is quite small relative to the severe instability found earlier. Indeed, just as the results for alternative policies cluster about those for the baseline simulation, given the same sample period, the same is true for other sample periods. For example, the absurd coefficient on social security wealth in the middle sample period is present regardless of which simulation is used. This suggests that, at least in the simulations compared here, the adoption of unfunded social security dominates other effects, and it is the behavior of the economy around the period of enactment that largely determines the regression results.

19.5 Conclusion

This chapter raises concerns with respect to actual and potential tests of the effects of social security on savings. Much of the empirical literature on social security and savings has proceeded without a precise statement as to what empirical results could definitively refute either the life-cycle or infinite-horizon consumption models. Many actual empirical tests appear to have very little power in deciding the issue they address. Time-series regression analysis of social security is a case in point. The simulation regressions presented here suggest that virtually any social security time-series coefficient, negative, zero, or positive, is potentially consistent with the life-cycle hypothesis.

Notes

We are grateful to the National Bureau of Economic Research for financial support and to David Reitman for excellent research assistance. The views expressed here do not reflect those of the National Bureau of Economic Research.

1. Robert Barro suggested this point in a recent conversation with one of the authors.

2. This presumes that the family members did not ex ante insure among themselves against such government behavior.

3. See Auerbach and Kotlikoff (1983) for a simulation analysis of debt policy.

References

Abel, A. B. 1979. *Investment and the Value of Capital.* New York: Garland Publishers.

Abel, A. B. 1982. Dynamic effects of permanent and temporary tax policies in a *q* model of investment. *Journal of Monetary Economics* 9:353–73.

Abel, A. B. 1985. Precautionary savings and accidental bequests. *American Economic Review* 75(4):777–91.

Abel, A. B. 1985. Precautionary saving and accidental bequests. *American Economic Review* 75:777–91.

Abel, A. B., and L. J. Kotlikoff. 1988. *Does the Consumption of Different Age Groups Move Together? A New Nonparametric Test of Intergenerational Altruism.* NBER Working Paper 2490. Cambridge, Mass.: National Bureau of Economic Research.

Adams, B. 1968. *Kinship in an Urban Setting.* Chicago, Ill.: Markham Publishing.

Adams, J. D. 1975. Estimates of the wealth elasticity of bequest. Ph.D. dissertation, University of Chicago, ch. 3.

Adams, J. D. 1977. *Personal Wealth Transfers.* Iowa State University Staff Papers Service 53. Ames, Iowa: Iowa State University.

Altonji, J., and A. Siow. 1986. *Testing the Response of Consumption to Income Changes with (Noisy) Panel Data.* NBER Working Paper 2012. Cambridge, Mass.: National Bureau of Economic Research.

Amemiya, T. 1983. Nonlinear regression models. In *Handbook of Econometrics,* Z. Griliches and M. D. Intriligator, eds. Amsterdam: North Holland, 333–85.

Ando, A. 1986a. Comment on Fumio Hayashi's paper. *NBER Macroeconomics Annual 1986.* Cambridge, Mass.: MIT Press, 211–20.

Ando, A. 1986b. Selected comments on current empirical evidence for or against the life cycle theory. Paper presented at the International Seminar on the Life Cycle Theory, Paris.

Ando, A., and F. Modigliani. 1963. The "life cycle" hypothesis of saving: Aggregate implications and tests. *American Economic Review* 53(1):55–84.

Aschauer, D. A. 1985. Fiscal policy and aggregate demand. *American Economic Review* 75:117–27.

Atkinson, A. B. 1971a. Capital taxes, the redistribution of wealth and individual savings. *Review of Economic Studies* 38(114):209–27.

Atkinson, A. B. 1971b. The distribution of wealth and the individual life-cycle. *Oxford Economic Papers* 23:239–54.

Atkinson, A. B., and A. J. Harrison. 1978. *The Distribution of Wealth in Britain*. Cambridge: Cambridge University Press.

Atkinson, A. B., and A. Sandmo. 1980. Welfare implications of the taxation of savings. *The Economic Journal* 90:529–49.

Atkinson, A. B., and J. Stiglitz. 1980. *Lectures on Public Economics*. New York: McGraw-Hill.

Auerbach, A. J. 1979. Share valuation and corporate equity policy. *Journal of Public Economics* 11:291–305.

Auerbach, A. J. 1981. *Evaluating the Taxation of Risky Assets*. NBER Working Paper 806. Cambridge, Mass.: National Bureau of Economic Research.

Auerbach, A. J. 1984. Social security and the economics of the demographic transition. In *Retirement and Economic Behavior*, H. Aaron and G. Burtless, eds. Washington, D.C.: The Brookings Institute.

Auerbach, A. J., and D. W. Jorgenson. 1980a. *The First Year Capital Recovery System*. Harvard Institute of Economic Research, Discussion Paper Series, no. 740. Cambridge, Mass.: Harvard University Press.

Auerbach, A. J., and D. Jorgenson. 1980b. Inflation-proof depreciation of assets. *Harvard Business Review* 58:113–18.

Auerbach, A. J., and L. J. Kotlikoff. 1983a. An examination of empirical tests of social security and savings. In *Social Policy Evaluation: An Economic Perspective*, E. Helpman, A. Razin, and E. Sadka, eds. New York: Academic Press, 161–79.

Auerbach, A. J., and L. J. Kotlikoff. 1983b. Investment versus savings incentives: The size of the bank for the buck and the potential for self-financing business tax cuts. In *The Economic Consequences of Government Deficits*, L. H. Meyer, ed. Boston, Mass.: Kluwer-Nijhoff, 121–54.

Auerbach, A. J., and L. J. Kotlikoff. 1983c. National savings, economic welfare, and the structure of taxation. In *Behavioral Simulation Methods in Tax Policy Analysis*, M. Feldstein, ed. Chicago, Ill.: University of Chicago Press, 459–98.

Auerbach, A. J., and L. J. Kotlikoff. 1983d. *Social Security and the Economics of the Demographic Transition*. Washington, D.C.: The Brookings Institution.

Auerbach, A. J., and L. J. Kotlikoff. 1985. Simulating alternative social security responses to the demographic transition. *National Tax Journal* 38(2):153–68.

Auerbach, A. J., and L. J. Kotlikoff. 1987. *Dynamic Fiscal Policy*. Cambridge: Cambridge University Press.

Auerbach, A. J., L. J. Kotlikoff, and J. Skinner. 1983. The efficiency gains from dynamic tax reform. *International Economic Review* 24:81–100.

Baily, M. N. 1977. Unemployment insurance as insurance for workers. *Industrial and Labor Relations Review* 30:495–504.

Baily, M. N. 1978. Some aspects of optimal umemployment insurance. *Journal of Public Economics* 10:379–402.

Bar-Llan, A., and A. S. Blinder. 1987. *The Life-Cycle Permanent-Income Model and Consumer Durables*. NBER Working Paper 2149. Cambridge, Mass.: National Bureau of Economic Research.

Barro, R. J. 1974. Are government bonds net wealth? *Journal of Political Economy* 48(6):1095–118.

Barro, R. J. 1978a. *The Impact of Social Security and Private Saving: Evidence from the US Time Series*. Washington, D.C.: American Enterprise Institute.

Barro, R. J. 1978b. Social security and private saving-evidence from the US time series. In *Studies in Social Security and Retirement Policy*. Washington, D.C.: American Enterprise Institute for Public Policy Research.

Barro, R. J., with a reply by M. Feldstein. 1978. *The Impact of Social Security on Private Saving: Evidence from the US Time Series*. Washington, D.C.: American Enterprise Institute for Public Policy Research.

Barro, R. J., and G. Becker. 1987. Fertility choice in a model of economic growth. Harvard University. Mimeo.

Barro, R. J., and G. Becker. 1988. A reformulation of the economic theory of fertility. *Quarterly Journal of Economics* 53:1–26.

Barro, R. J., and J. W. Friedman. 1977. On uncertain lifetimes. *Journal of Political Economy* 85:843–49.

Barro, R. J., and C. Sahasakul. 1983. Measuring the average marginal tax rate from the individual income tax. *Journal of Business* 56:419–52.

Barsky, R., G. N. Mankiw, and S. P. Zeldes. 1984. Ricardian consumers with Keynesian propensities. Mimeo.

Barsky, R., G. N. Mankiw, and S. P. Zeldes. 1987. Ricardian consumers with Keynesian propensities. *American Economic Review*. 76:676–91.

Bayer, R., et al. 1983. The care of the terminally ill: Morality and economics. *New England Journal of Medicine* 309:1490–4.

Becker, G. S. 1974. A theory of social interactions. *Journal of Political Economy* 82:1063–94.

Becker, G. S. 1981. *A Treatise on the Family*. Cambridge, Mass.: Harvard University Press.

Becker, G. S., and N. Tomes. 1976. Child endowments and the quantity and quality of children. *Journal of Political Economy* 84:S143—62.

Becker, G. S., and N. Tomes. 1979. An equilibrium theory of the distribution of income. *Journal of Political Economy* 87:1153—89.

Becker, G. S., E. M. Landes, and R. T. Michael. 1977. An economic analysis of marital instability. *Journal of Political Economy* 85:1141—87.

Behrman, J. R., R. Pollack, and P. Taubman. 1982. Parental preferences and provision for progeny. *Journal of Political Economy* 90:52—73.

Bernheim, B. D. 1982. Post retirement wealth decumulation. Mimeo.

Bernheim, B. D. 1986. Dissaving after retirement: Testing the pure life-cycle hypothesis. In *Issues in Pension Economics*, Z. Bodie, J. B. Shoven, and D. A. Wise, eds. Chicago, Ill.: University of Chicago Press, 237—82.

Bernheim, B. D., and K. Bagwell. 1985. Is everything neutral? Mimeo.

Bernheim, B. D., A. Shleifer, and L. H. Summers. 1986. Bequests as a means of payment. *Journal of Political Economy* 93(6):1045—76.

Bilson, J. F. O. 1980. The rational expectations approach to the consumption function. *European Economic Review* 13:273—99.

Black, F. 1981. *When Is a Positive Income Tax Optimal?* NBER Working Paper 631. Cambridge, Mass.: National Bureau of Economic Research.

Blanchard, O. J. 1985. Debt, deficits, and finite horizons. *Journal of Political Economy* 93:223—47.

Blinder, A. S. 1973. A model of inherited wealth. *Quarterly Journal of Economics* 87(4):608—26.

Blinder, A. S. 1975. Distribution effects and the aggregate consumption function. *Journal of Political Economy* 83:447—75.

Blinder, A. S. 1976. Intergenerational transfers and life cycle consumption. *American Economic Review* 66(2):87—93.

Blinder, A. S. 1981. Temporary income taxes and consumer spending. *Journal of Political Economy* 89:26—53.

Blinder, A, S., R. Gordon, and D. Wise. 1981. *Social Security, Bequests, and the Life Cycle Theory of Saving: Cross-Sectional Tests*. NBER Working Paper 1619. Cambridge, Mass.: National Bureau of Economic Research.

Boskin, M. J. 1975. Notes on the tax treatment of human capital. In *Conference on Tax Research*, US office of Tax Analysis. Stanford, Cal., and Cambridge, Mass.: National Bureau of Economic Research, 185—95.

Boskin, M. J. 1977. Social security and retirement decisions. *Economic Inquiry* 15:1–25.

Boskin, M. J. 1978a. Is heavy taxation of capital socially desirable? *Hearings before the Subcommittee on Economic Growth and Stabilization, the Joint Economic Committee.* 95th Cong. Washington, D.C.: US Government Printing Office.

Boskin, M. J. 1978b. Taxation, saving, and the rate of interest. *Journal of Political Economy* 86:3–27.

Boskin, M. J. 1982. Federal government deficits: Some myths and realities. *American Economic Review* 72:296–303.

Boskin, M. J. 1985a. The effect of social security of retirement in the early 1970s. *Quarterly Journal of Economics* 99(4):767–90.

Boskin, M. J. 1985b. *The Real Federal Budget.* Cambridge, Mass.: Harvard University Press.

Boskin, M. J., and L. J. Kotlikoff. 1986. Public debt and US saving: A new test of the neutrality hypothesis. *Carnegie-Rochester Conference Volume Series.* 23:55–86.

Boskin, M. J., and L. J. Lau. 1977. *Taxation and Aggregate Factor Supply: Preliminary Estimates.* NBER Working Paper 221. Cambridge, Mass.: National Bureau of Economic Research.

Boskin, M. J., and L. J. Lau. 1984. An econometric demographic model of postwar US consumption, saving, and wealth. Mimeo.

Boskin, M. J., and L. J. Lau. 1986. *An Analysis of Postwar US Consumption Saving.* Chicago, Ill.: University of Chicago Press.

Boskin, M. J., M. S. Robinson, and A. M. Huber. 1987. *Government Saving, Capital Formation, and Wealth in the United States, 1947–1985.* NBER Working Paper 2352. Cambridge, Mass.: National Bureau of Economic Research.

Bosworth, B. P. 1982. Capital formation and economic policy. *Brookings Papers on Economic Activities* 2:273–317.

Bradford, D. F. 1980. The economics of tax policy toward savings. In *The Government and Capital Formation*, George von Furstenberg, ed. Cambridge, Mass.: Ballinger, 11–71.

Bradford, D. F. 1981. The incidence and allocation effects of a tax on corporate distributions. *Journal of Public Economics* 15:1–22.

Brittain, J. A. 1978. *Inheritance and the Inequality of Material Wealth.* Washington, D.C.: The Brookings Institution.

Buiter, W. H. 1983. Measurement of the public sector deficit and its implications for policy evaluation and design. *International Monetary Fund Staff Papers* 30:306–49.

Bulow, J. I., and L. H. Summers. 1982. *The Taxation of Risky Assets*. NBER Working Paper 897. Cambridge, Mass.: National Bureau of Economic Research.

Burbridge, J. B., and A. L. Robb. 1985. Evidence on wealth-age profiles in Canadian cross section data. *Canadian Journal of Economics* 18(4):854–75.

Calvo, G. A. 1978. On the time consistency of optimal policy in a monetary Economy. *Econometrica* 46:869–74.

Calvo, G. A., L. J. Kotlikoff, and C. A. Rodriguez. 1979. The incidence of a tax on pure rent: A new (?) reason for an old answer. *Journal of Political Economy* 87:869–74.

Cambell, C. D., and R. G. Cambell. 1976. Conflicting views on the effect of old-age and survivors insurance on retirement. *Economic Inquiry* 14:369–88.

Cambell, J. Y., and A. S. Deaton. 1987. *Is Consumption too Smooth?* NBER Working Paper 2134. Cambridge, Mass.: National Bureau of Economic Research.

Chamley, C. 1980. Optimal intertemporal taxation and the public debt. Mimeo.

Chamley, C. 1981. The welfare cost of capital income taxation in a growing economy. *Journal of Political Economy* 89:468–96.

Chamley, C. 1982. Efficient tax reform in a dynamic model of general equilibrium. Mimeo.

Chan, L. K. C. 1983. Uncertainty and the neutrality of government financing policy. *Journal of Monetary Economics* 11:351–72.

Christensen, L. R. 1971. Entrepreneurial income: How does it measure up? *American Economic Review* 61:575–85.

Christensen, L. R., and D. W. Jorgenson. 1973. *US Income, Saving, and Wealth, 1929–1969*. Madison, Wis.: University of Wisconsin Press.

Cox, D. 1987. Motives for private income transfers. *Journal of Political Economy* 95:508–46.

Cuddington, J. T. 1982. Canadian evidence on the permanent income: Rational expectations hypothesis. *Canadian Journal of Economics* 15:331–5.

Daly, V., and G. Hadjimatheou. 1981. Stochastic implications of the life cycle–permanent income hypothesis: Evidence for the UK economy. *Journal of Political Economy* 89:596–9.

Danziger, S., J. Van der Gaag, E. Smolensky, and M. Taussig. 1983. The life cycle hypothesis and the consumption behavior of the elderly. *Journal of Post Keynesian Economics* 5(2):208–27.

Darby, M. R. 1979. *The Effects of Social Security on Income and the Capital Stock*. Washington, D.C.: American Enterprise Institute for Public Policy Research.

David, M., and P. L. Menchik. 1980. *The Effect of Social Security on Lifetime Wealth Accumulation and Bequests.* Discussion Paper 671. Madison, Wis.: Institute for Research on Poverty, University of Wisconsin.

David, M., and P. L. Menchik. 1985. The effect of social security on lifetime wealth accumulation and bequests. *Economica* 52(208):421–34.

David, P. A., and J. L. Scadding. 1974. Private savings: Ultrarationality, aggregation, and "Dension's Law." *Journal of Political Economy* 82:225–49.

Davidson, J. E. H., and D. F. Hendry. 1981. Interpreting econometric evidence: Consumers' expenditures in the UK. *European Economic Review* 16:177–92.

Davies, J. 1981. Uncertain lifetime, consumption and dissaving in retirement. *Journal of Political Economy* 89:561–77.

Deaton, A. 1986. *Life-Cycle Models of Consumption: Is the Evidence Consistent with the Theory?* NBER Working Paper 1910. Cambridge, Mass.: National Bureau of Economic Research.

Deaton, A., and J. Muellbauer. 1980. *Economics and Consumer Behavior.* Cambridge: Cambridge University Press.

Denardo, E. 1967. Contraction mappings in the theory underlying dynamic programming. *SIAM Review* 9:165–77.

Denison, E. F. 1958. A note on private saving. *The Review of Economics and Statistics* 40:261–7.

Diamond, P. A. 1965. National debt in a neoclassical growth model. *American Economic Review* 55:1126–50.

Diamond, P. A. 1970. The incidence of an interest income tax. *Journal of Economic Theory* 2:211–24.

Diamond, P. A. 1977. A framework for social security analysis. *Journal of Public Economics* 8:275–98.

Diamond, P. A., and J. A. Hausman. 1984. Individual retirement and savings behavior. *Journal of Public Economics* 23:81–114.

Diamond, P. A., and J. A. Mirrlees. 1978. A model of social insurance with variable retirement. *Journal of Public Economics* 10:295–336.

Dolde, W., and J. Tobin. 1981. *Mandatory Retirement Saving and Capital Formation.* Discussion Paper 594. New Haven, Conn.: Cowles Foundation, Yale University.

Domar, E. D., and R. Musgrave. 1944. Proportional income taxation and risk taking. *Quarterly Journal of Economics* 58:388–422.

Dooley, M. P., and P. Isard. 1980. Capital controls, political risk, and deviations from interest-rate parity. *Journal of Political Economy* 88:370–84.

Dreze, J. H., and F. Modigliani. 1972. Consumption decisions under uncertainty. *Journal of Economic Theory* 5 : 308–35.

Eaton, J. 1981. Fiscal policy, inflation, and the accumulation of risky capital. *Review of Economic Studies* 48 : 435–45.

Eaton, J., and M. Gersovitz. 1981. Debt with potential repudiation: Theoretical and empirical analysis. *Review of Economic Studies* 48 : 289–309.

Eaton, J., and H. Rosen. 1980. Taxation, human capital and uncertainty. *American Economic Review*. 70 : 705–15.

Eckstein, Z., M. Eichenbaum, and D. Peled. 1983. Uncertain lifetimes and the welfare enhancing properties of annuity markets and social security. Mimeo.

Eden, B., and A. Pakes. 1981. On measuring the variance-age profile of lifetime earnings. *Review of Economic Studies* 48 : 385–94.

Eisner, R. 1983. Social security, saving, and macroeconomics. *Journal of Macroeconomics* 5 : 1–19.

Eisner, R., and P. J. Pieper. 1984. A new view of the federal debt and budget deficits. *American Economic Review* 74 : 11–29.

Eisner, R., and P. J. Pieper. 1985. How to make sense of the deficit. *Public Interest* 78 : 101–18.

Evans, O. J. 1983. Tax policy, the interest elasticity of saving, and capital accumulation: Numerical analysis of theoretical models. *American Economic Review* 73 : 398–410.

Feldstein, M. S. 1974a. Incidence of a capital income tax in a growing economy with variable savings rates. *Review of Economic Studies* 41(4) : 505–13.

Feldstein, M. 1974b. *The Optimal Financing of Social Security*. Harvard Institute of Economic Research Paper 388. Cambridge, Mass.: Harvard Institute of Economic Research.

Feldstein, M. S. 1974c. Social security, induced retirement, and aggregate capital accumulation. *Journal of Political Economy* 82 : 905–26.

Feldstein, M. S. 1974d. Tax incidence in a growing economy with variable factor supply. *Quarterly Journal of Economics* 88 : 551–73.

Feldstein, M. 1976a. Social security and saving: The extended life cycle theory. *American Economic Review* 66(2) : 77–87.

Feldstein, M. S. 1976b. Social security and the distribution of wealth. *Journal of American Statistical Association*. 71 : 800–7.

Feldstein, M. S. 1977a. National saving in the United States. In *Capital for Productivity and Jobs*, E. Shapiro and M. White, eds. Englewood Cliffs, N.J.: Prentice Hall, 124–54.

Feldstein, M. S. 1977b. The surprising incidence of a tax on pure rent: A new answer to an old question. *Journal of Political Economy* 85:349–60.

Feldstein, M. S. 1978. The welfare cost of capital income taxation. *Journal of Political Economy* 86:S29–51.

Feldstein, M. S. 1980. *Social Security, Induced Retirement, and Aggregate Capital Accumulation: A Correction and Update.* NBER Working Paper 579. Cambridge, Mass.: National Bureau of Economic Research.

Feldstein, M. S. 1982a. Government deficits and aggregate demand. *Journal of Monetary Economics* 9:1–20.

Feldstein, M. S. 1982b. Social security and private saving: Reply. *Journal of Political Economy* 90:630–42.

Feldstein, M. S. 1983. Domestic saving and international capital movements in the long run and the short run. *European Economic Review* 21:129–51.

Feldstein, M. S., and C. Horioka. 1980. Domestic savings and international capital flows. *The Economic Journal* 90:314–29.

Feldstein, M. S., and A. Pellechio. 1979. Social security and household wealth accumulation: New microeconomic evidence. *Review of Economic Studies* 61:361–8.

Feldstein, M. S., and L. Summers. 1979. Inflation and the taxation of capital income in the corporate sector. *National Tax Journal* 32:445–70.

Fischer, S. 1979. *Dynamic Inconsistency, Cooperation and the Benevolent Dissembling Government.* MIT Working Paper 248. Cambridge, Mass.: Massachusetts Institute of Technology.

Flavin, M. A. 1981. The adjustment of consumption to changing expectations about future income. *Journal of Political Economy* 89:974–1009.

Fox, A. 1976. Alternative measure of earnings replacement rates for social security benefits. In *Reaching Retirement Age: Findings from a Survey of Newly Entitled Workers. 1968–1970* (Social Security Administration Report 47). Washington, D.C.: US Government Printing Office, 199–213.

Friedman, B., and M. Wahrshawsky. 1985. *The Cost of Annuities: Implications for Saving Behavior and Bequests.* NBER Working Paper 1682. Cambridge, Mass.: National Bureau of Economic Research.

Friedman, J., and J. Sjorgen. 1976. *The Assets of the Elderly as They Retire.* Abt Associates Report 79-142 to the Social Security Administration Report 47. Cambridge, Mass.: Abt Associates.

Friedman, J., and A. Spivak. 1986. Is there adverse selection in the demand for annuities? Mimeo.

Friedman, M. 1957. *A Theory of the Consumption Function.* Princeton, N.J.: Princeton University Press.

Friedman, M. 1962. *Capitalism and Freedom*. Chicago, Ill.: University of Chicago Press.

Friend, I., and M. E. Blume. 1975. The demand for risky assets. *American Economic Review* 65:900–22.

Froomkin, J. 1977. Tax Treatment of Tuition Expenses. *Hearings before the Committee on Ways and Means, House of Representatives*, 95th Cong. ser. 95–56. Washington, D.C.: US Government Printing Office.

Fuchs, V. R. 1982. Time preference and health: An exploratory study. In *Economic Aspects of Health*, V. Fuchs, ed. Chicago, Ill.: University of Chicago Press, 93–120.

Fullerton, D., J. B. Shoven, and J. Whalley. 1983. Replacing the US income tax with a progressive consumption tax. *Journal of Public Economics* 20:3–23.

Goldsmith, R. W., and R. E. Lipsey. 1963. *Studies in the National Balance Sheet of the United States*, vol. 1. Princeton, N.J.: Princeton University Press.

Gordon, R. H. 1981. *Taxation of Corporate Capital Income: Tax Revenues vs. Tax Distortions*. NBER Working Paper 687. Cambridge, Mass.: National Bureau of Economic Research.

Gordon, R. H. 1983. *Social Security and Labor Supply Incentives*. NBER Working Paper 986. Cambridge, Mass.: National Bureau of Economic Research.

Goulder, L. H., J. B. Shoven, and J. Whalley. 1983. Domestic tax policy and the foreign sector: The importance of alternative foreign sector formulations to results from a general equilibrium tax analysis model. In *Behavioral Simulation Methods in Tax Policy Analysis*, M. Feldstein, ed. Chicago, Ill.: University of Chicago Press, 333–64.

Grossman, S., and R. J. Shiller. 1980. Capital asset returns and consumption. Mimeo.

Grossman, S., and R. J. Shiller. 1981. The determinants of the variability of stock market prices. *American Economic Review* 71:222–7.

Hadjimatheou, G. 1987. *Consumer Economics after Keynes*. New York: St. Martin's Press.

Hall, R. E. 1968. Consumption taxes versus income taxes: Implications for economic growth. *Proceedings of the 61st National Tax Conference*. Columbus, Ohio: National Tax Association, 125–45.

Hall, R. E. 1978. Stochastic implications of the life cycle-permanent income hypothesis: Theory and evidence. *Journal of Political Economy* 86:971–87.

Hall, R. E. 1980. *The Importance of Lifetime Jobs in the US Economy*. NBER Working Paper 560. Cambridge, Mass.: National Bureau of Economic Research.

Hall, R. E. 1981. *Intertemporal Substitution in Consumption*. NBER Working Paper 720. Cambridge, Mass.: National Bureau of Economic Research.

Hall, R. E. 1985. *Real Interest and Consumption*. NBER Working Paper 1694. Cambridge, Mass.: National Bureau of Economic Research.

Hall, R. E. 1987. Consumption. In *The Handbook of Modern Business Cycle Theory*, R. J. Barro, ed. Amsterdam: North-Holland.

Hall, R. E., and F. Mishkin. 1982. The sensitivity of consumption to transitory income: Estimates from panel data on households. *Econometrica* 50:461–81.

Hansen, L. P., and K. J. Singleton. 1982. Generalized instrumental variables estimation of nonlinear rational expectations models. *Econometrica* 50:1269–86.

Hansen, L. P., and K. J. Singleton. 1983. Stochastic consumption, risk aversion, and the temporal behavior of asset returns. *Journal of Political Economy* 91:249–65.

Harberger, A. C. 1964. Taxation, resource allocation, and welfare. In *The Role of Direct and Individual Taxes in the Federal Revenue System*, J. Due, ed. Princeton, N.J.: Princeton University Press, 25–70.

Harberger, A. C. 1980. Vignettes on the world capital market. *American Economic Review* 70:331–7.

Harberger, A. C. 1983. The state of the corporation income tax. In *Directions in Federal Tax Reform for the 1980s*. Washington, D.C.: American Council for Capital Formation.

Hausman, J. 1979. Individual discount rates and utilization of energy using durables. *Bell Journal of Economics* 10(1):33–54.

Hausman, J. 1981. Labor supply. In *How Taxes Affect Economic Behavior*, H. J. Aaron and J. A. Pechman, eds. Washington, D.C.: The Brookings Institute, 27–83.

Hayashi, F. 1982. *The Effects of Liquidity Constraints on Consumption: A Cross-Sectional Analysis*. NBER Working Paper 882. Cambridge, Mass.: National Bureau of Economic Research.

Hayashi, F. 1984. *The Permanent Income Hypothesis and Consumption Durability: Analysis Based on Japanese Panel Data*. Discussion Paper 248. Tsukuba, Japan: University of Tsukuba Institute of Socio-Economic Planning.

Hayashi, F. 1985. *Tests for Liquidity Constraints: A Critical Survey*. NBER Working Paper 1720. Cambridge, Mass.: National Bureau of Economic Research.

Hayashi, F. 1986. Why is Japan's saving rate so apparently high? In *NBER Macroeconomics Annual 1986*, S. Fischer, ed. Cambridge, Mass.: MIT Press, 145–210.

Heckman, J. 1976. A life-cycle model of earnings, learning, and consumption. *Journal of Political Economy* 84:S11–44.

Heckman, J. 1977. *Sample Selection Bias as a Specification Error*. Report R-1984-HEW. Los Angeles, Cal.: Rand Corp.

Heckman, J. 1981. Heterogeneity and state dependence. In *Studies in Labor Markets*, S. Rosen, ed. Chicago, Ill.: University of Chicago Press, 91–139.

Hickman, B. 1966. Investment demand in the 60's. In *The Economic Outlook for 1966* (13th Annual Conference on Economic Outlook). Ann Arbor, Mich.: Department of Economics, University of Michigan, 91–111.

Hicks, J. 1942. Consumers' surplus and index numbers. *Review of Economic Studies* 9:126–37.

Historical Statistics of the United States, Colonial Times to 1970, pt. 1. 1975. Washington, D.C.: Government Printing Office.

Holden, K. C., R. V. Burkhauser, and D. A. Myers. 1986. *Pensioners' Annuity Choice: Is the Well-Being of Widows Considered?* Discussion Paper 802–86. Madison, Wis.: University of Wisconsin Institute for Research on Poverty.

Howrey, P., and S. Hymans. 1978. The measurement and determination of loanable-funds saving. *Brookings Papers on Economic Activity* 3:655–85.

Hubbard, G. R. 1983. Uncertain lifetimes and the impact of social security on individual wealth accumulation. Mimeo.

Hubbard, G. R. 1984a. *Precautionary Saving Revisited: Social Security, Individual Welfare, and the Capital Stock.* NBER Working Paper 1430. Cambridge, Mass.: National Bureau of Economic Research.

Hubbard, G. R. 1984b. *Uncertain lifetimes, pensions, and individual saving.* NBER Working Paper 1363. Cambridge, Mass.: National Bureau of Economic Research.

Hubbard, G. R. 1986a. Pension wealth and individual saving: Some new evidence. *Journal of Money, Credit, and Banking* 18:167–78.

Hubbard, G. R. 1986b. Uncertain lifetimes, pensions, and individual saving. In *Issues in Pension Economics*, Z. Bodie, J. Shoven, and D. Wise, eds. Chicago, Ill.: University of Chicago Press, 175–210.

Hubbard, G. R., and K. L. Judd. 1986a. Finite lifetimes, borrowing constraints, and short-run fiscal policy. Northwestern University. Mimeo.

Hubbard, G. R., and K. L. Judd. 1986b. Liquidity constraints, fiscal policy, and consumption. *Brookings Papers on Economic Activity* 1:1–51.

Hurd, M. D. 1986. *Savings and Bequests.* NBER Working Paper 1826. Cambridge, Mass.: National Bureau of Economic Research.

Hurd, M. D., and M. J. Boskin. 1984. The effect of social security on retirement in the early 1970s. *The Quarterly Journal of Economics* 99(4):767–90.

Hurd, M. D., and D. A. Wise. 1987. *The Wealth and Poverty of Widows: Assets before and after the Husband's Death.* NBER Working Paper 2325. Cambridge, Mass.: National Bureau of Economic Research.

Irelan, L., et al. 1976. *Almost 65: Baseline Data from the Retirement History Study.* Publication 76-11806. Washington, D.C.: Social Security Administration, Office of Research and Statistics.

Ishikawa, T. 1974. Imperfection in the capital market and the institutional arrangement of inheritance. *Review of Economic Studies* 41:383–404.

Ishikawa, T. 1975. Family structures and family values in the theory of income distribution. *Journal of Political Economy* 83:987–1008.

Johnson, S., L. J. Kotlikoff, and W. Samuelson. 1987. *Can People Compute? An Experimental Test of the Life Cycle Consumption Model.* NBER Working Paper 2183. Cambridge, Mass.: National Bureau of Economic Research.

Kaplan, R. S. 1976. *Financial Crisis in the Social Security System.* Domestic Affairs Study 47. Washington, D.C.: American Enterprise Institute for Public Policy Research.

Kimball, M. S., and N. G. Mankiw. 1987. Precautionary saving and the timing of taxes. Harvard University. Mimeo.

King, M. A. 1977. *Public Policy and the Coporation.* London: Chapman & Hall.

King, M. A. 1980. Savings and taxation. In *Essays in Public Policy,* G. A. Hughes and G. M. Heal, eds. London: Chapman & Hall.

King, M. A. 1983. *The Economics of Saving.* NBER Working Paper 1247. Cambridge, Mass.: National Bureau of Economic Research.

King, M. A. 1985. The economics of savings: A survey of recent contributions. In *Frontiers of Economics,* K. Arrow and S. Honkapohja, eds. Oxford: Basil Blackwell, 227–327.

King, M. A., and L. Dicks-Mireaux. 1982. Asset holding and the life cycle. *The Economic Journal* 92:247–67.

King, M. A., and D. Fullerton, eds. 1984. *The Taxation of Income from Capital: A Comparative Study of the US, UK, Sweden, and West Germany.* Chicago, Ill.: University of Chicago Press.

Kormendi, R. 1983. Government debt, government spending, and private sector behavior. *American Economic Review* 73:994–1010.

Kotlikoff, L. J. 1977a. Estimating the elasticity of bequests with respect to lifetime resources from a sample of potential decedents. Mimeo.

Kotlikoff, L. J. 1977b. Testing the theory of social security and life cycle accumulation. Harvard University. Mimeo.

Kotlikoff, L. J. 1978. Social security, time to reform. In *Federal Tax Reform,* M. Boskin, ed. San Francisco, Cal.: Institute for Contemporary Studies, 119–44.

Kotlikoff, L. J. 1979a. Social security and equilibrium capital intensity. *Quarterly Journal of Economics* 93:233–53.

Kotlikoff, L. J. 1979b. Testing the theory of social security and life cycle accumulation. *American Economic Review* 69:396–410.

Kotlikoff, L. J. 1980. Elasticities of labor supply and savings: Answers in search of questions. *Proceedings of the 73rd Annual Conference on Taxation*, S. J. Bowers and J. L. Staton, eds. New Orleans, La.: National Tax Association, Tax Institute of America, 96–9.

Kotlikoff, L. J. 1981a. The role of intergenerational transfers in aggregate capital accumulation. *Journal of Political Economy* 89(4):706–32.

Kotlikoff, L. J. 1981b. Some economic implications of life span extension. In *Aging: Biology and Behavior*, J. March and J. McGaugh, eds. New York: Academic Press, 97–114.

Kotlikoff, L. J. 1983a. Altruistic extended family linkages, a note. National Bureau of Economic Research. Mimeo.

Kotlikoff, L. J. 1983b. National savings and economic policy: The efficiency of investment vs. savings incentives. *American Economic Review* 73:82–7.

Kotlikoff, L. J. 1983c. Theoretical and empirical analysis of altruistic linkages within the extended family. Mimeo.

Kotlikoff, L. J. 1984. Taxation and saving: A neoclassical perspective. *Journal of Economic Literature* 22:1576–629.

Kotlikoff, L. J. 1986. Deficit delusion. *Public Interest* 84:53–65.

Kotlikoff, L. J. 1988. What microeconomics teaches us about the dynamic macro effects of fiscal policy. *Journal of Money, Credit, and Banking* (forthcoming).

Kotlikoff, L. J., and A. Pakes. 1988. Looking for the news in the noise: Additional stochastic implications of optimal consumption choice. *Annales d'Economie et de Statistique* (forthcoming).

Kotlikoff, L. J., and D. E. Smith. 1983. *Pensions in the American Economy*. Chicago, Ill.: University of Chicago Press.

Kotlikoff, L. J., and A. Spivak. 1979. *The Family as an Incomplete Annuities Market*. NBER Working Paper 362. Cambridge, Mass.: National Bureau of Economic Research.

Kotlikoff, L. J., and A. Spivak. 1981. The family as an incomplete annuities market. *Journal of Political Economy* 89:372–91.

Kotlikoff, L. J., and L. H. Summers. 1978. *Long Run Tax Incidence and Variable Labor Supply Revisted*. Working Paper 111. Los Angeles, Cal.: University of California.

Kotlikoff, L. J., and L. H. Summers. 1979. Tax incidence in a life cycle model with variable labor supply. *Quarterly Journal of Economics* 93:705–18.

Kotlikoff, L. J., and L. H. Summers. 1980. The role of intergenerational transfers in aggregate capital accumulation. NBER Working Paper 445. Cambridge, Mass.: National Bureau of Economic Research.

Kotlikoff, L. J., and L. H. Summers. 1981. The role of intergenerational transfers in aggregate capital formation. *Journal of Political Economy* 89:706–32.

Kotlikoff, L. J., and L. H. Summers. 1986. *The Contribution of Intergenerational Transfers to Total Wealth: A Reply.* NBER Working Paper 1827. Cambridge, Mass.: National Bureau of Economic Research.

Kotlikoff, L. J., T. Perrson, and L. Svensson. 1986. *Laws as Assets: A Solution to the Time Consistency Problem.* NBER Working Paper 2068. Cambridge, Mass.: National Bureau of Economic Research.

Kotlikoff, L. J., J. Shoven, and A. Spivak. 1987. Annuity markets, savings, and the capital stock. In *Issues in Pension Economics*, Z. Bodie, J. B. Shoven, and D. A. Wise, eds. Chicago, Ill.: University of Chicago Press, 211–34.

Kotlikoff, L. J., J. Shoven, and A. Spivak. 1986. The impact of annuity insurance on savings and inequality. *Journal of Labor Economics* 4(3), pt. 2, 5183–207.

Kotlikoff, L. J., A. Spivak, and L. H. Summers. 1982. The adequacy of savings. *American Economic Review* 72:1056–69.

Kurz, M. 1981. *The Life-Cycle Hypothesis and the Effects of Social Security and Private Pensions on Family Savings.* Technical Report 335. Stanford, Cal.: Stanford University, IMSSS.

Kurz, M. 1984a. Capital accumulation and the characteristics of private inter-generational transfers. *Economica* 51:1–22.

Kurz, M. 1984b. The life cycle hypothesis as a tool of theory and practice. Mimeo.

Kuznets, S. S. 1941. *National Income and Its Composition, 1919–1938*, 2 vols. New York: National Bureau of Economic Research.

Kuznets, S. S. 1946. *National Product since 1869.* New York: Arno.

Kuznets, S. S. 1961. *Capital in the American Economy: Its Formation and Financing.* Princeton, N.J.: Princeton University Press.

Kydland, F. E., and E. C. Prescott. 1977. Rules rather than discretion: The inconsistency of optimal plans. *Journal of Political Economy* 85:473–91.

Lauriat, P., and W. Rabin. 1970. Men who claim benefits before age 65: Findings from the survey of new beneficiaries, 1968. *Social Security Bulletin* 33:3–28.

Lawrence, E. 1983. Do transfers to the poor reduce savings? Mimeo.

Lebergott, S. 1976. *The American Economy, Income, Wealth, and Want.* Princeton, N.J.: Princeton University Press.

Leimer, D. R., and S. D. Lesnoy. 1980. *Social Security and Private Saving: A Reexamination of the Time Series Evidence Using Alternative Social Security Wealth Variables.* Working Paper 19. Washington, D.C.: Social Security Administration, Office of Research and Statistics.

Leimer, D. R., and S. D. Lesnoy. 1981. Comment on "Social security, induced retirement and aggregate capital accumulation: A correlation and update" by Martin Feldstein. Mimeo.

Leland, H. E. 1968. Saving and uncertainty: The precautionary demand for saving. *Quarterly Journal of Economics* 82:465–73.

Lesnoy, S., and D. R. Leimer. 1981. *Social Security and Private Saving: New Time Series Evidence with Alternative Specifications.* Working Paper 22. Washington, D.C.: Social Security Administration.

Leven, M., H. G. Moulton, and C. Warburton. 1934. *America's Capacity to Consume.* Washington, D.C.: Brookings Institute.

Levhari, D., and L. J. Mirman. 1977. Savings and consumption with an uncertain horizon. *Journal of Political Economy* 85(2):265–81.

Lillard, L. A., and Y. Weiss. 1976. *Analysis of Longitudinal Earnings Data: American Scientists 1960–1970.* NBER Working Paper 121. Cambridge, Mass.: National Bureau of Economic Research.

Lillard, L. A., and R. J. Willis. 1976. *Dynamic Aspects of Earnings Inequality.* NBER Working Paper 150. Cambridge, Mass.: National Bureau of Economic Research.

Lillard, L. A., and R. J. Willis. 1977. Inequality: Earning vs. human wealth. *The American Economic Review* 67(2):42–53.

Lipton, D., and J. Sachs. *Accumulation and Growth in a Two-Country Model: A Simulation Approach.* NBER Working Paper 572. Cambridge, Mass.: National Bureau of Economic Research.

Long, S. H., J. O. Gibbs, S. P. Crozier, D. J. Cooper, Jr., J. F. Newman, Jr., and A. M. Larsen. 1984. Medical expenditures of terminal cancer patients during the last year of life. *Inquiry* 21:315–27.

Loury, G. 1981. Intergenerational transfers and the distribution of earnings. *Econometrica* 49(4):843–67.

Lubitz, J., and R. Prihoda. 1984. The use and costs of medicare services in the last 2 years of life. *Health Care Financing Review* 5:117–31.

Lucas, R. 1976. Econometric policy evaluation: A critique. In *The Philips Curve and Labor Markets,* K. Brunner and A. H. Meltzer, eds. Amsterdam: North-Holland, vol. 1, 19–46.

MaCallum, B. 1984. Are bond-financed deficits inflationary? A Ricardian analysis. *Journal of Political Economy* 92:123–35.

McCall, N. 1984. Utilization and costs of medicare services by beneficiaries in their last year of life. *Medical Care* 22(4):329–42.

MaCurdy, T. E. 1981. An empirical model of labor supply in a life cycle setting. *Journal of Political Economy* 89:1059–85.

Mankiw, N. G., and M. D. Shapiro. 1985. Trends, random walks, and tests of the permanent income hypothesis. *Journal of Monetary Economics* 16:165–74.

Mankiw, N. G., J. J. Rotemberg, and L. H. Summers. 1982. *Intertemporal Substitution in Macroeconomics*. NBER Working Paper 898. Cambridge, Mass.: National Bureau of Economic Research.

Mankiw, N. G., J. J. Rotemberg, and L. H. Summers. 1983. Intertemporal substitution in macroeconomics. *Quarterly Journal of Economics* 100:225–51.

Manpower Report of the President. 1975. Washington, D.C.: US Government Printing Office.

Mariger, R. 1986. *Consumption Behavior and the Effects of Government Fiscal Policies*. Cambridge, Mass.: Harvard University Press.

Masson, A. 1982. A cohort analysis of wealth-age profiles generated by a simulation model (France 1949–1975). Mimeo.

Menchik, P. L. 1980. Primogeniture, equal sharing, and the US distribution of wealth. *Quarterly Journal of Economics* 94(2):299–316.

Menchik, P. L. 1985. Unequal estate division: Is it altruism, reverse bequests, or simply noise? Paper presented to the 1984 Seminar on Modeling the Accumulation and Distribution of Wealth, Paris, France, September.

Menchik, P. L., and DAVID, M. 1983. Income distribution, lifetime savings, and bequests. *American Economic Review* 83:672–90.

Merton, R. C. 1983. On the role of social security as a means for efficient risk sharing in an economy where human capital is not tradable. In *Financial Aspects of the US Pension System*, Z. Bodie and J. B. Shoven, eds. Chicago, Ill.: University of Chicago Press, 325–58.

Miller, B. 1974. Optimal consumption with a stochastic income stream. *Econometrica* 42:253–66.

Miller, B. 1976. The effect on optimal consumption of increased uncertainty in labor income in the multiperiod case. *Journal of Economic Theory* 13:154–67.

Miller, M. H., and C. W. Upton. 1974. *Macroeconomics: A Neoclassical Introduction*. Homewood, Ill.: Irwin.

Mirer, T. W. 1979. The wealth-age relation among the aged. *American Economic Review* 69:435–43.

Miron, J. A. 1986. Seasonal fluctuations and the life cycle–permanent income model of consumption. *Journal of Political Economy* 94:1258–80.

Mirrlees, J. 1974. Notes on welfare economics, information and uncertainty. In *Essays on Economic Behavior under Uncertainty*, M. S. Balch., D. L. McFadden, and S. Y. Wu, eds. Amsterdam: North-Holland, 243–58.

Modigliani, F. 1975. The life cycle hypothesis of saving, twenty years later. In *Contemporary Issues in Economics*, M. Parkin, ed. Manchester: Manchester University Press, 2—36.

Modigliani, F. 1983. The life cycle hypothesis and national wealth: A rehabilitation. MIT Discussion Paper. Cambridge, Mass.: Massachusetts Institute of Technology.

Modigliani, F. 1984. The contribution of intergenerational transfer to total wealth. Paper presented to the 1984 Seminar on Modeling the Accumulation and Distribution of Wealth, Paris, France, September.

Modigliani, F. 1988. The role of intergenerational transfers and life cycle savings in the accumulation of wealth. *Journal of Economic Perspectives* 2(1).

Modigliani, F., and R. Brumberg. 1954. Utility analysis and the consumption function: An interpretation of cross-section data. In *Post-Keynesian Economics*, K. K. Kurihara, ed. New Brunswick, N.J.: Rutgers University Press.

Modigliani, F., and R. Brumberg. 1980. Utility analysis and aggregate consumption functions: An attempt at integration. In *The Collected Papers of Franco Modigliani*, A. Abel, ed. Cambridge, Mass.: MIT Press, vol. 2, 128—197.

Moen, J. 1987a. Essays on the labor force and labor force participation rates: The United States from 1860 through 1950. Ph.D. dissertation, University of Chicago.

Moen, J. 1987b. The labor of older men: A comment. *Journal of Economic History* 47(3):761—7.

Mossin, J. 1968. Taxation and risk-taking: An expected utility approach. *Economica*, n.s., 35:74—82.

Muellbauer, J. 1982. Surprises in the consumption function. *Economic Journal*, suppl., 34—50.

Munnell, A. 1974. The impact of social security on personal savings. *National Tax Journal* 27:553—67.

Munnell, A. 1976. Private pensions and savings: New evidence. *Journal of Political Economy* 84:1013—32.

Musgrave, P. 1969. *United States Taxation of Foreign Investment Income: Issues and Arguments*. Cambridge, Mass.: Law School of Harvard University.

Myers, D. A., R. V. Burkhauser, and K. C. Holden. 1986. *The Transition from Wife to Widow: The Importance of Survivor Benefits to the Well-Being of Widows*. Discussion Paper 802-86. Madison, Wis.: University of Wisconsin Institute for Research on Poverty.

Nash, J. 1953. Two-person cooperative games. *Econometrica* 21:128—40.

National Longitudinal Survey 1966—69. Columbus, Ohio: Ohio State University.

Noguchi, Y. 1986. Demographic conditions, social security, and capital accumulation: A simulation analysis. NBER Summer Institute. Mimeo.

OECD Department of Economics and Statistics. 1983a. *Flows and Stocks of Fixed Capital, 1955–1980.* Paris: OECD.

OECD Department of Economics and Statistics. 1983b. *National Accounts, 1952–1981.* Paris: OECD.

Olson, M., and M. J. Bailey. 1981. Positive time preference. *Journal of Political Economy* 89:1–25.

Oulton, N. 1976. Inheritance and the distribution of wealth. *Oxford Economic Papers* 28:86–101.

Pellechio, A. 1978. Social security and retirement behavior. Ph.D. dissertation, Harvard University.

Phelps, E. S., and J. G. Riley. 1978. Rawlsian growth: Dynamic programming of capital and wealth for intergenerational 'maximin' justice. *Review of Economic Studies* 45:103–20.

Phelps, E. S., and K. Shell. 1969. Public debt, taxation, and capital intensiveness. *Journal of Economic Theory* 1:330–46.

Poterba, J. M. 1980. *Inflation, Income Taxes, and Owner Occupied Housing.* NBER Working Paper 553. Cambridge, Mass.: National Bureau of Economic Research.

Poterba, J. M. 1987a. Are consumers forward looking? Evidence from fiscal experiments. MIT. Mimeo.

Poterba, J. 1987b. Tax policy and corporate saving. In *Brookings Papers on Economic Activity*, A. M. Okun and G. L. Perry, eds. Ann Arbor, Mich.: Books on Demand UMI, 455–516.

Poterba, J. M., and L. H. Summers. 1986. Finite lifetimes and the effects of budget deficits on national savings. MIT. Mimeo.

President's Council of Economic Advisors. 1983. *1982 Economic Report of the President.* Washington, D.C.: US Government Printing Office.

President's Council of Economic Advisors. 1987. *The 1987 Economic Report of the President.* Washington, D.C.: US Government Printing Office.

Public Health Service. 1969. *Vital Statistics of the US Vol. 2, Part A, Mortality.* Washington, D.C.: US Government Printing Office.

Ransom, R. L., and R. Sutch. 1986. The labor of older Americans: Retirement of men on and off the job, 1870 to 1937. *Journal of Economic History* 46(1):1–30.

Ricardo, D. 1951. *The Works and Correspondence of David Ricardo*, Pierro Sraffa, ed. Cambridge: Cambridge University Press.

Roberston, A. H. 1978. Financial status of the social security program after the social security amendments of 1977. *Social Security Bulletin* 14:21–36.

Rossiter, L. F., and G. R. Wilensky. 1982. *Out-of-Pocket Expenditures for Personal Health Services* (National Health Care Expenditures Study). DHHS Publication (PHS) 82-3332. Washington, D.C.: US Department of Health and Human Services.

Runkle, D. E. 1983. Liquidity constraints and the permanent income hypothesis: Evidence from panel data. MIT. Mimeo.

Sachs, J. D. 1981a. *Aspects of the Current Account Behavior of OECD Economies.* NBER Working Paper 859. Cambridge, Mass.: National Bureau of Economic Researh.

Sachs, J. D. 1981b. The current account and macroeconomic adjustments in the 1970s. *Brookings Papers on Economic Activity* 1:201–82.

Salinger, M. A., and L. H. Summers. 1983. Tax reform and corporate investment: A microeconometric simulation study. In *Behavioral Simulation Methods in Tax Policy Analysis*, M. Feldstein, ed. Chicago, Ill.: University of Chicago Press, 247–87.

Sandmo, A. 1970. The effect of uncertainty on saving decisions. *Review of Economic Studies* 37:353–60.

Sargent, T. J. 1978. Rational expectations, econometric exogeneity, and consumption. *Journal of Political Economy* 86:673–700.

Schultz, T. W., ed. *Economics of the Family: Marriage, Children, and Human Capital.* Chicago, Ill.: University of Chicago Press.

Scitovsky, A. A. 1984. The high cost of dying: What do the data show? *Health and Society* 62:591–608.

Seidman, L. S. 1983. Taxes in a life cycle growth model with bequests and inheritances. *American Economic Review* 73:437–41.

Seidman, L. S. 1984. Conversion to a consumption tax: The transition in a life-cycle growth model. *Journal of Political Economy* 92:247–67.

Shapiro, M. 1986. The permanent income hypothesis and the real interest rate: Some evidence from panel data. *Economics Letters* 14:93–100.

Shavell, S., and L. Weiss. The optimal payment of unemployment insurance benefits over time. *Journal of Political Economy* 10:337–60.

Sherman, S. R. 1975. Assets on the threshold of retirement. *Social Security Bulletin* 36(8):

Sheshinski, E. 1978. A model of social security and retirement decisions. *Journal of Public Economics* 87:1347–62.

Sheshinski, E., and Y. Weiss. 1981. Uncertainty and optimal social security systems. *Quarterly Journal of Economics* 96:189–206.

Sheshinski, E., and Y. Weiss. 1982. Inequality within and between families. *Journal of Political Economy* 90 : 105−27.

Shiller, R. J. 1982. Consumption, asset markets, and macroeconomic fluctuations. *Carnegie-Rochester Conference Series on Public Policy* 17 : 203−38.

Shorrocks, A. F. 1975. The age-wealth relationship: A cross section and cohort analysis. *Review of Economics and Statistics* 57(2) : 155−63.

Shoven, J. B. 1983. Saving in the US economy. Mimeo.

Skinner, J. S. 1983a. Risky income and life cycle consumption. Mimeo.

Skinner, J. S. 1983b. Uncertain tax policy and economic efficiency. Mimeo.

Skinner, J. S. 1985a. The effect of increased longevity on capital accumulation. *American Economic Review* 75(5) : 1143−50.

Skinner, J. S. 1985b. Variable lifespan and the intertemporal elasticity of consumption. *Review of Economics and Statistics.* 67(4) : 616−23.

Skinner, J. S. 1986. Risky income, life cycle consumption, and precautionary savings. University of Virginia. Mimeo.

Social Security Administration. *Retirement History Survey.* Various years. Washington, D.C.: Social Security Administration.

Social Security Administration. 1966a. *Social Security Handbook*, third edition. Washington, D.C.: Social Security Administration.

Social Security Administration. 1966b. *US Population Projections for OASDHI Cost Estimates.* Actuarial Study 62. Washington, D.C.: Office of the Actuary.

Solow, R. M. 1956. A contribution to the theory of economic growth. *Quarterly Journal of Economics* 70 : 65−94.

Solow, R. M. 1982. Reflections on saving behavior. In *Saving and Government Policy* (Conference Series 25). Boston, Mass.: Federal Reserve Bank of Boston, 162−74.

Starrett, D. 1983. Long run savings elasticities in the life cycle model. Mimeo.

Stiglitz, J. E. 1969a. Distribution of income and wealth among individuals. *Econometrica* 37(3) : 382−97.

Stiglitz, J. E. 1969b. The effects of income, wealth and capital gains taxation on risk taking. *Quarterly Journal of Economics* 83 : 263−83.

Stiglitz, J. E. 1978. Equality, taxation and inheritance. In *Personal Income Distribution*, W. Krelle and A. F. Shorrocks, eds. Amsterdam: North-Holland.

Stiglitz, J. E. 1982a. *The Theory of Local Public Goods Twenty-Five years after Tiebout: A Perspective.* NBER Working Paper 954. Cambridge, Mass.: National Bureau of Economic Research.

Stiglitz, J. E. 1982b. Utilitarianism and horizontal equity: The case for random taxation. *Journal of Public Economics* 18:1–33.

Stiglitz, J. E., and D. Bevan. 1979. Intergenerational transfers and inequality. *Greek Economic Review* 1(1):8–26.

Summers, L. H. 1981a. Capital taxation and capital accumulation in a life cycle growth model. *American Economic Review* 71:533–44.

Summer, L. H. 1981b. Inflation, the stock market, and owner-occupied housing. *American Economic Review* 71(2):429–34.

Summers, L. H. 1981c. Taxation and corporate investment: A *q* theory approach. *Brookings Papers on Economic Activity* 1:67–127.

Summers, L. H. 1981d. Taxation and the size and composition of the capital stock: An asset price approach. Mimeo.

Summers, L. H. 1982. *Tax Policy, the Rate of Return, and Savings.* NBER Working Paper 995. Cambridge, Mass.: National Bureau of Economic Research.

Surrey, S. 1973. *Pathways to Tax Reform: The Concept of Tax Expenditures.* Cambridge, Mass.: Harvard University Press.

Sussman, M. B., J. N. Cates, and O. T. Smith. 1970. *Inheritance and the Family.* New York: Sage.

Thaler, R. H., and H. M. Shefrin. 1981. An economic theory of self-control. *Journal of Political Economy* 89:392–406.

Thurow, L. 1976. *Generating Inequality.* New York: Basic Books.

Tiebout, C. M. 1956. A pure theory of local expenditures. *Journal of Political Economy* 64:416–24.

Tobin, J. 1966. Liquidity preference as behavior towards risk. In *Monetary Theory and Policy*, Richard S. Thorn, ed. New York: Random House, 178–204.

Tobin, J. 1967. Life cycle saving and balanced growth. In *Ten Economic Studies in the Tradition of Irving Fisher*, W. Fellner et al., eds. New York: Wiley, 231–56.

Tobin, J. 1969. A general equilibrium approach of monetary theory. *Journal of Money, Credit, and Banking* 1:15–29.

Tobin, J., and W. Buiter. 1980. Fiscal and monetary policies, capital formation, and economic activity. In *The Government and Capital Formation*, G. M. von Furstenberg, ed. Cambridge, Mass.: Ballinger Press, 73–151.

Tobin, J., and W. Dolde. 1971a. Monetary and fiscal effects on consumption. In *Consumer Spending and Monetary Policy: The Linkages* (Federal Reserve Bank of Boston Conference Series 5). Boston, Mass.: Federal Reserve Bank of Boston.

Tobin, J., and W. Dolde. 1971b. Wealth, liquidity, and consumption. In *Consumer Spending and Monetary Policy: The Linkages* (Federal Reserve Bank of Boston

Monetary Conference Series 5). Boston, Mass.: Federal Reserve Bank of Boston, 99–146.

Tomes, N. 1981. The family, inheritance, and the intergenerational transmission of inequality. *Journal of Political Economy* 89:928–58.

Turnovsky, S. J., and W. A. Brock. 1980. Time consistency and optimal government policies in perfect foresight equilibrium. *Journal of Public Economics* 13:183–212.

US Department of Commerce, Bureau of Economic Analysis. 1973. *Long Term Economic Growth, 1860–1970*. Washington, D.C.: US Government Printing Office.

US Department of Commerce, Bureau of Economic Analysis. 1976. *The National Income and Product Accounts of the United States, 1929–1974, Statistical Tables*. Washington, D.C.: US Government Printing Office.

US Department of Commerce, Bureau of the Census. 1975. *Historical Statistics of the US Colonial Times to 1970*. Washington, D.C.: US Government Printing Office.

US Department of Commerce, Bureau of the Census. 1978. *US Statistical Abstract*. Washington, D.C.: US Government Printing Office.

US Department of Health, Education, and Welfare, Social Security Administration. 1966. *United States Population Projection for OASDHI Cost Estimates*. Actuarial Study 62. Washington, D.C.: US Department of HEW, Social Security Administration.

US Department of Labor, Bureau of Labor Statistics. 1978. *Employment and Training Report of the President*. Washington, D.C.: US Government Printing Office.

US Internal Revenue Service. 1970. *Statistics of Income*. Washington, D.C.: US Government Printing Office.

US Securities and Exchange Commission. 1977. *Statistical Bulletin*. Washington, D.C.: US Government Printing Office.

Varian, H. R. 1980. Redistributive taxation as social insurance. *Journal of Public Economics* 14:49–68.

Venti, S., and D. Wise. 1986a. IRAs and saving. Mimeo.

Venti, S. F., and D. A. Wise. 1986b. Tax deferred accounts, constraint choice, and estimation of individual savings. *Review of Economic Studies* 53:579–601.

Venti, S. F., and D. A. Wise. 1988. The determinants of IRA contributions and the effect of limit changes. In *Pensions in the American Economy*, L. J. Kotlikoff, ed. (Chicago, Ill.: University of Chicago Press), 9–47.

von Furstenberg, G. M. 1977. Corporate investment: Does market valuation matter in the aggregate? *Brookings Papers on Economic Activity* 2:347–97.

Weber, W. E. 1970. The effect of interest rates on aggregate consumption. *American Economic Review* 60:591–600.

Weber, W. E. 1975. Interest rates, inflation, and consumer expenditures. *American Economic Review* 65:843–58.

Weiss, L. 1976. The desirability of cheating incentives and randomness in the optimal income tax. *Journal of Political Economy* 84:1343–52.

Welch, F. 1979. Effects of cohort size on earnings: The baby boom babies; financial bust. *Journal of Political Economy* 87:65–98.

West, K. D. 1987. *The Insensitivity of Consumption to News about Income.* NBER Working Paper 2252. Cambridge, Mass.: National Bureau of Economic Research.

White, B. B. 1978. Empirical tests of the life-cycle hypothesis. *American Economic Review* 68:547–60.

Wilcox, D. W. 1987a. Income tax refunds and the timing of consumption expendituure. Federal Reserve Board of Governors. Mimeo.

Wilcox, D. W. 1987b. Social security benefits, consumption expenditure, and the life cycle hypothesis. Federal Reserve Board of Governors. Mimeo.

Williamson, S. H. 1987. The potential crowding out effect of social security transfers. University of California, Berkeley. Mimeo.

Williamson, S. H., and W. L. Jones. 1983. Computing the impact of social security using the life cycle consumption function. *American Economic Review* 73(5):1036–52.

Wright, C. 1969. Saving and the rate of interest. In *The Taxation of Income from Capital*, A. C. Harberger and M. J. Baily, eds. Washington, D.C.: The Brookings Institute.

Yaari, M. E. 1965. Uncertain lifetime, life insurance, and the theory of the consumer. *Review of Economic Studies* 32:137–50.

Zeldes, S. P. 1985. *Consumption and Liquidity Constraints: An Empirical Investigation.* Working Paper 24-85. Philadelphia; Pa.: Rodney L. White Center for Financial Research, Wharton School, University of Pennsylvania.

Zeldes, S. P. 1986a. Optimal consumption with stochastic income deviations from certainty equivalence. University of Pennsylvania. Mimeo.

Zeldes, S. P. 1986b. *Optimal Consumption with Stochastic Income: Deviations from Certainty Equivalence.* Working Paper 20-86. Philadelphia, Pa.: Rodney L. White Center for Financial Research, Wharton School, University of Pennsylvania.

Sources

"The adequacy of savings," with Avia Spivak and Lawrence H. Summers, *American Economic Review* 72(5):1056–69 (1982). © 1982 by the American Economic Association. [Chapter 17]

"Annuity markets, savings, and the capital stock," with J. Shoven and A. Spivak, in *Issues in Pension Economics*, Z. Bodie, J. B. Shoven, and D. A. Wise, eds (Chicago, Ill.: University of Chicago Press, 1987), 211–34. © 1987 by the National Bureau of Economic Research. [Chapter 5]

"Deficit delusion," *Public Interest* 84:53–65 (1986). © 1986 by Public Interest. [Chapter 10]

"Economic impact of deficit financing," *International Monetary Fund Staff Papers* 31(3):549–80 (1984). © 1984 by the International Monetary Fund. [Chapter 8]

"The effect of annuity insurance on savings and inequality," with J. Shoven and A. Spivak, *Journal of Labor Economics* 4(3), pt. 2, S183–S207 (1986). © 1986 by the University of Chicago. [Chapter 5]

"An examination of empirical tests of Social Security and savings," with Alan J. Auerbach, in *Social Policy Evaluation: An Economic Perspective*, E. Helpman, ed. (New York: Academic Press, 1983), 161–74. © 1983 by Academic Press, Inc. [Chapter 19]

"The family as an incomplete annuities market," with Avia Spivak, *Journal of Political Economy* 89(2):372–91 (1981). © 1981 by the University of Chicago. [Chapter 4]

"Intergenerational transfers and savings," *Journal of Economic Perspectives*, forthcoming. © by the American Economic Association. [Chapter 2]

"Investment versus savings incentives: The size of the bang for the buck and the potential for self-financing business tax cuts," with Alan J. Auerbach, in *The Economic Consequences of Government Deficits*, L. H. Meyer, ed. (Norwell, Mass.: Kluwer-Nijhoff, 1983), 121–49. © 1983 by Kluwer Academic Publishers. [Chapter 9]

"Public debt and United States savings: A new test of the neutrality hypothesis," with Michael J. Boskin, *Carnegie-Rochester Conference Series on Public Policy* 23:55–86 (1985). © 1985 by Elsevier Science Publishers B.V. (North-Holland). [Chapter 18]

"The role of intergenerational transfers in aggregate capital accumulation," with Lawrence H. Summers, *Journal of Political Economy* 89(4):706–32 (1981). © 1981 by the University of Chicago. [Chapter 1]

"Simulating alternative Social Security Responses to the demographic transition," with Alan J. Auerbach, *National Tax Journal* 38(2):153–68 (1985). © 1985 by the National Tax Institute–Tax Institute of America. [Chapter 13]

"Social Security and equilibrium capital intensity," *Quarterly Journal of Economics* 43(2):233–54 (1979). © 1979 by the President and Fellows of Harvard College. Reprinted by permission of John Wiley & Sons, Inc. [Chapter 12]

"Some economic implications of life-span extension," in *Aging: Biology and Behavior*, J. March and J. McGaugh, eds. (New York: Academic Press, 1981), 97–114. © by Academic Press, Inc. [Chapter 14]

"Taxation and savings: A neoclassical perspective," *Journal of Economic Literature* 22:1576–1629 (1984). © 1984 by the American Economic Association. [Chapter 7]

"Testing the theory of Social Security and life cycle accumulation," *American Economic Review* 69(3):396–410 (1979). © 1979 by the American Economic Association. [Chapter 15]

Index